The Critical Review: Or, Annals of Literature
by Tobias George Smollett

Address:
HardPress
8345 NW 66TH ST #2561
MIAMI FL 33166-2626
USA
Email: info@hardpress.net

THE

CRITICAL REVIEW:

OR,

Annals of Literature.

BY
A SOCIETY of GENTLEMEN.

VOLUME the FIFTY 6

——— *Nothing extenuate,*
Nor set down aught in malice.   SHAKSPEARE.

Ploravere suis non respondere favorem
Speratum meritis———   HOR.

LONDON,
Printed for A. HAMILTON, in Falcon-Court, Fleet-street.
MDCCLXXXIII.

574

CONTENTS.

CONTENTS.

CONTENTS.

CONTENTS.

CONTENTS.

CONTENTS.

THE

THE
CRITICAL REVIEW.

For the Month of *July*, 1783.

The Art of Poetry. An Epiſtle to the Piſos. Tranſlated from Horace. With Notes. By George Colman. 4to. 7s. 6d. Cadell.

THIS celebrated epiſtle, the delight and the torment of critics, has already been examined by the refined learning and the acute diſcernment of Dr. Hurd. It has not, indeed, eſcaped the enquiries of different ages ; and, as the opinions of authors have been ſo various, the moſt ſuperficial reader will be ready to conclude, that the arguments, which have been attended with ſo little ſucceſs, could not have been remarkable for their depth or their ingenuity. It was very generally allowed, that this *Art of Poetry* conſiſted of rules thrown together without art or connexion ; and the epiſtle, which ſtrongly inculcated the beauties of order and arrangement, was remarkably deficient in both. But the greater number of critics, as well as Scaliger, were miſled by the comparatively modern title, and tried the poet by a code of laws to which he could not with juſtice be ſubjected ; for, though a didactic poem, which profeſſed to teach the art of poetry, ſhould be regular and connected ; yet a familiar epiſtle on the ſame ſubject may be looſe and deſultory. In fact, however, Horace had probably a plan, to which, with few exceptions, he confined himſelf : Dr. Hurd has conſidered it with attention, and given a detail of it, in his commentary, with clearneſs and preciſion. Perhaps he has erred in the oppoſite extreme, and, as uſual, truth may lie in the middle.

Our preſent tranſlator, Mr. Colman, differs from the biſhop reſpecting the plan which it was ſuppoſed Horace had followed.

He

He thinks there is a violence and restraint offered to the composition, to accommodate it to the system of the commentator; and an attentive reader will not always be convinced of the existence of that very uniform regularity which Dr. Hurd has endeavoured to trace. We may be permitted to remark, for we do it with the utmost deference for the learning and talents of the very respectable commentator, that the discovery of a secret chain or an imperceptible link is frequently delusive. Of the infinite variety of plans, which a lively imagination or a fertile genius can invent, it will not be very difficult to find one which, with little ingenuity, may be adapted to the work in question; and in the ardour of discovery, slight objections will be despised, like ' the motes in a summer sun-beam.' We think also that Mr. Colman has, in some respects, been too much under the influence of a system; but, though he sometimes walks in fetters, yet they are neither too heavy, nor compress him so closely, as to prevent his wearing them with grace and apparent freedom. We shall give his opinion, in his own words.

' I conceive that one of the sons of Piso, undoubtedly the elder, had either writen, or meditated, a poetical work, most probably a tragedy; and that he had, with the knowlege of the family, communicated his piece, or intention, to Horace: but Horace, either disapproving of the work, or doubting of the poetical faculties of the Elder Piso, or both, wished to dissuade him from all thoughts of publication. With this view he formed the design of writing this Epistle, addressing it, with a courtliness and delicacy perfectly agreeable to his acknowleged character, indifferently to the whole family, the father and his two sons. Epistola ad Pisones, de Arte Poeticâ.

' He begins with general reflections, generally addressed to his three friends. Credite, Pisones !—Pater, & juvenus patre digni !—In these preliminary rules, equally necessary to be observed by poets of every denomination, he dwells on the necessity of unity of design, the danger of being dazzled by the splendor of partial beauties, the choice of subjects, the beauty of order, the elegance and propriety of diction, and the use of a thorough knowlege of the nature of the several different species of Poetry: summing up this introductory portion of his Epistle, in a manner perfectly agreeable to the conclusion of it.

> Descriptas servare vices, operumque colores,
> Cur ego si nequeo ignoroque, poeta salutor ?
> Cur nescire, pudens pravè, quam discere malo ?

' From this general view of poetry, on the canvas of Aristotle, but entirely after his own manner, the writer proceeds to give the rules and history of the drama; adverting principally to tragedy, with all its constituents and appendages of diction, fable, character,

character, incidents, chorus, meafure, mufic, and decoration. In this part of the work, according to the interpretation of the beft critics, and indeed (I think) according to the manifeft tenor of the epiftle, he addreffes himfelf entirely to the two young gentlemen, pointing out to them the difficulty, as well as excellence, of the dramatic art; infifting on the avowed fuperiority of the Græcian writers, and afcribing the comparative failure of the Romans to negligence and avarice. The poet, having exhaufted this part of his fubject, fuddenly drops a fecond, or difmiffes at once no lefs than two of the three perfons, to whom he originally addreffed his epiftle, and turning fhort on the Elder Pifo, moft earneftly conjures him to ponder on the danger of precipitate publication, and the ridicule to which the author of wretched poetry expofes himfelf. From the commencement of this partial addrefs, O major juvenum, &c. [v. 366] to the end of the poem, almoft a fourth part of the whole, the fecond perfon plural, Pifones!—Vos!—Vos, O Pompilius Sanguis! &c. is difcarded, and the fecond perfon fingular, Tu, Te, Tibi, &c. invariably takes its place. The arguments too are equally relative and perfonal; not only fhewing the neceffity of ftudy, combined with natural genius, to conftitute a poet; but dwelling on the peculiar danger and delufion of flattery, to a writer of rank and fortune; as well as the ineftimable value of an honeft friend, to refcue him from derifion and contempt. The poet, however, in reverence to the Mufe, qualifies his exaggerated defcription of an infatuated fcribbler, with a moft noble encomium of the ufes of good poetry, vindicating the dignity of the art, and proudly afferting, that the moft exalted characters would not be difgraced by the cultivation of it.

" Ne forte pudori
Sit tibi Mufa, lyræ folers, & cantor Apollo."

' It is worthy obfervation, that in the fatyrical picture of a frantic bard, with which Horace concludes his epiftle, he not only runs counter to what might be expected as a corollary of an effay on the Art of Poetry, but contradicts his own ufual practice and fentiments. In his Epiftle to Auguftus, inftead of ftigmatizing the love of verfe as an abominable phrenzy, he calls it ("levis hæc infania) a flight madnefs," and defcants on its good effects—" quantas virtutes habeat, fic collige!"'

' In another Epiftle, speaking of himfelf, and his addiction to poetry, he fays,

" —————————————ubi quid datur oti,
Illudo chartis; hoc eft, mediocribus illis
Ex vitiis unum, &c."

' All which, and feveral other paffages in his works, almoft demonftrate that it was not, without a particular purpofe in view, that he dwelt fo forcibly on the defcription of a man refolved

" —————————————— in fpite
Of nature and his ftars to write."

Though

Though our translator's opinion may seem one of those various hypotheses, which, on a subject so uncertain, may easily be made to put on the semblance of truth; yet we own the pointed application to the Elder Piso seems strongly to support it. It is remarkable that Dr. Hurd has not attended to this change of address, which is introduced by a personal compliment, and an allowance of every merit but that of a poetical genius; and from line 285, rather than from line 295, to the end of the epistle, he endeavours to inculcate a care and diligence in writing, and appears to have finished his observations on the drama. If then we examine the epistle to the Pisos, we shall find that of 476 lines not more than 112 relate to the subject, which Dr. Hurd has considered as the poet's end and aim. But we still think a more probable account may be given of the intention of our author; for to endeavour to dissuade from a favourite purpose was not with the utmost propriety attempted in an epistle, in which a soothing manner, often so necessary to convey an unpleasing truth, must lose much of its effect. We shall not dwell longer on this subject, because we do not consider it in a very important view; but would suggest to our translator, whether poetry may not have been the subject of a conversation between Horace and the Pisos, who, pleased with his opinions, may have wished to possess them in a less fugitive form, and consequently desired the poet's sentiments in that of an epistle. This will account for the peculiar addresses in different parts of the work, as each may have insisted on their particular opinions; not to add, that a person, purposely consulted, did not want the cover of a more general form, or the mask of a less pointed introduction.

The translation itself is, in many parts, neat and elegant; but it sometimes seems to have been executed in haste, and in a very few places to be less accurate than we had expected to find it. —— We shall endeavour to be more explicit. The elegant and easy negligence of the original is in general happily preserved; but the translator has not equalled his author in terseness and in energy. He has sometimes extended two words into as many lines, where more attention and greater care might have included their force in the former couplet; by which the vigour of the whole would have been increased. He has indeed avoided the error of Roscommon, who sometimes, as he was free from the shackles of rhyme, compresses his subject in concise and nervous language; but often omits passages, which perhaps he despaired of adorning: Mr. Colman is equally distant from the more poetical, though less accurate and discriminated

minated version of Mr. Francis. As a general specimen, we shall select the passage which appropriates to different subjects its peculiar numbers: the original is in every critic's hand, so that we shall not subjoin it.

    ' For deeds of kings and chiefs, and battles fought,
What numbers are most fitting, Homer taught:
    ' Couplets unequal were at first confin'd
To speak in broken verse the mourner's mind.
Prosperity at length, and free content,
In the same numbers gave their raptures vent;
But who first fram'd the Elegy's small song,
Grammarians squabble, and will squabble long.
    ' Archilochus, 'gainst vice, a noble rage
Arm'd with his own Iambicks to engage:
With these the humble Sock, and Buskin proud
Shap'd dialogue; and still'd the noisy croud;
Embrac'd the measure, prov'd its ease and force,
And found it apt for business or discourse.
    ' Gods, and the sons of Gods, in odes to sing,
The Muse attunes her lyre, and strikes the string;
Victorious boxers, racers, mark the line,
The cares of youthful love, and joys of wine.
    ' The various outline of each work to fill.
If nature gives no power, and art no skill;
If, marking nicer shades, I miss my aim,
Why am I greeted with a poet's name?
Or if, thro' ignorance, I can't discern,
Why, from false modesty, forbear to learn?
    ' A comic incident loaths tragic strains:
Thy feast, Thyestes, lowly verse disdains;
Familiar diction scorns, as base and mean,
Touching too nearly on the comic scene.
Each stile allotted to its proper place,
Let each appear with its peculiar grace!
Yet comedy at times exalts her strain,
And angry Chremes storms in swelling vein;
The tragic hero, plung'd in deep distress,
Sinks with his fate, and makes his language less.
Peleus and Telephus, poor, banish'd! each
Drop their big six-foot words, and sounding speech;
Or else, what bosom in their grief takes part,
Which cracks the ear, but cannot touch the heart?'

The most exceptionable parts of this quotation are the three last lines. ' *Six-foot* words' do not convey the proper meaning of '*sesqui* pedalia verba;' and ' cracks the ear' has no prototype in the original. In the subsequent lines he does not seem to have been equally happy:

    ' 'Tis not enough that plays are polish'd, chaste,
Or trickt in all the harlotry of taste,

They

They muſt have paſſion too ; beyond controul
Tranſporting where they pleaſe the hearer's ſoul.
With thoſe that ſmile, our face in ſmiles appears ;
With thoſe that weep, our cheeks are bath'd in tears ;
To make me grieve, be firſt your anguiſh ſhown,
And I ſhall feel your ſorrows like my own.
Peleus, and Telephus ! unleſs your ſtile
Suit with your circumſtance, I'll ſleep, or ſmile.'

In the two firſt lines we think the poet's meaning is—' 'Tis
not enough that your poems are ſplendid ; they muſt be *delight-*
ful and intereſting.' If ' dulcia' be ' paſſionate,' the epithet
is included in the ſubſequent line :

' Et quocunque volunt animum auditoris agunto.'

In the latter part the poet addreſſes the actors—' Male ſi
mandata loqueris'—' If you ſpeak your part *unfeelingly.*'
Roſcommon has given it this ſenſe ; but Dr. Hurd ſeems to
underſtand it in the ſame as our tranſlator, and, with
little probability, ſuppoſes two tragedies of the ſame name,
but of diſſimilar merit.

In ſupport of the opinion we have delivered, we ſhall ſelect
ſome inſtances where haſte probably has too far diminiſhed the
elegance and increaſed the extent of the preſent tranſlation.

' But, if the actor's words belie his ſtate,
And ſpeak a language foreign to his fate,
Romans ſhall *crack their ſides*, and all the town
Join *horſe and foot* to laugh the impoſtor down.'

The phraſes marked by Italics will be conſidered as too
familiar by the more refined reader ; and the latter is more
exceptionable, as Mr. Colman reads ' Equites *patreſque*' inſtead of the more common words ' Equites *pediteſque*.'
Again,

' He goes not back to Meleager's death
With Diomed's return, to *run you out of breath*,'

Beſides the more obvious exception, the learned reader will
find nothing in the original which relates to the laſt words.

' 'Till liberty grown *rank*, and *run to ſeed*—

is another error of the ſame kind, ſeemingly from too much
haſte. It is to this cauſe alſo we muſt attribute Medea's
murder of her children being called a ' *parricide*'—'*extended*'
for ' *crowded*' ſeats*, and ' *diurnal* bowl'—' vino diurno,

---

* If the tranſlator looks at the paſſage which refers to this word,
 ' Nondum ſpiſſa nimis, complere ſedilia flatu'—
he will find that his verſion is directly contrary to the ſenſe of the
author.

I

which in common language fignifies *daily*, inftead of ' by day.'

But we will not dwell too long on defects : there are other paffages where the original is rendered by a peculiar felicity of expreffion, as well as with harmony and energy.

  ' Aut famam fequere aut convenientia finge
  Scriptor'——

is happily tranflated——

  ' Follow the voice of fame ; or, if you feign,
  The fabled plan confiftently maintain.'

The old man, who ' res omnes timide gelideque miniftrat' is faid to be

  ' Timid and cold in all he undertakes,
  His hand from *doubt* as well as *weaknefs* fhakes'——

We are well aware that this may be confidered by fome as an affected antithefis ; but we own that it feems to us to add to the beauty as well as the fidelity of the picture.

Again, from the 108th line of the original, we have the following elegant verfion.

  ' For Nature firft to every varying wind
  Of changeful Fortune fhapes the pliant mind,
  Sooths it with Pleafure, or to Rage provokes,
  Or brings it to the ground by Sorrow's heavy ftrokes ;
  Then of the joys that charm'd, or woes that wrung,
  Forces expreffion from the faithful tongue.'

The laft line, the tranflation of ' Effert animi motus interprete lingua', is peculiarly beautiful.

The notes are taken from the beft commentators, or are the original obfervations of Mr. Colman. They are at once a proof of the good fenfe and ingenuity of the tranflator, and often firmly eftablifh his own opinion. Where he differs from Dr. Hurd, his remarks are dictated with that refpect which the exalted character of the prelate requires. We are forry that we are not able to purfue them at full length, but fhall felect our tranflator's obfervations on the chorus. Thofe who wifh to refer to Dr. Hurd's notes, will find the obfervations alluded to, page 129.

  ' Though it is not my intention to agitate, in this place, the long difputed queftion concerning the expedience, or inexpediency, of the chorus ; yet I cannot difmifs the above note without fome farther obfervation. In the firft place then I cannot think that the judgment of two fuch critics as Ariftotle and Horace, can be decifively quoted, as concurring with the practice of wife antiquity, to eftablifh the chorus. Neither of thefe two

        critics

critics have taken up the question, each of them giving directions for the proper conduct of the chorus, considered as an established and received part of tragedy, and indeed originally, as they both tell us the whole of it. Aristotle, in his poetics, has not said much on the subject ; and from the little he has said, more arguments might perhaps be drawn, in favour of the omission, than for the introduction of the chorus. It is true that he says, in his 4th chapter, that " Tragedy, after many changes, paused, having gained its natural form : πολλὰς μεταβολὰς μεταβαλοῦσα ἡ τραγωδία ἐπαύσατο, ἐπει ἔσχε τὴν ἑαυτῆς φύσιν. This might, at first sight, seem to include his approbation of the chorus, as well as of all the other parts of tragedy then in use ; but he himself expressly tells us in the very same chapter, that he had no such meaning, saying, that " to enquire whether tragedy be perfect in its parts, either considered in itself, or with relation to the theatre, was foreign to his present purpose." Τὸ μὲν οὖν ἐπισκοπεῖν, ἐ ἄρα ἔχει ηδη ἡ τραγωδία τοῖς εἴκασῶς, ἢ οὔ, αὐτό τε καθ᾽ αὐτὸ κρινόμε ον, καὶ πρὸς τὰ θεάτρα, ἄλλος γόλος. In the passage from which Horace has, in the verses now before us, described the office, and laid down the duties of the chorus, the passage referred to by the learned critic, the words of Aristotle are not particularly favourable to the institution, or much calculated to recommend the use of it. For Aristotle there informs us, " that Sophocles alone of all the Grecian writers, made the chorus conducive to the progress of the fable : not only even Euripides being culpable in this instance ; but other writers, after the example of Agathon, introducing odes as little to the purpose, as if they had borrowed whole scenes from another play." Καὶ τὸν χορὸν δὲ ἕνα δεῖ ὑπολαβεῖ τῶν ὑποκριτῶν. Καὶ μόριον εἶναι τῦ ὅλᾳ, καὶ συν γωνίζε θαι μὴ ὥσπερ παρ᾽ Εὐριπίδῃ, ἀλλ᾽ ὥσπερ παρα Σοφοκλεῖ. Τοῖς δὲ λοιποῖς τὰ διδόμε α μᾶλλον τῦ μύθε, ἢ ἄλλης Τραγωδίας εςὶ· δι᾽ ᾧ εμβόλιμα ἄδεσι, πρῶτε ἀοξαντος Αγράθωνος τῦ ποιήτε. Καὶ τῳ τῦ διάφερει, ἢ ἠμβόλιμα ἄδειν, ἢ ῥῆσιν ἐξ ἄλλε εἰς ἄλλο ἁρμόσειν, ἢ ἐπεισόδιον ὄκνος [περ. ποιντ. κ. ιη.]

On the whole, therefore, whatever may be the merits, or advantages of the chorus. I cannot think that the judgment of Aristotle or Horace can be adduced in recommendation of it. As to the probability given to the representation, by the chorus interposing and bearing a part in the action ; the public, who have lately seen a troop of singers assembled on the stage, as a chorus, during the whole representations of Elfrida and Caractacus, are competent to decide for themselves, how far such an expedient, gives a more striking resemblance of human life than the common usage of our drama. As to its importance in a moral view, to correct the evil impression of vicious sentiments, imputed to the speakers ; the story told, to enforce its use for this purpose, conveys a proof of its inefficacy. To give due force to sentiments, as well as to direct their proper tendency, depends on the skill and address of the poet, independent of the chorus.

Monsieur

* Monſieur Dacier, as well as the author of the above note, cenſures the modern ſtage for having rejected the chorus, and having loſt thereby at leaſt half its probability, and its greateſt ornament ; ſo that our tragedy is but a very faint ſhadow of the old. Learned critics, however, do not, perhaps, conſider, that if it be expedient to revive the chorus, all the other parts of the ancient tragedy muſt be revived along with it. Ariſtotle mentions muſic as one of the ſix parts of tragedy, and Horace no ſooner introduces the chorus, but he proceeds to the pipe and lyre. If a chorus be really neceſſary, our dramas, like thoſe of the ancients, ſhould be rendered wholly muſical ; the dancers alſo will then claim their place, and the pretenſions of Veſtris and Noverre muſt be admitted as claſſical. Such a ſpectacle, if not more natural than the modern, would at leaſt be conſiſtent ; but to introduce a groupe of ſpectatorial actors, ſpeaking in one part of the drama, and ſinging in another, is as ſtrange and incoherent a medley, and full as unclaſſical, as the dialogue and airs of the Beggar's Opera !'

The moral character of the chorus, which the biſhop conſiders in pages 141 and 146 of his notes, occaſions the following remarks from our tranſlator :

‘ One of the cenſurers of Euripides, whoſe opinion is controverted in the above note, is Monſieur Dacier ; who condemns the chorus in this inſtance, as not only violating their moral office, but tranſgreſſing the laws of nature and of God, by a fidelity, ſo vicious and criminal, that theſe women, [the chorus !] ought to fly away in the car of Medea, to eſcape the puniſhment due to them. The annotator above, agrees with the Greek ſcholiaſt, that the Corinthian women (the chorus) being free, properly deſert the intereſts of Creon, and keep Medea's ſecrets, for the ſake of juſtice, according to their cuſtom. Dacier, however, urges an inſtance of their infidelity in the Ion of Euripides, where they betray the ſecret of Xuthus to Creuſa, which the French critic defends on account of their attachment to their miſtreſs ; and adds, that the rule of Horace, like other rules, is proved by the exception. “ Beſides (continues the critic in the true ſpirit of French gallantry) ſhould we ſo heavily accuſe the poet for not having made an aſſembly of women keep a ſecret ?” D'ailleurs, peut on faire un ſi grand crime à un poete, de n'avoir pas fait en ſorte qu'une troupe de femmes garde un ſecret ? He then concludes his note with blaming Euripides for the perfidy of Iphigenia at Tauris, who abandons theſe faithful guardians of her ſecret, by flying alone with Oreſtes, and leaving them to the fury of Thoas, to which they muſt have been expoſed, but for the intervention of Minerva.

‘ On the whole, it appears that the moral importance of the chorus muſt be conſidered with ſome limitations : or, at leaſt, that the chorus is as liable to be miſuſed and miſapplied, as any part of modern tragedy.'

We

We muft now leave thefe flowery paths, and can only add, that if, in a future edition, Mr. Colman will revife his verfion with care, we fhall confider it as a refpectable addition to the Englifh tranflations of the ancient poets.

Differtations on Select Subjects in Chemiftry and Medicine, by Martin Wall, M. D. 8vo. 3s. 6d. Cadell.

THESE elegant Differtations, with an annexed fyllabus for a courfe of chemical lectures, are publifhed in order ' to promote the great caufe, which firft fuggefted their com-pofition,' viz. the eftablifhment of a proper plan of medical education at Oxford, in which the author holds an important office. We acknowledge the propriety of the attempt, but may be allowed to add our apprehenfions, refpecting its fuc-cefs. Dr. Wall muft be too well acquainted with the methods of ftudy both in Oxford, and the univerfities more peculiarly appropriated to medical inftruction, to be fanguine in his ex-pectations. Diligence and attention muft be rendered re-fpectable; a new ardor, and emulation to excel, muft arife; and every affiftance to ftudy become eafy and acceffible, or the moft ample funds and the moft able profeffors will exhauft their powers, without an adequate return. We wifh not, however, to difcourage the defign, but to affift it, by pointing out difficulties which will not be fo eafily overcome, as the appointment of a chemical profeffor, or a reader in chemiftry; for, in this refpect, the knowledge of the difeafe will materi-ally promote its relief.

This volume contains three differtations. I. An Inaugural Differtation on the Study of Chemiftry : read in the Natural Philofophy School, Oxford, May 7, 1781 —II. Conjectures concerning the Origin and Antiquity of the Ufe of Symbols in Aftronomy and Chemiftry.——III. Obfervations on the Dif-eafes prevalent in the South Sea Iflands, particularly the Lues Venerea, with fome Remarks concerning its firft Appearance in Europe.

The firft Differtation is a very fatisfactory and concife hif-tory of chemiftry. Dr. Wall's opinion of alchemy attracted our attention, on account of the late labours of Dr. Price. In our review of that performance, we endeavoured to infi-nuate, in the mildeft terms, our fufpicions of his having given to common appearances a new and unufual colour ; and we will frankly own, that we were not fufficiently credulous to truft implicitly the refult of every experiment. We find, in the fecond edition, which has not reached us, that he has made

made many alterations. Our readers will be fo good as to accept of them from Dr. Wall.

' In this edition he has ftudioufly omitted or altered every expreffion or fentence, which might be thought to betray an attachment to, or a belief in, the common opinions of alchemy. In a future more extenfive appendix, the author has promifed to explain his fentiments more fully on thefe fubjects : 'till then the candid and liberal fhould perhaps fufpend their judgment of his late publications, efpecially as he intimates an intention to illuftrate "the principles of fome of his proceffes, and to fhew their analogy to experiments related by chemifts of reputation." If in this line Dr. Price fpeaks explicitly and ingenuoufly, much inftruction may be expected from his chemical erudition and practical experience. In this work we may hope to fee the doctrine of the original and progreffive ftate of the bafes, or earths of metals clearly inveftigated ; and the balance held with an impartial hand between the two opinions, which have been maintained on the point.'

As the tract itfelf is an elegant account only of what is generally known, we fhall give a more interefting proof of the author's chemical knowledge, by inferting the reft of the note from which we have already tranfcribed a paffage, than by any other part of his hiftory.

' With regard to the origin and generation of metals, and the real nature of the earths that conftitute their bafes, naturalifts have held very different opinions. It is not within the compafs of my ability to difcufs the queftion fully, and in this place it would be improper. I fhall only therefore venture to introduce a few remarks in fome degree connected with that divifion of the fubject, which is more immediately before us. It has been often alledged, or implied by chemical writers, that there is really but one and the fame bafis or earth of all metals, which combined in different modes or various proportions with fome other principles, particularly the phlogifton (and fometimes the mercurial principle is adduced) gives all the forms of metallic fubftances. If this theory could be confirmed, it would be very favourable to the doctrine of the tranfmutation, as it gives a foundation to infer, that if certain principles could be in fome cafes taken away, or in others fuperadded, the qualities, that is the nature and effence of a metal, might be changed, or in other words, it might be tranfmuted into another metal. That the alchemifts maintained this hypothefis is obvious from thofe parts of their writings which are tolerably confpicuous. That many chemifts of much later date have entertained the fame fentiments is plain from the paffages of Becher and Stahl, to which I formerly referred (fee page 25), and particularly the fecond fupplement to the Phyfica Subterranea, Thef. I. " De tranfmutationis metallicæ neceffitate et connexione cum univerfo naturæ curfu." But
there

there is a fallacy in the defence of this thefis, which will perhaps be found in all the writings on the fame fide of the queftion, which proceed upon the fame mode of argument. The changes, which are there inftanced, in the courfe of nature, or the operations of art, are by no means applicable to the point in difpute: they only fhew that the world and all its conftituent parts are fubject to alterations and revolutions ; and that the animal, vegetable, and even mineral kingdom is influenced by fimilar laws : but they by no means prove, that in any one inftance any genus or fpecies of the natural productions, in the animal, vegetable, or mineral kingdom, has been changed into any other in that mode and degree, which the idea of tranfmutation implies. It holds perhaps throughout nature, that the genera and fpecies, which compofe the animate and inanimate world, are immutable and invariable ; that they cannot by any natural or artificial procefs be fo far deprived of their own effential qualities, as to affume abfolutely thofe of another fpecies or genus. Therefore it may be conceived, that the different metals are fubftances, as the naturalifts fay, fui generis, of a fpecific unalterable nature ; and though by various artificial or even natural means, by combination, folution, precipitation, their forms may be concealed and apparently altered, yet they continue perfectly diftinct however difguifed. And poffibly, it may be with truth alledged, that no mode of treatment, no addition, no procefs of reduction can really give to a metal or metallic earth any other fimple homogeneous metallic form, than that which is peculiarly appropriated to it.

If this doctrine be admiffible, and perhaps there are many good arguments to urge in its confirmation, the opinion of a tranfmutation of metals, either by art or nature, can have no foundation.'

The fecond tract is lefs important. Its chief object is to endeavour to demonftrate, that the chemifts adopted the hieroglyphic mode of writing from the aftronomers ; and confequently to depreciate the pretenfions of the alchemifts to any very high antiquity. The fymbol of Jupiter is fuppofed to reprefent the horn of Jupiter Hammon, with a crofs annexed. Venus, who, our author thinks, was the Ifis of the Egyptians, is reprefented by the fiftrum, which fhe ufually carried in her hand. The fymbol of Saturn is a falx ; and that of Mars a fpear and fhield. This is the outline of our author's fyftem ; but the fketch is very imperfect. It is fupported with much knowledge and learning ; but the uncertainty of the fubject, and its poffeffing little application to any ufeful purpofe, prevent us from enlarging on it.

In the third differtation, the author has chiefly confined himfelf to the confutation of Dr. Forfter's opinion, that the venereal difeafe was known to the inhabitants of the South
Sea

Sea iflands, before the vifits of the Europeans. Dr. Wall juftly obferves, that the arguments of the circumnavigator chiefly fhow, that it could not be imported from America; and, that even if his facts are credited, of which he fuggefts fome doubts, they will not prove that it was a difeafe, which exifted before the year 1688, and from that year to 1693. We have not lately engaged in this controverfy; but are convinced, from our former attention to it, that we do not owe this dreadful fcourge to America. This opinion rather multiplies than leffens the difficulties; for, in the hiftory of medicine, every difeafe which arifes from a fpecific contagion, appears to have been the peculiar product of a particular country, and to have been carried, only by infection, to others. We have little confidence in the philofophy of Fracaftorius, that the moft complicated productions are the lateft in their appearance;

‘ Tanta vi coeunt genitalia femina in unum.’

Indeed he forfakes his fyftem, as foon as he has formed it, and from his opinion of the eternity of the world, is obliged to allow that there has been a fufficient time for the union of particles moft diftinct in their nature, and diftant in their fituation: but it is rather neceffary to purfue our prefent author. This fubject is encompaffed with difficulties; and we own ourfelves unequal to the tafk of removing them. In fact, the older authors on the venereal difeafe are terrified and confufed. They fometimes confound other difeafes with the genuine fyphilis, and reprefent it with accumulated terrors; fo that we are often afraid of trufting even to their evidence, and we can meet with no other. Dr. Wall has, we think, fufficiently proved, that it firft appeared at the period which we have already mentioned; and that the inhabitants of the South Sea iflands are indebted for it to their intercourfe with the Europeans.

The fyllabus of the courfe of Chemiftry feems very complete; but, as the whole is divided only into twenty-four lectures, the time employed on each fubject muft be very inconfiderable. The path to fcience fhould allure by the pleafure of the attainments, rather than by its facility and eafe. The ftudent fhould be told, that it is thorny and intricate; or he will forfake it, on the firft appearance of difficulty and danger. Dr. Wall muft be well aware, that a courfe fo general and confined is adapted chiefly for the man of fafhion, who fips only the cup of fcience, as the ornament of polifhed converfation, and will not materially affift either the philofopher or the phyfician. Their enquiries muft be more varied and intricate: the femblance of fcience will flightly aid their re-

fearches,

searches, which must be pursued with unwearied toil; for nature will not yield her choicest treasures to the inattentive enquirer, or to the superficial observer.

---

*The Epistolary Correspondence, Visitation Charges, Speeches,
and Miscellanies, of the Right Reverend Francis Atterbury,
D. D. Lord Bishop of Rochester.   With Historical Notes.
2 Vols.   8vo.   12s.   Nichols.*

WE are again called on to attend the industrious author of
the Life of Hogarth, in the more humble capacity of an
editor.   Mr. Nichols, in these volumes, has collected the miscellaneous productions of the bishop of Rochester, and explained
them with notes so exact, that even if they were more interesting,
like the ' conviva satur,' we should scarcely have raised from our
elbows.   Yet we owe him our thanks for the entertainment
and instruction he has afforded us.   Collected from every
source, from the almost forgotten publications of Curl, from
Budgel, and the hitherto inviolated cabinets of individuals,
his mass of materials must necessarily be of a mixed kind, and
the value of each part consequently different.   But, on the
whole, they have given us some new and interesting information, respecting the character of this ambitious and turbulent
prelate.   As we have expressed our wishes, that the lives of
distinguished individuals should rather be looked on in a philosophical, than a chronological view; and that the aim of the
biographer should be to unfold the intricacies of the heart,
and add to the history of the human mind, instead of settling
the æras of a birth or a marriage, it may not be amiss to explain, in a general way, the opinions which the letters of
Dr. Atterbury have suggested, with respect to his character.

The mind of the bishop was, even in early life restless and
uneasy; he felt himself superior to his college engagements;
and his impatience was evident from the *accumulated* expressions of his first complaint, which a minor critic has condemned as inaccurate.   ' Mr. Boyle takes up *half my time*; college
business a *great deal more,* and I am forced to be useful to the
dean in a thousand particulars.'   A trait of this kind is worth
a volume of criticisms.   It points out the genuine efforts of
an ambitious mind, struggling with the obscurity of his situation.   The subsequent conduct of Dr. Atterbury fully showed
the effects of his turbulent ambition.   In every situation, either to support his dignity, to restore ancient privileges, or
for other reasons, he was involved in litigations and contests:
In every publication, he seemed to invite a dispute, by the pe-
culiarity

euliarity of his opinions; in short, while he appeared to court retirement, and to long for ease, he seemed to live only in contentions. This disposition seems also to have influenced his public conduct. His ambition, which would not acknowledge a superior, and even seemed uneasy at an equal, rendered him violent and intolerant. It was this disposition which influenced him in the convocation, and in the house of lords. It was his ambition which gives the fairest colour to those accusations of his enemies, which ended in his banishment. He was supposed to have aimed at the primacy; but really wished only for the bishoprick of Winchester: among the former possessors of that see, there was a character as enterprising and violent as his own, and in many respects resembled him, the famous William. If, as has been alledged, he was promised this preferment when it became vacant, as the price of his silence, we may conclude that a life of quiet would have been intolerable; or that, though this was the apparent extent of his ambition, he probably aimed at very different honours. His connection with the Pretender, during his banishment, cannot be eluded by ingenuity; though the guilt may be alleviated, by the apparent ingratitude of his former master, on the supposition, that he had not been guilty of the crimes imputed to him. These we cannot judge of; it will be at least evident, that he was condemned on such a foundation, as would now be rejected on the trial of the slightest culprit.

This was the general public character of the bishop of Rochester; yet we ought not to suppose, that he was invariably violent, or constantly ambitious. The human mind cannot support a continued contest, any more than the body an unremitted fatigue. The moments of sickness or distress, the reflections of disappointed pride, will point out the slight tenure, on which all our worldly prospects are founded, and the empty bubble which we are labouring to support. His advice to dean Swift was friendly and honest; yet to temporize, was not the common conduct of Atterbury. His deaneries were of the new foundation, where the deans consent to all proposals is absolutely necessary; yet this power did not content him, and his cautious advice to Swift was subsequent to his disappointments, after he had endeavoured to increase it. It may be worth the reader's while to contemplate his more rational resolutions, during the last sickness of his lady. Atterbury was not inconsistent; but, with him, as with all the world, external objects received their colour from the disposition of the mind; and we have scarcely met with any of his more moderate letters, but what may be traced to one of the sources which we have already mentioned. We shall insert one

one of these, and the subsequent passage, as a specimen:—both were written during this prospect of dissolution.

LETTER XXXVII.

The Bishop of Rochester to Mr. Pope.

March 16, 1721-2.

'As a visitant, a lodger, a friend (or under what other denomination soever), you are always welcome to me; and will be more so, I hope, every day that we live: for, to tell you the truth, I like you as I like myself, best when we have both of us least business. It has been my fate to be engaged in it much and often, by the stations in which I was placed: but God, that knows my heart, knows I never loved it; and am still less in love with it than ever, as I find less temptation to act with any hope of success. If I am good for any thing, it is *in angulo cum libello*; and yet a good part of my time has been spent, and perhaps must still be spent, far otherwise. For I will never, while I have health, be wanting to my duty in any post, or in any respect, how little soever I may like my employment, and how hopeless soever I may be in the discharge of it.

'In the mean time the judicious world is pleased to think that I delight in work which I am obliged to undergo, and aim at things which I from my heart despise. Let them think as they will, so I might be at liberty to act as I will, and spend my time in such a manner as is most agreeable to me. I cannot say I do so now, for I am here without any books, and if I had them could not use them to my satisfaction, while my mind is taken up in a more melancholy manner; and how long, or how little a while it may be so taken up, God only knows, and to his will I implicitly resign myself in every thing.

Fr. Roffen.'

'The givers of trouble one way shall have their share of it another; that at last they may be induced to let me be quiet, and live to myself, with the few (the very few) friends I like, for that is the point, the single point, I now aim at: though I know the generality of the world, who are unacquainted with my intentions and views, think the very reverse of this character belongs to me.'

In the more private life, the character of the bishop was more amiable; he seems to have been an affectionate husband, a fond father, and a sincere friend. The expression concerning Pope 'mens curva in corpore curvo,' may have been the accidental effusion of spleen or petulance. Perhaps it may have been deserved; for sincerity seems not to have been the most shining quality of the poet. But in general, he writes to him with the fullest affection, and the most unbounded confidence. The sincerity of Dr. Atterbury has received another wound, and, in our opinion, an unjust one, by the construction of a passage in one of the letters, written during

his

his exile, where he expresses his fondness for the constitution of his own country. It is well known that the Pretender always gave his friends the strongest assurances of his adhering inviolably to the English constitution, and of making no change in the established religion. The one would have necessarily followed the other; and the man, whom no promises of honour or advantage were able to detach from the latter, could not imagine that by the restoration of the lineal successor, the former would have been in danger. It is, indeed, highly probable, that Atterbury was deceived; and in that case, both the one and the other would have been involved in one common ruin.

The religion of the bishop has been also censured, for many reasons, and lately, on account of a story preserved by Dr. Maty, in his Memoirs of Lord Chesterfield. These letters, however, generally contradict this opinion; and we cannot more effectually combat it than in the words of an accurate and attentive correspondent of the editor.

'Dear Sir,   South Molton, Nov. 12, 1782.

'THE following anecdote was first communicated to the public by the late Dr. Maty, on the credit of lord Chesterfield: "I went (said lord Chesterfield) to Mr. Pope, one morning, at Twickenham, and found a large folio Bible, with gilt clasps, lying before him upon his table; and, as I knew his way of thinking upon that book, I asked him jocosely, if he was going to write an answer to it. It is a present, said he, or rather a legacy, from my old friend the bishop of Rochester. I went to take my leave of him yesterday in the Tower, where I saw this Bible upon his table. After the first compliments, the bishop said to me, "My friend Pope, considering your infirmities, and my age and exile, it is not likely that we should ever meet again; and therefore I give you this legacy to remember me by it. Take it home with you, and let me advise you to abide by it."—"Does your lordship abide by it yourself?" "I do."—"If you do, my lord, it is but lately. May I beg to know what new light or arguments have prevailed with you now to entertain an opinion so contrary to that, which you entertained of that book all the former part of your life?" The bishop replied, "We have not time to talk of these things; but take home the book: I will abide by it, and I recommend you to do so too, and so God bless you!"' Dr. Warton hath revived this story, which he justly calls an uncommon one, in his last Essay on the Genius and Writings of Pope. It was indeed very uncommon; and I have my reasons for thinking it equally groundless and invidious. Dr. Warton, though he retails the story from Maty's Memoirs, yet candidly acknowleges that it ought not to be implicitly relied on. That this caution was not unnecessary will, I apprehend, be sufficiently obvious, from the following comparison between the date of the story, itself and Mr. Pope's letters to the bishop.

'According to lord Chesterfield's account, this remarkable piece of conversation took place but a few days before the bishop went into exile; and it is insinuated that Mr. Pope, till that period, had not even entertained the slightest suspicion of his friend's reverence for the Bible: nay, it is asserted, that the very recommendation of it from a quarter so unexpected staggered Mr. Pope to such a degree, that, in a mingled vein of raillery and seriousness, he was very eager to know the grounds and reasons of the bishop's change of sentiment.

'Unfortunately for the credit of lord Chesterfield and his story, there is a letter on record that was written nine months before this pretended dialogue took place, in which Mr. Pope seriously acknowleged the bishop's piety and generosity in interesting himself so zealously and affectionately in matters which immediately related to his improvement in the knowlege of the Holy Scriptures. The passage I refer to is a very remarkable one; and you will find it in a letter dated July 27, 1722. It appears undeniably from this letter, that the bishop had earnestly recommended to Mr. Pope the study of the Bible, and had softened his zeal with an unusual urbanity and courtesy, in order to avoid the imputation of ill-breeding, and remove all occasion of disgust from a mind so "tremblingly alive" as Mr. Pope's. I will transcribe the passage at large. "I ought first to prepare my mind for a better knowlege even of good profane writers, especially the moralists, &c. before I can be worthy of tasting that supreme of books, and sublime of all writings, in which, as in all the intermediate ones, you may (if your friendship and charity towards me continue so far) be the best guide to, Yours, A. Pope."

'The last letter of Mr. Pope to the bishop, previous to his going into exile, was written (as you observe) very early in June, 1723. It must have been about this time that Pope paid his farewell visit to the bishop in the Tower. But whether such a conversation as that which hath been pretended actually took place, may be left to the determination of every man of common sense, after comparing lord Chesterfield's anecdote with Mr. Pope's letter.

'There must have been a mistake, or a wilful misrepresentation, somewhere. To determine its origin, or to mark minutely the various degrees of its progress, till it issued forth into calumny and falshood, is impossible. I have simply stated matters of fact as they are recorded, and leave it to your readers to settle other points, not quite so obvious and indisputable, as they may think fit. My motives in this very plain relation arose from an honest wish to remove unmerited obloquy from the dead. I should sincerely rejoice if the cloud, which in other respects still shades the character of this ingenious prelate, could be removed with equal facility and success. I am, dear sir, your faithful, humble servant,

SAMUEL BADCOCK.'

The

The literary character of Dr. Atterbury is sufficiently established. Mr. Nichols has preserved all the miscellaneous pieces which have been attributed to him, and they seem entirely to support what has already been advanced. Though despotic in his general temper, in letters he considered himself as a member of a republic; and of his candour and moderation in literature, these volumes afford repeated examples. Though not adorned with those original talents, which might have permitted us to style him a man of genius, he possessed extensive learning and great discernment. His language particularly united strength and elegance; but the former, in his political and controversial pieces, generally predominated. His Latin was elegant and classical; but his lighter poetical compositions wanted a taste and levity suited to the subject. They exhibit Hercules playing with a lap-dog, rather than combating with a lion; or wielding the distaff instead of a club. His taste, in general, was neither exact or refined; and, we fear, his noted criticism on the character of Iapis will be considered as a proof also, of failing judgement. But we cannot conclude our account without acknowledging, that the variety of literary remarks in these letters have afforded us considerable entertainment; and that the bishop's compositions, particularly during his exile, are both instructive and entertaining. The letters of his friends are often humorous and agreeable; and the separate pieces, which relate to Dr. Atterbury, are sometimes valuable for their intrinsic merit.

First Lines of the Practice of Physic, for the Use of Students in the University of Edinburgh. By William Cullen, M. D. & P. Vol. II. and III. 10s. 8vo. Johnson.

THOUGH we have felt some little anxiety at the delay of the slowly succeeding volumes of our respectable professor, we ought not to complain, since the necessary avocations of a precarious profession, the duty of his station, and his declining years, which require relaxation, may have prevented him from prosecuting a work whose difficulty would be felt even by the readiness and activity of a more early period*. In the second volume Dr. Cullen pursues his account of the Exanthemata, the Hæmorrhagies, and Profluvia. Of his opinions on each subject we shall give some account, in their proper order.

The order of exanthemata is almost strictly natural. It is only deficient by its comprehending diseases in which the

---

* See Crit. Rev. vol. xliii. p. 55, 131, for an account of the first volume.

matter

matter producing fever is sometimes received from *with-out*, and sometimes generated *in* the body. But this flight exception seems very immaterial, for the eruptions are generally subsequent to, and often in consequence of, the fever. The author first treats of erysipelas, as a general disorder. He describes it in the usual way, and recommends the application of dry powders only. The delirium and coma are, he thinks, seldom the effects of a metastasis, for the external inflammation does not disappear when they come on. The nature of the disease is commonly inflammatory, and Dr. Cullen doubts if it should be separated from phlegmasiæ. This opinion is probably the consequence of his practising in a northern climate, and his antiphlogistic method may be injurious in other situations: he indeed candidly allows, that it may be sometimes attended with putrid fever, and require other treatment; but, as these cases have not fallen under his observation, he does not enlarge on the subject.

On the plague we cannot expect much new information; but the method which he recommends for the prevention of the disease is so rational, and some of his rules apply so accurately to other infectious disorders, that we cannot resist the temptation of inserting it.

‘ With respect to the prevention: as we are firmly persuaded that the disease never arises in the northern parts of Europe, but in consequence of its being imported from some other country, so the first measure necessary, is the magistrate's taking care to prevent the importation; and this may generally be done by a due attention to bills of health, and to the proper performance of quarantains.

‘ With respect to the latter, we are persuaded, that the quarantain of persons may safely be much less than forty days; and if this were allowed, the execution of the quarantain would be more exact and certain, as the temptation to break it would be, in a great measure, removed.

‘ With respect to the quarantain of goods. it cannot be perfect, unless the suspected goods be unpacked, and duly ventilated, as well as the other means employed for correcting the infection they may carry; and if all this were properly done, it is probable that the time commonly prescribed for the quarantain of goods might also be shortened.

‘ A second measure, in the way of prevention, becomes requisite, when an infection has reached and prevailed in any place, to prevent that infection from spreading into other places. This can be done only by preventing the inhabitants, or the goods of any infected place, from going out of it till they have undergone a proper quarantain.

‘ The third measure for prevention, to be employed with great care, is to hinder the infection from spreading among the inhabi-

bitants

bitants of the place in which it has arisen. The measures necessary for this are to be directed by the doctrine already laid down; and from that doctrine we infer, that all persons who can avoid any near communication with infected persons or goods, may be saved from the infection.

' For avoiding such communication, a great deal may be done by the magistrate, 1. By allowing as many of the inhabitants as are free from the infection, and not necessary to the service of the place, to go out of it; 2. By discharging all assemblies, or unnecessary intercourse of the people; 3. By rendering some necessary communications to be performed without contact; 4. By making such arrangements and provisions as may render it easy for the families remaining to shut themselves up in their own houses; 5. By allowing persons to quit houses in which an infection appears, upon condition that they go into lazarettos; 6. By ventilating and purifying or destroying, at the public expence, all infected goods: lastly, By avoiding hospitals, and providing separate apartments for infected persons.

' The execution of these measures will require great authority, and much vigilance and attention, on the part of the magistrate; but it is not our province to enter into any detail on this subject of the public police.

' The fourth and last part of the business of prevention respects the conduct of persons necessarily remaining in infected places, especially of those obliged to have some communication with persons infected.

' Of those obliged to remain in infected places, but not obliged to have any near communication with the sick, they may be preserved by avoiding all near communication with other persons, or their goods; and, it is probable, that a small distance will answer the purpose, if, at the same time, there be no streams of air to carry the effluvia of persons, or goods, to some distance.

' For those who are necessarily obliged to have a near communication with the sick, it is proper to let them know, that some of the most powerful do not operate but when the bodies of men exposed to the contagion are in certain circumstances, which render them more liable to be affected by it: or, when certain causes concur to excite the power of it, and, therefore, by avoiding these circumstances and causes, they may often escape infection.

' The bodies of men are especially liable to be affected by contagions, when they are any how considerably weakened, as they may be by want of food, and even by a scanty diet, or one of little nourishment; by intemperance in drinking, which, when the stupor of intoxication is over, leaves the body in a weakened state; by excess in venery; by great fatigue; or, by any considerable evacuation.

' The causes which, concurring with contagion, render it more certainly active, are cold, fear, and full living.

' The several means, therefore, of avoiding or guarding against the action of cold are to be carefully studied.

' Against

' Against fear the mind is to be fortified as well as possible ; by insuring a favourable idea of the power of preservative means ; by destroying the opinion of the incurable nature of the disease ; by occupying mens minds with business or labour ; and, avoiding all objects of fear, as funerals, passing bells, and any notice of the death of particular friends.

' A full diet of animal food increases the irritability of the body, and favours the operation of contagion, and indigestion, whether from the quantity or quality of the food, has the same effect.

' Besides giving attention to obviate the several circumstances which favour the operation of contagion, it is probable, that some means may be employed for strengthening the bodies of men, and thereby enabling them to resist contagion.

' For this purpose it is probable, that the moderate use of wine, or of spirituous liquors, may have a good effect.

' It is probable also, that exercise, when it can be employed, if so moderate as to be neither heating nor fatiguing to the body, may be employed with advantage.

' Persons who have tried cold bathing, and commonly feel invigorating effects from it, if they are any ways secure against having already received infection, may possibly be enabled to resist it by the use of the cold bath.

' It is probable, that some medicines, also, may be useful in enabling men to resist infection ; but, amongst these, we can hardly admit the numerous alexipharmics formerly proposed, or, at least, very few of them, and those only of tonic power. Amongst these last we reckon the Peruvian bark ; and it is, perhaps, the most effectual. If any thing is to be expected from antiseptics, I think camphire, whether internally or externally employed, is one of the most promising.

' Every person is to be indulged in the use of any means of preservation, which he has conceived a good opinion of, whether it be a charm, or a medicine, if the latter be not directly hurtful.

' Whether issues be useful in preserving from, or in moderating the effects of contagion, I cannot determine from the observations I have yet read.

' As neither the atmosphere, in general, nor any considerable portion of it, are tainted or impregnated with the matter of contagion, so the lighting of fires over a great part of the infected city, or other general fumigations, in the open air, are of no use for preventing the disease, and may perhaps be hurtful.

' It would probably contribute much to check the progress of infection, if the poor were enjoined to make a frequent change of cloathing, and were suitably provided for that purpose ; and if they were, at the same time, induced to make a frequent ventilation of their houses and furniture.'

The small pox are considered at a great length ; and we receive a full examination of the circumstances which may render the inoculated small pox more mild than the natural ; but, that, though we would refer the reader to this very exact and accurate difcuffion, yet we do not find fufficient novelty to induce us to prefent our readers with any part of it.

The chicken pox and meafles are next confidered. In the latter Dr. Cullen admits of the ufe of opiates for quieting the cough, where there is no great dyfpnœa, and the inflammatory fymptoms have been before diminifhed by bleeding; and, with every other practitioner in the more ufual fpecies of meafles, advifes the antiphlogiftic regimen, in its utmoft ftrictnefs. He is doubtful about the application of cold air, and inclined to think it may be hurtful, in reprefling the eruption and increafing the pneumonic inflammation.

The fcarlet fever is frequently confounded with the ulcerous, fore throat : indeed, in many inftances, they cannot be diftinguifhed ; but Dr. Cullen thinks that they are really and fpecifically different difeafes. He forms this opinion from the following confiderations.

'There is a fcarlet fever entirely free from any infection of the throat, which fometimes prevails as an epidemic ; and therefore there is a fpecific contagion producing a fcarlet eruption without any determination to the throat.

'The fcarlatina, which, from its matter being generally determined to the throat, may be properly termed anginofa, has, in many cafes of the fame epidemic, been without any affection of the throat ; and, therefore, the contagion may be fuppofed to be more efpecially determined to produce the eruption only.

'Though in all the epidemics that I could alledge to be thofe of fcarlatina anginofa, there have been fome cafes which, in the nature of the ulcers, and in other circumftances, exactly refembled the cafes of the cynanche maligna ; yet, I have as conftantly remarked, that thefe cafes have not been above one or two in a hundred, while the reft have all of them been with ulcers of a benign kind, and with circumftances hereafter to be defcribed, fomewhat different from thofe of the cynanche maligna.

'On the other hand, as I have two or three times feen the cynanche maligna epidemically prevailing, fo among the perfons affected, I have feen inftances of cafes as mild as thofe of the Scarlatina Anginofa ufually are ; but here the proportion was reverfed ; and thefe mild cafes were not one fifth of the whole, while the reft were of the putrid and malignant kind.

'It applies to the fame purpofe to obferve, that, of the cynanche maligna, moft of the inftances terminate fatally, while, on the other hand, that is the event of very few of the cafes of the fcarlatina anginofa.'

The fcarlatina is, in our author's opinion, commonly inflammatory, and, in the milder inftances, his treatment of it is fuitable to his opinion of the complaint ; yet, in a few cafes,

C 4 particularly

particularly at its commencement, as an epidemic, it requires the remedies usually adapted to the cynanche maligna.

The miliary fever, in common with every system, has a distinct place; but the professor doubts whether it is an idiopathic disease. The chief symptoms, which have been found to attend it, are very generally those of fevers treated by a warm regimen; and it seems chiefly confined to patients who have suffered great losses of blood: it is therefore a common attendant on the fevers of child-bed, and those which have been attended with other similar evacuations. The chief care of the physician is consequently to prevent it by cool regimen: when it has come on, if the sweats be not critical, Dr. Cullen thinks that they should be stopped; and is even of opinion that the admission of cool air is safe and useful. It is necessary also to add, that the principal disease should be attended to, independent of the cuticular affection.

The urticaria, pemphigus, and aphtha, are shortly discussed, and the reader is chiefly referred to other authors.

The hæmorrhagies are those commonly styled by authors *active*, since these only are febrile diseases. As a natural order, they are very properly connected; indeed all the orders of the first class are seldom very exceptionable. An account of the general symptoms of hæmorrhagies first occur: Dr. Cullen then assigns the cause, viz. an inequality in the distribution of the blood, occasioning a congestion of it in particular parts. Next follow the several circumstances which influence the effusion from the different organs, in the successive periods of human life. The whole is too long for our insertion; but we have no scruple in adding, that we have never seen a more exact, comprehensive, and elegant system. The remote causes and cure of hæmorrhagies are next detailed; and, previous to the cure, Dr. Cullen considers whether, with Stahl, we should leave them to the conduct of nature. On the whole, he thinks that all præternatural hæmorrhagy should, as far as possible, be avoided. The general cure depends on avoiding plethora, by regulating the ingesta and egesta. Blood-letting, except in the emergency of an expected attack, often increases the plethora it was intended to prevent. The evacuation is to be moderated, by avoiding irritation, by refrigerant medicines, particularly acids and nitre, blood-letting, blistering, and astringents: he disapproves of ligatures on the limbs, and questions whether emetics and vomiting contribute to the cure of hæmorrhagies: the most powerful astringents are, he thinks, alum and cold water.

The

The hæmorrhage of the nose is of little consequence, except in the decline of life, when it indicates an apoplectic disposition. The cure affords little subject for remark.

The hæmoptysis is generally important, at least in its consequences. It often arises from a faulty proportion in the capacity or vessels of the lungs to the rest of the body. Our author adds some observations, to determine the source of blood thrown out of the mouth, which will be of service to the practitioner; but, in the cure, we meet with few peculiar remarks.

Though the phthisis scarcely finds a place in the author's system, it is too important to be omitted in a practical course of lectures. Dr. Cullen thinks that it always arises from an inflammation of the lungs; but the arguments of Dr. Reid, as we have already observed, raised in us some doubts, which reflection has rather strengthened than diminished. Dr. Cullen next proceeds to mention the distinguishing characteristics of pus, in opposition to mucus, and gives many circumstances by which the judgment may be assisted in the discrimination. He describes also the attending hectic, and thinks it owing to the acrimony of a vitiated pus, which increases the natural febrile exacerbations, at noon and night. The causes of an abscess in the lungs, and the circumstances which may corrupt the purulent matter, are next fully detailed; and, having considered the various circumstances which may influence both the disease and our opinion of its event, he proceeds to the cure. This depends in a great degree on the causes; but as the most frequent one is a tubercle, to that chiefly the observations of our author are directed. For tubercles, he thinks, a remedy may sometimes be found; but sea-water and mercury, the usual remedies for indurated glands, are, in his opinion, useless or injurious. Myrrh, he thinks, is seldom useful, and sometimes hurtful. The Peruvian bark, though in some cases it has seemed to relieve, yet more frequently fails; and, in the best circumstances, is but a partial palliative.

The hæmorrhois is next treated of, both as a general and topical affection: but, in our author's opinion, Stahl has too frequently considered it in the latter view; it is evident that Dr. Cullen very generally confines himself to the former. He does not think that the swellings are varicous veins, but tumors formed from an effusion of red blood in the cellular texture. The symptoms of piles, however, are not consistent with either of these opinions; we may be allowed to suggest another, which we shall probably, at some future period, have an opportunity of illustrating, viz. that they are the glands which usually separate the mucus, inflamed and enlarged. The
hæmor-

hæmorrhagy is said, by our author, sometimes to proceed from the arteries, and is then distinguished by a febrile state; but he observes that we have no other foundation for determining the source of the discharge. He thinks that females are peculiarly subject to this disease, for various reasons; and we have generally found his opinion supported by experience. In the cure he considers more fully the doctrines of Stahl, who generally trusted the disease to nature, and sometimes even endeavoured to procure it. Dr. Cullen, on the contrary, thinks that its first appearance should be guarded against; and, though it may become habitual, and not to be entirely cured without danger, yet that it may be moderated, and the necessity of it, if possible, superseded. The remedies are not very different from those commonly used.

The menorrhagia affords our author the chief support of his system of hæmorrhagies in general. He gives a very full account of the causes, and the means of relieving the disease, which we are sorry that the extent of this article will not enable us to follow with exactness. The leucorrhœa, which is often the consequence of menorrhagia, is relieved by those remedies which are chiefly calculated to restore the tone of the vessels. Every practitioner, however, is well acquainted with their uncertainty, and has often reason to lament that the most specious promises of authors are seldom supported by the event.

After these disorders Dr. Cullen considers the amenorrhœa, a disease opposite in its nature to those which it accompanies, but connected with the former in the functions which are affected. With amenorrhœa, or *retention* of the menses, the chlorosis is intimately connected; and, in our author's opinion, both are derived from the state of the ovaria, which, at the usual period, are deficient in their powers of exciting the action of the uterine vessels. The cure depends on restoring the tone of the system in general, and exciting the actions of the vessels of the uterus. The suppression is next considered; but we find few remarks sufficiently interesting to induce us to make any extract.

The next order is that of profluvia; and among its diseases the phthisis would probably, with propriety, have been arranged. Indeed he observes, that consumptions more frequently follow hæmoptysis than catarrh; but, in different situations, we are well convinced that he would have found a very different succession. Perhaps a more material reason was, that the diseases of this order are connected, in many cases, by the presence of a specific contagion.

The

The catarrh is seldom dangerous but in its consequences, and when it affects old people. It is not often an object of the practitioner's care, but when it appears, as a very general epidemic, with the name of influenza : under this title it has frequently been confidered in our Journal.

The dysentery is the last disease treated of in this volume. After a general, but exact description, the doctor proceeds to the causes. The remote causes are cold and contagion ; he doubts whether putrid animal effluvia will alone produce it. The proximate cause seems to be a praeternatural constriction of the colon, exciting spasmodic efforts, which are propagated to the rectum, and produce frequent stools, without any discharge of real faeces. The cure consequently consists in removing the constriction above, by gentle laxatives, which will promote a more uniform contraction of the whole canal. The mildest purgatives should be first tried. If these do not succeed, Dr. Cullen recommends emetic tartar, in small doses ; but rhubarb, he thinks, one of the most unfit purgatives for this purpose. Ipecacuanha seems chiefly useful, as it evacuates by stool. Opiates are sometimes used to diminish the griping, but they should not supersede the use of purgatives. The warm bath and blisters also materially assist in relieving the constriction of the colon ; but astringents, in the beginning, are useless. These are the outlines of the cure, but our author adds other particulars, which deserve the attention of the practitioner.

We shall pursue the third volume, just published, in a future Review. To give an extract from a sketch is to delineate the ' shadow of a shade ;' yet our very respectable author should be attended to with more than usual care. His accounts of diseases are often distinguished by an uncommon ingenuity, frequently by novelty, and always by an exact attention to nature, and an acute practical discernment. We have therefore seldom ventured to interpose our opinion ; we would not add to our other defects the imputation of a presuming confidence.

Aurelia ; or, the Contest. An Heroi-Comic Poem, in four Cantos. By the Author of Modern Manners. 4to. 2s 6d. Dodsley.

WE own, that we have been highly entertained by this elegant and poetical Contest ; but, though it possesses much merit, it is not entirely free from faults : some of these are almost unavoidable, from the peculiar delicacy of the subject, and some, we fear, have arisen from a little carelessness in the author.

The

The Mock Heroic muſt be confined by rules as ſtrict as if the 'Stagyrite o'erlooked each line;' for this obvious reaſon, that the pleaſure we receive from it chiefly ariſes from elevating a common ſubject, by heroic language. It has, on this account, all the diſadvantages of a parody; except, that it is not ſo cloſe as a real parody ought to be, and may be occaſionally enlivened by beauties peculiarly its own. If then we conſider this poem by the rules of the Epic, we ſhall ſometimes find it defective; but we would not arraign our author on ſo ſevere a ſtatute. It would be an ungrateful return for the pleaſure which we have received from his work; and we only mention theſe circumſtances to add that, on a careful reviſal, if he thinks it worth his attention, it might eaſily be made to ſatisfy the moſt faſtidious critic, freſh from the ſtudy of Ariſtotle and Boſſu.

It is perhaps a more unfortunate circumſtance, that our poet, in his path, has approached ſo near that of Pope, in the moſt perfect of his works. It has given the air of an imitation, where the author might claim the prize of originality, and degraded the animated obſerver to the rank of an humble copyiſt. The ſpirit Azaël has, indeed, too great a reſemblance to Ariel; and his nature and occupations are not ſufficiently diſcriminated; but the conſtantly varying faſhions, the changes of dreſs and manners, and the ſpirit with which they are deſcribed, add a luſtre even to a ſubject already treated of, and give to the airy nothings of the modern toilet, a local habitation and a name.

The ſtory of a poem, like this, is of little conſequence: the poet muſt raiſe a flame from ſmoke; but we may obſerve, that Aurelia, neglected by Florio, calls in the aid of rouge and coſmetics, to regain the wandering heart from Flavia. Azaël warns her, in a dream, to beware of dancing; but having attracted the attention of Florio, ſhe could not refuſe his requeſt; and, unfortunately, from the heat of the room and the exerciſe, the adventitious roſes and lilies of Aurelia ſuffered a change, which diſcovered the deceit. She is in deſpair at the event, and Azaël flies, for more permanent bluſhes, to the ſeat of Faſhion,—Paris; but, in the mean time, the Genius of Wiſdom appears in a dream, and converts her, from the fluttering, gaudy, and precarious regions of Faſhion, to thoſe of Worth and Virtue.

After a ſenſible introduction, and a deſcription of the ſpirit Azaël, the poem opens with the following elegant lines:

> 'Of Beauty long confin'd in Folly's chain,
> Miſled by Faſhion and her glittering train,
> Of evils ſpringing from that thirſt of praiſe
> Which fires the youthful dames of modern days,
> Which taught them all the various arts they know,
> " Brought Dreſs into the world, and all our woe,"
> I ſing; Ye Nine! the wonderous tale rehearſe,
> And lofty actions ſound in lofty verſe.'

Her firſt dream is full of poetry and fancy: we ſhall need no excuſe for tranſcribing it.

The

Aurelia; or, the Contest.

The sleeping maid her toilet now surveys,
Which taper pins, and sparkling gems displays;
Sudden the gems emit a burning light,
The pins spontaneous rife, and stand upright,
From the blue vase the conscious streams ascend,
And o'er the polish'd stand in fountains bend;
The combs and brushes from the table bound,
The boxes rattle, and the glass turns round;
She starts, some murmuring noise she seems to hear,
And three soft sighs steal gently on her ear;
Amaz'd she sees her crystal mirror show
The perfect image of a dazzling beau,
Who, gazing on her charms, with tender air
And voice melodious, thus address'd the fair.

"O Thou! the joy of every mortal eye,
Bright nymph, sultana, angel, deity!
A captive being in thy glass behold,
And hear his lips the hidden world unfold!
First know, when Death has seiz'd his pallid prey,
And drove the spirit from its house of clay,
Still dregs of sin man's airy substance stain,
And darling vices in the soul remain:
To purge this guilt away great Jove ordains
A tedious bondage, or consuming pains:
Some, clos'd in ice, beneath the northern sky,
Some chain'd in fires, or plung'd in ocean lie;
Some here on earth in various forms remain
Fast bound, and with a second death in vain:
The crafty trader in his warehouse lies,
Clos'd in a ponderous bale of merchandize;
The sleek churchwarden in a poor's-box lives,
And swallows still what liberal Pity gives;
The lawyer, turn'd to parchments, plagues the great
Stirs up dissention and litigious hate;
In golden coins the pinching miser bound,
Like Cæsar shines with regal laurel crown'd;
Serjeants, like rods, the master's hand employ,
And scourge that raw recruit, a truant boy;
While scolds, who once the shell of Discord blew,
Now clos'd in drum-sticks beat the loud tattoo;
Bold quacks, whose nostrums soon our fate decide,
Harden to pills, or into tinctures glide;
Drunkards preserv'd in fiery spirits lie,
And like rare lizards strike the wondering eye;
Gluttons to soups and oily turtles pass,
And the smooth flatterer shines — a looking-glass.

Such once was I, a dangler to the fair;
Still, as a glass, I praise their dress, their air;
I teach them how to make each youth a slave,
And heighten every charm which Nature gave;

That wretched maid who ne'er with me was blest,
Must stay at home, or go abroad undrest,
Ne'er gaze delighted on her blooming face,
And mark each rising morn some novel grace,
Ne'er the dear joy of admiration know,
Ne'er hear a sigh, or view a kneeling beau !—
    While fix'd on earth, o'er all the imprison'd bands
Superior demons wave their ruling wands ;
Of us, that near thy sex in bondage lie,
The great Azäel is the watchful spy ;
He, who of old, as learned rabbins say,
For Naamah forsook the fields of day :
Now round the fair his guardian wings he spreads,
And o'er the toilet fragrant odour sheds,
In thin pomatums thickening oil he pours,
And damag'd rouge to crimson bloom restores.
    At his command behold thy slave appear,
And thus, by me, his friendly counsels hear ;
O ! let not Reason's matron voice control
The gay emotions of thy polish'd soul,
Think not to quit dear Dissipation's bowers,
And waste in lonely wilds thy mournful hours,
But still through flowery paths delighted roam,
Nor bear, for one short night, to stay at home ;
What though one triumph grace a rival name,
A thousand triumphs have secur'd thy fame ;
Go on, nor heed though fops unhurt appear,
Though envious beauties chafe when thou art near ;
Fly to the play, the concert, and the ball,
Be true to Fashion's laws, and conquer all !
But, O ! beware ! nor let thy fancy stray
From her, whom every female should obey,
Still let thy soul her ruling power confess,
Great patroness of arts, and mighty queen of dress."

The modern dress, and the labours of the frifeur, are described in a lively and agreeable manner. The author cannot, in this part, be charged with plagiarism ; and his success sufficiently evinces his powers to be truly original, even when he attempts to bend the bow of Ulysses. The effects of her beauty are described in truly heroic strains.

    ' Ev'n Florio, kindling with the soft alarms,
    Forgot his Paris suit, and Flavia's charms ;
    Aurelia's brighter tints victorious prove,
    For soon he loves—as much as beaus can love !'

But we must not indulge this agreeable labour ; for we *feel* that we must insert the pleasing picture of the Dame of artless Life, represented by the Genius who converts the Heroine to Wisdom. Every reader, whose taste is not wholly depraved by
                                                                    fashion

fashion and by folly, will wish, that the original could be easily
found ; but it will shine more brightly by the contrast ;
' He said, and strait his opening robes reveal
Wide o'er his breast a plate of polish'd steel ;
On whose smooth face Aurelia casts her eyes,
And wondering sees a gorgeous chamber rise ;
The toilet first, in all its pomp array'd,
True to her sex, attracts the sleeping maid :
Transparent gauze enrich'd with spots of gold,
Hangs round the glass in many a studied fold ;
Close by its side another mirror lies,
Which swells each feature to gigantic size,
And shews what specks diminutive disgrace,
What coming pimples threat the beauteous face ;
Two marbled volumes on the toilet lay,
Their slender backs with golden letters gay,
Which words like these reveal in spreading pride,
The Master-piece of Art, and *Beauty's Guide* ;
Loose manuscript receipts around them lie
To bid warts, ring-worms, scurf, and morphews die :
Here, in array, the whole cosmetic band,
Face-papers, wash-balls, creams and tinctures stand,
Sultana water, the Circassian glow,
And the soft bloom of Ninon de l'Enclos.
Now to the bed the virgin turns her eyes,
Where, stretch'd in dirty pomp, a female lies ;
Around her head a circling bandage twin'd ;
Tied with white cords and fix'd with pins behind,
One clotted lump of hair beneath remain'd,
Stiff with hard grease, and all the pillow stain'd ;
Her thick complexion, like the stream that laves
The clay-bound soil when rains disturb the waves,
Look'd dark and muddy ; on her hand she wore
A glove, which seem'd too often worn before.
" Behold," the Genius cried, " a modish dame,
Whose bosom panted for ignoble fame,
The fame of beauty ; still intent to win
By outward charms, the nobler part within
She priz'd, as savage tribes th' unpolish'd gold,
When beads and glass their dazzled eyes behold ;
Tho' Nature gave her many a blooming grace,
The store of Art was ransack'd for her face ;
Now mark the fruit of all her toil and pains,
A sallow hag at thirty she remains,
Unable to forego the daily task,
And shew her well-known face without her mask.'
But now behold a dame of artless life,
Of equal years, a mother and a wife."
Soon as he spoke, the mimic mirror shows
A fair-one hush'd in undisturb'd repose ;

On the plain toilet, with no trophies gay,
Chapone's instructive volume open lay;
Low o'er her forehead, white as Lapland snow,
Her auburn locks in sweet disorder flow,
Nature's soft hands th' untortur'd curls adjust,
Unstain'd with perfum'd grease and colour'd dust;
On her soft cheek the blush of morning glows,
Her ruby lip reveals two pearly rows,
Her bosom, half uncover'd, brings to view
Such tints as Titian's pencil never knew;
While every speaking feature seems to shine
With peace serene, and purity divine."

We may be allowed perhaps to suggest to the author that, if the conversion of Aurelia had been the subject of the poem,—if the Genius of Wisdom had been a more discriminated character, and more frequently opposed to Azäel, it would have given a greater variety to his work, and brought it more nearly to the epic model. The change of fortune is not marked with sufficient distinctness, and the heroine's qualifications are not so striking as to interest us greatly in her favour. The moral is also, in some degree, exceptionable. It seems that Aurelia, like some other virgins, becomes good from despair; and submits to the austerity of a convent, only because she can no longer add to the brilliancy of a palace. We mention these circumstances not to detract from the great merit of the author, but to suggest those minuter particulars which, in our opinion, would contribute to embellish his performance.

The History of Sumatra. (*Concluded, from page* 439.)

AMONG the Sumatrans both sexes have the extraordinary custom of filing and otherwise disfiguring their teeth, which are naturally, on account of the simplicity of their food, very white and beautiful. Many of the women have their teeth rubbed down quite even with the gums, while others form them into points; but they almost universally have them stained of a black colour with the empyreumatic oil of the cocoa-nut shell. The great men sometimes cover the under row with a casing of gold; and we are told that this ornament, contrasted with the black dye, has, by candle-light, a very splendid effect.

Passing over the dress, the habitations, and the domestic economy of the Sumatrans, who, in those articles, generally resemble the other southern nations, we shall proceed to give a brief account of the chief productions of the island. Of these the most important and most abundant is pepper. This is so much the object of the East India Company's trade hither, that they keep it exclusively in their own hands. The pepper-
gardens

gardens are planted in even rows, running parallel and at right angles with each other; and their appearance, which is very beautiful, is rendered more striking by the contrast they exhibit to the wild scenes of nature which surround them. Once in every year a survey of all the pepper-plantations is taken by the Company's European servants. The number of vines in each particular garden is counted; accurate observation is made of its condition; orders are given, where necessary, for farther care, for completion of stipulated quantity, renewals, changes of situation for better soil; and rewards and punishments are distributed to the planters, according as they deserve.

We shall present our readers with Mr. Marsden's explicit and satisfactory information, relative to the culture of this valuable commodity.

' The inhabitants, by the original contracts of the head men with the Company, are obliged to plant a certain number of vines: each family one thousand, and each young unmarried man, five hundred; and, in order to keep up the succession of produce, so soon as their gardens attain to their prime state, they are ordered to prepare others that may begin to bear, as the old ones fall off; but, as this can seldom be enforced till the decline becomes evident, and as young gardens are liable to various accidents, which older ones are exempt from, the succession is rendered incomplete, and the consequence is, that the annual produce of each district fluctuates; and is greater or less in the proportion of the quantity of bearing vines to the whole number. To enter minutely into the detail of this business will not afford much information or entertainment to the generality of readers, who will however be surprized to hear that pepper planting, though scarcely an art, so little skill appears to be employed in its cultivation, is nevertheless a very abstruse science. The profoundest investigations of very able heads have been bestowed on this subject, which took their rise from the censures naturally expressed by the directors at home to the servants abroad, for a supposed mismanagement, when the investment, as it is termed, of pepper decreased in comparison with preceding years, and which the unfavourableness of seasons did not by any means account for satisfactorily. To obviate such charges, it became necessary for the gentlemen who superintended the business to pay attention to and explain the efficient causes which unavoidably occasioned this fluctuation, and to establish general principles of calculation, by which to determine at any time the probable future produce of the different residencies. These will depend upon a knowlege of the medium produce of a determinate number of vines, and the medium number to which this produce is to be applied; both of which are to be ascertained only from a comprehensive view of the subject and a nice discrimination.

Nothing general can be determined from detached instances. It is not the produce of one particular plantation, in one particular stage of bearing, and in one particular season, but the mean produce of all the various classes of bearing vines collectively, drawn from the experience of several years, that can alone be depended on in calculations of this nature. So in regard to the medium number of vines presumed to exist at any residency in a future year, to which the medium produce of a certain number, one thousand, for instance, is to be applied; the quantity of young vines of the first, second, and third year must not be indiscriminately advanced, in their whole extent, to the next annual stage, but a judicious allowance, founded on experience, must be made for the accidents to which, in spite of a resident's utmost care, they will be exposed. Some are lost by neglect or death of the owner; some are destroyed by inundations, others by elephants and wild buffaloes, and some by unfavourable seasons; and from these several considerations, the number of vines will ever be found considerably decreased by the time they have arrived at a bearing state. Another important object of consideration, in these matters, is the comparative state of a residency, at any particular period, with what may be justly considered as its medium state. There must exist a determinate proportion between any number of bearing vines, and such a number of young as are necessary to replace them when they go off, and keep up a regular succession. This will depend in general upon the length of time before they reach a bearing state, and during which they afterwards continue in it. If this certain proportion happens at any time to be disturbed, the produce must become irregular. Thus, if at any period the number of bearing vines shall be found to exceed their just proportion to the total number, the produce at such period is to be considered as above the mean, and a subsequent decrease may be with certainty predicted, and vice versâ. If then this proportion can be known, and the state of population in a residency ascertained, it becomes easy to determine the true medium number of bearing vines in that residency.'

White pepper, we are told, is manufactured by stripping the outer husk or coat from the ripe grains. This was, during centuries, supposed in Europe to have been the produce of a different plant, and to possess qualities superior to the common sort; on the strength of which idea it used to sell, for some time, at the India sales, for treble the price of the black. But it lost this advantage, as soon as it came to be known that the secret depended merely on the art of blanching the common pepper. For this purpose, it is steeped a certain time, about a fortnight, in water, in pits dug for the occasion in the banks of rivers, and sometimes in swamps and stagnant pools; till by swelling it bursts its tegument, from which it is

afterwards

afterwards carefully feparated by drying it in the fun, and rubbing it between the hands.

Mr. Marfden obferves, it has been much difputed, and is ftill undetermined, to which fort of pepper the preference ought to be given. The white pepper has this fuperiority, that it can be made of no other than the beft and foundeft grains, taken at the ftate of perfect maturity. But, on the other hand, it is argued, that by being fuffered to fteep the neceffary time in water, its ftrength is confiderably diminifhed; and that the outer hufk, which is loft by the procefs, has a peculiar flavour diftinct from that of the heart, and though not fo poignant, more aromatic. The white pepper, however, we are informed, ftands the Company in about three times the price of the black; owing to the encouragement they were obliged to give the planters, to induce them to deviate from their accuftomed track; but having been fold a few years ago at an equal, if not fometimes at an inferior rate, orders were fent for reftraining the manufacture to a very fmall quantity.

The feafon of the pepper vines bearing, as well as that of moft other fruits in Sumatra, is fubject to great irregularities, owing, as is conjectured,. to the uncertainty of the monfoons, which are not there fo ftrictly periodical as on the other fide of India. In general, however, the pepper produces two crops in the year; one called the greater crop, about the month of September; the other, called the lefs, or half crop, about the month of March. Sometimes, in particular dif-tricts, they will be employed in gathering it in fmall quantities during the whole year; bloffoms and ripe fruits appearing together on the fame vine; whilft perhaps in others the pro-duce is that year confined to one crop.

The pepper is moftly brought down from the country on rafts, which are ufually compofed of large bamboos. In the more rapid rivers they are fteered both at head and ftern, with a kind of rudder, or rather fkull, having a broad blade fixed in a fork or crutch. Notwithftanding the dexterity of the men, and their judgment in choofing the channel, the rafts are liable to meet with obftruction from large trees and rocks, which, from the violence of the ftream, overfet, and fometimes dafh them to pieces.

Camphor is a commodity for which Sumatra, as well as Borneo, has been in all ages much celebrated. The cam-phor-tree is a native of the northern parts of the ifland only, growing without cultivation in the woods near the fea-coaft, and is equal in height and bulk to the largeft timber-trees, being frequently found upwards of fifteen feet in circumference. The wood is much in efteem for carpenters purpofes, being

eafy

eafy to work, light, durable, and not liable to be injured by infects, particularly by the *coombang*, a fpecies of bee, which, for its faculty of boring timber for its neft, is called in common the *carpenter*.

The camphor, we are informed, does not exfude from the tree, or manifeft any appearance on the outfide; but the natives, from long experience, know whether any is contained within, by ftriking it with a ftick. In that cafe they cut it down, and fplit it with wedges into fmall pieces, finding the camphor in the interftices, in the ftate of a concrete cryftallization. Some have afferted that it is from the old trees alone that this fubftance is procured, and that in the young trees it is in a fluid ftate; but this, Mr. Marfden informs us, he has good authority to pronounce a miftake. The fame kind of tree that produces the fluid does not produce the dry, tranfparent, and fleaky fubftance; and many of the trees afford neither one nor the other.

Benjamin, or benzoin, is produced from a tree which grows in great abundance in the northern parts of the ifland. Mr. Marfden is of opinion that this drug is endowed with far greater medicinal virtues than have yet been difcovered.

The caffia is a coarfe fpecies of cinnamon, which likewife flourifhes chiefly in the northern parts of the ifland. The trees grow from fifty to fixty feet high, with large, fpreading, horizontal branches, almoft as low as the earth. No pains is beftowed on the cultivation of the caffia. The bark, which is the part in ufe, is commonly taken from fuch of the trees as are a foot or eighteen inches diameter. The difference of foil and fituation alters confiderably the value of the bark. Mr. Marfden informs us he has been affured by a perfon of extenfive knowlege, that the caffia produced in Sumatra is from the fame tree which yields the true cinnamon, and that the apparent difference arifes from the lefs judicious manner of quilling it.

In almoft every part of Sumatra two fpecies of cotton are cultivated, namely, the annual fort, and the fhrub cotton. The cotton procured from both appears to be of very good quality, and might, with encouragement, be obtained in any quantities; but the natives raife no more than is neceffary for their own domeftic manufactures. The filk cotton is alfo to be met with in every village. This, we are told, is, to appearance, one of the moft beautiful raw materials the hand of nature has prefented. Its finenefs, glofs, and delicate foftnefs, render it, to the fight and touch, much fuperior to the labour of the filk-worm; but, owing to the fhortnefs and brittlenefs of the ftaple, it is efteemed unfit for the reel and

boom,

loom, and is only applied to the unworthy purpofe of ftuffing pillows and mattraffes. Mr. Marfden thinks it has not undergone a fair trial in the hands of our ingenious artifts, and that we may yet fee it converted into a valuable manufacture. It grows in pods, from four to fix inches long, which burft open when ripe.

Coffee-trees are univerfally planted in Sumatra; but the fruit-proves not of very good quality, owing entirely, as is fuppofed, to want of fkill in the management of them. The plants are difpofed too clofe to each other, and are fo much overfhaded by other trees, that the fun cannot penetrate to the fruit. The berries likewife are gathered whilft red, which is before they have arrived at a due degree of maturity, and which the Arabs always permit them to attain, efteeming it effential to the goodnefs of the coffee,

The forefts of Sumatra contain a great variety of valuable fpecies of wood, which, it is conjectured, might, if properly attended to, be turned to account.

Befides almoft inexhauftible treafures in the vegetable kingdom, Sumatra has many other commodities of great value, among which are gold, tin, and other metals.

Our author next gives an account of the arts and manufactures of the Sumatrans. One of the principal of thefe, and which has been celebrated for its beautiful appearance, is the fine gold and filver fillagree; but it is, ftrictly fpeaking, the work of the Malay, and not of the original inhabitants of the ifland.

Mr. Marfden, after giving a general account of the languages and alphabets of the Sumatrans, proceeds to exhibit a comparative ftate of thofe iflanders, with refpect to their advancement in the arts of civil fociety. For this purpofe he delivers a particular detail of their government, laws, cuftoms, religion, &c. in all which he fhews a great acquaintance with the fubject. The work affords extenfive information, relative not only to the natural hiftory of Sumatra, but to the political ftate of the inhabitants; and the author has, more than is ufual in productions of this kind, thrown out fuch hints and obfervations, as, confidering his intimate knowlege of circumftances, may, we doubt not, be converted to great advantage by thofe who have the direction of the commerce with this valuable fouthern ifland.

Bibliotheca Topographica Britannica. No. XI. Containing the History and Antiquities of Croyland-Abbey, in the County of Lincoln. 4to. 7s. 6d. Nichols.

THIS Number contains the history and antiquities of Croyland abbey, and all the remaining charters and records relative to that religious foundation, with a view of the bridge, the church, &c.

Croyland is situated in the midst of a vast fenny level, on the south side of Lincolnshire. It is famous for its ancient abbey, and other monuments of antiquity. In the reign of Kenred, king of Mercia, between the years 704 and 709, Guthlac, a young man of a noble family, who had devoted himself to a monastic life, came hither, and built himself a miserable hut. In this solitude he was visited by Ethelbald, afterwards king, but then an outlaw. The prince received so much consolation from his counsel and encouragement, that he vowed, if he came to the throne, he would found a monastery on this very spot to the honour of God and Guthlac. In the year 716, when he became king of Mercia, though Guthlac was dead, he religiously performed his vow. The place where the monastery was erected was a horrid scene of bogs and brambles. The foundation was laid on piles driven into the ground, which was rendered firm and solid by earth and gravel brought from a considerable distance. The king endowed it with great liberality, granting it all the lands around it for several miles. In a short time miracles were said to be wrought at the tomb of St. Guthlac. This, according to the credulity and superstition of those ages, brought an influx of wealth to the shrine. In 868 the monastery was plundered by the Danes. About the year 966, lord Turketyl, a near relation of king Edward, accepting of the abbacy, made great additions to the original establishment, and raised it to a considerable degree of opulence and splendor. In 1075 Ingulph was appointed abbot, and was extremely active in settling the rights, and improving the state of the monastery. But in the year 1091 he had the mortification to see the whole range of buildings, the church, the chapter-house, the dormitory, the refectory, the infirmary, the library, &c. totally destroyed by fire. Ingulph was rebuilding and refurnishing the abbey when he died in 1109, and the care of it devolved upon his successor Joffrid, under whose administration the work was pursued with unremitted ardor. Some time between the years 1142 and 1170, the church with the offices was again burnt down : but the greatest part of it was soon afterwards rebuilt in a magnificent manner. In 1281 Richard

Richard Croyland, a native of the town, was elected to the abbacy, and began to rebuild the east end of the church with great expence, with a beauty and elegance superior to all the churches in the province. Between the years 1412 and 1427, William de Croyland, master of the works, under the direction of Richard Upton, abbot, built the north and south cross ailes of the choir, the lady chapel on the north side, the beautiful refectory house, and the lower part of the nave of the church to the west, and both its ailes, with their chapels. At present the north aile serves for the parish church. The west front, which proclaims the elegance of the builders, and is probably that built with the lower part of the nave and its ailes by William de Croyland above mentioned, is adorned with rows of most elegant and correct statues, representing, or supposed to represent, Adam and Eve, the Virgin Mary, the Apostles, St. Guthlac, St. Pega, Guthlac's Sister, king Ethelbald, Turketyl, Ingulph, and other saints, patrons, and benefactors. Mr. Willis and Dr. Stukeley say, all these groupes were formerly gilded. Some faint traces of colours may still be distinguished. The revenues of this abbey at the dissolution were valued at 1083l. 15s. 10d. or, 1217l. 5s. 11d. In 1643 the church was made a garrison for the king's forces. From this application of it we may date the ruin of what then remained. ' All the eastern part of the body of the church, says Dr. Stukeley, is entirely erazed to the foundation; and the ashes, as well as tombs, of an infinite number of illustrious personages, kings, abbots, lords, knights, &c. there hoping to repose, are dispersed, to the irreparable damage of English history. The monastic buildings, cloisters, hall, abbot's lodgings, and the like, which, no doubt, were very fine, are absolutely demolished, no traces of them being left, by which their extent may be guessed at. In the northwest corner of the church stands a strong tower, with a very obtuse spire, and a ring of small bells.' Our author, having described the remains of the ancient church, subjoins the following remark: ' Such is the present appearance of this once magnificent structure, still, in its ruins, the wonder of travellers. The ill-judged dilapidation of a large buttress on the south side, for materials to form buttresses to prop the present church, has occasioned an alarming settlement of the beautiful front. One of the upper south windows was on the point of being hauled down, had not the rope broken. One of the noble south pillars now gapes with a fearful crack, and large masses of stones continually crumble, or are blown down from the top. The present rector (the Rev. Mr. Moor Scribo) has influence enough to check further demolition; and may

his

his influence, or influence like his, long prevail!' We may add, that, as the town of Croyland has derived all its fame, and probably its very existence from the abbey, every principle of gratitude and piety should restrain such Goths and Vandals as bricklayers, surveyors, and churchwardens, from laying their impious hands on those venerable walls, and the reverend images of their ancient founders and benefactors. The bridge at Croyland is likewise one of the greatest curiosities in Britain, if not in Europe. It is of a triangular form, rising from three segments of a circle, and meeting in a point at the top. It seems to have been built under the direction of the abbots, rather to excite admiration, and furnish a pretence for granting indulgences, and collecting money, than for any real use; for, though it stands in a bog, and must have cost a vast sum, yet it is so steep in its ascent and descent, that neither carriages nor horsemen can pass over it. The rivers Nyne and Welland, and a stream called Catwater, on the sides of which the town is built, all meet under the great arch; and there forming one river, flow from thence through Spalding into the sea. The town consists of three *principal* streets, built on piles, and separated by three streams: these lead to the bridge, and there is no getting to them but by two narrow causeways. It stands not exactly in the centre of the north street, owing to the impossibility of using it for horses or carriages. On the south-west wing, which faces the London road, is placed, in a sitting posture, a stately image of king Ethelbald, founder of the abbey. This bridge is mentioned in the charter of Edred, king of Britain, in the year 943—' à ponte de Croyland triangulo.' It was most probably built in the time of king Ethelbald, who reigned from 716 to 755. [There is a small erratum in the work before us at p. 106, where the author says, Ethelbald was upon the throne from 856 to 860, inadvertently taking the grandson of Egbert for one of the kings of Mercia.]

Ingulph, who has left us an historical account of Croyland abbey, was born in London, and educated at Westminster and Oxford. He was for some time secretary to William duke of Normandy; and went to the Holy Land in company with several of the duke's court. On his return he took the vow, and was prior of the abbey of Fontanel in Normandy. When William embarked for the conquest of England, Ingulph brought him twelve young horsemen from the abbot; and on the deposition of Ulketul, abbot of Croyland, the conqueror sent for him to fill his place. He was appointed in 1075, and held his office till his death in 1109. "The relation which he bore to king William does manifestly bias him, says bishop Nicol-

Nicolfon, in the ill account he gives of Harrold.' He compiled his history, he tells us, from the most authentic documents he could meet with; the collections of the five senior brethren of the house; the life of abbot Turketyl, their first restorer, by his relation and successor Egelric; and the rest, including a period of little more than a century, from contemporary information. He concluded it at the year 1089, though he lived twenty years afterwards. The history was continued by Peter de Blois, archdeacon of London, to the year 1117. Peter died about 1200. Who took it up after Blesensis is not certain. It begins in the reign of Stephen, 1152, and goes on to 1486, 1 Hen. VII.

Ingulph was first published, with others of our historians, in 1596, and reprinted at Francfort, 1601, fol. by fir Henry Saville. Saville does not tell us where he had his manuscript, whether from the Cotton library*, Otho, B. xiii. z. since burnt, or from some other place. As it was imperfect in several parts, these defects were supplied from a manuscript in the possession of Mr. Marsham, eldest son of fir John Marsham, in a new edition of it by Mr. Fulman, among the Rerum Anglicarum Scriptores Veteres, Oxon. 1684, fol.

The present work is compiled from the printed accounts of this famous abbey by Ingulph and his continuators, from authentic manuscripts and registers of the abbey, from information received from the present rector, and from observations made upon the spot by former antiquaries, and by the editor, the very learned and accurate Mr. Gough.

An Historical View of the State of the Unitarian Doctrine and Worship, from the Reformation to our own Times. By Theophilus Lindsey, A. M. 8vo. 6s. Johnson.

IN a small tract intitled the Catechist, which was published in 1781, Mr. Lindsey endeavoured to shew, that the one Almighty Father of the Universe is the only God of Christians.' In a second part, which is intended to follow, he proposes to consider all the passages of scripture, supposed to favour the worship of Jesus Christ, and the Holy Spirit. This work is calculated to serve the same design. The author has, therefore, taken many opportunities to illustrate different portions of the sacred writings, which relate to this great subject; though his principal scheme is to exhibit an historical view of the state of the unitarian doctrine and worship, from the reformation to our own times.

---

* Founded about 1600.

The

The unitarian doctrine, he observes, was in a promising state in England at the time of the Reformation ; but many violent means were used to suppress it. In his account of that period, he has given us, from Strype, archdeacon Philpot's very singular Apology for spitting upon an Arian, with many observations on the intemperate zeal of its author ; he has likewise considered at large the sentiments and conduct of Socinus, relative to the present subject ; his controversy with Francis Davides, his harsh behaviour to Palæologus, his rigour in insisting on the worship of Christ, &c.

The opinion which Socinus maintained was, ' That in condescension to human weakness, in order that mankind might have one of their own brethren more upon a level with them, to whom they might have recourse in their straits and necessities, Almighty God, for his eminent virtues, had conferred upon Jesus, the son of Mary, some years after he was born, a high divine power, lordship, and dominion, for the government of the Christian world only, and had qualified him to hear, and to answer the prayers of his followers, in such matters as related to the cause of the Gospel.' To this reasoning Davides replied in general, ' That Socinus had mistaken the sense of the sacred writers, in those passages which he cited in support of his hypothesis ; and moreover, granting that such a perpetual power and government over Christians had been intrusted to Christ, it will by no means follow, that their prayers ought to be addressed to him on that account : for to constitute him an object of prayer, there needs an express command of Almighty God. But no authority of this kind is pretended.'

In this chapter the author has made some remarks on a charge by the late Bishop Newton, intitled a Dissuasive against Schism. From which we shall extract the following passage, as it may suggest a useful lesson to controversial writers, and serve to guard them against the use of intemperate language.

The bishop having produced some texts of scripture, in which our Saviour speaks of his having been in glory before the world was, of his coming down from heaven, of all men honouring the Son as they honour the Father, of his being the first and the last, &c. goes on in this manner : ' Nothing could justify such language, but its being the voice of a God, and not of a man. In any mere man it would be insufferable ; and such a man, so presumptuously affecting godhead, we could never with any reason believe to be a messenger of God, and a teacher of righteousness ; but must necessarily look upon him with abhorrence, as a gross impostor, or foul blasphemer, or downright madman at best. It is impossible therefore for

any

any consistent Socinian to be a true Christian.'—Mr. Lindsey proposes what he conceives to be the true import of such expressions, and adds, ' It is happy for us, that, whether we be true Christians or not, is not to be decided by each other's partial and prejudiced verdicts, but at a higher and more equitable tribunal. But whatever liberties men may think themselves allowed to take in censuring their fellow Christians, it is wholly unaccountable how they can bring themselves to use such terms as these, concerning the blessed Jesus ; that he must be thus undervalued and set at nought, as a gross impostor, or foul blasphemer, or downright madman, if he be not what some men take him to be, and do not come up to all that their warm imaginations have figured to themselves concerning him.'

In treating of the state of the unitarian doctrine, in the reign of Queen Elizabeth and the Stuarts, the author observes, that Elizabeth has for ever tarnished her memory by burning alive some unhappy Hollanders, Anabaptists, who had taken refuge in this kingdom ; and James, by his still more cool and wanton savageness towards Legatt and Wightman, and a Spanish unitarian, who happened unfortunately to be in his dominions, and within his reach.—Legatt was burnt in Smithfield, and Wightman at Litchfield, in 1611, for maintaining the divine unity.

From this time few or none ventured to avow and publish the same dangerous doctrine, till Mr. John Biddle rose up in its defence, towards the latter part of the reign of Charles I. Biddle narrowly escaped being burned by the assembly of Presbyterian divines, and died in prison in 1662. His disciple, Mr. Thomas Firmin, was a professed unitarian, but attended the trinitarian worship.

Our author, when he comes to the present century, gives us some account of the most eminent men, who have favoured the unitarian doctrine, some by professing the Arian, and others the Socinian scheme. In this list we find the names of Mr. Emlyn, Mr. W. Whiston, Dr. Samuel Clarke, Bishop Hoadly, Sir Isaac Newton, Abraham Tucker, Esq. of Beachworth Castle, near Darking, in Surry, author of the Light of Nature pursued†, and some others. Among those worthies, as he styles them, who have quitted the church of England, on account of the trinitarian forms of public worship, are the late Dr. Robertson, of Wolverhampton, Dr. John Jebb, Dr. Chambers, late rector of Achurch, in Northamptonshire, Mr. Tyrrwhit, of Jesus College, Cambridge, Mr. Evanson, Mr. Maty,

† Mr. Tucker died in 1776.

Mr.

Mr. Harries, late rector of Hanwood, near Shrewsbury, Dr. Difney, and a society of Unitarian Christians at Montrose, in Scotland.

In his account of Dr. Clarke, our author, on the testimony of Mr. Emlyn, Bishop Hoadly, &c. relates an idle story, propagated by Mr. Ramfay, and mentioned by Dr. Warton, in his Effay on the Genius and Writings of Pope, vol. ii. p. 121. concerning the doctor's repentance fome little time before his death, for having publifhed his book on the Trinity. In our Review for August, 1772, we have inferted a letter, written by Mr. Clarke, fon of Dr. Clarke, pofitively denying the truth of the foregoing report, which, indeed, is in itfelf utterly improbable.

As the Trinitarian Controverfy, including that part of it which relates to the object of divine worfhip, has been difcuffed by many learned writers, and occupies a thoufand volumes, we fhall not enlarge upon it in this place, but refer thofe readers, who wifh to know more of the fubject, to Mr. Lindfey's Hiftorical View. In this work they will find many ingenious criticifms, and undoubted proofs of the author's piety, induftry, and learning. The unitarian fcheme, let its merits be what they will, is conducted by this writer with decency and prudence. He never injures his caufe, like Socinus and many other controvertialifts, by intemperate zeal or paffionate invectives. Yet, notwithftanding all that he himfelf, his predeceffors, and his affociates, have advanced, every wife man will be extremely cautious in forming fchemes of feparation from the eftablifhed church. He will reflect, that infallibility is not to be expected in this imperfect ftate; that we are often deceived by the moft promifing appearances; that many doctrines, which have been for a time applauded and admired, have been afterwards found erroneous; and that, in a cafe like the prefent, piety, diffidence, and humility, are more amiable and meritorious qualities, than a hafty and pofitive fpirit of enterprize and innovation†.

Some of our readers will be furprifed, that the name of Dr. Prieftley does not appear in the foregoing lift of worthies, efpecially when they confider the diftinguifhed zeal of that writer, in favour of the unitarian doctrine, expreffed in various parts of his Opus Palmarium, the Hiftory of the Corruptions of Chriftianity. Our author however affigns a reafon for this omiffion, by obferving, that he would have fpoken of that work more at large, if lefs had been faid of himfelf in the dedicatory part of it.

† See the arguments for a feparation confidered, in our Review for Jan. 1778, p. 1.

Lectures on Rhetoric and Belles Lettres. In Two Volumes. By Hugh Blair, D. D. 4to. 1l. 16s. in Boards. Cadell.

THE author informs us, that he began to read these Lectures in the university of Edinburgh, in 1759; that several imperfect copies of them, composed of notes taken by students who had heard them read, were circulated*; and that he was induced to publish them, to prevent their being sent into the world under some defective or erroneous form.

In composing them, he says, he thought it his duty, as a public professor, to communicate to his pupils, not merely what was new, but what might be useful, from whatever quarter it came. He therefore freely acknowleges, that he has sometimes availed himself of the ideas and reflections of others, as far as he thought them proper to be adopted.

Before these Lectures appeared, we had many publications on subjects of oratory, criticism, and polite literature; such as Trapp's Prelections, Felton on the Classics, Miller's Translation of Batteux's Principles of Literature, Rollin on the Belles Lettres, Ward's System of Oratory, Lawson's Lectures on Oratory, Priestley's on Oratory and Criticism, lord Kaimes's Elements of Criticism, Campbell's Philosophy of Rhetoric, and others, which have their respective merits. But to such persons as are studying to cultivate their taste, to form their style, or to prepare themselves for public speaking or composition, the present lectures will afford a more comprehensive view of what relates to these subject than is to be received from any one book in our language.

In the first lecture the author sets out with some general observations on the study of eloquence and composition; in the second, he enters into some inquiries concerning taste.

Taste, he tells us, may be defined, ' the power of receiving pleasure from the beauties of nature and of art.'

Is this, we beg leave to ask, a just and adequate definition of taste? May not a stupid or an ignorant person, totally destitute of this quality, derive a transient and unaccountable *pleasure* from the beauties of nature and art? Does not taste imply discernment and discrimination, or a power of acutely and accurately distinguishing what is beautiful from what is inelegant, fantastic, absurd, or unnatural? If so, taste cannot be said to consist in the mere power of receiving *pleasure* from the beauties of nature and art.

' The first question, continues the author, which occurs concerning taste, is, whether it is to be considered as an internal

---

* See Biographia Britannica, Art. ADDISON.

sense,

sense, or as an exertion of reason?'—In answer to this enquiry, he says, ' Though taste, beyond doubt, be ultimately founded on a natural and instinctive sensibility to beauty, yet reason assists taste in many of its operations, and serves to enlarge its power.'

As we are no advocates for the doctrine of innate ideas, we cannot agree with our author, when he derives taste from feeling, from a certain natural and instinctive sensibility, and the like unaccountable principles. For what is taste, exclusive of understanding and reason? or, where shall we find any instinctive feelings, worthy of being distinguished by the name of taste, where reason does not operate? The truth is, the instantaneous decisions of reason, founded on experience, observation, and reflection, are frequently, but erroneously, considered as feeling and instinct.

Lect. III. *Of Criticism, Genius, Pleasures of Taste, and Sublimity of Objects.*—' True criticism, our author says, is the application of taste and of good sense to the several fine arts. The object which it proposes is, to distinguish what is beautiful and what is faulty in every performance. As no human genius is perfect, there is no writer but may receive assistance from critical observations upon the beauties and faults of those who have gone before him. No observations or rules can indeed supply the defect of genius, or inspire it where it is wanting: but they may often direct it into its proper channel; they may correct its extravagances, and point out to it the most just and proper imitation of nature. Critical rules are designed chiefly to shew the faults that ought to be avoided. To nature we must be indebted for the production of eminent beauties.'—Here our author, in a great measure, restrains the office of criticism to the business of shewing ' the faults which ought to be avoided.' This is an improper restriction. It falls within the province of criticism likewise to point out the beauties of composition, and the πηγαι της ὑψηγορίας, the sources of sublimity.

It has long been fashionable for petty authors to complain of critics and criticism. This superior writer very properly explodes all such complaints. ' Critics, says he, have been represented as the great abridgers of the native liberty of genius; as the imposers of unnatural shackles and bonds upon writers, from whose cruel persecution they must fly to the public, and implore its protection. Such supplicatory prefaces are not calculated to give very favourable ideas of the genius of the author. For every good writer will be pleased to have his work examined by the principles of sound understanding and true taste.'

Taste and *genius* are two words frequently joined together and confounded. Our author thus points out their difference.

' Taste,

' Taste consists in the power of judging; genius, in the power of executing. One may have a considerable degree of taste in poetry, eloquence, or any of the fine arts, who has little or hardly any genius for composition or execution in any of these arts. But genius cannot be found without including taste also. Genius therefore deserves to be considered as a higher power of the mind than taste. Genius always imports something inventive or creative, which does not rest in mere sensibility to beauty, where it is perceived, but which can moreover produce new beauties, and exhibit them in such a manner as strongly to impress the minds of others. Refined taste forms a good critic; but genius is farther necessary to form the poet or the orator.'

Having explained the nature of taste, the nature and importance of criticism, and the distinction between taste and genius, the professor proceeds to consider the pleasures of taste, or those pleasures which we receive from discourse or writing. In this inquiry he chiefly confines himself to sublimity and beauty.

Various hypotheses have been formed concerning that quality, in external objects, which is the foundation of sublimity. But all of them, he apprehends, are unsatisfactory.

' I am inclined to think, he says, that mighty force or power, whether accompanied with terror or not, whether employed in protecting or in alarming us, has a better title than any thing that has yet been mentioned to be the fundamental quality of the sublime; as there does not occur to me any sublime object, into the idea of which power, strength, and force, either enter not directly, or are not, at least, intimately associated with the idea, by leading our thoughts to some astonishing power as concerned in the production of the object.'

Lect. V. *Of Sublimity in Writing.*—Our author having observed, that a German critic, Johannes Gulielmus Bergerus, about the year 1720, composed a quarto volume, De naturali Pulchritudine Orationis, with an express intention to shew that Cæsar's Commentaries contain the most complete exemplification of all Longinus's rules relating to sublime writing, makes the following remarks on the last mentioned author.

' I am sorry to be obliged to observe, that the sublime is too often used in an improper sense by the celebrated critic Longinus, in his treatise on this subject. He sets out, indeed, with describing it in its just and proper meaning; as something that elevates the mind above itself, and fills it with high conceptions and a noble pride. But from this view of it he frequently departs, and substitutes in the place of it whatever in any strain of composition pleases highly. Thus many of the passages which he produces as instances of the sublime, are merely elegant, without having the most distant relation to proper sublimity; witness Sappho's famous ode, on which he descants at considerable length. He

He points out five sources of the sublime. The first is, boldness or grandeur in the thoughts; the second is, the pathetic; the third, the proper application of figures; the fourth, the use of tropes and beautiful expressions; the fifth, musical structure and arrangement of words. This is the plan of one who was writing a treatise of rhetoric, or of the beauties of writing in general; not of the sublime in particular. For of these five heads, only the two first have any peculiar relation to the sublime; boldness and grandeur in the thoughts, and, in some instances, the pathetic, or strong exertions of passion: the other three, tropes, figures, and musical arrangement, have no more relation to the sublime than to other kinds of good writing; perhaps less to the sublime than to any other species whatever; because it requires less the assistance of ornament. From this it appears, that clear and precise ideas on this head are not to be expected from that writer. I would not, however, be understood as if I meant, by this censure, to represent his treatise as of small value. I know no critic, ancient or modern, that discovers a more lively relish of the beauties of fine writing than Longinus; and he has also the merit of being himself an excellent, and, in several passages, a truly sublime writer. But, as his work has been generally considered as a standard on this subject, it was incumbent on me to give my opinion concerning the benefit to be derived from it. It deserves to be consulted, not so much for distinct instruction concerning the sublime, as for excellent general ideas concerning beauty in writing.'

Our author gives us the proper and natural idea of the sublime, in the following observations:

' The foundation of it must always be laid in the nature of the object described. Unless it be such an object, as, if presented to our eyes, or exhibited to us in reality, would raise ideas of that elevating, that awful, that magnificent kind, which we call sublime, the description, however finely drawn, is not entitled to come under this class. This excludes all objects, that are merely beautiful, gay, or elegant. In the next place, the object must not only in itself be sublime, but it must be set before us in such a light, as is most proper to give us a clear and full impression of it; it must be described with strength, with conciseness, and simplicity. This depends principally upon the lively impression, which the poet or orator, has of the object which he exhibits; and upon his being deeply affected and warmed by the sublime idea, which he would convey. If his own feeling be languid, he can never inspire us with any strong emotion.

' It is, continues he, generally speaking, among the most ancient authors, that we are to look for the most striking instances of the sublime. I am inclined to think, that the early ages of the world, and the rude unimproved state of society, are peculiarly favourable to the strong emotions of sublimity. The genius of men is then much turned to admiration and astonishment.

Meeting

Meeting with many objects, to them new and strange, their imagination is kept glowing, and their passions are often raised to the utmost. They think, and express themselves boldly, and without restraint. In the progress of society, the genius and manners of men undergo a change more favourable to accuracy than to strength or sublimity.'

In ancient writers we certainly meet with many striking instances of sublimity. But we cannot conceive, that their ideas were particularly elevated by any novelty or strangeness in the objects of nature. All objects are equally new and strange to every man, in every period of time, at his first entrance into life.—If the professor's argument is of any force, writers may be naturally expected to lose the spirit of sublimity, in proportion to their knowledge, or their distance from the days of Adam.

'The author produces several instances of the sublime from the Scriptures, from the writings of Homer, Ossian, Milton, Virgil; and gives us some examples of the faults opposite to the sublime, which, he observes, are chiefly two, the frigid and the bombast.

Lect. V. *Of beauty, and other pleasures of taste.*

' Beauty, he observes, next to sublimity, affords the highest pleasure to the imagination. The emotion which it raises, is very distinguishable from that of sublimity. It is of a calmer kind ; more gentle and soothing ; does not elevate the mind so much, but produces an agreeable serenity. Sublimity raises a feeling, too violent to be lasting ; the pleasure arising from beauty admits of longer continuance. It extends also to a much greater variety of objects than sublimity ; to a variety indeed so great, that the feelings, which beautiful objects produce, differ considerably not in degree only, but also in kind, from one another. Hence, no word in the language is used in a more vague signification than beauty. It is applied to almost every external object, that pleases the eye, or the ear ; to a great number of the graces of writing ; to many dispositions of the mind ; nay, to several objects of mere abstract science. We talk currently of a beautiful tree or flower ; a beautiful poem ; a beautiful character ; and a beautiful theorem in mathematics.'

The author enumerates several of those classes of objects, in which beauty most remarkably appears, and points out what he conceives to be the separate principles of beauty in each of them : he considers colour, figure, motion ; the beauty of the human countenance, and of certain moral qualities, the beauty arising from design or art ; and then proceeds to the consideration of several other principles, from which objects derive their power of delighting the imagination : as, novelty, imitation, melody, harmony, wit, humour, ridicule. He adds,

' If

' If the queſtion be put, to what claſs of theſe pleaſures of taſte, that pleaſure is to be referred, which we receive from poetry, eloquence, or fine writing ? My anſwer is, not to any one, but to them all. This ſingular advantage, writing and diſcourſe poſſeſs, that they encompaſs ſo large and rich a field on all ſides, and have power to exhibit, in great perfection, not a ſingle ſet of objects only, but almoſt the whole of thoſe, which give pleaſure to taſte and imagination ; whether that pleaſure ariſe from ſublimity, from beauty, in its different forms, from deſign and art, from moral ſentiment, from novelty, from harmony, from wit, humour, and ridicule. To which ſoever of theſe the peculiar bent of a perſon's taſte lies, from ſome writer or other, he has it always in his power to receive the gratification of it.'

Lect. VI. *Of the riſe and progreſs of language.*—The profeſſor having conſidered the difficulties attending the formation of language, the curious analogy, which prevails in the conſtruction of almoſt all languages, and that deep and ſubtle logic, on which they are founded, obſerves, ' that there ſeems to be no ſmall reaſon for referring the firſt origin of all languages to divine teaching or inſpiration.'

Many writers have attempted to prove the divine origin of language ; but the ſcheme is manifeſtly abſurd. For has there not been in former times, and is there not at preſent, a great variety of languages ſpoken by different nations ? And what greater difficulty is there in forming the principles of one language, than thoſe of another ? Why ſhould we have recourſe to inſpiration for giving a language to the firſt inhabitants of the earth, when we find, that ſubſequent generations have been able to form many new languages, without any ſupernatural aſſiſtance ?

Our author takes a middle courſe, in the determination of this queſtion.

' Suppoſing language, ſays he, to have a divine original, we cannot however ſuppoſe, that a perfect ſyſtem of it was all at once given to man. It is much more natural to think, that God taught our firſt parents only ſuch language, as ſuited their preſent occaſions ; leaving them, as he did in other things, to enlarge and improve it, as their future neceſſities ſhould require. Conſequently, thoſe firſt rudiments of ſpeech muſt have been poor and narrow ; and we are at full liberty to enquire, in what manner, and by what ſteps, language advanced to the ſtate in which we now find it.'

Here the buſineſs of inſpiration is reduced to that of teaching our firſt parents certain ' poor and narrow rudiments of ſpeech ;' and the curious ſtructure of language, together with the deep and ſubtle logic, upon which it is founded, is attri-

buted

buted to the inventions of men. But why may not we afcribe to human fagacity and contrivance the firft elements of language, as well as the glorious improvements, which it afterwards received? Our profeffor himfelf tells us, how the firft rudiments may be invented.

'Two men, fays he, at this day, would endeavour to make themfelves *be* underftood by each other, who fhould be thrown together on a defolate ifland, ignorant of one another's [each other's] language. Thofe exclamations, which by grammarians are called interjections, uttered in a ftrong and paffionate manner, were, beyond doubt, the firft elements or beginnings of fpeech.'

If thefe *interjections* were all the rudiments of fpeech, which, as our author fuppofes, God taught our firft parents, the divine infpiration of language amounts to nothing. And if we may draw any inference from the cafe here ftated, we may infer, that men might at firft communicate their feelings to one another, by thofe expreffive cries and geftures which nature taught them; and afterwards enlarge and improve their language, as their neceffities might require: and confequently, that the divine infpiration of language was unneceffary.

It may be imagined that thofe modes of expreffion, which are called figures of fpeech, are among the chief refinements of language, invented, when mankind were brought into a polifhed ftate, by orators and rhetoricians. Our author fhews that the contrary of this is the truth; that mankind never employed fo many figures of fpeech as when they had hardly any words for expreffing their meaning; that the want of proper names for every object obliged them to make ufe of comparifons, metaphors, allufions, and all thofe fubftituted forms of fpeech which render language figurative, &c.

'The ftyle of the Old Teftament, he obferves, is carried on by conftant allufions to fenfible objects. Iniquity, or guilt, is expreffed by a fpotted garment; mifery, by drinking the cup of aftonifhment; vain purfuits, by feeding on afhes; a finful life, by a crooked path; profperity, by the candle of the Lord, fhining on our head: and the like, in innumerable inftances. Hence, fays he, we have been accuftomed to call this fort of ftyle, the Oriental ftyle; as fancying it to be peculiar to the nations of the Eaft: whereas, from the American ftyle, and from many other inftances, it plainly appears not to have been peculiar to any one region or climate, but to have been common to all nations, in certain periods of fociety and language.

'Hence we may receive fome light concerning that feeming paradox, that poetry is more ancient than profe. The ftyle of all language muft have been originally poetical; ftrongly tinctured with that enthufiafm, and that defcriptive, metaphorical expreffion which diftinguifhes poetry.'

The

The paradox, which our author mentions, is not in the leaſt explained or illuſtrated by this obſervation. The ancients, with whom the queſtion originated, included *meaſure* under the idea of poetry. According to the account of Strabo and Pliny, poetry was older than proſe. Strabo tells us, that Cadmus, Pherecydes, and Hecatæus were the firſt, who diſcontinued the cuſtom of writing in verſe, λυσαντες το μετρον, τ᾽ αλλα δε φυλαξαντες τα ποιητικα, preſerving all the embelliſhments of poetry, except the *meaſure* *. Deſcriptions then and metaphorical expreſſions were ſome of the poetical ornaments, which thoſe writers retained, when they rejected the verſification of their predeceſſors. This is probably a mere vague and fabulous report ; but if it admits of any controverſy, we ſhould take up the queſtion on proper grounds, as Strabo has repreſented the matter, and not evade it, by obſerving, that the firſt productions of antiquity were written in poetic proſe.—Our author has treated the ſubject with more preciſion in his ſecond volume.

Lect. VII. *Of the riſe and progreſs of language.*—In treating of the arrangement of words in a ſentence, the author ſays,

'Let us figure to ourſelves a ſavage, who beholds ſome objects ſuch as fruit, which raiſes his deſire, and who requeſts another to give it to him. Suppoſing our ſavage to be unacquainted with words, he would, in that caſe, labour to make himſelf be underſtood, by pointing earneſtly at the object, which he deſired, and uttering at the ſame time a paſſionate cry. Suppoſing him to have acquired words, the firſt word which he uttered would of courſe be the name of that object. He would not expreſs himſelf, according to our Engliſh order of conſtruction, Give me fruit, but according to the Latin order, Fruit give me, Fructum da mihi. For this plain reaſon, that his attention was wholly directed towards fruit, the deſired object. This was the exciting idea, the object which moved him to ſpeak, and, of courſe, would be the firſt named. Such an arrangement is preciſely putting into words the geſture which nature taught the ſavage to make, before he was acquainted with words ; and therefore it may be depended upon as certain, that he would fall moſt readily into this arrangement. Accuſtomed now to a different method of ordering our words, we call this an inverſion, and conſider it as a forced and unnatural way of ſpeech. But though not the moſt logical, it is however, in one view, the moſt natural order ; becauſe, it is the order ſuggeſted by imagination and deſire, which always impel us to mention their object in the firſt place. We might therefore conclude, à priori, that this would be the order,

---

* Strabo, lib. i. p. 18. edit. 1620. Plin. lib. v. 27. vii. 56. Μετρον καλυμεν παν. το μη πεζον· εταν ειπω τα μεν Πλατωνος πεζα, τα δε Ομηρου μετρα. Metrum dicimus quicquid proſa non eſt ; ut cum ea quæ ſcripſit Plato, proſam ; quæ Homerus, metra nomino. Longin. Fragm.

in which words were moſt commonly arranged at the beginning of language; and accordingly we find, in fact, that, in this order, words are arranged in moſt of the ancient tongues; as in the Greek and the Latin; and it is ſaid alſo, in the Ruſſian, the Sclavonic, the Gaëlic, and ſeveral of the American tongues.'

This obſervation is ingenious. But if the order, in which the ſavage is ſuppoſed to place his words be ſo natural, how ſhall we account for the Engliſh order of conſtruction?—In this manner undoubtedly: a barbarous native of this country ſees an apple in the hands of his companion. The firſt idea, which ariſes in his mind, is the deſire of acquiſition or poſſeſfion, and he cries out, Give, give! Self is the next conſideration, and the fruit is the ultimate object of his wiſhes; he therefore exclaims, Give me that apple!

Our author very properly obſerves, that,

' In all modern tongues, the arrangement of the words is, in a great meaſure, limited to one fixed and determinate train, for this reaſon: we have difuſed thoſe differences, of termination, which, in the Greek and Latin, diſtinguiſhed the ſeveral caſes of nouns, and tenſes of verbs; and which thereby pointed out the mutual relation of the ſeveral words in a ſentence to one another, though the related words were disjoined, and placed in different parts of the ſentence. It was by means of this contrivance, that the Greek and Latin writers enjoyed ſo much liberty of tranſpoſition, and could marſhal and arrange their words in any way, that gratified the imagination, or pleaſed the ear.'

In his account of written characters, the profeſſor obſerves, that pictures were the firſt eſſay towards writing; hieroglyphics, which painted inviſible objects by analogies taken from the external world, the ſecond.

' It has been imagined, he ſays, that hieroglyphics were an invention of the Egyptian prieſts, for concealing their learning from common view; and that, upon this account, it was preferred by them to the alphabetical method of writing. But this, is a miſtake. Hieroglyphics, were undoubtedly employed, at firſt, from neceſſity, not from choice or refinement; and would never have been thought of, if alphabetical characters had been known.'

This is probable; but very uncertain. Hieroglyphics, on the walls and gates of their temples, and other buildings, might be preferred to alphabetic writing, for many reaſons. A ſymbolical figure carried with it a venerable air of myſtery; and might on that account be particularly agreeable to the taſte and genius of the Egyptians. An emblematic figure was likewiſe more ornamental; and, what was of great importance in public inſcriptions, was a more *compendious* method of ſug-

geſting

gefting moral or religious inftruction to people, who were certainly well acqnainted with the nature and import of thefe characters.

With refpect to the orign of alphabetic writing, our author fays : ' Moft probably, Mofes carried with him the Egyptian letters into the land of Canaan ; and there, being adopted by the Phœnicians, who inhabited part of that country, they were tranfmitted into Greece.'.

Some learned men have attempted to prove, that alphabetic writing was firft difcovered to Mofes, by divine revelation, on mount Sinai.   Dr. Winder, in his Critical Hiftory of Knowledge, has taken infinite pains to eftablifh this opinion.   But it is liable to many objections. And our author's hypothefis feems to be equally exceptionable.   As the firft fettlements of mankind are univerfally fuppofed to be in Afia, it is hardly credible, that the Afiatics fhould have no letters for above two thoufand five hundred years, and then at laft receive them from the Egyptians, who were fo far from being a learned people, that neither the Greeks nor the Romans ever thought any Egyptian book worth tranflating.

Lect. VIII. IX. *Of the ftructure of language.*—In thefe two lectures the author gives a general view of the chief principles, relating to this fubject, in obfervations on the feveral parts, of which fpeech or language is compofed, and more particularly on the genius of the Englifh language.

The following remark is worthy of notice.

' In the French and Italian there is no neuter gender. In the Englifh, when we ufe common difcourfe, all fubftantive nouns, that are not names of living creatures, are neuter without exception.   *He, fhe,* and *it,* are the marks of three genders ; and we always ufe *it,* in fpeaking of any object, where there is no fex, or where the fex is not known.   The Englifh is perhaps the only language in the known world (except the Chinefe, which is faid to agree with it in this particular) where the diftinction of gender is properly and philofophically applied in the ufe of words, and confined, as it ought to be, to mark the real diftinctions of male and female.'

Our author had no occafion to confine his obfervation to ' the *known* world.' There is no *terra incognita* on this globe, where there is the leaft probability of finding a philofophical language.

' In all our modern European tongues, fays the profeffor, conjugation is very defective.   They admit *few varieties* in the termination of the verb itfelf ; but have almoft *conftant* recourfe to their auxiliary verbs throughout *all* the moods and tenfes, both active and paffive.'

This

This obfervation fhould not have been expreffed in fuch general terms. In the Englifh language all the poffible variations of the original form of the verb are indeed not above fix or feven. But in the French and Italian the cafe is different. The French verb *aller*, for example, and the Italian verb *fapere*, have, each of them, above *forty* different terminations, and perhaps fome other verbs have more.

The profeffor fpeaks of the Englifh language with many juft encomiums. But we can by no means agree with him in this remark: ' Our verfe is, *after* the Italian, the moft diverfified and harmonious of any of the modern dialects.'

Let an impartial critic read the following lines in Taffo's Gerufalemme, and then judge how far the Italian language deferves this fuperior character:

' Canto l'arme pietofe, e'l capitano,
Che'l gran fepolro liberò di Chrifto.
Molto egli oprò col fenno, e con la mano,
Molto foffrì nel gloriofo acquifto;
E in van l'inferno a lui s'oppofe, e in vano
S'armò d'Afia, e di Libia il popol mifto.
Che il ciel gli diè favore, e fotto a i fanti
Segni riduffe i fuor compagni erranti.' Cant. i. v. 1—8.

In thefe lines the uniformity of the final fyllables, the perpetual repetition of a, e, i, o, chiming on, without any variety in the ftructure of the verfe, occafions a tirefome and difgufting monotony. This is the cafe with all Italian poetry. It is therefore no compliment to Englifh verfification to affirm, that it is fufceptible of more energy, dignity, harmony, and variety, than the Italian; and is entitled to a higher character, in every refpect, except in two departments, mufic and love.

Lect. X. *Of Style.*——All the qualities of a good ftyle, our author thinks, may be ranged under two heads, perfpicuity and ornament. Perfpicuity, confidered with refpect to words and phrafes, requires thefe three qualities in them, purity, propriety, and precifion. By purity, he means the ufe of fuch words, and fuch conftructions, as belong to the idiom of the language which we fpeak; in oppofition to words and phrafes that are imported from other languages, or are obfolete, or new coined, or ufed without proper authority. By propriety, he underftands the felection of fuch words in the language as the beft and moft eftablifhed ufage has appropriated to thofe ideas which we intend to exprefs by them, in oppofition to vulgarifms, or low expreffions, and to words and phrafes which would be lefs fignificant of the ideas that we mean to convey. In treating of precifion, he points out the different fignifications of many words which are reputed fynonymous.

This

This is a useful disquisition. But in such speculations as these, writers are apt to be too fond of subtle distinctions. The celebrated abbé Girard, in his Synonymes Françoises, has sometimes employed himself in splitting hairs.

Lect. XI. XII. XIII. *Of the structure of sentences.* — The properties, which the author thinks most essential to a perfect sentence, are, clearness and precision, unity, strength, and harmony.

First, clearness and precision. The least failure here, the least degree of ambiguity, which leaves the mind in any sort of suspence, as to the meaning, ought, he says, to be avoided with the utmost care. Ambiguity arises from two causes; either from a wrong choice of words, or a wrong collocation of them.

Secondly, unity. This, he observes, is a capital property. The very nature of a sentence implies one proposition to be expressed. During the course of the sentence, change the scene as little as possible. Never crowd into one sentence things which have so little connection, that they could bear to be divided into two or three sentences. Keep clear of all parentheses. Bring the sentence always to a full and perfect close.

Thirdly, strength. By strength the author means, such a disposition of the several words and members as shall bring out the sense to the best advantage; as shall render the impression, which the period is designed to make, most full and complete; and give every word and every member its due weight and force. Some of the rules, which the author gives for promoting the strength of a sentence, are these: prune it of all redundant words, and redundant members; attend particularly to the use of copulatives, relatives, and all the particles employed for transition and connection; dispose of the capital word or words in that place of the sentence where they will make the fullest impression; make the members of the sentence go on rising in their importance above one another; avoid concluding with an adverb, a preposition, or any inconsiderable word. In the members of a sentence where two things are compared or contrasted, where either a resemblance or an opposition is intended to be expressed, some resemblance, in the language and construction, should be preserved.

Fourthly, harmony, or musical arrangement. Under this head the author considers agreeable sound, in general, as the property of a well-constructed sentence; and observes, that there are two things on which the music of a sentence chiefly depends, the proper distribution of the several members, and the close or cadence of the whole. He then considers how the

the found may be fo ordered as to become expreffive of the fenfe.

Lect. XIV. XV. XVI. XVII. *Of the origin and nature of figurative language, of the metaphor, hyperbole, perfonification, apoftrophe, comparifon, antithefis, interrogation, exclamation, climax, &c.*—In treating of an hyperbole, the author has, among many others, this judicious remark :

' When a poet is defcribing an earthquake or a ftorm, or when he has brought us into the midft of a battle, we can bear ftrong hyperboles without difpleafure. But when he is defcribing only a woman in grief, it is impoffible not to be difgufted with fuch wild exaggeration as the following, in one of our dramatic poets :

————— " I found her on the floor
In all the ftorm of grief, yet beautiful ;
Pouring forth tears at fuch a lavifh rate,
That were the world on fire, they might have drown'd
The wrath of Heaven, and quench'd the mighty ruin."

LEE.

' This is mere bombaft. The perfon herfelf who was under the diftracting agitations of grief, might be permitted to hyperbolize ftrongly ; but the fpectator defcribing her, cannot be allowed an equal liberty : for this plain reafon, that the one is fuppofed to utter the fentiments of paffion, the other fpeaks only the language of defcription, which is always, according to the dictates of nature, on a lower tone : a diftinction, which however obvious, has not been attended to by many writers.'

Under the article of perfonification, he makes the following obfervations on a paffage in Mr. Pope's Epiftle from Eloifa to Abelard :

" Dear fatal name ! reft ever unreveal'd,
Nor pafs thofe lips in holy filence feal'd.
Hide it, my heart, within that clofe difguife,
Where, mix'd with Gods, his lov'd idea lies :
Oh ! write it not, my hand !— his name appears
Already written   Blot it out, my tears !"

' Here are feveral different objects and parts of the body perfonified ; and each of them *are* addreffed or fpoken to ; let us confider with what propriety, The firft is, the name of Abelard : " Dear fatal name ! reft ever," &c. To this, no reafonable objection can be made. For, as the name of a perfon often ftands for the perfon himfelf, and fuggefts the fame ideas, it can bear this perfonification with fufficient dignity. Next, Eloifa fpeaks to herfelf ; and perfonifies her heart for this purpofe : " Hide it, my heart, within that clofe, &c." As the heart is a dignified part of the human frame, and is often put for the mind, or affections, this alfo may pafs without blame. But, when from her heart fhe paffes to her hand, and tells her hand not to write his name, this is forced and unnatural ; a perfonified hand is low,

and

and not in the style of true passion: and the figure becomes still worse, when, in the last place, she exhorts her tears to blot out what her hand had written: " O! write it not," &c. There is, in these two lines, an air of epigrammatic conceit, which native passion never suggests; and which is altogether unsuitable to the tenderness which breathes through the rest of that excellent poem.'

In speaking of comparisons he remarks a fault, of which modern poets are very apt to be guilty.

' The antients, says he, took their similies from that face of nature, and that class of objects, with which they and their readers were acquainted. Hence lions, and wolves, and serpents, were fruitful, and very proper sources of similies amongst them; and these having become a sort of consecrated, classical images, are very commonly adopted by the moderns; injudiciously however, for the propriety of them is now in a great measure lost. It is only at second hand, and by description, that we are acquainted with many of those objects; and, to most readers of poetry, it were more to the purpose, to describe lions, or serpents, by similies taken from men, than to describe men by lions. Now-a-days, we can much *easier* form the conception of a fierce combat between two men, than between a bull and a tyger. Every country has a scenery peculiar to itself; and the imagery of every good poet will exhibit it. The introduction of unknown objects, or of a foreign scenery, betrays a poet copying, not after nature, but from other writers.'

The following caution, respecting the use of exclamations, is perfectly just.

' Nothing has a worse effect than the frequent and unseasonable use of them. Raw, juvenile writers imagine, that, by pouring them forth often, they render their compositions warm and animated. Whereas quite the contrary follows. They render it frigid to excess. When an author is always calling upon us to enter into transports which he has said nothing to inspire, we are both disgusted and enraged at him. He raises no sympathy, for he gives us no passion of his own, in which we can take part. He gives us words, and not passion; and of course, can raise no passion, unless that of indignation. Hence, I incline to think, he was not much mistaken, who said, that when, on looking into a book, he found the pages thick bespangled with the point which is called, 'punctum admirationis,' he judged this to be a sufficient reason for his laying it aside. And, indeed, were it not for the help of this ' punctum admirationis,' with which many writers of the rapturous kind so much abound, one would be often at a loss to discover, whether or not it was exclamation which they aimed at. For, it has now become a fashion, among these writers, to subjoin points of admiration to sentences, which contain nothing but simple affirmations, or propositions; as if, by an affected method of pointing, they could transform them in the reader's mind into high figures of eloquence.'

Lect.

Lect. XVIII. *Of the general characters of style, diffuse, concise, feeble, nervous, dry, plain, neat, elegant, flowery.*

Lect. XIX. *Of the general Characters of Style, simple, affected, vehement; with Directions for forming a proper Style.*—— With respect to simplicity in general, the author remarks, 'that the antient original writers are always the most eminent for it. This happens, continues he, from a plain reason, that they wrote from the dictates of natural genius, and were not formed upon the labours and writings of others, which is always in hazard of producing affectation. Hence among the Greek writers, we have more models of a beautiful simplicity, than among the Roman. Homer, Hesiod, Anacreon, Theocritus, Herodotus, and Xenophon, are all distinguished for it. Among the Romans also we have some writers of this character, particularly, Terence, Lucretius, Phædrus, and Julius Cæsar.'

The reason which the professor here assigns for that remarkable simplicity which appears in the style of some of the ancient writers, is not so very plain as he seems to imagine. Which of them were absolutely original authors, it is impossible for us to know. Terence * and Phædrus † wrote with great simplicity; but their works are professed imitations, ' formed upon the labours and writings of others.' It is therefore impossible that their simplicity should, in any respect, be owing to their originality. Besides, why an original author should write with more simplicity than one who imitates a prior model, is a paradox, which Dr. Blair has not sufficiently explained.

The English writers, which, in this lecture, he applauds for their simplicity, are archbishop Tillotson, sir William Temple, and Mr. Addison: the first for a certain negligent simplicity; the second for simplicity of a middle class; the third for the highest degree of ornament, which this character of style admits.

In his directions concerning the proper method of attaining a good style, he admonishes the young student to study clear ideas on the subject, concerning which he is to write or speak; to compose frequently; to render himself well acquainted with the style of the best authors; to avoid a servile imitation of any one author whatever; to adapt the style to the subject, and also to the capacity of the hearers, if he is to speak in public; and, lastly, not to let his attention to style engross him so much, as to detract from a higher degree of attention to the thoughts.

---

* Duæ [comœdiæ] ab Apollodoro translatæ esse dicuntur comico, Phormio & Hecyra; quatuor reliquæ à Menandro. Donatus.

† Æsopus auctor quam materiam reperit,
  Hanc ego polivi versibus senariis. Phæd. Prolog.

Lect.

Lect. XX. XXIV. Contain a critical examination of the style of Mr. Addison, in some papers of the Spectator, and of dean Swift, in his Proposal for correcting, improving, and ascertaining the English Tongue.

These, in general, are excellent criticisms, illustrating the author's preceding observations, and highly deserving the attentive perusal of every one, who wishes either to form a proper style, or improve his taste for the beauties of composition.

[*To be continued.*]

The Village, a Poem, in two Books. By the Rev. George Crabbe, Chaplain to his Grace the Duke of Rutland. 4to. 2s. 6d. Dodsley.

THOUGH this gentleman seems to have taken the hint of his poem from Goldsmith's Deserted Village, he does not represent it, like that writer ' as the seat of indolence and ease,' but describes it with more justice, and almost an equal warmth of colouring, as too commonly the abode of toil, misery, and vice. He begins with ridiculing the idea of shepherds, who

> ' in alternate verse,
> Their country's beauty, or their nymphs' rehearse;
> Yet still for these we frame the tender strain,
> Still in our lays fond Corydons complain,
> And shepherds' boys their amorous pains reveal,
> The only pains, alas! they never feel.
> On Mincio's banks, in Cæsar's bounteous reign,
> If Tityrus found the golden age again,
> Must sleepy bards the flattering dream prolong,
> Mechanic echos of the Mantuan song?'

Our pastorals are certainly in general unnatural and absurd. Neither are Virgil's exempt from censure on the same account. They but little agree with the Roman manners in his time, which in no respect coincided with those fancied ones of ' the golden age.' Theocritus alone, whom he copied, adhered to nature, and the prevailing customs of the country, and succeeded accordingly. The misery of the poor worn-out labourer and his family is thus described:

> ' Ye gentle souls, who dream of rural ease,
> Whom the smooth stream and smoother sonnet please;
> Go! if the peaceful cot your praises share,
> Go look within, and ask if peace be there:
> If peace be his—that drooping weary sire,
> Or their's, that offspring round their feeble fire,
> Or her's, that matron pale, whose trembling hand
> Turns on the wretched hearth th' expiring brand.
> Nor yet can time itself obtain for these
> Life's latest comforts, due respect and ease;
> For yonder see that hoary swain, whose age
> Can with no cares except its own engage;
> Who, propt on that rude staff, looks up to see
> The bare arms broken from the withering tree;

On

On which, a boy, he climb'd the loftiest bough,
Then his first joy, but his sad emblem now.
He once was chief in all the rustic trade,
His steady hand the straitest furrow made;
Full many a prize he won, and still is proud
To find the triumphs of his youth allow'd;
A transient pleasure sparkles in his eyes,
He hears and smiles, then thinks again and sighs:
For now he journeys to his grave in pain;
The rich disdain him; nay, the poor disdain;
Alternate masters now their slave command,
And urge the efforts of his feeble hand;
Who, when his age attempts its task in vain,
With ruthless taunts of lazy poor complain.
Oft may you see him when he tends the sheep,
His winter charge, beneath the hillock weep;
Oft hear him murmur to the winds that blow
O'er his white locks, and bury them in snow;
When rouz'd by rage and muttering in the morn,
He mends the broken hedge with icy thorn.'

The subsequent account of his sickness, death, &c. is, we fear, too true a picture. After enumerating the various vices prevalent in the country, which forcibly recalls Hamlet's observation, ' that the toe of the peasant comes so near the heel of our courtier, he galls his kibe,' we meet with the following striking reflection :

' Yet why, you ask, these humble crimes relate,
Why make the poor as guilty as the great ?
To show the great, those mightier sons of Pride,
How near in vice the lowest are allied ;
Such are their natures, and their passions such,
But these disguise too little, those too much :
So shall the man of power and pleasure see
In his own slave as vile a wretch as he ;
In his luxurious lord the servant find
His own low pleasures and degenerate mind ;
And each in all the kindred vices trace
Of a poor, blind, bewilder'd, erring race ;
Who, a short time in varied fortune past,
Die, and are equal in the dust at last.'

This poem deserves much approbation, both for language and sentiment. The subject is broken off rather abruptly towards the conclusion, where we meet with a long encomium on the Duke of Rutland, and the hon. Capt. Manners, who was killed in that memorable action in the West Indies, when the French fleet was defeated, and their admiral taken prisoner.

The Love of our Country, a Poem; with a Poetical Paraphrase of the 13th Chapter of St. Paul's first Epistle to the Corinthians. By the Rev. Henry Cha. Christian Newman, A. B. 2s. 6d. Faulder.

THE most exceptionable passages in this performance are probably contained in the dedications, addressed to the duke and duchess of Devonshire, and prefixed separately to each poem. The first begins with an assertion, that ' Englishmen have less of the *amor patriæ*, considered merely as an attachment to the soil, than most other nations of the globe.' This position cannot be allowed. A fond partiality and predilection for his country is the well-known characteristic of the home-bred Englishman. After this, we meet with some high encomiums on patriotism, and many higher ones on the illustrious patron, who is ' humbly desired to give the poem *un entré* (entrée) into the world.' This request is rather uncommon ; for publishers are usually considered as men-midwives to the Muses, on such occasions. We suppose the author meant to implore the protection of his performance ; but he should have known that though his Grace may protect him, his work must make its way by its own intrinsic merit only, and stand or fall by the judgment of the public.

The other dedication is more reprehensible. He observes, that ' as Vice therefore is ever drawn with deformed and distorted features to disgust us, so should Virtue, to win and engage our hearts, be described with an angelic symmetry of form and face. Our Saviour, while he was a pattern of perfection in his morals, was no less such in his manners, and these advantages and accomplishments were still heightened and improved by the most consummate beauty. Your Grace is only inferior in these qualities to an instance where inferiority is no diminution or disparagement of them.' Adulation is, in any respect, despicable ; but when it approaches to profaneness, deserves a harsher appellation. We fear the passage we have quoted is liable to censure on that account ; and, however amiable her Grace's person, however extensive her liberality may be, such a comparison ought to have been avoided.

In the poem on the Love of our Country we meet with no great depth of argument, nor strength of expression, much less novelty of thought, on a subject indeed sufficiently exhausted. It opens in the following manner :

   ' Ye chosen band ! whose well exerted zeal
Restores the public hopes and public weal,
Ye happy few ! whom Providence design'd
To vindicate the rights of human kind,
Whose stubborn virtue to its country true,
Nor interest nor pleasure can subdue.

Happy England, possest of such a treasure ! It may gratify the reader's curiosity to know of whom this chosen band consists ; and we are inform'd that

Ne'er,

'Ne'er, tho' greatly fall'n the mighty ſtate,
Shall total ruin on her empire wait,
While Portland, Cavendiſh, and Burke unite
With Fox, his country's idol and delight,
With Townſhend, and with Conway, friend to peace,
Bleſt race! who cauſ'd Britannia's tears to ceaſe.
Already union as a giant ſtands,
And joins Briareus like collected hands,
Already o'er the foe uplifts her arms,
And with a hundred deaths at once alarms,
Already humbled, Spain and France declare
How loſt is their ambition in deſpair;
How baffled all their mighty projects end,
And nought but ruin to themſelves portend,
While every Briton's boſom beats with joy,
And future triumphs all his thoughts employ.'

Poor Britannia! may thy tears be wiped off for ever from thy eyes, and our author's aſſertions be ſtrictly verified! But we have before now ſeen predictions of a ſimilar kind almoſt inſtantaneouſly defeated, and a ' firm united patriot band' diſunited and broken in pieces, almoſt as ſoon as their union was announced. One would almoſt ſuppoſe that, in the lines of our laſt quotation, the author had an eye to the concluding ſpeech in Shakſpeare's King John; at leaſt we think there is ſome reſemblance in the ſentiment.

' Thus England never did, and never ſhall,
Lye at the proud foot of a conqueror,
But when it firſt did help to wound itſelf.
Now theſe her princes are return'd again,
Come the three corners of the world in arms,
And we ſhall ſhock them.'

But notwithſtanding the too great predominancy of trite and puerile reflections in this poem, there are many paſſages in it deſerving our approbation; and the Paraphraſe is free from the faults which we obſerve in the original compoſition. The language is more nervous and correct, and the diction more animated.

FOREIGN ARTICLES.

Traité de l'Elaſticité de l'Eau & d'autres Fluides, par E. A. G. Zimmermann, Profeſſeur de Mathematiques, &c. au College Carolin de Brunſvic, 8vo. Amſterdam. Rey.

THIS famous queſtion has been ſo often agitated, that we can ſcarcely expect to derive either novelty or entertainment from another review of it. But our author, with the moſt extenſive knowlege of his ſubject, has enlivened his detail by an animated and agreeable manner of relating the ſeveral facts, ſo
that

that we are infenfibly drawn on to renew our acquaintance with the tutors of our youth, and the companions of our former ftudies. He has been chiefly induced to attempt this tafk, as a very ingenious German mechanic, Mr. Abick, has invented a machine, by which the elafticity of water is more fully afcertained, and more certainly eftablifhed, than by the experiments of former philofophers. It is, indeed, acknowleged, that M. du Hamel had before fuggefted a plan fimilar to that of Mr. Abick, but the German, attentive to his own refearches, confcious probably that his own refources were fertile and numerous, has been little acquainted with books; and actually, at the time his invention was completed, had never heard even of his name. But it muft be underftood, that we give this fact, on the authority of M. Zimmermann.

The Florentine experiments on the fubject are fully known, as well as thofe of Mr. Boyle: every fyftem is indeed more full than accurate, in the relation of thefe trials. We had long ago remarked, but have never met with the obfervation publickly, except in the work before us, that this experiment was greatly mifreprefented; for the globe, in which the water was comprefled, was made of filver; and the gentlemen of the experimental academy gave us explicit and fatisfactory reafons why they preferred that metal. On repeating it, another very material obfervation occurred; viz. that the water continued to ooze through the pores, *even* after the preffure was removed. We believe this circumftance was firft publifhed by Mr. Herbert of Vienna, in the year 1774. From the original experiment, which, with fome others, was made alfo by Mr. Boyle, it was for a long time concluded, that water was incompreffible. But, after fome period, it was fufpected that the refiftance of water was very great; and on that account, the conclufion might have been fallacious; or that, in an experiment fo rude, where a fmall diminution of fpace could not eafily be calculated, water might have been in fome degree compreffible, without any proof of its poffeffing fuch a property. Mr. Canton's trials feemed to fhow that it really was fo; yet in thefe, there was a flight fufpicion of error, which affected only the particular refult; while the general queftion was eftablifhed with fufficient certainty. It is almoft needlefs to remind the philofophical reader, that when the thermometer was at 50 degrees, and the barometor at 29½ inches, rain water was compreffed, 0.000046 parts of its bulk.

In this fituation the queftion was generally confidered to have remained; Mr. Zimmermann indeed has collected the opinions of feveral authors, who, from various experiments have endeavoured to demonftrate the compreffibility of water; and from the different teftimonies, we may conclude with Mr. Canton, that it really poffeffes a fmall degree of elafticity. We muft, however, confider this memoir in its proper order.

We fhall not dwell on the preface, in which with fome warmth, Mr. Zimmermann endeavours to fupport, the almoft exclufive

right

right of the Germans to the moſt important diſcoveries : he has enumerated ſeveral ; but the authors of ſome are ſtill diſputed. He explains, with propriety, the foundation of the diſcoverer's merits, by diſtinguiſhing between an accidental ſuggeſtion, and the conſequent reflections and experiments requiſite to complete the diſcovery. He next ſhortly conſiders the ſeveral experiments, by which the elements of earth, air, and water, are commonly ſuppoſed to be changed into each other ; but this we ſhall not enlarge on, as we find nothing very intereſting in his account. He then purſues his ſubject more particularly, and conſiders the arguments for the elaſticity of water, derived from the rebound of a ſtone or cannon ball, when it ſtrikes the ſurface, at an acute angle. A diſpute on this ſubject ſeems to have been carried on between two Italian philoſophers Bellogradi and Spalanzani, with great eagerneſs and acuteneſs. Our author determines in favour of the former, who ſupported the elaſticity of this fluid, both from reaſon, and the rebounding of drops of water from marble. He adds alſo the communication of ſound through water, which he properly conſiders, as a new proof of his favourite opinion. Experiments on this ſubject by the abbé Nollet and M. Arderon, are to be found in the French Memoirs and the Philoſophical Tranſactions.

M. Zimmermann then details the hiſtory of the various opinions on this ſubject. Having premiſed thoſe of Ariſtotle and Lucretius, he gives the ſyſtems of Bacon, Boyle, Fabry, Duhamel, Stair, Colbert, the Florentine academicians, De Lanis, Hamberger, Muchenbroek, Nollet, Hollman, Canton, Titius, Herbert, Fontana, and Abich. This very reſpectable liſt of names will be a convincing proof of his attention ; and we may add, that from the connected account, the hiſtory contributes to elucidate this difficult queſtion, as well as to trace the gradual evolution of the ſeveral opinions. For obvious reaſons, however, we muſt confine ourſelves to the experiments of the celebrated mechanic Mr. Abich.

He firſt tried to compreſs water in a gun-barrel, by means of a piſton, but the barrel burſt ; he then made a tube of braſs ¼ of an inch thick, in which the water was put, and the piſton driven by means of a ſcrew. The piſton was actually preſſed in, on the water ; and on increaſing the force of the ſcrew, the water appeared on the ſurface, as deſcribed by the Florentine academicians : but, on examination it ſeemed to be driven through ſome cracks in the tube itſelf. This obſervation has been made by other philoſophers ; and even when the globe was covered with an appearance like dew, it was found ſometimes to ariſe from the heated air, as the water was previouſly cooled as much as poſſible, and ſometimes from very numerous flaws in the metal.

The artiſt next made his cylinder more ſtrong. It was 1½ of an inch nearly in thickneſs ; and at the top and bottom, the cavity was diminiſhed, to render the deſcent of the piſton more viſible ; but a more particular deſcription will ſcarcely be intelligible

ligible without the plate. The power was commonly applied by a weight at the end of a long lever. The comparative compression of well water was 0.604 parts of a scruple (a scruple is $\frac{1}{12}$ of a line or $\frac{1}{144}$ part of an inch) of boiling water, 0.06687; of water saturated with salt, 0.06343; of milk, 0.05704; of aqua vitæ, 0.056194. The original length of the column of fluid was, 15 inches 3 lines and 9 scruples: the greatest compression of the well-water was 0.0723; and with an additional weight, it might be made to exceed in density, even sea-water. It is not easy to compare these experiments with those of Mr. Canton; from some rough calculations that we have made, they do not seem to differ materially, though there is a slight variation which should be accounted for. We wish that the experiments of Mr. Zimmermann may be repeated in different circumstances.

The author next endeavours to obviate some objections which may be made to these trials, as the piston might appear to sink from cavities in the metal, the compression of the leathers of the piston itself, the distention of the cylinder, and the air, either contained in the fluid, or in the machine. We cannot follow him in this tract; but must own that his observations and experiments have convinced us, that the effects of these different causes will be very inconsiderable. Mr. Zimmermann wishes that these experiments could be pursued, and recommends an iron, or a glass cylinder, if any one can be procured, that will be able to bear so great a pressure. He proposes, that the cylinder be previously exhausted of its air; the experiments made with water, from which the air has been drawn, or with water impregnated with fixed air; and that the apparatus of the lever be rendered more accurate and convenient. This memoir concludes with some observations on the different machines, which have been used for this purpose. The author, with unusual candour, seems to prefer the simple tubes of Hamberger and Herbert. But he also proposes an ingenious method of determining the pressure of the sea, at various depths; and then to calculate whether that is equal to a column of water, of the density of sea-water, without any compression. The idea undoubtedly deserves every praise that we can bestow; but his machine is by no means adapted to that purpose. Indeed, he seems only to have described it, in order to excite the attention of philosophers to pursue the plan, and to render it more perfect. On the whole, the present work is both instructive and entertaining. It conveys much useful information, and is written with greater elegance and spirit than we usually find in philosophical researches.

L: Produit et le Droit des Communes, et les Intérêts de l'Agriculture, Population, Arts, Commerce, Marine, Finances, et Militaire, à concilier pour le Salut des Individus et Propriétés, l'Amélioration des Domaines et autres Parties, la Richesse et Prospérité de l'Etat et des Citoyens. Paris.

Comprehensive as this title-page is, we have not copied the whole, in which the reader is, moreover, told that this is a treatise of political economy, in which patriotism, embracing

embracing all its branches, attempts chiefly to render, at once, the sovereign more powerful and happy, to connect the provinces more closely, to favour their trade, to render them less liable to epizootics, their inhabitants healthier and more fortunate, to get the armies better provided for, their convoys less slow and expensive, by culture and drains, by canals of navigation, as also for watering and draining; by converting the useless heaths and pestilential marshes and bogs into corn-fields, woods, and artificial meadows; that, at the same time, new forts of culture, and improvements of those already in use, are taught in it, with the general means relative to the soil, the manners, the industry, in order to raise the resources and power of France to the highest possible pitch of of superiority.

But even this is not yet enough for a title-page. The author, M. le Vicomte de la Maillardiere, Chevalier d'Honneur de la Chambre des Comptes de Bourgogne, Honoraire des Académies des Sciences d'Amiens, Arras, &c. de celles de Lyon & Metz, &c. who has dedicated his patriotic work to the French monarchy, adds, in the same title page, that the work also contains ' Un Tableau le plus étendu des Loix universelles et locales, fur les Communes et Terres vagues, et les Droits de Parcours, vaines Pâtures, Usages dans tout le Royaume, et particuliérement en Normandie et en Bretagne; en les rapprochant, on facilite les Jugemens qui doivent précéder la Mise en Valeur, et les Réclamations de chacun fur fon objet; le plan d'un Partage aux Profit des Communautés laïques, affurant la Conservation de leurs Communaux, celui d'une Inféodation par le Roi et les Seigneurs aux Sujets et Vaffaux, qui réunit fans inconvéniens les Avantages à quoi de trop grandes Concessions ont en vain tendu jufqu'à préfent.'

The wishes, pursuits, and hopes of the noble author are also in some measure pointed out by the following elegant verses of Voltaire, in his Épître fur l'Agriculture, adopted by M. le Vicomte de la Maillardiere for his motto:

. . . . Penfes-tu que rétiré chez toi
Pour les tiens, pour l'état tu n'a plus rien a faire?
La Nature t'appelle, apprends à l'obferver.
La France a des déferts, ofer les cultiver.
Elle a des malheureux; un travail néceffaire,
Ce partage de l'homme, et fon confolateur,
En chaffant l'indigence, amene le bonheur;
Change en épis dorés, change en gras pâturages,
Ces ronces, ces rofeaux, ces affreux marécages;
Tes vaffaux languiffans qui pleuroient d'être nés,
Qui redoutoient furtout de former leur femblables,
Vont fe lier gaiement par des nœuds défirables!
D'un canton défolé l'habitant s'enrichit,' &c.

Whether all or the greater part of the author's schemes are original, and whether he shall live to enjoy the pleasure of seeing them adopted, and rendered subfervient to the profperity of France, we must leave to be determined by time and by his own countrymen, as better acquainted with the local and

tem-

temporary circumſtances. But his patriotic ardor has a claim
to reſpect.

He obſerves, that one ſixth part of the lands of France conſiſts
in commons and waſte fields ; that nearly two-thirds of thoſe of
Bretagne only remain waſte, and that the greater part of them
conſiſts in commons. To cultivate and improve all theſe immenſe
tracts, to increaſe national population, ſafety, and proſperity by
ſuch peaceable and truly patriotic means, would hardly coſt a
tenth part of the immenſe ſums laviſhed in one ſingle war, with
a very precarious proſpect of uſeleſs or ruinous conqueſts. But
when we recollect that the very ſame reflexions may as juſtly be
applied to moſt parts not only of Europe, but of the globe :

     ' ——Animus meminiſſe horret, luctuque refugit.'

MONTHLY CATALOGUE.

POLITICAL.

*A conciſe Compendium of the Conſtitutional Part of the Laws of
England. By J. Peiſley, Gent. 12mo. 1s. 6d. Stockdale.*

THE author's intention is to give a conciſe view of the
Engliſh law, from the beſt authorities. He has ſelected
the conſtitutional part from the whole, and dedicated it to thoſe
able ſupporters of the conſtitution, the freeholders of the county
of York. We have no inclination to combat the juſtice or propriety of his conduct in this reſpect ; the execution, of which
we ought chiefly to judge, ſeems to merit the praiſe of accuracy
and conciſeneſs. This little work contains the *ſubſtance* of the
laws now in force relating to the liberty of the ſubject, freedom
of election and electors, power and privileges of parliament, diſ-
qualifications and diſabilities of its members, prerogative of the
crown, royal revenues, rights of peerage, and ambaſſadors.

*A Memorial addreſſed to the Sovereigns of America. By T. Pownal.
8vo. 2s. 6d. Debrett.*

Governor Pownal, after having, without any effect, publiſhed a Memorial to the Sovereigns of Europe, reſumes his political ſpeculations on the ſubject of America. The preſent memorial is chiefly congratulatory ; but the author likewiſe makes
a variety of general obſervations reſpecting the future government of the Trans-Atlantic republic. He appears to have a
ſtrong propenſity to the ſcience of legiſlation, mixed with no ſmall
degree of attachment to the American provinces.

*The Letters of Zeno to the Citizens of Edinburgh, on the preſent
Mode of electing a Member of Parliament for that City. 12mo.*

It appears that Scotland is at length infected with the ardour
of political reformation ; to promote which, as much as poſſible,
is the object of the Letters before us. Zeno endeavours to de-
monſtrate that the election of the repreſentatives for the Scottiſh
                                                      burghs

burghs has long been conducted in an arbitrary and iniquitous manner; and that those parts of the kingdom do not enjoy the rights of British subjects. He contends that all just power originates in the people; that magistrates are authorised by no principle of the constitution to exercise any power incompatible with the interest of the public; and that if any such has been usurped, the people have an undoubted right to procure its annihilation. Such are the arguments of Zeno, who zealously exhorts his countrymen to prosecute the abolition of their grievances; and in this he is both applauded and seconded by the authors of other letters in the collection, all of them industrious fellow-labourers in the popular vineyard of reformation.

DIVINITY.

A Course of Sermons upon Death, Judgment, Heaven, and Hell. By John Whitaker, B. D. Small 8vo. 2s. 6d. in Boards. Dilly.

The author of these discourses possesses a warm imagination, and represents to his readers, in the most striking colours, the awful circumstances of death, judgment, heaven, and hell. 'He enters, as he himself speaks, into the high regions of eloquence, he grasps the bolt, and darts the lightning of the gospel.' — So much may be said in his favour. On the other hand, when he attempts, 'to undraw the curtains of eternity, to lay open the secrets of the hall of spirits,' and to give a minute description of the general conflagration, the destroying angel, the seat of judgment, the throne of God, the dungeon of darkness, &c. 'he o'ersteps the modesty of nature,' astonishes and overpowers the mind of the reader, and inevitably misrepresents those tremendous scenes, which it hath not entered into the heart of man to conceive. It is, we apprehend, a known fact, that a few pathetic representations, at certain intervals, will have more effect on the mind, than a long continued series of the most dreadful descriptions.

A Sermon, preached at Chart Sutton, Kent, Nov. 3, 1782. At opening of the New Church; (the late Church being destroyed by Lightning.) By Henry Jones, A. M. 4to. 1s. Evans.

A rational sermon, very proper for the occasion on which it was delivered.

A Sermon; intended as a Dissuasive from the Practice of Duelling. 4to. 1s. Cadell.

A short, but well written discourse, highly deserving the attentive perusal of every man, before he sends or accepts a challenge.

A Discourse against the fatal Practice of Duelling. By the Rev. John Bennet. 4to. 1s. Wheeler, at Manchester.

The author exposes the mistaken notions of the duellist, and pathetically represents the pernicious consequences of duelling, as they are connected with humanity and religion.

F 3 *A Sermon*

A Sermon preached before the Humane Society, on March 30, and May 25, 1783. By John Hadley Swain. 8vo. 1s. Rivington.

Mr. Swain takes his text from St. Luke's account of our Saviour's restoring to life the widow's son at Nain; and after some general observations on that event, proceeds to recommend a spirit of Christian charity and benevolence, and more particularly that excellent institution, which gave occasion to this discourse.

A New Concordance to the Holy Scriptures of the Old and New Testament. By Thomas Taylor. 4s. 6d. Dilly.

The size, and the usual price, of Cruden's Concordance, very naturally suggested the idea of furnishing the public with one, upon the same plan, in a more commodious form, and at a less expence. The present compilation is sufficiently full and comprehensive for every ordinary purpose, and merits our recommendation as a useful index to the Bible.

Sacred History selected from the Scriptures, with Annotations and Reflections, suited to the Comprehension of young Minds. By Mrs. Trimmer. Vol. III. 12mo. 3s. sewed. Robinson.

In this volume the fair annotator has advanced as far as the twenty-first chapter of the second Book of Kings. To her reflections on the history of David she has very properly subjoined, in their respective places, all the psalms containing any circumstances, sufficient to ascertain the occasion on which they were composed. As her observations are calculated for young people, she uses the words, 'my dear', in almost every page. This, though in itself an insignificant circumstance, has a tendency to give her remarks an air of chit chat, and detracts from the dignity of a grave and learned commentator, whose expositions and practical improvements are suited to the capacities of old women, as well as young.

A concise History of the Kingdoms of Israel and Judah; connected with the History or chief Events of the Neighbouring States and succeeding Empires to the Time of Christ, and the Establishment of the Gospel Dispensation. By Ann Murry, in 2 vols. 8s. Dilly.

A general history for the use of young readers ought to be clear and concise, written in an easy and agreeable style, and filled with nothing but a regular narrative of the most important and interesting transactions. Bossuet's performance is encumbered with many dry, theological disquisitions. Miss Murry's has great merit.—We admire the intrepidity of this lady, who has ventured to enter into the depths of antiquity, and conduct her pupils through an intricate period of above four thousand years.

A curious Hieroglyphick Bible; or, Select Passages in the Old and New Testament, represented with near Five Hundred Emblematical Figures, for the Amusement of Youth. 12mo. 1s. Hodgson.

The following example will sufficiently explain the nature of these hieroglyphics: ' Thy *wife* shall be as a fruitful *vine* by the sides of thine *house*, and thy *children* like olive plants about thy *table*.' The wife, the vine, the house, the children, and the table, are represented by the figures of those objects, in wooden cuts;

cuts; the intermediate words are printed. The contrivance is rather calculated to amuse than instruct. The two gigantic faces representing the sun and moon must give children a strange idea of those objects; and surely there is a grofs impropriety in exhibiting the Holy Spirit in the shape of an overgrown dove, and the Supreme Being under the figure of an old man with a long beard.

POETRY.

Poetical Attempts; confifting of an Allegorical Poem in blank Verfe, intituled, The Sciences; An Ode to Pleafure; and fome other Pieces. 4to. 2s. Wallis.

This allegorical poem recalls to our mind the following lines in the Dunciad :

' Of darknefs vifible fo much be lent,
As half to fhew, half veil, the deep intent.'

Though we are forry to fay the refemblance does not always exactly hold ; for notwithftanding we now and then get a fhort view of the author's meaning, we find ourfelves foon loft in utter darknefs, and quite bewildered. The firft eleven lines, and the note fubjoin'd, will convey a fufficient idea of this myfterious performance.

' Down in a lone fequefter'd vale,* where all
The gay luxuriance of fpring, in foft
Profufion glow'd ; or fteril horrors reign'd :
Where rocks, woods, deep-ton'd cataracts, peaceful ftreams ;
Scenes form'd to footh to amorous delights ;
Teach Melancholy's gloomy brow to bend ;
Or wing the enraptur'd foul, on thoughts fublime,
O'er time and fpace ; fcenes more than poets yet
Have feign'd, or fancy form'd, in ample groups,
Magnificently rofe ; abforpt in thought,
Under a *platan*'s venerable fhade,
Reclin'd I fate.'

We think the author might have fpared himfelf the trouble of entering his book at Stationers-Hall.

Independence, a Poem, in Hudibraftic Verfe, addreffed to Richard Brinfley Sheridan, Efq. 4to. 2s. Flexney.

This is a pretty clofe copy of Hudibras, in every thing but wit and humour. As a fpecimen of that anti-elegance with which it abounds to a furprifing degree, take the following lines:

' For 'twas in vain to fue for *quarter*,
To ftop each conqueror's rage, and *flaughter*,

' * Ver. 1 to 11. A *lone fequefter'd vale*, &c.--- The Univerfe, which prefents fo vaft a variety of objects to the contemplative mind in its purfuit of knowledge.----*Sequefter'd*, or removed from the habitations of man, becaufe the way to intellectual accomplifhments is to remove from the general paths employed in the ordinary purfuits of life.----And *lone*, becaufe fo few fuffer their ideas to ftray beyond the moft obvious appearances and the furfaces of things.'

They

They therefore cried out to their *owners*
Help.—the Philistines are upon *us*."

Addison humorously commends Tom D'Urfey, in the Guardian, for 'enriching our language with a multitude of rhimes, and bringing words together that, without his good offices, would never have been acquainted with one another, so long as it had been a tongue.' Our author, however, shines forth superior to D'Urfey, in his peculiar excellency: for the concluding words of the last couplet have not even the least similarity of sound, and their whole resemblance consists in having the same final letter; a refinement in poetry hitherto unparalleled! But to proceed.

'And whilst his garters serv'd his *turn*,
He hop'd to be repair'd with *her'n*.'
'Barrocading door and *window*,
Resolv'd their fierce design to *hinder*.'
'In the next place these lusty *fellows*
With ale and beer well stock'd the *cellars*.'

We ask the reader's pardon for grating his ears with ribaldry and cockney rhimes. But let him consider what we have undergone in perusing this wretched performance, and we trust his pity will seal our pardon.

Drawings from living Models taken at Bath. 4to. 1s. Robinson.

In this little performance we meet with no great brilliancy of wit, or poignancy of satire. There is something, however, in it that approaches towards a resemblance of these characteristics. It is wrote in an easy gentlemanlike manner, with a tolerable degree of spirit; and will afford half an hour's amusement to readers in general, particularly those at Bath, where we suppose the characters in it are perfectly known.

The Rescue; inscribed to the Hon. C. J. Fox. 4to. 1s. 6d. Debrett.

This sprig of myrtle, in a female's lays, is intended to add to the wreath of olive and of bays, with which the head of the hero is surrounded. But the olive is the emblem of peace, and bays the crown of the poet, or the master of the revels, in the phrase of antiquity, the '*arbiter bibendi*.' We cannot therefore see any great propriety in either chaplet; but we must excuse slight improprieties in our fair author, for her admiration of the hero is so exalted, that she sees in him every thing that is great and good. Hear her own words:

'O thou! by all the patriot virtues fir'd,
By faction dreaded, by the world admir'd;
Who, form'd for all that bids mankind be great,
The prop and glory of a sinking state!
Whose genius ages shall transmit to fame,
And bless the sons of sires thy virtues shame!

The subject of the poem is the rescue of Britannia, from the despotic chains of a late chancellor, whose rugged virtue and inflexible integrity were little suited to the intrigues of party, or the changing views of a faction. We must not try poetry by the
code

code of truth : its profeſſors often ſucceed beſt in fiction ; but we dare not ſay that it is, on this account, that we have received much pleaſure in the peruſal of the work before us. The pencil of our author is light and elegant, rather than expreſſive and accurate ; and a few errors, ſometimes in language, and ſometimes in metre, are compenſated by animated deſcription, and harmonious poetry.' The ſpeech of a late negociator and quondam governor will afford a ſufficient ſpecimen.

> " Have I not been the Cerb'rus of the ſtate ?
> Have I not bark'd and mouth'd in each debate ?
> Whilſt frighted miniſters, my wrath to *ceaſe*,
> Sent me the gentle meſſenger of peace ;
> Like Amphiſbæna, did I not pronounce,
> From head and tail, two languages at once ?
> Let Suffrein tell the valour of my arms,
> And Liſbon maids bewail my ſofter charms ;
> Another Jaſon I triumphant came,
> Not with fleets captur'd, but the fleece and dame :
> E'en now, when France no more my arms employ,
> This tongue may yet a miniſter deſtroy ;
> Whilſt Burke to juſtice ev'ry guilt conſigns,
> I, more humane, may plead for H—ſt—ng's crimes.
> Or good or ill, no miniſter ſhall reſt,
> Whilſt ſcaffolds, ſwords,"—here wrath his words ſuppreſt.'

More Lyric Odes to the Royal Academicians. By Peter Pindar, a diſtant Relation to the Poet of Thebes, and Laureat to the Academy. 4to. 1s. Evans.

' Ecce iterum Criſpinus.'—In this manner our lively and ſatyrical author announces himſelf, before he draws the deſtructive ſword, which is again to overwhelm the members of the Royal Academy. His ſtrictures are more general, in this ſecond part, but though they are conveyed with additional force, we are perſuaded that the members will rather laugh at the wit than be hurt at the ſatire. The author ſeems to have been ſatisfied with the ſhare of praiſe which his former Odes had procured, but laments the loſs of the more ſubſtantial gratifications :

> ' The grave poſſeſſors of the critic throne
> Gave me, in truth, a pretty treat—
> Of flattery, mind me, not of meat ;'
> For they, poor ſouls, like me, are *ſkin* and *bone*.'

His criticiſms are chiefly levelled at the modern ſtyle of painting, which, while it aims at what is commonly ſtyled warm colouring, produces an unnatural and glaring effect ; and at the total neglect of the true appearance of diſtant objects, and the repreſentations of nature. His addreſs to Gainſborough is pleaſing and juſt,—we ſhall beg leave to inſert it.

> ' O Gainſborough, Nature plaineth ſore,
> That thou haſt kick'd her out of door,
> Who in her bounteous gifts hath been ſo free,
> To cull ſuch genius out for thee—

Lo! all thy efforts without her are vain!
Go find her, kiss her, and be friends again.'

But our author is not now uniformly satirical—we congratulate him on the change, and may probably find his future strains abounding in panegyric. Opie seems to deserve his praises; and his sonnet to Jackson is elegant and poetical. We should have selected a part of it, but we could not find one stanza preferable to the rest; the whole will certainly be agreeable to the reader of taste and feeling.

'Enchanting harmonist! the art is thine
Unmatch'd, to pour the soul-dissolving air,
    That seems poor weeping Virtue's hymn divine,
Soothing the wounded bosom of Despair!

O say, what minstrel of the sky hath giv'n
To swell the dirge, so musically lorn?
    Declare, hath dove-eye'd Pity left her heav'n,
And lent thy happy hand her lyre to mourn?

So sad thy songs of hopeless hearts complain,
Love from his Cyprian isle prepares to fly;
    He hastes to listen to thy tender strain,
And learn from thee to breathe a sweeter sigh.'

An Address from the Members of the Constitutional Body to their Sovereign, on the Change of the Ministry. 4to. 1s. Bladon.

The impotent efforts of a genius that seems qualified only for the office of a pandar to the stews.

NOVELS.

The Woman of Letters; or, the History of Miss Fanny Bolton. 2 vols. 12mo. 6s. Noble.

Whether this novel was meant to have any particular allusion, we shall not determine; but the moral of it seems not to be such as is often verified in female life. It inculcates, that genius and a learned education united, are insufficient to procure a woman a decent subsistence, or to prevent her from being entangled in the mazes of a plausible hypocrite. The novel, however, is undoubtedly superior to the common productions of the kind; and should it be attended with the effect of inducing ladies to cultivate the qualifications of domestic life rather than literary talents, it may prove of considerable advantage.

Burton Wood. 2 vols. 12mo. 5s. sewed. Dodsley.

The story of this novel is natural and pathetic, at the same time that it is rendered subservient to the introduction of moral and religious sentiments. Such qualities are the more entitled to approbation, as we are told this novel is the first attempt of a female author.

The Reconciliation; or, the History of Miss Mortimer and Miss Fitzgerald. 8vo. 5s. sewed. Lane.

This is entitled an Hibernian novel, but without any apparent reason for that appellation. It perfectly resembles English manufacture, and will therefore have an equal chance of sale among the purchasers of such commodities.

MISCEL-

MISCELLANEOUS.

A Tour to Cheltenham Spa; or, Gloucestershire Displayed: containing an Account of Cheltenham, the Natural History of the County of Gloucester, the City of Gloucester, &c. &c. 12mo. 1s. 6d. Dilly.

Those who have read the title-page will be surprised at the price, and look on the author as a mirror of generosity and disinterestedness. The information which it contains is collected from different sources, and from some authors who have not hitherto supported the reputation of accurate or industrious enquirers; so that the different parts are not equally valuable. Though announced with a pompous title, it is little more than a collection of circumstances which relate to Cheltenham Spa, and will be very interesting to those who frequent it. The reader must expect, as usual, that the virtues of the waters are much exaggerated; for they are generally taken from the common systems, assisted by the sentiments of an anonymous physician. The Display of Gloucestershire seems to be inserted as a temptation to the curious traveller, who might be supposed to visit Cheltenham with greater pleasure, on account of the vicinity of curious objects. It is needless to add, that the descriptions must be necessarily general and concise; but we have also, in many instances, found them imperfect. The most avaricious purchaser must, however, be contented with the *quantity*.

The Artist's Assistant in the Study and Practice of Mechanical Sciences. Calculated for the Improvement of Genius. Illustrated with Copper-plates. 12mo. 3s. in Boards. Robinson.

This is a collection of rules and receipts, of which we may assign the character from Martial; 'sunt bona, sunt quædam mediocria, sunt mala.' But it is not easy to give its proper character to each in particular. The chief defect which we have observed, after an attentive perusal, is a want of explicitness: this will, in many instances, materially affect the operation; so that the knowlege you *seem* to possess will, in actual practice, fail, without repeated trials, and an accurate attention to minuter circumstances than the author chuses to detail. The principal merit of the work is, that it collects many observations on a variety of subjects, and frequently gives very satisfactory information; yet we think it rather calculated for the assistance of an artist already accustomed to the subjects than for the instruction of a learner. It begins with drawing, proceeds with designing, perspective, colours, painting, enamelling, japanning, lacquering, staining, engraving, casting, bronzing, gilding, silvering, &c. and the more important subjects are illustrated by copper-plates.

Pictures of the Heart, sentimentally delineated in the Danger of the Passions, an Allegorical Tale; The Adventures of a Friend to Truth, an Oriental History; The Embarrassments of Love; and The Double Disguise, a Drama, in Two Acts. By John Murdoch. 2 Vols. 12mo. 6s. Bew.

This *pretty* title page introduces some entertaining adventures, which

3

which will agreeably amuse during the fashionable tortures of the frizeur. We can promise nothing more; but, if an attentive reader should probably think them worth his perusal, he will find the Adventures of a Friend to Truth superior to the other works. By a dexterous transposition of the letters, he will perceive the name of Voltaire under an apparently Chinese appellation, and some pointed and just satire both on literary and political subjects. Perhaps he will be able to develope some other hidden mysteries; but the author of this article resembles, in these respects, Davus rather than Œdipus.

The Life of Henry Chichelé, Archbishop of Canterbury, Founder of All Souls College, in the University of Oxford. 8vo. 6s. Walter.

Henry Chichelé, the subject of these memoirs, was born at Higham Ferrers in Northamptonshire, in the year 1362; was educated at Winchester school, and from thence removed to New College, in Oxford, where he took the degree of doctor of laws. By the favour of Richard Melford, bishop of Salisbury, and other patrons, he obtained several valuable preferments in the church. In 1408, he was made bishop of St. David's; and, in 1414, advanced to the see of Canterbury, where he continued to his death, which happened April 12, 1443. He was employed by Henry IV. in several embassies to foreign princes, in which he acquitted himself with integrity and address. He laid the foundation of All Souls College in 1437, and expended on that building four thousand three hundred pounds.

' The noblest exertions of Chichelé's liberality were dedicated to the service of literature, and the improvement of the university of Oxford: which at this time, and for some years before, laboured under very oppressive discouragements. Learning was fallen into general contempt; the number of students was much decreased, and many halls totally deserted. The ancient languages were not critically understood: Latin, the only one of the dead tongues in common use, was appropriated to the unintelligible jargon of schoolmen and metaphysicians; theology and philosophy were involved in a maze of intricate and unprofitable enquiries; and even the study of the civil and canon laws, overwhelmed with endless commentaries, was more calculated to exercise than improve the understanding. While genius, thus fettered by prejudice and prescription, was idly amused in subtle and uninstructive researches, the free exercise of judgment and reason was necessarily discountenanced and suppressed. What contributed perhaps to thicken the cloud of ignorance which enveloped this period, was an extreme scarcity of books: they were purchased at a great price, and lent with the utmost caution and reluctance.

' The manners of the students were as barbarous as their erudition. Each line, attached with bigotted partiality to their peculiar study, asserted its pre-eminence with intemperate zeal, and held every other branch of science in sovereign contempt. But the great factions which divided the university were those of the

northern

northern and southern members, whose inveterate prejudices, and unvarying animosity were displayed on many occasions in the most violent and sanguinary contests. Such was the state of the university, when Chichelé determined to enlarge its establishments by an addition to the number of its colleges. He began the execution of this design by erecting a house for the accommodation of the scholars of the Cistercian order, who at that time had no settled habitation in Oxford. It was built in the North-gate-street, and dedicated to the Virgin Mary and St. Bernard. To complete the plan, which he had thus far but partially effected, the archbishop, incited to it by motives of earnest solicitude for the welfare of the church, and compassion for those who had unfortunately fallen in the French war, erected the college of All Soulen (or All Souls) as it was commonly expressed, for the maintenance of certain persons, to pray in general for the souls of all the faithful deceased, and who might increase the number of the ministers of religion, and promote by their studies the knowledge of theology and of the civil and canon law.'

Having related the most memorable incidents of the archbishop's life, and his various acts of munificence, the author concludes with this sketch of his character:

' We have now seen Chichelé in the several situations in which a long and active life placed him. It is from his conduct in these that we are to collect his character. Of the early part of his life we know little more, than that his acquirements in it are indisputable proofs of his not having passed it unprofitably.

' As he grew into public notice by slow and gradual advances, his talents had time to acquire their full strength and maturity before they were brought into use: and it is to this circumstance probably that he owes the uninterrupted course of his success in the management of repeated negotiations. As he was able to acquit himself in these important commissions with the favour of his sovereign, and the approbation of his country, we may infer, that he possessed, besides extensive erudition, clear discernment, fertility of resources, solid judgment, and cool perseverance, recommended by general urbanity and politeness of manners. If we view him in the discharge of his ecclesiastical office, we shall find him to have been a man of undissembled piety, and who bore a sincere affection to the church. If his religion was tinctured with the superstition of the times in which he lived, we should recollect, that in passing judgment on the characters of men, we ought to try them by the maxims and principles of their own age.

' Fully persuaded of the truth of those doctrines which the catholic church professed, he maintained them with conscientious zeal. He knew the danger of innovation, and was vigilant to repress it; but he does not at any time appear to have been actuated by the spirit of persecution.

' Though warmly attached to the authority of the see of Rome in spiritual matters, and even to its exercise of civil rights founded on ancient usage, he still strenuously supported the liberties of the English church, and never forgot the respect due to the laws
and

and conſtitution of his country. Thus the doctrines and the privileges of the church were guarded by him with ſcrupulous fidelity; and, in whatever light we ſee his religion, there will ſcarcely be two opinions concerning his integrity.

‘ Of his benefactions a particular account has already been given; and if in ſumming up his character, to excellent natural abilities, liberal accompliſhments, and ſtrict piety and integrity, we add a charitable and benevolent heart, we ſhall not be guilty of exceſſive or blind partiality to his memory.’

The Life of Archbiſhop Chichelé was publiſhed in 1617 by Arthur Duck, fellow of All Souls. Our author has made that performance the ground work of his narrative; but he has enlarged his memoirs in every part by many additional anecdotes, extracted from the beſt authorities, both in print and manuſcript.

An Analyſis of the Principal Duties of Social Life. By John Andrews, LL. D. 8vo. 3s. 6d. Robinſon.

Theſe maxims are ſaid to be written in imitation of Rochefoucault’s. They are addreſſed to a young gentleman, in order to furniſh him with proper ſentiments and rules of conduct, on his entrance into the world. Many of them are undoubtedly founded on good ſenſe and experience. But few of them are either ſtriking or elegant. The firſt maxim may ſerve as a ſpecimen.

‘ Education is the manure that brings our innate qualifications to maturity; without it, the ſeeds of virtue and perfection implanted in us, inſtead of fructifying, are loſt or perverted: courage engenders ferocity; the ray of wiſdom that nature may have infuſed, is obſcured, or degenerates into pride; and if we are bleſt with a propenſity to goodneſs, we are liable to perpetual miſtakes and miſapplications.’

The metaphor, which our author has here adopted, is taken from a vulgar object; and is not properly ſupported. Education is repreſented as a dunghill; *ſeeds* are *perverted*; and a *ray degenerates into pride.*

An Eſſay on Education. By B. Webb. 8vo.

The author of this tract deſcribes the plan of education, which he purſues at Odiham ſchool; and makes ſome obſervations on the advantages of a public education, and the preference of the Engliſh language, in ſeveral inſtances, when compared with the Greek and Latin.

An Attempt to diſplay the Importance of Claſſical Learning. By Joſeph Corniſh. 8vo. 1s. Robinſon.

This tract is addreſſed to thoſe, ‘ whoſe circumſtances are ſuch, as render it improper for them to employ their ſons in manual labour; who muſt be kept at ſchool till they are fifteen or ſixteen years of age; who have a proſpect, from their fortunes and the employments to which they are deſtined, of filling up the higher or middle ranks of life, and are not likely to be ſo entirely engroſſed by buſineſs as to have hardly any time for relaxation or amuſement.’—The author’s deſign is to repreſent to them the uſe
and

and importance of giving their sons a classical education, or a competent knowlege of the Greek and Roman languages, as particularly calculated to open their minds, enlarge their ideas, amuse them in their solitary hours, and make them agreeable and respectable members of society.

In the latter part of this pamphlet the author makes some remarks on Mr. Knox's treatise on a Liberal Education; which, though he differs from that writer in some particulars, he nevertheless speaks of with the highest applause.

Thoughts on the Origin, and on the most rational and natural Method of Teaching the Languages. By John Williams, LL. D. 8vo. 2s. Robinson.

In this tract the author proposes two schemes for the advancement of learning, arts, and sciences.

First, that young gentlemen, designed for a learned profession, should, after an accurate grammatical knowlege of their native tongue, be taught the Hebrew, then the Arabic, the Samaritan, the Chaldee, the Syriac, the Greek, and then the Latin; and afterwards, the modern tongues, (which are derived from the Latin) as necessity or inclination may require. 'This, he says, is the most natural order, because it is the order, in which these languages have prevailed in the world.'

Secondly, he recommends the use of one universal language, and the publication of all works of science in that language. By this expedient, he observes, those who have a natural genius may acquire a knowlege of all modern discoveries and improvements, without the trouble of learning a variety of different languages. The Latin tongue, he thinks, is the best calculated for this important purpose, as its alphabet is familiar to all Europeans, and the language itself has been in common use for many ages.

These schemes would undoubtedly be attended with advantages, but not so many as the learned author seems to imagine. The former would engage young students in the acquisition of more languages than the generality of them would have either leisure or abilities to pursue. The latter would have a tendency to supersede the use of the English language in works of genius, and introduce in its place a barbarous latinity. We may add, that an Englishman, not intended for any learned profession, has very little reason to lament the want of books in any branch of science, in his own native language.

London's Gratitude. 8vo. 1s. Dilly.

This little pamphlet contains an account of such pieces of sculpture and paintings as have been placed in Guildhall at the expence of the city of London; with a list of those distinguished persons to whom the freedom of the city has been presented for public services, since the year, 1758. Part of these has already been printed in the Gentleman's Magazine, and is now accompanied with engravings of sculptures, &c.

The

The Saddle put on the Right Horse, &c. 8*vo.* 2*s.* 6*d.* Stockdale.

Under the cant appellation of this pamphlet, we meet with many acute observations on the present state of our affairs in the East Indies. The author appears to be well acquainted with the subject, and treats it in a strain of humour peculiar to the Vindication of General Smith, of which, it seems, he likewise is the writer.

The Order of Hereditary Succession to the Crown of these Kingdoms, on the Failure of immediate Heirs. 4*to.* 1*s.* 6*d.* Kearsley.

The British crown, however great, might be degraded into the subject of a catchpenny pamphlet; but the production before us appears too superfluous to answer even such an intention.

The Experienced Bee-Keeper. 8*vo.* 2*s.* Dilly.

The author of this pamphlet, whose name, we find, is Bryan I'Anson Bromwich, recommends the treatment of bees by a method, which, from long experience, he affirms to be easy and profitable. His observations are judicious, and merit the attention of those who would cultivate this too much neglected species of rural economy.

A System of French Syntax. By the Rev. Mr. Holder, of Barbadoes. 12*mo.* 3*s.* 6*d.* Dilly.

The professed design of this system is to illustrate, correct, and improve the principles laid down by Chambaud; and we must acknowledge that the author has effected his intention with success and ability. His observations are not only highly useful, but are exemplified by the best authorities. Those, therefore, who are desirous of attaining correctness and elegance in the French language, cannot use any grammatical guide, from which they may derive greater advantage.

Elegant Extracts. Small 8*vo.* 4*to.* 4*s.* Dilly.

These extracts, compiled from modern authors in prose, and disposed under various heads, are intended, we are told, for the improvement of scholars at classical and other schools, in the art of speaking, in reading, thinking, composing, and in the conduct of life. The extracts are selected with judgment, and well adapted to their various purposes.

The Bank of England's Vade-Mecum. 8*vo.* 1*s.* Becket.

Intended for the information of those who are unacquainted with the mode of transacting business at the Bank, and explaining the transactions relative to money, bills, the stocks, dividends, &c.

The London Directory, for 1783. 8*vo.* 1*s.* Lowndes.

A Guide to Stage Coaches, Waggons, Barges, &c. &c. 8*vo.* 1*s.*

Of these two productions the former contains a list of merchants and traders in and about London; and the latter, the rates of hackney coaches, chairs, boats, &c. Both of them appear to be compiled with care, and may therefore be useful.

THE

CRITICAL REVIEW.

For the Month of *August*, 1783.

Remarks, Critical and Illustrative, on the Text and Notes of the last Edition of Shakspeare. 8vo. 5s. 3d. Boards. Johnson.

CRITICISMS on Shakspeare have been so numerous, and sometimes so trifling, that curiosity is seldom excited by the copious, though important, additions of modern times ; and the attention is often fatigued, without any adequate gratification. It is indeed surprising that, after various efforts of conjecture, after refinement and learning had been exhausted in vain, the original text was only examined, and the poet's merit appreciated by his real works. From the early attempts of Rowe to the late accurate edition of Mr. Steevens, collation was more frequently promised than executed : though the path was generally acknowledged to be safe, it was rough and thorny ; and the critic, who could easily sport with conjecture, was unwilling to drudge in a work which required patient attention and laborious accuracy. Mr. Steevens' promises were ample, and, in the general opinion of the world, we believe that the expectations which he had excited were fully gratified ; but, after a long period, in which he has been in entire possession of the applause due both to his diligence and attention, our present author disputes his claim to, what seems the first duty of an editor, an accurate collation of the original copies. It is only after the most mature consideration that we have ventured to give our opinion on this subject ; and, while we avoid the meanness of adulation on one side, we shall endeavour, on the other, to deserve neither the imputation of blind prejudice or unjust severity.

The older impressions of Shakspeare possess different degrees of merit. It has been the usual custom to prefer those editions which were printed in the life-time of the author, where they can be procured ; while the folios, the labour of the players, are chiefly esteemed as the prototypes of those plays where no quarto impression has been found.——After a diligent examination, as far as our resources extend, the merits of the one set seem to have been too much exaggerated, and those of the other unjustly diminished : many valuable readings are to be recovered from the first folio, even where a previous quarto edition had existed.   The writings of Shakspeare were uncommonly fluent ; the blots and the corrections of sober criticism seldom obscured his first and most brilliant conceptions ; and, ' if the actor spoke more than was set down for him,' his gross additions did not probably pollute the copy at the theatre.   If, on this account, the folio may seem equally valuable with the quarto printed during the life of the author, it may appear more so, when we consider that it probably contained his mature reflections, and sometimes the result of his better judgment.   This attempt to ascertain the comparative merit of the several editions is not unnecessary ; for it will account for a part of the difference between our author and Mr. Steevens.   The editor of Shakspeare has endeavoured to establish the exclusive merit of the quartos, where they exist ; and we have principally considered his arguments in the opinion we have just delivered.   The author of the Remarks has in no instance endeavoured to combat them ; but, from his seldom mentioning the quartos, we may presume that they are not in his possession ; or that, in his judgment, they are of inferior merit.   The former may, therefore, think himself justified in recurring constantly to those which he considered as the most correct editions, the latter may accuse him on account of his different opinions.   Mr. Steevens will probably allege, that his frequent references to the folio shew that he has not been inattentive to the standard editions of his antagonist ; yet it must be acknowleged, that his complaisance for his coadjutor has sometimes prevented him from disturbing the text, where he probably had retrieved the genuine reading ; and, in a very few instances, the remarker has discovered it, where the editor had been totally silent.

As the foundation on which we have presumed that the dispute rests is now fixed, we shall next pay a little more attention to the author of the present Remarks.   As a critic on Shakspeare, he seems to possess diligence rather than accuracy, and judgment rather than candour.   His careful collation of the old folios has certainly recovered some genuine readings ; that they are not of great consequence cannot be imputed to our remarker's negligence ; the utmost efforts of
the

the gleaner's industry bear a very inconsiderable proportion to the rewards of the reaper. Even these, from the errors of the press, are not very advantageously conveyed; and, in several instances, he has already been anticipated. Remarks on the *last edition* of Shakspeare do not seem to have the Supplement for their object; and we should have candidly supposed that it had escaped his notice, if there were not some criticisms on it at the end. As he was sufficiently acquainted with these additional remarks, he ought to have suggested that he had, in many instances, been anticipated by them; nor plumed himself with the borrowed feathers of Mr. Malone, sir William Blackstone, and even of his antagonist Mr. Steevens. We could, in some respects, pardon an accidental coincidence; but in many of these remarks there is so striking and pointed a similarity, that we fear a careful comparison will not prejudice the public, either in favour of his accuracy or his candour.

Page 9. ' Now come I to my mother.' p. 12. ' to *leave* her token.' 13. ' Bear these letters *tightly.*' 14. ' *Curtail* dog.' 15. ' *Fortune thy foe.*' 46. ' I have found Demetrius, like a *jewel.*' 51. ' A *breed* of barren metal.' 56. ' As I remember.' 64. ' *Sure,* says Mr. Steevens.' 65. ' *Nettle* of India.' 67. ' *Vox.*' 69. ' *Some five.*' 99. ' A *Cotswold* man.' 112. ' Give me *thy* glove.' 120. ' I thank thee well.' 140. ' All the contagion.' 151. ' My friend when he *must* read me.' 181. ' Back foolish tears.' These, with many others which we have remarked, are taken from the Supplement of Mr. Malone, and are there attributed to their proper authors. The proportion in the subsequent pages is scarcely less.

The reader of this volume must soon observe the petulance and ill-humour of the author. He is anxious to discover the errors of the last editors, and eager to expose them; an established reputation seems the chief object of his satire; and to have deserved praise is the most probable method of attracting his vengeance. The merit of Dr. Johnson is too well established to be hurt by his unnerved arm. The learning and the judgment of this respectable commentator are unquestionable; his taste alone seems deficient; and his comments on Shakspeare, in this respect, frequently deserve some censure. He appears to have brought the learning and refinement of Warburton to elucidate a work, which required only an accurate investigation and plain common sense; and, as these failed in the attempt, their employment, and the merit of their author, has been unjustly diminished. As a specimen of

G 2   out our remarker's *manner*, we shall transcribe two or three notes; though ' Minnick,' in the sense of actor, has been very ably supported by Mr. Malone, in his Supplement.

' *Puck.* The shallowest thick-skin of that barren sort,
Who Pyramus presented in their sport,
Forsook his scene and enter'd in a brake :
When I did him at this advantage take,
An ass's nowl fixed on his head ;
Anon his Thisby must be answered,
And forth my *minnock* comes.

' *Minnock*, dr. Johnson says, is the reading of the old quarto, and, he believes, right. *Minnekin*, adds he, now *minx*, is a *nice trifling girl!* The folio, according to mr. Steevens, reads *mimmick*; perhaps for *mimick*, a word more familiar than that exhibited by one of the 4tos, for the other reads *minnick*. After all *minnock*, *mimmick*, and *minnick*, are onely, perhaps, misprints for *mammock*, which comes nearly to the same letters, and signifies *a huge misshapen thing* ; and is very properly applied by a Fairy to a clumsy over-grown clown. *Minnekin* is evidently a corruption of *mannekin* or *manikin*, properly *mankin*, a little man. Dr Johnson is so very imperfectly acquainted with the nature and derivation of the English language (and, in that respect, his dictionary, how valuable soever it may be on account of the explanation and use of English words, is beneath contempt ; there being scarcely ten words properly deduced in the whole work), that it is no wonder to find him making *minnekin* and *minx* the same word. But *minnekin* does *not* mean a *nice trifling girl* : and, though a substantive, is oftener used adjectively than otherwise : so in *Midas* (not John Lylies) : " *My* minikin *miss.*" The smallest sized pins are likewise called *minnekin*, or *minikin pins*. So Jerry Sneak, citizen and pin-maker, in the *Mayor of Garrat* :—" *as if I had been seeking for one of my own* minikins." As *mankin* got changed into *minnekin*, a little man, so they formed *minnekiness* a little woman, a girl ; which has since, by corruption, become *minx*. Thus *Laddess* (Ladess), from *Lad*, has, by a similar progress, become *Lass*.

' *Puck.* And at our *stamp* here o'er and o'er one falls.

' Dr. Johnson labours hard to prove this to be a vicious reading : " Fairies, says he, are never represented stamping, or of a size that should give force to a stamp, nor could they have distinguished the stamps of such from those of their own companions." He, therefor, reads :

' And at a *stump* here o'er and o'er one falls.

' To prove, however, that Fairies *could stamp*, mr. Steevens produces a passage from Olaus Wormius. He need not have gone so much out of his way : honest Reginald Scot could have i formed him, that our " grandams maides were woont to set a boll of milke before ' Incubus' and his cousine Robin good-
fellow,

I

fellow, for grinding of malt or muftard, and fweeping the houfe at midnight : and....that he would chafe exceedingly, if the maid or good-wife of the houfe, hauing compaffion of his nakednes, laid anie clothes for him, beefides his meffe of white bread and milke, which was his ftanding fee. For in that cafe he faith ; What haue we here ? Hemton hamten, here will I neuer more tread nor *ftampen.*" *Difcouerie of witchcraft.* 1584. p. 85.'

‘ *Shy.* ———— thou fhalt not *gormandize*
As thou haft done with me.

" The word [*gormandize*] is very ancient, and took its rife from a Danifh king. The Danes, towards the latter end of the ninth century, were defeated by king Alfred at Edendon in Wiltfhire ; and as an article of peace, Guthrum their king, commonly called Gurmond, fubmitted to be baptized, king Alfred being his godfather, who gave him the name of Athelftan, and took him for his adopted fon. During the ftay of the Danes in Wiltfhire, " they confumed their time in profufenefs, and bellycheer, in idlenefs and floth. Infomuch, that as from their lazinefs in general, we, even to this day, call them *Lur-Danes*; fo from the licentiousnefs of Gurmond, and his army in particular, we brand all luxurious and profufe people, by the name of *Gurmondizers.*" And this luxury, and this lazinefs, are the fole monuments, the only memorials by which the Danes have made themfelves notorious to pofterity, by being encamped in Wiltfhire. Vide, *A Vindication of Stone-Heng reftored*, by John Webb, efq. p. 227. Ben Jonfon in his *Sejanus*, act I.

" That great *Gourmond*, fat Apicius. G."

‘ After fuch a pompous difplay of learning, fo ftrangely introduced into the margin of Shakfpeare, how will this mr. G. (who has certainly fhewed, if not judgment, at leaft prudence, in concealing his name) be furprifed to hear that there is not a fingle jot either of fenfe or of truth from the beginning to the end of his laborious differtation ! *Gourmand*, a glutton, and *Gourmandife*, gluttony, whence Jonfons *Gourmond*, and our *gormandize* are immediately taken, are common French words to be found in every dictionary ; and *Lurdane*, properly *lourden*, is derived from *lourdin*, or *falourdin*, a word of the fame fignification, in the fame language, equally common. Either *Gourmond* or *Lurdane*, therefor, has no more (poffibly, much lefs) connection with the ancient Danes, than it has with this fame mr. G. the ftructor of the above ingenious, but, alas ! too eafyly demolifhed fabric.'

The hiftorical remarks of our author frequently deferve attention ; he feems familiar with the old chronicles, and has, in many paffages, elucidated Shakfpeare from them. We fhall felect two which cafually occur to our obfervation,

‘ *Cb.*

' *Ch. Just.* And *struck me* in the very seat of judgment.

' Sir John Hawkins subjoins an account of the insult given to the speaker by prince Henry, from Sir Thomas Elyot. But mr. Malone observes that there is no mention in it of the princes having *struck* him. " Speed however," adds he, " who quotes Elyot, says, *on I know not what authority*, that the prince gave the judge a blow on the face." That this most learned gentleman may, for the future, *know on what authority* Speed made the assertion, he has an opportunity to peruse the following extract.

" For imprisonments of one of his [prince Henrys] wanton mates and vnthriftie plaifaiers he *strake the chiefe Justice with his fiste on the face.* For which offence he was not onely committed to streyght prison, but also of his father put out of the preuy counsaill and banished the courte." Hall, Hen. IV. It is more than probable that Hollinshed has the same story; and the commentator might have likewise found it,—where Shakspeare did, —in the old anonymous play.'

' *A room in the Tower.* Enter Mortimer, *brought in a chair, and jailors.*

' Mr. Edwards, in his MS. notes, says mr. Steevens, observes, that Shakspeare has varyed from the truth of history, to introduce this scene between Mortimer and Richard Plantagenet. Edmund Mortimer served under Henry V. in 1422, and dyed unconfined in Ireland in 1424.

' The truth of this charge should have been established by some better authority than the dictum of mr. Edwards, adopted by mr. Steevens. In the third year of Henry the sixth (1425), and during the time that Peter duke of Coimbra was entertained in London, " Edmonde Mortymer," says Hall, " the last erle of Marche of that name (which longe tyme had bene restrayned frō hys liberty, and fynally waxed lame) diseased wythout yssue, whose inheritance discended to lord Richard Plantagenet, &c."

' This authority, even if the fact were otherwise, is sufficient to protect Shakspeare against the charge of having varyed from the truth of history to introduce the scene.'

The instances of his emendations from the older copies, which cannot be claimed by former authors, we have already observed, are not very important. We shall select a few, in the order in which they stand. The boatswain, in the Tempest, says, ' We will not *handle* a rope more.' The old word is ' *hand*,' and it is at present the sea-term. Our predecessor, Dr. Smollett, in his eulogium on lieutenant Bowling, the uncle of Roderick Random, introduces Jack Rattlin saying, ' Ben Block was the first man who taught him to reef, steer, and *hand* a rope;' yet *handle* is the word in all the editions. Prospero is said to ' be " wrapped" in secret studies;' the word in the old editions is certainly ' rapt;' but we have

observed

observed that Mr. Mason, in his Monody on Pope, has fallen into the same error. The remarker, in the following passage, viz.

'—————————— Urchins
Shall, for that vast of night that they may work,
All exercise on thee'——

seems to be mistaken by interpreting, ' spirits, perhaps, in the shape of *urchins* or *hedge-hogs.* In fact *urchin* is now frequent for a little creature ; and we find, from this circumstance of their size, fairies had acquired the name of urchins. Page says, in the Merry Wives of Windsor, that he will dress up children

' Like *urchins*, ouphes, and fairies.'

The remarker observes on that passage of Slender—' No, forsooth, he hath a " *little wee*" face'—that the meaning is extremely little ; and that the word is common in the North. But we apprehend that the proper word for *little* is *wee* ; and that, however diminutives are accumulated, he will never find *both* in one phrase. We have frequently heard ' wee bit housey,' for a very little house ; but do not recollect the expression of a little wee : it should probably be ' *little whey.*' The line which our remarker introduces from Cleveland is not connected with the subject ; a " Yorkshire *wee bit*," longer than a mile, is a way bit, or a bit of distance.—There is scarcely a passage in the poet which has excited so much attention as a speech of Leontes, in Much ado about Nothing ; it is simple and easy in itself, but confused by the attempts to explain it.

' If such a one will smile and stroke his beard,
And, sorrow wag ! cry hem, when he should groan.'

Even our remarker gives it up as inexplicable, though the present reading is that of the old copies, omitting only a comma after ' sorrow'. It must be observed that, in many provinces of England, ' wag' has the force of away—avaunt—and the reading is obviously, if such a one will hide his grief, drive off his sorrow, and when a groan involuntarily arises, obscure it by crying hem, &c. If the critics on Shakspeare had been more accustomed to provincial dialects, they would have found less difficulty in the ' God of their idolatry.' Thus, in Macbeth—we quote from the first folio—

' ——————No, this hand will rather
The *multitudinous* sea *incarnardine*,
Making the green one red'——————

G 4

The

The meaning is obviouſly, that his hand is ſo bloody, that the vaſt ſea (or the habitation of multitudes of living creatures) will be tinged with it, ſo that even the green one will become red.　An able critic explained ' multitudinous' by the variety of denominations which have been aſſigned to the different parts of the ocean ; but it is more probable that Shakſpeare alluded only to the ſea in general, and to the red ſea. It is a frequent means of diſtinction, in the provinces, to add the word *one* to the diſcriminating epithet, and even *that one* is very generally uſed in many counties.　But it is not our object to increaſe the number of annotators on Shakſpeare ; as we have already extended this article beyond its intended length, we muſt haſten to thoſe circumſtances which candor and propriety urge us to examine.

As a critic on Shakſpeare we have endeavoured to appreciate the merits of our author ; but, though his labours have deſerved our attention, and though we recommend them to Mr. Steevens, in his future publication, to be examined both with candour and caution, there are other ſentiments, artfully connected with his critical labours, which call for our ſevereſt reprehenſion.　That perjury itſelf *can* ever become a virtue, is a ſuppoſition too dangerous to be ſuffered to eſcape from the pen of a benevolent moraliſt.　His ſneers at myſteries, p. 23 ; his opinion that the revolution, in 1688, deſtroyed the conſtitution, p. 124 ; his indecent reflections on the conſequences of that meaſure, p. 84 ; will neither add to the credit of his head or his heart*.　We have by no means pointed out all, or even the moſt obnoxious paſſages of this kind ; nor uſed the language which is adequate to our feelings, and conviction of their pernicious tendency.　We need not, by our reproofs, diſſeminate what will be more properly conſigned to everlaſting oblivion ; or, by a violent condemnation, permit the reſentment due to virtue and juſtice to lie under the imputation of private pique or perſonal reſentment.

Our remarker adds ſome propoſals for preparing a genuine edition of the plays of William Shakſpeare, to be printed from the firſt folios, corrected by the quartos.　This edition is to be attended with ſhort notes and an accurate gloſſary. But, in this reſpect, we fear the editor will be under ſome peculiar diſadvantages.　His orthography is to us diſagreeable

* In ſome inſtances theſe paſſages are attributed to Mr. Collins. The annotator on Shakſpeare of that name has been ſome time dead ; but there is an author, diſtinguiſhed by this name, to whom theſe remarks ſhould probably be attributed :—His works are ſufficiently known ; and his ſentiments, in many reſpects, ſeem to be congenial to thoſe of the remarker.

　　　　　　　　　　　　　　　　　　　　　　　　　and

and uncouth; but it is not easy to enlarge on this subject: the several quotations, which we have printed exactly, will be sufficient examples of it. Besides this, we have already hinted, that the correctness of the present volume does not afford us the fullest proofs of his accuracy. The attempt, however, to give the genuine text of the author is proper and laudable; as the first editions are with difficulty procured, and, in many places, we are fully convinced that the author is more intelligible than *some* of his commentators.

First Lines of the Practice of Physic, for the Use of Students in the University of Edinburgh. By William Cullen, M. D. (Concluded, from p. 27.)

THE third volume of our respectable professor is distinguished, like the former, by the extent of its views, as well as the sagacity and discernment in their application. We shall, as usual, follow him with unequal steps; and, where we find a fault, or hesitate dislike, would wish to be acquitted of the imputation of presumption, or the remotest wish to detract from the very great and deserved reputation of the author.

The present volume includes the whole class of neurofes: the diseases of this class are frequently so dissimilar, as to admit of few general observations, which may be applied to any one family; and the several disorders are connected in consequence of their proceeding from an interruption, from a debility, or from an irregularity of the powers of sense and motion, under the titles of Comata, Adynamiæ, and Spasmi.

The diseases of the order comata are very nearly connected, and seem to differ only in degree; so that this order may be considered as strictly natural: these are apoplexy and palsy. Apoplexy is not limited to a *total* abolition of the powers of sense and motion, that the carus, cataphora, coma, and lethargus may be arranged under the same genus: it will be evident that they could not, with propriety, be separated. The author details, in a concise manner, the history and remote causes of the disease; and remarks, that the stertorous breathing is not always present, even in the most complete form, or the most violent degree of it. The proximate cause, or the interruption of the motion of the nervous power, is either owing to some compression of the origin of the nerves, or to something which destroys the mobility of the power itself. These two different and almost opposite sets of causes are considered very particularly; and they will be found to require the strictest attention, as the compression, from an effusion

effusion of fluids in the brain, is materially increased by those means which would restore the mobility of the nervous power. The defect of this distinction has often occasioned very dangerous consequences, and will account for all the confusion and contradiction in those authors who have treated of the cure of apoplexy and palsy. Though our author allows of the distinction of sanguine and serous apoplexies, he thinks it capable of little application in practice, except when the serous effusion may depend on hydropic diathesis. After Dr. Cullen has endeavoured to arrange the several particular causes, and to assign each its proper station, he proceeds to the prognosis and prophylaxis. The latter chiefly consists in preventing the plethoric state by exercise and diet; and accumulations in the head, by evacuations by stool, or a seton in the neck. In the course of apoplexies from effusion, he thinks vomits and stimulants precarious remedies; in other respects he does not materially differ from the common practice. In apoplexy from a sedative poison, besides vomits and acrid glysters, he recommends stimulants and repeated affusions of cold water.

Palsies, which are defined only by diminished motion, depend on an affection of the brain or of the nerves in their course; but the former is only treated of in this chapter, and our author's observations are confined to the most usual state of it, the hæmiplegia. The circumstances of the disease and its cure so nearly resemble those of apoplexy, that we shall not describe them. It will be only necessary to observe, that stimulants are allowed after the palsy has subsisted some time, when the compression is removed, or the disease is known to have proceeded from narcotic powers. The various kinds of stimulants are described in this place, and their different merits considered. In this part the professor is generally accurate; but seems more cautious in the use of stimulants than even his own system would allow.

The next order, the adynamiæ, consists of diseases arising from a weakness or loss of motion, either in the vital or natural functions. It contains only the syncope, dyspepsia, and hypochondriasis. Fainting, so commonly a slight complaint, sometimes arises from the most material and incurable topical affections of the heart and arteries; but our author chiefly confines his account to that species, which depends on the diminished energy of the brain, since this energy is equally necessary to the motion of the heart, as its own inherent muscular power. The causes of this diminished energy are either direct in their operation, or indirect; joy, violent exertion, and other similar causes, produce this effect from the constitution

of

of the nerves, by which every muscular action is alternated with relaxation. The organic affections of the heart are neither to be distinguished by their particular symptoms, or to be removed by medicine. The cure of the first and chief species of fainting, as it depends on removing the remote causes, which our limits would not permit us to enumerate, must be perused in the work itself.

The dyspepsia is so often a symptom of general weakness, that it may appear to have been improperly distinguished as an idopathic genus; but our author contends that all its symptoms frequently concur in one person, and therefore may be presumed to depend on one proximate cause: he might have also added, that it is very frequently hereditary, independent of any arthritic disposition. It may proceed from organic affections, from a diminished quantity, or a vitiated state of the gastric juices; that kind of dyspepsia is, however, chiefly considered which arises from a weakness of the fibres of the stomach. The causes and cure are detailed at full length; but we can find nothing that is sufficiently new or interesting to detain us.

The hypochondriac affection is considered as a disease by almost every author. It chiefly consists in a peculiar state of mind; and, as usual, this is connected with a particular condition of the body, resembling dyspepsia. This connection is, however, observed both in the sanguine flaccid temperament of young people, and the firm rigid melancholic temperament of those who have passed the meridian of life. In the former, the symptoms of dyspepsia prevail, and the disease is to be referred to the former genus; in the latter, those of melancholy; and it is consequently classed under that of hypochondriasis. This may be sufficient for a general account of the distinction, which Dr. Cullen considers with greater accuracy, and then proceeds to the cure. In hypochondriasis we chiefly follow the methods recommended in dyspepsia, except the diluents are more useful, and tonics more hurtful, in the present disease. Those remedies which also contribute to amuse the mind, are particularly serviceable. The management of the mind requires considerable attention. As we cannot easily abridge our author's account, we shall insert it entire.

' The management of the mind, in hypochondrias, is often nice and difficult. The firm persuasion that generally prevails in such patients, does not allow their feelings to be treated as imaginary, nor their apprehension of danger to be considered as groundless, though the physician may be persuaded that it is the case in both respects. Such patients, therefore, are not to be treated either by raillery or by reasoning.

' It

' It is said to be the manner of hypochondriacs to change often
their physician, and, indeed, they often do it consistently; for a
physician who does not admit the reality of the disease, cannot be
supposed to take much pains to cure it, or to avert the danger of
which he entertains no apprehension.

' If, in any case, the pious fraud of a placebo be allowable, it
seems to be in treating hypochondriacs, who, anxious for relief,
are fond of medicines, and though often disappointed, will still
take every new drug that can be proposed to them.

' As it is the nature of man to indulge every present emotion,
so the hypochondriac cherishes his fears, and, attentive to every
feeling, finds in trifles, light as air, a strong confirmation of his
apprehensions.   His cure, therefore, depends especially upon
the interruption of his attention, or upon its being diverted to
other objects than his own feelings.

' Whatever aversion, to application of any kind, may appear
in hypochondriacs, there is nothing more pernicious to them than
absolute idleness, or a vacancy from all earnest pursuit.   It is
owing to wealth admitting of indolence, and leading to the pursuit of transitory and unsatisfying amusements, or exhausting
pleasures only, that the present times exhibit to us so many instances of hypochondriacism.

' The occupations of business suitable to their circumstances
and situation in life, if neither attended with emotion, anxiety,
nor fatigue, are always to be admitted, and adhered to by hypochondriacs.   But occupations upon which a man's fortune depends, and which are always, therefore, objects of anxiety to
melancholic men, and, more particularly, where such occupations are exposed to accidental interruptions, disappointments,
and failures, it is from these that the hypochondriac is certainly
to be withdrawn.

' The hypochondriac who is not necessarily. by circumstances·
or habits, engaged in business, is to be drawn from his attention
to himself by some amusement.

' The various kinds of sport and hunting, as pursued with
some ardor, and attended with exercise, if not too violent, are
amongst the most useful.

' All those amusements which are in the open air, joined with
moderate exercise, and requiring some dexterity, are generally
of use.

' Within doors, company which engages attention, which is
willingly yielded to, and is, at the same time, of a chearful.
kind, will be always found of great service.   -

' Play, in which some skill is required, and where the stake is
not an object of much anxiety, if not too long protracted, may
often be admitted.

' In dyspeptics, however, gaming, liable to sudden and considerable emotions, is dangerous, and the long continuance of it,
with night-watching, is violently debilitating.   But in melan-
cholics,

cholics, who commonly excel in ſkill, and are leſs ſuſceptible of violent emotions, it is more admiſſible, and is often the only amuſement that can engage them.

' Muſic, to a nice ear, is a hazardous amuſement, as a long attention to it is very fatiguing.

' It frequently happens, that amuſements of every kind are rejected by hypochondriacs, and, in that caſe, mechanical means of interrupting thought are the remedies to be ſought for.

' Such is to be found in briſk exerciſe, which requires ſome attention in the conduct of it.

' Walking is ſeldom of this kind; though, as gratifying to the reſtleſſneſs of hypochondriacs, it has ſometimes been found uſeful.

' The required interruption of thought is beſt obtained by riding on horſeback, or in driving a carriage of any kind.

' The exerciſe of ſailing, except it be in an open boat, engaging ſome attention, does very little ſervice.

' Exerciſe in an eaſy carriage, in the direction of which the traveller takes no part, unleſs it be upon rough roads, or driven pretty quickly, and with long continuance, is of little advantage.

' Whatever exerciſe be employed, it will be moſt effectual when employed in the purſuit of a journey; firſt, becauſe it withdraws a perſon from many objects of uneaſineſs and care which might preſent themſelves at home; ſecondly, as it engages in more conſtant exerciſe, and in a greater degree of it than is commonly taken in airings about home; and, laſtly, as it is conſtantly preſenting new objects which call forth a perſon's attention.'

The order ſpaſmi is, in our opinion, very exceptionable. It naturally contains the tonic and clonic ſpaſms of different authors: it may be allowed alſo to contain the aſthma and pertuſſis, though terminated by an evacuation; but the diabetes, the diarrhœa, and the cholera, are very improperly arranged with the other diſeaſes. To ſuppoſe them to ariſe from increaſed motion, is to forſake the firſt foundation of an arrangement from ſymptoms, and to recur to an immediate cauſe. The firſt genus tetanus, including the locked jaw, is a diſeaſe of warm climates; and, though ſome of its leſſer ſpecies occur in theſe kingdoms, they are ſeldom violent or dangerous, but when they proceed from injuries, or appear in new-born children. Our author ſeems to add little to what has been hitherto ſaid by the practitioners of warmer ſituations, where the diſeaſe is more frequent.

The epilepſy is conſidered at great length: our author acknowledges, that he is not able to explain the peculiar ſtate of mind, which immediately occaſion thoſe violent and preternatural motions; but the remote cauſes, as they are more eaſily the ſubjects of obſervation, are fully detailed. The uſual ufual ftimulants, both in the brain and other parts, violent paffions and over-diftention of the veffels, have been fo often confidered as caufes of epilepfy, that we need not repeat them. Dr. Cullen feems anxious to point out another fet of caufes, or thofe whofe firft effect is to diminifh the energy of the brain, and which therefore are alfo frequent caufes of fyncope. Thefe are hæmorrhages, depreffing paffions, odors and fedative poifons, whofe effects are certain, but whofe mode of operation he is unable to explain. Another caufe, of an uncertain nature, is the partial affection of a nerve, propagated to the brain, and ftyled aura epileptica, from its effects, which our author feems willing to refer to a direct ftimulus. The prædifponent caufe is mobility, more particularly depending on debility, or on ' a plethoric ftate of the body.' There are fome obfervations on the ftate of the nerves which may probably be confidered as more curious than ufeful; we fhall therefore omit them; but ought to add, that the ftate of fleep frequently feems to prædifpofe to the complaint.

The cure of epilepfy, which depends on the aura, is directed to the part affected, to which blifters, or the actual or potential cautery are applied, to procure a fufficient difcharge. If thefe fail, or are inadmiffible, the nerve is directed to be occafionally compreffed, or, if poffible, to be divided. The cure of thofe cafes, in which no aura can be perceived, depends on obviating the remote caufes. The mobility, from over-diftention, is obviated by fpare diet, iffues, and occafional bleedings; that from debility, by tonics and antifpafmodics. Our author has found the cuprum ammonicale frequently ufeful; the flowers of zinc have feldom deferved this title: fome accidental inftances of the good effects of mercury are mentioned; and Dr. Cullen thinks, from the analogy of tetanus, that this metal may be alfo adopted to fome cafes of epilepfy. Of the antifpafmodics, our author chiefly depends on mufk and opium; but thinks that the animal oil (we fuppofe he means the highly rectified oil of Dippel), may be alfo an effectual remedy. Thefe antifpafmodics muft be only employed, when no marks of diftention have exifted, or after they have been removed. A total change of diet and air, as well as of every accuftomed habit, has been fometimes ufeful.

The dance of St. Vitus is generally cured by the bark and other tonics: bleeding, which, in plethoric patients, has been fometimes ferviceable, Dr. Cullen thinks has been frequently injurious.

Palpitation of the heart depends on many different caufes, which we cannot explain, from our author, in this place. His

His observations, however, do not contain the whole of Senac's very elaborate account of the disease; but he continues to point out those causes which operate by depressing the nervous energy. The cure consequently depends on obviating them, or on preventing their effects, by avoiding agitation of mind and plethora; and by correcting the general mobility of the system.

The dyspnœa, which depends on so many causes, and requires an attention to these only, is very shortly considered by our author; and we shall therefore proceed to asthma, or the asthma convulsivum, arising from a spasmodic constriction of the muscular fibres of the bronchiæ. The history of the disease is remarkably accurate, and comprehensive; indeed the difficulty, either in understanding or distinguishing the complaint, is inconsiderable, though it is seldom cured, and not greatly alleviated. Bleeding, except on the first attacks, is seldom useful; and, though the costiveness should be prevented, any considerable discharge by stool is frequently hurtful. Blisters and issues have little effect; and the chief remedies are occasional vomits, acids, and neutral salts. To correct the mobility, antispasmodics have been frequently tried; but the usual ones have been of little service. Our author has found opium effectual, and generally safe; if any doubts of its propriety have arisen, they have chiefly been in consequence of the physician's mistaking the genuine inflammatory dyspnœa for the true spasmodic asthma. For the minute and necessary rules of diet and exercise we must refer to the work itself.

The hooping cough, in Dr. Cullen's opinion, arises from a specific contagion; and he observes, that it is frequently attended with a slight fever of the remittent kind, and sometimes with a considerable dyspnœa. The history and prognosis are full and accurate. In the early stages the violent effects and fatal tendency of the disease are to be obviated, by bleeding, an open belly, and repeated blisters. Vomits are highly useful in many ways; and Dr. Cullen chiefly approves of the tartar emetic for this purpose, employed in the manner directed by the late Dr. Fothergill. After the beginning, our author thinks that the disease may proceed from habit; and in that case is principally relieved by medicines, suited to change the state and habits of the nervous system. The different antispasmodics, the hemlock, the cup moss, and misleto, have frequently disappointed Dr. Cullen in their effects. Opium has been useful in moderating the cough; but his chief dependence seems to be on the Peruvian bark, and the change of air.

The

The pyrosis, a disease known in England by the name of water-pang, has been seldom treated of. Dr. Cullen thinks it arises from a spasm in the stomach, terminated by a discharge of the contents of the exhalents. Opium and æther relieve the paroxysm; but these and every other medicine, given to prevent its recurrence, has been useless. He has never tried the nux vomica, recommended by Linnæus, and indeed the disease is so slight, as seldom to require the interposition of the physician.

Our author's account of the colic is full and satisfactory. His observations on the use of opium in this complaint deserve attention, and we shall therefore transcribe them.

' In all cases where the colic comes on without any previous costiveness, and arises from cold, from passions of the mind, or other causes which operate especially on the nervous system, opium proves a safe and certain remedy; but in cases which have been preceded by long costiveness, or where the colic, though not preceded by costiveness, has, however, continued for some days without a stool, so that a stagnation of fæces in the colon is to be suspected, the use of opium is of doubtful effect. In such cases, unless a stool has been first procured by medicine, opium cannot be employed but with some hazard of aggravating the disease. However, even in these circumstances of costiveness, when without inflammation, the violence of the spasm is to be suspected, when vomiting prevents the exhibition of purgatives, and when, with all this, the pain is extremely urgent, opium is to be employed, not only as an anodyne, but also as an antispasmodic, necessary to favour the operation of purgatives, and may be so employed, when, either at the same time with the opiate, or not long after it, a purgative can be exhibited.'

As a purgative he prefers the crystals of tartar, as least liable to be rejected; and thinks that, if a stronger purgative be required, jalap may be useful. Antimonials in small doses, and calomel, have each had their supporters; but our author does not decide on their merit from his own experience. Mechanical dilatation has been often unsuccessfully attempted; but large quantities of warm water thrown into the intestines by a syringe, both from his own experiments, and those of De Haen, he judges to be one of the most powerful and effectual remedies.

The cholera is confined to an evacuation of bile; by which means many of the species of Sauvages and Sagar are excluded. Our author adds little to our former experience: in warm climates the disease is often fatal, and the method practised by Mr. Schotte, at Senegal; and some other physicians, in the

more

more urgent circumstances, seems to promise the greatest success.

The several species of diarrhœa are fully explained, and the practical observations depend on their nature. Purging our author thinks superfluous or hurtful; but we apprehend that this opinion ought to be received with great caution. We have often found hardened scybala evacuated, after a continuance of a natural diarrhœa, and suspect that an obstruction may remain in the upper parts of the canal; though, from the quantity of the discharge from the lower parts, the contents of the whole may *seem* to be evacuated. Where there is time for the operation of a purgative, and a diarrhœa is not colliquative, we ought always to wait for the effects of a remedy of this kind. We agree with our author that opiates may frequently, and with great propriety, be employed in the cure of diarrhœa.

The causes of diabetes are considered at some length; but Dr. Cullen thinks they are all unsatisfactory. Even that of Dr. Dobson, which our author observes was first hinted by himself, is embarrassed with many difficulties. The practice is very shortly detailed, as he has found the several remedies fallacious; and we are informed that we may soon expect a more satisfactory account of this subject.

The hysteria next follows, and is supposed to have a great connection with the state of the uterus, though the spasms seem to begin from the alimentary canal. The chief part of the proximate cause is a mobility of the system, depending, generally, on its plethoric state; and the remedies are very nearly those of epilepsy. Of the hydrophobia, the account is short, as the disease in this country is little known; but Dr. Cullen observes, that the success of mercury is better supported by experience, than that of almost any remedy generally employed.

After this long and particular account of these last volumes of the very able and learned professor, it would be almost impertinent to give any opinion; yet we apprehend they will be generally allowed not to have detracted in the smallest degree, from the great and acknowledged merit of their author.

An historical Sketch of Medicine and Surgery, from their Origin to the present Time. By William Black, M. D. 8vo. 6s. sewed. Johnson.

TO delineate even the slightest sketch of the history of medicine and surgery; to trace the principal discoveries and improvements; to point out the authors, and to detect their

their imperfections and errors, must appear an object too extensive for the labour of an individual; and the bulk of the present volume seems very inadequate to it. But though our author's attempt was arduous, his success has not been inconsiderable: and, instead of captious exceptions at its imperfection, we are surprised at the numerous and various subjects which are included in the small compass of the present work. In many respects it is, indeed, necessarily a catalogue of names; but the principal circumstances, the various æras, which gave a new appearance to the art, are pointed out with precision; and the observations, though short, are generally candid, and sometimes interesting.

In the earlier periods, he had the assistance of Le Clerc, and, in the middle stage, of Freind; and of these authors he has given, what appears to us, an accurate abridgment:—We believe that he pretends to no more. It is in the subsequent period that he chiefly fails; for, though he has given, at length, the opinions of Hippocrates and Galen, he has very slightly mentioned Van Helmont, the most rational of the chemical sect. He has scarcely noticed Stahl, who produced a very material revolution in the practice of physic, in Germany, except as a chemist; and De Gorter, who was one of the most rational commentators on Hippocrates, and the author of the most judicious compendium of the practice of physic, independent of other works, is chiefly praised on account of a system of materia medica, written, or at least published, by his son. The account of the plague, and the history of quarantines, is, in general, accurate; but he has unaccountably omitted a very satisfactory treatise on it by De Haen, and the very rational observations of Chenot, on the Plague of Transylvania, who himself attended the victims of the epidemic, during the whole progress.

These are some of the more material omissions, which have occurred to us; we have not sought after faults, though our author's disrespect to Reviewers would have justified us, if we had been more eager in our researches. 'Those (he observes) who are acquainted with the *manufactory* of such anonymous criticisms, will think it prudent, very frequently, to distrust their panegyric and their censure.' We would give this confident young man a little *prudent* advice, that is, not to provoke the censure of those, whose opinion is sometimes regarded; or, at least, not wantonly to increase the number of even inconsiderable enemies. If these criticisms were manufactured in the manner which he seems to hint at, this sentence would have been a sufficient provocation for greater severity, and it would not have been difficult to find proper subjects.

- - The

The number of objects in the history of medicine, for the last three hundred years, has induced him to arrange them in regular classes. In this part we do not meet with many mistakes. His account is mostly deficient in the chemical and philosophical part; and there are some errors in the materia medica and natural history. The terra Japonica is said, for instance, to be the inspissated juice of a palm tree; and the seneka, to be only diaphoretic and diuretic. The turpith mineral is inserted among the despicable nostrums, constantly sold for curing the hydrophobia; but the utility of mercury is sufficiently established, and the turpith mineral has been frequently found to produce the peculiar effects of the remedy, sooner than any other preparation.

In the modern part he has very slightly mentioned either Dr. Hunter or Dr. Cullen; and his omission is more inexcuseable, as they have considerably improved their respective sciences. On the whole, we would recommend to him to revise this work with greater care, and to extend his account of the improvement of the *art* itself, as well as his *list* of authors.

Six Discourses delivered by Sir John Pringle, Bart. when President of the Royal Society; on Occasion of Six Annual Assignments of Sir Godfrey Copley's Medal; to which is prefixed the Life of the Author, by Andrew Kippis, D. D. F. R. S. and S. A. 8vo. 6s. Cadell.

WE have again perused, with fresh pleasure, these elegant Discourses, which appear to have been adapted to the circumstances, in which they were delivered, with the strictest propriety. They are light, easy, and eloquent; so that, while they point out the real merit of the candidate, by stating the advances which had been already made in that particular branch of science which has deserved the premium, they avoid the stiffness of a professed lecture, and the most remote suspicion of the society's want of information, even from a president. As they have been already published, the public have probably formed its opinion of their merits; we therefore, only mention, that the discourse was on factitious airs, when the medal was presented to Dr. Priestley;—on the torpedo, when Mr. Walsh received a similar compliment;—on the attraction of mountains, for Dr. Maskelyne;—on the means of preserving the health of mariners, for Captain Cook;—on the invention and improvements of the reflecting telescope, when Mr. Mudge received the honorary premium;

—and on the theory of gunnery, for Mr. Hutton. It may be also neceſſary to remark, that the diſcourſe on the health of ſeamen, is peculiarly perſpicuous and inſtructive;—that on the torpedo, entertaining, from the various quotations, both from the claſſics and former natural hiſtorians.

The Life of Sir John Pringle chiefly intereſts us in this publication. It is written by Dr. Kippis, with the affection of a friend, the preciſion of a philoſopher, and the moderation of a candid enquirer. A preſident of the Royal Society, the ſucceſſor of a Newton, is placed in a ſtation too conſpicuous to avoid the envenomed ſhafts of envy, or probably the detraction of an intereſted or ambitious competitor. If he was not equally converſant with every ſcience which forms the extenſive circle of human attainments, he was well acquainted with the moſt important, and profeſſed, with diſtinguiſhed reputation, one of the moſt valuable and intereſting. If he was impatient and reſtleſs, if he did not meet every intruder with equal complacency, or liſten with the ſame attention to the candid improver and to the viſionary reformer, he could only, like the reſt of mankind, be taxed with venial failings, or making a neceſſary diſtinction, which his detractors could not eaſily underſtand. His general conduct, as preſident of the Royal Society, was able and dignified; as a phyſician he was learned and ſagacious; and, as a friend, candid, ſincere, and affectionate. His life was not the ſubject of wonderful events, or diſtinguiſhed by important changes. Deſigned for merchandize, he adopted the profeſſion of phyſic, in conſequence of his having heard, by accident, a lecture from Boerhaave. He was early appointed profeſſor of moral philoſophy in the univerſity of Edinburgh; and, from the attention and reſpect of the patrons, we have reaſon to believe that he taught with reputation and ſucceſs. Even at that time, therefore, his abilities were not ſo inconſiderable, or his views ſo limited, as they been ſince repreſented. His appointment to the office of phyſician to the duke of Cumberland—the army in general—his ſettling in London—the reſpect paid to him by his gradual advancement to the higheſt honours both in philoſophy and phyſic—by foreigners as well as his own countrymen—if they are not common events, yet are ſcarcely of ſufficient importance induce us to enlarge this preſent article. We apprehend, however, that Dr. Kippis is miſtaken in one point; if we were not miſinformed, Sir John's deſign of reſiding, during the ſummer, in Scotland, originated from his viſit to it about the year 1773, which, we believe, was the firſt that he had paid to his native country ſince he attended the duke of Cumberland there, in 1745.

3

Dr.

Dr. Kippis's observations are frequently distinguished by their justness and propriety, and deserve a considerable share of attention. We would recommend the following remarks to the younger part of the profession, who are candidates for fame and fortune:

' It was to his knowledge, his application, and his attention alone, that he trusted for making his way in the metropolis. If any little artifices are ever made use of, in the city of London, to excite popularity, and to promote medical practice, Dr. Pringle was the last man to adopt such artifices. If he could not have built his success on the basis of substantial merit, he would not have succeeded at all. We cannot but think that such a conduct is highly deserving of approbation and applause. In every profession of life, there is no satisfaction that is equal to the consciousness of inward worth, and of a mind superior to the various contrivances for obtaining the notice and favour of mankind, to which insufficiency, vanity, or covetousness, sometimes have recourse.'

In a few passages the language of the biographer is in some degree exceptionable, from its familiarity; ' a *set* speech' and ' took the principal *lead*' with a few others, are forms of expression which are not suitable to the simple elegance of the rest of the performance. As a general specimen, however, of Dr. Kippis's work, we shall select the intellectual character of this eminent physician.

' Sir John Pringle's eminent character as a practical physician, as well as a medical author, is so well known, and so universally acknowleged, that an enlargement upon it cannot be necessary. He was distinguished, in this respect, by his attention and sagacity. For the recovery of his patients he was anxiously concerned; and his anxiety might, perhaps, be increased from his conviction, that the art of physic, though eminently useful, must ever, from unavoidable causes, be attended with a certain degree of uncertainty. His care was rewarded with much success in the course of his practice. In the exercise of his profession, he was not rapacious; being ready, on various occasions, to give his advice without pecuniary views. This he never denied to the poor; and, from many of his friends in better circumstances, and who were well able to afford the customary gratifications, he refused to accept of fees.

' The turn of Sir John Pringle's mind led him chiefly to the love of science, which he built on the firm basis of fact. With regard to philosophy in general, he was as averse to theory, unsupported by experiments, as he was with respect to medicine in particular. Lord Bacon was his favourite author; and to the method of investigation recommended by that great man he steadily adhered. Such being his intellectual character, it will not be thought surprising that he had a dislike to Plato. The speculations of that

sublime

sublime and ingenious, that elegant and beautiful, but at the same time fanciful writer, were by no means suited to the sober spirit of inquiry cultivated by Sir John Pringle. Indeed, whatever attention he might have paid, in his earlier days, and when he was professor of ethics at Edinburgh, to metaphysical disquisitions, he lost all regard for them in the latter part of his life; and though some of his most valued friends had engaged in discussions of this kind, with very different views of things, he did not choose to revert to the studies of his youth, but contented himself with the opinions he had then formed.'

We find that Sir John Pringle had little fondness for poetry, though himself the subject of an elegant ode ; and even thought the defects of Shakspeare not sufficiently compensated by his excellencies,

' In his youth, however, he had not been neglectful of philological inquiries ; and, after having omitted them for a time, he returned to them again ; so far, at least, as to endeavour to obtain a more exact knowledge of the Greek tongue, probably with a view to a better understanding of the New Testament. He paid a great attention to the French language ; and it is said that he was fond of Voltaire's critical writings. How far this might contribute to the honour of Sir John's taste, I shall not decide. However just that eminent Frenchman's observations may have been on some subjects of criticism, the truly ingenious and excellent Mrs. Montagu hath amply shewn, that he was absolutely unequal to the task of determining concerning the merit of Shakspeare. Among all his other pursuits, Sir John Pringle never forgot the study of the English language. This he regarded as a matter of so much consequence, that he took uncommon pains with respect to the style of his compositions ; and it cannot be denied, that he excels in perspicuity, correctness, and propriety of expression.

' Though our author was not fond of poetry, there was a sister art for which he had a great affection, and that was music. Of this art he was not merely an admirer, but became so far a practitioner in it, as to be a performer on the violincello at a weekly concert given by a society of gentlemen at Edinburgh. Music, if not too eagerly pursued, or permitted to engross an undue proportion of time, is a fine relief to the mind of a literary man. It is often neglected, as persons advance in years ; and this, I believe, was the case with my friend.

' Besides a close application to medical and philosophical science, Sir John Pringle, during the latter part of his life, devoted much time to the study of divinity. This was with him a very favourite and interesting object. He read many commentators on scripture, and especially on the New Testament, of which he was anxious to obtain an exact and critical knowlege. In this pursuit the learned and judicious bishop Pearce's Commentary and Notes gave him particular pleasure, and were

                                            -greatly

greatly fuited to his tafte. He correfponded frequently with Michaelis on theological fubjects; and that celebrated profeffor addreffed to him fome letters on Daniel's Prophecy of the Seventy Weeks, which Sir John thought worthy of being publifhed in this country. Accordingly he was at confiderable pains, and fome expence, in the publication, which appeared, in 1773, under the following title: " Joannis Davidis Michaelis, Prof. Ordin. Philof. et Soc. Reg. Scient. Goettingenfis Collegæ, Epiftolæ, de LXX. Hebdomadibus Danielis, ad D. Joannem Pringle, Baronettum; primò privatim miffæ, nunc vero utriufque confenfu publicè editæ." 8vo.

' Sir John Pringle was likewife a diligent and frequent reader of fermons; which form a valuable part of Englifh literature. Indeed, taken in their full extent, they conftitute a much more valuable part of Englifh literature than perhaps is commonly imagined; for, independently of their theological merit, in explaining the doctrines of natural and revealed religion, and throwing light on paffages of fcripture, we fhall fcarcely any where meet with a richer treafure of practical obfervation, or with reflections on life and manners, that are better calculated to improve the underftanding, mend the heart, and regulate the conduct.'

Memoirs of Albert de Haller, M. D.   By *Thomas Henry,* F. R. S,
    12mo. 2s. 6d.   Johnfon.

IF, in the eloges of fome foreign academies, the authors remember one part only of the duty of an hiftorian, ' ne quid falfi dicere audeat,' they are not fo careful of the other part, ' ne quid veri non audeat.' Every quality which commands refpect from the judgment, or allures the fancy, is detailed with a fcrupulous accuracy; and the perfect heroes of their tales are fuppofed to be even without the common failings of humanity. Thefe varnifhed hiftories are but indifferently calculated to lead the afpiring youth, or to inftruct the philofopher. The one will be cautious of attempting to attain a prize, which requires the union of fuch uncommon excellencies; the other will often reject the truth, becaufe he finds it mixed and almoft infeparable from improbabilities. We lately introduced the life of a refpectable phyfician, with confiderable applaufe; becaufe, though not wholly without the exaggerations of a zealous admiration, or entirely free from that colouring which friendfhip delights in beftowing, the amiable errors of an affectionate heart, it was diftinguifhed by candor and moderation, which added luftre both to the character of the biographer and of his fubject.

The prefent life has all the defects of the foreign panegyrics; it is a continued train of excellencies: induftry and genius, an active benevolence, and a perfevering ftudy, are almoft the

unvaried

unvaried views which are given of this celebrated professor. We will not deny that he deserved them in a considerable degree; but an attentive perusal of his writings will discover that his candor was sometimes mixed with a hasty petulance, and the effects of his learning and industry sometimes obscured by an obstinate attachment to former opinions. It must however be acknowleged, that his merits greatly counter-balanced his defects; and, if he has not added to our stock, by the ingenuity of his theories, the cobweb systems of a lively imagination, he has laid a more secure foundation, by an attentive collection of facts, and an industrious pursuit of accurate and well-digested experiments. The observations on his opinions of generation, the formation of the bones, and on irritability, are slight and inconsiderable; and, though we are now presented with some facts which were not very generally known, we wish to see a more accurate and finished picture of this very able physiologist. As a specimen we shall select his concluding character.

'M. de Haller was most agreeable in conversation. His elocution was free, strong, and concise; and his knowlege most distinguishedly diversified. His immense reading, fertile and faithful memory, and sound judgment, gave satisfaction to men of all dispositions. He was superior to the affectation of wit, and disdained to make a parade of the knowlege he possessed. His soul was gentle, and his heart replete with sensibility. All his writings are expressive of his love of virtue. Ever pure in his own morals, he beheld with regret the neglect of them in others, and sincerely lamented the influence which irregularities in private life seemed likely to produce on the manners of the state.

'Religion was the object of his most serious inquiries, even from his earliest youth. His comprehensive mind, ever capable of a just mode of thinking, had been happily impressed with the grand idea of a God, the great origin of all beings, and with the belief of eternity, "that ancient source as well as universal sepulchre of worlds and ages, in which the duration of this globe is lost as that of a day, and the life of man as a moment." Persuaded of a future life, he waited with confidence for that consummation which shall dissipate the mists of human wisdom, and display to us the universe such as it actually is, by the light of a new luminary, emanating from the Divinity himself. It was impossible that a spirit thus elevated, and constantly employed in researches after truth, could neglect to inquire into that most important one, the religion of his ancestors and of his country. Convinced of the reality of revelation, by diligently studying the scriptures, he could not behold, with indifference, any attacks on this fundamental law, this strongest band of society; and at a time when other illustrious men prostituted their fame and talents in making dangerous attacks upon religion, he thought it his duty to enter the lists as her avowed champion and defender.

'Few

' Few learned men have been born with fo active a difpofition, and few have loft fo little time as Haller. His life was fpent in his library, furrounded by his pupils, by his friends, by his fellow citizens, his children and his wife, whom he had infpired with a tafte for the fciences, and who all were employed, under his infpection, either in making extracts from books, or delineating plants and animals.

' A confiderable increafe in his bulk, weak eyes, and the habit of writing in fo fmall a character as to be almoft illegible, neceffarily rendered application to literary purfuits more difficult. Yet fo abfolute was the dominion of his tafte for ftudy, that he could not abftain from writing and reading, without referve, immediately after his meals, and at unfeafonable hours of the night. His impatience was even fo great under the conftrained abftinence from thefe purfuits, which ficknefs fometimes occafioned, that he appeared more anxious to curtail the duration than to eradicate the principles, of his malady. Nay, fuch was his activity, that, once, when he had broken his right arm, the furgeon, when vifiting him the next morning, was furprifed to find him writing, with fufficient facility, with his left hand. And it is furprifing, that with fuch intenfe application he fhould arrive at fo advanced an age; for his whole life was, in the ftricteft fenfe, one continued facrifice of his pleafures and health to his love of fcience.

' M. de Haller was, in his perfon, tall and well-proportioned. His countenance, which had acquired a ferious caft, from his fhort fight, and the habitual tenfion of his mufcles, was full of expreffion, and changed in proportion to the degree of energy in the ideas which occupied his mind.'

Some Account of the late John Fothergill, M. D. &c. &c. By John Coakley Lettfom. 8vo. 3s. Dilly.

AFTER repeated promifes, and an unaccountable delay, we receive a more full account of the life of an amiable and benevolent man, as well as of a very able and humane phyfician. We cannot yet take any notice of his works, for the third volume, which contains the only original performances, and therefore the chief object of our Review, is not yet publifhed. The Life of Dr. Fothergill, at prefent before us, is indeed a *part* of it; for the very *fame* impreffion feems to be intended to accompany the future volume. It is now publifhed, either to gratify the impatience of the public, who expected extraordinary information from a perfon fo intimately connected with him, or to accommodate thofe purchafers, who were unwilling to poffefs a collection of tracts, which, already, in different publications, are almoft entirely in their hands. The Life of Dr. Fothergill cannot furprife by its events, or

amufe

amufe by its variety. It was one continued feries of benevolent and ufeful conduct; for, in every circumftance which related to the benefit of mankind, he felt that he was a man, called on to render his fuperior ftation more eminently ufeful. A life, fubject to the calls of a precarious profeffion, could not be diftinguifhed by a connected feries of experimental enquiry, or indeed by any plan of ftudy, which would fuffer by occafional interruption. His works were, therefore, the fhort effays which his fituation would permit him to purfue, or obfervations, which might be continued in his abfence. Natural hiftory, which he has adorned by his labours, and the materia medica, which has been much elucidated by his enquiries, were the chief objects of his attention, when the practice of his profeffion would allow him to beftow his time on other fubjects. The hints of Dr. Fothergill on thefe branches of knowlege have been followed with confiderable fuccefs; and fucceeding ages will remember him with gratitude and with pleafure. We may be permitted to point out the benefits which he has, in this way, conferred on thofe, who formerly were proud to call themfelves Englifhmen, and on others who ftill acknowlege that title:—while they are ftriking examples of Dr. Fothergill's benevolence and affiduity, they will alfo convey fome curious information.

Such confiderations influenced Dr. Fothergill; and where he could not produce objects of equal importance, he exerted himfelf to accomplifh others of lefs, yet of great public utility. What he effected, and what he contributed to do, would fill a volume, were a grateful biographer to enlarge upon them: he pointed out what would fuit different foils, and formed a balance in the productions of the globe: from America he received various fpecies of catalpas, kalmias, magnolias, firs, oaks, maples, and other valuable productions, which became denizens of his domain, fome of them capable of being applied to the moft ufeful purpofes of timber; and, in return, he tranfported green and bohea teas from his garden at Upton, to the fouthern part of that great continent, now rifing into an independent empire: he endeavoured to improve the growth and quality of coffee in the Weft India iflands; the Bamboo cane (Arundo Bambos) calculated for various domeftic ufes, he procured from China, and purpofed to tranfplant it to our iflands fituated within the tropics. The laft time I was with him at Upton, I introduced Governor Nugent, who defervedly poffeffed the chief adminiftration of Tortola, to whom he expreffed the pleafure he fhould experience in being the means of furnifhing the Caribbæan Archipelago with this ufeful Afiatic; the very fhoots of which were marked for this defign. The elegant vegetable is now in my poffeffion; and I recollect with grateful pleafure, as often as I fee it, the wifh of his former proprietor, hoping, when the tumult of war fhall have fubfided, to carry his defign into execution.

† The

' The nutmeg-tree now flourishes in the Isle of France, and clove-trees have been transplanted from thence to Cayenne. The true cinnamon is a tree we have not hitherto been able to cultivate out of Asia, though the Doctor used many endeavours to introduce it into our West India colonies. The canella cinnamomæa I had from his garden; and the true cinnamon tree would have arrived here in health, had not the alarm of an enemy's ship induced my friend to throw it overboard, with other articles designed as a present: the war, however, may ultimately extend the cultivation of these exotics, which, like the inhabitants of a feraglio, are cautiously excluded from the eye of strangers.

' Intent as he was to promote so many articles of commerce, manufacture, and convenience, he could not lose sight of those departments of natural history, which were more immediately connected with medicine, in order to ascertain the knowledge of what was already acquired, and to expand it by experiment where deficient. Though he was not the first who administered hemlock internally, he was the first who accurately discriminated its virtues: by him we were made acquainted with the gummi rubrum astringens Gambiense; and by his endeavours, and the ardour of minds similar to his own, we know that terra Japonica is a vegetable extract; and to him and Dr. Russel we are indebted for the flourishing of genuine scammony in our soil, as if indigenous to it. He attempted to procure the tree which affords the Peruvian bark; and is said to have at length so far succeeded, as to have had one plant in his garden, but which I believe died with its possessor. This invaluable tree, which is so common in Peru and Chili, would doubtless thrive on the North American continent, and in the larger West India islands; it is perhaps already indigenous to the mountains of Jamaica; and by successive endeavours it may hereafter be cultivated in the colonies of different European states: we have seen in how short a period of time the true rhubarb (rheum palmatum) has been naturalized to our soil, furnishing us at home with so important an acquisition to the materia medica.'

The reader of this little volume, if he possesses the least sensibility, will be rouzed by the warm, active benevolence of its subject, which waited not for a call to be useful; but interposed, with eager zeal, when his knowlege, his influence, or his fortune, could promote any salutary undertaking. He will contemplate, with the highest satisfaction, this friend of mankind, who measured his life rather by good actions than by days; who, from his birth, laboured incessantly to support and assist. We will transcribe his sentiments on the lucrative emoluments of his profession, as they should be engraven on the *hearts* of those who desire to practise it, in the most liberal manner.

" My only wish, he declares, was to do what little business might fall to my share as well as possible; and to banish all thoughts

thoughts of practising physic as a money-getting trade, with the same solicitude, as I would the suggestions of vice or intemperance." And when the success of his practice had raised him to the summit of reputation and emolument, he seemed actuated by the same sentiment. "I endeavour, says this conscientious physician, to follow my business, because it is my duty, rather than my interest; the last is inseparable from a just discharge of duty, but I have ever wished to look at the profits in the last place, and this wish has attended me ever since my beginning."

"I wished at my first setting out, he observes, I wished most fervently, and I endeavour after it still, to do the business that occurred, with all the diligence I could, as a *present duty*, and endeavoured to repress every rising idea of its consequences; knowing most assuredly that there was a hand, which could easily overthrow every pursuit of this kind, and baffle every attempt, either to acquire fame or wealth. And with a great degree of gratitude, I look back to the gracious secret preserver, that kept my mind more attentive to the discharge of my present anxious care for those I visited, than either to the profits or the credit resulting from it: and I am sure, to be kept under such a circumscribed unaspiring temper of mind, doing every thing with diligence, humility, and as in the sight of the God of healing, frees the mind from much unavailing distress, and consequential disappointment."

It will not be expected that we should pursue the more uninteresting æras of the life of Dr. Fothergill, or point out various dates of his works. It is a disagreeable task to dwell on his imperfections, the necessary alloy of humanity, which his enemies have magnified into faults and crimes. But among the former, it may probably be proper to suggest that, during the year 1751, and some subsequent ones, he corresponded with the editor of the Gentleman's Magazine; and the experiments, on the contents of the air, signed "Investigator," in a later volume, were planned, if not executed and described by him.

The present work was read to the Medical Society of London, and thus seems intended to serve the triple office of a declamatory eulogium, a separate publication, and an introduction to the Miscellaneous Essays of Dr. Fothergill. To this alone we ought not to object; and indeed now mention it, as the chief apology that can be made—for tumid phrases, exaggerated description, and unnecessary quotations. The dignified simplicity of the subject does not suit with the pomp of language, and the tinsel of adventitious ornament. We must indeed own, that these defects do not very often occur, and might be less conspicuous on any other occasion; but the frequent quotations of very common passages, from the Latin poets, will not prove the strongest recommendation of the author's

thor's

thor's learning. It is an artifice below the dignity of a scholar, who knows with how much eafe whole pages may be filled with apparent learning, either by dullnefs or ignorance.

Lectures on Rhetoric and Belles Lettres. By Hugh Blair, D. D.
(Continued, from page 60.)

THE author, having finifhed that part of his courfe of lectures which relates to language and ftyle, proceeds, in the fecond volume, to examine the fubjects upon which ftyle is employed; and begins with what is properly called eloquence, or public fpeaking.

Lect. XXV. *Of Grecian eloquence.*—This lecture contains a fhort account of the principal orators of Greece, from Pififtratus, about five hundred and fixty years before the Chriftian æra, to Demofthenes, who poifoned himfelf, Ant. Ch. 322, after whofe days Greece loft her liberty, and eloquence degenerated into the feeble manner introduced by the rhetoricians and fophifts.

Lect. XXVI. *Of Roman eloquence, the eloquence of the fathers, and the ftate of eloquence in modern times.*—Several writers have employed themfelves in drawing elaborate parallels between Demofthenes and Cicero. Our author gives us his idea of thefe two orators very concifely, in the following terms: " The character of Demofthenes is vigour and aufterity; that of Cicero is gentlenefs and infinuation. In the one you find more manlinefs; in the other, more ornament. The one is more harfh, but more fpirited and cogent; the other, more agreeable, but withal loofer and weaker.'

None of the fathers, he obferves, afford any juft models of eloquence. Yet, afterwards, fpeaking of Chryfoftom, he fays: ' His language is pure; his ftyle highly figured. He is copious, fmooth, and fometimes pathetic. But he retains, at the fame time, much of that character, which has been always attributed to the Afiatic eloquence, diffufe and redundant to a great degree, and often overwrought and tumid. He may be read, however, with advantage, for the eloquence of the pulpit, as being freer of falfe ornaments, than the Latin fathers.' This is full as much as can be faid in favour of Chryfoftom. The encomiums beftowed upon him by father Gilbert are extravagant. He is by no means a pattern proper for imitation.

As to the ftate of eloquence in Great Britain, our author fays, ' It muft be confeffed, that, in moft parts of eloquence, we are undoubtedly inferior, not only to the Greeks and Romans, by many degrees, but alfo to the French.'

In

In confirmation of this last assertion, respecting our inferiority to the French, he mentions, with great applause, the pleadings of Patru, Cochin, and D'Aguesseau; and the sermons of Bossuet, Massillon, Bourdaloue, and Flechier ; telling us, that these pleaders and preachers have attained a much higher species of eloquence, than either British pleaders or preachers have in view. And in another lecture he says, 'Massillon is perhaps the most eloquent writer of sermons, which modern times have produced.'

Every country, we must observe, has its favourite species of oratory. The compositions of these writers are diffuse and declamatory. And there are perhaps few Englishmen of taste and ingenuity, in the present age, who would wish to write in the style of Bourdaloue or Massillon. Would the author of these lectures prefer the bishop of Clermont's discourses to those of Dr. Blair?

The professor, at p. 121, has quoted a passage from Massillon, as a specimen of his incomparable eloquence*. But were an English preacher to begin such an harangue, the more sedate and sensible part of the congregation would suppose him to be an enthusiast.

Lect. XXVII. *Of different kinds of public speaking, and the eloquence of popular assemblies, with extracts from Demosthenes.*

Lect. XXVIII. *Of the eloquence of the bar.*

' It must be laid down, says the professor, as a first principle, that the eloquence suited to the bar, whether in speaking or in law papers, is of the calm and temperate kind, and connected with close reasoning. It is purity and neatness of expression which is chiefly to be studied; a style perspicuous and proper, which *shall* not be needlessly overcharged with the pedantry of law terms, and where, at the same time, no affectation shall appear, of avoiding these, when they are suitable and necessary. He gives several other useful directions concerning the peculiar strain of speaking at the bar, and illustrates the subject by a short analysis of Cicero's oration for Cluentius. His principal design in this analysis is to furnish the young pleader with an excellent example of managing a complex and intricate cause, with order, elegance, and force.'

Lect. XXIX. *Of the eloquence of the pulpit.*——The end of all preaching, as the author justly observes, is to persuade men to become good.

' Every sermon therefore should be a persuasive oration. Not but that the preacher is to instruct and to teach, to reason and argue. All persuasion is to be founded on conviction. The understanding must always be applied to in the first place, in order

---

* See Encyclop. art. *Eloquence*, by Voltaire.

to make a lasting impression on the heart: and he who would work on men's passions, or influence their practice, without first giving them just principles, and enlightening their minds, is no better than a mere declaimer. He may raise transient emotions, or kindle a passing ardour, but can produce no solid or lasting effect. At the same time it must be remembered, that all the preacher's instructions are to be of the practical kind, and that persuasion must be his ultimate object. It is not to discuss some abstruse point, that he ascends the pulpit. It is not to illustrate some metaphysical truth, or to inform men of something which they never heard before; but it is to make them better men; it is to give them, at once, clear views, and persuasive impressions of religious truth.'

The chief characteristics of the eloquence, suited to the pulpit, as distinguished from the other kinds of public speaking, the professor supposes to be these two, gravity and warmth. ' The serious nature of the subjects, belonging to the pulpit, requires gravity; their importance to mankind requires warmth. It is far from being either easy or common to unite these characters of eloquence. The grave, when it is predominant, is apt to run into a dull uniform solemnity. The warm, when it wants gravity, borders on the theatrical and light. The union of the two must be studied by all preachers, as of the utmost consequence, both in the composition of their discourses, and in their manner of delivery. Gravity and warmth united form that character of preaching, which the French call *onction*; the affecting, penetrating, interesting manner, flowing from a strong sensibility of heart, in the preacher, to the importance of those truths, which he delivers, and an earnest desire, that they may make full impression on the hearts of his hearers.'

Here we will take the liberty to add, that when the preacher aims at what the French call *onction*, he should by all means take care not to be guilty of what is called, in Scotland, *soughing*; in England, *canting*.

Our author lays down and illustrates the following rules, respecting a sermon, as a particular species of composition: Attend to the unity of a sermon; that is, confine your observations to one main object: let your subject be precise and particular. Select the most useful, the most striking, and persuasive topics, which the text suggests, and rest your discourse upon these. Study above all things to render your instructions interesting to your hearers. And do not take your model of preaching from particular fashions, that chance to have the vogue. The servility of imitation extinguishes all genius, or rather is a proof of the entire want of genius.

With

With respect to style, he says, that which the pulpit requires should be very perspicuous. As discourses spoken there, are calculated for the instruction of all sorts of hearers, plainness and simplicity should reign in them. Yet the style may be abundantly dignified, and at the same time very lively and animated. The language of Scripture, when properly employed, either in the way of quotation or allusion, is a great ornament to sermons. But no points or conceits should appear in them. The preacher should never have what may be called a favourite expression.

The practice of reading sermons is one of the greatest obstacles to the eloquence of the pulpit. What is gained hereby in point of correctness, is not equal, he thinks, to what is lost in point of persuasion and force. They, whose memories are not able to retain the whole of a discourse, might aid themselves considerably by short notes lying before them, which would allow them to preserve, in a great measure, the freedom and ease of one who speaks.

The French and English writers of sermons proceed upon very different ideas of the eloquence of the pulpit. A French sermon is, for the most part, a warm animated exhortation ; an English one, is a piece of cool instructive reasoning. The French preachers address themselves chiefly to the imagination and the passions ; the English, almost solely to the understanding. It is the union of these two kinds of composition, of the French earnestness and warmth, with the English accuracy and reason, that would form, according to our author's idea, the model of a perfect sermon.

The professor, on this occasion, makes some remarks on the style of several French and English preachers, Saurin, Bourdaloue, and Massillon ; Clarke, Tillotson, Barrow, Atterbury, and Butler.

Lect. XXX. *contains a critical examination of a sermon of bishop Atterbury's*†.——Our author thinks bishop Atterbury deserves to be particularly mentioned, as a model of correct and beautiful style.——We see nothing in Atterbury's language which merits this *extraordinary* character.

Lect. XXXI. *Of the conduct of a discourse, in all its parts; the introduction, division, narration, and explication.*——The introduction, as the professor observes, should be easy and natural, bearing a peculiar relation to the subject in hand. Correctness should be carefully studied in the expression. The orator should set out with an appearance of modesty and calmness. No material part of the subject should be anticipated.

† Vol. I. Serm. 1.

And

And the preliminary obfervations fhould be fuited to the dif
courfe which is to follow, both in length and kind.

The prefent method of dividing a fermon, our author
thinks, ought not to be laid afide. Though it may give a
fermon lefs of the oratorical appearance, it renders it more
clear, more eafily apprehended, and of courfe more inftructive
to the generality of hearers, which is always the main object
to be kept in view.

The moft material rules for the divifion of any difcourfe
are, that the feveral parts be really diftinct; that the fimpleft
points be firft difcuffed; that the feveral members fhould exhauft the fubject; that the heads fhould be propounded as
clearly and concifely as poffible; and a multiplicity of divifions and fubdivifions avoided.

' In fermons, where there is feldom any occafion for narration,
explication of the fubject to be difcourfed on comes in place of
narration at the bar, and is to be taken up much on the fame
tone; that is, it muft be concife, clear and diftinct; and in a
ftyle correct and elegant, rather than highly adorned.'

Lect. XXXII. *Of the argumentative part of a difcourfe, the
pathetic part, the peroration.*——On thofe topics the author lays
down and illuftrates the following rules : avoid blending arguments confufedly together, that are of a feparate nature.
All arguments whatever are directed to prove one or other of
thefe three things, that fomething is true, that it is morally
right, or fit, or that it is profitable and good. Keep thefe
claffes of arguments feparate and diftinct. Advance in the
way of climax. Do not extend your arguments too far, nor
multiply them too much.

With refpect to the pathetic, confider carefully, whether
the fubject admit the pathetic, and render it proper; and, if
it does, what part of the difcourfe is the moft proper for attempting it. Never fet apart a head of difcourfe, in form,
for raifing any paffion; never give warning, that you are
about to be pathetic. Obferve the difference between fhewing the hearers that they ought to be moved, and actually
moving them. Be moved yourfelf. Attend to the proper
language of the paffions. Avoid interweaving any thing of a
foreign nature with the pathetic part. And, laftly, never attempt to prolong the paffions too much.

The great rule of a conclufion is, to place that laft, on
which you choofe that the ftrength of your caufe fhould reft.
Let the inferences rife naturally, and agree with the ftrain of
fentiment throughout the difcourfe. Endeavour to hit the
precife time of concluding. Clofe with dignity and fpirit.

Lect. XXXIII. *Of pronunciation or delivery.*—The great objects which every public speaker will naturally have in his eye in forming his delivery, are, first, to speak so as to be fully and easily understood by all who hear him ; and next, to speak with grace and force, so as to please and to move his audience. In order to be fully and easily understood, the four chief requisites, on which our author insists, are a due degree of loudness of voice, distinctness, slowness, and propriety of pronunciation. The higher parts of delivery, by which a speaker seeks to give grace and force to what he utters, are comprised under these four heads, emphasis, pauses, tones, and gestures.

In treating of pauses, the professor makes an observation, which the young speaker may possibly mistake. ' Many a sentence, he says, is miserably mangled, and the force of the emphasis totally lost, by divisions being made in the wrong place. To avoid this, every one, while he is speaking, should be very careful to *provide a full supply* of breath for what he is to utter.'—Is he to take in this *full supply* by an emotion of the breast, resembling the opening of a pair of bellows ? By no means. The speaker should relieve his voice at every stop ; slightly at a comma, more leisurely at a semicolon, or colon, and completely at a period ; and by these means should accustom himself to breathe freely and imperceptibly as he proceeds. This is the way, in which the voice is relieved in common discourse, and is all that nature requires.

Lect. XXXIV *Of the means of improving in eloquence.*— Among the means which the author considers as conducive to this purpose are, the virtuous and amiable qualities of the orator, a fund of useful knowlege, a habit of application and industry, attention to the best models, frequent exercise both in composing and speaking, and the perusal of the best critical and rhetorical writers.

Lect. XXXV. *Of the comparative merit of the ancients and moderns.*—Whatever superiority, says the professor, the ancients may have had in point of genius, yet in all arts where the natural progress of knowlege has had room to produce any considerable effects, the moderns cannot but have some advantage. Hence, in natural philosophy, astronomy, chemistry, modern philosophers have an unquestionable superiority over the ancient. The progress of society must be admitted to have given us some advantages in history. In dramatic performances we may be allowed to have made some improvements.

Lect. XXXVI. *Of historical writing.*—The author has very properly specified the various qualities required in a good historian, impartiality, fidelity, gravity, dignity, &c.

3

Lect.

Lect. XXXVII. *Of philosophical writing, dialogue, epistolary writing, fictitious history.*—This lecture consists of observations on these different kinds of composition, and on the ancient and modern writers, who have distinguished themselves in these departments of literature.

Lect. XXXVIII. *Of poetry, its nature, origin, progress, &c.*

Lect. XXXIX.—XLVII. *Of pastoral, lyric, didactic, descriptive poetry, of the poetry of the Hebrews, of epic poetry, and the most celebrated epic poets, of dramatic poetry, of Greek, French, English tragedy, and Greek, Roman, French and English comedy.*—In these lectures the professor gives his readers the common rules of criticism, relating to these different forms of poetical composition, and the characters of some of the most eminent poets.

Several writers † have taken notice of a conceit in Tasso's Aminta ; and, among others, Mr. Addison, Guard. No. 38. But our author defends the Italian poet. ' Tasso's Sylvia, says he, makes no such ridiculous figure as Mr. Addison pretends, and we are obliged to suspect, that he had not read the Aminta. Daphne, a companion of Silvia, appears in a conversation with Thyrsis, the confidant of Aminta, Sylvia's lover ; and in order to shew him that Sylvia was not so simple, or insensible to her own charms, as she affected to be, gives him this instance : that she had caught her one day adjusting her dress by a fountain, and applying now one flower, and now another to her neck ; and after comparing their colours with her own, she broke into a smile, as if she had seemed to say, I will wear you, not for my ornaments, but to shew how much you yield to me : and when caught thus admiring herself, she threw away her flowers, and blushed for shame.—This description, continues our author, of the vanity of a rural coquette, is no more than what is natural, and very different from what the author of the Guardian represents it.'

But, notwithstanding this ingenious observation, will it not be said, that Tasso is still chargeable with this conceit ?

' Ni porto voi per ornamento mio,
Ma porto voi sol per vergogna vostra.—Atto ii. 2.

' I do not wear you for my ornament, but only for your shame.'

Sylvia is indeed acquitted, because the witticism is ascribed to Daphne. But is it more excusable in Daphne than in Sylvia ? And is it not inconsistent with rural simplicity ? If it is, Tasso is blameable, and the professor has treated Addison too cavalierly, when he supposes, ' that he had not read the Aminta.'

---

† Bouhours, Fontenelle, Mr. Addison, Mr. Warton.

In

In his observations on Virgil, our author admits the force of an objection, which has been frequently urged against the Æneid. ‘ There are, he observes, almost no characters at all marked in the Æneid. In this respect it is insipid, when compared to the Iliad, which is full of characters and life.’—— The Iliad, we acknowlege, is full of characters; but they are chiefly *military* characters. In this circumstance, Virgil could not, with any prospect of advantage, follow the example of Homer, who had collected his heroes from every part of Greece, and pre-occupied almost every military character. He has therefore wisely pursued another course, and introduced a different species of characters. Æneas, Anchises, Acestes, Evander, Latinus, Ascanius, Pallas, Nisus, Euryalus, Turnus, Mezentius, Lausus, Sinon, Drances, Dido, Camilla, Creusa, Amata, Lavinia, and several others, form an agreeable variety of characters, many of which are totally different from any that appear in the Iliad.

In his account of Tasso, the professor says, ‘ The Jerusalem is, in rank and dignity, the *third* regular epic poem in the world, and comes next to the Iliad and Æneid ?——Has he forgot the Odyssey, or does he exclude it by design ?

Among philosophical writers, who have treated of dramatic poetry, it has been a question, how it comes to pass, that those emotions of sorrow, which tragedy excites, afford any gratification to the mind ? Our author, we conceive, gives the true solution, as follows :

‘ By the wise and gracious constitution of our nature, the exercise of all the social passions is attended with pleasure. Nothing is more pleasing and grateful than love and friendship. Whereever man takes a strong interest in the concerns of his fellow-creatures, an internal satisfaction is made to accompany the feeling. Pity, or compassion, in particular, is, for wise ends, appointed to be one of the strongest instincts of our frame, and is attended with a peculiar attractive power. It is an affection which cannot but be productive of some distress, on account of the sympathy with the sufferers, which it necessarily involves. But, as it includes benevolence and friendship, it partakes, at the same time, of the agreeable and pleasing nature of those affections. The heart is warmed by kindness and humanity, at the same moment, at which it is affected by the distresses of those with whom it sympathises ; and the pleasure arising from those kind emotions, prevails so much in the mixture, and so far counterbalances the pain, as to render the state of the mind, upon the whole, agreeable. At the same time, the immediate pleasure, which always goes along with the operation of the benevolent and sympathetic affections, derives an addition from the approbation of our own minds. We are pleased with ourselves, for feeling as we ought, and for
entering,

entering, with proper forrow, into the concerns of the afflicted. In tragedy, befides, other adventitious circumstances concur to diminifh the painful part of fympathy, and to increafo the fatisfaction attending it. We are, in fome meafure, relieved, by thinking that the caufe of our diftrefs is feigned, not real; and we are alfo gratified by the charms of poetry, the propriety of fentiment and language, and the beauty of action. From the concurrence of thefe caufes, the pleafure which we receive from tragedy, notwithftanding the diftrefs it occafions, feems to me to be accounted for, in a fatisfactory manner. At the fame rime, it is to be obferved, that, as there is always a mixture of pain in the pleafure, that pain is capable of being fo much heightened, by the reprefentations of incidents extremely direful, as to fhock our feelings, and to render us averfe, either to the reading of fuch tragedies, or to the beholding of them upon the ftage.'

The limits of our Review will not allow us to oblige our readers with more extracts from this work. We can therefore only recommend it to the perufal of all thofe who propofe to ftudy the belles lettres. The learned, who are well acquainted with the fubjects difcuffed in thefe lectures, will not find in them many new difcoveries; but they will find many judicious and important obfervations, delivered in clear and animated language.

We muft however obferve, that though Dr. Blair is, in many refpects, an excellent writer, he is not the moft correct. We fhall therefore take the liberty, in another Review, to point out fome of his inaccuracies of ftyle. Indifcriminate applaufe is abfurd. A perfon of tafte will read every thing with a diftinguifhing eye: and, as our author rightly obferves, 'it is perfectly confiftent with juft and candid criticifm, to find fault with parts, while, at the fame time, it admires the whole.'

Bibliotheca Topographica Britannica, *No XII.* 4to. 7s. 6d.
Nichols.

Bibliotheca Topographica Britannica, *No. XIII.* 4to. 2s. 6d.
Nichols.

NUMBER XII. contains an account of the town, church, and epifcopal palace at Croydon, in the county of Surry, from its foundation to the year 1783, by Dr. Ducarel. It was drawn up in 1754, at the requeft of archbifhop Herring, who, refiding almoft entirely at Croydon, was defirous of being acquainted with every thing relative to that town and palace. When the author had exhaufted all the materials which our old hiftorians afford, he obtained the archbifhop's permiffion to examine, in company with Mr. Mores, the regifters and records at Lambeth ; yet notwithstanding the laborious researches of these two able antiquaries, we find each of them, in their respective observations, complaining, that in many cases they could gain no satisfactory information.

There appears to have been a church at this town in the 10th century ; for to the will of Byrhtric and Ælfwyth, made abou the year 960, and printed in the perambulation of Kent, is wi ness Ælffie, the priest of Croydon.   The present structure is a handsome stone building, adorned with a lofty square tower and pinacles, and has a good ring of bells.   It is supposed to have been begun in the time of archbishop Courtney, and finished in that of archbishop Chichelé, who was archbishop from 1414 to 1443.

Mr. Mores supposes, that the manor of Croydon was given by Wi liam the Conqueror to Lanfranc, archbishop of Canterbury; and that Lanfranc was the founder of the palace.   It is however very certain from Domesday book, that the manor belong d to the see of Canterbury in the time of Lanfranc.

The author gives us an account of the archbishops who resided at this palace, the last of whom, for any length of time, was archbishop Herring, who expended upwards of six thousand pounds in repairing and adorning his palace and gardens here, and at Lambeth.   Since that time the house at Croydon has fallen to decay ; and on account of its unwholesome situation, and its unfitness to be the habitation of an archbishop of Canterbury, an act was obtained, in 1780, for selling it, and building a new palace, at a place called Park hill, pleasantly situated about half a mile from Croydon.   Accordingly, it was sold, Oct. 10, 1780, to Abraham Pitches, esq. of Streatham, now sir Abraham, for 2520l.

The value of this archbishopric, about the year 1599, is thus stated by archbishop Whitgift: ' The archbishopric is no better to me than it was to my late predecessors, who died not very wealthy, for any thing I can learn.   And I hope I bestow it as well as they did.   But whofoever faith, that this archbishoprick is yearly worth 6000l. or worth any way in ordinaries or extraordinaries 3000l. must answer to God, at the least for vain speeches, that I term them no worse.   And yet, out of that which every way I receive, there goeth in annuities, pensions, subsidies, and other duties to her majesty, 800l. at the least.   And then what remaineth is soon known.'

The following incident may serve to shew the bigotry and folly of the age in which it happened.

' Roland Philippis, vicar here from 1497 to 1538, preaching at St. Paul's against printing, then lately introduced into England, hath this passage : "We (meaning the Catholics) must

muſt root out printing, or printing will root out us." Fox, Martyrol. i. 804.'

This number is adorned with ten plates, neatly engraved.

No. XIII.—The late Mr. Mores, having formed a deſign to give ſome account of Great Coxwell, in Berkſhire, where his anceſtors had been lords of the manor, had ſix plates engraved, exhibiting a view of the church, the manor houſe, &c. The editor of the preſent work has made uſe of theſe plates, and collected from Mr. Mores's papers, from the communications of J. Richmond Webb, eſq. and other ſources of information, the moſt memorable circumſtances relative to the hiſtory and antiquities of the pariſh.

David Collyer, the author of the Sacred Interpreter, pub-liſhed in 1726, in two vols. 8vo. was vicar of this pariſh al-moſt fifty years. He died Oct. 21, 1724, aged 73.

Mons Badonicus is celebrated in Engliſh hiſtory on account of a bloody battle, which is ſaid to have been fought at that place, between king Arthur and the Saxons, A. D. 520. But authors are not agreed where this Badon hill is ſituated. Mr. Webb offers the following conjecture.

' On the top of Badbury Hill, on the North ſide of the turn-pike road leading from Farringdon to Highworth, and within a few yards of it, is a camp of a circular form, two hundred yards in diameter, with a ditch ten yards wide. About nine years ago, in levelling the north rampart, human bones and coals were found, and human bones are found every year in digging for peat in ſwampy ground about one mile ſouth of the hill. Le-land, in his Itinerary, vol. ii. page 20, ſays, that he " learned of certainty that a mile out of Farringdon, towards the right way to Highworth, appeared a great diche, wher a fortreſſe, or ra-ther a camp of warre, hath beene, as ſome ſay, diked by the Danes as a ſure camp." Mr. Wiſe, in his letter to Dr. Mead, concerning ſome antiquities in Berkſhire, page 49, ſuppoſes, that the battle of Mons Badonicus, or Badbury Hill, as he calls it, in the year 520, mentioned by Bede and Gildas, in which Arthur gained his twelfth victory, was fought near the White Horſe Hill; but, if from the ſimilitude of names it may be con-cluded that the battle happened in this neighbourhood, there is much more probability of this being the ſpot than of the Wilt-ſhire hills being ſo, as this camp is Daniſh, and nearer to the White Horſe than the other, the fortifications of which are Ro-man. Between this camp and the White Horſe Hills is a plain or dead flat, five miles wide, a very proper place for an engage-ment for two armies. Badbury Hill, in Wiltſhire, is more than ſix miles diſtant from the White Horſe, though Wiſe ſays only two or three.'

In order to determine this point, if it can be determined, we ſhall cite the words of ſome of our ancient writers. When

they

they speak of this battle, they mention it in the following terms:

' Ex eo tempore nunc cives, nunc hostes vincebant—usque ad annum obsessionis Badonici montis [qui prope Sabrinum ostium habetur.]' Gild. Hist. § 26. ' Duodecimum fuit bellum in Monte Badonis.' Nennius, c. 63. ' Ex eo tempore nunc cives, nunc hostes vincebant, usque ad annum obsessionis Badonici montis.' Bed. c. 16. ' In obsidione Badonici montis nongentos hostium profligavit Arthurus.' Will. Malm. lib. i. ' Duodecimum contra Saxones durissimè Arthur bellum in monte Badonis perpetravit.' Hen. Hunt. p. 313. ' Saxones usque ad Sabrinum mare depopulantur colonos: indè arrepto itinere versus pagum Badonis, *urbem* obsident. Arthurus *Sumersetensem* provinciam *ingressus* visâ *cominùs* obsidione.' Galf. Mon. ix. 3. ' Postremò in obsidione Badonici montis, nongentos hostium solus profligavit.' Hig. Polyc. p. 225. 'Ad ultimum urbem Badonis obsiderunt.' Mat. Westm. an. 520.

From these quotations it seems very evident, that Bath was the city which the Saxons besieged. It is called by our ancient writers Kaerbadun, Badus, Badon, Badonia, Bathon, Badecestre, Bathonia, &c. ' Bathoniam urbem, sive Badonem, construxit Bladud.' Higd. Polyc. l. i. p. 198.

Camden thinks, Mons Badonicus was Bannesdowne; ' Hic mons ille ipse videtur, qui nunc Bannesdowne dictus, Bathestone viculo juxta hanc urbem impendet, suosque etiamnum aggeres & vallum ostendit.' Camd. Brit. p. 201. ed. 1600. Arbishop Usher is clearly of this opinion: ' Nam urbem Badonis eandem esse rectè notavit in Dubricii Vitâ Johannes Tinmuthensis, cum eâ quæ nunc Bathonia vocatur. Hanc enim in Sumersetensi agro positam Britannis Caer Badon, & montem vicinum Bannesdowne, quod *excelsum collem* sonare dicitur, & *vallem* ad Avonam fluvium hic procurrentem *Nant* Badon appellari, à Camdeno præterea est observatum.' Brit. Eccl. Antiq. p. 476.

Leland entertains no doubt about it: ' Est autem Badonicus mons, quamvis aliter somniet Polydorus, ea civitas, quam Britanni Cair Badune; nostra verò ætas linguâ vernaculâ *Bath* appellat.' Leland de Script. Brit. c. 32.

If there can be any conclusion drawn from the Monkish historians above cited, or from the sentiments of Camden, Usher, and Leland, relative to an action, which is said to have happened in an obscure period of history, in which fable frequently supplies the place of truth, we must conclude, that the city which the Saxons besieged, under Cerdic, was Bath; and Badon hill, from which they were dislodged by Arthur, was Bannesdown, or some hill adjoining to that city. Mr.

Wise's

Wife's suppofition is evidently erroneous ; and the notion of a *Danish* camp, fuggefted in the foregoing quotation, is out of the queftion.

Evidence of our Transactions in the East Indies, with an Enquiry into the general Conduct of Great Britain to other Countries; from the Peace of Paris, in 1763. *By Mr. Parker, of Lincoln's-Inn.* 4to. 10s. 6d. *in Boards.* Dilly.

THE evidence collected by this author, on the fubject of Eaft India affairs, is too extenfive to be detailed to our readers ; but we fhall lay before them the fubftance of it, taken from a fhort view fubjoined to the numerous documents of which the narrative confifts.

It appears, therefore, that the provinces of Bengal, Bahar, and Oriffa were, in the year 1757, in a ftate of as great fertility and plenty as any country in Europe, and inhabited by about fifteen millions of people, under the government of Surajah Dowla, who had lately fucceeded his grandfather, Ally-Verdi Cawn, from whom he is faid to have received the following advice : " The power of the Englifh is great ; fuffer them not, my fon, to have factories or foldiers ; if you do, the country is not yours."

Dowla, on his acceffion to the government, required the Company's fervants to defift from fome works of ftrength, at their factory at Calcutta ; and, not being fatisfied with the anfwers he received, he led an army againft the place, of which he foon made himfelf mafter. Immediately on entering the fort, he difgraced the fuccefs of his arms by the inhuman act of committing a number of the Englifh to a dungeon, where only twenty-three remained alive next morning.

In confequence of thefe proceedings, war was begun with Surajah Dowla, on the arrival of a fufficient force ; but before the troops took the field, a treaty was made with Meer Jaffier, one of the firft fubjects of this prince, and a general in his army. The principal condition of the treaty was, that Jaffier fhould betray his mafter. He failed not to perform the terms of agreement ; and immediately after the defeat of Surajah Dowla on the Plaffey, in 1757, Meer Jaffier was placed in the government, by the commander of the Englifh army. On this occafion, it appears that the fum of one million two hundred and thirty-eight thoufand five hundred and feventy-five pounds was paid by Jaffier, out of his mafter's treafury, to the fervants of the Company, for themfelves, and the army and navy, with which they were affifted. At the fame time was paid the fum of one million eight hundred thoufand pounds,

pounds, as restitution to the Company, their servants, and other Europeans, for losses during the war.

In the year 1760, Meer Jaffier was deposed in favour of Cossim Ally Khan, a general in Jaffier's army; from whom the company's servants received two hundred and sixty-two thousand seven hundred and sixty-nine pounds. Cossim appearing to have designs of rendering himself independent, war was begun against him. On the commencement of hostilities, he put to death near three hundred persons, chiefly English; but he was soon obliged to retire with his army into the dominions of Shujah Dowla, a neighbouring prince, and one of the most powerful in that part of India.

In 1763, Meer Jaffier was restored to the government; and on this occasion divided amongst the Company's servants the sum of four hundred and thirty-seven thousand four hundred and ninety-nine pounds, exclusive of nine hundred and seventy-five thousand pounds received of him as restitution money.

It was demanded of Shujah Dowla that he should deliver up Cossim; but not complying with this requisition, the war was carried into his country. During its continuance Meer Jaffier died; and his second son, the eldest living, was advanced to the government, before an infant son of his elder brother. The Company's servants had the sum of one hundred and thirty-nine thousand three hundred and fifty-seven pounds divided amongst them; and about the same time the commander in chief received for himself, his family, and the army, the sum of sixty-two thousand six hundred and sixty-six pounds.

Shujah Dowla, after various disasters, cast himself upon the mercy of the commander. With this prince the servants of the Company got into their power likewise the heir or claimant of the Mogul empire; and obtained, by grant, the whole revenues of Bengal, Bahar and Orissa, in the name of the India Company; continuing the government in the name of the Nabob, Meer Jaffier's son, to whom the Company's servants gave a yearly allowance for the support of his dignity; appointing also a farther sum to be paid to the emperor, from whom they took the title to the revenues of the country. A treaty of peace was signed with Shujah Dowla, who was left in the possession of his dominions. The sum of five hundred and thirty-three thousand three hundred and thirty-three pounds was paid by him for the use of the Company; and the sum of ninety thousand nine hundred and ninety-nine pounds was received by two of the Company's servants, as presents from the emperor, the begum or queen of Bengal, and from one of the chiefs of the country.

The

The sums received by the servants of the Company, on the different occasions above mentioned, are stated to amount to five millions five hundred and ninety thousand one hundred and ninety-eight pounds; and the whole sum received for the use of the Company, from the beginning of the war in 1757 to 1771, is twenty-three millions eight hundred and ninety-two thousand seven hundred and fifteen pounds; amounting together to twenty-nine millions four hundred and eighty-two thousand nine hundred and thirteen pounds.

In 1765, when the Company's servants had adjusted their disputes with the country powers, they formed themselves into a society of trade, the capital stock of which was divided into sixty shares; and of these the civil and military servants of the Company were the sole proprietors. They now held the country in subjection by military force; they collected the revenues in the name of the East India Company; and they were merchants, possessed of an exclusive trade on their own account, in articles of common use, among the natives of the country.

This is the sum of the evidence contained in the papers to which Mr. Parker has had recourse in his investigation. He seems to have conducted his enquiry with great care; and has been prompted by a laudable desire of communicating to the public a clear account of the Company's transactions in the East Indies. The events which took place among the people in those provinces, after their surrender to the Company, have, Mr. Parker observes, been related on very good authority; but not having copies of such accounts transmitted from India, he has contented himself with giving a short narrative of what is believed to have happened since that period.

The Evidence of our Transactions in the East Indies is followed by an enquiry into the general conduct of Great Britain to other countries, from the peace of Paris, in 1763. Mr. Parker seems to be of opinion, that the measures of administration have neither been liberal nor politic; and, in contemplation of this subject, he introduces some texts of scripture, tending to evince the dangerous state of a country in which the principles of moral rectitude are disregarded. As we entertain no doubt of his meaning well, we shall not, by any remark of ours, insinuate the smallest disapprobation of a practice, which, however favourable to virtue, may perhaps be deemed unsuitable in a work of a political nature,

Two

Two Dialogues, concerning the Manner of Writing History. 12*mo*.
3*s*. 6*d*. *sewed*. Kearsley.

THE abbé de Mably, the author of this volume, has
been known for some years as an ingenious writer. He
has formerly exercised his talents in historical composition,
and now ventures on the arduous task of delivering critical
observations respecting the execution of this high department
of literature. In the first of these Dialogues, he considers the
different kinds of history, general and particular, and mentions the several studies which he regards as the necessary pre-
paratives for writing it. It seems to be his opinion, that the
historian, like the poet and the orator, must be born, not
made : but to discover what kind of narrative may best suit
the genius of a writer, he gives the following advice.

‘ Granting that you were born an historian, no person can
know better than yourself what kind of history you ought to
write. Recollect what particular ideas have made the greatest
impression upon your mind whilst you read over the accomplished
models of the art. If, for example, you have naturally, and,
as it were by instinct, rivetted your whole attention upon the
particular details of Livy, which serve to unravel and exhibit in a
striking form the genius of the Romans ; if the description of the
laws has powerfully engaged your notice ; and if the picture of
revolutions, which intervened amidst the government of the republic, has thrown you into a train of serious and deep reflections, you may relinquish all diffidence and distrust of the successful vigor of your talents, and enter upon a general history.
Have no circumstances affected you so much as the wars of the
Romans, their military discipline, and the atchievements of their
consuls ? Then, write only the history of some memorable war,
which may have changed the fortune of the contending states.
If, more interested by the various workings of the human heart,
you have particularly contemplated the passions, the vices and
the virtues of those men whose conduct or whose administration
has been explained to you, tread in the steps of Plutarch, and
strive to enlighten and to amend us by presenting to us the faithful portraits of distinguished characters, whose abilities have done
honour to humanity, and whose lives we should consider as an
instructive lesson to us for ever.’

Among the studies preparative to the writing of history, M.
Mably considers that of natural law as indispensable ; without which he thinks a writer cannot form a judgment of either
the justice or injustice of those enterprizes which may happen
to be the subjects of history.

‘ I know not, says he, whether I am mistaken ; but it appears
to me that, either to this ignorance of natural law, or to the abject disposition of the majority of the historians of the present
age,

age, which, driving them into a rebellion againſt the feelings of their conſcience, has forced them to flatter princes, we owe the diſguſting inſipidity of their writings. Why is Grotius ſuperior to ſuch authors as theſe ? Becauſe he has inveſtigated to their loweſt depth the laws and duties of ſociety ; and, therefore, do we trace in him the elevation and the energy of the ancients. I ſeize with eagerneſs ; I could devour his Hiſtory of the Low Countries ; whilſt the work of Strada, whoſe abilities were, probably, more equal to the power of entering into fine relations, is always dropping from my hands. Let me give you another example, from Buchanan, of the forcible effect of that ſtudy concerning which I am now ſpeaking to you. An attentive and well digeſted peruſal of his learned and ſagacious production, intituled, De Jure Regis apud Scotos, will not leave us in the leaſt ſurpriſed that this writer (the only perſon amongſt his contemporaries who knew how to think, as Locke has ſince thought, and, doubtleſs, in imitation of Buchanan) ſhould have compoſed an hiſtory which preſſes forward with that air of grandeur, liberality, and elevation, which eaſily inclines us to excuſe thoſe defects of order and congruity with which, otherwiſe, we might reproach him.'

We cannot help being of opinion, that a ſcientific knowledge of natural law, as ſuggeſted by M. Mably, is by no means abſolutely neceſſary for a hiſtorian. An acquaintance with the duties of man, in every moral relation, is an acquiſition far leſs difficult than our author appears to imagine, and is indeed impreſſed, almoſt intuitively, on the mind of every perſon of a ſound underſtanding. But the abbé, not ſatisfied with inculcating the neceſſity of a profound knowlege of natural law, pronounces the ſtudy of political law to be no leſs indiſpenſable. He is equally peremptory in requiring that a hiſtorian ſhould be perfectly converſant with the operation of the various paſſions. In fact, the abbé Mably would eſtabliſh it as a principle, that a great hiſtorian ought to be endowed, in a remarkable degree, with almoſt every human accompliſhment. Far be it from us to inſinuate, that a hiſtorian ought not to be a perſon of extenſive knowlege, and of the moſt improved underſtanding ; but theſe qualifications may, we think, be ſufficiently cultivated, for the purpoſe of ſuch a writer, without immerſing in the numerous and laborious ſtudies, which our author unjuſtly conſiders as indiſpenſable in a writer of hiſtory. In this, as in every other ſpecies of compoſition, good ſenſe is the primary requiſite †.

In the ſecond Dialogue the author proceeds to make obſervations on ſeveral eminent hiſtorians of the preſent time. We ſhall, for the gratification of our readers, ſelect what he has

---

† Scribendi recte ſapere eſt & principium & fons. Hor.

advanced relative to the hiſtorians of our country ; for whom it is evident that M. Mably has no predilection. The following remarks relative to Mr. Gibbon, are put in the mouth of Eugenius, the principal ſpeaker.

‘ A rational reader requires that the narration ſhould proceed rapidly, yet will not ſuffer the hiſtorian to omit any thing which may render it extremely clear, and perfectly intelligible. The principal art, therefore, conſiſts in preparing the reader for the events intended to be ſubmitted to his conſideration. What can prove more faſtidious than the method purſued by Mr. Gibbon, who, in his *eternal* Hiſtory of the Roman Emperors, ſuſpends, at every inſtant, his tedious and inſipid narrative, to explain to you the cauſes of the occurrences, the particulars concerning which you are on the point of reading ! No impediment ſhould croſs me during a recital ; and the author *muſt* be clear. This is the firſt law of all hiſtorians. But, he muſt be clear with art, leſt he diſcourage and check my attention ; and this ſecond law is not leſs requiſite than the firſt. I grow cold, I ſink into languor, if you ſuffer me to loſe ſight of that goal to which it is your buſineſs to conduct me. My memory is only tolerable ; and, doubtleſs, it behoves you to aſſiſt and to refreſh it, by calling up what, in the peruſal of a long work, I may have forgotten, and what I actually want, at this moment, in order that I may be able to underſtand your meaning. If the hiſtorian executes his taſk after the manner of Mr. Gibbon, I believe that, without *his* help, I ſhall remember what he has already told me, ſeveral times ; and, therefore, I ſhall reject his repetitions of intelligence with diſdain.’

In treating of *order* in hiſtorical compoſition, the author thus cenſures the conduct of Mr. Hume.

‘ *Order* is, of all points whatſoever, the moſt neceſſary to the compoſition of a work : nor need we produce a ſtronger proof of the juſtice of this aſſertion than that heap of books which, though filled with excellent things, afford not the leaſt inſtruction, becauſe they tire and diſguſt the generality of readers. *This* we have all experienced. A truth appears doubtful, unleſs it is prepared for by *that* truth which has preceded it ; and a beauty diſplaced becomes a defect ; but, *properly* arranged, grows more eſtimable.

> Ordinis hæc virtus erit et Venus, aut ego fallor,
> Ut jam nunc dicat jam nunc debentia dici ;
> Pluraque differat, et præſens in tempus omittat.

If *that* of which you have juſt informed me explains to me, before-hand, *what* you are going to relate, the attention of my mind will not meet with any interruption, and I ſhall eagerly run through the peruſal of a work which draws me on with pleaſure from the firſt page to the laſt. But, I know not whether an hiſtorian would not experience more difficulty than any other kind of writer, amidſt his endeavours to find out this *order* concerning which

which we are now speaking. The historian bends under the prodigious weight of his materials; and, if he cannot so arrange them as to form out of the whole one regular edifice, I shall lose myself in a labyrinth from whence no path is open to favour my escape. All this I have felt during the perusal of the History of the Stuarts by Mr. Hume. Instead of what was promised to me, I have found nothing except memoirs which might have served for the materials of his history; and how could I possibly regard with approbation a work which the historian, whether from an ignorance of his art, or from indolence, or from a dullness of comprehension, has only *sketched?* All these facts, unripped from each other, elude my recollection; I have wafted my time, and cannot form a proper judgment concerning those events of which the narrative is placed before me.'

On the subject of arrangement likewise he is led into some reflections with regard to the History of America.

' I have not perused the History of America written by Dr. Robertson: but, if the extract put into my hands was a faithful transcript from the original, I cannot avoid thinking that this work, replete with curious and even excellent matter, must not, however, be proposed as a model for unexceptionable historical writing. Why, let me ask you, does he waste all the first book in expatiating on the navigation of the ancients, their commerce, and their geographical discoveries? All this part of his publication may have been put together with great learning, fidelity, and precision. But, this is not what I want. I wish to know the nature of the reasons for imagining that a new world existed. I am anxious to become acquainted with the character of Christopher Columbus, and those uncommon and great qualities that enabled him to execute the prodigious enterprize which he had meditated. I am told that all the second book is set apart for the satisfaction of this curiosity, but those parts of it which have been described to me entitle me to ask whether Livy would not have treated the subject with more conciseness? Would *he* have suffered such a consumption of his time as must have gone, to the trouble of explaining to me a thousand things which it is, indeed, serviceable to know, but, concerning which I feel an absolute indifference, during my impatience to discover how the Europeans reduced to subjection an extensive country, that brought us to a state of poverty, by pouring in upon us immense quantities of gold and silver, of which the possession sowed the seeds of fresh wars, quarrels, and dissentions.

' The third book contains the history of the discovery and conquest of the islands, and the narrative of some attempts upon the continent. They tell me that, in the following book, the author treats concerning the mode of life among the savages, compares it to a state of civilization, and then begins to make mention of the manners of the Americans. I believe that all these different pieces are worthy of the greatest philosopher; but I am

I am always apprehensive left an eager desire to made a parade of philosophy and of literary knowledge should prove a detriment to history, which ought to move forward without ostentation, to reject all which is not necessary, and to wear only those ornaments which are suitable to its nature. Do you not perceive that, on this occasion, all *order* is overthrown? Had the historian placed the fourth book before the third, I think that I should have read, with more pleasure, and with more interested feelings, the narration of the exploits of Columbus and the Spaniards. It is true that, in such a case, Dr. Robertson would have refrained from a multitude of remarks which, at this moment, I should not wish to meet with ; but he would have entered into an excellent exposition, of which I, certainly, was desirous.

' It is in his exposition that an historian ought to manifest all that art which a great dramatic poet employs in order that he may prepare me properly to listen to either his tragedy or his comedy. Does a writer sacrifice every consideration to the pleasure which he feels in setting down, for the amusement of his reader, a variety of *fine things?* A judicious critic, without incurring the charge of severity, will laugh them to scorn ; and, for *this*, he shall have reason on his side. It is not possible that, even at the commencement of his work, an historian can make too much haste to proceed to the fact ; for the mind is impatient, and has not yet the least occasion to repose itself.

' The same disorder (as I am informed) prevails all through this work. The author devotes the first book to the conquest of Mexico, and the sixth to the conquest of Peru; then, travelling back his former ground, he, in the seventh book, entertains us with remarks touching the state of civilization at which the two kingdoms had arrived. Must it not have proved infinitely more suitable to the great plan of the historian if, having brought Columbus into Mexico, he had informed the reader that this captain would no longer find himself contending against a set of untutored, lazy, enervated and timid savages, like those inhabiting Saint Domingo, and the other islands ; but, against a civilized people, who had established for themselves a regular form of government, and who would have resisted the Spaniards and their courage inflamed with avarice, if, not being confounded by the novelty of the spectacle and the dangers which threatned them, they could have risen superior to that astonishment and those terrors which freeze up the mind, and of which the people of the ancient world have frequently become the victims. I I must repeat, Theodosius, that the author, by following the *order* to which I adverted, would feel himself reduced to the necessity of relinquishing a great part of his arguments, and of his reflections : and, so to employ the remainder that his narrative, continually clear, should not prove overburthened and slackened in his progress, might have become a task attended with a great deal of trouble. But, this is not my business, and, as Boileau boasted of having learned Racine to make verses *with difficulty*, so

I should

I should not feel the least concern at being reproached for having taught historians to write, *with equal difficulty*, their histories. It is scarcely possible too often to apprize them of the necessity of embracing all opportunities to collect together facts, and to follow them with suitable reflections; but it is a point of still greater importance to bring home to their conviction that they ought not to make use of *all* their riches, and (if you will allow me the expression) that the clippings of every work, and more especially of a good history, ought to be more considerable than the work itself.'

M. Mably is equally severe in his animadversions on some foreign writers, particularly Voltaire, of whom he speaks in terms that are even opprobrious. Whether jealousy of the fame of contemporary historians has warped the sentiments of the abbé on the present subject, we shall not determine; but most readers will, we believe, more readily acknowlege the justness of his remarks in what regards the ancient writers. In many parts of these Dialogues he discovers acuteness and good taste; and even where his critical decisions may appear to be tinctured with prejudice, we must approve of the general principles upon which they are conducted. Though the ingenious author has certainly much exaggerated the standard of learning requisite for the writing of history, he has made many observations on the execution of this species of composition, which are worthy of a judicious critic, and merit general attention.

Select Scotch Ballads. Vol. II. Small 8vo. 2s. 6d. sewed. Nichols.

IN our Review for September 1781, we gave an account of the former volume of this work, containing Tragic Ballads, accompanied with two prefatory dissertations, one on the oral Tradition of Poetry, and the other on the old Tragic Ballad. The present volume comprises the Scottish Ballads of the Comic Kind, and is introduced likewise by a dissertation on this species of poetry. The editor distinguishes those various pieces under the general denominations of Pastoral, Amatory, Ludicrous, and Convivial; on each of which he makes some ingenious observations. He remarks that the Love-verses in this volume are of almost every different kind, incident to that changeable passion; but a plaintive tenderness is the more general characteristic of them. We agree with him in opinion that the songs called *Lochaber*, *Ewhuchts Marion*, *Low down in the Broom*, and many others, have, when accompanied with their proper airs, an extraordinary pathos.

The editor, upon the authority of a gentleman who is said to have been born, and to have paſſed his early days in the ſouth of Scotland, adopts the idea that the beſt of the ancient Scottiſh airs were really compoſed by ſhepherds; becauſe, in the remembrance of the gentleman alluded to, there was, in almoſt every village of that diſtrict, a chief ſhepherd, who had acquired celebrity by compoſing better ſongs than others of the ſame profeſſion. Though we ſhall not diſpute the truth of this anecdote, we cannot conſider it as a ſufficient argument for aſcribing to thoſe of the paſtoral profeſſion the beſt of the ancient Scottiſh airs. Beſides that tradition has invariably attributed the moſt celebrated of thoſe compoſitions to ſome of the Scottiſh kings, the inference above mentioned is contrary to general experience. In other countries, the beſt lyric compoſitions, whether ancient or modern, have, we believe, been ſeldom produced by perſons in the loweſt ſtations. And though the life of a ſhepherd is, doubtleſs, not unfavourable to the cultivation at leaſt of paſtoral poetry, it is hardly to be imagined that the *Arcadian* ſpirit ſhould be ſo peculiarly prevalent among the ſhepherds in the ſouth of Scotland. Some allowance may perhaps be made for the gentleman's early prejudices. At any rate, his opinion, reſpecting the poetical genius of the Scottiſh Shepherds, ought to have been ſupported by more ample teſtimony than that of the following couplet,

> We'll a awa to the woods and murne
> Untill our Scotiſh joes come hame.

The editor afterwards makes another obſervation which alſo deſerves to be mentioned. In a book called The Complaint of Scotland, written by ſir James Inglis, and printed at St. Andrews, in 1548; the author, treating of a maſque, enumerates thirty-five ſongs, as forming part of the entertainment. It is remarkable, that not more than two or three of the pieces in the liſt are now known; and from this circumſtance the editor concludes, that not one of our Scottiſh popular airs is ſo ancient as 1548. It muſt be acknowleged, that the authority upon which this opinion is founded appears highly plauſible; but it ſeems not entirely ſatisfactory and deciſive. It is poſſible that in the maſque above mentioned, only the more rare, or more obſolete of the lyric compoſitions were admitted; that ſeveral of the ancient airs may have ſince received new names, and that in many, ſome variation of the original words may have been introduced. Without farther evidence than the liſt of ſir James Inglis, we cannot eaſily be reconciled to the opinion, that the whole of the Scottiſh muſic, previous to the middle of the ſixteenth century, ſhould be entirely obliterated. Such

an extinction seems the more improbable, when we consider
that several of the ancient Scottish songs were reputed to be
the production of their kings; a circumstance sufficient to
have impressed them indelibly on the memory of a nation so
much celebrated for attachment to its monarchs. What gives
still greater weight to the improbability of such an extinction
is, that Scotland continued to enjoy its independency; and
that the supposed revolution in its music must have taken
place, at a period when, as far as we can find, there happened
no considerable change either in the manners or language of
the people. These reasons, however, we only give as conjecture; for we should not desire to be thought dogmatical on
a subject of so much uncertainty.

The first ballad in the present volume was never before
printed. It is the production of James I. of Scotland, and
was communicated to the editor by Dr. Percy, who informs
him, that it is preserved in the Pepysian Library, at Magdalen
college in Cambridge, in an ancient manuscript collection of
Scottish songs and poems. For the satisfaction of our readers,
we shall lay before them a part of this curious specimen of ancient Scottish poetry, which consists of twenty-six stanzas.

'At beltane, quhen ilk bodie bownis
To Peblis to the Play,
To heir the fingin and the soundis;
The solace, futh to say,
Be firth and forreit furth they found;
Thay graythit tham full gay;
God wait that wald they do that stound,
For it was thair feist day,
       Thay said
Of Peblis to the Play.

'All the wenchis of the west
War up or the cok crew;
For reiling thair micht na man rest,
For garray, and for glew:
Ane said my curches ar nocht prest;
Than answerit Meg full blew,
To get an hude, I hald it best;
Be Goddis faull that is true,
       Quod scho,
Of Peblis to the Play.

'She tuik the tippet be the end,
To lat it hing scho leit nocht;
Quod he, thy bak fall beir ane bend;
In faith, quod she, we meit not.
Scho was so guckit, and so gend,
That dayis en byt scho eit nocht;
       Than

K 2

Than spak hir fallowis that hir kend ;
Be still, my joy, and greit not
Now.

Of Peblis to the Play.

' Evir allace ! than said scho,
Am I nocht cleirlie tynt ?
I dar nocht cum yon mercat to
I am so evvil sone brint ;
Amang yon marchands my dudds do ?
Marie I sall anis mynt
Stand of far, and keik thaim to ;
As I at hame was wont,
Quod sch

Off Peblis to the Play.

' Hop, Calyé, and Cardronow
Gaderit out thik-fald,
With Hey and How rohumbelow ;
The young folk were full bald.
The bagpype blew, and thai out threw
Out of the townis untald.
Lord sic ane schout was thame amang,
Quhen thai were our the wald
Thair we

Off Peblis to the Play.

' Ane young man stert in to that steid,
Als cant as ony colt,
Ane birkin hat upon his heid,
With ane bow and ane bolt ;
Said, Mirrie Madinis, think not lang ;
The wedder is fair and smolt.
He cleikit it up ane hie ruf sang,
Thair fure ane man to the holt
Quod he.

Of Peblis to the Play.

' Thay had nocht gane half of the gait
Quhen the madinis come upon thame ;
Ilk ane man gaif his consait,
How at thai wald dispone thame =
Ane said The fairest fallis me ;
Tak ye the laif and fone thame,
An uther said Wys me lat be.
On, Twedell syd, and on thame
Swyth,

Of Peblis to the Play.

' Than he to ga, and scho to ga,
And never ane bad abyd you :
Ane winklot fell and her taill up ;
Wow, quod Malkin, hyd yow

Qubat neidis you to maik it fua ?
Yon man will not ourryd you.
Ar ye owr gude, quod fcho, I fay,
To fat thame gang befyd yow
                              Yonder,
  Of Peblis to the Play ?

  ' Than thai come to the townis end
Withouttin more delai,
He befoir, and fcho befoir,
To fee quha was maift gay.
All that luikit thame upon
Leuche faft at thair array:
Sum faid that thai were merkat folk ;
Sum faid the Quene of May
                              Was cumit
  Of Peblis to the Play.'

After giving fuch an extract, it is proper to add, that the editor has fubjoined to the volume a gloffary of the Scottifh words.

The volume contains fifty-two comic ballads or fongs, of various lengths and meafures. The felection appears to have been executed with tafte ; and from the fuperior correctnefs with which the fongs are publifhed by this editor, the work, we doubt not, will afford great pleafure to the lovers of ancient poetry.

A Letter to the Right Reverend the Lord Bifhop of Landaff, in Anfwer to his Lordfhip's Letter to his Grace the late Archbifhop of Canterbury. By a Country Curate. 4to. 1s. 6d. Wilkie.

THIS writer fuppofes, that the evils, which the bifhop of Landaff wifhes to remove, do not exift ; or if they do, that they are evils in name and appearance only ; and that attempting to remove them, in the way his lordfhip propofes, would moft probably give birth to others infinitely greater.

The fcheme of equalizing the bifhopricks would, he thinks, have a tendency to deftroy that emulation, which is the fource of all great and generous efforts.

It was intimated by his lordfhip, that the income of the bifhops would be thought fufficient, if it were equal to the falary of the judges. This writer is of a different opinion. ' The world, he fays, does not expect as much from judges, as it does from bifhops and great churchmen. Judges are not particularly required to be given to hofpitality ; nor are they, like churchmen, particularly expected to contribute largely to all charitable focieties and inftitutions. In your

comparifon

comparison between the gains and the profits of the pulpit and the bar, your lordship seems wholly to have overlooked the immense profits of an extensive practice; some other still greater law-preferments than those you have enumerated; and almost all posts of high honour and profit in the state, to which, as matters are now ordered, the law is the fairest avenue.'

There is nothing, he thinks, exceptionable in commendams. The officiating clergymen in these cases have a motive for their attention peculiar to themselves, arising from the more enlarged abilities of their patrons. The clergy in general have the same pretensions to these livings as to the bishop-ricks; and the little preferment held in this manner is but as a drop in the ocean.

It has been observed, that the bishops promote the influence of the crown. Our author, taking up the argument on this ground, insists, that the little of this influence, which is still left, is our only security against a total *renversement* of our once glorious constitution.—' Influence, continues he, there undoubtedly is. I contend only, that it is not in the hands of the crown. The worst enemy your lordship has will not charge you with having contributed, in the smallest degree, to this supposed predominant influence of the crown; and yet your opposition to it has been no bar to your promotion.'

Part of his lordship's scheme was supposed to be calculated to promote the residence of the bishops in their respective dioceses. In opposition to this argument, our author observes, that levelling all the bishopricks could lay them under no greater obligations to residence than they are at present, and would deliver them from no particular temptations, to which they are now exposed.

Deanries, prebends, and canonries, he regards as useful institutions, as means of raising and rewarding men of learning. He adds, ' Supposing the rich deanries, the golden prebends of Durham, and every other dignitary, that will bear it, reduced according to your lordship's standard, no calculation I can make brings the sum they would yield to 30,000l. a-year. This divided among the 5597 livings under 50l. a year, would be but five pounds a piece. But there is good reason to believe, that on a closer investigation it would be found, that I am *more* than *one-half* above the mark. And I beg leave to submit it to your lordship, whether it would be worth while to hazard so great a change for the poor chance only of so small an advantage.'

Having

Having replied to all the bishop's arguments, the author remarks, that his lordship's plan is ' palpably copied from the Ordinances of Cromwell's parliament.'——See Hughes's Abridgement of the Acts and Ordinances of Parliament, between 1640 and 1656.

Near the conclusion of his letter, he suggests this idea for improving the condition of the lower clergy: that the Society, for propagating the Gospel in foreign Parts, or the Society for promoting Christian Knowledge, be enabled, by charter, annually to ask, collect, and receive, throughout the kingdom, the benevolent contributions of the well-disposed, for the single purpose of augmenting small livings in England and Wales. He likewise expresses a wish, in which he has certainly the concurrence of thousands, that the governors of queen Anne's bounty would lay before the world the whole history of their administration.

This letter, of which we have here given only some few imperfect strictures, appears to be the production of a respectable writer.

FOREIGN ARTICLES.

Winkelmann's Histoire de l'Art de l'Antiquité, (continued from vol. iv. page 485.)

WE return, with pleasure, to this curious and entertaining history; and, as we have introduced our author to the acquaintance of the reader, by tracing the peculiar traits of his mind, rather than the events of his life, we shall pursue the reflections of the intelligent antiquary, with additional pleasure. We have given a short analysis of the whole work; and, as we have promised a more copious detail of the uncommon and interesting particulars, we shall trace the progress of art among the Egyptians and the Greeks.

The peculiar situation of the Egyptians assisted their progress in many of the more useful arts; and, as they have, for many ages, been considered as the tutors of Greece, both in their mythology and philosophy, they have claimed a degree of attention, which was not deserved by their superior merits. An abject superstition, and an obstinate attachment to their original customs, prevented the progress both of art and science; after ages of civilization they were still the children of nature, without the capacity of improvement: the mind was fettered by habit, and the imagination checked by the aukward models which they were compelled to follow. Though this may, in a great degree, account for the defects of the statuary in the subsequent ages, when the superstitious Adrian introduced their deities into Rome,

K 4

and

and even Antinous was represented in the Egyptian manner—
'upright, without action, the hands hanging perpendicularly,
and attached to the sides, the feet placed parallel to each other,
and the back leaning against an angular column;' though, at this
period, the Egyptians were flattered by such rude and ill-formed
statues, from the causes just mentioned, yet our author pursues
the subject to its origin, and shows us the reasons for the first defects. The Egyptian form, their complexion, and their shape,
gave them very imperfect ideas of the beautiful. It is from comparing sensible objects, examining, selecting, and again com-
pounding, that the painter or statuary rises above real life, and
forms a beauty which, though taken from nature, is probably
superior to it. It may be useless to enter, with precision, into
disgusting particulars; it is enough to observe, that the ancient
Egyptians resembled the Chinese, so frequently represented on
the productions of China. There is a remarkable circumstance mentioned by prince de Radzivil, that, among a great
quantity of heads of Egyptian Mummies, which he had examined, there was not a single one which wanted a tooth, or
had any of their teeth corrupted. The reserved and gloomy
temper of the inhabitants of Egypt, was another cause of the little progress of the more polite arts. Music was held in contempt; and the most violent amusements were required to rouse
them from the melancholy, which seemed continually to devour them. It was this disposition which produced the great
number of hermits among them, for it is remarked by Fleury,
in his Ecclesiastical History, that towards the end of the fourth
century, Lower Egypt contained seventy thousand recluses.

Another cause of their deficiency was the obstinate attachment
to the ancient rules, relating to their customs and their religion.
Cambyses might probably have continued to govern them, if he
had not attacked the custom of embalming. It has been said, on
the apparent authority of Herodotus and Diodorus, that after
the conquest of Egypt by this monarch, it was discontinued;
but our author contends, that mummies of a subsequent date are
still preserved; and he thinks that they returned to this practice
during their revolts, under the successors of Cambyses. The
artists, even by the laws of their religion, were not permitted to
depart from the ancient style; and, as they were confined to the
representation of their gods, their kings, the royal family, as
well as their priests; and, as all these characters were united in
one family, for the ancient kings were their gods, there was little
variety of figure to animate their invention. The little esteem,
in which artists were held, impeded the progress of art. They
were of the lowest rank of the people, and confined to the laborious part of the profession. The son succeeded the father; and
both were contented, when they had equalled the copies from
which their statues were to be formed. They could neither hope
for recompence or honour, if they excelled. The only Egyptian statuary which the Greeks have recorded is, Memnon, probably

bably for the size of one of the statues, placed at the entry of a temple in Thebes. Another impediment was the want of science; and above all, the horror with which an anatomical diffection was confidered. Even the embalmers were obliged to efcape privately, from the revenge of their employers.

The abbé then proceeds to confider the different ftyles, viz. the ancient, the modern, and the imitations of the Egyptian artifts. The general character of the ancient ftyle, in naked figures, we have already mentioned. It is not true, as the ancient authors have obferved, that the feet are always parallel; that circumftance is confined to fitting figures. In the villa Albani, there is the ftatue of a man fourteen palms in height, whofe feet are three palms diftant from each other. In the female figures, the right hand only adheres to the fide, the left arm is folded on the bofom. The bones and the mufcles are but faintly reprefented; the nerves and the veins not at all. The fwellings of the body refemble nature; but are lefs free and flowing, which gives a harfh and embarraffed air to the whole. The female figures are alfo diftinguifhed by the flendernefs above the waift; animals are, however, differently reprefented. The execution of the Sphinxes is vigorous and elegant; the work-manfhip varied, and the outlines light and flowing. The fculptor was not here confined by cuftom and religion. He had the whole circle of nature, from which he might freely take what was moft beautiful; fo that the heat or cold, the moifture or drynefs of the climate, had little fhare in the defects of the Egyptian artifts.

In the fubfequent era, when the Grecians had introduced their divinities, the Egyptian fculptors feemed lefs attached to their former manners. The hands are more difengaged; the pillar, againft which they lean, is fometimes omitted; they hold fome-what in their hands, and they are more nicely finifhed; the feet are alfo rather more diftant. Thefe later ftatues have no hie-roglyphics, while thofe of the former period are generally cover-ed with them; nor is the fupporting column without thefe pe-culiar ornaments. But it is the ftyle, and not the hierogly-phics, which diftinguifh the works of the different ages; for many ftatues, undoubtedly ancient, are entirely without them.

The imitations of the Egyptian artifts refemble their ancient, rather than the modern ftyle. They are generally of Roman workmanfhip, when that complaifant nation admitted into Rome, the deities of the feveral kingdoms which they had annexed to their empire. There are fome ftatues of Ifis found at Pompeia; fo that they muft be more ancient than thofe dug from the villa of Adrian. This fuperftitious emperor built a temple, which he called Canopus; for the Egyptian deities, and the chief imita-tions of the arts of Egypt, have been dug from the ruins of Adrian. Thefe are of two kinds: in fome, he has exactly copied the ancient ftyle of the Egyptians; in others, he has united it with that of Greece. Unfortunately, the heads of many of thefe those recovered works have been loft, and antiquaries have confined their difcuffions to the labours of modern artifts. Thefe ftatues have frequently been referred to the earlieft ages, but they are eafily diftinguifhed by the intelligent antiquary. The cheft is high, the ribs diftinct, the body above the waift full, the articulations of the knees and the figure of the mufcles clear and ftriking, the fhoulder-blades round, and the feet of the Grecian form; the head alfo, and its pofition, have not the leaft refemblance to the Egyptian.

Thofe who are acquainted with our author, will at once fee the imperfection of our analyfis, and the reafon of it. We have chiefly confined our view of the different ftyles to the reprefentations of the naked body: our author confiders alfo the drapery and ornaments; but his language is fo expreffive, and his defcriptions fo comprehenfive, that it is not eafy to abridge them. We have, however, purfued him far enough, to give the reader a general idea of this part of his work, and of the very peculiar nation, which is the fubject of it; we fhall now proceed with him to the Hiftory of the Grecian Art.

The author enters on this Hiftory with all the fire and enthufiafm which a favourite fubject can infpire. In the Greeks, he faw every thing that is elegant and ufeful; and he expatiates, with pleafure, on every circumftance which relates to their art, without reflecting on the remotenefs of the connection. Their beauty, the ftatues which were erected to the conquerors in the field, and in the Olympic games, the contefts for the prize of beauty, the efteem which they entertained for their artifts, and the facred objects which they laboured to reprefent, were all adapted to increafe the progrefs of art. But their moral character, their love of liberty, their tendernefs and affection, and the warmth of their climate, had a much more remote tendency to the fame end, and fcarcely deferve, in this view, the attention of a moment.

In the chapter on the Effence of Art, he confiders the foundation of beauty, and endeavours to diftinguifh it from the effects of habit, as well as from that of the paffions. He talks of the grave and fublime ftyle of beauty, with the coldnefs of a connoiffeur, and fpeaks of ' a pretty figure, who can *fpeak* and *act*' with contempt.———This whole chapter, though laboured with precifion, and a philofophical accuracy, is exceptionable. He affumes the beautiful, before he attempts to analyfe it; and the perfon, who had twifted the Gordian knot, would have had no occafion to cut it with his fword. But as beauty is neceffarily an abftract idea, he would have given his reader greater fatisfaction, and equally eftablifhed his own principles, if he had analyfed the beauties which are moft generally interefting, and arifen from the fenfible form to the abftracted idea. We wifh it were in our power to purfue this fubject, but our limited article muft contain a more varied entertainment. It muft alfo be confeffed, that the reft of the fection

on

—on particular beauty, or the individual beauty of youth—on the ideal beauty, composed of different parts—on the beauty of eunuchs and hermaphrodites, and even on that which results from borrowing the appearance and expression of the nobler animals, and applying them to the human form, is accurate and entertaining.

In the next section of this chapter, the author treats of the discriminating circumstances of the age and the sex of the ancient statues. The acuteness of his penetration, is in these respects no less admirable, than the warm enthusiasm of his language. We can give but a small proportion of this engaging subject, yet we must transcribe the introduction.

‘ From extracting and uniting the most beautiful forms, we obtain, as by a new creation, a more noble substance ; and a perpetual youth is the chief result of our reflections on the beautiful.

‘ The soul of thinking beings has a natural desire to disengage itself from matter, and to dart into the intellectual world of ideas. It is most truly contented, when it can produce conceptions both new and elegant. The great artists of Greece, who may consider themselves as new creators, though they laboured rather for the feelings than the understanding, endeavoured to conquer the inflexibility of matter, and to impress it with life. In the dawn of art, this generous effort of the artists, occasioned the fable of Pygmalion and his statue. Their industry gave an existence to the objects of religious worship, which, to excite veneration, should be considered as types of a superior nature. The first founders of religion, the poets, furnished sublime ideas for the representations of divine intelligence : these ideas gave wings to the imagination, to raise the work both above itself, and above the sphere of the senses. The human conception, in bringing the divinities to our senses, could form nothing more worthy of, nothing more attractive to, the imagination, than the state of perpetual youth, than the spring of an unchangeable life ; by the remembrance of which, we are enchanted even in the more advanced age ! This picture was analogous to the idea of the immutability of a divine being : the beautiful shape of a young and blooming divinity excited love and tenderness, the only affections which can charm the soul in a delightful extasy. And is it not in this rapture of the sense that human felicity consists, which has been sought in every religion, understood or mistaken ?’

But alas ! this rapture, though expressed in strains so ambiguous, is merely intellectual ; and the religion, which has charmed the senses of our antiquary, is that of ancient Rome ; but his fire is still more equivocal, in his description of the Venus de Medicis. It is the lambent flame which seizes the heart, —far—far distant from the cold correctness of De Piles, alluded to in the article of Mason's translation from Du Fresnoy.

‘ Among

Among the divinities, Venus, as the goddess of beauty, justly assumes the first rank. She alone, with the Graces and the deities of the Seasons. or Hours, has the privilege of appearing without attire. She is more often represented in this manner, than the other goddesses, and this is the representation of different ages. I shall give here a short description of the statue of this goddess, preserved at Florence.

'The Venus de Medicis resembles a rose, which appears at the close of a beautiful morning, and blows at the rising of the sun. She is entering on the period of her life, when the vessels begin to distend, and the bosom to assume some firmness. When I contemplate her in her attitude, I fancy I see the Lais, whom Apelles instructed in the mysteries of love: I think I see her, as she appeared, when she was obliged, the first time, to throw off her clothes, and to appear naked to the eyes of the enchanted artist.' Those who have once looked at the ancient statue, will feel the full force of the description; but the abbé will elude the conclusion, and still appear to be enraptured with the statue alone. After speaking of the celestial Venus, whose attributes and appearances are different, he adds, that 'the eyes of both are full of sweetness, with a languishing and amorous look, which, the Greeks call ὑγρον,' or more properly with swimming eyes; but he adds, for his distinctions are often nice, 'that this kind of look is very different from those lascivious expressions with which some modern sculptors have pretended to characterize their Venus; for, among the ancients, love was looked on by the artists, as well as by the more rational philosophers, as the colleague of wisdom, τα σοφια παρεδρος Ερωτας.'

We wish to transcribe the picture of Juno, which is still distinguishable by her large eyes—of the grave and modestly reserved Pallas—of the eager and lively Diana, or of the mild and gentle Graces. Our author too, impresses terror with equal success. 'The Parcæ' are described, as 'three old women, overcome with old age, their limbs trembling, their faces wrinkled, their bodies bent, and their look harsh and severe;' but we must leave this very pleasing spot, for we can scarcely select a beautiful passage, without feeling a regret for what we must necessarily omit. It is like a delightful prospect, where the eye is never satisfied in one place, because there are many others which have an equal claim to the attention, and where the mind is never at rest, on account of the continual recurrence of equal or superior beauty.

To descend from descriptions, dictated by the warmest enthusiasm, to attitudes and proportions, may seem unsuitable; yet we must follow our author. It is the air of calmness and repose, which is most favourable to beauty, and in the way the ancient deities are represented. Yet we have representations of Jupiter, in all the pangs of child-birth, when, by the rude untutored operation of Vulcan, he produced a Pallas from his brain; and another of Apollo, after killing the Python with expressions of anger

anger and difdain; anger againft the ferpent which lay at its feet, and a contempt of fo defpicable a victory. The attitude of the legs croffed is chiefly adapted to perfons in pain, and to lefs dignified characters. It is never found, where the objects are entitled to our efteem and our reverence. A Chefterfield could not have explained this point with more feeling and precifion than our author. The general expreffions of the faces, in the heroic ages, was that referved and dignified calmnefs, which fignifies, in the ftrongeft manner, wifdom and difcretion. In the torments of Laocoon, and the grief of Niobe, the artift forms their reprefentatives, not with the weaknefs of a man who feels diftrefs, but with the appearance of a ftrength of mind fuperior to complaint, which is able to bear it. The figure of Philoctetes fhows a *concentrated* grief; and that of Ajax, the heart-felt forrow, which muft arife from reflecting on the confequences of his madnefs.—The female figures were feldom divefted of their peculiar foftnefs, even in fituations where they had deferted their own characters. Clytemneftra feems to run away from the murder of her hufband, inftead of bathing her own hands in his blood; and Medea fometimes appears irrefolute, and fometimes even foftened with compaffion, in the horrid fcene of flaughter. The complaifance of the artift was permitted to facrifice truth to beauty: the aged Hecuba, and the mother of Medea, in a few inftances, appear in blooming youth.

The emperors and empreffes are always reprefented with a noble confidence, and great firmnefs. They are the firft only of their citizens, for art long fupported its independence, after an effeminate and corrupted fenate had fubmitted to the groffeft flattery, and the moft fervile obedience. Nothing is prefented to them on the knee; and they could not be diftinguifhed, if they had not been in the center of the picture, or difcriminated by the peculiar action, which occafioned the reprefentation.

Our author's obfervations on the proportion of the ancient ftatues, and the compofition of the artift, cannot be eafily abridged; and as we muft not enter into any very copious details, fhall proceed to the fourth chapter, on the beauty of the different parts of the human body.

It will not be eafy to purfue our author, with minutenefs, but we fhall defcribe in general, the perfon which he would call beautiful, after the Grecian model, without always delaying the reader with his particular reafons.—The line which marks the profile, from the front to the tip of the nofe, fhould be nearly ftrait, or with a very flight inflection; for ftrait lines mark out the fublime ftyle of beauty, and a light flowing contour the delicate. The forehead rather low, the hair turned back, and round towards the temples; the eyes large, but in ftatues they are deeper than is confiftent with beauty, that the arch of the eye-brow may be more confpicuous. The fhape of the aperture varies on different bufts, to exprefs the different characters. In Jupiter, Apollo, and Juno, the eyes are large, round, and open;

in Pallas, large, but apparently turned towards the ground; in Venus small, with the lower eye-lid raised, to express the swimming eye, the eye-brows raised, arched, and the hairs fine and delicate. Our author contends, in spite of some seeming authorities, that the ancients did not consider their junction over the nose, as a beauty: in fact, this appearance is very unusual, in a face resembling the Grecian model. Beautiful mouths are generally known; yet the abbé generally thinks, that the upper lip should be a little more full than the lower one. The heads of the emperors and heroes have generally the mouth apparently shut; those of the gods, slightly opened. It is the Fauns and Satyrs only, who are represented as laughing; the chin is generally full and round, without any dimple; the ears, executed with the nicest care, frequently, by this means, distinguish an ancient from a modern head. The hair is differently represented; when the head is carved in brittle materials, it is generally short; but in others, and particularly in female figures, it is flowing, frequently turned in graceful curls, and tied behind.

The ancients were not less careful in representing the extremities. The hands are of a moderate fullness, the fingers diminishing in a beautiful proportion, the joints slightly represented, the last joint seldom bent, and the nails generally short; the knees are scarcely distinguished but by a gentle eminence, which is gradually lost both in the leg and thigh; and the feet are executed, like the hands, with nice attention, but the nails are somewhat flatter.

The beauty of the chest in the statues of men, seems to consist in the gradual diminution of its elevation; in those of women, it has seldom too great fullness. The ancients endeavoured to represent the appearance of the bosom, at that age when its swellings begin to be observed, when its risings, though obscure, may yet be distinguished.

'Crinis ad *obscuræ* decurrens cingula mammæ.'

The other parts afford little variety to occasion the discussions of the artist, and the chapter concludes with a few slight observations on the representations of animals.

We must now leave our engaging author, though we fear, instead of having gratified the curiosity of the reader, we have only excited it. We have pursued the arts of Greece, as far as we proposed, and as far as we pursued those of the Egyptians. The drapery, a subject which deserves and shares the attention of the antiquary, we must necessarily omit, as it would detain us longer than our other avocations will allow. We must omit too many engaging speculations on the mechanical part of the Grecian arts, and the styles of the different periods: we can only apologize for the omission, by our having endeavoured to extract the more interesting, and the more useful passages. If we can again resume this work, we shall chiefly attend to the third volume, on what may be more strictly called the History of Art.

We

We shall now close this article with some remarks on our author and his translator.

The character, the attention, the learning, and above all, the situation of Mr. Winkelmann, have peculiarly adapted him for the present work; and we have reason to think, that his most sanguine admirers have not been disappointed in their expectations of it. It is indeed true, that his extravagant admiration of antiquity, and his eager desire to approve of what the ' sacred rust' had sanctified, has sometimes led him into errors, and in a few instances, occasioned absurdities. But in a work like this, the critic who could stop to mark them, would deserve a worse epithet than fastidious. They are fully compensated by the extent of his learning, and the acuteness of his discernment: there are few sciences which have not lent their assistance to his enquiries, and contributed to the ornament of the work.

The translator's diligence deserves also our praise. We have no reason to distrust his accuracy, though we have no foundation on which we can commend it, as we have never seen the original History. The language is frequently deformed by German idioms; but it is nervous and clear, and from its very defect, is more intelligible to an English reader. This edition is considerably corrected from the different publications of Mr. Winkelmann; and the editor has availed himself of all the additions which the abbé had intended to adopt in the French translation, the object of the unfortunate journey in which he was assassinated. The head and tail-pieces are taken from the former editions, and the other works of the author; they are also better adapted to the subject of each chapter which they are intended to adorn. On the whole, we have received considerable entertainment and instruction from these volumes, and we have not the slightest hesitation in bestowing the warmest commendations on them.

Des Fürsten Michael Schtscherbatowo Russische Geschichte von den Ältesten Zeiten an; or, *Prince Mich. Schtscherbatowo's Russian History, from the earliest Times. Translated from the Russian, by M. C. H. Hase. Vol. I. and II. 8vo. Danzig.* (German.)

THE author, who is now privy counsellor to the empress of Russia, and president of the board of finances, has far excelled his predecessors, especially in point of completeness. The Russian archives are opened to him by her majesty's command; he has also carefully collected his materials from sources hitherto inaccessible to foreigners, and pointed out in his preface; he has arranged them, he has noticed the variations of the annalists from one another, has sometimes attempted to reconcile their discordant relations, has given his own opinion, and supported it by arguments, and thus obliged the public with a variety of useful materials for a future regular history of his country. His work, as it proceeds to later times, will no doubt become incomparably more interesting and valuable, on account of the facts to be be drawn from authentic records. It is to consist of ſeven voiumes, of which four are said to be already publiſhe , in the Ruſſian language.

It opens with an introduction, containing fragments of the earlieſt hiſtory of the nations who either formerly inhabited or now inhabit Ruſſia: this introduction is ſucceeded firſt by an enquiry on ſeveral ancient nations, who formerly reſided in Ruſſia; and then by the body of the work itſelf, of which the firſt part carries down the hiſtory to the year 1053, and the ſecond part to the year 1237, when Ruſſia was conquered by the Tartars.

MONTHLY CATALOGUE.

D I V I N I T Y.

Divine Revelation impartial and univerſal. By the Rev. John Bennett. 8vo. 3s. in Boards. Cadell.

THE imperfect and ſeemingly partial propagation of the Goſpel, has furniſhed unbelievers with ſome popular objections againſt Chriſtianity. The ingenious author of this tract has therefore attempted to obviate theſe objections, by ſhewing, that the diffuſion of religion and happineſs to all mankind has been the uniform plan of the Deity; that his mode of doing this, or the nature, degree, and extent of his revelations, have been varied in accommodation to the diſpoſitions and circumſtances of mankind, in different ages and nations, on the principle of that free-will or free-agency, which is an eſſential characteriſtic of intelligent creatures; that Chriſtianity would probably have been communicated ſooner, in its fullneſs and perfection, if men in earlier times had been able to receive it; that a religion, full of ceremonious inſtitutions, was the only one, which a hardened and unrefined people were capable of bearing, and the moſt effectual barrier againſt idolatry; that the intellectual darkneſs, in which many nations are now ſituated, is owing either to their miſuſe of divine information, to our indolence and remiſſneſs in not promoting their converſion, to their want of proper laws, diſcipline, and education, to their luxury and ſenſuality, or to ſome other circumſtances, for which the juſtice and benevolence of the Deity cannot be impeached; and that, if the mercy of heaven were not reſtrained by human vices, the neceſſary conſequences of free-agency, ' the earth, at this moment, would probably be full of the knowledge of the Lord, as the waters cover the ſeas.'

This writer, as he candidly acknowleges, has derived conſiderable aſſiſtance from the biſhop of Carliſle's excellent Theory of Religion.—He has illuſtrated his text by a great variety of curious and uſeful notes, ' which have coſt him, as he himſelf informs us, infinitely more pains than the compoſition itſelf.'

Au.

An Attempt to explain certain Passages of Scripture generally misunderstood. 8vo. 1s. 6d. Dilly.

The author of this tract has explained a great number of metaphorical expressions in the New Testament, such as, 'dead in trespasses and fins, the old man, the new man, a new creature, born again, regenerated,' &c. by referring them to the state of mankind in the heathen world, and afterwards under the Gospel dispensation, respectively. This work may be read with advantage by those young students in theology, who have not Taylor's Key to the Apostolic Writings, where these and the like phrases are explained more at large, upon similar principles.

A Call to the Jews. 8vo. 3s. 6d. sewed. Johnson.

The author of this tract, in a warm and peremptory manner, contends, that the genuine Christian Scriptures, and the Jewish prophecies, uniformly concur in representing Jesus Christ as a mere man, the son of Joseph and Mary, or the feed of David; and that the passages, on which the doctrine of his supernatural generation is founded, viz. Mat. i. 18, 20, 25. Luke i. 34, 35. iii. 23. are forgeries. Having thus removed what he considers as an obstruction to the conversion of the Jews, he proceeds to shew them, that Jesus was their promised Messiah; and that their dispersion will continue as long as they reject him. He then endeavours to convince them, that if they embrace Christianity, they will be admitted to the rights of citizens, in the countries where they choose to reside; but that as many of them as prefer a return to their own land, will obtain the divine blessing in this enterprize; that all of them at last will be restored in joy and triumph; and, finally, that the Messiah will reign over them in great splendor and felicity, in Jerusalem.

This glorious restoration, he calculates, will commence in the year 1793, or 1794; and he is so sanguine in his expectations, that if a thousand Jews are willing to engage in this adventure, he offers to be their leader. 'Yea, verily, says this pious projector, I mean to accompany you into your own land, where, as I would wish to be considered as a member of your civil community, as one of your people, when they acknowledge Jesus to be the Messiah, I doubt not but you will give me a possession in your future division of the land. Nay, I repeat what I have before said, that if a considerable number of you, my countrymen, the British Jews, or of the foreign Jews, should, on your conversion, be at a loss for a leader to conduct you thither, I intend, under God's direction, to undertake that to me most agreeable office, and will endeavour to remove every obstacle which may be thrown in the way of your return. I therefore hold myself prepared to meet any man of a fair character among you, who shall be pleased to honour me with a line post paid, addressed to the Author of a Call to the Jews, at Mr. Johnson's, bookseller, St. Paul's Churchyard, signifying his heart-felt conviction, that Jesus was the Messiah, expressing a wish of an interview with the author, and signed with his real name and residence.'

As it is very necessary that he and his associates should not engage in a long and dangerous expedition, without some assurance of success, he has given several copious extracts from a treatise published in 1747, On the future Restoration of the Jews and Israelites to their own Land, in which the author has attempted to confirm the certainty of this great event by a variety of passages collected from the prophets.

If this author has not seen The eighth Treatise of Rabbi Sahadias the Excellent, concerning the last Redemption, we would recommend it to his perusal. It will be a delightful amusement to him and his associates in their march to the Holy Land. — But, let him remember, that all their hopes must depend on the right interpretation of the prophecies, which are highly *figurative* and *hyperbolical*; and if those which he applies to the restoration of the Jews in a future period were actually fulfilled in their return from the Babylonian captivity (as we have no doubt they were) he is only deluding himself and his brethren with a RABBINICAL DREAM.

A Sermon on the Blessings of Peace. By the Rev. Charles Cordiner.
4to. 1s. White.

A laboured and florid discourse, in the style of the following paragraph: ' The louring combination of terror and distress, which hung over the nations ; a gloomy storm that overshadowed all the blessings of life, is now appeased ; we have the pleasure of beholding a clearer azure diffused over the horizon of life.'

A Sermon on the Excellency of the Christian Religion. 8vo. 6d.
Law.

A performance, which the author might have preserved in manuscript, without any disadvantage to the republic of letters.

A Rational Defence of Scripture Mysteries ; attempted in a Discourse on the Doctrine of the Trinity. By the Rev. John Walker, A. B.
8vo. 6d. Lowndes.

What we have said on the foregoing article is applicable to the present.

POLITICAL.

Thoughts on the Naval and Military Establishments of Great Britain. 4to. 1s. Elmsly.

The design of this writer is to abridge the enormous expence of raising men for the navy and army, in the time of war ; to man the navy without an impress ; to recruit and augment the army as effectually in war as in peace ; and to maintain a militia, that shall invigorate, not embarrass the nation. — For the purpose of manning the fleet, he proposes a registration of all ships in Great Britain and Ireland, including under the denomination of ships every vessel that navigates the sea. He suggests that the register should express the port ; the ship's name or number ; the owner or owners names ; the tonnage ; the number of hands ; distinguishing seamen from apprentices ; the trade ; the year in
which

which the ship was built; the builder's name and abode.   That ships not registered within the time limited should be charged with a duty of so many shillings per ton, monthly, ships at sea excepted.   That an allowance of a certain number of days be made to such, after they come into port; and that ships falsely registered be deemed and charged as unregistered ships.   That returns be made twice a year by the owner or master of the vessel, to the custom-house of the port or district; and these returns to be transmitted to the Admiralty, where they ought to be reduced into proper order, for the inspection of the board.   That builders in private yards return the number of hands employed by them, in the same manner.   That the number of seamen being collected from these returns, when men are wanted for the navy, a requisition, founded on the just proportion of the seamen at each port to the whole, should be made by the Admiralty to the several ports of Great Britain and Ireland.   That this requisition should be accompanied with a general embargo; from which, however, any port or single vessel may be released, by furnishing their proportion of seamen required.

The author's plan for the regulation of the army is, that the portion of it which is allotted to the English counties shall be recruited and augmented out of the males who have been, or may hereafter be maintained by the parish rates.   That they be drawn by ballot from among those who are above seventeen years of age, and under thirty-five, unmarried, and not apprentices. That, after completing a certain term of service, they shall be entitled to their discharge, either totally, or into the militia, at their option.

These are the outlines of the plan proposed by this author, for levying a sufficient number of seamen and land-forces on any emergency.   It is unnecessary for us to mention the subordinate regulations which he suggests; but we cannot avoid observing, that his proposal appears to be dictated with judgment.

Two Letters to the Right Hon. Edmund Burke. 8vo. 1s. 6d. Bew.

These Letters are written in reply to the insinuations in the Ninth Report of the Select Committee, which affect the character of Mr. Hastings.   The author expostulates with Mr. Burke, in warm and pointed terms, respecting his declared opposition to the governor-general of India, whose conduct he likewise vindicates in a clear and satisfactory manner.

The Speech of the Right Hon. William Pitt. 1s.

An imperfect copy of the Speech made by the late chancellor of the exchequer in the house of commons, on the 21st of February last.

A State of Facts, &c. 1s. 6d. Cadell.

The author of this pamphlet endeavours to delineate the character and political conduct of the right hon. Charles James Fox; but the description is neither sufficiently complete, nor expressive.

POETRY.

The Disbanded Subaltern; an Epistle from the Camp at Lenham. 4to. 1s. 6d. Flexney.

In an advertisement prefixed to this performance, the author informs us, that "the subject upon which the epistle is founded, occurred to him from seeing the halls of the inns of court so constantly filled with cockades, as they have been during the course of this war." We, however, rather suspect it to have been written by an officer; and that the character of a disbanded subaltern, which he assumes in the poem; and where, like Othello, he bids adieu to the "pride, pomp, and circumstance of glorious war," is his real one: obliged to quit the noble science of arms, for the harsh drudgery, and, as some may think, no less destructive profession of the law. We at least observe many striking traits of a soldier's character, and lively descriptions of military manners, that could not have been acquired merely by contemplating the "cockades in the inns of court," nor indeed by a conversation with the greater part of those who wore them. The following description of a march is of this kind.

'When orient day first glimmers in the skies,
Wak'd by the general's lively call we rise,
And while with active vigour we prepare
To breast the keenness of the morning air,
The sun-burnt soldier at an alehouse door
Pays from his scanty purse his last night's store,
And, as his host a parting draught bestows,
The cumb'rous belt o'er his broad shoulders throws,
Adjusts his knapsack, shakes his landlord's hand,
His musket grasps, and takes his silent stand.
Now to the martial band's enliv'ning sound,
In duely-measur'd steps we beat the ground;
But not unmindful of the window's height,
Which courts on either side the glancing sight,
We pass along — for there, all unarray'd,
Sweet as the morn appears the lovely maid,
The well-adjusted curtain half reveals
Those charms which yet no cruel robe conceals,
For at the drum's rude sound she left her bed,
By punctual love, or idle fancy led,
Perhaps her eyes with vacant pleasure stray
O'er the well-form'd battalions proud array,
Perhaps she seeks, repentant, to renew,
With kinder token the last night's adieu.
Up the steep hill, or through the drizzly grove,
Or clayey vale, with sturdy step, we move,
While jocund as the party winds along,
Burst the loud laugh, or swells the chearful song.
Can I forget, with emulation fir'd,
When my steps led them, and my mirth inspir'd,

How

How the men ftrove, with tale or carrol gay,
To fmooth the deftin'd labour of the way,
Proud to divert, and grateful to my care,
How oft they vied th'approving laugh to fhare,
While the joke feign'd to feek a comrade's ear
Was juft told loud enough for me to hear?'

This is painted with fpirit and truth. The ferjeant's portrait is equally characteriftic and natural.

' His port erect, his firm, commanding air,
The hoary honours of the well-club'd hair,
His furr-coned helmet worn with ftudied grace,
The plumage waving o'er his burnifh'd face,
The well expanded fafh of varied dye,
Whofe fringe rode graceful on his manly thigh,
The well-clean'd belts which crofs'd his ample breaft,
His ftrutting chitterlin, and fnowy veft;
Sweets which alone the wedded foldier proves,
The darling labour of the girl he loves.
When (as we march'd the gazing crowd among)
He caught th' applauding murmurs of the throng,
I faw his mien elate with honeft pride,
I faw him woo the glance from fide to fide,
With more expreffive note his ready feet
Refponfive echo'd the drum's chearful beat,
Stern glanc'd his eye, full rofe his fwelling cheft,
And all the martial coxcomb ftood confeft.'

We meet with fome paffages liable to cenfure; but we fhall wave the ungrateful tafk of pointing them out in a performance, the perufal of which has afforded us much entertainment.

The Peafant of Auburn, or the Emigrant, a Poem. By J. Coombe, D. D. 4to. Elmfly.

The author tells us that ' the hint of this little poem is taken from Dr. Goldfmith's Deferted Village.' That gentleman's ftyle is likewife imitated with great fuccefs; fometimes, indeed, too clofely in regard both to the thought and expreffion. An inftance occurs in the beginning of the poem.

' Dark was the fky, and fatal was the morn,
When firft from Auburn's vale I roam'd forlorn.
The neighbouring fwains came penfive o'er the lea,
And parting breath'd their laft kind prayers for me,
Ah! gentle fouls, your prayers for me how vain,
The man of forrow, penury, and pain.
Thus Edwin mourn'd, pale, melancholy, flow,
Where wild Ohio's founding waters flow.'

The two laft lines nearly refemble thofe with which the Traveller opens.

' Remote, unfriended, melancholy, flow,
Or by the lazy Scheld, or wandering Po.'

L 3 Edwin

Edwin proceeds to contrast his present miserable state with the happiness he formerly enjoyed, and gives the following pathetic description of his sensations when he quitted his native country—

'Good heaven! what anguish wrung this boding heart,
When the rough boatswain gave the word to part.
Then first the tear, at nature's bidding, fell,
As bleeding friendship press'd its long farewel.
Pale on mine arm connubial mildness hung,
Fond filial duty round my bosom clung.
Firm for their sakes, along the surf-beat strand,
And whispering peace, I led the weeping band;
Deceiv'd their thoughts from Auburn's much-lov'd plain,
And talk'd of happier seats beyond the main.
Poor aged man! since that eventful day,
Despair and terror mark'd thee for their prey.
War, sickness, famine, bursting on thine head,
Mock thy vain toils, and weigh thee to the dead.'

The remainder merits our warmest approbation; and we know not which to commend most, his lamentation for the death of his wife, his terror on account of the Indians who had carried off his only surviving daughter, or the following affecting conclusion.

'Ah my poor Lucy! in whose face, whose breast,
My long lost Emma liv'd again confest,
Thus robb'd of thee, and every comfort fled,
Soon shall the turf infold this wearied head;
Soon shall my spirit reach that peaceful shore,
Where bleeding friends unite, to part no more.
Then shall I cease to rue the fatal morn
When first from Auburn's vale I roam'd forlorn.
He spoke—and frantic with the sad review,
Prone on the shore his tottering limbs he threw.
Life's crimson strings were bursting round his heart,
And his torn soul was throbbing to depart;
No pitying friend, no meek-ey'd stranger near,
To tend his throes, or calm them with a tear.
Angels of grace, your golden pinions spread,
Temper the winds, and shield his houseless head.
Let no rude sounds disturb life's awful close,
And guard his relicks from inhuman foes.
O haste, and waft him to those radiant plains,
Where fiends torment no more, and love eternal reigns.'

The Skull, a true, but melancholy Tale, inscribed to the prettiest Woman in England. 4to. 2s. Bowen.

A surgeon passing through the wards of St. George's Hospital perceived a dead body, and was struck with the whiteness of the teeth; he preserved the skull, and Leon, 'who to science had a claim,' remarked with rapture their beauty. He enquired after the person who had been formerly distinguished by such charms, and found that it was Laura, seduced by him, and abandoned.
The

The unhappy fair one, for a time procured a precarious and distressing living, as a prostitute; by an accident broke her leg; and died, after amputation, in the hospital. 'Leon's distress wanted little aggravation, and will not easily admit of description. The story is told in an artless manner; but the poem is neither pathetic nor interesting, though the subject seems almost sufficient ' to harrow up the soul.' The lines are harmonious and pleasing; though not without slight errors in metre and language: we can, however, forgive greater failings, for the benevolence of the intention.

Arx Herculea Servata, or Gibraltar Delivered, a Poem. 8vo. 1s. M. Davis.

The principal part of this performance is taken up in celebrating the praises of Elliot, and his brave garrison, but the subject deserves a better muse. Though two languages are employed for that purpose, we can scarcely discern any marks of genius in either. The Latin is frequently barbarous; the translation not always correspondent to the original, and an air of burlesque is too often conspicuous. In the following passage, the victorious Briton is described as *sticking* to the fortified rocks:

> ' Quam sibi vicinæ vario certamine gentes
> Quæsierant, victor pridem, sedet arce Britannus,
> Munitisque jugis, expelli nescius, *hæret.*'

The translation varies from the original, and, what could scarcely be supposed, is inferior to it: instead of a Briton, &c. we have Britain herself turned to, and enshrined in a rock.

> ' Lo! on these rocks, whose blood-disputed right,
> Contending nations long engaged in fight,
> Victorious Britain sits enshrined in stone;
> Herself a *rock*, and not to be o'erthrown.'

Elliot, in the next page, is addressed in the following manner:

> ' Salve, *sancte* senex, nulli cessure priorum,
> Elliade? rapido pugnantes dejicis igni,
> Dejectos idem *lachrymans* amplecteris hostes.'

Can any thing be more improper than the epithets we have marked with Italics? We ask pardon; the correspondent ones in the translation at least vie with the original:

> ' Hail Elliot, hail, time-ever-honour'd sage!
> Second to none in history's fair page;
> Whether to launch the red hot fiery blow,
> Or pitying snatch from fate the wave-o'er-whelmed foe.'

' Time-ever-honour'd sage' is as unfortunately applied to our gallant veteran as ' sancte senex;' and the ' launching a red-hot fiery blow,' breathes a genuine spirit of true bombast, not easy to be paralleled.

Poetical Effusions of the Heart. 8vo.

This author complains of having met with an ' early misfortune in life, by which he was precluded many advantages and

opportunities of improvement.' A lift of fubfcribers, chiefly inhabitants of Dover, where we apprehend he refides, is prefixed;
from whence we think it not improbable that he labours under
pecuniary diftreffes, and that within the circle of his acquaintance
there are many friends who wifh to alleviate his calamity. We
mean no ill-natured reflection by the fuppofition; nor, whatever
his misfortunes are, will we add frefh preffure to them, by pointing out fome faults in the compofition with critical feverity. Indeed, the principal ones are to be attributed to the author's want
of a claffical education, which had he enjoyed he would probably
have made a very refpectable figure in the poetic department.
Not that we would be underftood to deny many of thefe poems
real merit: fome of the elegies particularly are truly pathetic,
and expreffive of the genuine feelings of nature.

The Cumbrian Feftival, a Poem, by a Cumbrian. 4to. 1s. 6d.
Robfon.

This author defcribes a politico-poetical vifion, in which the
Genius of Cumbria, Liberty, and Britannia, meet together in a
very fociable manner: at leaft the interview concludes quite ami-
cably; for Britannia appears at firft a little afhamed on account
of the treatment fhe gave and received, from ' her daughter' on
the other fide the Atlantic. Liberty, however, confoles her upon
the occafion, tells her,

 ' The fault was others, the misfortune thine.'

This leads to, what we apprehend to have been the author's principal object, an encomium on our prefent illuftrious premier.

 ' Yet let me now fpeak comfort to thy foul,
  And tell the joys which yet await thy land:—
 No more the tranfatlantic thunders roll,
  And here my Portland leads the patriot band.

 ' Portland, the friend of freedom and mankind,
  New luftre adds to Bentinck's honour'd name;
 Defies all foes in flav'ry's caufe combin'd,
  All fears renouncing, but the fear of fhame.

 ' Soon fhall perfidious France and haughty Spain
  Revere his counfels, or incur their fate;
 In the great fcale of empire yet again
  Britannia fhall affert her priftine weight.'

The author is at laft awakened by ' Jove's own thunder,' and
a grand chorus of fairies, who fing,

 ' That Britons never fhall be flaves.'

And his ' wild conjectures' at what the vifion can portend, are
cleared up by the information that,

 ' Portland, the lord and patron of our plains,
  Is rais'd to lefs alone than fov'reign power:
 Hence on each village-green the nymphs and fwains
  With feftive garlands deck the feftal bow'r.

           The

' The tidings *flash conviction* on my mind,
Thither with beating heart I speed my way :
The nymphs, the swains, the feſtal bow'r I find,
And to the votive wreath thus add the votive lay.'

There are ſome marks of genius and animation in this poem ; but puerility is its predominant characteriſtic.

The Imperfection of Human Enjoyments, a Poem. By the Rev. Thomas Moſs, A. B. 4to. 2s. 6d. Dodſley.

The title is a palpable miſnomer: the poem contains many juſt religious ſentiments and moral reflections, but ſcarcely a ſingle ray of poetic fire illuminates the heavy, ungenial maſs. The concluſion is flat and inſipid : reduce it to proſe, or rather break the metre, and it runs in the following manner. ' Would we have riches, let it be our care to dig for thoſe that will not create pain ; that neither wax old, nor ſuffer decay. *Let us ſeek* an intereſt in the everlaſting God : the deep unfathomable mine, filled with endleſs wealth and infinite bleſſings. The portion of that man who, by actions uniformly great and good, has ſought for a long time to find this hidden treaſure of the deſire of his heart. Would we have friends ? let us ſeek him, whoſe ſmiles are truth itſelf ; whoſe love is unbounded ; who will not diſappoint, if he promiſes. Whoſe wiſdom will direct our ſteps, if they wander : whoſe fulneſs can ſupply our wants ; whoſe power can ſhield us from every ill ; and who can give happineſs when other friends frown, and all creation is our foe. Would we then lay hold of the immortal palm, and reign victorious over a hoſtile world, let us be virtuous, and the prize is acquired.'—This would be no bad concluſion to a ſermon, but bears little reſemblance to the language of poetry ; and we are ſorry to add, that we can find few paſſages ſuperior to what we have already quoted.

MEDICAL.

Practical Obſervations on the Human Teeth. By R. Woofſendale, Surgeon Dentiſt, Liverpool. 8vo. 3s. Johnſon.

Theſe Obſervations are ſometimes judicious ; but we cannot avoid remarking, that our author ſtrongly inculcates the unremitted attention of the operator ; and ſeems, in general, to conſider the growth of the teeth to be more advantageouſly conducted by art than by nature. It is indeed a common error in every branch of the faculty : practitioners are copious in their inſtructions when activity is required, but ſeldom inculcate the more uſeful leſſon of waiting on the operations of nature, after the ſeveral impediments which may oppoſe them are removed. In another view, our author ſeems not to deſerve the attention of the more liberal part of the profeſſion ; for there are many marks of an uncandid reſerve, where we expect inſtruction ; and ſometimes he is entirely ſilent, when we had been induced to look for the moſt ſatisfactory information. The intention of the treatiſe is not to give an accurate anatomical deſcription of the teeth, but to collect the observations which long practice has procured: The author has, however, confined himself to censuring many parts of the usual customs of dentists, frequently without substituting any thing but the recommendation of a *concealed* preparation, which we may therefore properly call a nostrum.

Mr. Woofendale's sentiments, in other respects, scarcely deserve our attention. He seems to doubt whether the teeth are supplied with nerves; but if he looks into Dr. Monro's new work on the Structure and Functions of the Nervous System, he will find an accurate delineation of those of one of the larger teeth. Another opinion, which seems peculiarly his own, is, that the teeth are marked by the small pox. It is not easy to say how a man of the slightest medical knowlege could, for a moment, entertain one so little consonant both to the disorder, and the laws of the animal economy. His explanation is given with confidence, but with unusual obscurity; we had almost said confusion. It seems that the second set of teeth are sometimes pitted by this disorder, in their shell; and sometimes in their softer state, as soon as they emerge from the gum. It is not in our power to be more particular, but we could not convey a more successful refutation of this visionary opinion than the words of its fondest admirer.

On the whole, we have derived but little entertainment or instruction from this performance; but this cannot affect the author's character as a practical operator. In his profession he may possess merit: we are sorry that we cannot add to it, by giving him the title of an enlightened philosopher, or a rational physician.

Observations on the General Bills of Mortality, by W. Hawes, M. D. Author of the preceding Address, &c. Together with farther Hints for restoring Animation. By A. Fothergill, M. D. 8vo. 3s. Dodsley.

The Observations are intended to accompany the Address to the King and Parliament, on the subject of general receiving-houses. They are too crude, trifling, and insignificant, to delay us a moment in their consideration. We have the highest respect for Dr. Hawes as a man of humanity, but can pay no compliment to his abilities; and, like Trebatius, shall in one word give him a salutary lesson.—' Quiescas.'

Dr. Fothergill's Hints are more accurate and correct than those which formerly attracted our attention. He seems to have availed himself of our information, respecting De Haen, and Van Helmont; and condescends to obviate our objections against the different and opposite effects of electricity. Of this latter subject, he has given a new and somewhat different view; and has cleared it from those inconsistencies of which we complained. It is not so much the different *force* with which the electrical fluid passes through the body, as its different *direction*, which occasions the seeming opposition of its effects. Nor is it surprising that violent shocks, which are capable of destroying the organization of the important contents of the thorax, should be less effectual than those slight ones, which operate only as simple stimuli.

The

The hints on the use of dephlogisticated air deserve attention; but we think that, like all new discoveries, its importance has been exaggerated. The other means are, electricity and heat: the latter is an ambiguous remedy, and Dr. Fothergill's limitations are accurate and just.

To the whole some queries are subjoined, whose chief tendency are to suggest, that dephlogisticated air may be a very important agent in the animal œconomy. But the different functions, which are attributed to it, must result from the union and relation of the solids and fluids of which the body consists, and can never be the effect of any one power. The queries are, however, acute and ingenious; and have led us to expect matter of greater importance.

A Catalogue of the British Medicinal and Agricultural Plants cultivated in the London Botanic Garden. By William Curtis. To which are prefixed, Proposals for opening it by Subscription. 12mo. 3s. 6d. White.

Mr. Curtis has had the address to make a mere catalogue of plants both entertaining and interesting. The medical plants, which are authorised by the college of London or Edinburgh, are selected from the rest; and others, which have been used without their sanction, are subjoined. To both these catalogues the English and the Linnæan names are added. In the last class we have observed some omissions, and a few mistakes: the omissions we cannot, in our limited circle, supply; but shall mention a few seeming errors. The gum ammoniac is probably produced from a plant similar to, if not of the same genus with, the ferula assa fœtida; but, instead of leaving the usual blank, Mr. Curtis has filled it up with a name, ammoniacum, which expresses neither a genus or species. The ipecacuanha is not a species of the viola, but of the psycotria. It is a creeping plant, characterised by Linnæus (Lin. filius) in his supplement, p. 144. The hyoscyamus *niger* is the species commonly used in medicine. The sago is taken from the cycas circinalis of Linnæus. There are a few others of less consequence, which it is needless to mention. These are only pointed out, to induce Mr. Curtis to revise this part of the catalogue.

The British plants are arranged in a calendar, according to their time of flowering; and a dry subject is enlivened by some apposite quotations from Milton and Thomson. This method gives a material assistance to the younger botanist; and the physician, as well as the rational agriculturist, will attain some useful information, from this humble unassuming tract. The library consists of the most valuable authors; and we doubt not but that the garden, an institution which so intimately unites instruction and amusement, will find a liberal support.

A sovereign Remedy for the Dropsy, published by Desire, for the public Benefit. 4to. 6d. Dodsley.

This benevolent tract deserves the warmest praises. A drachm of broom-seed finely powdered is to be steeped twelve hours in a

glass

glass and a half of rich white wine, and to be taken, every other
morning, fasting. After each dose, the patient must walk for
an hour and a half, and then take two ounces of olive oil, without eating or drinking any thing else, for an hour more. We
mean, at a future period, to give some observations on this remedy, from experience. At present we can only observe that the
dropsy, as it so commonly proceeds from some of the most obstinate and intractable internal diseases, is seldom cured; and the
best remedies must be far from infallible, or even generally successful. Broom-ashes have been commonly employed; but it
has been supposed that their efficacy proceeds from the alkali
produced by the burning: the present remedy seems to suggest
another opinion, which experience rather than reason must ultimately appreciate. It is necessary to add, that it seldom produces any sensible discharge; and that its indiscriminate praises,
both for dropsy and other diseases, give it an appearance in some
degree suspicious.

*A Treatise upon Ulcers in the Legs, with an Introduction on the
Process of Ulceration and the Origin of Pus laudabile. To which
are added, Hints on a successful Method of treating some scrophulous Tumours, &c. By Michael Underwood, Surgeon to the
British Lying-in Hospital. 8vo. 3s. in Boards. Mathews.*

We are not willing to decide on the method recommended
by our author. It is the business of experiment rather than
reason; and the ingenuity of a critic is never employed to
less advantage than when he combats experience, without being
able to adduce his dictates from the same salutary source. Mr.
Underwood recommends the very free use of stimulant applications to almost every kind of ulcer; and, over them, he
binds a tight bandage of thin flannel. With these assistances, he
encourages his patients to walk as far as their strength will permit; and remarks, that the pain is not increased, after the first
two or three days. The diet should be nourishing, and any medicine, that may be required to correct the obvious disease in the
general habit, should be freely used: the chief dependence
is, however, on the topical applications and free exercise. The
strong suppuratives, or rather stimulants, are not unfrequently
applied in common practice, in those ulcers, where a foul slough
sticks at the bottom, and the discharge is thin and ichorous. Our
author's method is peculiar to himself, by *extending* the use of
these applications, and by *enjoining*, rather than permitting, the
exercise of walking. This is the outline of a plan, which we dare
not, for the reasons already assigned, object to; yet we own that
its singularity at first led us to suspect its utility. We are willing
to rely, at present, on the credit of its author; but we are sure
that we shall not offend him, when we recommend it to a cautious trial, and reserve our final judgment, till we can have the
same method of forming it.

Me.

Mr. Underwood's theoretical opinions are more exceptionable. The chief difficulty of healing old ulcers, he thinks, depends on the nervous energy in the legs being less, in proportion to their distance from the center. But, while this opinion may be at least pronounced uncertain, the consequence which he draws is erroneous. Though the nervous energy may be really less, on the extremities, the healing of wounds does not entirely depend on it. When the sacro-sciatic nerve of a frog had been divided, wounds in the same leg were found to heal with as much facility as before. There is another opinion, which, as it may be more dangerous, we must necessarily mention, viz. that old ulcers may be safely healed. It is, indeed, afterwards limited, by the author's observing, if there is no disease of the viscera; but, even with this restriction, it may mislead. We have seen both asthma and palsy repeatedly brought on and cured, by healing an old ulcer, and again opening it; nor would any remedy prevent the recurrence of these dangerous disorders, or cure them, without restoring the usual discharge; and from the *very same* part. Mr. Underwood follows De Haen in thinking, that pus is a secreted fluid, and not the effused serum, changed by fermentation.

Scrophulous swellings are treated in the same manner, brought to a suppuration, and filled with præcipitate. If they do not suppurate easily, Mr. Underwood advises us to draw a seton through them, and occasionally soften the thread, with a stimulating ointment. We have more than once seen the good effects of this treatment; but it is severe, and frequently, if the lower part of the sore can be brought to suppurate, it will disperse the rest of the hardness and swelling.

The observations on sore nipples and mammary abscess are important and instructive, though concise; and we would recommend them to the attention of the faculty.

Letters on the Medical Service of the Royal Navy, with occasional Remarks, &c. 8vo. 2s. Newbery.

Many of these Letters have already been published in the newspapers; they relate to the scanty provision for the surgeons of the royal navy, with some remarks on the practice. We readily concur with our author (Mr. Renwick) in thinking, that the neglect of useful and deserving officers materially injures a country, and reflects an indelible disgrace on it: policy, if humanity had no share in administration, would dictate a different conduct. The medical remarks are of little consequence; but the story of Eugenius is highly pathetic and interesting. The language is frequently exceptionable.

The Appendix is addressed to Dr. Hawes, on the subject of burying alive. Our author very properly expostulates with the doctor, that his directions, if they were pursued either in the army or the navy, and the bodies kept till signs of putrefaction are discovered, might be very injurious by propagating putrid fevers. We

We are aware that the natural feelings and the humanity of the world will powerfully support Dr. Hayes; but have no scruple in owning, that we think his directions in this respect should be received with great limitations.

MISCELLANEOUS.

An Essay on Landscape Painting, with Remarks general and critical on the different Schools and Masters, ancient and modern. 12mo. 2s. 6d. sewed. Johnson.

Though this little tract is chiefly intended for the artist, it may be read with equal advantage by the connoisseur; but to those who are neither, it must appear uninteresting, and perhaps unintelligible.

The author, very judiciously, in our opinion, recommends the study of English nature to English painters. To the realizers of pictures, the modern embellishers of ground, he offers some useful advice, and endeavours to rescue a beautiful tree from indiscriminate destruction.

' The ash is the most elegant of all trees, affording to the painter an opportunity of displaying the neatness and precision of his pencil more than any other: for it is seldom so massy in its foliage, as to give only a general effect of light and shade; its slender and graceful branches admit the light through all parts, the eye may distinguish every leaf, and, when well handled upon canvass, affords a sharpness and delicacy not to be equalled. I am sorry to understand, that Mr. Browne, and the modern improvers of land, are at declared enmity with this tree, and make it feel their displeasure wherever they meet wit, as being pernicious to every thing within its influence; but as that influence is confined to the circumference of its own branches and roots merely, I cannot conceive it a sufficient reason for its extirpation.'

To the purchasers of pictures he gives the following advice:

' I would caution every young collector against the buying dark and obscure pictures: he may have many inducements to commit this error, from the pleasure and self-gratulation he receives, in finding something to admire in pictures, which, before his mind had imbibed a passion for the art, and before his taste began to form, appeared to him as mere blots; an imperfection in judgment, from not having yet seen the better and clearer pictures of the same artists, whose works he is beginning to admire, may be another cause of his falling into this mistake. It is a gross taste that is easily satisfied. It is not to be supposed, that these pictures came as they now appear, originally from the easel: no painter could be pleased with obscurity and indistinctness; and the ignorant in the art, may justly look with ridicule on the man who is peering for beauties in midnight, and admires a chaos instead of a representation of the graces of the creation.'

*An Essay on Landscape, or the Means of improving and embellishing
the Country round our Habitations. Translated from the French
of R. L. Gerardin, Vic. D'Ermenonville. 12mo. 3s. sewed.
Dodsley.*

If we reflect on the various discoveries in science, and the useful arts with which Europe has been so happily enlightened, within the three last centuries, we shall find, that the French have
contributed a very small proportion. But what they want in
reality is abundantly supplied by their pretensions; for, though
they have a just title to a little only, they claim the whole.
This remark has been suggested by the work before us; and,
though apparently illiberal, because it is general and national,
will be found to be dictated by experience, and supported by
facts. It is well known to all Europe that the English were the
inventors of the modern art of gardening. They have suffered
all the scandal and ridicule which is the usual lot of discoverers;
they have been considered as wild and visionary innovators, and
now begin only to reap the reward. Till within these few years,
the French have been their chief opponents in the pursuit; but at
last truth has prevailed and all those who wish, in their gardens,
to realize the conceptions of great landscape painters, imitate the
English, both in their arrangement and their ornaments. We
appeal to the public, in the most general sense, for the truth of
this assertion. The viscount D'Ermenonville, and, what is still
more fatal and treacherous, his translator, are determined to deprive us of this honour. The latter, in his preface, finds in the
ancients all our principles, and the former finds them in nature.
We readily agree that there are many descriptions of places in the
Greek and Roman writers, which equal all our wishes; but, in
these passages, the poet found, and described, in the most animated language, a beautiful and romantic view. He described
the *country*, not a *garden*; but it is our chief boast that we have
neglected the usual decorations of the latter, and by adorning the
former, have supplied the beauties which uncultivated nature
could not afford. It wanted not the discernment of the viscount
to discover, that our principles are from nature; we own the imputation, if it be one, while we glory in the first application of
those principles, and that we alone invented the art of landscape gardening. Even the Chinese are but weak competitors in
this path; since they are not acquainted with the art of perspective, or the true principles of painting.

Having thus established our just pretensions to this beautiful
art, as well as our short limits will permit, we make no scruple of
recommending this Essay, as worthy the perusal of those, who
are engaged in the pleasing employment of a picturesque improvement of their ground. It contains many hints extremely advantageous both to the artist and the gentleman. A view of Rousseau's tomb, in the Island of Poplars, near the seat of the viscount, is prefixed; the design is elegant, but we cannot highly
commend the execution.

An

An Easy Introduction to the Arts and Sciences. By R. Turner, jun. 12mo. 3s. Crowder.

This publication consists of definitions, and some of the first principles of religion, morality, rhetoric, grammar, poetry, painting, natural philosophy, astronomy, chronology, geography, history, mythology, &c. and is calculated to give children a *general* idea of these arts and sciences. The design is laudable, and the scheme comprehensive and useful. But the sentiments and the language are frequently inelegant. For example : to the question, Who is the author of the Christian religion? The answer is, ' The Son of God, who left the bosom of the Father, and all his glories there, to dwell in flesh and blood : He became the child of a poor maid in Galilee ; when grown up he appeared as a *young carpenter*, and *sweat* and *laboured* in the trade of his father Joseph.'

Elegance of sentiment and language is perfectly consistent with ease and perspicuity. But this representation is coarse and vulgar ; and, even supposing it to be *true*, unnecessary.

A New Description of Europe. Long 8vo. 2s. 6d. Dilly.

Mr. Charrier, the author of this compendium, appears to be a very industrious person, and must have bestowed great pains in composing the present system ; but we are not without apprehension, that it is digested in a method too complex to be generally approved.

A Collection of Tales and Essays on the most curious and amusing Subjects. 8vo. 2s. 6d. Moore.

This collection, so far from meriting the favourable title with which it is decorated, is, in every respect, extremely ill qualified to afford entertainment to any reader.

Themidore and Rozette ; or, Authentic Anecdotes of a Parisian Counsellor and Courtezan. 2s. 6d. Hookham.

A mixture of dullness and obscenity, too despicable to gratify even the most profligate character.

ERRATA in Critical Review, for July.

Page 11, l. 43, *for* conspicuous *read* perspicuous. Page 44, l. 5, *for* relates *read* refutes. Page 55, l. 22, *for* suor *read* suoi.

THE
CRITICAL REVIEW.

For the Month of *September*, 1783.

Observations on the Structure and Functions of the Nervous System,
illustrated with Tables. By Alexander Monro, M. D. President
of the Royal College of Physicians, and Professor of Physic, Ana-
tomy, and Surgery, in the University of Edinburgh. Folio.
2l. 12s. 6d. Creech, Edinburgh; Johnson, London.

THERE is probably no part of physiology which will with
such constancy elude the most diligent investigation, as
the functions of the nerves. Their powers are so considerable,
instantaneously exerted, executed with force and energy, and,
though occasionally remitted, yet capable of being renewed
and continued for many years with a vigour almost unimpaired, that, since our observations can furnish us with few
similar phænomena, we can only in a very remote degree investigate their analogies and relations. But there is still a
more powerful obstacle to our researches; these exertions, so
numerous and varied, have sometimes no perceptible origin,
or one little proportioned to the effects. Volition, a simple
act of the mind, impels the muscles to exert a force which no
mechanical power can imitate; and, in the human body, there
is a circle of motions, depending on each other, in which we
cannot distinguish the cause or the effect, nor trace their source
from any operation of a distinct principle. These are difficulties which must necessarily remain; for a power, different from
matter, in its common forms, or possibly in its nature, can neither be an object of the sense, or even of the intellect: a visionary philosopher may pursue his airy castles, but they will
be always the phantoms of a heated imagination, which the
torch of truth will immediately dissipate.

M Modern

Modern physiologists almost constantly use the term vibrations, to express the mode of communication in the nervous system; and, though this word has been the subject of much debate, and of some confusion, we shall continue to employ it. But we mean not to be confined by the fetters of a system, or implicitly to follow those philosophers who think the vibrations exist in the solid substance of the nerves; or those who, with more reason, suppose them to be a peculiar state of a fluid inherent in that system. It is also necessary to remark that, when in the future article we speak of the communication in the brain, and the effects resulting from it, we do not mean to exclude an immaterial principle.—The subject is already sufficiently embarrassed, without any additional difficulties; and, though the communications of fibres in the many different parts of the brain may sometimes be supposed to exclude the necessity of such a principle, yet a true philosopher will not, on that account, deny its existence. Indeed there are many other inexplicable phænomena, which require its assistance, if we had not another and a better foundation for believing it.

The present work is splendid in its appearance; for, independent of the printing, which is very elegantly executed, it is adorned with forty-seven tables. We must, however, confess that, in the latter, we were much disappointed; they are generally deficient in elegance, and sometimes even in distinctness; but the curiosity of the subjects compensates for the former defect, though it makes us feel the latter with additional force. In a work like this, the favourite subject of its author, the labour and the amusement of many years, we cannot easily allow of an apology—like, 'want of time obliging him to trust the dissection to other hands,' or, 'an imperfect sketch from memory;' yet these and similar excuses sometimes occur. After some appearances too have been allowed to be microscopical deceptions, the delineations of these appearances must add to the bulk, rather than to the value of the work. A minute criticism might detect many other defects; but we would equally avoid indiscriminate commendations, or an anxiety to discover errors.

The Observations are chiefly confined to those facts and remarks which have escaped the attention, or which have not been clearly ascertained by other anatomists and physiologists. The first section of the first chapter relates to the circulation in the head, and is illustrated by a table of the rete mirabile Galeni, which is found to be a division of the internal carotid into small serpentine branches.

This

This arrangement is peculiarly useful in brutes, who are destined to the prone position of the head, and it is confined to them ; in men the same effect is chiefly produced by the ascent of the blood, and by the turns and angles of the carotids. Our author then examines the structure and uses of the sinuses. He considers them as veins calculated, from their structure, to prevent either too great accumulation of blood in the head, or obstruction to the circulation.   The practical remarks are, that cutting the temporal artery may be of service, by changing the course of the blood, if its quantity is not much diminished ; and that the proposal of trepanning the head in apoplexy, phrenitis, &c. to obtain the pressure of the air on the over-distended vessels, can be of no service, and may be injurious.   The chapter concludes with an account of an experiment to prove, that a person hanged dies rather from a stoppage of respiration than fullness of the vessels of the head, as Petit and others supposed.

The second chapter, on the membranes of the brain, contains little remarkable, except that the pia mater, when it covers the ventricles, has fewer blood-vessels than when it is extended over the other parts of the brain.   The third and fourth chapter, on the communications of the ventricles, will not be intelligible in an abridgment.   The author has discovered the communication of the two lateral ones ; and finds that *all* the ventricles communicate with each other, but that they have no communication with the spinal marrow.   The plate, however, which relates to this part, cannot be said to add to the clearness of the description.——The next chapter relates to the lymphatics of the brain.   The author endeavours to establish their existence by analogy rather than by observation ; yet there are many facts, both in Haller and Hewson, that are more pointed and satisfactory, in this view, than the arguments of Dr. Monro.   The infundibulum, he thinks, is a hollow tube ; and the glandula pituitaria of the conglobate kind.   The ventricles, by our author's account, seem to be chiefly serviceable in extending the surface of the brain, and probably of the pia mater.   But this affords little room for deduction ; if their surfaces had been cineritious, it might have materially assisted our enquiries, but they are chiefly medullary.   We meet, indeed, with cineritious matter in the substance of the brain and nerves, as within the fornix, &c. it is therefore probable that in that situation its purposes are answered as well as if it were on the surface.   This part of the brain is probably very important ; and from whatever source its energy may be derived, the cortical part seems to be a very necessary assistant.   It ends abruptly, and the division between it and the medulla is accurately defined.

The

The eighth chapter is ' on the fuppofed origin and formation of the nerves.' Dr. Monro obferves, that the brain not only fupplies the nerves with their medulla, but probably ferves fome other ufeful purpofe ; for there are many tranfverfe bundles of fibres in it, and animals which have this organ very fmall, feem to feel as acutely, and exert their mufcles as violently, as the human fpecies. Indeed he feems willing to fuppofe that the brain is rather connected with the nerves, than the fource and origin of them, and that the latter may exift independent of the former. We fhall felect his arguments, as they contain fome curious facts.

' 1. In children delivered at the full time, plump and well formed in their trunk and limbs, I have obferved the fubftance which fupplied the place of the brain not more bulky than a fmall nut, and, inftead of containing a white medullary fubftance, it was of a red colour refembling a clot of blood : and fmall cords, occupying the place of the optic nerves, were likewife of a red colour. Yet the fpinal marrow, and all the nerves from it, had the ordinary fize and appearance.

' 2. In a monftrous kitten, with two bodies and the appearance of one head, I found the fpinal marrow of one of the bodies connected with a brain and cerebellum of the common fhape and fize. But the fpinal marrow of the other body, though equally large, had only a fmall button of medullary fubftance at its upper end, without a fuitable brain or cerebellum.

' 3. In living frogs, I have repeatedly cut acrofs the fpinal marrow, or the trunk of the fciatic nerve, and fed the animal for upwards of a year thereafter. In fome of them, the fciatic nerves were rejoined ; but in none of my experiments did the nerves under the incifion recover their powers; yet the nerves under the incifion feemed, at the end of that period, as large in the limb in which the experiment was made, as they were in the found limb.

' Whilft thefe facts feem to prove that the nerves may exift without the brain, and that they are not to be confidered, according to the common idea, as being merely ducts which convey a fluid from a gland to diftant parts, they feem alfo to fhew, that there is an energy of the nerves, independent of the energy of the brain ; and, therefore, lead us to attempt to prove more fully that the nerves poffefs fuch an energy, and to difcover the ftructure on which the poffeffion of the energy depends.'

In the ninth chapter, which is not eafily abridged, and which our limits will not permit us to tranfcribe, we are prefented with a very accurate defcription of the fpinal marrow, and the nerves arifing from it. It is remarkable, that nature feems to have united every bundle of nerves, as they come from the fpine, with a peculiar anxiety, to thofe above or below, by means of fome detached fibres, or by thofe of a ganglion. The confequences of this union is explained in a future chapter ; and the plate, which illuftrates it, is one of the moft diftinct and ufeful of the whole collection. Another circumftance which deferves attention is, the deep fiffures between the fides of the fpinal marrow, which, our author thinks, may explain the partial affection in hæmiphlegiæ.

The fubftance of the nerves is more brown than that of the medullary part of the brain, and they are larger in their progrefs than at their fuppofed origin. The optic nerve, and the portio mollis of the auditory nerve, feem to acquire cineritious matter from the pia mater, which is continued through their whole courfe, fo foon as they reach the organs on which they are to be difperfed. It is alfo evident, that the nerves receive fupport and nourifhment in their progrefs ; for a nerve, after it has been long divided, does not appear to fhrink, or to have loft its fubftance : and the blood-veffels perform every function, though the mufcles are paralytic.

Dr. Monro next defcribes the appearance of the nerves in their courfe : they feem to confift of ' a femipellucid fubftance, in which a more white and opake fibrous-looking matter appears to be difpofed, in tranfverfe and ferpentine lines ;' but when the nerve is ftretched, thefe lines difappear. They are, in our author's opinion, folds or joints, to adapt them for different ftates of flexion or diftention ; and probably the ftructure is, in no degree, connected with their peculiar functions. Our author, who has obferved thefe folds to be numerous within the cranium, and where the nerve is nearly fixed in its place, thinks, that they may be alfo ufeful in increafing the furface of the nerve ; but, by his defcription, the furface is no more increafed by thefe ferpentine fibres, than that of a leaf by the fpiral fibres in its fubftance, which have been called the tracheæ or vafa aërea.

The connexion of the nerves is the next fubject of attention ; they are joined at acute angles, when they purfue the fame courfe ; at obtufe angles, when they run in oppofite directions ; and they are alfo united in hard bodies, which have been frequently defcribed by anatomifts, under the name of ganglia. The firft mode of communication, which has been ftyled plexus, was examined many years ago by our author, in that of the arm. He found, as he expected, that ' in the plexufes the fibres of the different trunks were intermixed, and that every nerve, under the plexus, confifted of fibres of all the nerves, which were tied together above its origin from the plexus.' The optic nerves, though intimately united, are fo foft, that it is not eafy to trace their fibres ; but our author

M 3 thinks

thinks he has seen a partial decussation of them. It is, indeed, highly probable that the union is far from being complete. The connection of nerves in opposite directions, seems to be of a similar kind. The principal example is the portio dura of the auditory nerve, which is united to the second and third branches of the fifth pair, in the face : these our author has traced, both in a man and an ox. The nerves are also very intimately united in their course, while they run in one common sheath. The reasons for this arrangement are judiciously detailed by our author ; and we shall need no apology for inserting his remarks.

‘ The chief intention of nature, in this very solicitous intermixture of the nervous fibrils, is, I apprehend, to lessen the danger with which accidents or diseases, affecting the trunks of the nerves, would, without these combinations, have been attended.

‘ Thus, let us suppose that two nerves are sufficient to supply the flexors and extensors of the fore arm ; it is evidently better for us, that the one-half of each nerve goes to the flexors, and the other half of each to the extensors, than that the whole of the first nerve should have gone to the flexors, and the whole of the second to the extensors. For if, by accident or disease, one of these nerves should be cut across, or lose its powers, we should, on the first supposition, preserve one half of the power both of flexion and extension, which would surely be preferable to our possessing fully the flexion, without any power of extension.

‘ If a still greater number of nerves is employed to supply the flexors and extensors, the loss of power, arising from an accident happening to one of the trunks of the nerves, will be felt in a much smaller degree ; thus, in the arm, where five trunks are found, a fifth part only of the power would be lost.

‘ 1. Notwithstanding we have observed that the fibres of the nerves, in this course, are much more intimately intermixed than has been supposed, still as their branches do not anastomose, there is little or no reason for believing that the energy of one fibre can directly affect that of a neighbouring or contiguous fibre, or that the sympathy of nerves can depend directly on their connection in their progress. We are, therefore, led to refer it, in the first place, to their connections in the brain, where we have found there are many more medullary fibres than are sufficient to form a bulk equal to all the nerves, and where, besides, many of the fibres seem evidently intended to connect opposite sides of the brain.

‘ 2. But although we cannot, from the intermixture of the nervous fibres in their course, account for their sympathy, but are obliged to refer the cause to their connections in the brain, in which the feeling principle is seated ; yet, from finding that each small branch of a nerve is derived from various sources, we perceive,

perceive, that an injury done to it may affect and irritate the brain in various and diftant places, and, thefe reacting, we underftand better how a fufferance by fympathy may become extenfive or univerfal, than we do, when we conceive that each nerve is derived from a fingle fmall portion only of the brain.

' 3. As different nerves, intermixed, are fupplied by branches of the fame artery, and that the arteries furnifh pia mater and cortical matter to the nerves in their progrefs, and evidently influence their energy, it may be a queftion meriting attention, whether fympathy of nerves may, in fome meafure, depend on the irritation and reaction of their accompanying blood-veffels ?'

We muft purfue our account of this fplendid work in another article, and fhall conclude the prefent with a few remarks. The chief additions which are made to the anatomy of the brain afford little room for reflection, or for deduction. While we are ignorant of the ufes of the ventricles, their communications are of lefs importance ; and the only confequences which we can derive from our improved ftate of fcience are, that, in the brain, the nerves are united, and the communication between each part of the body, in this common receptacle, is apparently free and unembarraffed. But even this general remark muft be received with great limitations. The hæmiplegia affects one eye and ear ; the hæmicrania is fo nice in its diftinctions, that the patient can frequently draw a line between pain and eafe, between difeafe and health. If we look more nearly, we fhall probably find, that this free intercourfe is ufeful rather to the corporeal than the mental functions ; and that it is only in an intellectual view that the brain can be ftyled the common fenforium. In this way it will materially affift the doctrine of the affociation of ideas ; and the mere materialift will find fome difficulty in excluding the vibrations of fenfation, while thofe of intellect maintain a free paffage. It is evident, however, that this paffage muft really exift ; for, in hæmiplegia, while one part is only injured in fenfe and motion, the intellects are more flightly and more generally affected ; while the nerves of one fide have their peculiar functions almoft entirely deftroyed, the internal fenfes remain, but with diminifhed vigour. If thefe wellknown facts be compared with the reafoning of our author, which we have juft tranfcribed, they will probably be found to give a very important affiftance to our opinion.

With refpect to the origin of the nerves, Dr. Monro has not, we think, fully availed himfelf of the arguments which may be drawn from the comparative anatomy. Perhaps he was afraid that it might lead him into more important metaphyfical difquifitions ; into thofe dangerous fyftems of materiality,

M 4

riality, where narrow limits bound truth and falfhood ; and one improper ftep may plunge the author into, at leaft apparent, infidelity. But, if Reafon be not abufed, if it be permitted to purfue its paths with candour and with caution, it may be followed with a fteady confidence, with a defiance of danger. In the prefent cafe, if our limits would permit, we could more clearly fhow, from the above mentioned fources, that the brain and the nerves are almoft diftinct fyftems ; and that, though they are connected, the operations and functions of each are peculiarly appropriated, and independent of the other.—But we fhall defer the reft of our remarks, which are more nearly connected with the fubfequent parts of this volume, till the appearance of a future Number.

An Effay on Laborious Parturition, in which the Divifion of the Symphyfis Pubis is particularly confidered. By William Ofborn, M. D. 8vo. 5s. in Boards. Cadell.

THOUGH novelty attracts by its fplendor, and apparent improvements are eagerly caught at by the reftlefs and impatient fpirit, which difdains a common tract, yet the cool dictates of reafon will be at laft attended to, and every pretenfion valued at its true rate. We have already ventured to predict the downfall of the new operation, viz. the divifion of the fymphyfis ; and the refpectable publication now before us will very materially contribute to it. As we had formerly been mifinformed on this fubject, we have undefignedly mifled our readers, by faying that the operation had been performed in fome parts of Great Britain ; but this was a miftake, which, as it arofe from the relation of fome experiments on the dead body, candour obliges us to point out. This is a fubject, however, which decorum will not permit us to enlarge on : we fhall therefore give a concife, and we hope an exact, view of our author's opinion.

Dr. Ofborn begins with obferving, that the efforts of nature do not fo much require affiftance, in this function, from our eagernefs to interfere, as from fome real difference in the conformation of the human fpecies, when compared with brutes. On account of the operation of gravity, the human fœtus is fecured by an irregular contexture of bone, and the pelvis expofed to deformity, from its bearing, in different parts, almoft the whole weight of the body. It is obvious, therefore, that parturition is impeded by many caufes, which cannot affect the brute creation. Where, however, neceffity demands the facrifice of one life, for obvious reafons, he thinks
that

that of the child lefs valuable; but, both in the divifion of the fymphyfis, and in the Cæfarean feetion, the prefervation of the child is very uncertain, and the life or health of the mother in the greateft danger. Dr. Ofborn confequently propofes, where the pelvis is very much diftorted, the operation of embryotomy, in preference to either; and endeavours to fupport it by arguments, to prove that, in this fituation, the child is either dead or infenfible to pain; and by recurring to his former pofition, that we at leaft facrifice a life lefs valuable, to preferve one which, in comparifon, is infinitely more fo. We fhall not ftop to confider the only argument which appears to us exceptionable, the infenfibility of the child, becaufe the reafoning is decifive without its affiftance; but proceed to the principal part of this work, which endeavours to fhew, that embryotomy is fuperior either to the Cæfarean feetion, or to the new operation of Monf. Sigault.

The repeated failure of the Cæfarean feetion, in the modern attempts, muft in a great meafure decide our judgment of its propriety. The earlier experiments are, we own, fufpicious; but they are related with fo much confidence, that we were not furprifed to fee a profeffor in a neighbouring univerfity, Dr. Hamilton, of Edinburgh, fupporting his recommendation of the operation on their credit. We have had many proofs of his abilities and judgment; but it requires a little boldnefs to impeach the credit of medical records, in a public work. We mean to throw no imputation on Dr. Ofborn; for we own that, in ancient medical authors, we find more room for fufpicion, at leaft, than for belief; and that we are often incredulous, when we are obliged, apparently, to affent.

The new operation has been much commended: as Dr. Ofborn was therefore convinced of its danger and inutility, it required no common attention to the feveral experiments, which have been made, to oppofe the confidence with which it has been recommended. All the feveral attempts have, on this account, been particularly confidered; and he finds that, in the beft circumftances, the recovery has been flow; that the patient has been weakened by exfoliations, or more nearly endangered by lacerations and inflammations from the preffure. He thinks it has fometimes been wantonly employed, when nature could have effected the delivery without its affiftance; and that it will not enlarge the pelvis, in a fufficient degree, when it really becomes neceffary. Even Dr. Leake's fuppofition, that the aperture of the divided bones will receive the hind-head of the child, he thinks, may be injurious, as, in that cafe, the interpofed parts muft receive

considerable

considerable preſſure, and probably injury : And Dr. Hunter's argument, that it may make room for the crotchet, is, in his opinion, inadmiſſible.

On theſe accounts he contends for the preference of embryotomy; for while, from Sigault's operation, the ſpace of about ſix or ſeven lines, at the utmoſt, can be obtained, though one inch and a half is ſometimes wanted ; by this, the head of the child can be brought within the ſize that is, in almoſt any inſtance, neceſſary. We own ourſelves entirely of the ſame opinion, and think that Dr. Oſborn's attempt deſerves the higheſt commendation.——This work is written with accuracy, candour, and good ſenſe, and will add conſiderably to his reputation. If we can perceive any fault, we think he has truſted too little to the efforts of nature, and limited her powers by ſtating, that the greateſt compreſſion which the head can with ſafety bear, will not reduce its tranſverſe diameter to leſs than about two inches and three quarters. But this is a trifling blemiſh, and we rather point it out as a ſubject of his future conſideration, than reprehend it as a real error.

Letters and Papers on Agriculture, Planting, &c. ſelected from the Correſpondence-Book of the Society inſtituted at Bath for the Encouragement of Agriculture, &c. Vol. II. 8vo. 5s. in Boards. Dilly.

A Society, inſtituted on liberal principles, for the encouragement of one of the moſt uſeful ſciences, deſerves both ſupport and commendation ; but while we contribute our praiſes, we ought not to conceal its defects. A laudable ambition to ſerve his country, and contribute to the aſſiſtance of its inhabitants, will frequently incite either the philoſopher or agriculturiſt to communicate the reſult of his experiments ; an eagerneſs for diſtinction will often induce thoſe who are leſs qualified for the taſk, to attempt it ; and the only compenſation, for the crudeneſs of their remarks, will be an affected importance, frequent exaggeration, and we fear ſometimes fiction. As theſe papers are *ſelected*, we do not frequently meet with exceptionable ones ; but no ſociety can be always aware of the arts of ingenuity, or diſtinguiſh between the probable and the true ; between the ornaments of fancy and the dictates of experience.

This collection, like every other, will conſequently be found to be of various merit ; if it is not diſtinguiſhed by any very ſplendid diſcovery, we find few obſervations that we can, with propriety, reprehend. There are many proofs of the attention of the various correſpondents ; and, where we

have

have room for doubt, the determination muft neceffarily be left to future experience.

There are fome obfervations on the culture of carrots, by Mr. Young, which deferve attention ; others on manure, which will probably be advantageoufly followed. As the article on planting feems correct and ufeful, we fhall infert it. The appearance of the country, in many fituations, is much injured by the devaftation which, from various caufes, have been made among the trees.

'*On Planting barren Lands with Wood.*—Among all the improvements which a lover of his country would naturally wifh to fee take place, there are none which feems to want, or to merit encouragement, more than that of planting barren foils and wafte lands with wood. One principal caufe of this improvement having made a flower progrefs than many others is, that the firft expence is confiderable, and the profits, although certain in the end, are remote ; and therefore I have for feveral years wifhed to fee your premiums increafed on this article.

' As I have made confiderable plantations in my time, and always found the future profits, as well as the prefent pleafure attending it, to exceed my expectations, I do not offer my advice on an uncertain theory, but *know* what I take the liberty of recommending to you.

' There are three kinds of land ufually termed barren ; and with refpect to almoft every purpofe but that of planting, they are, and muft remain fo, unlefs an expence, greater than moft people chufe to be at, be fubmitted to, in improving them.

' The firft kind is mere fand. This foil, unlefs there is clay or marle at a few feet depth under it, (as is the cafe in the Weft part of Norfolk, about Thetford and Brandon) will pay better by being planted with Scotch firs and larches than any thing elfe ; efpecially, if in making the plantations, a little clay or marle be mixed with the fand in the holes where each tree is planted ; and this may be done at a fmall expence.

' Thefe trees will grow here very well. I know feveral large plantations, where the foil has been fo perfectly fandy, that there was not grafs enough to keep one fheep on an acre, and yet after being planted twenty years, there have been two thoufand trees on an acre, worth at the loweft eftimate one fhilling each as they ftood. A few acres of fuch land thus planted would be a pretty fortune for the younger branches of a family.

' The fecond kind is boggy or wet moors, which are fometimes fo fituated as not to be drained without too great an expence. Wherever this is the cafe, fuch foils may be planted to greater advantage, as Mr. Fletcher, in his letter on this fubject, printed in your firft volume, has juftly remarked. Afh for poles or copfing, will thrive here beyond expectation ; and alders, with feveral fpecies of the fallow tribe, will grow rapidly, and in twenty years after planting pay a profit of three

pounds

pounds per acre per annum, for the whole time. The expence attending it is confined almoſt wholly to the firſt five or ſix years; for after that time little more is required than to keep up the fences, and the profit is certain.

'The third ſoil on which planting anſwers better than any thing elſe, is barren rocky hills, which cannot be ploughed on account of the ſtones lying level with the ſurface, or growing above it. In ſuch places there are numerous little clefts or fiſſures in the rocks, filled with veins of earth to a conſiderable depth, which the roots of trees will follow and find ſufficient nouriſhment in. Many inſtances of this may be found in the counties of Somerſet, Glouceſter, and Dorſet, where the wiſdom of our forefathers induced them to try the experiment. On the north ſlope of Mendip hills in particular, (a ſituation as unfavourable as moſt, on account of its being a bed of rocks expoſed to the bleak north and eaſt winds) we ſee beautiful woods of large extent hanging over the pariſhes of Compton-Martin, Ubley, Blagdon, Hutton, and Churchill. In theſe woods, although the timber is not large, the growth of the pollard trees and copſe wood muſt every twelve years bring in conſiderable ſums to the owners, although the land for any other purpoſe would not be worth one ſhilling an acre.

'In planting barren mountainous ſituations, full of ſtone, no particular directions can be given as to the number of trees per acre, for you muſt follow the veins of earth where they are deepeſt; but in general plant as thick as you can, for this will beſt prevent the bad effects of tempeſtuous winds, by the interior parts being ſheltered from them.

'In theſe ſituations intermix Scotch firs, which will ſecure leſs hardy trees from the fury of the winds, eſpecially if a double row of them form the boundary. As the ſurfaces of ſuch places are moſtly craggy and uneven, be careful to plant your trees in the little hollows, for two reaſons; firſt, becauſe there is moſt earth and moiſture; and ſecondly, becauſe in theſe cavities the plants will, while young, be moſt ſheltered from the winds. Fear not to plant too thick, for as the plants increaſe in ſize and hardineſs, you may thin them at pleaſure, and the wood will pay for the labour.

'Your young plants ſhould be raiſed in a ſituation as ſimilar as poſſible to that where you intend they ſhould continue; for if they are tranſplanted out of a rich warm nurſery, it would prove their deſtruction. As there is ſeldom ſufficient depth of ſoil among the rocks to receive long tap-roots, the plants which naturally have them ſhould be cut off when they are firſt taken from the ſeed beds and planted in the nurſery. By treating them in this manner, although their vigour will be checked for the firſt year or two, until they have ſent forth a number of lateral roots, they will recover their ſtrength, and prove equally thrifty with others.

'Theſe

' These plantations may be made with beach, birch, oak, afh, fycamore, and black poplar ; always obferving to place the tendereft trees in the leaft expofed fituations, where they are fheltered from north and eaft winds. In places where the foil is very thin, raife little hillocks about the young plants, which will greatly encourage their growth.

' In fuch bleak fituations, plant as late in the fpring as you can with fafety. April is a month in which it may be expected the moft ftormy weather is over, and all the kinds of trees I have mentioned may fafely be replanted at that time. But your nurfery fhould always be near the fpot you intend to plant, or elfe the roots of your young trees will get dry, and their buds be rubbed off in carriage.

' During the firft three months after planting, they fhould frequently be examined, and the earth made faft about their roots, otherwife they will be loofened by the winds ; but after that time they will have put forth new roots fufficient to hold them fecurely.

' The upright Englifh elm, and the wich elm, may alfo be properly introduced in thefe fituations, for they are hardy trees, and, when once rooted, grow well on rocky foils. The timber of the latter is very valuable for naves of carriage wheels, boring for water-pipes.

' If oaks, chefnuts, or beech, or indeed any other tree that fheds its leaves in winter, grow crooked, make incifions with the point of a knife from top to bottom in the hollow part. This will occafion the tree to increafe in bulk more in thofe parts than in any other, and by this fimple eafy method, I have known many a crooked tree grow ftrait and handfome. R. E.'

There is a paper from the late Dr. Fothergill, refpecting the rhubarb, in which he feems to object to the cultivation of this drug in England. The Englifh root *may*, he thinks, be as good, but it may alfo differ, and fubject practitioners ' to the rifque of difappointment, or the folicitude of attending numerous experiments.' What can be raifed cheaper and better, by other nations, who will exchange their products for thofe articles in which we can excel, fhould, he thinks, ' from motives of juft policy and humanity,' be imported.

Another paper, from Dr. Pultney, on the different fpecies of rhubarb, attracted our attention. The rheum rhaponticum, though the rhubarb of Diofcorides, and probably of the ancients, is certainly, as Dr. Pultney fuppofes, at prefent known *not* to be the true fpecies. The rheum palmatum was at laft believed, by Linnæus himfelf, to be that from which the officinal medicine is commonly procured, though he formerly gave the preference to the undulatum. Monf. Pallas, the lateft obferver, appears to confider it as indifferent, whether it be the root of the rheum palmatum or undulatum.

latum. Dr. Pultney fays, that he feems to have determined, that the Ruffian rhubarb is of the former kind, and the Chinefe of the latter. From the accounts of Monf. Pallas, which we have infpected, he feems to give the preference to the latter. They are probably fo nearly fimilar, that the difference is trifling : thefe two fpecies, we find, have produced a mongrel plant, which our author feems to expect will excel either. We have feen a hybrid, from the rheum palmatum & compactum, which had very active purgative virtues. Bergius, he obferves, recommends taking them up in autumn ; Dr. Pultney rather gives the preference to the fpring, from the general analogy of the virtues of roots. Bergius thinks that they require to be eleven or twelve years old ; Dr. Hope, that they are fufficiently good at the end of four or five years. The young roots, it is faid, are more purgative, the older ones more aftringent ; and it is probably owing to this circumftance, that our rhubarb yields to the foreign in aftringency, while it excels it in the other quality.

The fifty-fixth article, by Mr. Rack, on the origin and progrefs of agriculture in different ages and nations, deferves attention. We fhall felect that part which relates to the early ftate of hufbandry in this country. It is curious, and not unentertaining.

' We are very much in the dark with refpect to the ftate and progrefs of agriculture in Great Britain previous to the fourteenth century. That it was pretty generally practifed, efpecially in the eaftern, fouth, and midland parts of England, is certain : but of the mode, and the fuccefs, we are left almoft totally ignorant. In the latter end of the fifteenth century, however, it feems to have been cultivated as a fcience, and received very great improvement.

' At this time our countryman, Fitzherbert, Judge of the Common Pleas, fhone forth with diftinguifhed eminence in the practical parts of hufbandry. He appears to have been the firft Englifhman who ftudied the nature of foils, and the laws of vegetation, with philofophical attention. On thefe he formed a theory confirmed by experiments, and rendered the ftudy pleafing as well as profitable, by realizing the principles of the ancients, to the honour and advantage of his country. Accordingly, he publifhed two treatifes on this fubject ; the firft, intitled "The Book of Hufbandry," appeared 1534 ; and the fecond, called "The Book of Surveying and Improvements," in 1539.

' Thefe books, being written at a time when philofophy and fcience were but juft emerging from that gloom in which they had long been buried, were doubtlefs replete with many errors ; but they contained the rudiments of true knowledge, and
revived

revived the ſtudy and love of an art, the advantages of which were obvious to men of the leaſt reflection. We therefore find that Fitzherbert's books on agriculture ſoon raiſed a ſpirit of emulation in his countrymen, and many treatiſes of the ſame kind ſucceſſively appeared, which time has however deprived us of, or at leaſt they are become ſo very ſcarce as only to be found in the libraries of the curious.'—

' During the reign of Charles the firſt, our fatal domeſtic diſſentions and wars reverſed the true order of things, changing our ploughs and pruning hooks into martial weapons. But in the general revolution of affairs, which took place on the death of that unfortunate monarch, artful and avaritious men crept into the confiſcated eſtates of ſuch of the nobility and gentry as had ſteadily adhered to the royal cauſe ; and as many of theſe new incroachers had riſen from the plough, they returned with pleaſure to their old occupations, being chiefly animated with the love of gain. About this time, Tuſſer, Platt, Plattes, Hartlib, Blythe, and ſome others, ſeized this favourable opportunity of encouraging the diſpoſition of the common people, by writings, which have been equalled by few in later times.

' This revival of the art of huſbandry received conſiderable encouragement from Cromwell himſelf.

' Sir Hugh Platt was one of the moſt ingenious huſbandmen of the age in which he lived ; yet ſo great was his modeſty, that all his works, except his Paradiſe of Flora, ſeem to be poſthumous. He held a correſpondence with moſt of the lovers and patrons of agriculture and gardening in England ; and ſuch was the juſtice and modeſty of his temper, that he always named the author of every diſcovery communicated to him. Perhaps no man in any age diſcovered, or at leaſt brought into uſe, ſo many new kinds of manure. This will be evident to thoſe who read his account of the compoſt and covered dung-hills, and his judicious obſervations on the fertilizing qualities lodged in ſalt, ſtreet-dirt, and the ſullage of ſtreets in great cities, clay, fuller's earth, mooriſh earths, dung-hills made in layers, fern, hair, calcination of all vegetables, malt-duſt, willow-tree earth, ſoaper's aſhes, urine, marle, and broken pilchards.

' Gabriel Plattes may be ſaid to have been an original genius in huſbandry. He began his obſervations at an earlier period, in the reign of queen Elizabeth, and continued them down to the commonwealth. But notwithſtanding the great merit of this writer, and the eſſential ſervice he had rendered his country by his writings, the public ungratefully ſuffered him to ſtarve and periſh in the ſtreets of London ; nor had he a ſhirt on his back when he died.

' Samuel Hartlib, a celebrated writer on agriculture in the laſt century, was highly eſteemed and beloved by Milton, and other great men of his time. In the preface to the work entitled

titled his Legacy *, he laments that no public director of huſbandry was eſtabliſhed in England by authority ; and that we
had not adopted the Flemiſh method of letting farms upon improvement.

' This remark of Hartlib's procured him a penſion of 100l.
a-year from Cromwell ; and the writer afterwards, the better
to fulfil the intention of his benefactor, procured Dr. Beatti's
excellent annotation on the Legacy, with other valuable papers
from his numerous correſpondents.'

---

*Archæologia : or Miſcellaneous Tracts relating to Antiquity. Vol.
IV. Publiſhed by the Society of Antiquaries of London.* 4to.
1l. 2s. *in Boards.* Brown.

THIS volume commences with a farther account of ſome
remains of Roman and other antiquities, in or near the
county of Brecknock, in South Wales. By John Strange, eſqr.

In Mr. Strange's former paper on this ſubject †, he mentioned the diſcovery of a Roman ſtation at Cwm, in the pariſh of Llanier, on the borders of Brecknockſhire. This ſtation he then thought much more likely to be the Bullæum of
Ptolemy, than either Buahlt or Kaereu, where he found no
ſigns of the Romans ; but he is ſtill more inclined to fix Mag-
nis of Antoninus at Cwm ; and in this opinion he is confirmed, by the circumſtances reſpecting its ſituation and di-
ſtance from other places. Among the conjectures formerly
ſuggeſted by Mr. Strange, one was, that a Roman road had
led from Gaer, near Brecknock, along the valley weſtward,
and ſo over Trecaſtle-hill into the vale of Llanimdovery, in
Carmarthenſhire. In ſupport of this conjecture, he informs
the Antiquarian Society, that ſince the communication of his
former account, a ſtone with a Roman inſcription engraved
upon it has been dug up on the top of Trecaſtle-hill. This
ſtone was found about two feet under ground. It is a coarſe
ſort of lime-ſtone, flat on the ſide where the moſt imperfect
part of the inſcription is engraved, and round on the other,
tapering towards the edges, and the thickeſt part of it hardly
meaſuring three inches. In reſpect of the inſcription, as the
characters are not very good, and only a part of them intelli-

---

* ' It muſt here be obſerved, that the famous work attributed to Hartlib,
and called his Legacy, was not written by him. It was only drawn up at
his requeſt by one R. Childs, and after undergoing Hartlib's correction and
reviſal, was publiſhed by him. It conſiſts of a general anſwer to this queſtion : " What are the actual defects and omiſſions, and what the poſſible
improvements, in Engliſh huſbandry ?"

† See vol. xliv. p. 88.

gible,

gible, we must of neceffity refer our readers to the engraving. Mr. Strange alfo gives an account of fome other remains of antiquities, lefs remote, which occurred to him on his journey in thofe parts.

Art. II. On the term Lavant. By the Hon. Daines Barrington.——Camden, in treating of the city of Chichefter, obferves, that ' it is wafhed on every fide but the north by the little river Lavant;' and of the fame fubject Philemon Holland adds, ' the courfe of which ftream is very unaccountable, being fometimes quite dry, but at other times (and that often in the midft of fummer) fo full as to run with fome violence.' Mr. Barrington obferves, in explanation of the term Lavant, that, in various parts of England, it is applied to all brooks, or fea-fands, which are dry at fome feafons.

Art. III. An Enquiry into the Nature and Caufe of King John's Death. By the Rev. Mr. Pegge.——Mr. Pegge endeavours to prove, by hiftorical teftimony, and a variety of arguments, that the death of king John was not effected by poifon, as fome writers have reprefented; and we think, that, as far as a negative queftion can be determined, he has fucceeded in his attempt.

Art. IV. Illuftration of a gold enamelled Ring, fuppofed to have been the property of Alhftan, bifhop of Sherburne; with fome account of the ftate and condition of the Saxon Jewelry in the more early ages. By the Rev. Mr. Pegge.—— This ring was found by a labourer on the furface of the ground, on a common, at a place called Llys Faen, in the north-eaft corner of Catnarvonfhire. It is gold, enamelled, of good workmanfhip, and in fine prefervation. It weighs about an ounce, and has upon it a Saxon infcription.

Art. V. An Account of Human Bones filled with Lead. By Mr. Worth, late of Difs.——Thefe bones were found in making a grave in the chancel of Badwell Afh, near Waltham le Willows, in Suffolk, in the year 1774. On one of them, which is the lower half of an adult thigh-bone, the following obfervations have been made by the late Dr. Hunter.

' The metal contained appears to be genuine unmixed lead; that is, not reduced to an amalgam, or mixed with any thing that would make it melt with a fmall degree of heat: and it appears to be but little corroded on its furface.

' Little more of the bone itfelf remains than the fpungy internal part which had contained the marrow; the folid, cortical or external part of the bone being every where removed, except at the lower part forwards, and a little of the furface which had made the joint, and efpecially at the cavity between the two condyles.

'The lead is all granulated, corresponding to the medullary cavities and pores; and the interstices contain the bony remains, which are of the common brown colour of church-yard bones, and do not appear burnt.

'At the enlarged extremity of the bone the cells are more partially filled; some containing lead, some being quite empty, and many of them containing a hard, brittle, whitish stony substance, which effervesces with a spirit of sea salt.

'At the lower extremity, the lead had run upon the surface of the bone, in some parts forming thin plates, and in one place making an irregular mass, closely covered with earth and gravel.

'From the appearance, the natural supposition would be that the lead had been poured into the medullary canal after the marrow had been consumed by time.'

Mr. Worth supposes the bones to have been thus impregnated with lead, either from lightning, or some subterraneous vapour taking fire in the vault. But the most probable opinion is that suggested by Dr. Hunter. Perhaps the filling of bones with lead was a method sometimes used to preserve relics. Bones so filled, however, have been met with in other places; and there are some, in the same state, in the library of St. John's college, in Cambridge.

'Art. VI. erroneously marked VII. Remarks on the Antiquity of the different Modes of Brick and Stone Buildings in England. By Mr. James Essex, of Cambridge.——From the accurate view exhibited by Mr. Essex, of the various kinds of masonry used in England in different periods, it appears very difficult to determine the age of a building by the materials or the methods of using them, when no other circumstance concurs to assist in the determination; and this is observed to be particularly the case in respect of those buildings which were erected with new materials, either before or soon after the Conquest. The age of ancient buildings, however, Mr. Essex observes, may sometimes be nearly ascertained by the fragments of pillars, voussoirs of arches, and other members of Gothic architecture, worked into the walls of ancient edifices. But to judge by this circumstance, a person must be well acquainted with the various modes of Gothic architecture which prevailed in different ages.

Art. VIII. Observations on Kit's Cotty House, in Kent. By the Rev. Mr. Pegge.——With regard to the occasion on which this monument was erected, antiquaries have formed different conjectures; but they are agreed in opinion that it has been intended as sepulchral.

Art. IX. Account of a singular Discovery of a Quantity of Birds Bones, buried in Christ Church Priory, Hampshire. By

By Guftavus Brander, Efq.—The cavity in which thefe bones were depofited was under the pavement of what is fuppofed to have been the prior's private oratory. They amounted to the quantity of at leaft half a bufhel, confifting of the bones of herons, bitterns, cocks and hens, many of which have long fpurs, and moftly well preferved. Mr. Brander obferves, that the foundation of the ancient priory in which thofe bones were difcovered, feems to be of a very early date. According to Tanner, this place, in the time of Edward the Confeffor, was the refidence of a dean and twenty-four fecular canons, afterwards changed into regulars, of the order of St. Auguftine. But Mr. Brander, from the circumftance of the above mentioned bones, thinks it not improbable that the building was of a more remote origin, and had once been a Pagan temple.

Art. X. An Account of the Great Seal of Ranulph Earl of Chefter, and of two Infcriptions found in the Ruins of St. Edmund Bury Abbey. By Edward King, Efq.—Ranulph earl of Chefter was one of the moft powerful barons in the time of king Stephen. This, which there is ftrong prefumption to think was his great feal, is made of lead, and has a fort of handle, with a hole, by which it might be faftened to a ftring, or ribband. It is ill defigned, but tolerably well cut, according to the unimproved ftate of the arts at that time.

Of the two infcriptions mentioned in the title of this article, the former is remarkable on account of the fhape of the letters, and the fubftance on which they are executed. They are raifed in a very bold relief, and inftead of being cut, or carved, have been evidently caft, with the whole mafs, in a kind of clay, which had afterwards been burnt in the manner of tiles. The other fragment, which is larger, is of a coarfe, foft ftone, and fuppofed to be a part of the tomb of the poet Lydgate, whofe name is legible upon it.

Art. XI. Obfervations on a Coin of Robert Earl of Gloucefter. By Mr. Colebrook.

Art. XII. On the Origin of the Word Romance. By the Rev. Mr. Drake.—The ingenious Mr. Warton, in his Hiftory of Englifh Poetry, has confidered the word Romance as of French extraction; but Mr. Drake endeavours to prove that it is of Spanifh original.

Art. XIII. Some Obfervations on Lincoln Cathedral. By Mr. James Effex.

Art. XIV. Account of the Difcoveries at Pompeii, communicated by Sir William Hamilton.—One of the parts difcovered is a colonade, encompaffing a fquare court, not yet

cleared

cleared from the rubbish of pumice stones and ashes, by which the city was overwhelmed. The columns are of coarse stone, coated with plaster or stucco, and coloured. On many of the columns the soldiers have idly scratched their names, some in Greek, and some in Latin. In the rooms in which the soldiers had been quartered, were found the skeletons of some of them, besides several helmets, and pieces of armour for the arms, thighs, and legs, but none for the breast. These pieces of armour are mostly ornamented with dolphins and tridents, in relievo, and some are encrusted with such ornaments in silver; whence it is conjectured that they had been destined for sea service.

'The helmets, says sir William Hamilton, are singularly formed, not unlike the hats used by the firemen in London. Some are very richly ornamented, and one particularly beautiful and interesting, with the principal events of the taking of Troy admirably executed in relievo. Some have vizors, like the helmets of the lower ages, with gratings or round holes to see through. From their size and weight, it has been disputed, whether they had been really worn, or were only intended as ornaments for trophies; but, as I was present at the discovery of some of them, and saw distinctly part of the linings which were then adhering to them, and are now fallen out, I have no doubt as to their having been worn. A curious trumpet of brass, with six ivory flutes attached to the outside of it, and all communicating to one mouth-piece, was found in one of these rooms. The flutes are without holes for the fingers. A chain of bronze hung to it, probably that the trumpeter might sling it over his shoulder. It might be a very proper military instrument, and produce a spirited *clangor tubarum,* but not much variety or harmony.'

The plan of most of the houses at Pompeii is a square court, with a fountain in the middle, and small rooms round, communicating with the court. Sir William Hamilton observes, that, by the construction and distribution of the houses, it seems the inhabitants of Pompeii were fond of privacy. They had few windows towards the street, except when, from the nature of the plan, they could not avoid it; but, even in that case, the windows were placed too high for any person in the streets to overlook them. The rooms are in general small, from ten to twelve feet, and from fourteen to eighteen feet; few communications between room and room; almost all without windows, except the apartments situated to the garden, which are thought to have been allotted to the women. No timber was used in finishing their apartments, except in doors and windows. The floors were generally laid in Mosaic work. One general taste prevailed of painting the sides

7   and

and cielings of the rooms. Small figures, and medallions of low relief, were sometimes introduced. Their great variety consisted in the colours, and in the choice and delicacy of the ornaments, in which they displayed great taste. Their houses were some two, others three stories high. Among the discoveries made at Pompeii, is a temple dedicated to Isis. These curious remains of antiquity are illustrated by a number of engravings.

Art. XV. Some Account of a curious Seal Ring, belonging to Sir Richard Worsley, of Appledore-combe, in the Isle of Wight, Bart. By the Rev. Dr. Milles, Dean of Exeter.—This curious ring, set in gold, and of exquisite workmanship, is said to have been in the family of Worsley ever since the time of Henry VIII. whose property it is supposed to have originally been.

Art. XVI. Conjectures on Sir Richard Worsley's Seal. By John Charles Brooke, Esq. of the Herald's College.

Art. XVII. A Dissertation on a most valuable Gold Coin of Edmund Crouchback, Son of Henry III. By the Rev. Mr. Pegge.

Art. XVIII. An Account of the Events produced in England by the Grant of the Kingdom of Sicily to Prince Edmund, second Son of King Henry III. With some Remarks upon the Seal of that Prince.

Art. XIX. Of the Wisdom of the Ancient Egyptians; a Discourse concerning their Arts, their Sciences, and their Learning; their Laws, their Government, and their Religion. With occasional Reflections upon the State of Learning among the Jews, and some other Nations.—This treatise, which occupies almost a hundred pages, was written by the late Dr. John Woodward, and having come into the possession of Mr. Lort, the latter presented it to the Society of Antiquaries.

In this treatise, which discovers a great extent of knowlege, Dr. Woodward produces many strong arguments, calculated to refute the general opinion that the ancient Egyptians were remarkable for the cultivation of the arts and sciences. The author likewise opposes, by many just and forcible observations, the idea which a few writers have maintained, that some parts of the Mosaic institution were taken from the polity of the Egyptians.

Art. XX. The Ceremonial of making the King's Bed. Communicated by Mr. Brooke, of the Herald's Office.—Among the injunctions relative to this important operation, it is ordered, that a yeoman with a dagger shall search the straw of the king's bed, 'that there be none untreuth therin.' It is further enjoined, that no person shall set any dish upon the bed, ' for fere of hurtyng of the kynge's ryche counter-poynt that lyeth therupon.'

Art. XXI. Obfervations on the Apamean Medal. By the Hon. Daines Barrington.——This celebrated medal has already been the fubject of much difpute among antiquaries. Mr. Barrington partly admits the obfervations made by Mr. Bryant refpecting this medal, but cannot agree with him in opinion that it alludes to the Mofaical account of the deluge. The latter of thefe gentlemen has thus defcribed the emblem of the medal,

" Upon the reverfe is delineated a kind of fquare machine floating upon the water. Through an opening in it are feen two perfons, a man and a woman, as low as the breaft, and upon the head of the woman is a vail. Over this ark is a kind of triangular pediment, on which there fits a dove, and below it another, which feems to flutter its wings, and holds in its mouth a fmall branch of a tree. Before the machine is a man following a woman, who, by their attitudes, feem to have juft quitted it, and to have gotten upon dry land. Upon the ark itfelf, underneath the perfons there inclofed, is to be read, in diftinct characters, ΝΩΕ."

On this defcription Mr. Barrington makes the following re-marks.

' The fquare machine is reprefented as fo fmall, that the man and woman have but juft room to ftand in it; and how can this be applicable to Noah's ark, confifting of three ftories, and which was to contain fo many animals with the provifion ne-ceffary to fubfift them for more than twelve months? I allow indeed that mint-mafters do not pique themfelves upon accuracy in fuch particulars; but that there would not have been fuch a grofs mifreprefentation in the apparent fize of the ark, I can appeal to the engraving of the Argo, prefixed to Mr. Bryant's Differtation, which is confiderably larger than the fuppofed ark of Noah.

' The roof of this ark is open, and the very top cannot much exceed fix feet, by comparing it with the height of the two per-fons inclofed. How likewife does the removal of the roof agree with the Mofaical account of the ark's having but one window? and Mr. Bryant himfelf fuppofes the patriarchal family to have ufed torch-light whilft the ark floated.

' With regard to the two figures alfo conceived to be Noah and his wife, it muft be recollected that not only the patriarch and his wife, but his three fons, with their wives, are exprefsly ordered both to go into, and remove from the ark; nor is there any one animal following them.

' As for Noah's wife, fhe bears fo inconfiderable a part in the Mofaical hiftory, that we do not know even what was her name; but if fhe was really of importance, there is a pannel

left

left for γομ, or και γυμ, which it was equally proper to inscribe, as ΝΩΕ under the patriarch.

' This man and woman when they have left the ark are raising up their right hands; but to what part of the Mosaical history does this relate? In Mr. Crofts', Dr. Hunter's, and the Pembrokian medal, the man is represented as rather young, and with a fort of Phrygian cap; whereas in Mr. Bryant's engraving he hath a venerable beard, and no covering on his head. The Philip likewise on the other side of the medaglion is very different from Mr. Bryant's.

' The next circumstance is a bird perched upon the top of the ark, which cannot be either Noah's dove or raven; for the latter does not return at all; and the former, when it comes back, is taken immediately into the ark by the patriarch.

' As for the bird on the wing with a branch of a tree in its claws, this also is not agreeable to the book of Genesis, which expressly states that it was a *leaf*, and not a *branch* of an olive-tree, which is much more probable, as it is more easily carried by a bird of so small a size as a pigeon. This leaf is also said to be placed in the pigeon's mouth, and not in its claws.'

Mr. Barrington, having endeavoured to show that the Apamean medal is not properly applicable to the Mosaical account of the deluge, proceeds to support the opinion suggested by Vaillant, that it relates to Deucalion's flood, as described by Ovid and Plutarch. The doctrine he maintains is, in substance, that the deluge was not general; but that there had been a great flood at Apamea, whilst Alexander was high-priest; and that the event was commemorated by a medallion.

Art. XXII. Observations on the Apamean Medal. By the Rev. Dr. Milles, Dean of Exeter.—In these observations, Dr. Milles takes no part in the controversy; though he seems not to be so much satisfied with Bryant's remarks on this, as on other subjects. The principal object of his attention is to describe the different state of the medals under consideration, to distinguish the spurious from the genuine coins, and rather to show what consequences cannot be drawn, than to establish any positive determination on so conjectural a subject.

Art. XXIII. Remarks upon Mr. Bryant's Vindication of the Apamean Medal. By the Abbé Barthélemy and Mr. Charles Combe.—These remarks tend to corroborate the opinion, that the letters ΝΩΕ, which have been deemed so essential in the explanation of this medal, are not genuine, but have been fabricated for the purpose of imposition.

Art. XXIV. Account of Coins, &c. found in digging up the Foundations of some old Houses near the Church of St. Mary Hill, London, 1774. By the Rev. Dr. Griffith.—Between three and four hundred of these coins being carefully

examined, they were found to confiſt entirely of the printies
of Edward the Confeſſor, Harold II. and William the Conqueror.

Art. XXV. Obſervations on Ancient Caſtles. By Edward
King, Eſq.

Art. XXVI. Mr. Pegge's Remarks on the Bones of Fowls
found in Chriſtchurch-Twynham, Hampſhire.

These are the ſeveral articles contained in the preſent volume of the Archæologia, which is, as uſual, illuſtrated with
a great number of engravings relative to the various ſubjects.

---

*Ruſſia: or, a Compleat Hiſtorical Account of all the Nations
which compoſe that Empire. Vol. IV. 8vo. 5s. in Boards.*
Nichols.

THIS volume begins with the Mongol nations, which are
ſuppoſed to be of very ancient origin. It is thought
that they formerly perambulated the deſerts on both ſides of
the mountains that ſeparate Dauria from the preſent Chineſe
Mongelia, and the ſouthern parts of the Sayane hills. At
leaſt the names of the mountains and rivers of theſe parts, as
well as of thoſe about Tibet, are of Mongol derivation. The
Mongols being driven out of China in the year of our Lord
1368, they, in conjunction with the Tartar hords, after ſub-
duing their weſtern neighbours, ſpread into Ruſſia, and other
European countries, and formed in them new colonies. In
proceſs of time, the princes of the two nations ſeparating,
their empire was disjoined in the ſixteenth century, ſince
which the Mongols and Tartars have continued diſtinct tribes.
Though the cloſe confederacy which had long ſubſiſted between the two nations produced a ſimilarity in their manners
and ſpeech, their governments are conſiderably different from
each other; the Tartarian being democratical, while that of
the Mongols inclines to the monarchical form.

The Mongols at preſent divide themſelves into three collateral branches, dependent on each other; the Mongols properly ſo called, the Olrats, and the Buráts. The Oirats are
commonly called Kalmucs. According to their own hiſtory,
their firſt reſidence was in the Mongol empire, between the
Kokonoor or Blue Sea, and Tibet. In after-times ſome
branches of them came weſtward to the banks of the Irtiſch,
the Urol, and at length even upon the Volga. On the diſ-
memberment of the Mongol-Tartarian monarchy, they divided
themſelves into the following hords and headſhips, viz. the
Khofchoots, the Soongarians, the Derbets, and the Torgots.
The

The firft of thefe, called alfo the Warriors, on account of their bravery, comprehends fifty thoufand bows, or fighting men. This nation dwells near Tibet, and acknowleges the fovereignty of China.

The Soongarians, in very remote times, made one hord with the Durbets ; but the difputes of two brothers occafioned their feparation. Their firft known refidence was about the Balkafchmoor, and the upper part of the Irtifch. They can raife fifty thoufand men. From a few years before the clofe of the laft century, to near the middle of the prefent, the Soongarians were the terror of all the Mongol hords, and were formidable even to China. The eaftern towns of Bucharia, and the Burats, or great Kirguinan hord, were tributary to them. They took Budala, the capital city of the Dalai Lama, and ravaged Siberia ; where they obliged feveral nations, in fubjection to Ruffia, to pay them tribute. The Soongarians, however, are now fo far declined, that they have been obliged to feek protection from other hords.

The refidence of the Derbets has generally been about the fource of the rivers Ifchim and Tobol. In 1673, they furrendered themfelves, to the amount of five thoufand tents or families, to the khan of the Torgots, on the river Urol, a people who pay homage to Ruffia. In 1723, the Derbetan princes forfook the territory of the Torgots, and migrated to the parts about the Don ; at which time they were computed to amount to fourteen thoufand families. But when it appeared to the Ruffian government that the Derbetan prince, Lava Dondue, was putting himfelf under the protection of the Krim, the Derbets were obliged to repafs the Volga to the Torgots again.

The Turgots appear not to have formed themfelves into a hord fo early as the nations above mentioned, and take their rife from a fmall beginning. At prefent they inhabit about the Yemba, and perambulate as far as the Urol. So long ago as 1662 they were fifty thoufand ftrong. They are called the Volgiac as commonly as the Torgotan hord.

The deferts which the Kalmucs inhabit, with their hords, lie between the Don and the Volga, and on the river Urol, from Irgis to the Cafpian fea. They confift of a ftrong loam, are quite arid, deftitute of wood, abound in falt, contain many frefh-water lakes and brooks, and numbers of lakes that are perfectly falt. They produce wholefome plants and good herbage ; fo that the cattle are in general vigorous, and fpeedily become fat. The remaining Kalmucs confift of upwards of twenty thoufand tents, or families. The eftablifhment of the hord is entirely military. Their weapons are the bow, in the

Tungurian

Tungurian form. The quiver is a neat flat earthen bag. They carry alſo lances and ſabres, and for ſome time paſt fire-arms, which they procure from Bucharia; but being ſeldom furniſhed with locks, they are obliged to diſcharge them with a match. Thoſe who are rich among them have coats of mail of wire rings. A complete equipage coſts from forty to fifty horſes.

The army is compoſed of regiments of unequal numbers, and every regiment is divided into hundreds. Each regiment has its colours, painted with the idol-gods of war, dragons, ſerpents, tygers, lions, &c.

The perſons of the Kalmucks are thus deſcribed by the author of the preſent hiſtory.

' The Kalmucs are of a middling ſtature, ſeldom large; for the moſt part, raw-boned and ſtout. Their viſage is ſo flat, that the ſkull of a Kalmuc may eaſily be known from that of any other man. The eyes too are ſmaller, and the corners of them flatter, than among the Europeans. They have thick lips, a ſmall noſe, a ſhort chin; and their beard is ſcanty, and appears late. Their teeth are even and white. Their complexion is a reddiſh brown; generally indeed from the wind and ſun, and their neglect of cleanlineſs, it is of a yellowiſh brown. Their ears are very large and prominent; their hair is black. Their knees always ſtand outwards, like a bow: this proceeds from their cuſtomary manner of ſitting on their ancles, and their being almoſt conſtantly on horſeback. Their ſenſes of feeling and taſte are dull; but thoſe of ſmell, ſight, and hearing, are wonderfully quick. The women are of the ſame ſhape and make with the men, only the ſkin of their face is very clear, and of a wholeſome white and red.'

The cloathing of the men is entirely oriental, and their heads dreſſed exactly in the Chineſe faſhion. They wind li-nen about their feet, and draw over it their buſkins, which are of black, or yellow, or ſome other coloured leather. Their breeches are large; their under-garment is of light ſtuff, with narrow ſleeves, and a girdle, to which is ſuſpended the ſabre, a knife, and the implements for making tobacco. Their up-per garment is of cloth, with wide ſleeves. They let the beard grow, but ſhave the head all to one lock, which they plait into three ſtrings. The covering for the head is a flat yellow bonnet, with a ſmall round brim, ſet off with a taſſel. The dreſs of the women is preciſely the ſame with that of the men; only, inſtead of the upper garment, they wear a veſt without ſleeves. They let their hair grow, and plait it like the Tartar girls in ſeveral treſſes, which hang about their necks; but when married, they divide it into only two. Their ears, which are ſmaller than thoſe of the men, are

adorned

adorned with pendants, and their fingers with rings. Great finery is beſtowed on their upper veſt.

The principal food of the Kalmucs is animals, both tame and wild, except dogs, and beaſts and birds of prey; and next to animal food, they prefer cheeſe, butter, greaſe, and blood. According to the doctrine of the metempſychoſis, they ought not to ſlay any healthy beaſt; but they do not obſerve this very ſtrictly, eſpecially with regard to ſheep. Even the firſt people among them feed upon cattle that have died of diſtemper or age; and though the fleſh ſtinks ever ſo much, they eat it without any diſguſt.

Their ordinary drinks are ſour milk prepared after the Tartarian manner, butter-milk, milk ſpirits or koumiſs, and broths; but for the moſt part only water. They are alſo much addicted to tea, which they make either of the Chineſe teas, or by an infuſion of their own plants, with ſalt and milk. Of late they are become immoderate lovers of mead and brandy. Both ſexes ſmoke tobacco at an enormous rate.

The editor of the work, beſides giving a particular account of the manners and cuſtoms of the Kalmucs, has preſented us with ſeveral ſpecimens of their poetry, of part of which the following is a traſlation.

'Ah thou, mine unparalleled darling!
How elegant is thy quiver of arrows, O thou, my darling
The only food of my ſoul art thou, my darling!
Without anger, without falſhood, and full of mildneſs art
    thou, my darling!
Without pride, without any ridiculous reſtraint, art thou,
    my darling!
Thou, whoſe heart with mine is but one kernel!
Who has any thing to reproach thee with?
Any one that does it muſt do it from jealouſy.
Ah let them ſay what they will,
The reproach will lie upon their own taſte.
Let the glorious ſun and moon dart their light from the
    heavens,
And let all men upon earth ſee thee and me, both of us
    alone;
And even then would we never remove from one another,
But enjoy the deliciouſneſs of life together.'

After the ſpecimens of the Kalmuc poetry, follows the Legend of Gheſſur Khan, which occupies no leſs than fifty pages; but for the entertainment ariſing from this ſtory, if, indeed, it afford any ſuch, we muſt refer our readers to the work; as we ſhall likewiſe for the ample narrative contained in the Kalmuc Chronicle.

The

The subjects which next occur in the history are a description of Tzaritzin, and its confines ; the colony of Sarepta; the Caspian sea ; towns and fortresses between Tzaritzin and Astrachan ; the history of Astrachan ; the Volga, and the Armenians. Concerning the latter of these we shall lay before our readers the following short extract, upon the authority of the editor.

' The Armenians, in the time of Tournefort, must have been quite different people from those of the present times, or the polite Frenchman was the dupe of his gallantry in the description he gives. According to the observations of M. Gmelin, which a long residence and commerce among them enabled him to make, they are almost all knaves, acting intirely as circumstances require, either with the most assuming pride, or the most abject meanness ; but always with a view to interest. An Armenian (according to him) is capable of selling his father and his brother, if he thinks it to his advantage. He does not hesitate a moment about taking a false oath, if he can escape a merited punishment, or save a portion of his money by perjury. He will come and throw himself at your feet, if he has need of your assistance ; nay, he will offer you his house, and all he is worth ; but the instant he is out of the scrape, he not only forgets his deliverer, but will do him every mischief that lies in his power. The Armenians have even a gloomy and secret antipathy for each other, the source of continual disagreement, and constantly cherish in their hearts the poison of hatred.'

The editor of this work has, in our opinion, stretched it to an extent that far surpasses the limits to which the subject had any just claim; but we must acknowledge at the same time, that he has amassed a large stock of information ; though by what authorities it is supported, we are not explicitly told.——The present volume is ornamented with several plates, and a map of the new discoveries in the northern sea.

The Works of the Right Rev. Thomas Newton, D. D. late Lord Bishop of Bristol, and Dean of St. Paul's, London. With some Account of his Life, and Anecdotes of several of his Friends. Written by himself. In three Volumes. 4to. 3l. 15s. in Boards. Rivington.

WHEN we consider the various accidents and disasters to which literary productions are usually exposed; after the decease of their respective authors, the depredations of raw and trunk-makers, the ignorance or the negligence of executors, and the carelessness or the mistakes of editors; we

cannot

cannot but think it a wise precaution in every voluminous writer (provided his finances, or the faith of his bookseller, will permit) to print a complete edition of his works, adorned with his effigy, and accompanied with an account of his own life and writings.

By this expedient he will be able to communicate them to the public in the most advantageous form; he will prevent his genuine performances from being disgraced by the addition of spurious publications; he will obviate any false or unfavourable accounts, which may be given of his parentage, or his conduct in particular cases; he will save the editors of biographical dictionaries, in future times, the inconceivable trouble and expence of collecting the memoirs of his life from tradition, from a register, from an epitaph, and from other imperfect sources of information; and, lastly, he will have the satisfaction to see his own monument erected, before he leaves the world.

The learned author of these volumes has taken this method to secure his works against all disasters, and has written the story of his own life. In the general opinion, this may have an appearance of vanity; but the same thing has been done by many grave and respectable writers; and, for the reasons we have assigned, is a prudent scheme.

As the literary world has been long acquainted with his lordship's writings, and the volumes now before us have been some time published, we shall only extract some of the most memorable facts and dates from his memoirs, and specify the principal articles, which compose this collection.

Thomas Newton was born at Litchfield, Dec. 21, 1703. His father was a considerable brandy and cyder merchant. He received the first part of his education in the free school of Litchfield, under Mr. Hunter. In 1717 he was sent to Westminster school; and six years afterwards, to Trinity college, Cambridge. In 1744, by the interest of Lord Bath, he was presented to the rectory of St. Mary le Bow, in Cheapside, and the year after took the degree of D. D. In 1747 he was chosen lecturer of St. George's, Hanover-square, and married the eldest daughter of Dr. Trebeck. In 1749 he published his edition of Milton's Paradise Lost, and about three years afterwards, Paradise Regained, and the other poems of Milton. In 1754 he had the misfortune to lose his wife. The same year he published the first volume of his Dissertations on the Prophecies. In 1757 he was made prebendary of Westminster, sub-almoner, and precentor of York. About the beginning of the next year he published his second and third volumes of Dissertations. In 1761 he married his second wife,

Mrs.

Mrs. Hand, relict of the Rev. Mr. Hand, and a daughter of
Lord Lisburne. In September the same year he was appointed
bishop of Bristol, and residentiary of St. Paul's. And in
1768 he was promoted to the deanry of St. Paul's, on which
he resigned his living in the city.

As he was disabled by ill health from performing his duty
in the pulpit, and even from attending the service of the
church, he employed several years in revising, correcting,
and preparing his works for the press. One of the last things
of his writing was the account of his own life; and this he
continued till within a very few days before his death, which
happened at the Deanery, Feb. 14, 1782, in the 79th year of
his age. He was buried, by his own desire, in a vault, under the south aile of St. Paul's.

In this narrative the bishop has introduced a variety of
anecdotes, relative to his friends and contemporaries, viz.
bishops Smalridge, Atterbury, Berkeley, Hoadly, Green,
Pearce, Warburton, Secker, Dr. Lockyer, Dr. Bentley, lord
Tyrconnel, lord Bath, lord Chesterfield, the duke of New-
castle, lord Chatham, lord Mansfield, sir Thomas Clarke,
Mr. Andrew Stone, and some others.

On several occasions his lordship reminds us of the venerable old Nestor, and takes notice of incidents, which he would
have passed over in silence, if he had not been writing on a
favourite topic; such as the compliments which were paid
him at court, and the voluntary zeal of men in power to load
him with preferments. In the same manner, if we rightly recollect, the good bishop Pearce was persecuted and oppressed
by the gracious offers of royal favour, and the obliging im-
portunities of his friends, entreating him to accept of the
mitre. Happy days! when palaces and cathedrals opened
their gates to the learned, and men of merit were compelled
to come in!

In his account of the year 1780, the bishop severely repro-
bates the principles and practices of the Protestant associators,
and the leaders of opposition.

In the year 1781 he employed some of his leisure hours in
reading Mr. Gibbon's History of the Decline and Fall of the
Roman Empire, Dr. Johnson's Lives of the Poets, Dean
Milles's edition of Rowley's Poems, and Mr. Bryant's Remarks
on the same.

Mr. Gibbon, he tells us, ' by no means answered his expectation : for he found his history rather a prolix and tedious
performance, his matter uninteresting, and his style affected,
his testimonies not to be depended upon, and his frequent scoffs
at religion offensive to every sober mind.' Dr. Johnson's Lives,
he

he fays, 'afforded more amufement; but candour was much
hurt and offended at the malevolence that predominates in
every part. Some paffages, it muft be allowed, are judicious and well written, but make not fufficient compenfation
for fo much fpleen and ill humour. He was, therefore, furprifed and concerned for his townfman; for he refpected him
not only for his genius and learning, but valued him for the
more amiable part of his character, his humanity and charity,
his morality and religion.'——The bifhop perhaps would have
read thofe performances with more complacency, if they had
been publifhed, and fallen into his hands, in 1761, and not
at a time when ill health had embittered all his enjoyments.

By what he could learn and collect at Briftol, he was of opinion, that it was utterly impoffible for Chatterton to be the
author of the poems afcribed to Rowley; and he was pleafed
to have his judgment confirmed by the concurrence of two
fuch able writers as Dean Milles and Mr. Bryant.——His lordfhip probably had not fufficiently confidered the wonderful
productions of many early geniufes, or the pieces which were
confeffedly written by Chatterton himfelf.

Befides the Author's Life, the firft volume contains,

I. A Speech defigned for the Houfe of Lords, on the fecond
reading of the Diffenters Bill, 1772.

II. The Sentiments of a moderate Man concerning Tolera-
tion, 1779.

III. A Letter to the new Parliament, with Hints of fome
Regulations, which the Nation hopes and expects from them,
1780.

IV. Differtations on the Prophecies.

In thefe Differtations the bifhop has difplayed great learning and judgment, has difcovered an extenfive knowlege of
ancient and modern hiftory, and thrown light upon many obfcure paffages of fcripture. The moft entertaining part of
his work are thofe, in which he treats of the prophecies relating to Nineveh, Babylon, Tyre, Egypt, and Jerufalem; the
leaft interefting or fatisfactory are thofe differtations, in which
he endeavours to unfold the myfteries of the Revelation. In
this undertaking he has fucceeded better, perhaps, than any
of his predeceffors: but the book itfelf is fo obfcure, fo
much involved in figures and allegories, that the beft
explanations of it are mere conjectures. Accordingly, in
the numerous lift of commentators, who have attempted to
expound the vifions of the apocalyptical divine, there are
fcarcely two who concur in the fame opinion; and we have
seen

seen many of them grosly mistaken in their most positive calculations †.

The second volume consists of Dissertations on the Writings of Moses, the Creation, and the Fall, the Antidiluvian World, the Deluge, the Confusion of Languages, the History of the Patriarchs, and the Transactions of David and Nathan:—On religious Melancholy, Self-Love, God's Omnipresence, the Divine Goodness, the Pleasure and Comfort of Religion, the Government of our Thoughts and of the Tongue, Happiness and Misery, a chearful and a wounded Spirit, Flattery, Reproof, Agur's Wish, Public Worship, Dreams, the Abuse of Names and Words, Modesty and Shame, learned Pride, the Philosophy of Scripture:—Sermons on public Occasions, and five Charges, on reading the Scriptures, the Increase of Popery, the Licentiousness of the Times, the late Attempts against the Church, and a Dissuasive from Schism.

In the first dissertation his lordship proves, that Moses was the author of the Pentateuch, from general fame and tradition, from citations by other ancient authors, from being delivered to a whole nation together, from internal proofs and arguments, and the refutation of objections. He then shews, that he is deserving of peculiar regard and attention from his being the oldest author now extant, from his fame among heathen writers, from the importance of his subjects, his qualifications, his learning, his style, his impartiality, and his inspiration.

In his account of the fall, he says, the language of Moses is extremely figurative, being taken from the ancient pictures and hieroglyphics, wherein these transactions were first recorded. In conformity to this idea, he supposes the serpent to be only the symbol of the tempter; the eating of the forbidden fruit to be nothing more than a continuation of the same hieroglyphic characters, denoting a violation of a divine prohibition, the indulgence of an unlawful appetite, and the aspiring after forbidden knowlege; that the tree of life is a figurative expression, like the rest, an emblem only of a happy immortality, and no more to be understood of a real tree in this place, than it is in Revelation, ii. 7. xxii, 2, 14.

It is commonly said, that God ' set a mark upon Cain,' Gen. iv. 15. and the conjectures concerning this mark, have been various and ridiculous. Our author supposes that the true meaning of the text is, ' that God gave him a sign or token to confirm his promise; such as was frequently asked,

---

† Whiston assured the world, that the restoration of the Jews, and the Millennium, would commence on or before the year 1766.—Pag. 322.

and

and frequently granted in fucceeding times, as we read in other parts of Scripture; and fuch, whatever it was, as allayed and quieted Cain's fears and apprehenfions.'

In the fame chapter we meet with a very obfcure paffage concerning Lamech, on which his Lordfhip offers the following conjecture:

' Of this Lamech Mofes has thought fit to preferve (ch. iv. ver. 23, 24.) a fhort fragment, which was handed down by tradition, and appears to have been compofed in metre, to be fung, perhaps, to fome of his fon Jubal's inftruments of mufic. As we knew not the occafion, we cannot be certain of the meaning of this little fketch of ancient poetry. But what appears to me the moft probable account of it is, that the family of Cain, having long lived under apprehenfions of Adam's family coming, and taking revenge for the murder of Abel, and Tubal-Cain having lately invented weapons and inftruments of war, Lamech therefore proclaims unto his wives, who were more liable to thefe fears and apprehenfions, that they might now reft in peace and fecurity. What reafon is there for thefe fears and apprehenfions? Have I flain a man that I fhould be wounded, and a young man that I fhould be hurt? For with the Arabic verfion I would read the fentence interrogatively? Which interrogation is equivalent to a negation, as the Chaldee paraphrafes it, " I have not flain," &c. If then the murder of Cain, who committed the fact, fhall be amply avenged, " avenged fevenfold," as God hath declared, furely the murder of Lamech, or any of his innocent family, fhall be more amply avenged, " avenged feventy and fevenfold." Wherefore be of good courage, I have done no violence, and I fear none.'

Commentators have been much divided in their explanations of thefe words, in Gen. xi. 4. ' Let us make us a *name*.' Our author, with Perizonius and other learned men, takes the Hebrew word שֵׁם *Sem* in the fenfe of the Greek word σῆμα, *fema*, which probably was derived from it, and underftands by it a fign, a monument, a land-mark. This interpretation renders the fenfe clear and obvious. The builders of Babel intended to erect a landmark to prevent their difperfion.

Many learned men have afferted, that the primitive and original language was the Hebrew. But, upon this fuppofition, his lordfhip thinks, ' that it will be very difficult to account how the Hebrew came to be the language of Canaan, and why the wicked pofterity of accurfed Ham fhould be fuffered to retain their firft language, and be more exempted from the confufion at Babel than any other people. For, fays he, that the Hebrew was the language of Canaan, appears not only from all the remaining monuments of the Canaanitifh

or Phœnician language, but is exprefsly fo called by the prophet Ifaiah, ch. xix. 18.—The utmoft that we can allow to the
Hebrew is, that it might be a dialeft of the primitive language, as alfo might the Chaldee, Syriac, and Arabic, which,
as being the daughters of the fame parent, have fome family-
likenefs and refemblance to one another. What appears moft
probable is, that the primitive and original language was loft
in the confufion at Babel, fome few words, perhaps, and names
only, being retained in other languages.'

In his account of Lot's wife, our author fuppofes, ' that
looking behind, contrary to the exprefs order of the angel,
and lingering on the plain, fhe was overtaken by the fhower,
fo that her body was all incrufted over with a mixture of falt
and fulphur, and was left ftanding there like a pillar.' Jo-
fephus, he obferves, affirms, that this pillar was to be feen in
his time; and the Jerufalem Targum afferts, that it will en-
dure till the refurreftion. His lordfhip very properly adds,
' There is fomething that the inhabitants of the country fhew
now-a-days to ftrangers for this pillar of falt; but the moft
intelligent and judicious travellers pay no regard or attention
to it; they look upon it in the fame light as upon other fuperftitious relics.'—It may be curious to obferve, how the author of a poem, entitled *Sodoma*, printed among the works of
Tertullian, embellifhes the ftory. The image, fays he, is
perpetually preferved, without diminution:

> ' Dicitur et vivens alio jam corpore, fexûs
> Munificos folito difpungere fanguine menfes.'

Such outrages on common fenfe ought to be treated with
the utmoft contempt.

In his Differtation on Dreams, the bifhop prefers the hypothefis of Mr. Baxter, who fuppofes them to be caufed by fpiritual agents. This opinion, however, he allows, is liable to
inexplicable difficulties; and therefore he chiefly employs himfelf in pointing out the proper ufes to which dreams may be
applied. Our dreams, he thinks, will fhew us our natural difpofition and temper; will afford us no inconfiderable arguments for the immateriality and immortality of the foul; and
convince us of the neceffity of preferving a good confcience,
by fearing God, who has an abfolute power over the foul, and
can either ravifh it with the moft pleafing images, or torment
it with the moft terrible vifions; and, if there were no other
heaven or hell, could conftitute one in the human bofom.—
The laft of thefe three leffons is, perhaps, the beft we can
learn from our dreams: the firft is inconfiftent with Baxter's
hypothefis.

　　　　　　　　　　　　　　　　　　　　　　　The

The third volume contains Diſſertations on the Expediency of the Chriſtian Revelation, on John the Baptiſt, on our Saviour's Incarnation, the Time of his Appearance, the Names of Jeſus and Chriſt, his private Life, Temptation, Faſting, Miracles, the Lord's Prayer, the Service of the Church, the Demoniacs, the Blaſphemy againſt the Holy Ghoſt, Swearing, the Parable of the Tares and the Talents, Hereſies and Schiſms, the two great Commandments, the Import of Mark ix. 49, 50, the Parable of the Prodigal, Luxury, our Saviour's Diſcourſe with the Woman of Samaria, his Eloquence, his Sufferings, his Reſurreċtion, Aſcenſion, Chriſtianity our true Liberty, the Infidelity of the Jews, the Chriſtian Sacraments, the Uſe of Reaſon in Religion, Myſteries, the long Life of St. John, St. Paul's Eloquence, St. Paul at Melita, Confirmation, the Love of Novelty, running in Debt, St. Paul's Deſcription of Charity, Self Knowledge, Anger, the Beauty of Virtue, Converſation, abſtaining from all Appearance of Evil, the Prevalence of Popery, the Nature of Angels, Infidelity of the preſent Age, the Recompence of the Reward, the Sin which eaſily befets us, the Romiſh Clergy, the Ceſſation of Miracles, the Difficulties of Scripture, the intermediate State, the Reſurreċtion, the general Judgment, and the final State of Men.

In theſe Diſſertations the biſhop maintains the orthodox opinion relative to Jeſus Chriſt ; he aſſerts, that our Lord's temptation was not a viſionary, but a real tranſaċtion ; that the demoniacs were perſons really poſſeſſed by evil ſpirits ; that miracles were performed after the days of the apoſtles ; that the ſouls of men exiſt in an intermediate ſtate ; that the dead will not riſe with the ſame bodies ; that repentance is not impoſſible even in hell ; and that there may be a univerſal reſtitution.

We could extraċt many paſſages from theſe very learned Diſſertations, which would be highly acceptable to the curious and intelligent reader ; but the limits preſcribed to this article will not allow us to enlarge.

Thirty-Two Sermons on Plain and Practical Subjects. By the late Rev. Thomas Pyle. Vol. III. 8vo. 5s. 6d. Boards. Robinſon.

THomas Pyle, the author of theſe diſcourſes, was the ſon of a clergyman, and was born at Stodey, near Holt, in Norfolk, in 1674. He was educated at Caius college, Cambridge, where he took the degree of M. A. was near fifty years leċturer and miniſter of King's Lynn, and was alſo prebendary of Saliſbury.

He firſt diſtinguiſhed himſelf as a writer in the famous Bangorian controverſy, and afterwards acquired a more confiderable reputation, by his excellent Paraphraſe on the Acts of the Apoſtles, the Epiſtles, the Revelation of St. John, and the Hiſtorical Books of the Old Teſtament.

Mr. Pyle was intimately acquainted with biſhop Hoadly, who gave him his preferment in the church of Saliſbury, Dr. Samuel Clarke, and Dr. Sykes. He was a learned, rational, and judicious divine, and an admired preacher.

The two former volumes of his diſcourſes were publiſhed in 1773; and four ſermons on the Good Samaritan, and the Nature of Chriſt's Kingdom, were printed in 1777.

The manuſcripts, from which this third volume is printed, was ſent to the editor, Mr. Philip Pyle, by the executrix of Dr. Edmund Pyle, and by his brother, Mr. Thomas Pyle, Prebendary of Wincheſter.

Theſe diſcourſes contain a fund of ſolid ſenſe and rational piety, adapted to the underſtanding of every reader, with a remarkable perſpicuity of ſtyle and method.

The following extract from a plain practical ſermon on Covetouſneſs, will confirm this obſervation.

' This idolatrous power of riches is but too viſible, from daily experience, in the conduct of all people, who have ever addicted themſelves to the purſuit of them. Wherever a paſſionate fondneſs for earthly treaſures has once taken poſſeſſion, the man becomes deaf to all arguments, that concern his Chriſtian life, or the treaſures of another world. And the attempting to perſuade him, or to make him a convert, is exactly like offering addreſſes of love to a heart, whoſe whole affections are previouſly engaged.

' If you would attack him in his ſenſible part, and make ſure of his attention, you muſt talk to him in a different ſtile, upon quite other topics ! Tell him he is in danger of having his houſe broke open, and all his bags rifled. Tell him there are ſome ſhrewd ſuſpicions lately ſtarted, touching the validity of his title to one of his eſtates. Tell him of a profuſe young heir, who much wants preſent caſh, and will give him exorbitant intereſt for his money, upon undoubted ſecurity. Offer him a bribe with a decent grace : or put him into the way of making a bargain ; ſomewhat illegal indeed, but highly advantageous. Inform him that you are acquainted with a proficient in the law, who will undertake his cauſe at all events ; and is maſter of ſuch rhetoric, as to render any cauſe, juſt or unjuſt, victorious. On all theſe points, you ſpeak intelligibly, the man's ear is open : he thoroughly underſtands every ſyllable you ſay.

' But

' But difcourfe to him, with the tongue of an angel, upon difinterefted virtue. Affure him, that this life is only a paffage to another ; that riches are only talents, committed to him by Providence, for the exercife of his bounty ; that to love money too much, is not to love himfelf at all ; that to difpenfe it in acts of charity, will procure him the favour of God, and " bags in heaven, that never wax old ; where no thief approacheth, nor moth corrupteth." In what light, think you, will fuch doctrines appear to him ? Why, as the empty vifions of moralifts and divines ! Or perhaps he will fee them in a different view, and refolve them into the artifice of priefts or politicians, to enflave the world ! However, in all probability, he will not hear one half of what you have to alledge. Or if he does, it will be juft fuch a hearing as the Jews gave their prophet Ezekiel. " He will hear thy words, but he will not do them : and his heart will turn back, after his covetoufnefs."

' Thus proceeds the life of a worldly-minded man, and thus it moftly ends ! Thoughtlefs of what is heavenly, and clofely tied down to the earth that bare him ! Till either an early death fnatches him from all the joys he had fet his poor heart upon ; or elfe old age comes, to augment the evil, and to fink him ftill lower in every qualification. For age generally encreafes that diftemper of mind, above all others. Jealoufy, needlefs fufpicion, exceffive caution, are the infirmities that grow up with advancing years. And, at laft, the approach of death renders him totally unable to look, either backward or forward. Behind him he fees what he would fain carry away with him ; but that is impoffible. Before him lies a ftate, for which he has made no kind of provifion ; which therefore affords him not the fmalleft glimpfe of hope, and prefents to him many moft fubftantial fears. So he leaves the world, as the young man in the Gofpel left our Saviour ; " very forrowful, becaufe he had great poffeffions."

In this volume the author treats of the following ufeful fubjects : All Men are Sinners,—Againft Covetoufnefs,—How Men darken the Light within them,—Abftinence from all Appearance of Evil,—How Chriftians have their Names written in Heaven,—Religious Contemplation,—The Sin of Achan, Jof. vii. 13.—The Sinfulnefs of evil Thoughts,—The Crime of covering our Sins,—Confeffion of Sin,—The Wifdom of the Serpent,—The Innocence of the Dove,—How God gives Men to Chrift,—The Neceffity of Herefies,—The promifcous Diftribution of prefent Good and Evil,—The Profperity of the Wicked,—The Adverfity of good Men,—And the fupreme Good of Man.

This volume completes the collection of Mr. Pyle's difcourfes.

A Hiftory

A History of the English Law, from the Saxons to the End of the Reign of Edward the First. By John Reeves, Esq. Barrister at Law. 4to. 1l. 4s. Brooke.

WHEN a lawyer suffers any part of his time to be broke in upon by a literary pursuit, he claims an attention in proportion to the sacrifice he makes. The profits and honours of the profession are such a temptation, and the attendance necessary to attain them so unremitting, that few are disposed to look farther than these scraps of knowlege that are more directly useful. If any carry their researches farther, and attempt to furnish assistance to the studies of others by any publication, it is a work of supererogation, that must be received with great indulgence, whatever the real merit of it may be : our author in this light has a claim to some consideration ; but the praise he may acquire must depend on the subject he has chosen, and the manner in which he has treated it.

It has been the taste of the present age to look into the history of our constitution and laws ; and several treatises upon parts of our old jurisprudence have been published. These have contributed to open a subject which was capable of much more discussion. Dalrymple's Feudal Tenures is an essay towards a larger work, which the author seems to have had in contemplation. Sullivan's Lectures are principally confined to the same subject as the foregoing work, that is, the origin and progress of the feudal constitution ; but it is done more fully, and without any allusion to the Scotch law, which so frequently obscures the former : it contains also much discourse upon other parts of our law, and is a very valuable introduction. In Dr. Henry's History, the progress of our laws is made a part of his plan ; and this subject is handled by that author with the same ability with which he treats the others. To these modern authors may be added Nathaniel Bacon's Historical Discourse on the Laws and Government of England, Hale's History of the Common Law, and others of less note.

Notwithstanding the public were in possession of these performances, our author thought the history of our law was a field still open to new adventurers, and has hazarded an attempt of his own, to exhibit it in a new light. The method in which he has done this will best appear from his own words, in the dedicatory preface to the late lord chancellor Thurlow.

' The plan on which I have pursued this attempt is wholly new. I found that modern writers, in discoursing of the ancient law, were too apt to speak in modern terms, and always with reference to some modern usage : hence it followed, that

what

what they adduced was strangely distorted and misrepresented, with a view of displaying, and accounting for, certain coincidences in the law at different times. As this produced very great mistakes, it appeared to me, that, in order to have a right conception of our old jurisprudence, it would be necessary to forget, for a while, every alteration which has been made since; to enter upon it with a mind wholly unprejudiced, and peruse it with the same attention that is bestowed on a system of modern law. The law of the time would then be learnt in the language of the time, untinctured with new opinions; and when that was clearly understood, the alterations made therein in subsequent periods might be deduced, and exhibited to the mind of a modern reader in as simple and intelligible a form, as they were to persons who lived in those several periods. Farther, if our statutes, and the interpretations of them, with the changes that have happened in the maxims, rules, and doctrines of the law, were related in the order in which they severally took place; such a history, from the beginning of our oldest memorials down to the present time, would convey to the reader a tolerably just and complete account of our whole law as it stands at this day, with that advantage which an arrangement conformable with the *nature* of the subject, enjoys over one that is merely *artificial.*'

The time of the Saxons is thrown into an Introduction; and the author seems hastening to a period, which he considers as the proper point of departure from whence a juridical historian should set out, namely, the establishment made in consequence of the Conquest. What he says of the Saxons is entirely confined to their judicial polity; not entering into the grand question of the constituent members of the legislative assembly of the witenagemote, nor even that concerning the existence of tenures. He seems to disregard those questions, which have detained so many authors in the labyrinth of Saxon antiquity, and to confine himself to such as are less obscure, but, in his opinion (and perhaps justly), more worthy of notice. He is therefore more full upon the law of private rights and of criminal justice than former writers, who have been more diffuse upon the Saxon customs in general.

After stating the writers who have maintained the affirmative and negative of the question about the existence of feuds, he goes on thus.

' After this difference of opinion, some later writers have taken a middle course. Dalrymple and Sullivan endeavour to compromise the dispute, by admitting an imperfect system of feuds to have subsisted before the Conquest. Perhaps the latter of these opinions may be nearest the truth. A system of policy that had prevailed over all parts of Europe, it is most probable, got footing in England, inhabited by persons descended from

the

the same common stock, and possessed of the country they then enjoyed under like circumstances with the nations on the continent. But the feudal law, in the time of our Saxon kings, was in no part of Europe brought to the perfection it afterwards received; and in this country, separated from the world, and receiving by slow degrees a participation of such improvements as were made in jurisprudence on the continent, we are not to look for a complete system of feudal law. At the later part of this period, feuds were very little more than in their infant state; they were seldom more than estates for life. It appears there were estates of this kind, under a species of tenure, among the Saxons; and it has before been said, that there was the relation of lord and vassal. Without engaging in a controversy of this extent and difficulty, it will be more satisfactory to observe what facts we really know of the property of their lands, than hunt after conclusions which have eluded the greatest learning and sagacity. We know that the lands of the Saxons were liable to the *trinoda necessitas*; one of which was a military service on foot; another, *arcis constructio*; and another, *pontis constructio*. They were in general hereditary; and they were partible equally among all the sons: they were alienable at the pleasure of the owner; and were devisable by will. They did not escheat for felony; and landlords had a right to seize the best beast or armour of their dead tenant as a heriot. This is the outline of landed property among the Saxons.'

The author's sentiments upon the study of such remote antiquity are conveyed in the following paragraph, which closes his account of the Saxon laws and customs.

' This is a sketch of that system of jurisprudence which subsisted among our Saxon ancestors. The materials which furnish any knowledge of it are so few and scanty, that it is with the utmost difficulty any thing consistent can be collected from them. This must give rise to a variety of opinions, according to the prejudices and different turns of thinking in antiquarians. However, though the accounts given of this people and their legislation may be different, where so much depends on conjecture, perhaps the clearest opinion that can be formed respecting such distant and obscure times, is not worth defending with much obstinacy.'

It is not easy to say how far the author's want of earnestness in this particular may be relished by the lovers of Saxon antiquities. Certain it is, that when the changes in our laws are to be deduced from a known period, the remains we have of Saxon customs seem very little capable of application or inference.

The Conquest, then, is considered by our author as the period from whence his history is to begin; when, to use his own words, ' a new order of things commenced, the nature of
landed

landed property was changed, the rules by which personal property were directed were modified, a new system of judicature was erected, new forms of proceeding were devised, and new modes of redress conceived.'

In the same temper in which he passed over the two questions about the witenagemote and tenures, he now dismisses that about the term *conquest*, with this remark : ' That the tyranny of a prince who lived seven hundred years ago cannot be a precedent for the oppressions of his successors ; or any length of time establish a prescription, against the unalienable rights of mankind.'

Having in this manner disengaged himself from all unnecessary discussions, he proceeds to the subject which he had particularly in view ; that is, an account of the establishment made in our judicial polity, either immediately or in consequence of the Norman invasion ; such as tenures and their kinds, the nature of descent, of the judicature of the *aula regis*, justices itinerant, of the bench, the chancery, and council, the division of the spiritual from the ecclesiastical court, the introduction of the Roman and canon law, of trials by duel and by jury, of fines, of the nature of writs and records. All these constitute the materials of the first chapter, and comprise such progress as was made in forming our judicial polity between the time of William the Conqueror and Henry the Second.

Of these objects of enquiry none more engages the attention than the origin of the trial by jury, which our author has investigated minutely, so as to exhibit a clear and curious history of its first formation. Want of room prevents us from transcribing the whole, but the following particulars are too curious to be omitted.

' The earliest mention we find of any thing like a jury, was in a cause where Gundulph, bishop of Rochester, was a party, upon a question of land, in the reign of the Conqueror. The king had referred it to the county, i. e. the *sectatores*, to determine in their county court, as the course then was, according to the Saxon establishment ; and they gave their opinion of the matter. But Odo, bishop of Baieux, who presided at the hearing of the cause, not being satisfied with their determination, directed, that if they were still sure that they spoke truth, and persisted in the same opinion, they should chuse twelve from among themselves, who should confirm it upon their oaths. It should seem the bishop had here taken a step which was not in the usual way of proceeding, but which he ventured upon in conformity with the practice of his own country, the general law of England being, that a judicial enquiry concerning a fact should be collected *per omnes comitatûs probus homines*. Thus it

appears

appears, that in a cause where this same Odo was one party, and archbishop Lanfranc the other, the king directed *totum comitatum confidere*; that all men of the country, as well French as English, particularly those of the latter, learned in the law and custom of the realm, should be convened: upon which they all met at Pinendena, and there it was determined *ab omnibus illis probis*, and agreed and adjudged *à toto comitatu*. In the reign of William Rufus, in a cause between the monastery of Croyland and Evan Talbois, in the county court, there is no mention of a jury; and so late as the reign of Stephen, in a cause between the monks of Christ Church, Canterbury, and Radulph Picot, it appears from the acts of the court that it was determined *per judicium totius comitatus*.'

The second and third chapters of this work contain a complete view of our laws, as they stood at the close of Henry the Second's reign; for which our author is principally indebted to Glanville, who is supposed to have compiled his treatise by the command of that prince. This account is divided into the rights of persons, the rights of things, and the proceedings of courts.

As little is said by Glanville upon the first of these heads, our author does little more than take notice of the distinction between freemen and villains, and then proceeds to those rights of property claimed by individuals, under particular circumstances. The first of these is Dower, which is discussed very fully; in the illustration of which the law of Alienation and Succession is necessarily stated. The title of Maritagium properly introduces an account of the order of Descent, of the nature of Testaments, of the restrictions laid on Heirs during their minority by Wardship and Marriage; then of Legitimacy and Escheat. The Right of Lords to the Service of their Tenants by Homage and Relief, with a mention of Aids, closes the second division.

The manner in which justice was administered requires a more minute and circumstantial discourse, as it is the foundation upon which great part of our present judicial process is built. The natural division of the subject is into Civil and Criminal Pleas. Both these were farther artificially divided by the separate jurisdictions to which causes of certain descriptions belonged. In both the sheriff had cognisance of such as were of lesser importance; while causes of difficulty and consequence, or crimes which required any severity of punishment, were appropriated to the king's courts.

The most important civil suit was that of a Writ of Right, of which, and its process, our author gives a very circumstantial account, from the summons to the judgment. The only ancient way of decision in this action was by the duel. The alteration

alteration made by Henry II. in this part of the law claims our attention; not only as difcountenancing that abfurd mode of trial, but as tending to avoid the formal delays, to which the parties, according to the old procefs, were fubject. By this provifion alfo the trial by jury was eftablifhed, and brought into frequent ufe, if not inftituted. The mutual connections between the lord and tenant, in relation to their refpective rights, which they loft or acquired by this action, are, in the next place, clearly examined. The method of recovering other fpecies of property, fuch as Advowfons, Villains, and Dower, which, from their nature, required a diftinct procefs, concludes the fecond chapter.

From the incroachments of the Ecclefiaftical Court, in claiming jurifdiction over all pleas relating to the firft of thefe three heads, originated, probably, the writ of Prohibition now in fuch frequent ufe; which is the ftrongeft proof of the controul of the civil courts over the ecclefiaftical.

Thofe amicable compofitions called Fines, which conftitute fo effential a part of modern conveyancing, fall next under our author's confideration. The notoriety and validity of this, proceeding, tranfacted in open court, and confirmed by its record, foon brought it into frequent ufe. The mention of fines naturally leads to a brief inquiry into the nature of Records, and the courts which had the power of thus regiftering their proceedings. The remedies given to the lord againft his tenant, who either withdrew his fervices, or incroached on his manerial rights, conclude the hiftory of the actions then in ufe for afferting rights to lands, and their appendant fervices.

The univerfal prevalence of the civil law, when it did not interfere with the doctrine of tenures, is no where more apparent than in the divifion and diftinction of the feveral forts of debts, which our author next proceeds to treat of; in the courfe of which fubject fomething is faid on the law of Mortgages, buying and felling, and other commercial or confidential tranfactions. Thefe were all the actions which might be originally commenced in the *curia regis*; to which is properly fubjoined fome account of Attornies, by whom all bufinefs of a civil nature might be transacted in the abfence of the parties.

The *curia regis* had a jurifdiction over the inferior courts, temporal as well as fpiritual; when the former failed in juftice, the caufe was removed: when the latter interfered in temporal matters, their proceedings were ftayed by prohibition.

A full and accurate account of the feveral forts of affizes, which were inftituted by Henry the Second, clofes the Difcourfe on Civil Pleas, one of which, namely, that *de morte anteceforis,*

teceſſoris, was an original proceeding.   The others, in our author's opinion, were reſorted to, by the aſſent of the parties,
for ſettling ſome collateral point, on which they each reſted
their cauſe.

The criminal laws in thoſe days were ſhort and ſimple.
Our author, in treating of them, having premiſed ſome few
obſervations on the laws made before Henry the Second's time,
explains the modes of proſecution, and the nature of the ſeveral crimes cognizable in the king's court; to which he ſub-
joins an account of the proceedings before the juſtices itinerant.

Thus ends what may be called the Hiſtory of the Law in
this period, which is done with accuracy and perſpicuity.
—What follows is valuable; and though not immediately within the ſcope of our author's plan, is cloſely connected with it.   However, the reader will peruſe with pleaſure the hiſtory of our conſtitution at this early period; of
thoſe famous charters, the corner-ſtones and foundations upon
which our preſent conſtitution has been erected, the characters
of our firſt kings in their legiſlative capacity, their laws, and
their ſtatutes.

This chapter concludes with a view of the law-treatiſes of
that period, and particularly of Glanville, to whom our author is under great obligations.   The length of this article
muſt be our excuſe for not giving our readers any more extracts; we ſhall therefore to refer them to the work itſelf,
which contains a fund of legal and conſtitutional inform-
tion.   [*Correſp.*

[*To be continued.*]

---

*Obſervations on the Commerce of the American States.   With an
Appendix.*   8vo.   2s. 6d.   Debrett.

WHEN a nobleman enters upon the inveſtigation of an
intricate, political, or commercial ſubject, with the
view only of promoting the intereſts of the community, he
certainly is entitled to the grateful acknowledgments of the
public.   Such is the ſituation of lord Sheffield in the pamphlet now before us, which diſplays a more extenſive acquaintance with the American commerce than we have hitherto found
in any other writer.   His lordſhip ſets out with remarking,
that we ought henceforth to conſider America entirely in the
light of a foreign country; and that great ſacrifices to her intereſts, on the part of Great Britain, are neither requiſite nor
expedient.   He condemns the impatience with which we have
endeavoured to pre-occupy the American market; an eagerneſs which has likewiſe been indulged by our rival nations,
and

and has proved the means of already stocking, or most probably overstocking America, with European commodities. In confirmation of this opinion, we are told that British goods of several kinds were cheaper last year in New-York than in London; and that the last letters from Philadelphia mention several articles twenty-five per cent. cheaper.

Lord Sheffield is firmly of opinion, that the British merchants, from their superior power of accommodating the American traders, will, notwithstanding the utmost efforts of the other maritime nations, obtain, almost exclusively, that important branch of commerce; an idea which we are glad to find his lordship establish upon a more solid basis than that of sanguine expectation alone. With this view the noble author points out what are the wants of America; what this country can provide her with, which cannot be procured elsewhere on terms equally advantageous; and what are the productions of America to give in return. His lordship observes, that the imports and exports of the American States must in general, from many causes, be, for a long time to come, the same as formerly. Beginning with the imports from Europe, lord Sheffield divides them into those in which Great Britain will have scarce any competition; those in which she will have competition; and those which she cannot supply to advantage. In the first of these classes are woollens; iron and steel manufactures of every kind; porcelain and earthen ware of all qualities, except the most gross and common; glass; stockings, shoes, buttons, hats, haberdashery, and millenery; tin in plates, lead in pigs and in sheets; copper in sheets, and wrought into kitchen and other utensils; painters colours; cordage and ship-chandlery; jewellery, and ornamental as well as useful articles of Birmingham manufacture; materials for coach-makers, sadlers, and upholsterers; medicinal drugs; steel in bars; Indian trade; and books.

The second class, or that in which there may be competition, consists of the following, viz. linens, sail-cloth, paper and stationary ware, laces, callicoes and printed goods, silks, salt from Europe, tea and India goods in general, salt-petre and powder, lawns, thread, and hemp.

The third class comprises the after-mentioned, viz. wine, brandies, geneva, oil, raisins, figs, olives and other fruits, and cambrics.

Lord Sheffield observes, that the principal part, at least four-fifths, of the exports from Europe to America were at all times made on credit: that the American States are in a greater want of credit now than at former periods; and that it can only be had in Great Britain, the French merchants not

not being able, and the Dutch not willing, to afford it, except on the beſt ſecurity. His lordſhip thence infers, that nearly four-fifths of the American importations will be from Great Britain directly; that where articles are nearly equal, the ſuperior credit given by England will always enſure the preference; and that many foreign articles will probably go to America through Great Britain.

The noble author afterwards gives a ſimilar detail of the articles exported from America to Europe and the Weſt Indies, upon each of which, as well as on the imports above enumerated, he makes judicious obſervations. The reſult of his lordſhip's enquiry is the eſtabliſhment of the doctrine, that nothing can be more weak than the idea of courting commerce with the Americans; that a regard to their own intereſts renders ſuch conduct unneceſſary; and that by endeavouring to gain their attachment in particular, we ſhall diſguſt nations with which we have great intercourſe, and prejudice the beſt trade we have.

After giving the above general account of this judicious and intereſting pamphlet, we ſhall preſent our readers with two ſhort extracts, which highly merit the attention of thoſe in power.

' This (tobacco) being the principal article of American commerce, deſerves much attention from government. It was exported from Virginia, Maryland, and North Carolina, to Great Britain only, where it was ſorted and re-exported unmanufactured, except a quantity not very conſiderable. The exportation being now free to every part, it remains to be determined by experience, if it be more advantageous to tranſport it to every country where it is conſumed, or to carry it firſt to one general market to meet the purchaſer, and to be ſorted for the different markets. This buſineſs is underſtood in Great Britain only, and to encourage America to make this country the general market, the tobacco ſhould be permitted to be put into the king's warehouſes, and there only, without paying any duty, a bond being only given by the importer to pay the duty for ſuch part as ſhould be ſold for home conſumption; what is exported ſhould go out free of all duty. It will be ſent in large quantities in return, or payment for our manufactures, and we can afford to give the beſt price in this manner, by taking it in return. Before the war it was imported on a double bond, and the merchant, on paying 3l. per hogſhead, took it into his own poſſeſſion, and had eighteen months to export it, or pay the duty, then 7d. per pound. Since the war new regulations have been made, and the duty has been encreaſed from 7d. to 1s. 4d. per pound, and the tobacco is locked up by the officers of the cuſtoms till the duty is paid, or an entry made for exportation.

' By

' By a late order of the king and council, every importer of tobacco depositing tobacco in the king's stores, must pay 4l. per hogshead, by way of pledge or deposit, to make a part of the duty if used for inland sale, or to be drawn back if exported : this measure certainly will operate strongly against making Great Britain an entrepot for tobacco, because its subjects the importer to an advance of 50 per cent. on the value, without any benefit whatever to government, and on the supposition that two-thirds of the tobacco of America would center in Britain to be assorted for other markets, it would divert from the capitals of the merchants 200,000l. to lie dead in the custom-house, which might otherwise be usefully employed in the trade. This restriction, while Dunkirk, Holland, &c. are open without any advance whatever, will, if not speedily altered, divert the carrying trade of tobacco to those ports, by way of deposit. It is the worst policy to throw the Americans into new tracts. If they are encouraged, by equal advantages, to bring their tobacco to Britain to be assorted there, ships will consequently load from Britain in return, in place of Holland and Dunkirk. The tobacco will be left to pay for the goods, or to form a fund of credit, which will attach and rivet the trade to this country.

' The idea of obliging a merchant to advance 4l. for liberty to store a hogshead of tobacco, which costs eight or nine pounds, appears too absurd not to meet the immediate attention of his majesty's ministers.'

' Free ports at Bermuda, the Bahamas, the West Indies, &c. have been suggested, as a means of assisting commerce, but they will be dangerous to our carrying-trade ; they will undoubtedly be the means of dividing it with others. America, or the shipping of any nation, would carry from them our West India produce where they pleased. They may be advantageous to individuals ; but if a free port is in any case necessary, or proper, it must be at Bermuda, or one of the Bahama islands, for those articles only that it may be absolutely necessary for the British West India islands to have from the southern American States, viz. Indian corn and rice, and rum only should be received in return. The laws of Congress could not prevent the Americans from running to Bermuda with their provisions, &c. In many respects free ports are exceptionable ; but the allowing the produce and merchandise of the American States (imported only in ships of that country or of Britain) to be stored, until a sale can be made of them at home, or in some other part of Europe, might be of great advantage to both countries. The produce and merchandise when landed should, if sold for consumption in the kingdom, be subject to, and pay, when taken from the warehouses, the duties and taxes which are, or may be, laid upon such articles ; but such part as shall be re-exported to foreign markets, should be subject to no burthen whatever, excepting the usual store-rent, and unavoidable charges at the custom-house. By this means the British merchant will have the

management,

management and advantages to be derived from the sales ; and the American, without running the risk, and incurring the expences of going from one port to another, will be at all times sure of the best market to be had in Europe. The American commerce, especially for the most necessary and the most bulky articles, would, in a great measure, center in this kingdom ; and the merchants in America, not being able to make remittances in advance, but, on the contrary, obliged to go in great part on credit, being able thus to deposit her effects at the disposal of her correspondents, at the highest market which can be had in Europe, and in case they are universally low on the arrival of the produce, to wait a demand, and rise of them, will derive a very essential advantage ; and the British merchant being secured in his demands, will be induced to answer the American orders for goods, previous to the sale of the articles shipped to him for payment. By adopting this plan we should have the carrying from hence of the several articles, or great part of them, in British ships. This might in a great degree prevent the ships of the American States from going to other countries, and taking from thence produce and manufactures merely for a freight, though not so advantageous ; and it would promote the taking through Britain such articles as the American States may want from other countries, which this country does not supply. The articles should be placed in public stores, and only certain ports should be allowed to receive them. France is not without the idea of opening ports in the manner now mentioned. The idea is suggested for consideration, and may be worthy attention ; and it is the opinion of some, that it might be extended to goods from other countries as well as from America, to promote an increase of the trade and navigation of this country.'

We have only to add, in favour of the observations of lord Sheffield, that they appear to be the result of great enquiry and information ; which has been so extensive, that, in a large Appendix, a particular account is given of the exports and imports of America, at different periods, with the quantity of shipping, and the number of seamen employed.

Joseph : A Poem. In Nine Books. Translated from the French of M. Bitaubé. In Two Volumes. 12mo. 6s. Cadell.

THE story of Joseph has been always accounted a beautiful and interesting narrative. ' Voltaire thought it a subject highly proper for the Epic Muse.' In the same view M. Bitaubé has made choice of it for the ground-work of this poem. Though his work is in prose, he has preserved the usual arrangement of the epopea. That is, he has quitted the historical order, and transported his readers at once into the

the middle of the fubject. At the beginning of the firft book, we find his hero attending the flocks of Potiphar, in a lonely retreat, on the banks of the Nile. Here Zaluca, Potiphar's wife, accidentally fees him, conceives a paffion for him, and engages him to tell her his ftory. In the fecond book he relates to her his misfortunes, and his attachment to Selima, a young fhepherdefs, who had been adopted into Jacob's family. The third book defcribes the progrefs of Zaluca's paffion, her difappointment, and revenge. The fourth contains an account of Jofeph in the dungeon; the fifth his interpretation of the dreams of Amenophis, Darval, and Pharaoh; his advancement, and the death of Zaluca. The fixth prefents the reader with a defcription of Egypt. The feventh is an account of the famine, of Jofeph's adminiftration, and his difcovery to his brethren. In the eighth, Benjamin relates to Jofeph the hiftory of his father and his brethren, during the time of Jofeph's captivity. And the laft contains an account of Jacob's defcent into Egypt, his interview with Jofeph, the fettlement of his family in Gofhen, and the nuptials of Jofeph and Selima.

Thefe are the principal events; and this is the order in which they are arranged. A variety of defcriptions and epifodes, or lefs important incidents, fubordinate to the principal action, are occafionally introduced, in order to diverfify and embellifh the ftory. In feveral inftances the author has recourfe to fupernatural machinery. In the ninth book, Jofeph is tranfported to the fources of the Nile, and explores the caufes of its fertility; he is then carried through the etherial regions, and inftructed in the myfteries of nature, This aerial tour is fuppofed to be performed in a vifion, under the conduct of Ithuriel, the genius of Egypt. But this vifion is not conducive to the main action; and is a contrivance which does not feem agreeable to the nature of the epopea.

The moral of this work is unexceptionable; and the author has difplayed a lively imagination in many of the epifodes and fictitious occurrences, which he has introduced. But by attempting to embellifh every part of his work, and even the moft trivial circumftances, he difgufts us with his florid language, and pompous defcriptions.

Poetical ornaments are undoubtedly neceffary. But every thing will not bear embellifhment. And continual fplendor dazzles and fatigues the reader's imagination. The following incident is related with great fimplicity in the original: 'They took Jofeph's coat, and killed a kid of the goats, and dipped the coat in the blood.' But obferve how it is beautified by this writer:

' Simeon takes the robe, spreads it on the ground, snatches the kid from its fostering mother. In vain she runs to its aid ; he strikes the harmless kid, and its reeking blood distains the garment. Thus this innocent animal, instead of being offered on the altar of the God of the universe, to celebrate the birth of a son, or some other happy event, becomes the victim of the hand of cruelty, and perishes with the loss of a brother.'

In the description of the famine, the author says, ' While the animals perished in the woods, and in the dry channels of the Nile, the happier birds assembled in clouds around the edifice where the corn was distributed. The grain scattered on the ground became immediately their prey, and they repaid Joseph with their song, the only pleasure which nature, difpoiled of her charms, could afford him.'

These are affected ornaments and puerilities, below the dignity of an epic poem. The author has profeffedly imitated Gefner's Death of Abel ; and his performance may be very properly placed on the same shelf with that production.——M. Bitaubé has also published a tranflation of Homer.

Orlando Furioso, tranflated from the Italian of Lodovico Ariofto. With Notes. By John Hoole. 5 Vols. 8vo. 1l. 11s. 6d. Cadell.

IN the year 1773, Mr. Hoole published a translation of the first ten books of Orlando Furioso, and has now completed his arduous undertaking by the addition of four others : the life of the author, and a preface, originally annexed, are likewife confiderably enlarged and improved. The two former versions of this celebrated poem are by no means to be confidered as juft obftacles to the prefent attempt. That of fir John Harrington, in the reign of queen Elizabeth, though not deftitute of merit, at the time in which it was written, is now too obfolete in its language, too rugged in its diction, to afford the reader much fatisfaction ; and that of Mr. Huggins, publifhed in the year 1757, though executed with great fidelity, is too flat and profaic to convey a proper idea of the original.

To point out the merits and defects of Ariofto, is no difficult talk ; they ftrike at the firft view, and form a ftrong and glaring contraft. His ftyle is pure and elegant ; his defcriptions rich and wonderful ; his fancy and invention prodigious; his wit brilliant ; his fatire ftrong, and humour exquifite : to this muft be added almoft all the learning of his age. The reverfe of the medal exhibits to our view a multiplicity of low,
indelicate

indelicate ideas, or puerile conceits, that often intermingle
with, and debafe the moſt ſublime and affecting paſſages; a
variety of ſtories ſtrangely involved in one another, which
generally break off in an intereſting part, and leave the reader
in the moſt provoking ſuſpence; ' another and another ſtill
ſucceeds,' modo Thebis modo ponit Athenis. As we begin
to loſe fight of the firſt ſtory, or recollect it with indifference,
it burſts upon us when leaſt expected; and thus we are perplexed till the poem concludes. But this ſtrange method has
met with its admirers, as tending to excite attention, and prevent ſatiety; and Arioſto ſeems perfectly ſatisfied with his conduct in this reſpect.

> ' As at the board, with plenteous viands grac'd,
> Cate after cate excites the ſickening taſte;
> So while my Muſe repeats her vary'd ſtrains,
> Tale following tale the raviſh'd ear detains.' B. 13.

We cannot, however, but conſider it as a fault, and thank
the tranſlator for his marginal directions, referring us to the
page where the ſtory is continued. This tantalizing mode of
relation, generally adopted by the old Romance writers, is
finely ridiculed by Cervantes, in his account of Don Quixote's
combat with the Biſcayan. Butler, who likewiſe frequently
laughs at the abſurdities of knight-errantry, has the ſame object in view, when he abruptly breaks off his ſtory of the bear
and fiddle. Even Arioſto himſelf, in ſome places, ſeems to
treat as a jeſt the plan he has adopted. Thus, in a highly-
intereſting paſſage, at the end of the 14th book, we are
deſired to wait for the commencement of another, till he can
inform us of the event. The reaſon aſſigned is, that ' he can
fing no more, being extremely hoarſe, and wiſhing for a little
repoſe.'

> ' ——— non più di queſto canto;
> Ch' io fon già rauco, e vò poſarmi alquanto.'

It is not, indeed, always clear when he means to be ludicrous, and when ſerious*. Many paſſages are of ſo equivocal
a nature as to defeat conjecture; and both are often ſo intimately blended, that they ſpoil the moſt affecting narratives.
This muſt have rendered the tranſlator's taſk extremely difficult; and ſometimes the tranſlation ſeems to require ſuch allowances to be made for it.

---

* See canto 42. ſt. 20, 22. where he vindicates the truth of his narrative,
moſt probably by way of jeſt, from the objections of Fulgoſo, archbiſhop of
Salerno, who blamed him for his deviations from probability.

We

We find not in Ariosto, as in Homer, a connected, well-regulated plan, where the separate parts act in unison, and tend to produce the great event. His plan is confused and irregular. From the opening of the poem we are taught to suppose, that Agramant's invasion of France, and overthrow by Charlemain, would form the principal part: excepting, however, the siege of Paris, we hear but little of these monarchs' transactions. From its title, Orlando Furioso, and from that hero's being represented in many places as the Christian's most eminent champion, and that their success depended on his recovering his senses, we should naturally expect the greatest exploits would be performed by him, and the war terminated by his single valour. Instead of this, the last account of him is, that he fixed on Rogero's spurs (*gli sproni il conte Orlando a Ruggier strinse*), just before that warrior concludes the performance, by killing in single combat the Christian's most formidable enemy. Indeed Rogero appears throughout the most interesting character, and performs the most brilliant exploits. Though some characters in this poem are strongly drawn, we do not meet with that discrimination which appears so wonderful in the Iliad. Ariosto's knights, like Homer's heroes, are all brave and enterprising; but we do not perceive those nicely-blended tints, that diversify their manners, and render them more distinct the more closely they are examined. We are not ignorant that Ariosto has been applauded for drawing a variety of characters; but we cannot, at least comparatively speaking, subscribe to that opinion: not that he is destitute of merit in this respect. The boastful and impious Rodomont, whose name is become proverbial, the original of Tasso's Argantes, the sagacious and elegant Sabrino, Ariosto's Nestor, the tender and affectionate Isabella, the noble-spirited and accomplished Bradamant, the prototype of Spenser's Britomartis, are highly coloured, and delineated with the utmost justice and propriety. Yet still we must think that there is too great a uniformity in the heroic characters—fortemque Gyan, fortemque Cloanthum:—and the translator has contrived to strengthen the idea by applying the epithet *good*, without any warrant from the original, often indiscriminately, and almost constantly, to Rogero and Rinaldo, who, in some places, are not represented as patterns of moral virtue.

To carry on a comparison between the Grecian and Ferrara Homer, is idle and superfluous. The latter spurns at the Stagyrite's laws, and appeals to fancy, whim, and genius. They bear, indeed, little more resemblance to each other than a Chinese pagoda does to a Grecian temple: in the latter, art, elegance,

elegance, and simplicity unite ; the more exactly we contemplate the edifice, the more it excites our admiration : in the former, objects grotesque and disproportioned strike us at once with astonishment, sometimes perhaps with disgust ; yet many inferior ornaments offer themselves occasionally to our view ; and an air of magnificence, an irregular kind of splendor, captivates the eye, and dazzles the imagination, which, if more nicely examined, could not satisfy the judgment.

Yet, after allowing all that may be detracted from Ariosto's poetical merit, he still possesses our high esteem and admiration. We perceive something in him more consonant to the idea which Shakspeare, no incompetent judge, seems to have entertained of a true poet, than in any other author we can recollect. How truly descriptive of him are the following lines in the Midsummer Night's Dream !

‘ The poet's eye, in a *fine frenzy* rolling,
Doth glance from heaven to earth, from earth to heaven,
And as *imagination* bodies forth
The forms of *things unknown*, the poet's pen
Turns them to *shape*, and gives to *airy nothing*
A *local habitation*, and a *name*.’

‘ These tricks of strong imagination’ are peculiarly characteristic of the Italian bard. If any could dispute with him the precedence, in point of fancy and invention, it is Spenser. But let it be considered that, according to his own words, though otherwise applied, in Ariosto,

‘ The pure well-head of poesy did dwell,’

from whence himself and Milton often quaffed the richest draughts of inspiration.

Yet, great and wonderful as Ariosto's creative powers certainly were, we must not attribute all his stories, allusions, &c. to the fertility of his own imagination. He drew from a variety of sources. The Greek and Roman authors, historians as well as poets, supplied him with ample materials. To Boyardo's Orlando Inamorato, an unfinished romance, the substance of which is given us by Mr. Hoole, he is indebted for the ground-work of his story. The romantic history of Charlemain, and the twelve Peers or Paladins of France, written by a monk about two hundred years after the death of that prince, furnished him likewise with some of the great outlines of this performance. The name of Turpin, archbishop of Rheims, the friend and companion of Charlemain in his wars, is prefixed to the forgery ; and to this ideal prelate Ariosto often gravely appeals, for the confirmation of his most marvellous stories. Others are borrowed from Morte Arthur, an old French Romance translated into English, and published by

Caxton,

Caxton, in the year 1484. Some probably from romances now forgot; and even the sacred writers have been ransacked to furnish materials for this variegated composition. But, by additional strokes, either of the humorous or sublime, by altering the conduct or conclusion of his borrowed narratives, he generally makes them peculiarly his own: and though, like Theseus†, in the speech we have already quoted,

       ' We never may believe
Thefe antic fables, nor thefe fairy toys;
Such shaping fantasies that apprehend
More than cool reason ever comprehends.'

Yet still, when once fairly dipt in this enchanting poem, in spite of all its absurdities, and the disappointment we sometimes must expect to find, we are never able to lay it aside without the utmost reluctance: or, to adopt the language of romance, when once entered the lists, we cannot prove so recreant as to decline the combat, though we have the melancholy prospect of a discomfiture before the tournament concludes.

In respect to the translator's merit, we before observed, that he had undertaken no easy task. The romantic turn of the story, the simplicity of the language in which it is conveyed, a certain *naiveté* that characterises the author, are sometimes the principal, or only merit of the original, for several succeeding pages; destitute of poetic ornaments and moral reflections, and sometimes abounding with low and ludicrous ideas. To preserve this simplicity, and characteristic features, without descending into vulgarity, is extremely difficult. That Mr. Hoole sometimes fails is no wonder; that he generally adheres closely to the original, and yet avoids, or softens its absurdities, redounds greatly to his literary reputation. We shall present the reader with a specimen of Ariosto's ludicrous talents, in a passage where they are most improperly applied, as the other part of the story is sublime and pathetic. Orlando is represented as approaching, in a skiff, to the rescue of a distressed damsel, exposed to be devoured by the *Orc*, a strange kind of sea monster:

---

† Shakspeare's Theseus, like his namesake in Chaucer's *Knight's Tale*, and Fletcher's *Noble Kinsmen*, is a character quite consistent with the laws of chivalry. What is more remarkable, his life in Plutarch reads like an old romance, and the actions ascribed to him by the Grecian poets are as extravagant as any performed by Ariosto's heroes. The leading character of knight errantry is to *redress grievances*, and *punish the wicked*: and this Theseus very solemnly professes, in *the Suppliants* of Euripides.

    "Εθος τοδ᾽ εις Ἑλληνας εξελεξαμεν
Ἀει ΚΟΛΑΣΤΗΣ ΤΩΝ ΚΑΚΩΝ καθιςαται.

                                  ' When,

' When, hark ! the feas, the woods, the caverns roar !
The billows fwell ; and from the depth below,
In open view appears his monftrous foe.
As from the humid vale black clouds afcend,
When gathering ftorms their pregnant wombs diftend ;

So through the liquid brine the monfter prefs'd
With furious courfe ; beneath his hideous breaft
Vex'd ocean groans—Orlando, void of fear,
Nor chang'd his colour, nor his wonted cheer ;
Firm in himfelf, to guard the weeping maid,
And her dire foe with powerful arm invade,
Between the land and Orc his courfe he ply'd,
But kept undrawn the falchion at his fide.'

C. xi. f. 35, 36.

Thefe preparatory lines are equally beautiful in the original and tranflation : but mark what follows.

' L' ancora con la gomona in man prefe,
Poi con gran cuor l' orribil moftro attefe.

Tofto, che l' Orca s'accoftò, e fcoperfe
Nel fchifo Orlando con poco intervallo,
Per inghiottirlo tanta bocca aperfe,
Ch' entrato un uomo vi faria à cavallo ;
Si fpinfe Orlando innanzi, e fe gl'immerfe
Con quella ancora in gola : e, s'io non fallo,
Col batello anco, e l'ancora attaccolle
E nel palato, e ne la lingua molle.'   C. xi. f. 36, 37.

Who but muft exclaim with Defdemona, ' Oh, lame and
impotent conclufion !'   It is thus rendered in the tranflation :

' Soon as the monfter, that to fhore purfu'd
His deathful way, the boat and champion view'd,
He op'd his greedy throat, that might enhume
A horfe and horfeman in its living tomb !
Near and more near Orlando dauntlefs rows,
Then in his mouth the ponderous anchor throws,
Whofe width forbids the horrid jaws to clofe.'

Though the paffage ftill appears a little ridiculous, we
cannot but acknowlege that Mr. Hoole has acquitted himfelf
as well as its nature would allow, and judicioufly omitted
Ariofto's remark, that ' Orlando, the boat and anchor,
(e s'io non fallo) hung on the tender tongue of the monfter.'
We know not on what account fhe is converted into a male,
contrary to the original, but it is of little confequence.   A
mode, quite reverfe to that Mr. Hoole has adopted, prevails
among the Italians, who, when they mean to be particularly
polite, addrefs men in the feminine gender.

P 4

The

The following paffage is likewife much foftened, where Orlando perceives, as he fuppofes, Angelica at a window, imploring his affiftance.

> ' Pargli Angelica udir, che fupplicando,
> E piangendo gli dica, aita, aita,
> La mia virginità ti raccommondo
> Più, che l'anima mia, più che la vita.
> Dunque in prefenzia del mio caro Orlando
> Da quefto ladro mi farà rapita?
> Più tofto di tua man dammi la morte,
> Che venir lafci à fi infelice forte.'　　　　　C. xii. f. 15.

Nothing can be more ridiculous than fome of the above lines, thus tranflated by fir John Harrington:

> ' Helpe, now or never helpe; alas fhall I
> In mine Orlando's fight loofe my virginitie?'

Mr. Hoole's verfion has a very different effect.

> ' High at a window ftood the feeming maid,
> And thus, in moving words, implor'd his aid;
> Ah! help!—I give to thy protecting care
> My honour, dearer than the vital air!
> Shall this vile-ravifher his will purfue
> Unpunifh'd, in my dear Orlando's view?
> Ah, rather let thy fword prevent my fhame,
> And fave by timely death my virgin fame.'

Sometimes Mr. Hoole is inferior to the original. The 35th ftanza, canto 24, is thus rendered:

> ' Rage kindling rage with many a wrathful word,
> Againft the king Alceftes bar'd his fword,
> And flew him fpight of each furrounding friend,
> Who with drawn weapon would his prince defend.
> That day th'Armenians fled before his hand,
> And his brave followers aided with a band
> Of Thracians and Cilicians by his pay *maintain'd.*'

The ftrength and fpirit of the firft five lines in Ariofto are but weakly exprefled in the tranflation, and the concluding Alexandrine halts moft miferably. We have fome others of the fame nature.

> ' Whence never could her tidings reach my ear again.'
> ' Not one remains with him, his deareft friend to take.'

Such lines bring too forcibly to our recollection Pope's idea of the wounded fnake, and bear no kind of refemblance to ' the long-refounding march and energy divine.'

The paffage which defcribes Rodomont, when inclofed alone in the walls of Paris, and probably borrowed from Virgil's gil's account of Turnus, in a similar situation, though not void of merit, seem likewise inferior to the original.

'Non sasso, merlo, trave, arco, ò balestra,
Nè ciò che sopra il Saracin percuote,
Ponno allentar la sanguinosa destra,
Che la gran porta taglia, spezza, e scuote,
E dentro fatto v'ha tanta finestra;
Che ben vedere, e veduto esser puote,
Da i visi impressi di color di morte,
Che tutta piena quivi hanno la corte.

Suonar per gli alti e spaziosi tetti
S'odono gridi, e femminil lamenti.
L'afflitte donne percuotendo i petti
Corron per casa pallide e dolenti;
E abbraccian gli usci; e ì geniali letti,
Che tosto hanno, à lasciare à strane genti.' C. xvii. s. 12,13.

'Not beams, nor rafters, from the fabric rent,
Not stones, nor arrows on the Pagan *sent*,
Nor whirling slings, his dreadful arm can stay:
The crashing portal to his stroke *gives way*,
While from within the pale and haggard crew
Through many a breach the dire besieger view!
The court is fill'd with death; loud clamours rise;
The shrieking females join the soldiers cries;
They beat their breasts, they fly from place to place,
The portals and the genial beds embrace;
Now threatned to receive a foreign race.'

The distinct enumeration of the various instruments with which the besieged annoy their enemy; his different efforts to burst open the gate, and the 'colour of death' impressed on the Christians' countenances, are but faintly imaged in the translation.

The following lines are feeble and trifling; but they become worse by being dilated.

'Giunsero al loco il dì; che si dovea
Malagigi mutar ne i cariaggi.'   C. xxv. s. 95.

'The hour approach'd, when either Pagan train
Prepar'd to bring each car, and loaded wain,
With Malagigi, Vivian, and the gold
For which the wretched chiefs were *bought* and *sold*.'

In the 26th book some knights are introduced, as contemplating a mystical sculpture fabricated by Merlin: among other figures an allegorical monster is represented, by which the commentators suppose Avarice is typified; and Francis the First is complimented with a prophetic description of his signalizing himself in checking her incursions: a delicate and
just

just encomium on that monarch, who always distinguished himself as a munificent patron of the arts and sciences.

‘ A la Fera crudele il più molesto
Non farà di Francesco il Re de’ Franchi ;
E. ben convien, che molti ecceda in questo,
E nessun prima, e pochi n’ abbia à fianchi ;
Quando in splendor real, quando nel resto
Di virtù farà molti parer manchi,
Che già parver compiuti, come céde
Tosto ogn’altro splendor, che’l sol si vede.

L’anno primier del fortunato regno
Non ferma ancor ben la corona in fronte,
Passerà l’Alpe ; e romperà il disegno
Di chi à l’ incontro avrà occupato il monte.
Da giusto spinto, e generoso sdegno
Che vendicate ancor non sieno l’onte,
Che dal furor da’ paschi, e mandre uscito
L’ esercito di Francia avrà patito.’   C. xxvi. f. 43, 44.

These lines are thus rendered :

‘ Not one shall more the cruel beast appal
Than Francis, whom the Franks their sovereign call.
He, first of men !—with happy omens led,
The crown scarce settled on his youthful head,
Shall cross th’opposing Alps, and render vain
Whate’er against him would the pass maintain ;
Impell’d by generous wrath, t’ avenge the shame,
Which from the rustic folds, and sheep cotes came,
With sudden inroad on the Gallic name.’   }

Four lines of the first stanza are, by a kind of chemical operation, condensed into four words, ‘ He, first of men !’ The beautiful comparison of Francis to the sun, before whom ‘ the stars hide their diminish’d heads,’ taken probably from Horace’s *velut inter ignes luna minores*, is totally omitted, and the conclusion feeble and obscure.——To point out defects, in a writer of eminence, whose performance has given us singular pleasure, is no agreeable part of our office ; but having discharged this duty to the public, we shall proceed with pleasure to considerations of another kind.

[*To be continued.*]

Remarks on the French and English Ladies, in a Series of Letters, interspersed with various Anecdotes, and additional Matter arising from the Subject. By John Andrews, LL.D. 8vo. 6s. Robinson.

THESE Remarks are extended through a volume, of a size little proportioned to their importance.—We were with difficulty able to follow our author, and, at last, congratulated
ourselves

ourselves at 'the sight of land'.—We must, indeed, acknowledge, that some of the Remarks are new, and some of them
entertaining; but candour will own, that they are in general
the hackneyed representations of every traveller, or the casual observations of an occasional visitant.

The anecdotes, interspersed in this volume, are not always
interesting in their nature, or related with the sprightliness
which these little histories generally require. The story of
Louisa and Narcissa is less exceptionable than some others.—
The account of the celebrated Ninon de l'Enclos is, in some
respects, different from that which has usually been given;
we shall therefore present it to our readers.

'She was in all respects, but that of gallantry, a woman
of irreproachable character: her behaviour was a model of
perfect decency and good breeding; her sentiments were noble and generous in the sublimest degree, and her actions entirely corresponded with them. Many are the anecdotes recorded of her magnanimity and beneficence. What was particularly remarkable, her loves always ended in the strictest
and sincerest friendships; her fidelity had frequent trials in
the troublesome time she lived in, but always remained invio-
lable. As her attachments were indiscriminately among the
celebrated personages that divided France into factions at that
day, she became of course acquainted with many of their secrets, and was often entrusted with deposits of the highest value. But she never betrayed the confidence of any man; and
while the spoils of her numerous lovers, friends, and acquaintance, lay at her option, either to secure for their owners, or to waste or embezzle without fear of detection, she was
never known to swerve in one single instance, from the strictest
rules of disinterestedness and integrity.

'This was the more singular and praise-worthy, as she was
surrounded by examples of perfidy and baseness. The ministry of cardinal Mazarin was an æra of the most shameful ve-
nality. Public spirit and private probity received a dreadful
shock under his government; and the French were become
loose and profligate beyond the precedents of former periods.

'When we view Nimon de l'Enclos in this illustrious and
exemplary light, when we reflect that she was admired, beloved, and caressed by all that was great and exalted in
France, royalty itself not excepted, and that casting the veil
of oblivion on one single frailty, she was a pattern of every
accomplishment that dignifies her sex; when all these considerations are duly weighed, we need not be surprised, that
her name is so respectfully remembered in her country, and
that

that her failing is loſt and forgotten in the enumeration of
the many virtues and eminent qualities that compoſed her
character.

‘ Unhappily, however, for the generations that followed,
the ſplendour that accompanied her public life and actions,
ſeemed in ſome meaſure to apologize, and even to atone for
her private irregularities. They of courſe who felt an inclination to imitate her in the leaſt meritorious part of her conduct, did not fail at the ſame time to propoſe to themſelves
an adequate imitation of her excellencies.

‘ Determinations of this kind have doubtleſs helped to
people France with numerous copies of this celebrated original. Neither ſhould it be denied, that many of them have
been remarkably ſucceſsful. They have had the art of al-
lying a ſyſtem of voluptuous immorality with the exerciſe of
many valuable qualifications, and have often proved very beneficial members of that ſociety, which their actions did not
always edify.

‘ But in the midſt of thoſe freedoms, in which Ninon thought
proper to indulge herſelf, ſhe had an excuſe to plead (if any
excuſe can be admitted), which is not always in the power of
her followers to alledge. She was a ſingle woman, and remained ſuch all her life, notwithſtanding the ſolicitations of
men of the firſt conſequence in the realm, to favour them with
her hand.

‘ She knew her own nature ; and being diſpoſed to perſiſt
in the indulgencies ſhe had granted it, ſhe had too much honour to deceive any man by falſe appearances.

‘ Such probably was the motive that kept her out of the
pale of matrimony. Had ſhe ever been prevailed upon to alter her condition, it is equally probable, from the native great-
neſs of her ſoul, that ſhe would have proved a model of conjugal fidelity.

‘ It were ſincerely to be wiſhed, for the honour and happineſs of her ſex in France, that ſhe had conſented to become
a wife, as every reaſon concurs to render it likely that ſhe
would have done the higheſt credit to that appellation.’

---

*Memoirs of the Baſtille ; containing a full Expoſition of the myſte-
rious Policy and deſpotic Oppreſſion of the French Government,
in the interior Aaminiſtration of that State Priſon.* Tranſlated
from the French of Mr. Linguet. Small 8vo. 3s. ſewed.
Kearſley.

JUST eſcaped from the horrors of a priſon, from the ſnares
of tyranny and oppreſſion, it may be expected that our
author feels the dangers to which he has been expoſed ; and
deſcribes,

defcribes, with peculiar fenfibility, the diftrefs of his confinement, and the refined torment of his perfecutors. In
this fituation, we cannot blame the force of his defcriptions, the energy with which they are repeated, nor the accumulated expreffions with which each repetition is overwhelmed; but, though his peculiar fituation furnifhes the
true and only reafon for this animation, yet we may be allowed to fuggeft, that they detract, in fome degree, from the
authenticity of his narrative. We would not be underftood
to defend the police which eftablifhes a ftate-inquifition of
this kind, or to blame the fenfibility of the author, who
feels acutely, and expreffes his feelings with uncommon force;
but to a man in this fituation we cannot look for cool obfervation, or accurate defcription, except in objects conftantly
before him.

We purpofely avoid the confideration of the crime for which
he was compelled to vifit thefe infernal abodes. Even from
his own account there was a *fufpicion* that he had violated the
terms on which he was firft recalled; but to inflict a punifh-
ment fo very difproportioned to the crime, unlefs there was
another foundation befides fufpicion, cannot be defended.
A defcription of the cell, in which the unfortunate prifoner
is confined, will at once fhew the powers and the fufferings
of the author.

‘ Thefe cells are all contained in towers, of which the walls
are at leaft twelve, and at the bottom thirty or forty feet thick.
Each has a vent-hole made in the wall; but croffed by three
grates of iron; one within, another in the middle, and a third
on the outfide. The bars crofs each other, and are an inch in
thicknefs; and, by a refinement of invention in the perfons who
contrived them, the folid part of each of thefe mefhes anfwers
exactly to the vacuity in another; fo that a paffage is left to the
fight, of fcarcely two inches, though the intervals are near
four inches fquare.

‘ Formerly each of thefe caves had three or four openings,
fmall indeed, and ornamented with the fame gratings. But this
multiplicity of holes was foon found to promote the circulation of
the air; they prevented humidity, infection, &c. A humane
governor therefore had them ftopped up; and at prefent there
remains but one, which on very fine days juft admits light enough
into the cell to make “ darknefs vifible.”

‘ So in winter thefe dungeons are perfect ice-houfes, becaufe
they are lofty enough for the froft to penetrate; in fummer they
are moift, fuffocating ftoves, the walls being too thick for the
heat to dry them.

‘ Several of the cells, and mine was of the number, are
fituated upon the ditch into which the common fewer of the Rue
St. Antoine empties itfelf; fo that whenever it is cleared out, or

7   in

in fummer after a few days continuance of the hot weather, or after an inundation, which is frequent enough both fpring and autumn in ditches funk below the level of the river, there exhales a moft infectious, peftilential vapour; and when it has once entered thofe pigeon-holes they call rooms, it is a confiderable time before they are cleared of it.

‘ Such is the atmofphere a prifoner breathes : there, in order to prevent a total fuffocation, is he obliged to pafs his days, and often his nights, ftuck up againft the interior grate, which keeps him from approaching, as defcribed above, too clofe to the hole cut in the form of a window, the only orifice through which he can draw his fcanty portion of air and of light. His efforts to fuck a little frefh air through this narrow tube ferve often but to increafe around him the fetid odour, with which he is on th point of being fuffocated.

‘ But woe to the unfortunate wretch, who in winter cannot procure money to pay for the firing, which they diftribute in the King’s name! Formerly a proper quantity was fupplied for the confumption of each prifoner, without equivalent, and without meafure. They were not ufed to cavil with men in every other refpect deprived of all, and fubjected to fo cruel a privation of exercife, on the quantity of fire requifite to rarefy their blood coagulated by inaction, and to volatife the vapours condenfed upon their walls. It was the will of the fovereign, that they fhould enjoy the benefit of this folace, or this refrefhment, unreftrained as to the expence.

‘ The intention, without doubt, is ftill the fame ; yet is the cuftom altered. The prefent governor has limited the proportion for each prifoner to fix billets of wood, great or fmall. It is well known, that in Paris the logs for chamber ufe are but half the market fize, being fawed through the middle : they are no more than eighteen inches in length. The economical purveyor is careful to pick out in the timber-merchants’ yards the very fmalleft he can find, and, what is as incredible as it is true, the very worft. He chufes in preference thofe at the bottom of the piles, which are exhaufted by time and moifture of all their falts, and for that reafon thrown afide to be fold at an inferior price to the brewers, bakers, and fuch other trades as require a fire rather clear than fubftantial. Six of thofe logs, or father fticks, make the allowance of four and twenty hours for an inhabitant of the Baftille.

‘ It may be afked, what they do when this allowance is exhaufted? They do as the honourable governor advifes them; they put up with their fufferings.

‘ The articles of furniture are worthy of the light by which they are exhibited, and the apartments they ferve to decorate. I muft firft obferve, that the governor contracts with the miniftry to fupply them ; and this is one of the trifling perquifites attached to his immenfe revenue, which I fhall take notice of prefently. He may frame excufes for himfelf, with regard to the inconveniences

niences of the prifon, becaufe he cannot change the fituation of places; he may palliate the niggardly diftribution of wood, under the pretext of faving the king's money. But on the head of furniture, which is entirely his own affair, and for which he is paid, he can have neither excufe nor palliation: his parfimony in this particular is at the fame time both cruel and difhoneft.

‘ Two mattraffes, half eaten by the worms, a matted elbow chair, the bottom of which was kept together by pack-thread, a tottering table, a water pitcher, two pots of Dutch ware, one of which ferved to drink out of, and two flag-ftones to fupport the fire, compofed the inventory of mine. I was indebted only to the commiferation of the turnkey, after feveral months confinement, for a pair of tongs and a fire-fhovel. I could not poffibly procure dog-irons; and whether it may be confidered as the effect of policy, or want of feeling, what the governor does not think proper to furnifh, he will not fuffer the prifoner to provide at his own expence. It was eight months ere I could gain permiffion to purchafe a tea-pot; twelve before I could procure a chair tolerably fteady and convenient; and fifteen ere I was allowed to replace, by a veffel of common ware, the clumfy and difgufting pewter machine they had affigned me.

‘ The fole article I was allowed to purchafe, in the beginning of my imprifonment, was a new blanket; and the manner by which I obtained this privilege was as follows:

‘ It is well known that in the month of September the moths which prey upon woollen ftuffs are transformed into butterflies. On the opening of the cave into which I was introduced, there arofe from the bed, I will not fay a number, or a cloud, but a large thick column, which inftantly overfpread the whole chamber. The fight caufed me to ftart back with horror; when I was confoled by one of my conductors with the affurance, that before I had lain there two nights, there would not be one left.’

The hours of ficknefs, which require the confolations of humanity, if the tender foothings of friendfhip be denied, are in the Baftille fpent in accumulated diftrefs.

‘ Firft, as to thofe tranfitory complaints, or fudden attacks, which can only be obviated by ready affiftance and immediate application, a prifoner muft either be perfectly free from them, or muft fink under them if they are fevere; for it would be in vain to look for any immediate fuccour, particularly during the night. Each room is fecured by two thick doors, bolted and locked, both within and without; and each tower is fortified with one ftill ftronger. The turnkeys lie in a building entirely feparate, and at a confiderable diftance: no voice can poffibly reach them.

‘ The only refource left is, to knock at the door; but will an apoplexy, or an hæmorrhage, leave a prifoner the ability to do it? It is even extremely doubtful, whether the turnkeys would hear the knocking; or whether, once lain down, they would think proper to hear it.

‘ Thofe,

' Those, nevertheless, whom the disorder may not have deprived of the use of their legs and voice, have still one method left of applying for assistance. The ditch, with which the castle is surrounded, is only an hundred and fifty feet wide: on the brink of the opposite bank is placed a gallery, called the passage of the rounds; and on this gallery the centinels are posted. The windows overlook the ditch; through them, therefore, the patient may cry out for succour; and if the interior grate, which repels his breath, as was before explained, is not carried too far into the chamber; if his voice is powerful; if the wind is moderate; if the centinel is not asleep, it is not impossible but he may be heard.

' The soldier must then cry to the next sentry: and the alarm must circulate from one sentry to another, till it arrives at the guard room. The corporal then goes forth to see what is the matter; and, when informed from what window the cries issue, he returns back again the same way, (all which takes up no inconsiderable time) and passes through the gate into the interior of the prison. He then calls up one of the turn-keys; and the turnkey proceeds to call up the lackey of the king's lieutenant, who must also awaken his master, in order to get the key; for all, without exception, are deposited every night at that officer's lodging. There is no garrison where in time of war the service is more strictly carried on than in the Bastille. Now against whom do they make war?

' The key is searched for: it is found. The surgeon must then be called up; the chaplain must also be roused, to complete the escort. All these people must necessarily dress themselves; so that, in about two hours, the whole party arrives with much bustle at the sick man's chamber.

' They find him perhaps weltering in his blood, and in a state of insensibility, as happened to me; or suffocated by an apoplexy, as has happened to others. What steps they take, when he is irrecoverably gone, I know not: if he still possesses some degree of respiration, or if he recovers it, they feel his pulse, desire him to have patience, tell him they will write next day to the physician, and then wish him a good night.'

' Now this physician, without whose authority the surgeon-apothecary dare not so much as administer a pill, resides at the Tuilleries, at three miles distance from the Bastille. He has other practice: he has a charge near the king's person; another near the prince's. His duty often carries him to Versailles; his return must be waited. He comes at length: but he has a fixed annual stipend, whether he do more or less; and, however honest, he must naturally be inclined to find the disorder as slight as may be, in order that his visits be the less required. They are the more induced to believe his representations, inasmuch as they are apt to suspect exaggeration in the prisoner's complaints: the negligence of his dress, the habitual weakness of his body, and the abjection no less habitual of his mind, prevent them from observing any alteration in his countenance or in his pulse;

both

both are always those of a sick man: thus he is oppressed with a triple affliction; first, of his disorder; secondly, of seeing himself suspected of imposture, and of being an object of the raillery or of the severity of the officers, for the monsters do not abstain from them even in this situation of their prisoner; thirdly, of being deprived of every kind of relief, till the disorder becomes so violent as to put his life in danger.

' And even then, if they give any medicines, it is but an additional torment to him. The police of the prison must be strictly observed: every prisoner shut up by himself, by day and night, whether sick or in health, sees his turnkey, as I have before observed, only three times a day. When a medicine is brought him, they set it on the table, and leave it there. It is his business to warm it, to prepare it, to take care of himself during its operation; happy, if the cook has been so generous as to violate the rules of the house, by reserving him a little broth; happy, if the turnkey has been possessed of the humanity to bring it, and the governor to allow it. Such is the manner in which they treat the ordinary sick, or those who have strength enough to crawl from their bed to the fire-place.

' But when they are reduced to the last extremity, and unable to raise themselves from their worm-eaten couch, they are allowed a guard. Now let us see what this guard is. An invalid soldier, stupid, clownish, brutal, incapable of attention, or of that tenderness so requisite in the care of a sick person. But, what is still worse, this soldier, when once attached to you, is never again permitted to leave you; but becomes himself a close prisoner. You must first, therefore, purchase his consent to shut himself up with you during your captivity; and if you recover, you must support, as well as you can, the ill-humour, discontent, reproaches, and vexation of this companion, who will be revenged on you in health for the pretended services he has rendered you in sickness. Judge now of the sincerity of D'Argenson, the lieutenant of the police, when he insisted on the temporal comforts prisoners experienced in the Bastille, and on the charity of the governors.'

The whole tenor of the narrative is of the same kind. The reader will observe, that our author's descriptions are animated by the still bleeding wounds of persecution, by the reflection that he has been the innocent victim of perfidy and cruelty. But, though somewhat may be allowed for his recent escape, though humanity may severely sympathize in his sufferings, yet every true-born Briton will exult, with peculiar pleasure, on his own comparative situation. The language of faction and aspiring democracy, which has not only predicted our falling liberty, but even announced the event, will necessarily be silent, when it is remembered, that suspicion must be supported by proofs, and proofs produce a full conviction, before personal liberty can be abridged, or guilt receive its proper punishment.

The Miscellaneous Works, in Verse and Prose, of Gorges Edmond Howard, Esq. Three Volumes. 8vo.

THIS gentleman informs us, in his preface, that the present work will 'make his publications *fifteen volumes*, four in quarto, and eleven in octavo.' The greater part, we find, consists of discourses on law and politics; and, we hope, those subjects have proved sufficiently advantageous, as there is a dreadful discount on the article of poetry. He assures us, 'but for that unfortunate talent, he might have been worth many thousands more than he has ever been possest of.' At the same time he declares himself to have been amply recompensed by the innate pleasure he felt when employed in such kind of compositions; and that he feels 'the satisfactory comfort of never having published a line in the least offensive to religion and virtue.'——Indeed a goodness of heart, no less than a singularity of manners, characterises almost every article of this *very* miscellaneous performance, in which we have odes and epigrams—three tragedies—a large collection of apophthegms and maxims, digested in alphabetical order—observations and queries on the popery laws and libels—actions and sayings of great and wise men—advice to a member of parliament; (poetical addresses from others to himself) and *other* tracts, calculated for the benefit of society.* The author's memoirs, contained in the preface, are extremely entertaining: no great elegance or accuracy of style, however, must be expected; their principal merit consists in unfolding, without any affectation of disguise, the events of his life, and the genuine sentiments of his heart. By them we find that a cacoethes scribendi has always been his predominant passion, though constantly engaged in a very laborious employment, or, as he somewhere expresses it, 'the most *insipid* of all businesses, that of an attorney.' Of this the following passage is a striking instance:

'Thus plunged in the pleasures of the imagination, it is easy to conceive, that the business or study of my profession, so diametrically opposite to them, could not fail of growing very irksome, if not quite disgusting; for if there be a being in the creation, to which, above all others, the Muses bear an especial antipathy, it must be a deep read, plodding, special pleader; nor is the sophister behindhand in his aversion to them; however, I thought, whilst I retained my occupation in the profession, the closest attention thereto was not only a moral, but a religious and indispensable duty; wherefore, as I ever

* Some of these performances have been mentioned with approbation in our former Reviews.

was

was a moft early rifer in the morning, fome hours before many of the men of bufinefs in this kingdom have a thought of ftirring, and but very feldom wafted an evening in the way that numbers of them do, fo that in general I laboured about fourteen hours, fometimes fifteen, of the four and twenty, I determined with myfelf that after nine or ten at fartheft in the forenoon, I would not pay any farther court to the Mufes; but, alas! I found I had undertaken what I could not execute; an unfinifhed thought when I broke off intruded on me whilft I walked the ftreets, fo that I have often flipped into fhops and entries, and fcribbled for minutes; on which account, I was actually, in the laft war, feized in the Caftle-yard by the centinel as a fpy, and brought to the guard-room, to the high entertainment of all who heard of it: and many are the accidents my limbs have met with when in this mufing mood.'

The reader will fometimes fmile at this gentleman's peculiarities, but he muft always refpect the honefty of his intentions, and benevolence of his heart. The prefent heterogeneous collection feems to flow from that fource, though a little excufable vanity had probably fome fhare in it. The publication was announced with a view of raifing, by fubfcription, a fum of money for the Lying-in Hofpital at Dublin; but the fuccefs by no means anfwered his wifhes, or expectations. As the author's account of this affair, though not very happily or clearly exprefled, is fomewhat amufing and characterftic, we fhall give it in his own words.

' I did conceive that the bare mentioning that I intended the benefit, which I might have expected by this work, for that firft of charities, the Lying-in Hofpital, would have brought in ten fubfcribers for one I have had: but, notwithftanding this my intention has been fo fignified thefe two years paft and upwards, not only in difperfed printed propofals, but in advertifements in public papers at no fmall expences for fubfcriptions, and that when I was told the finances of the charity would not afford to rifk advancing the expence of publifhing, had offered it myfelf, yet not any have been procured thereby; and the number of fubfcribers which I have myfelf been able to get (not having time to folicit in perfon) has been fo fmall, and the expence of publifhing fo heavy, that, but for my good-will to the charity, and my refpect to thofe who gave me the honour of their names, as my propofals were not to print until three hundred fubfcriptions were had, I would have returned them to each of the fubfcribers as had paid.

' Wherefore, and as I had intended a legacy for this charity in my *will,* but, for reafons, chofe this method of giving it

in

in my life-time, I fhall fend into it one hundred and thirty fets, bound and lettered on the back, according to the publifhed propofals, clear of all expences to it, which will produce about one hundred and fix pounds for its benefit, and is almoft double the amount of the fubfcriptions paid and to be paid; (for I am to obferve, that feveral of the names therein are of perfons to whom I had prefented them) and, as I have printed much more than I purpofed at the time of my propofals, I hope to be enabled to give fome advantage alfo to fome other charities or charity.'

We hope our brother-fubjects on the other fide the Channel will wipe off this national reflection, by buying up all the bound and unbound fets of Mr. Howard's Works; and that they will not permit him to affume the merit of being the *fole* protector of the fair fex, in their moft helplefs and diftreffing fituation. What an indelible ftain will it fix on their characters, if they ungeneroufly neglect thofe who, in this kingdom, are univerfally fuppofed to bear towards them a moft difinterefted attachment!

MONTHLY CATALOGUE.
POLITICAL.

A Plain Letter to the Common People of Great-Britain and Ireland, giving fome fair Warning againft transporting themfelves to America. 12mo. 2d. Brown.

IT has for fome years been a current opinion, that, as foon as the war with America fhould terminate, great numbers of people would be encouraged to refort thither from thefe kingdoms. The author of the prefent Letter, however, paints in a ftrong light the danger of fuch emigrations. He affirms, from his own experience, that, before the commencement of the late commotions, many perfons, who had been allured by the artifices of mafters of fhips and kidnappers, to quit the northern parts of England, Scotland, and Ireland, and to fettle in America, were actually, upon their arrival on that continent, reduced to the condition of flaves: that, contrary to exprefs ftipulation, an unexpected and exorbitant charge of pretended expences of paffage was made upon them, which being abfolutely unable to liquidate, they were reduced to the dreadful alternative of being either thrown into prifon, or engaging themfelves for a long term of years in the fervice of fome planter: that they generally had accepted the latter, as the leaft horrible of the two evils; and that they were fent into remote parts of the provinces, where they were treated with all the feverity ufually practifed towards the Negroes, and entirely deprived of the poffibility of communication with their native country. The author

author preſſes forcibly upon the imagination of his readers the danger of ſimilar treatment to future emigrants, and earneſtly exhorts them againſt a meaſure which may terminate in the irremediable ruin of themſelves and their families.

Beſides the repreſentation above mentioned, the author urges a variety of other powerful arguments, to diſſuade his countrymen from all thoughts of riſking their fortune in the territory of the American States. He deſcribes the provinces, in general, as far from being entitled to the favourable opinion commonly entertained of them, in point either of produce or of climate. In ſome of them the heat is exceſſive; fevers and dyſenteries are almoſt perpetually endemic; and the annoyance of gnats, not to mention venomous ſerpents, is almoſt intolerable. He obſerves, that even the more temperate are not exempt from ſudden and violent viciſſitudes of the atmoſphere; and that all of them, in their back-ſettlements, are expoſed to the depredations of capricious ſavages.

Other arguments, which the author uſes againſt emigrations, are the extreme unſettled ſtate of the American government, and the weight of the taxes which muſt be impoſed in the ſeveral provinces, not only for defraying the public debt, but for the ſupport of a civil, and if not of a military, at leaſt a naval eſtabliſhment.—Upon the whole, though we think the author of this letter has exaggerated both the moral and natural diſadvantages of America, we muſt acknowledge that he has enforced his well-meant purpoſe with laudable energy; and we heartily concur with him in the homely, but honeſt advice, he gives his countrymen, by all means to 'look before they leap.'

A plain Reply to the Strictures of Mr. Cumberland and the Country Curate, on the Biſhop of Landaff's Propoſal. 4to. 2s. Murray.

The author of this tract ſtrenuouſly defends the biſhop of Landaff's propoſals, and endeavours to obviate, not only the objections of Mr. Cumberland and the Country Curate, but of every other writer on that ſide of the queſtion; inſiſting, that his lordſhip's letter is calculated to ſerve, if not abſolutely to ſave, the church, in an unpropitious criſis; and expreſſing his aſtoniſhment, that any of the clergy, even the dignitaries themſelves, ſhould be averſe to his propoſals.

In the Poſtſcript he ſhews, that the church of England is not ſupported by any direct contribution from the lords of manors, or from the patrons of livings; but by a general tax, levied by the legiſlative authority, on the public at large; that biſhops had originally the ſole right of nomination veſted in them; that they parted with this right on particular occaſions, and only for the lives of thoſe by whom churches were built and endowed; that through the indolence of the biſhops, and the ignorance of the people, this right was uſurped by the heirs of thoſe perſons; and, in general, that patronage is not a property, but a privilege; that patrons are no more than truſtees for the public, and, as ſuch, are not to fill their own purſes, by betraying the intereſt of the community.

From these considerations he proceeds to demonstrate the injustice, the bad policy, and the immoral tendency of bonds of resignation. It was of late years become 'a common method, he says, of evading the act and the oath against simony, to give a bond of resignation, under a certain penalty. After the clerk was instituted, the patron demanded, as matter of form, the resignation of the living, and the incumbent of course chose rather to pay the penalty. Thus actual perjury was committed, and the law of the land was shamefully trifled with.' If this custom, continues the author, had been allowed, the property of the church would have been made the property of individuals ; the clergy would have been reduced to a state of dependence, deprived of their rights, and their influence in the pulpit. But these and other ill consequences, which he mentions, have been happily prevented by a late decision in the house of lords.

A Letter of Advice, addressed to the Merchants, Manufacturers, and Traders of Great-Britain. 8vo. 6d. Kearsley.

The advice contained in this letter is, that the public in general should firmly determine against paying the tax on receipts, a tax which the author considers as extremely oppressive and reprehensible. He observes, that the names of two witnesses, subjoined to any receipt upon unstamped paper, will always prove a sufficient controul to the stratagems of the dishonest ; and that, even without any witness, the hand-writing of the receiver alone may fully answer the purpose ; as, though it might not establish the validity of the receipt, it would certainly, if attempted to be denied, afford unexceptionable proof of perjury. Such are the arguments used by this author, who, at the same time that he declares himself vehemently against this obnoxious tax, is no less a violent enemy to the administration which devised it.

A Speech, intended to have been spoken on Thursday, April 13, 1783. 8vo. 1s. Murray.

The supposed auditors of this speech are the electors of Westminster, assembled at the Shakspeare Tavern in April last. The author's design is to vindicate Mr. Fox's conduct in uniting with Lord North ; and this purpose he attempts by arguments which, at least, are ingenious and plausible.

DIVINITY.

A Sermon preached at the Meeting in Monkwell-street, at the Ordination of the Rev. James Lindsay, by the Rev. Henry Hunter, D. D. To which are added, the Questions proposed by the Rev. Andrew Kippis, D. D. F. R. S. and S. A. together with the Answers to the same ; and the Charge, by the Rev. James Fordyce, D. D. 8vo. 1s. 6d. Buckland.

The ordination of ministers among Protestant Dissenters seems to be a tedious process : for the theological documents now before us fill a hundred pages. And on these occasions little is to be expected but pious exhortations, and common-place reflec-

tions,

tions, on the duty of Gospel ministers. Here however we find men of eminent learning and ingenuity engaged in the ceremony; and we attend to their instructions with patience and complacency. Dr. Hunter preaches on the grounds and evidences of Christianity; Dr. Kippis proposes a series of important questions to the candidate, which are answered by the latter with great propriety; and Dr. Fordyce delivers the Charge. Mr. Lindsay, the gentleman who is ordained, is called to succeed Dr. Fordyce as minister to the congregation in Monkwell-street; the doctor therefore seems to have exerted himself with peculiar energy and eloquence, in describing the character of a faithful minister, and in recommending ' the lambs of the flock, his dear young friends,' to the pastoral care of his successor.

CONTROVERSIAL.

A Reply to the Animadversions on the History of the Corruptions of Christianity, in the Monthly Review for June, 1783; with additional Observations relating to the Doctrine of the Primitive Church, concerning the Person of Christ. By Joseph Priestley, LL. D. F. R. S. 8vo. 1s. Johnson.

A writer in the Monthly Review, in his account of Dr. Priestley's History of the Corruptions of Christianity, begins his remarks with this tragical exclamation : ' When we review the passages we have now transcribed, we are equally grieved and astonished. We are grieved to see a writer of Dr. Priestley's eminence, and who hath long stood very high, even in the opinion of his enemies, for integrity of character, laying himself so open to the charge of perversion and misrepresentation. We are astonished at his rashness,' &c. In this publication Dr. Priestley recriminates, charging his criticiser with misconstructions, misrepresentations, and the exaggeration of some insignificant errors. He does not however confine himself to those points, which are the immediate objects of his dispute with the Reviewer; but makes some additional observations, relating to the doctrine of the primitive church, concerning the person of Christ.

To this reply he has subjoined a few small alterations, which he has found it necessary to make in his history. In our Review for March we took notice of a slight mistake, into which the doctor had fallen, in speaking of the eucharist; we therefore think ourselves obliged to subjoin his correction of it, which is as follows :

Vol. ii. p. 11, read, ' In this age the table on which it was celebrated was called the mystical table; and Theophilus, to whom Jerom (if the epistle be genuine) writes, says, that the very utensils,' &c.

The author, with a spirit of genuine candour and liberality, adds, ' For this correction I am obliged to the writer of the Critical Review. I shall be thankful for the notice of any other oversight, which in a work of this extent I did not expect to escape.'

Remarks

Remarks in the Vindication of Dr. Priestley, on that Article of the Monthly Review for June, 1783, which relates to the First Part of Dr. Priestley's History of the Corruptions of Christianity. 8vo. 6d. Johnson.

The author of these Remarks considers seven charges, which the Monthly Reviewer has alleged against Dr. Priestley; and having pointed out some of ' the perversions and misrepresentations' of the former, concludes, that none of his objections are of any importance. The principal point in debate is this passage in Justin Martyr's Dialogue with Trypho: ἰς ου συνιθεμαι· ἠδ᾽ αν πλειςοι ταυτα μοι δοξασαιες ειποιν. p. 267. ed. 1686.

This tract appears to be the production of a learned and ingenious writer, well acquainted with theological systems, and the writers of antiquity.

A Reply to the Vindication of Observations on the Decline of the Clerical Credit and Character. 8vo. 1s. 6d. Brett.

The first pamphlet, which appeared on this subject, was, Observations on the Decline of the Clerical Credit and Character. This publication was followed by a Letter to the late Rector of Bourton. The Letter occasioned a Vindication of the Observations; and the Vindication has induced the author of the Letter to publish this Reply. In this dispute, it may be naturally supposed, that the two opponents are the principal persons concerned in the affair of the rectory. But this, we are told, is not the case. The vindicator has declared, ' that he never had the most remote design upon the living at Bourton:' and the author of the Reply affirms, ' that the present rector does not know who the letter-writer is.' We are therefore to believe, that they are volunteers, actuated by the most noble and disinterested motives; the former, by a laudable zeal for the church of England; and the latter, by a generous indignation, excited by the appearance of a publication, in which, he says, ' religion was made a pretence for personal malice and abuse.' But whatever their motives were, the contest has produced many reciprocal invectives; and is not likely to afford much entertainment to the uninterested reader.

MEDICAL.

Observations on Hepatic Diseases incidental to Europeans in the East-Indies. By Stephen Mathews, Surgeon in the Honourable United East-India Company's Service, &c. 8vo. 5s. Cadell.

These Observations chiefly relate to the hepatitis, putrid bilious fever, and hepatic dysentery. The descriptions seem to be accurate, and the general method of cure judicious; so that we have no hesitation in recommending them to the attention of practitioners, in similar situations. The putrid fever seems of the remittent kind; but our author first uses the cooling method, before he employs the bark: in the most urgent cases he waits for the appearance of remission, and generally wishes it to be considerable. He remarks, that petechiæ are sometimes critical. This subject has already occasioned some disputes, which we we cannot now purſue; and ſhall only add, that, in theſe ſituations, there are many ſources of deluſion, and in no inſtance can obſervation be more truly ſaid to be fallacious. Our author's practice, in the dyſentery, ſeems peculiarly pointed and proper: we cannot give it a greater encomium than to obſerve, that it very much reſembles the conduct of Zimmerman. His attempt to eſtabliſh the ſimilarity between the ſyphilis and hepatitis, from the ſimilar appearances of the blood, and the ſucceſs of the ſame remedy, mercury, in both, is more exceptionable. It has, indeed, very little foundation; for, by this mode of reaſoning, we could connect ſome of the moſt diſſimilar diſeaſes of the whole ſyſtem. The uſe and the management of mercury in hepatitis are, we believe, now ſufficiently underſtood; but we would refer thoſe, who wiſh for information on this ſubject, to the preſent author.

The language is frequently perplexed, ſometimes not explicit, and, in a few inſtances, incorrect; unleſs the laſt error be attributed to the corrector of the preſs, who ſeems, in general, to have executed his taſk with little attention or accuracy.

An Eſſay on the various Cauſes and Effects of the diſtorted Spine, and in the improper Methods uſually practiſed to remove the Diſtortion; to which are added, ſome Obſervations on the Treatment of Ruptures. By T. Sheldrake, jun. 8vo. 2s. Dilly.

Mr. Sheldrake, who unites a competent knowlege of anatomy to his mechanical abilities as an inſtrument-maker, endeavours to recommend an improved inſtrument to remove diſtortions of the ſpine. Mr. Jones, ſome years ſince, propoſed an inſtrument, which was very ſimilar to one formerly deſcribed by Mr. Vacher of the French Academy, without acknowledging its original, though it was probably borrowed from Mr. Vacher. This machine frequently failed; and we muſt own, that we ſhould, in ſuch caſes, rather prefer 'the ills we have—than fly to others that we know not of.' The improved inſtrument by Mr. Sheldrake is certainly free from many of the inconveniencies of that of Jones; and we are convinced, from other reaſons, beſides thoſe employed in the preſent pamphlet, that it can have no effect in diſtorting the pelvis. It may therefore be cautiouſly uſed, though it ought always to be laid aſide, if it give the leaſt pain: its principles are rational, and its execution is generally proper. We need not inform our readers, that Mr. Pott has only propoſed a method of curing the paralyſis of the lower extremities, without any means of removing the diſtortion. He ſeems to think that it ſhould remain; but Mr. Sheldrake is of opinion, that its removal may be ſafely attempted by his machine; and, with the reſtrictions juſt mentioned, we can ſee little objection to it.

The Obſervations on Ruptures are intended to point out the impracticability of curing them without proper truſſes. They undoubtedly recommend thoſe made by Mr. Sheldrake; but the ſuperior excellence of his works muſt be determined by experience.

Eſſay

Essay on the Bite of a Mad Dog. By John Berkenhout, M. D. 8vo. 1s. 6d. Baldwin.

We have renewed our acquaintance with this lively and entertaining author, and received considerable entertainment by it. His object is to prove, that the dread of water in hydrophobia is only a symptom of the complaint, and that its removal has little tendency to restore health. 2dly, That the several preservative remedies are generally useless, sometimes dangerous or pernicious.—He has fully attained this end, and his little work is not less instructive than amusing. The solemn pedantry and pompous nonsense of physic is ridiculed with humour, and opposed with judgment; but there is a vast field yet open for his talents, and we wish him to extend his attacks. If this essay, however, appears in a second edition, and he is willing to correct some parts of it, or to enlarge his views, we would recommend to him Sauvages' Treatise ' sur la Rage.'—— We shall extract a single paragraph from this pamphlet, as we wish it to be generally known, and firmly inculcated. ' The best medicines are often the most simple, and those which are nearest at hand. We are too apt superciliously to overlook the dictates of nature and common sense, to the discredit of our profession, and the loss of our patients. Art, chemistry, compounds and systems, are the hobby-horses of young physicians; and it is not till they have grown old in the profession, that they return to nature and Hippocrates.'

POETRY.

An Essay on Modern Agriculture. 8vo. 1s. Cadell.

The loyal and benevolent subject, who began his poem with

' God prosper long our noble king,
Our lives and safeties all'——

is by no means superior in these excellent qualities to our author.—Hear *his* concluding prayer:

' May Industry prevail, and Virtue smile,
The guardian angel of the British isle;
With Commerce may Integrity increase,
And Britons pious long be blest with peace.'

Amen and Amen.

Having thus discharged our duty to the author's morality and to our country, we must attend to the poem, which very carefully recommends several weighty concerns. A lawn, with a painted rail before the house; a running stream; a good warm stable for the horses and calves, and, we believe, excellent hay, in winter. We had almost forgotten that the corn mows are to be raised on conical stones, ' large at the basis, lessening on the top,' for fear of Norway rats. But it will not be easy to mention all the valuable hints contained in this poem.—For ' the goodness of sediment, the fruitful nature of the mud of ponds and ditches,' and similar instructions, we must refer to the work itself.

In a little more serious strain, we ought, however, to observe, that though the observations are sometimes trifling, and the

the sentiments trite, yet there is a great degree of benevolence, and many marks of tenderness and good nature, in this poem. The author seems to hint, that his mind has sought relief from the Muse when oppressed with a ' heavy woe,' which ' blasted the promise of his future years.' We sincerely commiserate his misfortunes, but cannot bestow very high commendations on his poetical talents. Yet the following lines are picturesque,—we had almost said beautiful ;—perhaps, in a happier state of mind, they might have been improved and polished, so as to have deserved that title.—We shall insert them as a specimen.

' Sometimes, as Science her fair reign extends,
And public spirit's bold attempts befriends,
We view, surpriz'd, the innovating tide,
Thro' unknown countries in new channels glide.
Thro' open'd hills the floods their currents steer,
Or roll suspended in the fields of air ;
Th' affrighted Dryad, lost in wonder, sees
The white sails moving midst her mountain's trees ;
Th' astonish'd traveller, with inward dread,
Now hears deep torrents rolling o'er his head ;
Now rais'd on high, he casts a look below,
And sees thro' vallies borrow'd waters flow ;
The vessel from the lofty cliff depends,
And, wond'rous, from the height with ease descends,
From town to town her ready way she plies,
And carriage safe at easy rate supplies.'

The State Coach in the Mire, a Modern Tale, in four Parts. By Thomas Brice. Small 4to. 1s. Scatcherd and Whitaker.

This industrious author, who, we are informed, is also a provincial printer and publisher, deserves our applause.—His limited education and obscure situation have not entirely repressed the excursions of fancy, or the efforts of genius. The poem is allegorical, and the metre Hudibrastic: it abounds with irregular rhymes, but the observations are frequently acute ; and if the ear is sometimes disgusted by rhymes which are the consequence of provincial pronunciation, the mind is frequently gratified by the shrewd sagacity of the poet. The description of the coach itself, though rather too long, ought not to be omitted, on account of its original merit. It is supposed to be the speech of general Conway, which produced the dissolution of lord N—h's administration.

' See, Britons, what a sad disaster,
These men have brought upon their master !
His coach, late wonder of the world,
They've split and int' a quagmire hurl'd.
The paintings fair that grac'd its pannels
Are worn away or splash'd in kennels ;
And piece from piece 'tis separating,
E'en whilst we thus stand here debating.
—Here, on the left, of late was seen
The diligent American,

With

With busy Commerce on her quay,
While British bales unnumber'd lay:
But ere the coach reach'd yon rough summit,
These drivers shook that pannel from it.
Now in its stead a patch appears,
Whereon the clumsy painter smears
Two armies fierce of kindred brood,
Who deluge all the scene with blood:
And e'en this patch with mud's so smeared,
The British army's almost buried.
—On this next pannel, lately shone
The Genius of the Torrid Zone,
Whose countenance express'd in smiles
The bliss of our West Indian isles.
Now in her cheeks are seams and furrows,
Which render her the queen of sorrows;
And here, behold, a hideous crack
Hath rent her robe, and broke her back.
—Here, on the right, we might behold
Hibernia with her harp of gold,
Whose silver strings appear'd to move
In notes of harmony and love;
Whilst, on this pannel, at her side,
Britannia seem'd to lift with pride.
But now the scene's annihilated;
The peaceful harp's obliterated;
The warlike drum Hibernia beats,
And calls her sons to martial feats:
In steady phalanx rang'd, appears
A troop of sturdy volunteers,
Whose sullen aspects seem to say,
Our Mother only we'll obey;
And, spite of all who dare resist her,
Own no proud mistress in her Sister.
—And here, in heart of oak, behind,
To which the coach's springs are join'd,
Two stout sea-horses plac'd astride on,
Ride British Neptune and his Triton,
Denoting Albion's boundless reign
Over the globe-encircling main.
But Neptune, see, has lost his trident;
And Triton, batter'd, looks quite frighten'd.
—And here too, carv'd in oaken stocks,
T' uphold the fore-springs and the box,
Stand Mars and Palls, emblems fit
Of courage true and sterling wit.
But Pallas, see, hath lost her head,
And Mars holds G—rm—e's broken blade!
—Such, such, dear Briton's, is the fate
Of this once-envied coach of state

—Can any fay, 'twas want of purfe
Reduc'd it to a plight fo curft?
No.—'Twas well known to each accountant,
(Let thofe examine it who doubt on't)
Sufficient cafh was duly furnifh'd,
To greafe its wheels and keep it burnifh'd.
I've got each item in my mind,
And dare aver 'fore all mankind,
One hundred millions and a furplus
They've fquander'd to this hopeful purpofe!'

Select Poems, and fhort Effays in Profe, from Dr. Watts. 12mo.
3s. Blamire.

The moral tendency of Dr. Watts's writings in general muft fecure veneration to his name. His piety and benevolence are confpicuous in the prefent collection, which therefore cannot fail of being received by the public with complacency.

Annus Mirabilis; or, the Eventful Year Eighty-Two. By William Tafker, A. B. Second Edit. 4to. 2s. 6d. Baldwin.

This fecond edition is confiderably more correct than the former, and has evinced what we lately obferved, that Mr. Tafker's publications are, in general, too rapid. The Georgium Sidus, or, as it ought to be called, the Neptune, is not the difcovery of this celebrated year, though it is added, to make wonders more wonderful. The author wifhed alfo to praife Dr. Johnfon, for reafons which he can beft explain: but even poetic licence could not *add him* to this period; fo that the lines, which have already appeared in every newfpaper, are fubjoined to, rather than make a part of the poem.

The Order of St. Patrick. 4to. 1s. Debrett.

An Ode on the Reftoration of the Rights of Ireland, not written with correctnefs, but, at the fame time, not without fpirit.

The Difmembered Empire. 4to. 1s. 6d. Johnfon.

It appears that this poem was written under circumftances of fuch perfonal diftrefs as ought to procure its author the indulgence of criticifm. But its own merit co-operates fo ftrongly with our fympathy, that we can, without any violation of juftice, affign it a favourable character.

MISCELLANEOUS.

Phyfical Prudence, or the Quack's Triumph over the Faculty. Infcribed to Lord J. Cavendifh. Small 8vo. 1s. 6d. Wilkie.

The triumph which the quacks have obtained, by the legal fanction of a licence, is celebrated in this tract. What Cæfar faid to a perfon who did not read with propriety: 'Si cantas, male cantas; fi legis, cantas,' we may apply to the prefent author. If it be poetry, it is very bad; if profe, it is too poetical. There is, indeed, fome little appearance of irony; but, if it was intended to be ironical, the defign is obfcure, and the execution not happy.

Letters

Letters from a celebrated Nobleman to his Heir, never before published. Small 8vo. 2s. 6d. sewed. Bowen.

We have met with so many similar publications, that we were almost tempted to throw the present work aside with disdain; but a superior motive induced us to read it, and we can truly say, that we have received much pleasure from the perusal. The public will not expect us to enquire into its authenticity; and on this subject we have not bestowed a moment's reflection. The work rather consists of extracts of letters, and, in many places, of detached thoughts, sometimes in French, and sometimes in English. They are generally animated and elegant, strictly moral, and frequently entertaining. A letter at the end, to be delivered to his heir after his return from travel, and after the death of the author, supposed to be the late earl of Chesterfield, is very interesting and instructive. On the whole, the present publication deserves our commendation; though, as the Letters are addressed to a very young correspondent, the subjects are sometimes trifling.

A Letter to Dr. Toulmin, M. D. relative to his Book on the Antiquity of the World. By Ralph Sneyd, LL. B. 8vo. 1s. 6d. Rivington.

This writer censures, with great severity, the abusive terms, the gross invectives, the impious notions, and the speculative dreams, which he had observed in Dr. Toulmin's Dissertation on the Antiquity of the World*. He exposes the preposterous fable of Burmha or Bruma†, which, the doctor tells us, carries with it more appearance of probability than any other account of the creation: he shews, by a ludicrous theory, that it is easy to invent other visionary systems, which will appear as plausible as Dr. Toulmin's; and, lastly, he points out the futility of some of the doctor's principal arguments.

Calendar of the Weather for the Year 1781, with an Introductory Discourse on the Moon's Influence at common Lunations in general; and on the Winds at Eclipses in particular, founded on a regular Series of Observations. By B. Hutchinson, Vicar of Kimbolton, and Prebendary of Lincoln. 8vo. Fielding.

This very sensible and candid observer concludes, both from reason and observation, that the moon, at its conjunctions, has little influence on the weather; its attraction of the air being frequently affected or counteracted by various other causes. The appearance of the moon,—the pointed and obtuse horns, are to be attributed to the state of the atmosphere; and the consequences of these appearances will have little connection with the planet itself.

The observations on the winds, about the time of the eclipses, were first suggested by Lord Bacon, who thought that they might, in some degree, determine the question concerning the influence of the moon on the weather. Our author has therefore observed, with particular attention, the weather two days

---

* Crit. Rev. vol. I. p. 34.   † Vide Hist. of Relig. Cerem. vol. iii.

previous

previous and subsequent to that on which the eclipse happened. Out of seventeen successive eclipses, there are but two instances of high winds pointedly at the time. In six instances, there was no wind in the period observed; and in nine there was wind, but at such different times, that it could afford little foundation to determine the question.

The Calendar is kept in the usual manner, but the observations on the barometer and thermometer should have been more frequent. The situation of the latter must have been exceptionable, for 80 and 81 are frequent numbers; but, during the heat of the last sultry summer, a good thermometer, in a proper situation, did not exceed 75: the lowest point of the thermometer was 17, the highest 82. The dryness of March and October of the year 1781, were very considerable; but, in the whole year, 21.65 inches of rain fell, though the average quantity of six years, in a similar situation, was only 19.14 inches, according to Derham. Our author is therefore surprised at the uncommon effects of drought which appeared in this year; but accounts, in our opinion, very satisfactorily for it. The barometer on February 27th, 1781, fell to 28.6; and it is remarkable, that in the southern parts of this island, we have been informed, it was at this point, the 9th of February last, the day after the most violent commotions at Messina. In both cases, this remarkable fall of the mercury was attended with violent gusts of wind.

Method of constructing Vapor Baths, so as to render them of small Expence, and commodious Use, in private Families; with a Design and Description of a convenient Hot Water Bath. By James Playfair, Architect. 8vo. 1s. Murray.

This method of our author is, indeed, cheap and convenient. The disagreeable circumstances attending public baths, as well as the expence, often preclude their use, when most wanted. We would, therefore, strongly recommend the plans of Mr. Playfair, though the description of the two last plates is remarkably deficient. In the form of a pamphlet, like this, there is little room for censure or praise. He recommends as little water as possible, both from convenience, and the practice of the ancients. If Archimedes, he observes, had not used a small bath, he would not have found the gradual elevation of the water, as he stepped in; and consequently the component parts of Dionysius's crown would have been still unknown.

Stenography: or, the most easy and concise Method of writing Short-Hand. By M. Nash. 4to. 10s. 6d. Richardson.

The variety of alphabets of this kind leave the learner little trouble but that of choice. They have all peculiar advantages and disadvantages; for what is gained in dispatch, is always lost in distinctness.

The greater number of systems are fully equal to the task of following an extempore oration; though few, except in the hands of a very skilful artist, can copy the more condensed substance of a premeditated one, or the more rapid articulation of of a reader. It is therefore probable that, in either view, much is not gained by a choice; and that any system, written with readiness and accuracy, will answer the purpose. Distinctness should be in general a very material object; for it is much more easy to write with dispatch, than to read it with ease when written.

Mr. Nash's alphabet is simple and clear; but, though he objects to points in particular places for the vowels, the distinction of many of his letters depend on points. It is certain that, in taking the pen from the paper much time is lost; but when the vowels are formed by the *position* of the succeeding letter, rather than by points, distinctness will fully compensate for the loss. We do not, on the whole, perceive any great improvement in this work, though there are no material defects in it. We would, however, recommend to every learner not to study arbitrary marks in any author. He may introduce them by degrees; and while they are of his own invention they will never be forgotten. We ourselves can, by this means, read, with ease, the short-hand, which we have not seen or practised these fifteen years.

The History of the Life of Tamerlane the Great. 12mo. 1s. 6d. Law.

This translation is superior to what had before been published of the Life of Tamerlane, and may afford both entertainment and instruction.

Laws for regulating Bills of Exchange, Inland and Foreign. By *J. Blagrave.* 12mo. 1s. Nicoll.

Beside the Laws of Exchange, this little manual contains abstracts of the several acts lately passed, for levying a stamp-duty on promissory notes, drafts, receipts, &c. with the additional duties upon bonds, bills of sale, wills, powers of attorney, ecclesiastical preferments, &c. To these are subjoined forms of promissory notes, bills of exchange, indorsements, and receipts, as prescribed by the late acts of parliament. The compilation appears to be made with care, and may, undoubtedly, be useful to people in business.

A Description of the Island of Madeira. 12mo. 1s. Kearsley.

This description of the island is accompanied with an account of the manners and customs of the inhabitants. The whole is comprised in exceeding small compass; but its shortness is, we doubt not, compensated by its fidelity.

An Account of the Loss of the Grosvenor Indiaman. 8vo. 1s. Nourse.

This account, which is published with the approbation of the Court of Directors, is founded upon the report given by Alexander Dalrymple, esq. and contains a circumstantial narrative of the melancholy event, with the subsequent history of the survivors.

The Trial of Lieutenant Colonel Cockburne, late Governor of the Island of St. Eustatia, &c. 4to. 3s. Faulder.

The issue of this trial has confirmed the suspicion that had, from the beginning, been entertained of colonel Cockburne's delinquency at the last capture of St. Eustatia.

THE
CRITICAL REVIEW.

For the Month of *October*, 1783.

Orlando Furioso. (*Concluded, from p.* 218.)

AFTER fubfcribing to the general cenfure on Afiofto for
the wildnefs of his plan, indecency of fome paffages,
and extravagance of others, much ftill remains to be faid in
his favour. The manners defcribed in his poem, however
extraordinary they now appear, were painted from the life,
and confonant to the ftate of fociety which prevailed in Europe for many centuries, and were not totally abolifhed long
after the Orlando Furiofo was compofed. A fhort fketch,
therefore, of this period, fo far as it proves explanatory of
the performance, may not be unacceptable to the reader.

Chivalry was not entirely unknown among the northern nations at a very early æra. It was not uncommon for warriors to travel in queft of adventures, to proclaim themfelves
protectors of the fair fex, and challenge each other to fingle
combat. Thefe cuftoms were ftrengthened by fimilar ones,
interwoven in the nature of the feudal conftitution ; and when
expeditions began to be undertaken for the conqueft of the
Holy Land, chivalry rofe to its higheft perfection. Impelled
by a kind of military fanaticifm, the martial nobility engaged
in the moft daring and extravagant enterprizes. To acquire
the honour of knighthood was more grateful to the high-fpi-
rited and ambitious than any other reward. It was conferred
with great pomp and folemnity, and kings themfelves were
eager for that diftinction. In thefe times, and even afterwards, it is well known that the feudal fyftem was of fo loofe
a texture, that powerful barons frequently fhook off the yoke
of their fovereigns, and formed little independent principalities.

lities. The state of the Highlands not long since was a representation of Europe in miniature, during the dark ages. These self-appointed princes erected castles, for the sake both of grandeur and security; were generally engaged in war, either to defend their own territories, or invade those of others; and military adventurers, consequently, were highly respected. Tilts and tournaments were instituted from political views, and exhibited with magnificence, to draw them to the several castles, and exercise them in the use of arms. This incited emulation, and proved the respective force and address of the combatants. From thence proceeded the custom so often mentioned by Ariosto, of knights encountering each other, when they met accidentally; which did not originate from a brutal and causeless animosity, but merely to make trial of their skill and prowess. The savage and cruel flocked to the courts of the proud and ferocious, from a congeniality of temper, and to indulge their lust for rapine and slaughter. On the other hand, the castles of the noble-spirited, where elegance and refinement were cultivated, became receptacles of the brave, and asylums for the fair. The latter, according to the feudal system, were often heirs to principalities, or large domains; and it is not surprising that, in such turbulent times, they were frequently expelled from them by some powerful and rapacious neighbour. Hence the description we so often meet with of their wandering in deserts, flying from their foes, or accompanying their protectors, appears consistent with historic truth. It is natural to suppose, that the most spirited knights were emulous to obtain such ladies' favours, and proclaim themselves their champions: and from hence a refined gallantry, and invincible resolution, became their characteristic.

The odd mixture of religious zeal and thirst for slaughter, not only in Ariosto's knights, but those of all old romances, took its rise from the crusades; and the highly-coloured accounts which he gives of splendid equipages, martial processions, rich pavillions, and immense armies, have their foundation in truth; for in those frantic expeditions, kings, knights, and ecclesiastics, were inflamed with one spirit of emulation, to 'exceed' each other in magnificence as well as valour. The different insignia of arms, and devices on shields, which our author so frequently describes, were probably invented in those times. Women warriors, from whom we have Bradamant and Marphisa, impelled by the same enthusiasm, frequently signalized themselves in these crusades; and hermits, so often mentioned by Ariosto, were then as common in real life. People who, from religious motives,

forsook

forſook the world, and retired to the wildeſt ſolitudes, ſoon acquired not only the reputation of ſuperior ſanctity, but of ſupernatural powers in conſequence of it. In regard to his marvellous ſtories, it may be obſerved, that the times he deſcribes was the age of credulity : an age in which Dryden's hyperbolical expreſſion,

    ' Portents and prodigies are grown ſo frequent,
    That they have loſt their name,'

ſeems to have been almoſt literally verified. The power of magic was univerſally credited. Numberleſs improbable fictions were propagated over Europe by thoſe who returned from the cruſades, either from their own credulity having been impoſed upon, or a deſire to deceive others. At the ſame time the exiſtence of dwarfs, giants, dragons, and other monſters of Gothic origin, was never diſputed. Superſtition likewiſe, no leſs powerful than poetic fancy, aſſiſted in peopling the world with ideal beings ; and none were infidels enough to deny the interference of angels, ghoſts, and evil ſpirits.

We mean not to vindicate Arioſto's extravagancies in general, but to obſerve, that many paſſages which ſeem fantaſtic and ridiculous in this noble, though eccentric poem, would, if traced to their ſource, appear in a very different light. The peculiar manners which he deſcribes, and which prevailed over Europe for many centuries, are now vaniſhed like ' the baſeleſs fabric of a viſion.' The retroſpect, however, on what has been, is amuſing to the imagination, and grateful to curioſity ; and however outré ſome parts of Orlando Furioſo may be, yet others give us a lively picture of the manners of an age but little known ; when barbariſm and courteſy, a religious zeal and luſt for ſlaughter, refined gallantry and brutal outrage, united to form a remarkable æra in the progreſs of human ſociety.

In order to convey ſome idea of the many beauties contained in this poem, we ſhall not take upon us to trace any particular ſtory through its confuſed mazes, though ſome are worked up in a highly dramatic* manner ; but ſhall ſelect, as they are extremely various, examples from thoſe of very different kinds.—Of that *animation* and *fire* which Arioſto ſo frequently exhibits, the following will prove a ſufficient ſpecimen. The battle is truly Homeric.

---

* A fine inſtance occurs in the 36th book, where Bradamant ſuſpects Rogero to be in love in Marphiſa, who is afterwards diſcovered to be his ſiſter. A maſterly ſcene, in which the different paſſions of rage, love, and jealouſy, are depicted in the moſt ſtrong and vivid colours.

Shrill

' Shrill trumpets mix'd with many a barbarous sound,
Join the hoarse drums ; wheels clatter o'er the ground:
Huge engines creak ; stones rattle from the sling :
From twanging bows unnumber'd arrows sing ;
While louder clamours seem to rend the skies,
Triumphant shouts, and groans, and dying cries :
Such is the din where falling Nilus roars,
And deafens, with his surge, the neighbouring shores !
From either army storms of arrows fly,
Whose dismal shadows intercept the sky ;
While sultry vapours mix'd with dust ascend,
And black as night in clouds condens'd extend.
Now these, now those to fickle chance give way ;
Lo ! this pursues, and that deserts the day.
One breathless here is stretch'd, while near him slain
His foe beneath him there has press'd the plain.
When spent with toil one squadron seems to yield,
Another hastens to sustains the field.
Now here, now there, the throng of arms *increas'd* ;
There thrust the foot, and here the horsemen *press'd*,
The earth on which they fought impurpled grew,
And chang'd her green for robes of sanguine hue :
Where flowerets lately deck'd th' enamell'd way,
Now horse and man in mingled carnage lay.'

Of the *terrible*, the subjoined is a striking instance. Rinaldo is represented as wandering in the dreary shades of Arden.

' From towns and cities far remote, expos'd
To perils dire, with deepening wilds enclos'd ;
A sudden darkness o'er the sky was spread,
Th' affrighted sun in clouds conceal'd his head,
And from a cavern, veil'd in darkest night,
A female monster rush'd, abhor'd to sight !
Her thousand eyes a watch eternal keep,
No lids were seen to close their orbs in sleep :
As many ears her head terrific bears,
And hissing snakes supply the place of hairs.
A horrid serpent for her tail appears,
That o'er her breast his curling volumes rears.
From hell's dire gloom *, where howling fiends lament,
This dreadful demon to the world was sent.
What ne'er till then had touch'd Rinaldo's breast
In many a field of death, he now confess'd.
Soon as the monster met his startled view,
And swift t' assail him near and nearer drew,
A terror, more than mortal can sustain,
Congeal'd his blood, and crept thro' every vein ;

---

* De le diaboliche tenebre.

Yet

Yet wonted courage in his looks he feign'd,
And drew his weapon with a trembling hand.
The cruel fiend, well practis'd in the field,
Began th' assault, and round the warrior wheel'd.
Her venom'd snake she brandish'd as she came,
And at Rinaldo bent her baneful aim:
She leaps upon him with a furious bound;
Now here, now there, Rinaldo shifts the ground:
He deals direct, and sidelong many a blow,
But none he deals can reach his hated foe.
The fiend applies her serpent to his breast:
Beneath his mail he feels the dreadful pest
Cold at his heart: now on his helm it rides;
Now o'er his face, now round his neck it glides.
Rinaldo, terrify'd, his fiery steed
Gores with the spur, and urges all his speed:
But the dire fiend, that follows like the wind,
Vaults with a bound, and grasps him close behind:
Whether direct or short his course he wheels,
Still at his back the pest accurs'd he feels;
In vain each art to shake her thence he tries,
And with arm'd heel his rapid courser plies.
Trembles, like autumn-leaves, Rinaldo's heart;
The freezing snake clings close to every part:
He groans—he howls—and shuddering with affright,
He calls aloud for death, and loaths the light.
Thro' bogs, thro' brakes, thro' thorny ways and rude,
Thro' thickest covert of th' entangling wood,
He flew, in hopes to loosen from behind
Th' infernal fiend, whose snake his limbs entwin'd.'

There is something very horrid in this passage, that makes
us ' feel it cold at the heart.' This allegorical monster, so it
proves, is emblematic of JEALOUSY, and at last conquered by
DISDAIN. Their combat is finely related in the same style.
It is needless to observe, though we meet with two or three
defective rhymes, that Mr. Hoole has done ample justice to
the original in what we have quoted: nor less so in the following passage, which gives full testimony to Ariosto's abilities in the *pathetic.*—Brandimart and Flordelis are represented
as united in the bonds of marriage and affection. With Orlando and Olivero he engages three Pagan champions, and
though the Christians prove victorious, falls in the action.—
Flordelis is thus introduced:

' As Flordelis at night in slumber lay,
The night preceding that unhappy day,
She dreamt the mantle, which her pious care
Had fashion'd for her Brandimart to wear,

His

His ornament in fight, now, strange to view,
Was sprinkled o'er with drops of sanguine hue;
She thought her erring hand the veil had stain'd,
And thus in slumber to herself complain'd.
" Did not my lord command these hands to make
His vests, his mantle, all of mournful black?
Why have I then, against his bidding, spread
The sable ground with fearful spots of red?"
Ill omens hence she drew.—Th' ensuing night
Arriv'd the tidings of the glorious fight;
Astolpho yet conceal'd, with tender fear,
A truth too dreadful for a wife to hear:
Till now, with Sansonetta join'd, he came
(A mournful pair) before the boding dame.
  Soon as she view'd the face of either chief,
In such a conquest, clouded o'er with grief,
No more was needful—her distracted thought
Too well divin'd the fatal news they brought:
Chill grew her heart, and sickening at the sight,
Her closing eyes were cover'd o'er with night:
Senseless and pallid, stretch'd on earth she lay,
And look'd a wretched corse of lifeless clay.
Her sense returning, frantic with despair,
She call'd her much-lov'd lord—she rent her hair—
She bruis'd with cruel hands her groaning breast,
She rav'd as if some fiend her soul possess'd.
So seem'd the Menades, when wide were borne
Their shouts and clamours with the maddening horn.
From this, from that, she begg'd some sword or dart,
Some weapon's point, to pierce her to the heart.
Now would she seek the ship, that to the shore
The corse of either Pagan monarch bore,
On their remains, with momentary rage,
To glut her vengeance, and her grief assuage:
Now would she pass the seas, to seek where dy'd
Her better half, and perish by his side.
Why did I leave thee, O! my Brandimart!
On such a day without me to depart!
I saw thee go—I fainted at the view—
Why did not Flordelis her lord pursue?
Had I been present in the hour of fight,
My eyes had watch'd thee with a lover's sight;
When fell Gradasso rais'd behind his blade,
My single cry had giv'n the saving aid;
My speed, perhaps, had rush'd between, and found
The happy time to take thy threaten'd wound.
My head, for thine, had met the Pagan sword,
A worthless ransom for my bosom's lord!
Yet will I die, though now my parting breath
Avails not thee, nor profits aught my death.

But

But had I dy'd for thee, what heavenly power
To better use could bless my dying hour?
Had cruel fate, or heaven averse, withstood
My pious aid, to save thy dearer blood,
At least I had obtain'd the mournful bliss,
To bathe with tears, to press with many a kiss
Thy ashy cheek; and ere with sons of light
Thy soul had to her Maker wing'd its flight,
I might have said—To heavenly peace ascend;
Thy flight ere long shall Flordelis attend!
Thus canst thou, Brandimart, thy consort leave,
And is it thus thy sceptre I receive!
With thee at Damogeia thus I meet!
And thus thou shar'st with me thy regal seat!
How, ruthless fortune! hast thou clouded o'er
My future prospects—hope is now no more!
Since I have lost this good, all comfort dies!
And not another with the world supplies!'

The preparatory dream; the wild agitations of her mind; at first burning for revenge, then wishing she had been present to have averted the blow, or at least consoled her Brandimart in the hour of death, are evidently wrought by the hand of a master.

Of all the passages, however, in this poem, that from whence it takes its title, and is descriptive of the progressive steps of Orlando's phrenzy, is probably the finest; it is at least the most exact draught from *nature*. Angelica, daughter of the king of India, with whom he is deeply in love, neglects his passion, and that of many other gallant knights, but becomes herself enamoured of a young Moor of obscure race, called Medoro: she marries him, and, regardless of her exalted station, dwells with him in a sequestered spot, which is beautifully described, and at which Orlando accidentally arrives. He observes, on the bark of trees, inscriptions by the hand of his mistress; and again,

' Angelica and her Medoro twin'd,
In amorous posies, on the sylvan rind,
He sees, while every letter proves a dart,
Which love infixes in his bleeding heart.
Fain would he, by a thousand ways, deceive
His cruel thoughts; fain would he not believe
What yet he must—then hopes some other fair
The name of his Angelica may bear.
But, ah! (he cry'd) too surely can I tell
These characters, oft seen and known so well:
Yet should this fiction but conceal her love,
Medoro then may blest Orlando prove.

R 4

Thus

Thus self deceiv'd, forlorn Orlando strays
Still far from truth, still wanders in the maze
Of doubts and fears, while in his breast he tries
To feed that hope his better sense denies.
So the poor bird, that from his fields of air
Lights in the fraudful gin or viscous snare,
The more he flutters, and the subtle wiles
Attempts to scape, the faster makes the toils.'

His catching at the least shadow of hope, his giving way to
self-delusion, contrary to his better judgment; and his endeavours to reason against conviction, when he afterwards reads
Medoro's verses in praise of Angelica, display an intimate
knowlege of the workings of the human heart.

' Three times he reads, as oft he reads again
The cruel lines; as oft he strives, in vain,
To give each sense the lie, and fondly tries
To disbelieve the witness of his eyes;
While at each word he feels the jealous smart,
And sudden coldness freezing at his heart.
Fix'd on the stone, in stiffening gaze, that prov'd
His secret pangs, he stood with looks unmov'd,
A seeming statue! while the godlike light
Of reason nearly seem'd eclips'd in night.
Confide in him, who by experience knows,
This is the woe surpassing others woes!
From his sad brow the wonted cheer is fled,
Low on his breast declines his drooping head;
Nor can he find (while grief each sense o'erbears)
Voice for his plaints, or moisture for his tears.'

As the night advances he mounts his horse, and proceeds
to a neighbouring cottage.

' No nourishment the warrior here desir'd,
On grief he fed, nor other food requir'd.
He sought to rest, but ah! the more he sought,
New pangs were added to his troubled thought:
Where'er he turn'd his sight, he still descry'd
The hated words inscrib'd on every side.
He would have spoke, but held his peace, in fear
To know the truth he dreaded most to hear.'

The cottager, in order to relieve his melancholy, gives
him an account of the loves of Angelica and Medoro; and, in
proof of his veracity, shews the bracelet she had bestowed
on him, as a reward for his hospitality. This bracelet had
been given her by Orlando, whose doubts and fears are now
confirmed. What follows describes the effects of violent passions operating on an elevated mind and robust body, ' a frame
of adamant, a soul of fire,' in a most affecting manner. We
                                                        trace

trace every ſtage of the diſtemper, from his firſt ſtruggle, through indignation and ſhame, to conceal his anguiſh, till it terminates in abſolute phrenzy.

‘ At length, from every view retir’d apart,
He gives full vent to his o’er-labour’d heart :
Now from his eyes the ſtreaming ſhow’r releas’d,
Stains his pale cheek, and wanders down his breaſt ;
Deeply he groans, and ſtaggering with his woes,
On the lone bed his liſtleſs body throws,
But reſts to more than if in wilds forlorn,
Stretch’d on the naked rock, or pointed thorn.
While thus he lay he ſudden call’d to mind,
That on the couch, where then his limbs reclin’d,
His faithleſs miſtreſs, and her paramour,
Had oft with love beguil’d the amorous hour :
Stung with the thought, the hated down he flies ;
Not ſwifter from the turf is ſeen to riſe
The ſwain, who, courting grateful ſleep, perceives
A ſerpent darting thro’ the ruſtling leaves.
Each object now is loathſome to his ſight ;
The bed—the cot—the ſwain—he heeds no light
To guide his ſteps ; not Dian’s ſilver ray,
Nor cheerful dawn, the harbinger of day.
He takes his armour, and his ſteed he takes,
And through ſurrounding gloom impatient makes
His darkling way, there vents his woes alone,
In many a dreadful plaint and dreary groan.
Unceaſing ſtill he weeps, unceaſing mourns ;
Alike to him the night, the day returns ;
Cities and towns he ſhuns ; in woods he lies,
His bed the earth, his canopy the ſkies.’

A pathetic lamentation, though debaſed by ſome puerile conceits, enſues ; but what follows is ſtrongly expreſſive of the wildeſt infanity, and makes us almoſt ſhudder at the repreſentation.

‘ Through the ſtill night the earl from ſhade to ſhade
Thus lonely rov’d, and when the day diſplay’d
Its twilight gleam, chance to the fountain led
His wandering courſe, where firſt his fate he read
In fond Medoro’s ſtrains ; the ſight awakes
His torpid ſenſe, each patient thought forſakes
His maddening breaſt, that rage and hatred breathes,
And from his ſide he ſwift the ſword unſheaths.
He hews the rock, he makes the letters fly ;
The ſhatter’d fragments mount into the ſky :
Hapleſs the cave whoſe ſtones, the trees whoſe rind
Bear with Angelica Medoro join’d ;
From that curs’d day no longer to receive,
And flocks or ſwains with cooling ſhade relieve ;

While

While that fair fountain, late fo filvery pure,
Remain'd as little from his arm fecure :
Together boughs and earthen clods he drew,
Crags, ftones, and trunks, and in the waters threw;
Deep to its bed, with ooze and mud he fpoil'd
The murmuring current, and its fpring defil'd.
His limbs now moiften'd with a briny tide,
When ftrength no more his fenfelefs wrath fupply'd,
Prone on the turf he fhrunk, unnerv'd and fpent,
All motionlefs, his looks on heav'n intent,
Stretch'd without food or fleep, while thrice the fun
Had ftay'd, and thrice his daily courfe had run.
The fourth dire morn, with frantic rage poffeft,
He rends the armour from his back and breaft :
Here lies the helmet, there the bofly fhield,
Cuifhes and cuirafs further fpread the field ;
And all his other arms, at random ftrow'd,
In divers parts he fcatters through the wood ;
Then from his body ftrips the covering veft,
And bares his finewy limbs and hairy cheft ;
And now begins fuch feats of boundlefs rage,
As far and near th' aftonifh'd world engage.'

These feats we fhall not enumerate ; for though many are
finely imaged, the fublime at laft becomes too much blended
with the extravagant. This did not efcape Cervantes, who
has ridiculed Orlando's fury, by making Don Quixote propofe him as his model, during his penance among the mountains of the Sierra Morena ; but, at the fame time, he has
appropriated many ftriking paffages, in his defcription of Car-
denio's madnefs.

We meet with nothing that more fully difplays the richnefs
of Ariofto's imagination, or his various powers, than Aftol-
pho's flight on the Gryphon horfe (the Hippogriff of Efchylus)
to the terreftrial paradife, and the moon. A moft wonderful
mixture of fenfe, keen wit, and abfurdity ; but altogether fo
delightful, that, according to Mr. Hoole's obfervation, ' we
are hurried along by the ftrength and livelinefs of the poet's
defcriptive powers, and have no leifure to attend to the cold
phlegm of criticifm.'——Without taking notice of the terreftrial paradife, which is difplayed in the richeft colouring,
and from whence the Mahometan one, fo beautifully drawn
by Mr. Hughes, in his Siege of Damafcus, feems partly to
have been borrowed, let us fuppofe him arrived at the moon,
accompanied by St. John, in order to reftore Orlando's fenfes ;
for we are told that every thing loft on earth is to be found
there : the knight being conducted by the Apoftle, perceives
in a deep valley

Here

' Here safely treasur'd : each neglected good
Time squander'd, or occasion ill bestow'd.
Not only here are wealth and sceptres found,
That, ever changing, shift th' unsteady round:
But those possessions, while on earth we live,
Which Fortune's hand can neither take nor give.
Much fame is there, which here the creeping hours
Consume, till time at length the whole devours.
There vows and there unnumber'd pray'rs remain,
Which oft to God the sinner makes in vain.
The frequent tears that lovers eyes suffuse ;
The sighs they breathe ; the days that gamesters lose,
The leisure giv'n, which fools so oft neglect ;
The weak designs that never take effect.
Whate'er desires the mortal breast assail,
In countless numbers fill th' encumber'd vale.'

A much larger list follows, equally descriptive and laughable. The conclusion wittily insinuates how * blind we are
to our own faults, and quick-sighted in discerning those of
others.

' There his past time misspent, and deeds apply'd
To little good, Astolpho soon espy'd ;
Yet these, though clear beheld, had ne'er been known,
But that his guide explain'd them from his own.'

We are next told,

' At length they came to that whose want below
None e'er perceiv'd, or breath'd for this his vow ;
That choicest gift of heav'n, by wit exprest,
Of which each mortal deems himself possest.'

This wit we find bottled up in different vases, with the
owners' names inscribed ; and Astolpho is rather surprised at
perceiving some of his own there, as well as that of many
people whom he had admired for their wisdom. Being willing to reap some benefit from his travels,

' The vase that held his own Astolpho took,
So will'd the writer of the mystic book,
Beneath his nostril held, with quick ascent
Back to its place the wit returning went.
The Duke (in holy Turpin's page is read)
Long time a life of sage discretion led,
Till one frail thought his brain again bereft
Of wit, and sent it to the place it left.'

Our last quotations, we believe, will sufficiently prove
Ariosto's *humorous* and *satyric* powers : from such passages

---

* Ben mi si potria dir, Fratre, tu vai
L'altrui mostrando, e non vedi il tuo fallo.   C. 24. s. 3.

aa

as thefe, from his fometimes blending the low with the fublime, as well as from his ftrange exaggerations, he has been
fufpected of an intention to ridicule the old romances, and the
Orlando Furiofo accounted merely a Don Quixote in verfe,
But this we cannot allow; too many ftriking relations of a
different kind prevent our adopting fuch an opinion. That he
had no fettled plan to proceed upon, we can eafily fuppofe.
He followed entirely the impulfe of his genius: when fublime
ideas rofe on his imagination, he gave way to his feelings;
when ludicrous ones offered, he thought it by no means neceffary to reject them. To readers who prefer variety, this may
be no unpleafing circumftance; but he would not have funk,
in our opinion, had he proceeded in a more uniform manner;
at leaft thrown the laughable, for we fhould be forry to have loft
it entirely, into an underplot, and kept it diftinct from the
ferious.——The poem itfelf may not be unaptly compared to a
mine of gold, which, though fometimes mingled with drofs,
contains a vein of the richeft ore, that will amply repay the
labour of the fearcher. The extracts we have given are fufficient proofs of the tranflator's abilities, and the explanatory
notes he has fubjoined are fenfible and judicious.

Obfervations on the Structure and Functions of the Nervous Syftem.
(Concluded, from p. 168.)

THE nerves, in their progrefs to different parts, which are
animated, and, in fome degree, fupported by them,
have been found to communicate with each other. The fibres
are mixed in different proportions, as their union is more or
lefs complete; but in the brain only is the communication
general and confiderable. On this account it has been
called the common fenforium of the body; and the various
intellectual faculties depend probably on the fize, and the
freedom with which the motions are propagated through it.
But it is not only on cafual communications of nerves,
either in the fame or different directions, nor on the more general, but diftant union in this organ, that the valuable purpofes, mentioned in our laft article, depend: there are alfo
bodies, called ganglia, in different parts of the nervous fyftem, where the different fibres are more generally intermixed,
than in the tranfitory decuffations. Our author has defcribed
their ftructure, and delineated it, though not with elegance,
at leaft with diftinctnefs. The fixth pair, the portio dura of
the feventh, the eighth and the ninth pairs, though fuppofed
without ganglia, have been found to fend filaments to the

7

ganglia of the great fympathetic nerves ; and indeed it may be obferved in general, that the more important nerves are mixed with others, and their office is feldom expofed to the chance of accidents or difeafes, which may happen to a fingle one. The obvious confequence of this diftribution is indiftinct fenfation, refpecting the fource of pain, or the part affected ; the other confequences drawn by our author we fhall infert from the work itfelf.

‘ From thefe feveral facts I apprehend we may draw the following conclufions.

‘ Firft, Several branches of the nerves, which enter a ganglion, run upon its furface, feparating from each other, and joining again, fo as to form new combinations of threads at the other end of the ganglion.

‘ Secondly, When we cut a ganglion, we are fo far from finding that the courfe of the nerves is interrupted within it, or that it is a fubftance totally different in its nature from the nerves that enter it, that we are able to trace, in every part of the ganglion, nerves diftinguifhable by fuch folds or joints as are feen in them in all other places.

‘ Thirdly, In the fubftance of the ganglion, we fee nervous cords leading from any one nerve, connected to the ganglion, to the greater number of, if not to all, the other nerves connected with it, from which we may conclude, that various other combinations of the nervous threads take place within it.

‘ Fourthly, It appears very difficult, in many inftances, to diftinguifh all the nerves which enter a ganglion, from thofe which are fent off from it. And, of courfe, it is difficult or impoffible to determine all the fources from which any branch fent off from the ganglion is derived. For example, although the nerves at the upper end of a thoracic ganglion of the great fympathetic nerve are compofed chiefly of defcending branches, and, in like manner, the two nerves which tie it to the proper dorfal nerve, are chiefly derived from the dorfal, yet there feem to be afcending branches from the nerves below, and others, fent outwards, from the ganglion, to the proper dorfal nerve, and, probably, the fplanchnic nerves receive threads from all thefe fources.

‘ Fifthly, The nerves which iffue from ganglia feem, as authors have alledged, to be more bulky than the nerves we may fuppofe to enter the ganglia ; yet I have not been able to difcover that the coats of the nerves going out were thicker, or different from the coats of the nerves going into the ganglia : hence there is juft reafon to fuppofe, that nervous matter is furnifhed by the ganglia.

‘ Sixthly, To ftrengthen the fuppofition that the ganglia are to be confidered as fources of nervous matter and energy, I would obferve,

‘ That

' That the yellowish or brownish matter of ganglia has numerous vessels conveying red blood, as in the cortical substance of the brain, dispersed upon it: that its colour, especially in man, very much resembles that of the cortical substance of the brain : that in several children, in whom the brain had either been originally imperfect, or compressed by accident, its colour and consistence still more closely resembled that of a ganglion. As to the greater hardness of the ganglia than of the cortical substance, which to Dr. Meckel has appeared to afford sufficient reason for denying that they serve for secretion, that, I apprehend, will evidently appear necessary to defend them from external violence, or the pressure of the muscles and other organs.

' To which I would add an observation on the first pair, or olfactory nerves, which seems to carry with it considerable weight, to wit, that, in man, the trunk of the olfactory nerve has, adhering to its end, a cineritious bulb, situated within the cranium, and which is evidently of the same texture with the cortical matter of the brain.   Now, in fish, I have found, that the olfactory nerve has no such bulb within the cranium ; but when we trace that nerve forward towards the nose, which is, in them, at a great distance from the cranium, we find a ganglion near the nose, which supplies the place of this bulb, and from which more nerves come out than enter in.

' Seventhly, We shall more readily receive the opinion that the ganglia are additional sources of nervous energy, if we are persuaded, from what has been before observed, that every nerve is, in its course, covered with cineritious matter, from which energy is added to it.

' Eighthly, When we compare a lymphatic conglobate gland with a ganglion, we remark a striking resemblance.   The lymphatic vessels form a net-work on the surface of these glands, in which we can readily trace their whole course.   Other lymphatics enter into the substance of the gland, which, in its number of blood-vessels, its colour, and consistence, very much resembles a ganglion : thus, till we trace the splanchnic nerves into the semilunar ganglia, we are apt to mistake them for conglobate glands.   Yet no person, who understands the subject, can doubt, that, in the conglobate glands, the arteries make a secretion of matter, which is added to the lymph, although the nature of that matter has not yet been fully ascertained by experiment.'

In the next chapter the author treats of the sphæroidical bodies, in different parts of the nervous system of some fishes. (the genus, Gadus, Lin.)   They resemble, in some measure, an egg; for they possess the albumen, but instead of the yolk, there is a serpentine white body, which our author suspects to be cretaceous.   Their use is not known : they are, probably, not ganglia, because they are partially confined to a few species.

Dr.

Dr. Monro then mentions feveral nerves, which have not been properly defcribed by authors. They are chiefly thofe of the eye, the ear, the nofe, the teeth, and the larynx. He defcribes a fmall, but conftant nerve, fent to the ligament of the wrift. The plates, which reprefent them, and which are neceffary to the explanation, are diftinct, and feemingly accurate. As the larynx receives a pair of nerves from above, as well as the recurrent nerves, the voice is not loft, though the latter are cut through, or deftroyed. When the experiment was tried on a dog, the tone of his voice was altered, and it became weaker; but it was afterwards in a great degree recovered.

Our author next defcribes the appearance of the nerves, when viewed through a microfcope. He preferred the compound reflecting one, which increafed the diameter of objects 146, or their furface 21,316 times. It will be obvious, that a glafs of this kind is liable to mifreprefent; and, in fact, each nerve feemed convoluted and ferpentine. Though this may really have been the ftructure of nerves, yet it was found that almoft every folid body put on the fame appearance, particularly melted wax when cooling, folutions of falts when fhooting, &c. It was however plain, from various reafons, that they were optical deceptions, and we are furprifed that the learned author could for a moment hefitate on the fubject. In profeffor Robifon's opinion, they arofe ‘ partly from the unavoidable aberration of light in the microfcope, and partly from the irregular difperfion of it from bodies, whofe inequalities are neither incomparably greater, nor incomparably fmaller, than the diftance, at which light is acted on by bodies.’ We have obferved, that our author has delineated thefe deceptions; but has partly compenfated for this ufelefs addition, by his remark on a probably fimilar deception of Mr. Hewfon; though it fhould be obferved, that *be* ufed only a fingle lens. We fhall tranfcribe the paffage.

‘ In material anatomical points, I fufpect that this deception, produced by the microfcope, has mifled fome authors, particularly the late Mr. Hewfon and Mr. Falconer. In Mr. Falconer's Experimental Inquiries, plate iv. fig. 4. cells are delineated, fuch as are faid to be obferved in the lymphatic glands, which cells will, I apprehend, be found to exift in the microfcope only, this figure being merely an imperfect reprefentation of the deception produced by that inftrument.

‘ The fize and fhape of cells in the fpleen, we are told by Mr. Falconer, fo nearly refemble thofe we have before defcribed in the lymphatic glands, that a tolerably accurate idea of them may be obtained, by referring to the above mentioned plate.

‘ I would

' I would here repeat my obfervation made on the fuppofed
cells of the lymphatic glands, adding to it, as a decifive proof
that a miftake was committed by thefe authors, either in fact,
or in theory, about the fpleen, that the diameter of thefe cells
reprefented, is not larger than the fixtieth part of an inch,
when viewed through a lens of one-fiftieth of an inch focus, fo
that their real diameter fhould not exceed the 24,000th part of
an inch, yet the red particles, the diameter of one of which is
faid by Mr. Hewfon to be almoft equal to the 1-2000th part of
an inch, are by them fuppofed to be contained and completed
within thefe cells.

' Nay, in plate iv. fig. 2. the veficles of the red particles of
the blood, viewed though a lens of 1-23d of an inch focus, are
delineated nearly double the diameter of the cells of the fpleen,
though viewed by a lens 1-50th of an inch focus, reprefented
in fig. 4; fo that one veficle of the blood is reprefented by Mr.
Falconer himfelf above fixty times the fize of one of the cells
of the fpleen, within which, he teaches, it was contained and
formed.'

On the whole, we may be allowed to fuggeft, that an ample
field is ftill open for a dexterous microfcopical obferver.   Dr.
Monro acknowledges, that the nature of the energy of the
nerves is ftill uncertain ; fo that we fhall not follow him on
this very obfcure and ufelefs fubject.   The nerves, in their
courfe, if not attended by the dura mater, are at leaft covered
by a membrane equally capable of refifting preffure, or guarding the nerve againft injury.   The vafcular pia mater is conftantly obferved, and, in their courfe, we frequently find cineritious matter.   The uniform appearance of veffels, both in
the brain, and in every part of its appendages, furnifh the
moft powerful arguments for thofe who think the nervous fluid
is feparated by it from the blood.   But the hypothefis is gra-
tuitous, fince the veffels may ferve other important purpofes.
Their fullnefs certainly contributes to increafe the energy of
the nerves, though there is little fufpicion that this peculiar
fenfibility is the confequence of an increafed fecretion, for it
is the effect of a partial, as well as of a general fullnefs.   We
can fee clearly that the veffels fupply the vifcid fluid which
furrounds them, and which affifts their operations ; fince paralytic nerves have been found dry and fhrivelled.   Their
other effects we are not able to explain, and fcarcely to conjecture.

That the nerves are the media, by which we feel and act, is
certain ; but it is by no means clear that they perform any
other office.   They have been fuppofed to be the organs of
nutrition, and this opinion is examined in the fucceeding
chapter.

The

The anfwers, which are given by our author to the arguments of the oppofite fect are, fhortly, that the brain probably does not exift before the heart ; but that, from reafon and obfervation, every part of the body feems coeval. 2dly, That the fhrinking of palfied limbs is very inconfiderable, and fcarcely more than can be accounted for, from their inactivity. 3dly, That the proofs of the glandular ftructure of the brain, with its attendant ducts or nerves, are not fufficiently eftablifhed. On the other hand, by various arguments, and fome obfervations fufficiently fatisfactory, for which we muft refer to the work itfelf, he concludes, that the arteries prepare and directly fecrete the nourifhment in all our organs; and that the nerves do not contain nor conduct the nourifhment, but, by enabling the arteries to act properly, contribute indirectly to nutrition.

We muft be allowed to obferve, that this is, on the whole, an incomplete view of the queftion. It is probably correct, in the extent here mentioned ; but if we reflect on the various matter depofited, the probability of a glandular apparatus, and the effects of the nervous influence on the various fecretions, we may allow a larger fcope to the operations of the nerves. There is however another circumftance, which was firft attended to in this queftion by the vifionary, but eloquent and attentive Buffon,——that is, the power which determines the appofition of new matter, to affume the peculiar form of the animal. This ' moule interieure,' as it is called by the French naturalift, muft, in a great degree, depend on the original ftamina, which are probably entirely nervous. But the fubject is, in general, fo obfcure, that we may be excufed from enlarging on it. We may probably receive fome elucidation from the labours of Dr. Hamilton, Profeffor of Midwifery in Edinburgh, who has formed, we are told, an elegant fyftem on this foundation. The opinions of Mr. Bonnet are probably known to the greater part of our readers.

Dr. Monro next confiders the termination of nerves in mufcular organs. It is well known that they have been lately fuppofed to be the continuation of nerves only, and, by Dr. Cullen, called the moving extremities of nerves. Our author oppofes this opinion ; but his arguments are by no means conclufive, fince mufcles are evidently bodies of a very peculiar ftructure and organization, whofe mafs is compofed of many blood-veffels, much cellular fubftance, and comparatively few fibres. On this account they can admit of no comparifon with the nerves, either in their appearance, bulk, feeming ftrength, or peculiar properties. Their bulk, compared with the attendant nerve, is fufficiently accounted for ; nor can the mufcle be expected to shrink considerably, though its principal nerve be divided, while the blood-vessels remain unhurt.

The vis insita and vis nervea, as distinguished by Haller, next share the author's attention. He concludes, from various experiments, that they are increased and diminished by the same means, and therefore are probably the same. Indeed the subject would not admit of a moment's doubt, if it were accurately stated. The power of the muscle itself is certainly the same as that of its leading nerve; but, if a power exists in the muscle, independent of the nerve, it must be understood to be that which results from its own organization, distinct from the power it receives from the act of the brain, which we term volition. The one is a necessary consequence of life, while any portion of it remains; the other may be influenced, impeded, or prevented, by different accidents.

The Doctor proceeds to consider the manner and causes of the actions of the muscles, and, as usual, divides them into voluntary and spontaneous. In some of the latter he observes, that we are conscious of a stimulus; and it is probable if, for stimulus, we substitute the terms uneasiness or anxiety, that all our involuntary motions were primarily attended by a similar sensation. He objects, with reason, against the opinion of those who think these motions arise from sympathy, in consequence of any communications of nerves in their course, or in the several ganglia, as well as against the sentiments of others, who suppose that the mind, intimately acquainted with the texture of the body, reasons on, and consequently performs the several actions. There is still another sect, to which Dr. Whytt is referred, who think that the mind, though it be not acquainted with the texture, acts *necessarily* from the several impressions. The opinion is certainly intricate; but our author opposes it as almost unintelligible, or contradictory. Dr. Monro's conclusion may be styled religious, rather than philosophical; but in a state so uncertain, where the ground constantly eludes either a firm or a cautious step, the most intelligent philosopher will be distinguished by a rational scepticism, or an awful reverence, and conclude with our author, that

' When we throw into the scale the various effects of what has been commonly called the instinct of animals, does it not appear, that the most just, as well as most becoming conclusion we can draw, is, that the power which created all things, which gave life to animals, and motion to the heavenly bodies, continues to act upon, and to maintain all, by the unceasing influence of a living principle pervading the universe, the nature of which our faculties are incapable of duly comprehending.'

We

We have already said, that the numerous plates of this volume, frequently on subjects which awaken curiosity, though they may not improve the judgment, are seldom elegant, and sometimes not clear. Those whose expectations were not raised so high, will probably not suffer equal disappointment. We have mentioned some of the most important ones, in the progress of this article, and have assigned them, in our opinion, their true character. The enumeration only of the others would exceed our limits.

The text, in general, evinces the author's diligence and attention, in the pursuit of anatomical knowlege. It contains, frequently, important information; and its application to practice seems to be inculcated with peculiar anxiety. Though Dr. Monro confines his observations to those parts which former physiologists have neglected or mistaken, yet the reader will sometimes suspect that the author has been anticipated. In fact, his situation as a public professor, and his desire of promoting the progress of science, has induced him to explain what others might have selfishly concealed; and the publications of his pupils, as well as his own lectures, have already communicated some of the experiments and observations. But this circumstance rather adds to than detracts from his merit; and we must wish that, with equal knowlege, every author possessed equal candour. We have freely given our opinion of some disputed passages; and if we have not mentioned the work with the enthusiastic warmth, and zealous admiration, which the fondness of an author might have expected, our excuse must be that which we have so often alleged, the necessity of giving an impartial opinion, equally free from indiscriminate praise, or wanton invective.

Doctrines and Practice of Hippocrates in Surgery and Physic; with occasional Remarks. By Francis Riollay, M. B. 8vo. 5s. in Boards. Cadell.

IT is not easy to write on this subject with candour and propriety; for the human mind seldom knows the medium between blind admiration and contemptuous neglect. Hippocrates deserves neither; for, though he affords us much to wonder at, rather than admire, his works teach us to observe the efforts of nature, with little assistance to enable us to regulate or supersede them. Indeed our author seems to have appreciated them with justice; and, if the balance rather inclines in favour of the object of his commentary, we ought to excuse the slight partiality, while we reflect on his candour and moderation. Dr. Riollay thinks, from the complacency

S 2

with

with which Hippocrates speaks of some of the less important
parts of his works, ' that he himself has not done much towards the investigation of diseases, or the introduction of
essential remedies :' and, ' that through a great deal of uninstructive, unnecessary matter, appear evident marks of extensive knowlege, strong understanding, genius for observation,
an enlarged manner of thinking, and professional candour.'

With this opinion of his author, Dr. Riollay has given an
abstract of his more useful works, with a translation of the first
book of Epidemics, and the cases which relate to it.   He has
omitted the tracts on the Diseases of Women, on Dentition,
and the Nature of Children, &c. as their contents are trifling,
and frequently suspicious.   These are accompanied with critical remarks, generally lively, and frequently acute and sensible.   He thinks, that almost all the opinions of the elder
physicians are to be found in Hippocrates ; and that from
him the student, to whom he chiefly writes, may acquire a
competent knowlege of the ancient systems and practice.   He
indeed allows, in the subsequent pages, that ' the others
contain some useful observations, and the traces of a few steps
towards improvement ;' but that they are ' concealed under a
heap of repetitions.'   We look on this opinion as rather too
partial and confined ; but the author has supported it by a
slight sketch of their several merits, drawn with spirit, if not
always with justice.

To those who are acquainted with the writings of Le Clerc,
the present work may appear superfluous.   We shall therefore insert our author's own explanation of their difference.

' Should any body think that, after the sensible account this
gentleman (Mr. Le Clerc) has given of our founder's doctrines,
there was no great occasion for this ; I will answer ingenuously,
that if this reflection should occur after reading both, I have
nothing to say for my justification : but that, if it arises only
from an averseness to perusing new publications on the same
subject, the two plans are not the same.   The main object of
his, as an historian, was to represent, in a general manner, the
state of physic in the time of Hippocrates.   The main object of
mine is to enquire, by entering into greater particulars, how
far a study of his writings is useful at present ; and, at the same
time, by freeing them, in a great measure, from the unnecessary
minuteness, frequent obscurities, contradictory passages, endless
repetitions, and confused manner with which their worth is mingled and disfigured ; to spare to others a good part of the labour I
once thought myself bound to undergo.   His province was confined to facts ; mine extends to opinions : in one word, to examine
impartially whether the cause is equal to the effect ; or whether
the facts deserve the opinions they have occasioned, is the object

ject of this attempt. The name of Mr. Le Clerc renders it unneceffary to fay, that the hope of equalling his fuccefs is not fo
great as the wifh.'

Dr. Riollay's obfervations, in oppofition to the influence of
critical days, deferve our attention, as we have profeffed a
very different opinion; but they are too long, and the fubject not fufficiently interefting, to induce us to tranfcribe them.
We agree with the commentator, that the difpute is not to be
determined by quotation, or by reafoning, but by obfervation
alone: we may therefore be allowed to repeat, that the
more careful and accurate our own obfervations have been, the
more clearly we have feen falutary changes occur, on the days
commonly called critical. This is the only meaning which,
in thefe climates, we can affign to the term; and this explanation will, we think, obviate a little miftake in our author's
idea of it.

As a fpecimen of his manner, we fhall conclude this article
with his remarks on Hippocrates' Tract on Diet, &c.

' There are undoubtedly many ingenious obfervations in the
three preceding chapters, which, though not always connected
with the fubject, nor always juft, fhew, however, a confiderable knowledge of nature, very comprehenfive views, and a liberal manner of thinking. Thefe writings alone fufficiently
prove, that fo far from having feparated medicine from philofophy, he cultivated both with great diligence. His opinions,
concerning the caufe of the different effects of winds, would not
difgrace a Newton; nor would his ideas of government feem
mifplaced in the writings of Locke. If, in endeavouring to
account for the different genius of nations, he afcribed too much
to the influence of climates; the number of thofe who have
fallen into the fame error, will, perhaps, appear a fufficient excufe: or it will not, at leaft, be denied, that an error which
the illuftrious Montefquieu committed, ought to be overlooked
in Hippocrates. No Hume had then remarked, that the fame
people, living in the fame places, had, at different times, a
quite different character and turn of mind, according to the
nature of their political conftitution. Therefore, inftead of
cenfuring him on this head, we will not hefitate to conjecture,
that had he lived in our days, he would not, like fome
moderns, have filled up a number of fheets on this obfolete
fubject.

' As to the rules which he delivers concerning the diet of
healthy people, though they were all as true as he believed
them, it ftill would be fuperfluous to beftow much time in explaining their ufe, or enforcing their practice. It is not from
ignorance that we commit pernicious exceffes, but from the
ftrength of our paffions, and the weaknefs of our reafon: a
complicated caufe, which perfonal experience alone, not pre-

cepts

cepts, has the power of preponderating. Every body knows the salutary effects of sobriety, regular hours, and moderate exercise ; but a citizen at a banquet, a young woman at a masquerade, and a scholar in his study, equally disdain thoughts of this kind ; till apoplexies, consumption, and the gout, have marked them for an example, unavailing to others. Thus, by a remarkable fatality, we neglect the assistance of the art, when it would be serviceable, and never fail to implore it, when it can have no effect.

' His principles for the dietetic management of the sick are so general and so vague, that the young practitioner must apply somewhere else for proper instructions on this point. His regimen does not seem to have been strict enough in acute fevers, nor is he sufficiently explicit (though prolix enough) in other complaints, to enable us to form a judgment of his practice in this respect. It is not, in my apprehension, an arduous part of our profession to inform oneself of these particulars ; but whoever is desirous of perusing some sensible observations on this subject, made by a celebrated admirer of Hippocrates, may, with advantage, consult the works of Dr. De Haen.

' A French author, speaking of his treatise on Air, Waters, and Places, has the following words: " 'Tis a master-piece of the art which contains, I will not say the foundation of physic, but a degree of perfection, almost equal to that of our times." If, instead of attributing to the power of aspects, many effects and accidents little subjected to their influence, Hippocrates had, like Dr. Hales and Dr. Priestley, ascertained the properties of air, by a numberless series of ingenious experiments : if, instead of asserting at random, that rain water, though the purest of all, putrifies sooner than any ; that snow-water is the very worst sort, &c. &c. he had, like Mr. Marggraf, and the illustrious Dr. Heberden, or the ingenious Dr. Percival, found out the sameness of these two kinds, constated their superior purity, and instructed the public on a number of interesting particulars, I wonder what eulogic expressions Mr. Diderot would then have employed ! I believe I shall have occasion to mention again this declamatory gentleman, and the honour he does our art, by modestly erecting himself judge of its founder's merit, without having ever learned its first rudiments ; therefore will defer, to another opportunity, the pleasure of entertaining any reader with more samples of his judicious eloquence.'

Torberni Bergman Chemiæ Prof. &c. Sciagraphia Regni Mineralis, secundum principia proxima digesti. 8vo. 3s. Murray.

THE progress of science is considerably impeded, while its current is restrained, or directed in partial channels ; for the philosopher, who contemplates one spot, though rich and fertile, is not able to comprehend, with accuracy, the whole region,

region, and probably labours to produce what the attentions of others have already effected. We therefore confefs our obligation to the editor of this little tract, for conveying to us that knowlege, which we could not otherwife have eafily acquired. Though fmall in bulk, it is rich in information ; but it is only in our power to afford a little profpect of the contents : the inquifitive chemift will eafily be enabled to obtain a more extenfive view.

Though naturalifts long contended concerning the proper method of claffing minerals, yet it was at laft determined, that they could only be, with propriety, arranged from their chemical properties. Indeed thofe who obftinately adhered to the ufual mode of claffing, from their external appearance, tacitly confeffed the fuperiority of the other method, by purfuing it when the chemical properties were commonly known, or eafily inveftigated ; and feemed to acknowlege, that their plan was principally owing to their imperfect knowlege of the nature of the feveral minerals. The chemical naturalifts do not, on the other hand, entirely neglect external appearances. They attend to them with care, as they may fuggeft the proper experiments, which will ultimately determine the place of the object in their fyftem ; and the varieties are ftill allowed to depend entirely on the more obvious properties. This is a fhort, but pretty accurate ftate, of the conduct of different mineralogifts : the firft who purfued the chemical plan with more accuracy, and to a greater extent, was Cronftedt, whofe work on that fubject is ftill highly valuable ; though, as our author obferves, the improving ftate of mineralogy, in which, we may add, the Swedes have chiefly diftinguifhed themfelves, has enabled us to obferve feveral blemifhes in that fyftem. Even the works of the celebrated Pott, fays Mr. Bergman, have added little to our knowlege of the principles of bodies ; and he probably wifhed rather to confufe than to enlighten the chemift, fince his chief aim was to difcover the porcelain, which has fince been manufactured at Drefden with great applaufe : and he was permitted only to publifh fome of his experiments, on the exprefs condition, that they fhould not enable other chemifts to rival this beautiful fabric.

Our prefent author, in this ' fhadow,' conftantly refers to the work of Mr. Cronftedt, which he in many places corrects. His introduction gives a fhort account of the different methods of purfuing mineralogy, and of the opinions which have guided him in the prefent attempt.

In this part he has rather yielded to cuftom, than determined from reafon ; but we have frequently obferved, that the con-

S 4 fufion,

fufion, which arifes from an oppofite conduct, would be more detrimental to fcience than even flight errors.

The foffil kingdom is divided, by our author, into falts, earths, bitumens, and metals. Of thefe, with their feveral *chemical* combinations, he gives a concife, but a very exact and comprehenfive defcription. The *mechanical* union of thefe feveral bodies are, he obferves, fcarcely the object of this fketch ; but as it is fometimes of fervice in a phyfical as well as an œconomical view, to be acquainted with them, he has added two appendices. To thofe who are in poffeffion of our author's Opufcules, this work will not convey much additional information, though there are feveral analyfes, which have not yet been publifhed : thofe who have not been able to procure them, will find many valuable obfervations, extracted from that work, in this little tract. Our attention was in fome degree attracted by two peculiar minerals, arfenic and black lead. Thefe fubftances acquire a metallic form, as ufual, by the addition of phlogifton ; but, when dephlogifticated, feem only to poffefs the properties of an acid. It has been fuppofed that other metals alfo contain an acid ; though, from the obftinate adherence of the phlogifton, chemifts have never been able entirely to feparate it. But the acid of thefe two minerals feems to be more diftinct, and to be encumbered with little, if any, earth. The black lead, in its acid ftate, ftill retains fome portion of phlogifton ; for it poffeffes both an acid and a metallic tafte ; is capable of tinging both borax and the microcofmic falt ; of being decompofed by a phlogifticated alkali ; has a concrete form, and a confiderable fpecific gravity. Befides, we are told, that it has been actually reduced by Mr. Hielm ; but the regulus has not yet been particularly examined.

Mr. Bergman informs us, that the acid of phofphorus, which occurs in the animal kingdom, is *more plentiful* in the *vegetable,* and very rare in the foffil. This is very different from the ufual opinions ; but the limits of his tract does not permit him to explain it. We find the fedative falt has been found diftinct from its alkali, in a lake near Siena, in Tufcany.

We fhall beg leave to extract, as a fubject not generally known, our author's account of the terra ponderofa, commonly found united to the vitriolic acid, and then called fpathum ponderofum ; by Cronftedt, marmor metallicum.

‘ Ut hæc, quantum fieri poteft, pura obtineatur, fpathum, quod vulgo ponderofum audit, in fubtilem comminuatur pulverem, qui cum alkali fixo et pulvere carbonum in proportione anatica commixtus in crucibulo claufo per horulam igniatur. Maffæ pulveratæ adfundatur acidum nitrofum vel muriaticum dilutum,

dilutum, donec omnis ceſſat effervefcentia et liquor acidus ma-
net, qui dein addito alkali fixo aërato, demittit terram ponder-
ofam aëratam. Si vel acidis vel fali alkalino quidquam ineſt
acidi vitriolici, mox ſpathum regeneratur ponderofum. Quod
in hac operatione remanet acido intactum eſt ſpathum nondum
decompofitum, operationis repetitione divellendum, ſed quæ
tum obtinetur terra martiali et interdum argillaceo vaſis conta-
minata reperitur, præſtat igitur qua puritatem primæ operationis foboles.

' Terra ponderofa aërata gravitate ſpecifica gaudet 3, 773,
in centenario continens aquæ circiter 28, acidi aërei 7 et terræ
puræ 65. Acida cum effervefcentia illam adgrediuntur : vitri-
olicum generat ſpathum ponderofum, aqua non folubile, nitrofum et muriaticum connubia præbent, quæ in cryſtallos ægre
folubiles facile rediguntur, fed hæc terra acetata deliquefcit.
Igne vix fluit, fi omni caret inquinamento acido vel alcalino,
fed ponderis $\frac{1}{18}\frac{1}{5}$ amittit. Mediante materia caloris adfixa 900
partes aquæ unam folvunt; quæ dein fub forma cremoris, in
acidis effervefcentis, fecernitur, fi aëri atmofphærico aditus
patet. Uſtam acida fine effervefcentia, fed cum æſtu fufcipi-
unt, tardius tamen, quam aëratam. Uſta quoque e fale am-
moniaco alkali volatile expellit caufticum et cum fulphure he-
par conficit, cujus tamen folutio aquofa acido nitrofo vel muria-
tico non nifi imperfecte decomponitur ob infignem attractionem
terram inter et acidum in fulphure, cujus ope etiam alkali ve-
getabili hoc acidum eripitur.

' Hifce proprietatibus cum illis comparatis quæ mox de calce
memorabuntur tam convenientia, quam difcrepantia facile elu-
cet.'

The ruby, fapphire, topaz, and emerald, are faid to confift of clay, with rather lefs than half their quantity of flint,
and a little mild lime-ſtone, coloured by iron. The diamond
is feparated from them, and claſſed with the bitumens; and,
though this mode of arrangement feems unnatural, yet our author's reaſons for it are very fatisfactory. We fhall infert
them.

' Primo forfan intuitu mihi vitio vertetur, quod a gemmis
principem fegregem et heic inferem, at fingulis rite penfitatis,
magis convenientem locum me ignorare fateor. Nemo hacte-
nus via humida decomponere valuit, et igni expofitus in vafe
aperto totus confumitur cum nimbo vel flammula, ambitum
lambente. Hæc deflagratio quamvis lenta, cum inflammabili-
bus tamen diſtinctam evincit adfinitatem. Præterea in foco
vitri cauſtici fuliginis exhibet veſtigia. Nova experimenta, fi
in poſterum meliora docent, errorem lubentur corrigam.'

We have thus felected a few intereſting particulars,
to excite rather than to gratify curiofity : the work itſelf
will fully repay the attention of a very diligent and careful
examination.

examination. We could eafily have extended our article by extracts, but might still have left fomething ufeful, unlefs we had tranfcribed the whole.

An Essay on the Ufefulnefs of Chemiftry, and its Application to the various Occafions of Life. Tranflated from the Original of Sir Torbern Bergman. 8vo. 2s. 6d. Murray.

THIS entertaining and popular effay is a proper companion for the Sciagraphia of the fame author; for, though fome parts of it have been already publifhed in that work, there are others which were not the objects of a mineralogift. The application of chemiftry to the different arts, which have contributed either to the pleafures or the conveniencies of mankind, deferves the attention of thofe who are interefted in the increafe of either. Our author enumerates them, without any anxiety for the credit of his fcience, by unjuft exaggerations; nor have we difcovered any material omiffion. He next defcribes the general properties of the feveral chemical fubftances; and, in this part, he has repeated fome of thofe circumftances which are more fully mentioned in his former work. Air, though found in the earth, was omitted, on account of its chiefly occurring in compofition; and water has never yet made a part of any mineralogical fyftem. The obfervations on thefe fubjects are therefore new, and frequently interefting. His account of the air is fyftematic and ufeful; but fometimes lefs exact, and, in a few inftances, deficient, on account, probably, of his diftance from the fource of more recent difcoveries. We fhall felect, as a fpecimen, his remarks on heat and light, which are connected with his obfervations on air. Though not entirely new, they are diftinguifhed by their fimplicity, and probably by their juftnefs.

' Although pure air, combined with a certain quantity of phlogifton, feems to conftitute the fame fort of noxious fubftance which depraved air is; we have, notwithftanding, reafon to believe, that the matter of heat (that fubftance which is fo indifpenfably neceffary to all living creatures) is no otherwife produced than by the union of pure air with a certain different proportion of phlogifton. That the fame elements, combined in different manners, or in different proportions, may produce different bodies, is already pretty well proved in various inftances.

' It is alfo, at this time, by a multitude of experiments, put out of doubt, that heat confifts merely in an internal motion taking place among the particles of the feveral forts of fubftances that are fufceptible of it. It is, on the contrary, a fubftance *fui generis*, a particular fubtle kind of fluid, which penetrates or pervades all, even the denfeft bodies, and thereby,

according

according to its quantity, produces thofe particular fenfations in animals, which are called cold, warmth, and heat.

'Fire is therefore neither more nor lefs than that ftate of inflammable bodies, in which the greater part of the phlogifton, which enters into their compofition, is torn away by means of the pure air, with great force and violence, from thofe particles with which it was before combined. This, then, is the way in which a great quantity of heat, or what comes to the fame thing, what we call fire, muft neceffarily be produced; as to the flame, it is, properly fpeaking, generated from inflammable air, which, in thefe circumftances, is detached from all inflammable bodies in great quantity, and very readily takes fire.

'As to the light, which in thefe circumftances is alfo always generated, it appears probable, from a variety of experiments and obfervations, that this fubftance is compofed of heat, charged with a certain over-proportion of phlogifton. He who confiders in what different forms water fhows itfelf, when in a liquid ftate, and when in a ftate of vapours, and that owing to no other caufe than the different quantities of heat which it contains, will hardly pronounce it abfolutely incredible, that a different proportion of phlogifton fhould convert heat into light; although he fhould not yet have been informed of the reafons by which that propofition is made out.

'Heat, then, being a fubftance, is, like other fubftances, fubject to the laws of attraction. Accordingly, when it is prefent in bodies in fuch a manner as to form a conftituent part of them, that is, to be in a ftate of chemical combination with the other elements of which they are compofed, the power which it has, in other circumftances, of exciting the fenfation of warmth, is found to be compleatly mafked, as it were, and fufpended, in the fame manner as the characteriftic properties of an acid are by combination with an alkali. Hence it comes, that, upon the decompofition of fuch bodies, a fenfible heat or warmth is produced: the matter of heat, which before was fixt, being now difengaged or fet at liberty, by a more powerful attraction.'

The tranflator feems rather to have aimed at accuracy than elegance; we can with juftice praife the former, and, in the other refpect, he has not been remarkably deficient.

Illuftrations of Maxims and Principles of Education, in the fecond Book of Rouffeau's Emile. Small 8vo. 1s. 6d. Dodfley.

ROmantic and vifionary as the fyftem of education, which we have received from Rouffeau, may appear, it certainly abounds with falutary maxims as well as ufeful leffons; and it difcovers an intimate acquaintance with the heart. Thefe leffons are frequently obfcured by an affectation of paradox,

and

and by visionary refinements: they are sometimes debased by folly and absurdity. It is not worth a moment's attention, whether the present author be anxious to remove a suspected blemish from the works of his favourite, or whether he really found a mother who admired the precepts, while she was alarmed by the character of the preceptor; who discerned, through fancies and speculations, a sound judgment, though incapable of drawing a proper line between the one and the other. Our illustrator steps forward, to obviate either difficulty: he confines himself to the second book, the period of infancy, when the young ideas begin to shoot; and the mind, with its various passions and propensities, to be developed.

The objections which have been made to the man, independent of the author, are opposed in the following manner, by his advocate.

' But you say, the tendency of some parts of his writings to inflame passions, of themselves sufficiently warm, and the authentic dishonour cast on his name by the confessions he has left of the secret transactions of his youth, are objections which you cannot meet, consistent with the delicacy you would cherish in your own mind, and the reputation you would wish to preserve.

' I do not see that you have the slightest concern in those objections, whether justly or unjustly founded. Mr. Rousseau may have delineated a scene in a novel, over which most men would have drawn a veil. He has confessed to the world a series of puerile errors, follies, and vices, in connection with their causes and motives, which most men would have concealed. The only difficulty, or even matter of conversation, on these subjects, is, whether the author was right or wrong, blameable or commendable, in the publication of them? This is a question in which you are not interested in the remotest degree; and, in your place, I would never suffer it to perplex me.

' You are told Rousseau was a bad man: the tendency of his writings is therefore to be suspected; and his principles to be regarded as dangerous and pernicious.

' I do not believe Rousseau was a bad man: but I would not have you enter into a discussion of the subject; for you are not concerned in it. You might even admit the most uncandid and reproachful opinion of him. For you are not to make him your husband, your friend, or to entrust any thing to his heart or his passions. You find lessons, directions, and principles in his works, which approve themselves to your judgment; and therefore you adopt them. His understanding may be of use to you; though his temper may have been a dishonour and a torment to himself.

' Besides, the inference from character to principles, and from the incidents or habits of a man's life to the utility of his productions,

productions, is not candidly or juſtly drawn. It is uſed among the common artifices of defamation ; and very weak minds are impoſed upon by apparent connections, like thoſe of cauſes and effects. But you can certainly have no great difficulties in combating ſuch modes of reaſoning, or in defeating ſuch artifices, if you ſhould think yourſelf obliged to attend to them.

‘ No man ſits down to write any thing beyond trifles, until thoſe paſſions which form the peculiarities of his character have paſſed the meridian, and have determined their orbits. It muſt be on the experience he has had, that he aranges his opinions and principles. If the rules and maxims he recommends are in oppoſition to thoſe on which he has been educated, the irregularity of his life, and the defects of his character, give them weight and authority, inſtead of furniſhing objections to them. For the meaſures purſued in his education having produced a vicious and unhappy diſpoſition, he ſeems to conceive it a duty to warn the public againſt thoſe meaſures, and to adviſe others of different tendencies. The vices and miſeries of his mind, ſo far from diſqualifying him for theſe ſervices, are the circumſtances which entitle him to peculiar attention.

‘ The caſe of Rouſſeau ſeems to be of this kind. Though I am myſelf firmly perſuaded, that if all men were to make confeſſions equally ſincere, we ſhould find Rouſſeau in the favourable minority ; yet he had committed errors of a nature to embitter his recollections ; his paſſions were capriciouſly formed ; and his temper became acrimonious by the effects of diſappointments on a lively and irritable fancy. Theſe circumſtances rendered him unhappy, in ſpite of a vigorous, penetrating, and comprehenſive genius. It was the favourite employment of his leiſure hours (I ſpeak on his own authority) to trace his miſeries to their cauſes : and this is the origin of his hints, directions, and leſſons on education.

‘ To apprehend danger from Rouſſeau, there ſhould be ſome reaſons to ſuppoſe he wiſhed his diſciples to be like himſelf, and ſuch meaſures adopted as had produced his temper and character ; but his utmoſt zeal and eloquence are employed to deter men from thoſe meaſures : and he has conſigned his name to popular reproach and diſhonour, by publiſhing the private follies of his life, to give the greater weight and effect to his admonitions. The faults of Rouſſeau are, therefore, particular reaſons for giving attention to his precepts and directions on education.’

Theſe ſenſible remarks will probably, in ſome degree, eſtabliſh the character of Rouſſeau’s defender ; and, in every part of this little volume, he appears to be equally candid and intelligent.

The ruling idea, through the whole of Emile, is certainly what our author repreſents it ; that every ſpecies of care, with reſpect to man, has its ſeaſon ; that a certain time is requiſite

to

to develope or form the faculties of the body and mind; and
that simple sensations are necessary, before the mind can reflect
or reason, before it can have ideas of a moral obligation and
a moral character. This opinion is undoubtedly just; but, if
not wholly theoretical, is, we fear, impracticable in its utmost extent. The treasures of the mind are seldom of its
own acquisition; we must necessarily attain general rules of
conduct from instruction, from imitation, or from caprice:
in short, while the mind is still a blank, there is no source to
which it will not stoop for materials. This can scarcely be
an objection to Rousseau, who endeavours to strengthen it,
and to prevent the access of every image, except of its own
acquiring; but, on that account, he wishes that the mind
should continue a blank, till this office can be performed to
advantage. There is, indeed, another and more formidable
objection, which we can only hint at, since to pursue it would
lead us into dangerous and doubtful paths. Without following those gloomy moralists, who think that we are by nature
incapable of any good, there is some reason to suppose, that
there is an original diversity of mind, not only with respect to
strength and weakness, but to goodness and depravity. We
are, probably, in no situation, that rasa tabula which has been
supposed rather from imagination than observation: the soul is
no more without passions and properties, frequently amiable,
though sometimes different, than the body is without its peculiar beauty or deformities. On his own principle however he
opposes a too early pursuit of moral or scientific acquirements,
for which he has been frequently condemned. It would be
too much to transcribe the passages of the author, or the arguments of his opponents; we shall only insert a few of the
observations here alleged in his defence. They will be a
sufficient specimen of his advocate's abilities, and probably
recommend the present work to the attention of those who are
employed in the important business of education.

' It is true, that nothing is ever lost in the processes of nature; and therefore, all plans which imply waste and loss of
time are unnatural, and unjustifiable. Rousseau seems to have
been fully convinced of this truth as any of those persons who
have blamed him. And in the present passage he certainly
does not mean that time should actually be lost, and children
neglected; for he immediately subjoins, that " the interval
from the birth of a child to the age of twelve, is the most dangerous of his life." The obscurity of his general maxim, and
consequently the merit of the paradox which it forms, is owing
to an inaccurate use of the word education, through the whole
treatise. The design of the work is to recommend a prudent,
and, on the whole, an admirable species of attention to children;

dren ; a mode of affifting the developement of their faculties, which he calls education. In order to heighten the advantages of his fyftem, he throws the cuftoms and meafures in common practice into a fhade ; and yet he denominates them education. When he is feducing your judgment, it is in behalf of education ; and when he is ridiculing your folly, it is for the employment it finds in education. Thefe double and oppofite meanings, in the application of the fame term, create a perplexity which might have a good effect in comedy, or fatire ; but is diftreffing, and perhaps contributes more than any thing to defeat the great purpofes of the author, in an elementary and important work.

' I have no difficulty however in affirming, that nothing could have been further from Rouffeau's intention, than what is commonly afcribed to him—a defire that the time between the birth of a child and the age of twelve might be funk, loft, or fpent at random. He fays forcibly, it had better be loft than mifemployed ; and his directions to thofe who entertain the common notions of education are always to this effect : "Do not gain this time in your manner, but rather lofe it. Your meafures are fo injurious to the future happinefs of your children, that they will be benefited by the lofs ; for ignorance is preferable to error and the moft aukward fimplicity, than habits of artifice, fervility, and vice."

' To give the objection under confideration its full force, I will tranflate the following paffage, which, from the vague and perverfe ufe of words, is, I think, the moft exceptionable in the whole work. "The firft education fhould therefore be purely negative ; it confifts not in teaching virtue and truth, but in guarding the heart from vice, and the mind (l'efprit) from error. If you could abftain from doing any thing, and would fuffer nothing to be done ; if you could lead your pupil healthy and robuft to the age of twelve, without having diftinguifhed his right hand from his left, at your firft leffons the eyes of his underftanding would open to reafon. Without prejudice, and without habit, he would have nothing in him to deftroy the effect of your cares. He would, very foon, become in your hands the wifeft of men ; and in commencing by doing nothing, you would produce a prodigy of education."

' There is not a fentence of this paragraph which he does not obfcure by equivocal terms. His general principle is, that children not having judgment, reafon, or any reflective faculty, fhould not have maxims and rules which require reflection forced on their memories. He therefore means their education fhould be negative, as far as verbal leffons are concerned. As he always diftinguifhes between the mind (l'efprit) and the foul (l'ame) he is too unguarded in affirming that, by his own method ; by preferving the child's conftitution and health in a ftate to receive juft impreffions, and to form accurate, though fimple ideas, we do not teach the rudiments of truth and virtue.

tue. But the moſt ſingular and offenſive conceit is, that if the child be preſerved from mental empiriciſm ; in ſo much ignorance as not to diſtinguiſh his right hand from his left ; his underſtanding, like ſome periodical planet, when the hand of time points to twelve on the circle of life, will riſe in full glory, and exhibit a prodigy. This, unqueſtionably, is the language of romance ; but it may, in a great meaſure, be rendered into that of truth and common life. Rouſſeau wiſhes, and I think with reaſon, that the animal or ſenſitive powers of children ſhould be firſt exerciſed and perfected in their ſimple operations. The proceſſes he recommends would give his pupil a greater command of his limbs (of his hand for inſtance) than thoſe commonly obſerved ; but never having been required to compare or reaſon on the relation of objects to each other, he might without injury be literally ignorant of ſuch relative denominations as right and left. This, however, being only poſſible, the author's phraſe alarms, or is treated with ridicule. He is deemed much more inexcuſable in the poetic licence of fixing on the preciſe period of twelve ; and giving an inſtantaneous and miraculous birth to the underſtanding at that period. The ſtock of ſimple ideas, and that maturity of ſenſitive faculties which firſt gave birth and exerciſe to the underſtanding and judgment, are obtained at very different periods in different conſtitutions. However, if it be near the age of twelve, Rouſſeau may plead the example of the Pſalmiſt, who ſays, " the days of man are three ſcore years and ten," though great multitudes drop on each ſide of that period. Whether, in particular inſtances, the faculties are in a condition to give the firſt employment to reaſon, at the age of five, or twelve, or twenty, the general doctrine of Rouſſeau is true, that until they arrive at that period, all leſſons by maxims, whether ſcientific or moral, will not be juſtly apprehended, will be miſunderſtood, and form prejudices and errors which may never be removed.'

Lectures on Rhetoric and Belles Lettres. By *Hugh Blair,* D. D.
(*Concluded, from p.* 117.)

THIS ingenious writer has analyſed ſome of the compoſitions of Atterbury, Swift, and Addiſon ; and his obſervations on their inelegant and ungrammatical expreſſions will be uſeful to every one, who wiſhes to write the Engliſh language with purity and preciſion. We hope therefore he will excuſe us, if we take the liberty to point out SOME of the inaccuracies, which we have obſerved in theſe Lectures.

We ſhall not always attempt to correct his expreſſions, as it may frequently be neceſſary to alter the ſtructure of the ſentence ; and, in ſome caſes, the beſt emendation is not to ſubſtitute one word for another, but to omit the whole period, or at leaſt the moſt exceptionable part of it.

' TERMS

' TERMS and PHRASES, which border too much on VULGAR and COLLOQUIAL language, to be proper for being employed in a polished composition.' pag. 427.

Bating these two slight inaccuracies. 458. *Bating* this expreffion, there is nothing that can be subject to the least reprehenfion. 480. ii. 294. 437.——*Excepting* is preferable to *bating* in these paffages.

Neither are the abilities of any human writer sufficient to supply a continued *run* of unmixed sublime conceptions. 76.——a continued *series*.

In this, and other inftances, a more attentive review may probably suggeft better emendations than those, which we fhall occafionally fubjoin.

This general idea muft direct the *run* of our compofition. 265.——the *tenor* of our compofition; or, the *modulation* of our periods.

Such attentions as these are requifite in the common *run* of ftyle. 285.——requifite in *compofition*.

A fentiment, which is expreffed in a period clearly, neatly, and happily arranged, makes always a ftronger impreffion on the mind, than one that is *any how* feeble or embarraffed. 245.——in *any respect* feeble.

If these be *any how* connected. 333.

The French language furpaffes ours, *by far,* in expreffing the nicer fhades of character. 174.——*by far* may be omitted.

More inftances of the true language of nature *can* [may] be quoted from Shakefpeare, than from all other tragic poets *put together.* ii. 511.——all other tragic poets *united.*

We are *every now* and *then* interrupted by unnatural thoughts. ii. 523.

Some circumftance *pops out,* which ought to have been omitted. 223.——*appears.*

When, to our furprife, a new MEMBER *pops out* upon us. 490.——*presents itself,* or *appears.*

Agamemnon *pitches upon* Brifeis. ii. 429.——*demands* Brifeis.

All *pitch upon* fome one beauty. 28. I *pitched upon* it for the fubject of this exercife. 495. He *pitched upon* the war of Troy. ii. 408. Some great enterprize, which he *pitches* upon. ii. 409. *Pitch upon* fome moving and interefting ftory. ii. 480.——*Choofe,* or, *felect.*

Eloquence rejoices in the *burfts* of loud applaufe. ii. 35.——rejoices in loud applaufe.

Poetry included then the whole *burft* of the human mind. ii. 322.——the whole *effufion* of the human mind, or all the *productions,* &c.

The refponfe is made by the *burft* of the whole chorus. ii. 390.——by the whole chorus.

It is the *burft* of infpiration. ii. 399.——the *language* of infpiration.

More inſtructive to the *bulk* of hearers. ii. 170. The *bulk* of readers. ii. 287, 347, 356.—The *generality.*

Milton has *chalked out* for himſelf a new road in poetry. ii. 471.

No ſubject *bids fairer* for being favourable to poetry. ii. 337.—*ſeems* to be more favourable. To *bid fair* is a vulgariſm.

What is called the *antepenult.* 178. To reſt either on a long, or on a *penult* long ſyllable. 260, &c.—The word *penult* is an abbreviation, as barbarous as *phyz* and *plenipo.*

AUKWARD PHRASES.

This much may ſuffice to have ſaid concerning witticiſm. 401. *This much* is ſufficient to have ſaid upon the ſubject of beauty. 91. *Before concluding* this lecture. 79. A ſick or *drunk* perſon. 74.

The moſt uſeful art, *of* which men are *poſſeſſed.* 125.—It would be much better, in general, to uſe this verb in the active form: ' which men *poſſeſs.*'

In order to extend *ſome farther* the firſt method. 128. The firſt rude inventors of language would be long *of* arriving at ſuch general terms. 151. The excuſe can rarely, if ever, be *ſuſtained.* 185. With reſpect to this diſtribution, *ſomewhat* ſingular hath obtained in the ſtructure of language. 145. Which is left *lagging* behind, like a *tail* adjected to the ſentence; *ſomewhat* that, as Mr. Pope deſcribes the Alexandrine line,

' Like a wounded ſnake, drags its ſlow length along.' 223.

I juſt expreſs my thoughts in the ſimpleſt manner *poſſible.* 273.—A conciſe writer compreſſes his thoughts into the feweſt *poſſible* words. 371. Only *before* proceeding to this. 276. It is the ſentiment or paſſion, which lies under the figured expreſſion, that gives it *any* merit. 277.

Make the application of it *be underſtood.* 210. To make his ſubject *be* better *underſtood.* 344.—To *illuſtrate* his ſubject.

He was fonder of *nothing* than of wit and raillery. 397. In his reaſonings, *for moſt* part, he is flimſy and falſe. 400. 451. For *in place of meaning* to ſay, that the Latin ſpoken in Britain was not ſo debaſed as *what* was ſpoken in Gaul and Spain, he means juſt the contrary. 485. In order to make it *be* diſtinctly apprehended. 488. *Before entering* on any of theſe heads. ii. 1. Dionyſius of Halicarnaſſus has given us upon the orations of Iſocrates, *as alſo* upon thoſe of ſome other Greek orators, a full and regular treatiſe. ii. 17. The diſguiſe can *almoſt never* be ſo perfect, *but* it is diſcovered. ii. 55. 330. But *for* the truths of religion, *with* the greater ſimplicity and the leſs mixture of art they are ſet forth, they are likely to prove the more ſucceſsful. ii. 104. Some things, which he may *only ſhortly* touch. ii. 110. The extreme of *overdoing* in accuracy. ii. 118. I would *adviſe it* to be always treated with brevity. ii. 131.

The French writers of ſermons ſtudy neatneſs and elegance in *laying down their heads.* ii. 173.—The author means, *in the diviſion of their ſubjects.*

The

The middle pitch is that which he employs in common conversation, and which he should use *for ordinary* in public discourse. ii. 205.—*For ordinary* is a Scoticism.

He who should tell another that he was very angry, or *very grieved*. ii. 217. Nature must always have done *somewhat*. ii. 228. That *profession* to which he *addicts* himself. ii. 234. It may be fit, therefore, that *before proceeding* farther, I make some observations. ii. 247. When an historian is much *given to dissertation*. ii. 270. Fewer had the means and opportunities of distinguishing themselves *than now*. ii. 255. We *will read* him without pleasure, or most probably we shall soon *give over* to read him at all. ii. 274. They are *much formed* upon the ancients. ii. 283. She *broke into* a smile, *as if* she had *seemed* to say, I will wear you, &c. ii. 351. He must *reckon upon* finding characters. ii. 429.

The best French tragedies make not a *deep enough* impression on the heart. ii. 518.—*do not make a sufficient* impression.

The plays of Plautus and Terence, both of *whom* were *formed upon* the Greek writers. ii. 537.—*The plays, which* were formed.

REDUNDANCIES.—' Sentences, as the author rightly observes, should be cleared of redundant words, and redundant members.' p. 227.

The small stock of words, which men *as yet* possessed. 106. Let us proceed to consider *of* the style of language. 111. The main design of this lecture is to consider *of* the means to be used for improvement in eloquence. ii. 228. To unite *together* copiousness and precision. 203. Going before them, or following *after* them. 281. What goes before, and immediately follows *after*. 293. 415. What goes before may give light to what follows *after*. ii. 169. Inserted into what follows *after*. ii. 262. The more exactly *that* this track is pursued, the more *that* eloquence is properly studied, the more shall we be guarded, &c. ii. 5. Provided always *that* so much unity be preserved. ii. 109. He must always take care, that *any* such allusions be natural and easy. ii. 116. But *for you*, whenever I hear you, I go away displeased with myself. ii. 126. It must needs give pleasure, if *we shall* find the beauty and dignity of the composition adequate to the weight and importance of the matter. ii. 385. The more *that* this unity is rendered sensible to the imagination, the effect will be the better. ii. 413. The nearer *that* a poet can bring the representation to an imitation of nature, the impression will be the more perfect. ii. 516.

Passages, in which things are supposed to be in ONE CLASS, and, at the same time, represented as belonging to ANOTHER.

The relations, which, of all *others*, we have the most frequent occasion to mention. 150. The relations which, of all *others*, is *by far* the most fruitful of tropes. 293. Our past misfortunes afford a circumstance, the most favourable of all *others*, to our future hopes. ii. 63. Sure of acquiring that fame, and even

veneration,

veneration, which is, of all *other* rewards, the greatest incentive to genius. ii. 255.

The SUPERLATIVE degree instead of the COMPARATIVE.

Which of these two, methods is of the *greatest* utility and beauty. 152. Of the two it is the *safest* extreme. 217. When our sentence consists of two members, the *longest* should, generally, be the concluding one. 238. It remains, to this day, in doubt, whether his beauties or his faults be *greatest*. ii. 523.

DOUBLE COMPARATIVES.

Lesser differences. 27. Attend to all the *lesser* and more refined graces. 43. ii.-22. The *lesser* forms of poetry. ii. 335.—*Lesser* is a corruption of *less* ; but the author has innumerable authorities for the use of it.

Adjectives having a SUPERLATIVE signification, improperly used in a COMPARATIVE sense, or compared by *more* and *most*.

The characters of taste, when brought to its *most perfect* state, are reducible to two, delicacy and correctness. 23.—*Most perfect*, though a common, is not an eligible expression ; because *perfect*, being an absolute term, cannot with *strict* propriety be used comparatively. In this passage it would be better to say, its *perfect*, or, its most *improved* state.

Nothing that belongs to human nature is *more universal* than the relish of beauty. 17. The foundation, upon which they rest, is what has been found from experience to please mankind *most universally*. 31. We can conceive no motive, which would *more universally* operate upon men, 102. The vehement manner of speaking by tones and gestures became not *so universal*. 116. Music is known to have been a more extensive art among them, than it is with us ; *more universally* studied. 252. The practice of reading sermons has prevailed *so universally* in England. ii. 43. Nothing has *so* great and *universal* a command over the minds of men as virtue. ii. 230. The reputation of *great* ancient classics being *so* early, *so* lasting, *so universal*, among all the most polished nations. ii. 252. Thuanus has, by attempting to make the history of his own times *too universal*, fallen into the same error. ii. 266.—We may say, more *general*, more *extensive*, &c. but we cannot, with any propriety, say *more universal*.

ADJECTIVES instead of ADVERBS.

We can *much easier* form the conception of a fierce combat between two men, than between a bull and a tiger. 351.—We can *more easily*.

It might be requisite for them to be *exceeding* full. ii. 110.

ANY instead of EITHER.

The verse marches with a more slow and measured pace, than in *any* of the two former cases. ii. 330.

EITHER instead of EACH.

Truth, duty, and interest. But the arguments directed towards *either* of them are generically distinct. ii. 184.—*Either* refers to *two* things only.

The

The diftributive pronoun NEITHER, improperly followed by the poffeffive pronoun in the PLURAL number.

Sight and feeling are, in this refpect, perfectly on a level; *neither* of them can extend beyond *their* own objects. 413.—*its own objects. Neither* relates to two perfons or things, taken feparately.

EACH improperly followed by a verb in the PLURAL number.

Here are feveral different objects, and *each* of them *are* addreffed or fpoken to. 335.—*is* addreffed.

EACH OTHER inftead of ONE ANOTHER.

By what bond could any multitude of men be kept together, *until once*, by the intervention of fpeech, they could communicate their wants and intentions to *each other*. 100. Objects could not be diftinguifhed from *each other*. 156. A great number of governments rivals of *each other*. ii. 11.

ONE ANOTHER inftead of EACH OTHER.

Two men, ignorant of *one another's* language. 102. The clofe relation of any two words to *one another* in meaning. 122. Where two things are compared or contrafted to *one another*. 243. Which two opinions are entirely confiftent with *one another*. 490. The characters of Corneille and Racine are happily contrafted with *one another*. ii. 520.—*Each other*, like the word *bath*, ought only to be ufed when we are fpeaking of two things; *one another*, when we are fpeaking of more than two.

ONE followed by a pronominal adjective in the PLURAL number.

It has been advifed by writers on this fubject [action] to practife before a mirror, where *one* may fee, and judge of *their* own geftures. ii. 222.

THEM BOTH.

The reprefenting *them both* as fubject, at one moment, to the command of God, produces a noble effect. 62. The fingle word 'afcertain' conveys the import of *them both*. 418. Ezekiel, in poetical grace and elegance, is much inferior to *them both*. ii. 403.—*Them both* is an aukward pleonafm.

The RELATIVE not agreeing with its ANTECEDENT.

That ingenious *nation, who have* done fo much honour to modern literature. ii. 284.—*The writers of* that ingenious nation.

Verbs in the PLURAL NUMBER inftead of the SINGULAR.

A great *mafs* of rocks, thrown together by the hand of nature, with wildnefs and confufion, *ftrike* the mind with more grandeur, than if they had been adjufted to *each other* with the moft accurate fymmetry. 52.—The author might have faid, *vaft* rocks thrown together. *Mafs* is not a noun of multitude.

My heart begins to be touched; my gratitude *or* my compaffion *begin* to flow. ii. 192.—*begins* to flow.

The fmart, *or* the fneering manner of telling a ftory, *are* inconfiftent with the hiftorical character. ii. 273. Neither the one,

nor

nor the other, *find* a proper place in history. ii. 280. What the heart *or* the imagination *dictate*. ii. 299. There was much genius in the world before there *were* learning or arts to refine it. 343.—before there *were arts* or learning.

You was instead of you were.

You *was* in distress circumstances; you *was* pushed to the utmost. ii. 185. When you *was* most in earnest. ii. 219.—*You* in English, *vous* in French, and *voi* in Italian, are uniformly and indisputably pronouns of the *plural* number. The use of them, in speaking to one person, is a modern refinement, intimating, that we regard the person we are speaking to, as much as we do a multitude of other people.

The subjunctive mode instead of the indicative.

I must observe, that, although this part of style *merit* attention, and *be* a very proper object of science and rule; although *much* of the beauty of composition *depends* on figurative language; yet we must beware of imagining, that *it* depends *solely*, or even chiefly, upon such language. 277.—That figurative language merits attention, and is a very proper object of science and rule, are positions which do not admit of the least doubt, and therefore should not have been expressed in the subjunctive mode; more especially as the verb *depends*, in the same sentence, and in the same circumstances, is used in the indicative.

We shall be disgusted if he *give* us too much of the servile employments, and low ideas of actual peasants; and if he *makes* his shepherds discourse as if they were courtiers, &c. ii. 338.

It *were* much to be wished, that some such work were undertaken. 201. It *were* to be wished, for the honour of his memory. ii. 301.—' It *were* to be wished' is an absurd phrase. There is no pretence for the use of the subjunctive mode in this case. ' It *is* to be wished' is the proper expression.

Sermons are always the more striking, and commonly the more useful, the more precise and particular the subject of them *be*. ii. 109.—Here is likewise no pretence for the use of the subjunctive mode; and *be*, in the indicative, is obsolete.

Verbs which ought to be in the active, or the passive voice, employed as neuters.

The mist *dissipates*, which seemed formerly to hang over the object. 21.—The mist *is dissipated*, *evaporates*, or, *disappears*.

This manner of writing *obtained* among the Assyrians. 134, 145, 146, 151, 187, &c.—*Obtained* is frequently used as a neuter verb; but *prevailed* is preferable.

This readily *connects* with the flourishing period of a plant. 282. The reader soon *wearies* of this play of fancy. 313. To keep up the reader's attention, and to prevent him from *tiring* of the author. 382.—By *tiring of* the author, the professor means, *being tired* of him. But in this sentence, the expression can only signify the reader's tiring or fatiguing the author.

Such authors as those one never *tires of* reading. 395. Lest the reader should *tire of* what he may consider as petty remarks:

467:

467. Every audience is very ready to *tire*. ii. 60. They begin to *tire*. ib. He will *tire of* it, and forget it. ii. 175.—The verb *tire*, like the word *fatigue*, is generally used in the passive form : as, he *is tired* with reading, or, he begins to *be tired*.

The use of the word APPLIES.

The word ' nature' would have equally *applied* to idea and to soul. 448.—have been equally *applicable*.

The epithet ' stately' *applies*, with more propriety, to ' palaces.' 466. My other observation, which *applies* equally to dean Swift and Mr. Addison. 495. The saying *applies* to the subject now before us. ii. 503.—This expression is a Scoticism, which has been lately introduced into the English language, by some careless writers.

HAD instead of WOULD, attended with some other improper phrases, or a faulty arrangement.

Metaphors, which need this apology of an ' as it were,' *had* generally *be* better omitted. 305. In this case, figures *had* much better *be wanted*. 365. This sentence *had* better *been wanting* altogether. 425. He *had* better *have* omitted the word. 334. It *had* better *have been* expressed by, &c. 436. This member of the sentence *had* much better *have been* omitted. 449. 450. ii. 159. *Had* better *have been* dropped. 450. The parenthesis *had* better, far better, *have been* avoided. 457—By omitting the adverbs, the reader will perceive the gross absurdity of these phrases, *had be wanted*, *had have been* dropped, *had have been* avoided, &c. The author should have said, this sentence *would* have been better omitted, &c.

WILL instead of SHALL.

Without having attended to this, we *will* be at a loss in understanding several passages of the classics. 109. What we conceive clearly, we *will* naturally express with clearness. 402. As this sentence contains several inaccuracies, I *will* be obliged to enter into a minute discussion of its structure and parts. 447. We *will* always be able to give most body to that pitch of voice, to which in conversation we are accustomed. ii. 206, &c.

WILL instead of MAY.

There are few great occasions of public speaking, in which one *will* not derive assistance from cultivated taste, and extensive knowledge. ii. 234.

SHALL instead of SHOULD.

If it *shall* now be required, What are the proper sources of the sublime? 75.

WOULD instead of SHOULD.

The Asiatics at no time relished any thing but what was full of ornament, and splendid in a degree, that we *would* denominate gaudy. 26. There are no two words we *would* more readily take to be synonymous than ' amare' and ' diligere.' 196. ' Tutus' and ' securus' are words which we *would* readily confound. 196. Without a careful attention to the sense, we *would* be naturally led, by the rules of syntax, to refer it to the rising and setting of the sun. 213. We *would* be greatly at a loss, if we could nor borrow assistance from figures. 285. If I should mingle in one discourse arguments for the love of God, and for the love of our neighbour, I *would* offend unpardonably against unity. ii, 109.—If I were to mingle, I *should.*

From whom [Horace] we *would* be led to form a very high idea of the taste and genius of the Augustan age. ii. 258. The heroes glorying, as we *would* now think very indecently, over their fallen enemies. ii. 429.

CAN and COULD instead of MAY and MIGHT.

The difference between them *can* be clearly pointed out. 40. Some trivial, or misjudged circumstances, *can* be overlooked by the reader. 72. If it be of that elevating, solemn, and awful kind, which distinguishes this feeling, we *can* pronounce it sublime. 75. The history of the English language *can*, in this manner, be clearly traced. 171. A plain native style *can* be made equally strong and expressive with this Latinised English. 188. Language *can* be rendered capable of this power of music. 248. How easily *could* it have been mended by this transposition! 260. This *can* be sometimes accomplished. 266. Even gloomy and dismal objects *can* be introduced into figures. 302. In solemn discourse this *can* often be done to good purpose. 328. This inaccuracy *could* have been remedied. 484. Most, or *all* of the matters, which *can* be the subject of public discourse. ii. 47. Formal introductions *can*, without any prejudice, be omitted. ii. 159. Passages *can* be produced. ii. 455. Ghosts, angels, and devils, *can* be conceived as existing. ii. 469.

The PAST time instead of the PRESENT.

If any should maintain that sugar *was* bitter, and tobacco *was* sweet, no reasonings could avail to prove it. 30. Old Horatius is reminded, that his son stood alone against three, and asked, What *he would have had him to have done?* 53.—The wish of Horatius must be referred either to the time of the combat, or to the time when the question is asked. In the former case, would it not be sufficient to say, ' What he would have wished him *to do.*' In the latter, ' What he would wish him to *have done.*' The sentiment, as our author has expressed it, is embarrassed, and requires some emendation.

Twisted columns always displease, when they are made use of to support any part of a building that is massy, and that *seemed* to require a more substantial prop. 89. The sentence contains three separate propositions, which *required* three separate sentences to *have unfolded* them. 447.—to *unfold* them.

OF instead of FROM.

In an author's writing with propriety, his being free *of* the two former faults seems implied. 189. The style of dean Swift is free *of* all affectation. 476. There may be writers much freer

freer *of* such inaccuracies. 495. Chryſoſtome may be read with advantage, as being freer *of* falſe ornaments than the Latin Fathers. ii. 37. It is not free *of* the fault which I imputed to Pliny's Epiſtles. ii. 301. Taſſo's Aminta is not wholly free *of* Italian refinement. ii. 350. Racine wanted the copiouſneſs and grandeur of Corneille's imagination; but is free *of* his bombaſt. ii, 519.

ON inſtead of IN.

By the cuſtom of walking often *on* the ſtreets. 197. The ſpectator ſpeaks only the language of deſcription, which is always *on* a lower tone. 321. The capital of all nations, ſuddenly involved *on* one conflagration. 359. To place any modern writer *on* the ſame rank. ii. 38,

AMONG inſtead of IN.

Among a nation ſo enlightened and acute, *and where* the higheſt attention was paid to every thing elegant in the arts, we may naturally expect to find the public taſte refined and judicious. ii. 12.——The prepoſition *among* implies a number of things, and therefore ſhould not be prefixed to a noun, which either denotes one ſingle object, or an aggregate of many, taken collectively.

NEVER inſtead of EVER.

Let a ſpeaker have *never* ſo good a reaſon to be animated. ii. 56.

THAT inſtead of AS.

A direction the more neceſſary, *that* the preſent *taſte* of the age in writing, ſeems to *lean* more to ſtyle than to thought. 407. The harmony is the more happy, *that* this diſpoſition of the members of the period, which ſuits the ſound ſo well, is no leſs juſt and proper, with reſpect to the ſenſe. 411. Theſe rules are the more neceſſary, *that* this is a part of the diſcourſe which requires no ſmall care. ii. 161.

INVERTED SENTENCES, which have an air of ſtiffneſs and affectation.

Conſiderable merit doubtleſs he has. 396. Of figures and ornament of every kind he is exceedingly fond. 397. Great virtues certainly he had. 14. No contemptible orator he was. ii. 16. Living examples of public ſpeaking, it will not be expected that I ſhould here point out. ii. 236. Imperfections in their works he may indeed point out; paſſages that are faulty he may ſhew. ii. 250. *Orators,* ſuch as Cicero and Demoſthenes, we have *none.* ii. 257. Of orations, or public diſcourſes of all kinds, I have already treated fully. ii, 259. With digreſſions and epiſodes he abounds. ii. 266. In Dodſley's Miſcellanies ſeveral very beautiful lyric poems are to be found. ii. 360. Of parables the prophetical writings are full. ii. 398. Of lyric poetry, or that which is intended to be accompanied with muſic, the Old Teſtament is full. ii. 401. Than Terence nothing

nothing can be more delicate, more polished and elegant. ii. 538.

In these sentences the grammatical order of words would be much more natural and agreeable, than this inverted arrangement.

Suppose a man should gravely and seriously ask a friend to take a walk into his garden, in some such language as this:—— ' Into the garden let us walk, of flowers it is full, of fruit I think you are fond, on the trees some peaches are to be found, apricots this year I have none, to tea we shall return,'——he would be thought a coxcomb, or a pedant. Why then should such inverted expressions be used in our compositions?

METAPHORS.

' From the *influx* of so many *streams*, from the *junction* of so many dissimilar *parts*, it naturally follows, that the English, like every compounded language, must needs be somewhat *irregular*. We cannot expect from it that correspondence of parts, that complete analogy in *structure*, which may be found in those simpler languages, which have been formed in a manner within themselves, and built on one foundation.' 172.—In this passage the English language is considered as a river and a structure. But these two images are inconsistent.

' Rules tend to *enlighten* taste, and to lead genius from unnatural deviations into its proper *channel*.' 6.—What has genius to do in a *channel*, which is literally the bed of a river?

' Good hopes may be entertained of those whose minds have this liberal and elegant *turn*. Many virtues may be *grafted* upon it.' 12.—We can form no idea of grafting on a turn, or a tendency, which is neither a visible, nor an intellectual object.

' As Dr. Young's imagination was strong and *rich*, rather than delicate and *correct*, he sometimes gives it too loose *reins*. Hence, in his Night Thoughts, there prevails an *obscurity* and a *hardness* in his style. The metaphors are frequently too bold, and frequently too far *pursued*; the reader is *dazzled* rather than enlightened, and kept constantly on the stretch, to *comprehend* and *keep pace* with the author. We may observe how the following metaphor is *spun out*.' 313.—The imagination is confounded by this mixture of literal and figurative expressions, and this rapid transition from one metaphor to another.

' *Dryads* and *Naiads*, the *genius* of the wood, and the *god* of the river, were, in men of lively imaginations, in the early ages of the world, *easily grafted* upon this turn of mind.' 326.— The grafting of nymphs and genii is a new mode of propagation, which has never been thought of before, even by the celebrated Dr. Graham; and yet our professor represents it as an easy process.

' Comparison is a *sparkling ornament*; and all things that sparkle, dazzle and fatigue, if they recur too often. Similies should, even in poetry, be used in moderation; but in prose writings much more: otherwise, the style will become disgust-

ingly

ingly *luscious,* and the *ornament* lose its *virtue* and *effect.*' 348.—
We may represent similes as sparkling ornaments of style,
which dazzle and fatigue the reader's imagination ; but we
cannot at the same time, with any propriety, represent them as
things unpleasing to the palate, or ' disgustingly luscious.'

' The real and proper ornaments of style are *wrought* into
the *substance* of it. They flow in the same *stream* with the *current* of thought.' 365.—The ornaments of style are here considered as capable of being wrought into a solid *substance* ; and,
in the next sentence, represented as a *stream* flowing with a
current.

There is the same confusion of ideas in the following passage :
' In his humorous pieces, the plainness of his manner gives his
wit a singular *edge,* and sets it off to the highest advantage.
There is no *froth,* nor *affectation* in it ; it *flows* without any studied preparation ; and while he hardly appears to smile himself,
he makes his reader laugh heartily.' 382.

' Lord Shaftesbury is ever in *buskins, full of circumlocutions,*
and artificial elegance.' 397.—We may say, Lord Shaftesbury's
writings are ' full of circumlocutions.' But if we substitute
the author for his works, and introduce him in *buskins,* or in a
personal character, we cannot so properly say, he is *full* of circumlocutions, as that he is *fond* of them.

' In that region which it [eloquence] occupies, it admits
great scope; and to the defect of zeal and application, more
than to the want of capacity and genius, we may ascribe its not
having hitherto *risen higher.* It is a *field* where there is much
honour yet to be reaped ; it is an *instrument,* which may be
employed for purposes of the highest importance.' ii. 44.—Eloquence is here described as something capable of *rising,* as a
field, and as an *instrument* ; but these are representations, from
which it is impossible to form any consistent idea.

In our Review for August we observed, that there were many
inaccuracies of style in these Lectures. The passages, which we
have now cited, will be sufficient to justify this observation ; and
may serve perhaps in some respects to shew, that the Eloquence
of this country has not yet fixed her residence on the north side
of the Tweed. Some of these improprieties may be thought
too trivial to deserve the attention of a celebrated author, and
others may probably be defended by analogy, or the example of
preceding writers. But the greater part of them are real viola-
tions of grammar, or of that purity, propriety, and precision,
which Dr. Blair himself has very justly recommended.

We shall conclude with the following extract from the ninth
Lecture, which will be a sufficient apology for all the freedom
we have taken with our author's performance in this article.

' Whatever the advantages or defects of the English language
be, as it is our own language, it deserves a high degree of our
study and attention, both with regard to the choice of words
which we employ, and with regard to the syntax, or the arrangement

rangement of these words in a sentence. We know how much the Greeks and the Romans, in their most polished and flourishing times, cultivated their own tongues. We know how much study both the French and the Italians have bestowed upon theirs. Whatever knowledge may be acquired by the study of other languages, it can never be communicated with advantage, unless by such as can write and speak their own language well. Let the matter of an author be ever so good and useful, his compositions will always suffer in the public esteem, if his expression be deficient in purity and propriety. At the same time, the attainment of a correct and elegant style is an object which demands application and labour. If any imagine they can catch it merely by the ear, or acquire it by a slight perusal of some of our good authors, they will find themselves much disappointed. The many errors, even in point of grammar, the many offences against purity of language, which are committed by writers who are far from being contemptible, demonstrate, that a careful study of the language is previously requisite, in all who aim at writing it properly.'

Travels to the Coast of Arabia Felix, and from thence by the Red Sea and Egypt, to Europe. 8vo. 2s. Blamire.

MR. Rooke, the author of these letters, sailed in the small squadron, which proceeded southward in 1781, under the command of commodore Johnstone. It had been sent out by the government with the view of attacking the Cape of Good Hope; but the commodore, finding that the place had been succoured by the arrival of a French fleet, was obliged to abandon the design. The destination of the major (for such he then was) had been for the East Indies; but after a tedious voyage, on which many of the crew were cut off by sickness, the fleet, standing in need of water and refreshments, put into Morebat bay about the end of November. Here Mr. Rooke, finding his health much impaired, resolved on returning to Europe; and with this view embarked in an Arabian vessel, which carried him to Mocha. Before this period, the letters contain an account of the various places which had been visited by the fleet, as well as of the occurrences in its progress; and in those which are subsequent, the author gives a narrative of his own travels.

From Mocha Mr. Rooke proceeded in a vessel to Juddah, and thence to Suez, the Arsinoe of the ancients, which is situated at the top of the Red Sea. This town stands surrounded by the Desert, and is, as he informs us, a shabby, ill-built place. The ships anchor at the distance of a league from the town, to which the channel that leads is very narrow, and has only nine or ten feet depth of water. From Suez the traveller arrives at Cairo, after a journey of no more than

than a day and a half, performed with a caravan across the Desert. Being come thither, the Egyptian pyramids, as may be supposed, were the first objects of his attention. Though these have been repeatedly described, it may not be unpleasing to our readers to see the author's account of the largest.

' After having gazed at them with wonder for some time, we prepared to pry into the inmost recesses of the larger pyramid, into which only of the three there is an entrance: having lighted our candles, we crept in at a small aperture in one of the sides, about one-fourth of the way up from the base of the pyramid: crawling along on our hands and knees for some way down a sloping and rugged path, we came to the lower apartment, where discovering nothing that engaged our curiosity, we soon left it, and ascended by a more regular passage up to the great chamber: being arrived there, we found it a spacious, well-proportioned room; at one end is a tomb or sarcophagus of granite, thought to have contained the body of the prince who built this pyramid, as his sepulchral monument: the chamber is lined with granite throughout, the cieling being formed of nine long stones: this room is thirty six feet long, eighteen feet wide, and twenty feet high; the sarcophagus is seven feet long, four feet wide, and four feet deep. There is a room above this, but no way to go up to it. There is likewise supposed to be one below that which we first went into; the way to it is by a deep kind of hole or well, which probably leads down to the island, formed by the water of the Nile at the time of the annual inundation, according to Herodotus's account, who says that there was a tomb on the island.

Having attentively viewed these inner regions, we crept out again half choaked with dust, and almost suffocated with the closeness of the air: after a short repose, we scaled the sides of the pyramid, which have the appearance of a flight of steps or rows of benches decreasing to a point, for the original smooth and polished surface having mouldered away, the stones placed in regular rows, bear the form I describe, serving by that means as steps to the very summit, from whence the view is extensive and noble, taking in the Nile, and fertile country on each side of its banks, for a considerable tract, numberless villages, Old Cairo, Giza, the pyramids of Sacara, where are the catacombs, &c. &c. Although there are pyramids without number scattered all over the country, yet these are the three that we call emphatically *the* pyramids, and are here termed *El Haram di Giza*, from their vicinity to that place; they stand about nine miles from the banks of the Nile, and on the verge of the fertile country, being placed on elevated ground, up to the foot of which the water flows on the annual inundation: they are of different sizes. The large one, according to Greaves's measurement, is 700 feet square, covering about eleven acres of ground; the inclined plane is equal to the base, so that the an-

gles

gles and bafe make an equiateral triangle; the perpendicular height is 500 feet. The apex is thirteen feet fquare.'

Mr. Rooke reprefents the Egyptian government as extremely undefined and tyrannical. On one hand, the pacha or viceroy, fent by the grand fignior, to whom the country is tributary, claims the fovereignty; on the other, twenty-four beys exercife an oppreffive power, alike independent not only, of each other, but of the former. Of the capricious government of thofe defpots, we meet with the following remarkable inftance.

' In one of my rides about the city, I was met by a party of Turkifh foldiers, who accofting me, and fome European friends who were of my party, faid, that by order of their mafter Muftapha Bey, they were come in fearch of us, and that they muft immediately conduct us to him. We did not at all relifh this falutation, and would gladly have been excufed the honour of paying a vifit to a bey, but having no alternative, we proceeded quietly under their efcort. We were not, you may be fure, extremely comfortable in this fituation, and in our way endeavoured to divine the caufe of it, but in vain: we found we had nothing elfe to do but fubmit patiently, and wait the event. Being arrived at the bey's palace, my companions were fet at liberty, and I only was detained; one of my friends, however, ftayed with me, to act as interpreter, and plead my caufe. We were now ufhered into the prefence chamber, and found this potentate fitting crofs-legged on a carpet, fmoaking a pipe feven or eight feet long; he was a middle-aged man, rather corpulent, had a black and bufhy beard that reached below his breaft, and his countenance was handfome, although ftern and fevere; his myrmidons, who were bearded like himfelf, ftood in a circle round him, into the midft of which we were introduced.

The Bey, being informed that I was the perfon whom he had fummoned, furveyed me attentively, and with an imperious tone of voice, pronounced my crime and my fentence in the fame breath, telling me, an Armenian merchant having reprefented to him that an Englifhman, who had paffed through Cairo two years before, owed him a fum of money, his orders were, that I fhould immediately difcharge the debt incurred by my countryman. I heard with aftonifhment this extraordinary charge and verdict, and in reply endeavoured to explain the hardfhip and injuftice of fuch a proceeding, telling him, that, in the firft place, I doubted much whether the debt claimed by the Armenian was juft; and in the fecond, fuppofing that it was, did not confider myfelf by any means bound to difcharge it: but all endeavours to exculpate myfelf on the principles of reafon or juftice were totally ufelefs, fince he foon removed all my arguments by a fhort decifion, which was, that, without further ceremony, I muft either confent to pay the money, or

remain

remain prisoner in his castle. I began then to enquire what the sum was, which the Armenian pretended to be due to him, and found it to be near five hundred pounds, at which price, high as it was, I believe I should have been induced to have purchased my liberty, had not my friend advised me to the contrary, and given me hopes that it might be obtained without it, recommending to me rather to suffer a temporary confinement, than submit to so flagrant an extortion. Accordingly, I protested against paying the money, and was conducted under a guard into a room, where I remained in arrest.

It was about noon, the usual time of dining in this country, and a very good pilau with mutton was served up to me; in short, I was very civilly treated in my confinement, but still it was a confinement, and, as such, could not fail of being extremely unpleasant: my only hopes were founded in the good offices of Mr. R———, an Italian merchant, whose services to me and many of my countrymen, who have been embroiled in affairs of the like nature here, deserve our warmest gratitude.

My apartment was pleasantly situated, with a fine view of the Nile, and a rich country; but I should have enjoyed the prospect much more upon another occasion. On a kind of lawn, shaded with trees, in front of the castle, two or three hundred horses stood at piquet, richly caparisoned, belonging to the bey and his guards. His principal officers and slaves came to visit me, and, in talking over my case, they agreed that it was very hard, but, to comfort me, said, that their master was a very good prince, and would not keep me long confined. I found several of them pleasant liberal-minded men, and we conversed together very sociably through my Arabian servant, who remained with me.

The people in this country always sleep after dinner, till near four o'clock; they then rise, wash and pray; that time of prayer is called by them *asser*, and is the common hour of visiting; the beys then give audience, and transact business: Mustapha Bey now sent for me again, and seeming to be in good humour, endeavoured to coax me into payment of the demand he made; but I continued firm in my refusal, on which he changed the subject, and smiling, asked me if I should not like to be a Mussulman, telling me it was much better than being a a Christian, and hinted that I should be very well off if I would become one of them, and stay at Cairo, using likewise other arguments to effect my conversion, and all this in a jocular laughing manner: while he was proceeding in his endeavours to bring me over to his faith, two officers came from Ibrahim Bey to procure my release. I have before told you that he is the chief bey, and luckily Mr. R———, having very good interest with him, had made application in my behalf, and in consequence thereof, these two ambassadors were sent to request that Mustapha Bey would deliver me up to them; but he seemed by no means inclinable so to do, and resuming his

former

former sternness of look, remained for some time inexorable; till at length, wrought on by their entreaties, he consented to let me go, observing at the same time, that whenever he had an opportunity of making a little money, Ibrahim Bey always interfered, and prevented him; a pretty observation! From which you may infer, that they look upon us as fair plunder, and do not give themselves much trouble to find out a pretence on which to found their claims.

' The English seem particularly to have been victims to this species of rapine, owing, I believe, to the facility with which they always submit to it: and many of our wealthy country-men having returned by this road laden with the spoils of India, these beys have frequently fleeced them, allured by the temptation of that wealth, which these nabobs are so fond of displaying: various are the instances of extortions practised on them. You may form an idea of all, when I mention one of a gentleman, who, passing by Suez in his way to England, that he might not be detained there by the searching of his baggage, prevailed on the custom-house officers to dispense therewith, and only put their seals on his trunks, to exempt them from being visited till his arrival at Cairo, where being come, fatigued with his journey, and impatient to shift himself, he would not wait for the inspection of the officers, but broke the seals to get his clothes, and paid a thousand pounds for the luxury of a clean shirt, an hour before he otherwise would have had it.'

On quitting Egypt, the master of the vessel in which Mr. Rooke took his passage, according to the practice of those Mediterranean sailors, ran up among the islands of the Archipelago, without putting into any but that of Rhodes. Our author's curiosity was thus only partially gratified; but he was soon afterwards unexpectedly landed on the coast of Barbary, where he had the pleasure to view the site of ancient Carthage, and some other celebrated places.—These Travels, in general, are written in a style that partakes equally of ease and vivacity; and, as they give an account of objects either interesting or not much known, they are likely to afford the reader entertainment.

The History of Ireland, from the earliest Period to the present Time. In a Series of Letters, addressed to William Hamilton, Esq. By William Crawford, A. M. In Two Volumes. 8vo. Robinson.

THE history of Ireland may, with greater justice than that of any other country, be distinguished into the legendary and the authentic. The former of these has found warm abettors among several Hibernian annalists; and the latter has

has been accurately treated by the faithful and judicious Dr. Leland. The author of the work now before us difcovers equal zeal in profecuting both thefe divifions of the Irifh hiftory; in one of which he gratifies the national vanity of his countrymen; and in the other, he endeavours no lefs to fupport their patriotic ardour, than to develope the occurrences tranfmitted by hiftorical documents. We muft acknowledge, however, that his plan would have appeared to us lefs exceptionable, had he totally avoided intermixing with his narrative all fuch fentiments and obfervations as ferve rather to inflame the prejudices of the people of Ireland, than to elucidate the hiftory of the kingdom. At the fame time we are ready to make allowances for an author, who wrote amidft the ferment of national exertions and the flufh of emancipated liberty.

Of the manner in which thefe hiftorical Letters are executed, we fhall lay before our readers a fpecimen, extracted without any felection.

' Victory at Wakefield, where the Duke of York was flain, having declared in favour of Margaret of Anjou, opened to her a fair profpect of retrieving her paft misfortunes. It brightened. Near St. Albans fhe obtained a fecond triumph over the army of York, commanded by the Earl of Warwick. Short lived were her hopes. At Santon, Warwick obtained a decifive victory, and Edward, eldeft fon of the duke of York, was placed on the throne. Upon his acceffion, the earl of Kildare, appointed to the office by the Irifh council, was confirmed lord juftice of this kingdom. Shortly after, the duke of Clarence was created, for life, viceroy of Ireland. Victory too often inflames refentment and triumphs over the beft propenfities of the heart. The earl of Ormond, a fteady friend of the family of Plantagenet, had died in England by the hand of the executioner. Our parliament imitating this fhameful example of inhumanity, attainted feveral lords, and a number of the family of Butler, as guilty of high treafon. Sir John Butler, reprefentative of the houfe of Ormond, being fo imprudent as to engage to difadvantage the troops of the earl of Defmond, was entirely defeated. His towns and territories became a prey to the conquerors. In reward of this fuccefsful effort againft the only attempt of confequence made in this country in favour of the houfe of Lancafter, Edward created Defmond lord lieutenant of Ireland. Never before had an Irifh chieftain obtained this honour. He was delighted with it. But a cloud foon darkened the agreeable profpect which it prefented to his view.

' Petit, an ancient Englifh fettler, made incurfions into the territories of Melachlin, a branch of an Irifh fept, diftinguifhed by their confequence in Munfter. Melachlin collected forces, repulfed the invader, and kept his army together, for the annoyance of his enemies. This was confidered by the deputy as an infult upon his authority. He attacked Melachlin in battle. Fortune deferted his ftandard. He was defeated, and taken prifoner. One of Melachlin's leaders, on this occafion, was the fon of O'Connor, who, when his father was expofed in battle to the moft imminent danger, had exerted himfelf for his fafety with fuch tender and generous fenfibility. Once more he appears to us in a diftinguifhed and amiable point of view. Young O'Connor remembered with gratitude the kindnefs with which his father had been treated by a former deputy, and determined to return the obligation to Defmond. He took him under his protection, with a number of his followers, preferved them from infult, and was the means of their being reftored to liberty.

' This affair leffened the deputy in the opinion of the natives. They made incurfions into Munfter, and even threatened an invafion of the pale. To avert this danger, Defmond entered into a treaty with them, the terms of which were not favourable to his authority.

' He was now obliged to defend himfelf from an attack of a different nature. From the time, in particular, of his being created deputy, he had many enemies. Thefe refolved to embrace the prefent opportunity of gratifying their refentment. They reprefented to the king that Defmond was difloyal, and an oppreffor of his fubjects; that inftead of oppofing his enemies with fpirit, he had purchafed peace by difhonourable treaties.

' A parliament fummoned to Wexford, probably to fruftrate this accufation, tranfmitted an addrefs to Edward, in which they entreated him to pay no regard to any accufations made to him of the deputy, affuring his majefty that he had been a zealous and a fuccefsful oppofer of his enemies of the Ormond faction, and well qualified for difcharging with propriety the duties of his office. Thus fupported, Defmond paffed over into England, vindicated his character, and returned triumphant.

' To fecure the favour of the king, whofe interpofition in his behalf had faved him from deftruction, he refolved to exert himfelf, in fupport of the Englifh intereft in this kingdom.

' It has been mentioned, that numbers of Irifh had continued to live in different parts of the pale. Parliament now determined that they fhould, in a year, become liegemen of the king; that they muft take Englifh furnames, and wear the Englifh garb. Defmond had not that attachment to the rights of the natives which, as an Irifh chieftain, might have been expected. Befides this encroachment on their privileges, they had experienced, foon after his appointment to the government, an act of arbitrary power in the legiflature difgraceful to juftice, and fhocking to every fentiment of humanity.

' In 1463, the parliament had enacted, that any of the natives, without legal procefs, might be killed, if engaged in

                                                        ftealing

ſtealing or robbing, provided they had no perſons in their company cloathed in Engliſh apparel.

' The parliament of 1465 was diſtinguiſhed by a law, which
enacted, that all ſtatutes made by authority of the parliament
of England be ratified and confirmed, and held in full force in
Ireland, from the ſixth of March preceding.

' At this period earl Rivers, father-in-law to the king, was
dignified with the office of lord high chancellor of England.
To make way for this promotion, Tiptoft, earl of Worceſter,
was created, with extenſive power, deputy of Ireland. Before
him the enemies of Deſmond renewed their complaints. Tiptoft gave them a favourable hearing. In a parliament met at
Drogheda, under the influence of the oppoſite faction, not only
Deſmond, but the earl of Kildare and Edward Plunket, on
account of various crimes and miſdemeanors, were attainted of
high treaſon. Kildare eſcaped. Deſmond, through the violence of his enemies, loſt his head upon the ſcaffold. Kildare
went immediately to England. In the preſence of the king he
complained of the injuries he had received. Edward admitted
him to favour, and, at his majeſty's deſire, the Iriſh parlia-
liament reverſed his attainder. From the condition of a ſtate
criminal, in which his life had been expoſed to imminent danger, he was veſted with the dignity of lord lieutenant of Ireland,
and Tiptoft, recalled to England, and condemned of partiality and injuſtice, paid for his miſconduct the forfeit of his life,
by a public execution.'

We cannot help remarking that, in our opinion, Mr.
Crawford has been too careleſs with reſpect to elegance of
ſtyle. He has, in general, adopted a precipitate retrenched
kind of narrative, well calculated indeed for conciſeneſs, but
flowing neither with the dignity of hiſtorical, nor the poliſhed
eaſe of epiſtolary compoſition. The work, however, affords
a competent view of the Iriſh hiſtory through its different periods, and will, we doubt not, give ample ſatisfaction to all
who are warmly intereſted in the legiſlative independency of
Ireland.

---

*Archæologia : or Miſcellaneous Tracts relating to Antiquity. Vol.
VI. Publiſhed by the Society of Antiquaries of London. 4to.
1l. 6s. 6d. in Boards. White.*

THE preſent volume begins with an account of ſome Roman antiquities diſcovered at Exeter. By the Preſident
of the Society.—Theſe antiquities conſiſt of five elegant Roman penates, in bronze, which were diſcovered in 1778, in
digging a cellar. The firſt, a female figure, four inches and
a half high, is dreſſed in a long looſe garment, now greatly
corroded with ruſt. Her hair, which is tied behind, and

falls

falls down her back, is adorned with a diadem, resembling those on Livia and Trajan's queens. Her left hand is broken off, and in her right she holds a cornucopia of fruit.

Among the remaining figures are two statues of Mercury, one four inches and a half long, the other four inches and a quarter. The former is said to be a perfect and well proportioned figure. Instead of a bonnet, or petasus, the wings on his head shoot out between his hair, and he has no wings on his feet. A long loose garment, doubled on his left shoulder, passing under the upper part of the arm, is brought over it below the elbow, and hangs half way down his leg. His right hand, though turned upward, as if meant to contain something, is empty; in his left he holds a purse. The other statue of Mercury has the petasus, and wings on his feet. He is more clothed than the former figure, his garment covering his right arm and side, and reaching down almost to his feet. His left hand is in a similar attitude, but the shape of the purse in his right is different. The fourth figure, two inches and a half high, represents either Mars or a Roman warrior, completely armed, with a high helmet, a coat of mail, and boots covering the whole front of the leg. Both the arms are truncated at the hands. The last, and most elegant of these figures, is only two inches and a quarter in height. This, which is a male figure, is, from the delicacy of its shape, the turn of countenance, and the dress of the hair, supposed to be an Apollo. The right hand is broken off at the elbow; the left holds something like a linen cloth, but so covered with rust, that it is impossible to ascertain its form. These five penates were found with, or rather surrounded by a considerable quantity of large oyster-shells, which, from their size and form, are known to come from Budleigh, a village on the coast, twelve miles south-east of Exeter.

Art. II. Remarks on the Rev. Mr. William Harris's Observations on the Roman Antiquities in Monmouthshire, and the neighbouring Counties of Wales; with an Account of some curious Remains of Antiquity in Glamorganshire. By John Strange, Esq. his Majesty's Resident at Venice.

Art. III. An Illustration of a Saxon Inscription remaining in the Church of Aldbrough in Holderneffe, in the East Riding of the County of York. By John Charles Brooke, Esq. Somerset Herald.——The inscription expresses, that ' Ulf commanded this church to be erected for the souls of Hanum and Gunthard.' From this and other circumstances it is inferred, that the church of Aldbrough was built by the Saxons, though it now has a more modern appearance, owing to the succession of repairs it has undergone, and the addition of windows very different from the original lights.

Art.

Art. IV. An Account of a fingular Stone among the Rocks at Weſt Hoadley, Suſſex. By Thomas Pownall, Eſq.—The object which Mr. Pownall deſcribes is a penſile ſtone ,about twenty feet in height, known in the neighbourhood by the name of Great upon Little.

Art. V. Obſervations on Reading Abbey. By Sir Henry Charles Englefield, Bart.

Art. VI. Obſervations upon a Paſſage in Pliny's Natural Hiſtory, relative to the Temple of Diana at Epheſus. By Joſeph Wyndham, Eſq.—Theſe Obſervations relate to the ancient architecture, of which Mr. Wyndham appears to have a clear idea.

Art. VII. Remarks on the Ancient Pronunciation of the French Language. By the Rev. Mr. Bowle.

Art. VIII. Obſervations on the Plague in England. By the Rev. Mr. Pegge.—This paper was written in October, 1778, about which time the plague raged violently at Conſtantinople, in the Levant, and in Africa. Mr. Pegge therefore expreſſes an apprehenſion leſt that dreadful calamity ſhould be imported into Great Britain ; but happily the nation has remained many years uninfected with the peſtilential contagion. The few obſervations which Mr. Pegge has made on this ſubject are rather expreſſive of his regard for the public ſafety, than diſtinguiſhed by any importance, either in a political or medical point of view.

Art. IX. A farther Deſcription of Ancient Fortifications in the North of Scotland. By Mr. James Anderſon.—Some remarks on this ſubject, by the ſame gentleman, were publiſhed in the preceding volume of the Archæologia. In the preſent article, which is written in the form of a letter, Mr. Anderſon informs his correſpondent, that he had examined ſeveral other hills fortified after the ſame manner as that at Knockferrel, and had found that they differed from each other in ſome particulars. At Knockferrel the vitrified cruſt ſurrounded the wall only on the outſide ; but at Tap-o-noath, in Aberdeenſhire, where a large fortification of this kind has been, the vitrified cruſt is only diſcoverable on the inner ſide of the wall, except at one place, where the whole of the conical wall is incruſted on both ſides.

On the top of the hill called Dun-o-deer, in Aberdeenſhire, are alſo veſtiges of a fortification of this kind. Here likewiſe are the remains of another ancient ſtructure of ſtone and lime, ſuppoſed by the vulgar to have been the palace of one of the kings of Scotland. This caſtle, Mr. Anderſon informs us, has been originally a ſquare, ſixty feet on each ſide, the walls about twelve feet in thickneſs, with ſmall windows,

U 3

in

in the common ftyle of building in thofe days. It is now in rubbifh, except a fmall part of the weft wall, which, to keep it from falling, was lately repaired, at the expence of the neighbouring gentlemen, who wifhed to preferve it on account of its picturefque appearance, being feen from afar.

It has been alleged, that thofe vitrified walls are no where to be found, but where the rock on which they ftand is of the plum-pudding kind ; but this remark, Mr. Anderfon affures us, is a miftake. The hill of Tap-o-noath confifts chiefly of fmall fragments of rotten granite ; that of Dun-o-deer is a mafs of flaty iron gravel.

Mr. Anderfon, in his former account of vitrified walls, had hazarded a conjecture, that the circular towers called duns were of Norwegian extract. Since that time he has made enquiry if they were common in the Orcades, which, he concluded, muft be the cafe, if his conjecture was well founded. By a letter from Arthur Nicolfon, efq. junior, of Lerwick, he learns that buildings of that kind are extremely frequent through all thofe iflands.

Art. X. Obfervations on the vitrified walls in Scotland. By the Hon. Daines Barrington.—As this paper fcontains a fingular conjecture relative to the origin of thofe walls, we have extracted it for the fatisfaction of our readers ; though we muft acknowledge at the fame time, that the prefent hypothefis of the honourable and ingenious gentleman appears to us not very probable.

'Thefe fuppofed forts, thus built, have lately much engaged the attention of the Scotch Antiquaries, particularly Mr. John Williams (a mineral engineer), who publifhed a pamphlet on the fubject in 1777, as alfo Mr. Freebairn, whofe fentiments on the fame head are to be found in the minutes of the fociety, June 17, 1779. To thefe I may add a Differtation of Mr. Anderfon's, in the fifth volume of our Archæologia, p. 255. and a fecond by the fame gentleman immediately preceding the prefent paper.

'All thefe ingenious antiquaries agree in fuppofing, that thefe walls were once vitrified, becaufe the natives of North Britain, at that time, did not underftand how to make what we at prefent call cement ; that, in moft of the few which remain, the vitrification only takes place on one fide ; that they are fituated upon infulated hills of a very confiderable height, and that they were ufed as places of defence.

'With regard to the firft of thefe particulars, I fhould conceive, that if one fide of the wall only was heated, and to any height, the matter in fufion would all drop down to the bottom, and therefore could not operate as a cement to fill the interftices of the loofe ftones.

'In

' In relation to the second circumstance, I have myself been twice in the Highlands of Scotland, and have seen very few hills of any height which were cloathed with wood; the trouble therefore of carrying it up to the top of such a mountain would be considerable; nor do I very well understand how the wells being vitrified on one side only, added much to the strength of the post against an enemy.

' Mr. Williams, indeed, after having observed the third particular of their being intended as fortresses, was sensible that water was requisite, if the place was to be held for any time; he therefore informs us, that there are dried wells within these forts. In answer to which I would observe, that shelter from the weather is also necessary (during a siege) upon the top of a bleak Scotch hill, whilst whisky (or a succedaneum for it) would be often in greater request than the bare element of water.

' As I therefore cannot entirely subscribe to the opinions of the before mentioned antiquaries, though supported with much ingenuity, I shall without difficulty state my own hypothesis, be it never so erroneous; for, in many matters of antiquity, he who guesses best does best; nor is demonstration often to be produced on any side.

' As I have travelled the most mountainous circuit of Wales for more than twenty-one years, I have frequently seen stone walls like those in the present drawing, and upon inclosures of a much smaller compass. There is a long tract of such in the western part of Merionethshire, very near to the sea.

' When I first observed these small inclosures made with thick walls of loose stones, I could not comprehend how it could be worth while to make so formidable a fence to such a small compass of ground. Upon examining, however, the adjacent country, I found it almost entirely covered with such loose stones, and that therefore the smaller the piece of ground to be cleared the less expensive the removal. For the same reason, such dry walls are often of a great thickness, and sometimes the corners of the inclosure are filled with stones to a great width, this being the only possible means of procuring pasture.

' Thus likewise, and for the same reasons, this practice is very common in the Highlands of Scotland; and lord Bredalbane (at his most capital place of Taymouth) hath for many years employed a labourer solely in blasting large pieces of stone dispersed over some of his fields, which then became manageable, and may be used in the stone enclosures of the same piece of ground.

' But it will be urged, that the stones of the fences in question are vitrified; which observation, indeed, is unanswerable, if the expence of vitrification was incurred merely to make these supposed fortresses more strong. But may not this vitrification have been occasioned either by volcanoes, or what are called bloomeries? The same effect may be produced likewise on dry

walls

walls of ftone, by lightning paffing along them. The loofe
ftones in either cafe would not be rejected, becaufe they were
glaffy, and would be piled up in the fences of the inclofure ;
as the great point upon thefe occafions is to clear the ground,
and remove the incumbring ftones to the fmalleft diftance.

‘ One of the advocates for the defigned and not fortuitous
vitrification, fays, that the pieces he had procured did not refemble what is called lava ; but every volcano is not neceffarily
an Ætna, or a Vefuvius ; and confequently, the matter difengaged from the crater muft perpetually vary, both in fubftance
and form. Vitrific maffes, larger or fmaller, will likewife be
produced by the fame means.

‘ It may be contended indeed, that pafture thus procured,
by clearing the ground, would be more convenient at the bottom or fides, than on the top of the hill. But to this I anfwer, that in rocky countries you muft get what pittance you
can of foil, and often it will happen, that the only detached
and removable ftones are on the fummit.

‘ When fuch inclofures have been made, they become very
convenient for putting cattle into ; and hence perhaps fome of
the wells which Mr. Williams hath mentioned.

‘ I fhall conclude thefe obfervations by fuggefting, that if
vitrification anfwered the purpofe of cement, it is very extraordinary that the ancient inhabitants of Scotland did not apply it
to the houfes or huts in which they conftantly lived, but referved this expenfive and troublefome procefs merely for a fortification, which might not perhaps be ufed in a century againft
an enemy.’

Art. XI. Obfervations by Sir Henry Charles Englefield,
Bart. on the ancient Buildings at York, &c.

Art. XII. An Account of certain Earthen Mafks from the
Mufquito Shore. By Charles Rogers, Efq.

Art. XIII. An Account of fome Druidical Remains on
Stanton and Hurtle Moor, in the Peak, Derbyfhire. By
Hayman Rooke, Efq.

Art. XIV. Obfervations on the word Efnecca. By John
Topham, Efq.—In an ancient Englifh charter, bearing no
date, but which Mr. Topham, from certain circumftances,
concludes to have been granted by Henry II. between the
year 1162 and 1169, there occur thefe words, ‘ minifterium
meum de *efnecca* mea.’ The word efnecca, in this charter,
clearly relates to fome office under the crown ; and Mr. Topham feems to have evinced, by good authorities, that the office
alluded to, was that of mafter or keeper of the kings’s own fhip
or veffel.

Art. XV. Obfervations on the Roman Earthen Ware taken
from the Pan-Pudding Rock. By Edward Jacob, Efq.

Art.

Art. XVI. Obfervations on the Roman Earthen Ware found in the Sea on the Kentifh Coaft, between Whiftable and Reculver, on the Borders of the Ifle of Thanet. By George Keate, Efq.

Art. XVII. Nummi Palmyreni illuftratio, per Rev. Carolum Godofredum Woide.—From the attempts formerly made to afcertain the alphabet ufed by the inhabitants of Palmyra, the characters on three of thefe coins, preferved in the mufeum of the late Dr. Hunter, are fuppofed to form the names of Haththil, Joheth, and the great Creator. Who Haththil and Joheth were, the defect of Palmyrenian records muft leave for ever in obfcurity. The interpretation of a fourth coin, in the fame valuable collection, is referved by Mr. Woide as the fubject of future enquiry.

Art. XVIII. Four Letters from Beaupré Bell, Efq. to Roger Gale, Efq. on the Horologia of the Ancients, with Mr. Gale's Anfwer.

Art. XIX. Account of a Hiftorical Monument in Britanny. By Monf. D'Auvergne.

Art. XX. The Commencement of Day amongft the Saxons and Britons afcertained. By the Rev. Mr. Pegge.

This paper being fhort, and the fubject of it curious, we fhall give it in the anthor's own words.

' The beginning of day amongft the ancient Greeks and Romans (meaning by a day the νυχθήμερον, or the fpace of twenty-four hours accomplifhed by a fingle revolution of the fun, to fpeak vulgarly) feems to be very clearly underftood and determined, and is of great ufe and importance in regard to the innumerable paffages of their authors.

' The fame may be faid in refpect of the Hebrews ; but as to the Britons and Saxons, the matter appears to be very dubious and uncertain, or at leaft is made fo by the fuggeftions of a confiderable antiquary, who declares, "When our anceftors the Saxons, or before them the Britons, began the day, I have no books to inform me." This, however, is a point which ought to be afcertained amongft them, as well as other nations, and for the fame reafon ; and therefore it fhall be the bufinefs of this fhort memoir to illuftrate this doubtful problem in the beft manner I can.

' The learned antiquary, in the uncertainty under which he laboured, offers a conjecture in the following terms : "But, from the word noon, I conceive one or other of them, if not both [Britons and Saxons], began the day at twelve of the clock. The word noon, if I underftand it right, fignifies as much as novus dies." And to make way for this new etymology, he rejects the old one for nona, i. e. hora nona, in thefe words : "Minfhew, I fee, derives it from hora nona, the ninth canonical hour, which anfwers to our three of the clock in the afternoon.

afternoon. But this derivation I cannot agree to, becaufe, from time immemorial, the very ufe and acceptation of the word hath been otherwife. For, according to the common acceptation, and according to the fenfe of all the Englifhmen or books I ever read or met with, it is as fully noon when the fun has once reached the meridian, as when the clock has ftruck three."

' But other authors, as well as Minfhew, and very refpectable ones, deduce the word noon from nona, as fir Henry Spelman, bifhop Kennet, and Mr. Johnfon. Many write it accordingly none, as Skelton the poet, Hall in his Chronicle, and Dr. Plott. The Saxon non has the fame original, and it amounts to the fame thing whether our word noon be the Saxon non, or the Latin nona, fince they both import the ninth hour of the day, and of confequence had no relation originally to the fun in his meridional altitude, but to the ninth hour, fuppofing the day to begin at fix o'clock in the morning.

' I conceive then, that this term came to denote the time of dining ; firft, becaufe it was the hour when, in fafting, people were allowed to break their fafts, or the monks to eat their dinner, which was after noon-fong ; and fecondly, that by an eafy abufe or catachrefis the word was brought to fignify twelve o'clock, the common hour of dining, in all cafes. It is remarkable that, for fome fuch reafon, eleven o'clock is noon at Trent ; fo arbitrary are things of this nature.

' The ground or foundation of Mr. Peck's conjecture being thus overturned, by eftablifhing the old etymology of the word noon, in oppofition to the fanciful one of novus dies, the conjecture itfelf muft confequently fall ; or at leaft we are at liberty to inveftigate the commencement of the day among the Saxons and Britons upon a different and more probable hypothefis. And this, indeed, is the main queftion in agitation.

' Now it fhould feem that the Saxons reckoning by nights and not by days (whereby the nights evidently preceded the days), their day began at evening ; hence our fe'nnight and fortnight ; and fee Tacitus, Du Frefne, fir Thomas Brown, Verftegan, and Thorefby.

' As to the Britons, ftill more anciently their practice may be collected with fome degree of certainly from Cæfar's Commentaries, where it appears that the Gauls began their day at the fame time as the Saxons did, viz. with the evening ; and it is always allowable to argue from the cuftoms of the Gauls to thofe of our Ifland-Britons, where it follows, that thefe laft began their day at the fame time. But though this may feem to be fufficiently conclufive, I fhall neverthelefs refer you, as a further fupport of the argument, to Mr. Camden, Sheringham, Sammes, Wilkins, Richards's Britifh Dictionary, and the following infertion in Du Frefne, concerning the Armoricans : " Armorici Seifun vel Seifhun, i. e. feptem fomni, dicunt, pro feptimana, et henos vel henoas pro hodie, quod proprie

hæc

hac nocte significat." I shall only add for a conclusion, that this argument, from night's preceding day both among the Saxons and Britons, will appear very forcible to all those who infer from the words of Moses, in the first chapter of Genesis, as I think all do, that the Hebrews began their nucthemeron with the evening.'

Art. XXI. Remarks on the Sumatran Languages. By Mr. Marsden.

Art. XXII. Observations on the Indian Method of Picture-Writing. By William Bray, Esq.

Art. XXIII. Observations on the Origin and Antiquity of Round Churches, and of the Round Church at Cambridge in particular. By Mr. James Essex.

Art. XXIV. A Description of an Ancient Picture in Windsor Castle, representing the Embarkation of King Henry VIII. at Dover, May 31, 1520, preparatory to his Interview with the French King Francis I. By John Topham, Esq.

Art. XXV. On the Cubical Contents of the Roman Congius. By Henry Norris, Esq.

Art. XXVI. Some Observations on Dr. Bernard's Cubic Contents of the Roman Amphora. By Henry Norris, Esq.

Art. XXVII. Sequel to the Observations on Ancient Castles. By Edward King, Esq.

Art. XXVIII. Additions to Mr. King's Account of Lincoln Castle. By Sir Henry Charles Englefield, Bart.

Art. XXIX. Observations on Rochester Castle. By the Rev. Mr. Samuel Denne.

Art. XXX. Governor Pownall on Roman Earthen Ware, and the Boundary Stone of Croyland Abbey.

This volume of the Archæologia is enriched with an uncommon number of well executed engravings, which form a considerable addition to a work intended to illustrate objects of antiquity, whether natural or artificial; as, without such assistance, adequate ideas of these cannot always be so clearly communicated by the most accurate verbal descriptions.

☞ An account of the first volume of Archæologia was given in the Crit. Rev. for Jan. 1771; of vol. II. in that for July, 1773; of vol. III. in Aug. and Sept. 1775; of vol. IV. in Aug. and Oct. 1777; and of vol. V. in Oct. and Nov. 1779.—It is necessary to mention, that the fourth volume was again examined, in the last Review; from which inadvertency, however, no great mischief can arise; for the reader who thinks the *first* article too severe, will probably approve of the *second.*

Adelaide

Adelaide and Theodore; or, Letters on Education. Translated from the French of Madame la Comtesse de Genlis. 12mo. 9s. in Boards. Cadell.

IT is not easy to adapt even the most judicious precepts to other manners, and a state of society different from that in which they were dictated. The name and the reputation of Madame de Genlis are well known; and these little volumes will not be found to detract from the praises which she has hitherto merited. They are indeed sensible, judicious, and clear; but we dare not recommend them to an English family, without the exact attention of a careful mother, who possesses both sensibility and judgment to adapt them to our own customs. Even the elegant and judicious precepts of the late amiable Dr. Gregory, whose country was so near to our own, and allied to it by a similarity of government, of religion, and, in some respects, of manners, will scarcely form an English woman, who would be styled attracting. The reserve which he so strongly inculcates, and which is a striking feature in the characters of our fair neighbours, would be considered in this country as an affected distance, or a blameable timidity. This difference must be more striking in another kingdom; and to hear of a married woman's lover, without its being followed by marks of infamy and disgust, might blunt that acute sensibility, which makes every approach to vice, and every hint of impropriety, so painful to a female of delicacy and virtue. We have mentioned only one circumstance; but there are many that have occurred to us, which render this work, in some degree, unfit for the purpose probably designed by their translator. We think that he would have performed an acceptable task, if, when he had given it an English dress, he had expunged every exceptionable passage: his task would have been easy, for there are very few.

While we make this objection to the present volumes, we must own, that it is daily diminishing, and probably is of little consequence to those who wish to lose their native distinctions, in the frivolity of the continent. To see other countries and different manners, enlarges the mind, makes it capable of valuing what is truly excellent, enables it to despise what is trifling, and detest what is vicious. Unfortunately, however, this is not the object of the greater number of travellers; and though France affords men of learning and genius, as well as women of exquisite taste and sensibility; though the vivacity of their manners, and their general strict attention to decorum, might furnish useful lessons, either to the diffident or bashful Englishman; yet we find their foibles preferred

ferred

ferred to their virtues, and the trifles of fashion courted, inftead of their knowlege or their virtues. This work indeed gives a pleafing picture of the intelligent and delicate inha-bitants of that kingdom; and, if we fometimes recognize the little vanities of the nation, we receive ample amends by their elegance and information. But we muft ftill add, that there are fome things which we wifh. to correct, before it fhould hold the mirror to our own countrywomen.

The precepts of Madame de Genlis are animated by the de-fcription of her fituation, by various incidents and anecdotes, by entertaining or pathetic hiftories. It might be miftaken for a novel, if it had a different title; but is much fuperior to the ufual novels, in the general ftrictnefs and purity of its precepts, and the exquifite delicacy with which the moft im-portant leffons are inculcated. The different precepts are alfo adapted for young men; and leffons, fuitable even to royalty, are introduced. As we find no particular fyftem of education, we cannot eafily give an idea of the whole; and perhaps we might appear partial, if we felected any portion. We fhall therefore give a fpecimen of the work, by tranfcribing the author's obfervations on Parifian manners. They are put into the mouth of a kind of mifanthrope, for we apprehend the fpecies is not yet extinct in Paris, and addreffed to a young man, who had been fome time abfent from his native country.

' This is a charming room, faid I, and the more fo, as it gives one fuch ideas of the perfons to whom it belongs. The black man fhrugged up his fhoulders, faying, from whence do you come, fir? From Mofcow, fir?—From Mofcow! Oh then you are my man, I will inftruct you. This apartment, which you may well imagine to be a temple confecrated to friendfhip, to ftudy, and meditation, is only a room for parade; all thefe books fpread on the defk are merely defigned for ornament, like china on a chimney-piece. Moliere ridiculed the learned women of his age, who were to be fure very abfurd, but at leaft they knew fomething. Inftead of which, ours, at this time, pretend to great knowledge, when they labour under the moft profound ignorance. By this difcourfe I fufpected the man to be an original, a kind of fatirical, whimfical jefter; and I was not deceived in my opinion. But, fir, anfwered I, the ladies of our time, though it is true they cultivate the fciences, yet they cannot be accufed of pedantry. They make ufe of no learned expreffions, they do not make a parade of what they know.—But, fir, once more, they know nothing. That fort of pedantry, of which you are fpeaking, at leaft fuppofes fome degree of knowledge. But none is neceffary to go and fee experiments in electricity, to attend a courfe of chymical lec-tures, and to be infinitely amufed by it: in fhort, to liften with an appearance of underftanding, and at the fame time by now

7

and

and then putting in a word, to difcover their total ignorance. They have in general received very different educations; and, as foon as they are their own miftreffes, they read nothing but foolifh pamphlets and plays, which completes the corruption of their tafte. They lead the moft diffipated lives, and pretend to univerfal knowledge. They affect to underftand painting and architecture. They fuppofe themfelves judges of the principal opera-fingers, or performers, without knowing a note of mufic. They go to court, ride on horfeback, play at billiards, go out hunting, drive about in their carriages, fpend the night at affemblies, or playing at pharo, write at leaft ten billets in a day, receive a hundred vifits, and fhew themfelves every where in the fpace of twelve hours; at Verfailles, at Paris, at the millener's, the minifter's levee, the public walks, at the fhop of a ftatuary, at the market, the academies, the opera, and the rope-dancers; equally delighted with, and applauding Reville, and Jeannot; d'Auberville, and the Little Devil. Doing fo many things, purfued he, how would you have them fucceed in any one? Neverthelefs, they are peremptory in their decifions, and particularly Madame de Surville, who knows not the meafure of a verfe, and is even ignorant of grammar, or fpelling; yet fhe gives her opinion on works of literature, and is vain enough to imagine the letters fhe writes to her friends will defcend to pofterity, like thofe of Madame de Sevigny.

' With regard to their fenfibility, it is true they have ornaments made with their friends hair; they have galleries with their pictures; they have altars and odes dedicated to Friendfhip; they are conftantly embroidering cyphers, they talk only of love, friendfhip, gratitude, and the charms of folitude, &c. and they every one fancy themfelves poffeffed of fuperior talents.

' But do they employ themfelves more in the education of their children? Do they live more retired lives than the women of former times; are they more ufeful, more fenfible, or more amiable, than des Houlieres, the Sevignys, the Grafignys? Have they fewer whims, or are they lefs extravagant, fince they are become fo benevolent and fo learned? You may compare the irregularities of their conduct to thofe hypocritical devotees, whofe religion confifts only in outward fhew, who keep an oratory and relics, and pray to the faints, without any love for the Divine Being; who preach to others without correcting their own faults, and blame with great feverity thofe who do not imitate their examples.'

In thefe Letters we think the merit of the celebrated Rouffeau is properly appreciated. His fentiments are often retained, when they are juft, and as freely cenfured when vifionary or abfurd. Indeed, in almoft every view, Madame de Genlis deferves our warmeft praifes. Her errors are thofe of her nation, and of the cuftoms of her country. Her virtues are

are her own. Her affection, her care, and her unremitted attention, circumstances essentially necessary in teaching the young ozier to bend, are probably the characteristics of her sex, and of her situation. But her discernment in tracing the first deviations, the exquisite address with which she teaches us to rectify them, and the judgment of her general conduct, will confer on her the highest credit. If it was meritorious to save the life of one citizen, it is infinitely more so to form the morals, and correct the errors of a nation.

Reeves's History of the English Law. (*Concluded, from p. 204.*)

IN the reign of Henry the Third the History of the Law becomes more precise and certain ; our author, therefore, adopts a different method, and divides his history ' conformably with the nature of the materials from which it is formed into the alterations made by statute, and those made by usage and the decision of the courts.' He begins with the statutes, which are Magna Charta, the statute of Merton & de anno bissextili. These, though very important, would afford little amusement to our readers : they are arranged very methodically, not according to the order of the chapters as they stand in the statute-book, but according to the matters the respective parts treat of.

The great length of this king's reign makes it necessary that some account should be given of the common law before the statutes passed in the latter years of it are examined, for which Bracton supplies an ample fund of materials.

The ranks of persons come first under consideration, which is followed by a view of the different sorts of tenures, that now began to be better understood, the services more accurately reserved, and the several species more precisely distinguished.

The methods of acquiring property by gift, by will, and by succession, are next considered in their order ; the first is largely explained, as contributing to the knowledge of, and being closely connected with, the present system of conveyancing.

The law relating to wills had received very little alteration, except that the ecclesiastical court had gained an unrestrained jurisdiction of all testamentary causes.

A short explanation of the principles of descent, in which the doctrine of representation began to gain ground, closes this chapter.

From the next chapter no reader, but a professional one, can expect much amusement, as it is confined to the examination of the different sorts of actions which had gradually

become

become the subject of much learning and refinement. As real actions, which are now nearly disused, were the most important at that time, we hear very little either of mixt or personal. The proceedings in each are stated minutely and accurately.

A view of the criminal law completes the legal history of this reign : it is the subject of the sixth chapter, which begins with a curious and interesting account of the eyre, the duty of the itinerant justices, and the jurors of the several hundreds who met them ; and which, but for its length, we would insert. The law respecting the several degrees of crimes is then treated of, in order. The first is leaze majesty. The account of the steps to be taken by the person who had discovered an offender, is curious, and shews the anxiety of the legislature on this head.

‘ The law required an accusation of this crime to be made with all expedition. A person who knew another to be guilty, was to go instantly, says Bracton, to the king himself, if he could, or send, if he could not go, to some *familiaris* of the king, and relate the whole matter. This was to be done instantly ; for he was not, says Bracton, to stay two nights nor two days in one place, nor to attend the most urgent business of his own ; he was hardly permitted, says he, to turn his head behind him ; and the dissembling the charge for a time by silence, made him a sort of accomplice and betrayer of the king ; and afterwards, should he prefer his accusation, he could not by law be heard, unless he could shew some very good reason for his delay.’

Homicide follows next : in regard to this crime, the tendency of the law of that time to encourage forfeiture, had introduced this curious determination ; that ‘ if a man, in the endeavour to do some hurt to another, killed himself, the felonious intention he meditated against another would be punished in himself, and his inheritance was by law forfeited.’

A digression (if it may be called so) is here introduced, concerning the office of coroner, whose duty it was to make inquisition upon almost all such breaches of the peace, as were criminally punishable ; upon which, if the party could not find pledges, he was to be imprisoned. Breach of prison, whatever might be the cause of commitment, was capital, though the innocence of the person could be proved.

Trial by ordeal was now entirely disused ; nor was that by duel encouraged ; the proceedings upon the latter are related. Common report was sometimes a ground of prosecution ; but this was to be presented by the jurors, and the reasonableness of it was always examined into.

The lesser order of crimes were frequently prosecuted civilly ; among which was the taking and unjust detention of cattle,

cattle, which introduces the law of replevin, with which the account of the common law is concluded.

Some of the statutes passed in the latter part of this reign relate to the regulation of the market, and the returns of the terms. The statute, among other points of less consequence, put the law of replevin and distresses upon a more certain footing, guarding equally against the oppression of the lord, and the fraud of the tenant; the remedy by writ of entry was also enlarged.

The history of this reign is concluded with the character of Henry the Third, who, during the course of a long reign, seemed always to be endeavouring to evade the privileges which he had been compelled to grant and confirm. Bracton's Treatise was published in his reign, and, probably, before the latter end of it, of which book a very useful and accurate view is given by the author, which will be of very great service to any future editor.

The clergy in this reign laid the foundation for a regular body of canon law; and though they were forbidden to appear in the king's courts as advocates, they continued to be eligible as judges.

The reign of Edward the First has long been considered by lawyers as the most distinguished period in our law, owing to the great number of statutes then made, and the great advancement supposed to be thereby effected in our whole legal polity. He has been thence called the *English Justinian.* However, the reign of this king does not fill so great a space in our author's work, as might be expected from the materials furnished by so many statutes; indeed it is comprized in less compass than that of Henry the Third: the reason for this is given by the author himself.

' With all the importance, says he, which is so deservedly attributed to these statutes, and notwithstanding the space which the learning upon them fills, when viewed in retrospect by a modern lawyer; yet, in the historical account that has been here attempted of our ancient legal polity, they appear comparatively small. It is true, that in the reign of this prince many more statutes were made in a few years, than in many reigns of his predecessors; and those statutes were very important in their object, and very beneficial in their consequences to posterity; but, antecedent to that period, the slow hand of time and experience had been long moulding our laws and judicature into a form capable of receiving the finishing touches that were made by Edward; and in that respect, perhaps, the turbulent and unprosperous reign of his father, Henry, was more productive than his. This consideration of the subject will account for the appearance which these statutes, and indeed this whole reign, makes in point of length, when compared with the former.'

The manner in which our author treats these statutes may, perhaps, surprise, and disappoint those, who are conversant with the second Institute of lord Coke; for our author contents himself with a short mention of them (not omitting any of their contents) and refers to the former parts of the History for the previous state of the law; and sometimes, if necessary, introduces them, with such remarks as are necessary to connect them with what went before, and to point out the object of the statute: when he has done this, he dismisses them, without adding any observation upon the consequences that have been since derived from them. We had been taught by his Preface to expect this; for he says, ' as an account of the revolutions in our law, antecedent to the making of those acts, must, altogether, contain an account of the law, as it stood when they were made, it follows, that the reader enters upon them with a previous information, that will enable him to comprehend their import, on a bare statement of their contents. As to the opinions and principles that were founded on them, in after-ages, to take any notice of them would be anticipating the materials which are to constitute the subsequent part of the history.'

The method pursued by our author in laying these statutes before the reader, is this: he selects from them such as are of a political nature, as the *statutum Wallicæ, ordinatio pro statu Hiberniæ,* the *confirmationis chartarum,* that *de tallagio non concedendo,* and the like, and throws them together, in a way that is consistent enough with the subject-matter, and sufficiently clear to the reader. Having done this, he considers the other statutes of this king in the order in which they were made. The principal of these are the statute of Westminster 1st; the statute of Gloucester; statute of Westminster 2d; statute of Westminster 3d; and the statute of *articuli super chartas.* These contain those improvements in the administration of justice, that have reflected so much honour upon this king's memory. Out of the various mass of matter, with which these statutes are filled, we shall select one article, because our author has treated it in a different manner from any that have gone before him; this is the singular punishment called *peinè forte et dure,* which used to be inflicted on felons, who refused to plead, and is supposed to be ordained first by stat Westminster 1st. c. 12.

After stating the common opinions on this point, he goes on thus: ' If a conjecture may be hazarded upon a point, that has

has created much debate, this statute may be considered as auxiliary towards the establishment of trials by jury, in preference to all others then in use. It may be remembered, that *Magna Charta*, in declaring the privilege every man shall have of being fairly tried, mentions two modes; that *per judicium parium suorum*, and that *per legem terræ*; these being methods of trial much more ancient, as we have before seen, than that by jury, and such as therefore might be more properly called the *lex terræ*, than the latter invention of trial *per pares*. It is remarkable that Fleta uses the like expression, after reciting at length the judgment of penance; *hæc diæta*, that is, this is the course, *omnibus legem refutantibus*, with all those who refuse to be at the law, or common law; and the particular case he there states, as an instance in which that judgment should be passed, is, of a criminal, who, having said that he would defend himself *per corpus*, *vel per patriam*, as the court should award, would not, as he ought by law to do, make a specific declaration by which of those modes he would be tried. This was therefore to be considered as putting himself upon no trial at all, which was totally renouncing the decision of the law, and consequently, by the old course (that is, before the statute, according to our author's opinion), he was to be sentenced to the penance.

'To apply this to the statute before us. The trial by inquest had of late been encouraged, as we have seen in the last reign, and was in more esteem than the barbarous practice of the old jurisprudence; nor was there any object of judicial reformation that more deserved the countenance of a wise legislator, than this mode of enquiry. We have seen that Bracton, in his account of the proceeding *per famam patriæ*, says, that a person so indicted might make his purgation, or put himself upon the country; though it does not appear from that passage, nor from any other of that author, whether the country there meant was the same, that had indicted him, or some other. Indeed it should seem, that a person indicted was to stand or fall by the verdict of that single jury, unless he made his purgation. However, it should seem that it was intended by the present statute to make an alteration in this point; and that as a person appealed might put himself upon the country to prove his innocence, so one indicted should no longer make purgation, but should be compelled to put himself on an inquest of the country, to try the charge brought against him by the indictors.

' If the statute is read with these sentiments, and a knowlege of these circumstances in the then state of criminal judicature, it will receive a new light, and appear in a point of

X 2

view

view that it never was before ſeen in. It will then very plainly ordain, that perſons charged, or indicted of crimes, and who will not put themſelves on inqueſts, that is, on the particular mode of trial which it is ſeen fit to encourage, as the moſt rational, ſhall be ſent to priſon, and treated with the ſame ſeverity as thoſe ſuffer, who refuſe to put themſelves on the old method of inquiry, long uſed by the law of the land. The ſtatute certainly reads as intelligibly in this way, as in any other, and perhaps more ſo ; and whether this ſenſe of it does not agree with the cotemporary hiſtory of the trial by jury, which grew now every day to be more reſorted to, will be for the reader to judge.'

This is our author's opinion upon this ſtatute. Perhaps there is not a book to which the reader may more properly recur for a refutation, or confirmation of it, than the former part of this hiſtory ; where there is brought together more information on the ſubject of juries, aſſizes, ſectatores, proofs, and other modes of trial both in civil and criminal actions, than in any writer upon Engliſh law.

At the cloſe of this reign he has made mention of Fleta, Britton, and others, as he had before of Glanville and Bracton ; and, after conſidering their diſtinct merits, he makes this comparative view of theſe old authors. ' The great copiouſneſs, learning, and profoundneſs of Bracton, place him very high above the reſt : it is to him that we owe Fleta and Britton, which would probably never have exiſted without him. To him we are indebted for a thorough diſcuſſion of the principles and grounds of our old law, which had before lain in obſcurity. But while we give to Bracton the praiſe that is due to him as the father of legal learning, we muſt not forget what Bracton, as well as poſterity, owe to others. Britton delivered ſome of this writer's matter in the proper language of the law, and Fleta illuſtrated ſome of his obſcurities ; while Glanville, who led the way, is ſtill intitled to the veneration always due to thoſe who firſt open the paths to ſcience.

While our author beſtows ſuch deſerved praiſe on his favourite Bracton, every lover of legal antiquities feels ſome obligation to him, for bringing forward that venerable ſage in a more modern, and more pleaſing dreſs. The moſt uſeful and curious parts of this Hiſtory, is that where our author has taken Bracton for his guide. What diſtinguiſhes this from other books upon our old conſtitution, is, the ſtrict and religious adherence to this and other ancient writers. The conſequence of which has been, that the author has not given us a ſelection of ſplendid topics, eaſily inveſtigated, and of little uſe when found, ſet off with ill-grounded conjectures and ſpe-

ious

cious obfervations, with a certain difplay of things calculated for the amufement of idle readers; but a cautious and laborious enquiry into the origin of our whole law, containing much ufeful and found knowlege. With all the pains beftowed on the collecting and arranging his materials, it muft be obferved, that he has many negligences of compofition, that are evident marks of hafte; and it may be pardoned, if he has fometimes in his language a little tincture of the ftyle contracted from thofe books, with which he muft have been converfant. [*Correfp.*

MONTHLY CATALOGUE.

POETRY.

Jephthah's Daughter; a Dramatic Poem. By Mrs. Ann Wilfon. 8vo. 1s. 6d. Flexney.

IN the Preface to this performance we have the following paffage. ' My giving her (Jephthah's daughter) a lover, is a piece of anachronifm which I hope will be forgiven me, love having been ever looked upon as the refiner and harmonizer of human nature.' But this lady has been guilty of another *piece of anachronifm*, as fhe calls it, by giving her a ravifher, at leaft an intentional one, and that no lefs a perfonage than an *Elder of Ifrael:* he, however, expreffes fome remorfe on the occafion, and tells Jephthah,

' I was the people's angel late,
· But a devil am tranfmew'd.'

This ' fmall fpark of grace,' as Jephthah calls it, effects a reconciliation, and all things at laft conclude happily; for ' as the high prieft lifts up the facrificing knife, an angel defcends down within the curtain, and pulls him by the fleeve.' This marvellous interpofition, this *dignus vindice nodus*, may be confidered by ill-natured critics as a piece of anachronifm fimilar to thofe already mentioned; but no matter—the eminent virtues of Jephthah's daughter entitled her to a hufband, and we cannot be difpleafed at the good-natured author's beftowing one upon her, though it is not quite confiftent with hiftoric probability. The father, like a Proteftant divine, bids Ibzan

' Take this maid to be thy wife;'
and the high prieft, in the fame ftyle, joins their hands with the following words:

' O, great Jehovah! look down upon
This virtuous pair:
Regard their fidelity, and crown their lives
With eternal happinefs.'

A chorus of Levites and virgins conclude the drama very properly with an epithalamium.

X 3

The Diſtreſs of Integrity and Virtue, a Poem, in Three Cantos. By Ambroſe Pitman, Eſq. 4to. 1s. 6d. Becket.

The author of this little allegorical performance ſtyles it, in his Dedication, a juvenile attempt ; and it pretty evidently appears to be ſo. It is written in an unequal manner, is in ſome places defective in point of harmony and diction, and in others the ſentiments are weak and puerile. The dawnings of genius are however evidently diſcernible; and if this gentleman thinks proper hereafter to cultivate his abilities in the poetic line, we have little doubt but that his future publications will merit and receive our approbation.

Occaſional Epiſtles, written during a Journey from London to Buſſorah. To William Haley, Eſq. By Eyles Irwin, Eſq. 4to. 3s. Dodſley.

The firſt epiſtle opens in the following manner :

   ' The Rhine and Danube paſt, the Alps o'ercome,
Venice ſurvey'd—and yet the traveller dumb !
Not light the labor, to a vacant mind,
To fill the ſketch which Addiſon deſign'd :
Nor will ſucceſs more juſtify the aim,
Tho' friendſhip lean on ſome eſtabliſh'd name.
   Yet, while poetic ſcenes my ſong invite,
To thee, my Hayley, I preſume to write ;
Hayley, whoſe genius bold on Learning's ſhore
Has touch'd, like Cook, where bard ne'er touch'd before ;
Whoſe muſe, like Pallas from the Thunderer's brain,
Iſſu'd adult, the faireſt of the train.'

The firſt ſix lines appear rather obſcure : we know not what is meant by the ' ſketch which Addiſon deſign'd ;' but are certain, travellers have not been ſilent in reſpect to obſervations on the ſame ſubjects which this author conſiders. The ninth and tenth are extremely flat, and the compariſon unhappy. We mean not to detract from Mr. Hayley's acknowledged merit but what line of compoſition has he adopted which has not been purſued before ? The two laſt lines are beautiful, the thought new, and the application juſt ; for that gentleman's firſt public performance entitled him to a ſeat among our moſt diſtinguiſhed poets. The following Addreſs to him has likewiſe conſiderable merit.

   ' Fix'd in this maxim be my Hayley found,
To pay due homage to his native-ground.
Abroad for ſubjects ſhould the Druid rove,
Who draws the Muſes to his haunted grove ?
Can fabled charms allure, who boaſts a fair,-
The ſoul of grace and virtue's darling heir ?
Bleſt in his hopes, he views with pitying eye
The ſweet deluſions of a milder ſky.
Nature herſelf ſubmits to chaſten'd taſte,
And Eartham blooms, while Tempe lies a waſte.

Mute are the lyres that charm'd th' Ægean main,
While Eartham's fhades refound with freedom's ftrain.
O! oft entreated, be that ftrain renew'd,
By fancy fofter'd, and by praife purfu'd.
Since Britain glows with liberty divine,
To rival claffic poefy be thine:
So fhall thy portion of the fpoils of Greece
Tranfcend the value of her golden fleece;
As far as wit refpect o'er wealth can claim,
Or Homer foars beyond Atrides' fame!'

The obfervations contained in thefe Epiftles are fenfible, the lines fmooth, and the diction elegant; yet fome of the real fcenes defcribed in Mr. Irwin's voyage up the Red Sea, are more animated and affecting than any we here meet with, though invention and poetry are called upon to embellifh them. A ftriking inftance of the fuperiority of nature to art. We may admire the one, but we *feel* the other.

Columba, a Poetical Epiftle, heroic and fatirical, to the Right Hon. Charles Earl Cornwallis. By Miles Parkin; A. B. 4to. 2s. 6d. Debrett.

In explanation of the title, which appeared rather myfterious, the author informs us, that ' he makes ufe of it not only in juftice to the great Columbus, the difcoverer of the weftern world, but becaufe the word America is too trite and feeble to be admitted into a chafte Englifh couplet.' Now, though we commend his zeal for eftablifhing the glory of that'illuftrious navigator, we can perceive nothing anti-harmonious in the found of America, that would debafe the chafteft elegy, or militate againft the dignity of epic verfe. The poem is written in a ftrange defultory manner; is replete with encomiums on lord Cornwallis, and other officers of diftinction, invectives againft the enemies of our country, and eulogies on thofe who perifhed in defence of it. Above all, the author expreffes great anxiety that a reconciliation might be effected between the daughter and mother country; for which purpofe he wifhes,

O! was I bleft with each heart-melting trope,
The wing of Milton, and the flow of Pope,
Was all the melody of Warton mine,
And all the mufic of the tuneful Nine;
To thee, Columba, ever, ever true,
My fofteft fong fhould flow, to foften you.'

Some paffages are extremely enigmatical.

' By dire difeafe to fad dilemma driv'n,
See! Murray yields his corps to God and heav'n;
Dread fate of things! that e'er that haughty foul
Should bow indignant to infulting Gaul;
Yet fate of things more dreadful ftill await,
Lo! Murray ftands a criminal of ftate;

X 4

Trial

Trial how perilous to Draper's fame,
To Murray's glory, and the British name!'

By Murray's 'yielding his corps,' &c. we at firſt ſuppoſed
that the author meant to expreſs the death of the general, and
that his dilemma was, whether he ſhould yield his body to God
or heaven; but our doubts increaſed as we proceeded in our inveſtigation, and found him afterwards arraigned as a ſtate
criminal: on a re-examination we were led to conjecture,
that by *corps* we ſhould underſtand his garriſon forces. Not
that we venture to aſſert it poſitively. His yielding to God
and heaven may be figuratively true, but he certainly did not
ſurrender to the French, but Spaniſh army. The following
paſſage likewiſe is almoſt equally obſcure.

' See Pitt in council; Thurlow at the bar;
See Burgoyne languiſhes and burns for war;
See Lowth in learning; ſee Southampton, brave;
Coote on the herbage; Rodney on the waye.'

It is evident theſe names were introduced as proper ſubjects
for panegyric, but conjecture muſt ſupply what kind of praiſe
was intended to be conferred upon them. Southampton has
the only poſitive encomium, and he is ſaid to be ' brave;' for
we can annex no abſolute idea of merit to Burgoyne's ' burning and languiſhing.' We ſhall conclude with a very ſtriking
anticlimax, not ſo much in the poetry, as liſt of the poets;
whether it is ſimilar in ſome reſpects as to the heroic line, we
ſhall not preſume to determine.

' Great Homer drew Achilles fierce in fight,
Whilſt Maro ſung the Trojan's matchleſs might;
Our Addiſon great Marlb'ro's potrait drew,
Phillips ſung Eugene's praiſe, and I ſing—you:
Thus, in degree, each chief has had his bard,
To chaunt the hero, and the man reward.'

The Diſjointed Watch. By Francis Okely. 12mo. 2d. Lackington.
The well-meaning author of this two-pennyworth of poetry
laments the diviſions of the church under the ſimilitude of a
diſjointed watch. We ſincerely wiſh, with him, that the diſ-
arrangements of both could be corrected with equal facility;
but, alas! this is more than can be expected.

Vis-a-Vis of Berkeley Square. 4to. 1s. 6d. Murray.
A diſguſting attempt of impudence to counterfeit ingenuity.

*The Amours of Florizel; or, the Adventures of a Royal Red Cap.
1s. 6d.* Rich.
The Effuſions of Love. 4to. 1s. 6d. Liſter.
Never have we ſeen any thing more deſpicable than theſe two
productions, in which the moſt daring impudence vies with the
moſt abject ſtupidity.

PO-

POLITICAL.

*History of the Political Life and Public Services, as a Senator and
a Statesman, of the Right Hon. Charles James Fox, one of his
Majesty's Principal Secretaries of State.* 8vo. 7s. in Boards.
Debrett.

If, as we suspect, the author of the Life of the Earl of Chatham
has become the eulogist of Mr. Fox, we may congratulate him
on his improvements.—The swelling pomp of the former work
has given way to a more manly and rational style, while the reflections, introduced with less dignity, are frequently more valuable. We still, however, perceive the veteris vestigia flam-
mæ: the author is sometimes too flowery, and the sentiments,
in a few instances, are trite or trifling. If we are mistaken in
our suspicion of the author, our opinion may be easily collected
from the article referred to.

But though the manner may deserve commendation, we cannot allow that he has furnished us with new information. In
this respect he is probably rather to be blamed for the choice of
his subject than for the deficiency of those facts which the
news-papers of the day will not supply. It was not easy, at
this time, to be explicit in censure, if the author had not been
resolved to praise; and it will be obvious, that a character can
be only drawn with justice, when the whole truth can be
spoken with impunity. Our author has collected the several
circumstances which relate to the public life of his subject,
and detailed them with precision, and we believe with accuracy. Every effort of Mr. Fox excites his admiration; and even
the celebrated coalition draws forth his abilities in its defence.
The reflections may be said to be his own; and, if they are
not just, they are always ingenious. Reflections indeed are the
manufacture of every historian; they are the connecting media
of facts, the apologies of the panegyrist, and the weapons of
the satirist. They exalt the fortunate commander into a hero,
or depress the politician, who was probably able but unlucky,
into a blundering pretender. They are so much in the power
of the historian, that we no longer wonder, when we find an
opposite conclusion from the same premises. We need not mention the tendency of those of our author: if the principles were
those of Mr. Fox, they will confer the highest honour both on
his head and his heart; if they proceed from his eulogist, they
will be equally creditable to *his* judgment and ingenuity.

*A View of the Constitution of the British Colonies in North Ame-
rica and the West Indies, at the Time the Civil War broke out on
the Continent of America. By Anthony Stokes, his Majesty's
Chief Justice of Georgia.* 8vo. 7s. White.

In America and the West Indies, the mode of proceeding, in
matters of law, is different from that established in Great Britain; and no precedents having hitherto been collected on the

subject, an unacquaintance with the legal forms is almost universally prevalent. To remedy this inconvenience, Mr. Stokes engaged in the present work, which he appears to have executed with great industry and attention. He begins with an account of the British colonies in America; the nature of their dependance on the mother-country, at the breaking out of the civil war; with such alterations as have taken place down to the present period. He next treats of the regulations to which the commerce of the British American colonies had been subjected; with such alterations as have also taken place, to the present time. He afterwards proceeds to take a view of the civil jurisdiction in those countries, under the different heads of the governor, council, and general assembly. He next enquires into the constitution of the inferior and superior courts of civil jurisdiction, the courts of criminal jurisdiction, the judges of the superior courts in the colonies, the counsel and attornies, and the court of vice-admiralty.

The author, having thus far taken a view of the several courts, and related the usual method of proceeding in each of them, turns his attention to the more practical part of the work. He delivers the method of authenticating letters of attorney, and affidavits in Great Britain, for the recovery of debts in America, with forms of both sorts; and the method of authenticating letters of attorney, which are to be transmitted without affidavits of debt; with forms of letters of attorney adapted to various cases. He next treats of the Negroes in those countries, and the mode of conveying and manumitting them; of the manner of docking estates tail, reversions and remainders; and of barring dower; with directions for authenticating and registering deeds; to which are added, abstracts from several acts of assembly. The eighteenth chapter is employed on conveyances of land and Negroes in Barbadoes, Antigua, St. Christopher's, and Jamaica; and in an appendix, the author recites three orders of the king in council (relative to the trade between the subjects of his majesty's dominions, and the inhabitants of the United States of America) made in pursuance of the powers granted to his majesty, by the act of parliament passed the 12th of May, 1783.

The mere enumeration of the various articles contained in this volume is sufficient to evince its usefulness to those who have occasion to execute legal transactions with America and the West Indies; and we need only to add, that Mr. Stokes appears to have compiled the whole with judgment and accuracy.

A Letter of his Grace the Duke of Richmond, 8vo.   1s. 6d.
Stockdale.

This Letter is written in consequence of a request from the Committee of correspondence in Ireland, that the duke of Richmond would be pleased to favour them with his sentiments respecting a parliamentary reform in that kingdom. His grace
accordingly

accordingly has delivered his opinion on the subject with freedom and perspicuity, upon the same principles which he adopted a few years ago, in a bill presented to the British house of peers. Though we approve the liberality of the noble duke's sentiments in many points, we cannot help thinking, that, in suggesting the propriety of admitting the whole body of the people, and even paupers, to vote at the election of members of parliament, his grace has extended his idea of popular rights beyond what can be justified by sound policy. The avowed intention of reform being to restrain, as much as possible, the exercise of corruption, nothing seems to be worse calculated for answering that purpose than such regulations as would invest a numerous and dependent class of people with the power of sacrificing the public interest to an aristocratic influence, which their necessities would not permit them to resist. This intelligent senator, so conversant in political speculations, must certainly know that principles, however generous and benevolent, which tend to establish a universal equality in the privileges of a great nation, are far more likely to prove detrimental than serviceable to the community. With regard to a foederal union between Great Britain and Ireland, which the duke of Richmond has cursorily mentioned in this Letter, his grace's sentiments are marked with a just discrimination; and he has also shown a prudent reserve in respect to his opinion concerning the religious principles of electors.

A Letter to his Grace the Duke of Richmond. 8vo. 1s. Smith.

This author, in reprehending the principles maintained by the duke of Richmond on the subject of parliamentary reform, attacks his grace with an asperity and petulance which merit the severest reprehension. Excluding, however, those illiberal parts of the writer's remarks, his arguments are not destitute of foundation. He contends, with justice, that the extension of the privilege of voting at elections, as proposed by the duke of Richmond, would be productive of great disorder, and might ultimately render the assembly of representatives not only disgraceful, but odious and pernicious to the nation. The duke, in his plan of reform, was inclined to exclude only ideots from the privilege of voting; but the letter-writer thinks there are numbers of persons, in the lower class of the people, hardly any thing superior to ideots in the capacity of judging with regard to the qualifications of members of parliament.

At the same time that this writer discovers great animosity against the duke of Richmond, he expresses so high an opinion of Mr. Fox, as to affirm that he is the only person in the kingdom equal to the important task of amending the constitution. Though we hold the talents of that right honourable gentleman in no small degree of esteem, we cannot help regarding such exclusive panegyric as extravagant; and, for the honour of our country, should even be sorry if it were not unjust.

A Let-

A Letter to the Court of Directors of the East-India Company, from Warren Hastings, Esq. Governour-general of Bengal. 8vo. 1s. 6d. Robinson.

Different opinions have been for some time entertained respecting the public conduct of the governor-general of Bengal; and so far were the directors of the East India Company influenced against him, that in the summer, 1782, they came to several resolutions, plainly indicating the necessity of a change in the government of the British possessions in that country. In consequence of the prejudice confirmed by those resolutions of the board of direction, the character of Mr. Hastings daily sunk in the public estimation; and it was not without symptoms of apparent diffidence, that even his friends could persevere in the attempt of vindicating the rectitude of a man so flagrantly criminated by representations, which obtained general credit in proportion to the effect they had-produced on the minds of the directors. The present Letter of Mr. Hastings, however, promises to dissipate entirely the injurious opinions which had been formed of his administration in India. He vindicates his own conduct with a manly boldness, a consistency, and a force of argument that places both his public virtue, and his political exertions, as a governor, in the most respectable light. Having said thus much, it is unnecessary for us to enter into a more particular account of the Letter. It is sufficiently known at the India-House, where it can alone be of any use, either for approving or condemning the conduct of Mr. Hastings.

An Address to the Proprietors of East India Stock. 8vo. 1s. Wilkie.

The author of this Address is a violent opponent of Mr. Hastings, whom he not only accuses of temerity in entering into the Mahrattah war, but of unjustifiable misconduct during the prosecution of it. Whether the representation adduced in support of this weighty charge be founded in justice, or be only the artful colouring of invidious obloquy, we shall not determine. When the affirmations of hostile parties clash so violently with each other, there remains no other method of ascertaining the truth, but by a full and impartial enquiry. That in an affair of so much importance such an enquiry will be instituted, there cannot be any reason to doubt. Until that can be deliberately effected, it is more adviseable to suspend opinion, than rashly to adopt measures which in the end may be found to have been not only prejudicial to the affairs of the East India company, but disgraceful both to the discernment and the justice of the nation.

The Letters of a Citizen on India Affairs. 8vo. 1s. Bew.

The author of these Letters, who writes in the character of a plain man, makes many just and shrewd remarks on some of those who have appeared the most forward in condemning the conduct of the Company's servants in India. In the most essential

tial

tial parts of the Letters, the principal object of his censure is Mr. Burke, of whose professed disinterestedness and patriotism he entertains a very unfavourable opinion. The dispatches lately received by the directors of the East India company, from Mr. Hastings, afford a strong and explicit vindication of the governor-general; and the Letters now before us are calculated to enforce the impression which the former, we believe, have universally made on the public.

A Capital Mistake of the Legislature. 8vo. 6d. Kearsley.

This author warmly censures the receipt-tax as oppressive and impolitic; but the principle upon which he chiefly condemns it is, that it will prove the means of opening an immense channel to forgers, both foreign and domestic, who may engross the whole profits of the revenue; while the public must be burthened with some additional tax, to compensate the deficiency of this unproductive and odious impost. We must acknowlege that the author's arguments appear to us in a very strong light; and there is reason to think that they will operate towards a repeal of the tax in question.

D I V I N I T Y.

Seventeen Sermons on Practical Subjects. By the late Rev. Joshua Parry. 8vo. 6s. Rivington.

Mr. Parry treats of the following subjects:—The Causes of neglecting Public Worship; Christ's Look directed to Peter; the Nature, Reward, and Honour of Christian Obedience; the mutual Aid of the Virtues; the Guilt and Danger of Hypocrisy; the Nature and Danger of ill Company; the Influence of corrupt Example; the Nature, Guilt, and Danger of Censoriousness; the Amiableness of Childhood; the Moral Conquest; the Causes and Danger of Religious Procrastination; the Folly and Impiety of Human Presumption; the Treachery of worldly friendship; no Happiness without Religion; the Divine Goodness to the Unthankful; the peculiar Guilt and Punishment of perverse Sinners.

These sermons were preached at Cirencester, in Gloucestershire, between the years 1745 and 1772. As they were addressed to a plain country audience, the author has not entered into any critical disquisitions, or speculative enquiries; nor has he attempted to entertain the reader's imagination by florid language or poetical imagery. His arguments are plain and obvious, accompanied with practical observations; his style, for the most part, simple and unaffected, yet, in general, sufficiently animated.

A Discourse on Predestination, &c. By the Rev. John Walker, A.B. 8vo. 6d. Lowndes.

In this discourse Mr. Walker endeavours to evince what he terms ' the impropriety and impertinence of the doctrine' of predestination; he then proceeds to point out its ' inconveniencies.'

7

W

We shall present our readers with one of his arguments, which is *new*, and must have been perfectly *satisfactory* to his auditors.

' If we hurry ourselves into voluntary danger, God hath no where promised to work a miracle to effect our escape. If any given congregation, induced by this their belief, were absurd enough to hang themselves up before the porch of the Lord's house, on supposition, that if this should not be their appointed time, the Deity would, by immediate descent, or a miracle, prevent their suicide; would the thinking part of mankind, when acquainted with their creed, be at a loss to account for their conduct?'

The author doth not seem to have aimed at *any* degree of *elegance*, either in his composition, or in the appearance of his publication.

A Charge delivered to the Clergy of the Archdeaconry of St. Alban's, at a Visitation holden May 22, 1783. By the Rev. Samuel Horsley, LL. D. 4to. 3s. Robson.

The object of this Charge is Priestley's account of the doctrine of the Trinity, in his History of the Corruptions of Christianity.

The general view, which our author has given us of the Doctor's notions concerning this article, is as follows:

' That the doctrine of the Trinity, in the form in which it is now maintained, is of no greater antiquity than the Nicene council. That it is the result of a gradual corruption of the doctrine of the Gospel, which took its rise in an opinion first advanced in the second century by certain converts from the Platonic school; who, expounding the beginning of St. John's Gospel by the Platonic doctrine of the Logos, ascribed a sort of secondary divinity to our Saviour, affirming that he was no other than the second principle of the Platonic Triad, who had assumed a human body to converse with man. That before this innovation, of which Justin Martyr is made the author, the faith of the whole Christian church, but particularly of the Church of Jerusalem, was simply and strictly Unitarian. The immediate disciples of the apostles conceived our Saviour to be a meer man, whose existence commenced in the womb of the Virgin; and they thought him in no respect the object of worship. The next succeeding race worshipped him indeed, but they had however no higher notions of his divinity, than those which were maintained by the followers of Arius in the fourth century. In short the first race of Christians, in Dr. Priestley's opinion, were Unitarians in the strictest sense of the word; the second, Arians. As Dr. Priestley follows Zuicker in these extravagant assertions; so the arguments, by which he would support them, are in all essential points the same which were alleged to the same purpose either by that writer or by Simon Episcopius.'

Our modern historian, according to this writer, ' in support of his imaginary progress of opinions from the Unitarian doctrine, to the Nicene faith, hath produced few, if any, arguments, which

which make directly for his purpose, but what are to be found
a the writings either of Zuicker or Epifcopius. Nor is a fingle argument to be found in the writings either of Zuicker or
Epifcopius, which is not unanfwerably confuted by bifhop Bull.'

As this is the cafe, it is no wonder the learned archdeacon
has undertaken to fhew, that Dr. Prieftley's fundamental propofitions reft upon precarious affumptions, perverted hiftory,
mifconftrued and mifapplied quotations, &c.

In the profecution of this defign our author difplays a very
confiderable knowlege of ecclefiaftical antiquities, and a zealous
attachment to ' the catholic doctrine of the Trinity.'

NOVELS.

Memoirs of the Manftein Family. Two Vols. 12mo. 6s. Lowndes.

An interefting narrative, accompanied with virtuous fentiments, renders this novel fuperior to the common productions
of the kind. It exhibits a pleafing picture of characters and
manners, calculated to afford rational entertainment, and may
be read without any danger of the pernicious infection fo often
communicated to the heart by the productions of fancy.

The Orphan. Two Vols. 12mo. 6s. Hookham.

This novel is not deftitute of agreeable qualities, though it
abounds with defects. The incidents in general are neither
interefting nor new, and the attention is frequently fatigued
with a fimilarity of defcription. But thefe blemifhes are in
fome degree compenfated by the marks of an unvitiated difpofition, and of natural fenfibility, obfervable in many parts of
the narrative.

DRAMATIC.

*The Recript Tax. A Farce in Two Acts, as performed at the The-
atre Royal in the Haymarket. 8vo. 1s.* Stockdale.

Though farce and comedy be equally compofitions intended to
excite the laughter of the audience, they are widely different in
refpect of the means by which they endeavour to produce that
effect. In legitimate comedy there are certain laws of decorum,
which even the greateft eccentricity of character ought never to
violate ; but in farcical productions, a more extenfive latitude
may be allowed ; always excluding, however, what is obvioufly
immoral or profane. The author of the prefent farce has not
been extremely fcrupulous with regard to this circumftance ;
nor has he happily infufed that ftrain of humour, and laughable abfurdity, which is calculated to atone for defects.

*The Prince of Arragon. A Dramatic Piece, with Songs, as per-
formed at the Theatre Royal, in the Haymarket. By J. O'Keefe.
8vo. 1s.* Cadell.

An elegant compliment to the Prince of Wales on his birth-
day ; now publifhed with the beft of *all poffible* dedications—for
which, we hope, the author has received an acknowledgment
proportioned to its merit.

Triftram

Tristram Shandy. A Farcical Bagatelle; as it is now performing at the Theatre Royal, Covent Garden. By L. Macnally, Esq. 8vo. 1s. Bladon.

The author, by a judicious and liberal use of his pruning knife, and a proper distribution of the incidents, has rendered this little piece much more pleasing and dramatic than it appeared to us when first performed at Covent Garden theatre.

MISCELLANEOUS.

Advice to the Universities of Oxford and Cambridge, and to the Clergy of every Denomination. Small 8vo. 2s. Kearsley.

In ancient times many customs were observed in our Universities, which were absurd and ridiculous; and others, which were mean and illiberal. Among the former, we may reckon some of those which Pointer has mentioned, in his Antiquities of Oxford; among the latter, we may include the custom of capping the quadrangle, the office of servitors, the use of the small round cap, and other tokens of servility, unsuitable to the character of gentlemen, who go to the university for the benefit of LIBERAL education.

As some of these customs are still retained at Oxford and Cambridge, we imagined that they might be the objects of our author's animadversions. But his satire, we find, consists only of ironical advice to the vice-chancellor, the proctors, the heads of colleges, the fellows, the undergraduates, and certain academical wights, included under the denomination of Quiz, Raph, or Buck.

The first bears a general resemblance to the character of a pedant; the second is a sloven or blackguard; the third is a turbulent and ungovernable rake.

The latter part of this work is addressed to the clergy; and, like the former, contains some USEFUL ADVICE.

The Beauties of Shakspeare. 12mo. 2s. 6d. sewed. Kearsley.

This is not the first time that the beauties of the celebrated English poet have been extracted. A selection of the same kind, under the title of 'Shakespeariana,' was made by Gildon, who arranged the several passages under distinct heads. Dr. Dodd, in executing a similar work, conducted the arrangement, not by classification, but by adhering to the order in which the parts which he selected occur in the writings of the great dramatist. The editor of the present selection has adopted the method of Gildon, which is doubtless the most useful for those who would have recourse to the poet's sentiments concerning particular situations in human life.

The Trial of Christopher Atkinson, Esq. M. P. 8vo. 2s. Debrett.

The crime imputed to this delinquent was perjury, of which he was clearly convicted. He had been cornfactor to his majesty's victualling board; and his name, until formally erased, still disgraces the list of the House of Commons.

Narrative of Two Sailors. 8vo. 1s. Pownal.

This narrative relates to the Grosvenor Indiaman, which was wrecked on the coast of Caffraria, in August, 1782.

THE
CRITICAL REVIEW.

For the Month of *November*, 1783.

Philofophical Tranfactions of the Royal Society of London. Vol.
  LXXII. Part II. *For the Year* 1782. 4to. 8s. *fewed.*
  L. Davis.

THIS part of the annual volume is fmall, but, in many
  refpects, important. We mention this with particular
pleafure, fince the Society have been fometimes accufed of
compenfating by the bulk, for the value of their materials:
but we muft proceed in the ufual manner.

Article XIX. An Attempt to make a Thermometer for meafuring the higher Degrees of Heat, from a red Heat up to the
ftrongeft that Veffels made of Clay can fupport. By Jofiah
Wedgwood.—This article appears to us of confiderable importance; though the philofopher was not wholly deftitute of affiftance. Sir Ifaac Newton inveftigated with care the heat of bodies; and, by applying the thermometer when it would bear
that of iron, which had been allowed to cool gradually from a
red heat, calculated what was the higheft point, from that which
he was able to meafure. The experiment by which he endeavoured to eftablifh his propofition is related in a former volume
of the Philofophical Tranfactions. (Abridgment, IV. z. p. 3.)
He fuppofed that the quantities of heat loft, in given fmall
times, would be always proportional to the heats fubfifting in it,
reckoning the heat to be juft the excefs, whereby it is warmer
than the ambient air. If then the times be in an arithmetical
progreffion, the heats will be in a geometrical. Principia, lib.
ii. lem. 1. The fuppofition was however to be more exactly
limited; and, when his experiments were repeated, the refults were different. Other methods were afterwards invefti-

gated, but they require frequently so much attention, and sometimes so long calculations, that they have been seldom practised. The most ready method, though by no means an exact one, is to heat a cube of iron in the fire, whose heat is to be measured, and to plunge it into a given quantity of water, of a given heat; the increase of heat, allowing for the different densities of the iron and water, gives the degree required. Still it was necessary to attain both a more easy and exact method of measuring high degrees of heat; and we think that Mr. Wedgwood, who has modestly styled his paper an 'attempt' only, has in general succeeded.

The experiment is founded on the property of clays diminishing in bulk from fire. He finds that this diminution is regular and gradual, from a low red heat, to the greatest degree that clay can bear, without being vitrified. That the clay may be repeatedly cooled and heated, yet, in higher degrees, its diminution shall go on as regularly as if it had not before been exposed to the fire. The method of making a thermometer of this kind is therefore obvious; either a cylinder or a paralelopiped is formed of this clay, and hardened in the lowest red heat. After it is hardened, it must be ground down to a given size, and its length should be about an inch; a gage is then made, twenty-four inches long, divided into inches and tenths; this gage consists of two upright pieces of brass, fixed on a base. The distance between them, at the top, is exactly equal to the size of the clay in its hardened state, and the sides converge, so that, at the bottom, their distance is equal to what it will assume from being exposed to the greatest heat which it will bear; consequently, at any intermediate degree, the converging sides will prevent it from falling down, and the marks on the brass will point out the diminution.

The contrivance is elegant and ingenious, though not described so minutely as to enable a workman to follow it; but, when the principle is once understood, the minuter directions are easily supplied. It will be obvious, that the clay must be of the same kind, to compare observations made with it; our author observes, that the Cornish porcelain clays are best adapted to this purpose, and offers to the Royal Society enough of it to supply the world with thermometers for numerous ages. But as he has given an accurate analysis of it, and finds that five parts of this clay affords three parts of pure argillaceous earth, and two parts of an earth of a very different kind, probably siliceous, we think there will be little difficulty in imitating it. A piece of burnt earth, four-tenths of an inch deep, six-tenths broad, and an inch long, may be cheap enough, if even alum is decomposed to procure the

z
clay

clay pure; while nearly one-half is supplied by a substance so cheap, and so easily procured, as common flint. All clays have a large proportion of flint; sometimes it exceeds one-half of the whole quantity.

It is an inconvenience in all thermometers, that their degrees are arbitrary, and subject to many alterations, which we can neither foresee or prevent; so that their real utility arises only from these circumstances affecting every observation, by which we certainly attain the *relative* heats. We cannot therefore object to Mr. Wedgwood's attempt on this account; nor is it of more importance to observe, that a scale of this kind can never be very minute. It must begin above a low red heat; and, though the scales of thermometers are sometimes carried farther than this point, they certainly cannot be employed to measure with accuracy heats which are so intense. His thermometer, he observes, shows the change, when it is equal to $\frac{1}{600}$ part of its bulk, which is fully equal to every exigency either of the chemist or the potter. To compensate these seeming disadvantages, it possesses some material conveniencies; but on this occasion we must use Mr. Wedgwood's own words.

' The thermometer-pieces possess some singular properties, which we could not have expected to find united in any substance whatever, and which peculiarly fit them for the purposes they are here applied to.

' 1. When baked by only moderate degrees of fire, though they are, like other clays, of a porous texture, and imbibe water; yet, when saturated with the water, their bulk continues exactly the same as in a dry state.

' 2. By very strong fire, they are changed to a porcelain or semi-vitreous texture; nevertheless. their contraction, on further augmentations of the heat, proceeds regularly as before, up to the highest degree of fire that I have been able to produce.

' 3. They bear sudden alternatives of heat and cold; may be dropped at once into intense fire, and, when they have received its heat, may be plunged as suddenly into cold water, without the least injury from either.

' 4. Even while saturated with water in their porous state, they may be thrown immediately into a white heat, without bursting or suffering any injury.

' 5. Sudden cooling, which alters both the bulk and texture of most bodies, does not at all affect these, at least not in any quality subservient to their thermometric uses.

' 6. Nor are they affected by long *continuance* in, but solely by, the *degree* of heat they are exposed to. In three minutes or less, they are perfectly penetrated by the heat which acts upon them, so as to receive the full contraction which that degree

Y 2

of

of heat is capable of producing equally with thofe which had undergone its action during a gradual increase of its force for many hours. Strong degrees of heat are communicated to them with more celerity than weak ones: perhaps the heat may be more readily tranfmitted, in proportion as the texture becomes more compact.

'Thefe facts have been afcertained by many experiments, the particulars of which are omitted, becaufe they would fwell this paper much beyond the bulk intended.

'The ufe and accuracy of this thermometer for meafuring, *after an operation*, the degree of heat which the matter has undergone, will be apparent. The foregoing properties afford means of meafuring it alfo, eafily and expeditioufly, *during the operation*, fo that we may know when the fire is increafed to any degree previoufly determined upon. The piece may be taken out of the fire in any period of the procefs, and dropped immediately into water, fo as to be fit for meafuring by the gage in a few feconds of time. At the fame inftant, another piece may be introduced into the place of the former, to be taken out and meafured in its turn; and thus alternately, till the defired degree of heat is obtained. But as the cold piece will be two or three minutes in receiving the full heat, and correfponding contraction; to avoid this lofs of time, it may be proper, on fome occafions, to have two or more pieces, according to convenience, put in together at firft, that they may be fuccefsively cooled in water, and the degrees of heat examined at fhorter intervals. It will be unneceffary to fay any thing further upon precautions or procedures which the very idea of a thermometer muft fuggeft, and in which it is not apprehended that any difficulty can occur, which every experimenter will not readily find means to obviate.

'It now only remains, that the language of this new thermometer be underftood, and that it may be known what the heats meant by its degrees really are. For this purpofe a great number of experiments has been made, from which the following refults are felected.

'The fcale commences at a red-heat, fully vifible in daylight; and the greateft heat that I have hitherto obtained in my experiments is 160°. This degree I have produced in an air-furnace about eight inches fquare.

'Mr. Alchorne has been fo obliging as to try the neceffary experiments with the pure metals at the Tower, to afcertain at what degrees of this thermometer they go into fufion; and it appears, that Swedifh copper melts at 27, filver at 28, and gold at 32.

'Brafs is in fufion at 21. Neverthelefs, in the brafs and copper founderies, the workmen carry their fires to 140° and upwards: for what purpofe they fo far exceed the melting heat, or whether fo great an additional heat be really neceffary, I have not learnt.

'The

' The welding heat of iron is from 90 to 95; and the greatest heat that could be produced in a common smith's forge 125.

' Cast iron was found to melt at 130°, both in a crucible in my own furnace, and at the foundery; but could not be brought into fusion in the smith's forge, though that heat is only 5° lower. The heat by which iron is run down among the fuel for casting is 150°.

' As the welding state of iron is a softening or beginning fusion of the surface, it has been generally thought that cast iron would melt with much less heat than what is necessary for producing this effect upon the forged; whereas, on the contrary, cast iron appears to require, for its fusion, a heat exceeding the welding heat 35 or 40°, which is much more than the heat of melted copper exceeds the lowest visible redness.

' Thus we find, that though the heat for melting copper is by some called a white heat, it is only 27° of this thermometer. The welding heat of iron, or 90°, is likewise a white heat; even 130°, at which cast iron is in fusion, is no more than a white heat; and so on to 160° and upwards is all a white heat still. This shews abundantly how vague such a denomination must be, and how inadequate to the purpose of giving us any clear ideas of the extent of what we have been accustomed to consider as one of the three divisions of heat in ignited bodies.

' A Hessian crucible, in the iron foundery, viz. about 150°, melted into a flag-like substance. Soft iron nails, in a Hessian crucible in my own furnace, melted into one mass with the bottom of the crucible, at 154°: the part of the crucible above the iron was little injured.

' The *fonding* heat of the glass furnaces I examined, or that by which the perfect vitrification of the materials is produced, was at one of them 114° for flint-glass, and 124° for plate-glass; at another it was only 70° for the former, which shews the inequality of heat, perhaps unknown to the workmen themselves, made use of for the same purpose. After complete vitrification, the heat is abated for some hours to 28 or 29°. which is called the *settling* heat; and this heat is sufficient for keeping the glass in fusion. The fire is afterwards increased, for working the glass, to what is called the *working* heat; and this I found, in plate-glass, to be 57°.

' Delft ware is fired by a heat of 40 or 41°; cream-coloured, or queen's ware, by 86°; and stone ware, called by the French *pots de grès*, by 102°: by this strong heat, it is changed to a true porcelain texture. The thermometer-pieces begin to acquire a porcelain texture about 110°.

' The above degrees of heat were ascertained by thermometer-pieces fired along with the ware in the respective kilns. But this thermometer affords means of doing much more, and going further in these measures than I could at first even have expected; it will enable us to ascertain the heats by which many of the porcelains and earthen wares of distant nations and differ-

ent

ent ages have been fired: for as burnt clay, and compofitions in which clay is a prevailing ingredient, fuffer no diminution of their bulk by being re-paffed through degrees of heat which they have already undergone, but are diminished by any additional heat, if a fragment of them be made to fit into any part of the gage, and then fired along with a thermometer-piece till it begins to diminifh, the degree at which this happens points out the heat by which it had been fired before. Of feveral pieces of ancient Roman and Etrufcan wares, which I have examined, none appear to have undergone a greater heat than 32°, and none lefs than 20°; for they all began to diminifh at thofe or the intermediate degrees.

' By means of this thermometer fome interefting properties of natural bodies may likewife be difcovered or more accurately determined, and the genus of the bodies afcertained. Jafper, for inftance, is found to diminifh in the fire, like an artificial mixture of clay and filiceous matter; granite, on the contrary, has its bulk enlarged by fire, whilft flint and quartzofe ftones are neither enlarged nor diminifhed. Thefe experiments were made in fires between 70 and 80° of this thermometer. A fufficient number of facts like thefe, compared with each other, and with the properties of fuch natural or artificial bodies as we wifh to find out the compofition of, may lead to various difcoveries, of which I have already found fome promifing appearances; but many more experiments are wanting to enable me to fpeak with that certainty and precifion on thefe fubjects which they appear to deferve.

' A piece of an Etrufcan vafe melted completely at 33°; pieces of fome other vafes and Roman ware about 36°; Worcefter china vitrified at 94°; Mr. Sprimont's Chelfea china at 105°; the Derby at 112°; and Bow at 121°; but Briftol china fhewed no appearance of vitrification at 135°. The common fort of Chinefe porcelain does not perfectly vitrify by any fire I could produce; but began to foften about 120°, and at 156° became fo foft as to fink down, and apply itfelf clofe upon a very irregular furface underneath. The true ftone Nankeen, by this ftrong heat, does not foften in the leaft; nor does it even acquire a porcelain texture, the unglazed parts continuing in fuch a ftate as to imbibe water and ftick to the tongue. The Drefden porcelain is more refractory than the common Chinefe, but not equally fo with the ftone Nankeen. The cream-coloured or queen's ware bears the fame heat as the Drefden, and the body is as little affected by this intenfe degree of fire.

' Mr. Pott fays, that to melt a mixture of chalk and clay in certain proportions, which proportions appear from his tables to be equal parts, is " among the mafter pieces of art." This mixture melts into a perfect glafs at 123° degrees of this thermometer.

' The whole of Mr. Pott's or any other experiments may, by repeating and accompanying them with thefe thermometric
pieces,

pieces, have their respective degrees of heat ascertained, and thereby be rendered more intelligible and useful to the reader, the experimenter, and the working artist.

' I flatter myself that a field is thus opened for a new kind of thermometrical inquiries; and that we shall obtain clearer ideas with regard to the differences of the degrees of strong fire, and their corresponding effects upon natural and artificial bodies; those degrees being now rendered accurately measurable, and comparable with each other, equally with the lower degrees of heat which are the province of the common mercurial thermometer.'

We have been more than usually full on this article, because it seems to deserve attention. It adds not only to the *bulk*, but to the *stock*, and contributes to extend our enquiries, by facilitating the means of ascertaining the powers of our instruments.

Article XX. An Analysis of Two Mineral Substances, viz. the Rowley-rag-stone and the Toad-stone. By William Withering, M. D.—Dr. Withering appears to be both an industrious and an accurate chemist. He purposes to investigate the nature of all those ' substances which are known to exist in the earth in large quantities.' The attempt is laudable, and, in pursuing it, he will probably add more to our knowlege than all the systems of cosmogony which have been hitherto invented.

' The Rowley-rag-stone forms a range of hills in the southern part of Staffordshire. The lime-stone rocks at Dudley bed up against it, and the coal comes up to the surface against the lime-stone. The highest part of the hills is near the village of Rowley. The summit has a craggy, broken appearance, and the fields on each side to a considerable distance are scattered over with large fragments of the rock, many of which are sunk in the ground. In a quarry near Dudley, where a pretty large opening has been made in order to get materials for mending the roads, the rock appears to be composed of masses of irregular rhomboidal figures: some of these masses inclose rounded pebbles of the same materials. At the distance of four, five, or six miles from the hills, as at Bilston, Willenhall, and Wednesbury, the rag-stone is frequently found some feet below the surface in rhomboidal pieces, forming an horizontal bed of no great depth, and seldom of more than a few yards extent.—

' Its more obvious properties are a dark grey appearance, with numerous minute shining crystals. When exposed to the weather gets an ochry colour on the outside; strikes fire with steel; cuts glass; melts, though not easily, under the blowpipe. Heated in an open fire becomes magnetic, and loses about 3 in 100 of its weight.—

' It consists of siliceous earth, clay, or earth of allum, and calx of iron. From the latter must be deducted $11\frac{1}{2}$ for the

quantity

quantity of calciform iron, found by experiment to be contained in the quantity of phlogisticated alkaly made use of, and then the proportions in 100 parts of the stone will be these:

Pure siliceous earth	—	$47\frac{1}{2}$
Pure clay, free from fixable air	—	$32\frac{1}{2}$
Iron in a calciform state	—	20

$$100$$

'From this view of the component parts of this stone, it is not improbable, that it might advantageously be used as a flux for calcareous iron ores. The makers of iron are acquainted with such ores, but never could work them to advantage, for want of a cheap and efficacious flux.'

The toad-stone forms large strata in Derbyshire, which are fully described in Mr. Whitehurst's very valuable and intelligent work. It is of a dark brownish grey; 'a granulated texture, with several cavities filled with crystallized spar. It does not strike fire with steel; it melts to a black glass.' From the experiments 100 parts of this species of toad-stone appeared to contain

Siliceous earth	—	—	56 } $=63\frac{5}{10}$
More ditto	—	—	$7\frac{5}{10}$
Calciform iron	—	—	16
Calcareous earth	—	—	$7\frac{5}{10}$
Earth of allum	—	—	$14\frac{5}{10}$

$$101\frac{5}{10}$$

'From the addition of $1\frac{5}{10}$ of weight it is probable, that the substances capable of uniting with fixable air were not in the specimen used fully saturated with it, as they would be after their precipitation by the mild alkaly.

'Upon repeating these experiments with different portions of the toad-stone, the quantities of the calcareous earth were found to differ a little; but nothing further appeared to invalidate the general conclusions.'

The experiments seem to have been planned with judgment and executed with dexterity. They are also related with remarkable clearness. Dr. Withering has added a table, showing the solubility or insolubility of certain saline substances in alcohol, taken from Macquer and his own experiments. But his table would have been more useful, if he had noticed also the degrees of these qualities.

Article XXI. New Fundamental Experiments upon the Collision of Bodies. By Mr. John Smeaton, F. R. S.—We entirely agree with the attentive and judicious author of this article, that simple principles of science cannot be too critically examined. To be accurate in the elements is the first step in improvements; but this accuracy is only to be attained by a master of the science, because he alone can be aware

of

of the different sources of fallacy. Mr. Smeaton, with this view, introduced his Tract on Mechanic Power to the Society, and it was published in the LXVIth volume, for the year 1776. This paper was intended as a supplement to it ; but different circumstances prevented its appearance at that time. His present purpose is to show, that whether bodies are gradually put in motion from rest, and uniformly accelerated to any given velocity, or suddenly moved in consequence of collision, the principle of motion and its laws are the same ; or, at least, have the same relation to mechanic power defined in the paper just mentioned. It is not necessary in this place to state the opinions of philosophers on the communication of motion ; the point at present in dispute is concerning non-elastic bodies. It has been always said that, when one non-elastic body either perfectly soft, or perfectly hard, impinges on another at rest, that both will proceed with *one half* of the velocity of the impinging body.

Mr. Smeaton, in his Experiments on Mills, was misled by this doctrine, and now endeavours to support a very different one. It is well known that there are no bodies *perfectly* hard, soft, elastic, or non-elastic ; and that water only comes nearest to the description of a non-elastic soft body. The want of subjects for a proper experiment, has occasioned endless confusion ; since philosophy, without the assistance of facts to guide it, degenerates into fanciful and groundless hypothesis. Mr. Smeaton therefore properly observes, that this subject can be only determined by an *indirect* experiment, so limited, as clearly to prove that the velocity, after the collision of *non-elastic soft* bodies, must be very different from that which appears after the collision of non-elastic hard ones. In fact, to show that by the change of figure, which a soft body suffers in an experiment of this kind, that *one-half* of the original power is lost. In the case of elastic bodies, a force seemingly equal to that lost in changing the figure of soft bodies, for a time disappears, but is again capable of being exerted without any original accession.

These opinions are brought to their proper test by means of a machine, for which we must refer to the volume itself. The principle on which the experiments depend is, the comparison of elastic bodies with non-elastic ones, by the action of the springs being allowed, or suspended at pleasure. The experiments on this machine fully show, that one half of the mechanic power, residing in the striking body (when both are non-elastic and soft) is actually lost in the stroke. We shall insert Mr. Smeaton's conclusion respecting inelastic hard bodies, which he thinks cannot exist, because their properties

involve

involve a contradiction. We particularly infert it for the confideration of our philofophical readers, who will find in it fome curious fubjects of fpeculation.

'Refpecting bodies unelaftic and perfectly hard, we muft infer, that fince we are unavoidably led to a conclufion concerning them, which contradicts what is efteemed a truth capable of the ftricteft demonftration, viz. that the velocity of the center of gravity of no fyftem of bodies can be changed by any collifion betwixt one another, fomething muft be affumed that involves a contradiction. This perfectly holds, according to all the eftablifhed rules, both of perfectly elaftic and perfectly non-elaftic *foft* bodies; rules which muft fail in the perfectly non-elaftic *hard* bodies, if their velocity after the ftroke is to the velocity of the ftriking body as one is to the fquare root of 2; for then the center of gravity of the two bodies will by the ftroke acquire a velocity greater than the center of gravity the two bodies had before the ftroke in that proportion, which is proved thus.

' At the outfet of the ftriking body, the centre of gravity of the two bodies in our cafe will be exactly in the middle between the two; and when they meet it will have moved from their half diftance to their point of contact, fo the velocity of the center of gravity before the bodies meet will be exactly one half of the velocity of the ftriking body; and, therefore, if the velocity of the ftriking body is 2, the velocity of the center of gravity of both will be one. After the ftroke, as both bodies are fuppofed to move in contact, the velocity of the center of gravity will be the fame as that of the bodies; and as their velocity is proved to be the fquare root of 2, the velocity of their center of gravity will be increafed from 1. to the fquare root of 2.; that is, from 1. to 1.414 &c.

' The fair inference from thefe contradictory conclufions therefore is, that an unelaftic hard body (perfectly fo) is a repugnant idea, and contains in itfelf a contradiction; for to make it agree with the fair conclufions that may be drawn on each fide, from clear premifes, we fhall be obliged to define its properties thus: that in the ftroke of unelaftic hard bodies they cannot poffibly lofe any mechanic power in the ftroke, becaufe no other impreffion is made than the communication of motion; and yet they muft lofe a quantity of mechanic power in the ftroke; becaufe, if they do not, their common center of gravity, as above fhewn, will acquire an increafe of velocity by their ftroke upon each other.

' In a like manner the idea of a perpetual motion, perhaps, at firft fight, may not appear to involve a contradiction in terms; but we fhall be obliged to confefs that it does, when, on examining its requifites for execution, we find we fhall want bodies having the following properties; that when they are made to *afcend* againft gravitation their abfolute weight fhall be

lefs

lefs; and that when they *defcend* by gravitation (through an equal fpace) their abfolute weight fhall be greater; which, according to all we know of nature, is a repugnant or contradictory idea.' [*To be continued.*]

Pharmacopœia Collegii Regii Medicorum Edinburgenfis. 8*vo.* 5*s.* in Boards. Robinfon.

A S fcience has advanced, and medicine acquired a greater fimplicity, and probably fuperior efficacy, the members of a college, which has contributed to fome of thefe improvements, would have been unpardonable, if they had not availed themfelves of the new æra which they have adorned. Different editions of this Pharmacopeia have confequently been publifhed; but, though none have been faultlefs; and though, in fome inftances, we have obferved alterations rather than improvements, yet they have evinced their attention to the fcience itfelf, and have laudably aimed at a degree of perfection which human frailty can probably never attain. In the edition of 1774, the lift of the articles of materia medica was very confiderably fhortened; but it was obfervable, that fome new remedies were adopted, from fufpicious fources, with a facility which is feldom confpicuous in an experienced phyfician. The prefent edition probably will not be thought materially defective, though the different preparations of the flammula jovis, pulfatilla nigricans, ftramonium, and white dittany, are expunged. The ambergris, calcined bones, faffron, Curaffoa orange, eryngo, St. John's wort, afh-coloured liver-wort, opoponax, oyfter fhells, and comfrey, have fhared the fame fate; and it will by no means difgrace the art, or injure the diftreffed, if they are never recalled. But the fame complaifance which induced them to attend to M. Storck, has ftill in fome degree influenced them. The new medicines are probably only fuggefted for the fake of a cautious experiment; but thefe refpectable phyficians ought to have confidered, that, in their Pharmacopeia, they acquire an eftablifhment, at leaft for the period of the prefent impreffion; and that, while the world, with reafon, complains of the inftability of the art, they add to its uncertainty, by fuffering themfelves to be wafted, 'arbitrio populario auræ.'——The additional remedies in this edition are the arnica, balf. Gileadenf. cardamine pratenfis, caffia lignea, cinera hortenfis, cubebæ, curfuta, a root of which we have never heard, digitalis purpurea, elaterium, filix mas, dolichos pruriens, geoffræa inermis or cabbage bark, gratiola, ginfeng, lichen Iflandicus, lobelia, olivæ, palmæ fructus & oleum, capficum, pix liquida, quaffia, rad. Indica

Indica Lopez, rhododendron cryfanthemum, fal alcalin. fof-filis, falicis cort. fang. draconis, fapo alb. Hifpanus, fpigelia Marylandica or Indian pink, vipera & ulmi cortex.

Some of thefe medicines are reftored from former catalogues, from which they had been expunged, by a rage for reformation: a very few extepted, we receive them with pleafure. The learned reader will recollect, that the others have been adopted from authors of credit; though we are forry to obferve, that we cannot yet expect any regular importation of them. The rad. Indica Lopez, which was firft mentioned by Gaubius, has not, we believe, been fince procured.

In this edition the feveral fpecies are afcertained with accuracy from Linnæus, and thofe authors who have feverally defcribed them. This part is very material: it often points out a remarkable affinity between medicines little known and thofe in our poffeffion, and fometimes fhows that we have rejected and admired remedies which refemble each other. It is probably by attending to the natural orders, and other relations, that we fhall complete our reformation of the materia medica.

The great change, which influences every part of this edition, is the direction of the College, to determine every thing by weight. The liquid menftrua are therefore never meafured, and the quantities are confequently apparently varied. The names of the neutral falts are changed, and better adapted to their real nature. The cupr. ammoniacale and the tart. emet. which they have called tartarus antimonialis, with fome others, are differently prepared. As the latter is very frequently employed, and, as the recipe feems remarkably accurate, we fhall infert it.

' ℞ Caufticum antimon. vel butyri antimon. q. v. infunde in aquam fervidam, in quâ falis alkalini fixi vegetabilis purificati tantundem prius fuerit folutum, ut præcipitatur pulv. antim. qui, probe ablutus, exciccetur. Dein aquæ libris quinque, adde hujus pulveris, drachmas novem, cryftallor. Tart, pulv. uncias duas, cum femiffe; coque paulifper donec folvantur pulveres. Solutio cocta lente vaporet in vafe vitreo, ad pelliculam ut cryftalli formentur.'

We fhall alfo beg leave to infert a neat and expeditious method of preparing the animal oil, which we have great reafon to expect will be a very efficacious medicine.

' Oleum e Cornubus Rectificatum, five Oleum Animale.

' R. Olei empyreumatici e cornubus animalium deftillati recentis, q. v.

' Diftillet ex matracio, capitello inftructo, igne leni, quamdiu prodit oleum tenue coloris expers, quod ope aquæ a fale et fpiritu spiritu alcalino purgetur. Ut limpidum et sincerum restet hoc oleum, in phialis parvis omnino repletis et inversis servari debet, cuique vasculo prius instillatis aliquot aquæ guttis, ut, inverso vasculo, hæc inter oleum et vasis obturaculum interjaceat.

The external remedies are almost entirely changed in their forms, as well as more systematically described. But while it is impossible even to hint at all the alterations, or to point out the several improvements, it is no less difficult, in our confined limits, to offer those remarks which have occurred to us. This Dispensatory, though a strong proof of the attention of that respectable school to the improvement of their art, is still in some parts defective; but, in general, the forms are neat and elegant, frequently accurate, and well adapted to their particular purposes.

Observations on the Management of the prevailing Diseases in Great Britain, particularly in the Army and Navy; together with a Review of that of other Countries, and Arithmetical Calculations of the comparative Success of different Methods of Cure. By John Millar, M. D. 4to. 16s. in Boards. Johnson.

THIS volume has been printed since the year 1778, but is only now published. It contains a variety of different observations, from which we were willing to have extracted something valuable, but cannot boast of the success of our researches. The conduct of the Westminster Dispensary is not at present our object; and, though we may be astonished at seeing 138 cases of consumption cured, out of 212, or nearly ⅔, we shall not contend with the author, that, by some inadvertency, probably catarrhal complaints, have been invested with this formidable title. The contest with Dr. D. Monro is in abler hands; though it will detain us, for a short time, in the subsequent article.

The principal intention of our author is to show, that fevers are very generally of one kind only; that the bark is the general specific, and alone, or with a cordial regimen, equal to the cure. These are the propositions which in different parts of the work are considered in different views. Dr. Millar leaves them with anxiety and reluctance, and returns to them with pleasure. It would not probably be deemed an objection to observe, that propositions so general will become the refuge of indolence or of ignorance: they must be examined with candour and with caution, and ultimately determined by experience. The subject is not new; so that we can enter on it with greater facility and confidence. Dr. Millar's first position is not generally true, that inflammatory

and

and mixed fevers rarely occur, and that the putrid is the more uſual type. We have examined the hiſtories of epidemics for this purpoſe; we have attended to the operations of nature with care and attention; but we muſt confeſs that, if we except fevers attended with *fixed* local inflammation, they were generally of the mixed kind; and we can find very few that did not appear to be, in the beginning, of an inflammatory tendency. Violent heat of the ſkin, a firm or hard pulſe, red urine, local pains, and fullneſs of the eyes, we conſider as ſymptoms of this kind. We are aware of *one* objection, and therefore add, that we now ſpeak of the *general nature* of epidemics, not of the appearances in a few individuals. Let then Dr. Millar come out on this ground, adduce the various hiſtories related by real obſervers, and collect with caution from them. The ſubject is not to be determined by general aſſertions or declamation.

There are indeed various circumſtances which will account for the opinions of our author. A populous city, where the inhabitants are crowded, with little air, and leſs attention to the circumſtances which may prevent or impede putrefaction: the phyſician, placed in a ſituation where the acceſs of fevers is probably ſeldom obſerved, and frequently obliged to depend on the reports of ignorant, and ſometimes of intereſted attendants: in theſe circumſtances he probably ſees nothing but thoſe putrid ſymptoms which announce extreme debility; and, on theſe accounts, the beneficial effects of the bark may be more conſiderable. But, though this may excuſe in ſome meaſure the confidence with which this remedy is recommended, it will not excuſe the Doctor's want of candour, in extending his praiſes, without excepting different ſituations, and other appearances.

In a late Review, when conſidering Dr. Robertſon's treatment of putrid fevers, we had occaſion to ſtate this queſtion in an exact but comprehenſive manner. It was not the opinion of the moment, but the reſult of ſome attention. The uſe of the bark we there confined to the malignant remittents, the fevers of camps and ſhips, ſometimes of hoſpitals and priſons. We had too much reſpect for our medical readers to mention the diſtinguiſhing circumſtances which are certainly ſometimes obſcure; but, that the diſtinction was well founded, appears from this fact, that the bark is more uſeful, the more nearly a fever approaches in its ſymptoms to an intermittent form. There certainly are malignant fevers, where it is pointedly and decidedly uſeful; there are others, where *alone* it is ſometimes uſeleſs, and ſometimes prejudicial. Reaſon and experience points out the diſtinction which we have made;

and

and we cannot recede from it, in consequence of a general, indiscriminate recommendation, though supported by positive assertions.

Dr. Millar will probably, in his turn, deny our assertion, that the bark is either useless or prejudicial in continued fevers of the putrid kind. It is therefore the opposition of facts, which must be determined by farther experience; but he will allow us to add, that if his cases resemble those which he has adduced under the title of Dr. Fothergill, Dr. Heberden, or Sir John Pringle's testimony, in favour of the bark, they will afford him very little assistance. Evidence, related in a manner so crude and so trifling, is at once a disgrace to the author, and an insult to the reader. There are other arguments on which we have as little dependence, as on the uncircumstantial facts which we have just reprehended. Fevers are, it seems, now less fatal than in some past periods; but is there no *other* change in their treatment? are there no variations in diet, and the manner of living? The same questions may be asked, when the records of public hospitals are produced with similar intentions. But, when our author adduces the testimony of practitioners which has been published, in support of his system, except Dr. Lettsom, all his evidence is taken from authors, who have treated of the malignant remittents.

His observations on the fevers of his majesty's navy are chiefly collected from Dr. Robertson's Journal, which has been already noticed, with respect, in our Review; and those, on infection, are useful; but we have met with nothing which has not been already mentioned by Dr. Lind, and other authors. Indeed this very concise account will not admit of a comparison with many which have been long since public.

Part of this volume contains an answer to our observations on his ' Account of the Prevailing Diseases of Great Britain *.' But, while we have no reason to retract a syllable which we there advanced, we must express our regret, that, in this more mature work, Dr. Millar seems not to have acquired either more candour or more knowlege. With this evidence of the irritability of our author, we should not have willingly opposed him, if we were not sensible that our duty required our interposition, and had not found that these opinions and this practice had already gained some ground, and been materially injurious to the public. As we neither wish for a dispute, nor fear it, we would advise him, in such circumstances, to adduce the experience of others rather than his own. Many practitioners have used the bark in continued fevers, and have given a candid testimony of its success.

---

* Crit. Rev. vol. xxix. 332—340. and 408—419.

Observations on the Management of Diseases in the Army and Navy, during the American War; together with some Account of the Loss of Senegal, and of the Army at York in Virginia. In Reply to Dr. Monro. By John Millar, M. D. 4to. 3s. Johnson.

THIS Supplement to the preceding work appeared with it; and the publication of both was probably occasioned by Dr. Monro's Reply to Dr. Millar, in the last edition of the Diseases of the Army. We are by no means inclined to take any part in the dispute. The difference between the returns cited by Dr. Monro and Dr. Millar seems to depend on this circumstance, that the one includes the sick of the whole army, the other the returns only of the general hospitals; but it may be added, that Dr. Monro's are the public returns from the War-office, and that we cannot judge of those of Dr. Millar: from the nature of the information, his source must necessarily be secret. As we have already mentioned that epidemics are generally of the mixed kind, we may expect to find inflammatory symptoms in a greater degree in the robust soldier, exposed to cold and wet, than in the enervated inhabitant of a crowded and dirty city. Yet, in the last situation, the first appearance of fevers has been so imposing, their shape so questionable, that there is no one circumstance which has so much perplexed us, as the propriety of early bleeding in small quantities. Every author speaks of it, with so much hesitation, that there is little foundation to determine; and though we have generally refrained from the lancet, we are not, at this moment, satisfied of the propriety of our conduct. A degree of inflammation probably increases the subsequent debility more than a cautious evacuation: but it is so difficult to determine in doubtful circumstances; the true path is so narrow, and so easily mistaken, that, on the whole, it has appeared more safe to abstain from a measure, which it is not easy to regulate. In the army however the diseases are very different; and an early bleeding, with an emetic and a laxative, will be often necessary. It adds no credit to Dr. Millar or his assistant, that at the end of one of his monthly returns, it is added, ' no antimonial medicine has been prescribed in the physician's department,' though there are thirteen remittent fevers, eleven consumptions, besides asthmas, dysenteries, &c.

Dr. Millar next resumes his former subject; and from the late publications of Dr. Robertson, Dr. Dancer, and Mr. Rollo, endeavours to support the credit of the bark. There is a great deficiency in his candour, when Mr. Schotte is added to this list. In *his last three* patients, as we have already mentioned in that article, he quieted the vomiting by opium,

opium, and then gave the bark. In two it fucceeded, and in the third failed; but, he very properly adds, that, ' at this time, the ravage of the difeafe had much abated; nor do I know, fays he, whether the fuccefs is to be afcribed to this mode of treatment, or perhaps to a wholefome change taking place in the air' (p. 139). But we are informed by Dr. Millar, in a comparative table, ' Fevers treated with bleeding, &c. at Senegal, *all* died; with opium and bark, *all* recovered.'—Indignation has fcarcely words to exprefs its feelings at a mifreprefentation fo flagrant.

We muft now take our leave of Dr. Millar, who has afcribed the furrender of York Town and Senegal to the number of fick, and confequently to the mifconduct of the phyficians. We fhall probably again meet him; but fhould wifh to find a greater degree of candour, and a more intimate acquaintance with the works of real obfervers.

Experiments and Obfervations in Electricity. By *Thomas Milner,* M. D. 8vo. 2s. Cadell.

THE chief defign of this fhort work is to explain the conftruction of a little portable apparatus, which may be readily made, and eafily carried even in the pocket, to fhow the common properties of the electric fluid. Though no great power can be excited, yet the tender and exact balance of the different parts are proportioned to the weaknefs of the materials. We were confequently pleafed with the neatnefs of the contrivances, and recommend the work to thofe gentlemen who think that philofophical amufements, and the exercife of a mechanical genius, are preferable to the pleafures of the chace, or of the bottle.

While we leave the particular defcriptions to thofe who can follow them more fatisfactorily by the affiftance of the plates, it may be expected that we fhould enlarge on the opinions of the author, and the refult of his experiments. The tendency of thefe is, to illuftrate the Franklinian fyftem of contrary ftates of electricity; a fyftem which has flourifhed from oppofition, and acquired ftrength even from thofe efforts which were calculated for its deftruction. Every body, whether an electric or conductor, in our author's opinion, feems to be attracted by the electric power, though *properly* only the oppofite powers attract each other; and, in every circumftance, the fubftance attracted is only influenced from its acquiring a ftate contrary to that of the fubftance which attracts. This general power of attraction is, in fome refpects, different from the received opinions; and it became neceffary to account for

the feeming repulfion. In this part our author appears rather
deficient, and probably the fubject may be elucidated by his
future labours. At prefent he feems to think, that the repulfion is owing to a change in the electricity of the air, which
attracts, in a different direction, the body which appears to be
repelled. Dr. Milner frequently mentions the ' permanent'
and ' influential' electricities : if we properly underftand him,
he means a real difference in the fides of a phial, or a plate
of glafs; which they preferve, even after the fuperadded power,
communicated by the charge, has been diffipated. This is a
little inconfiftent with the permeablility of glafs by this fluid,
which he endeavours to fupport; but the force of feveral facts,
as well as the explanation which it affords of Mr. Volto's elec-
trophorus, induce him to adopt it. The oppofite nature of
the pofitive and negative powers, he thinks, produces the
different phænomena of the univerfe; and that all our electrical experiments are only different modes of deftroying or reftoring the equilibrium,—he might have added, with their
different appearances and effects.

We have given this fhort analyfis of the more material parts
of the prefent work, with the defign of drawing the attention
of thofe whofe leifure will permit them to follow fimilar purfuits. The fimplicity of our author's views, and the elegance
of his experiments, deferve our commendations.

Dr. Milner has added fome obfervations on the analogy
between electricity and magnetifm, to fhow thofe who are
fond of deducing them from fimilar principles, that they are
frequently oppofite in their appearances. We fhall tranfcribe
them, as they feem to be equally intelligent and accurate.

'Several writers have mentioned the fimilar appearances of
electricity and magnetifm, in particular experiments; and the
analogy will be rendered ftill more ftriking, by confidering the
effects of an electric power on different fubftances, formed into
proper needles. It is however the influential electricity, and
that only in particular circumftances, which bears the neareft
refemblance to magnetifm. The experimental philofopher may
find it of fome ufe to remember thefe fimilitudes : but a regard
to truth requires alfo his attention to other circumftances,
which plainly fhow thefe powers to be effentially different.
Some of the moft remarkable circumftances of this kind are
contained under the following particulars :

'I. Electricity may be raifed in a great variety of very different fubftances, and is then capable of being communicated to
all bodies in general : but magnetifm is confined to one particular kind of matter, both in its origin and communication.

'II. The tourmalin, and a few other ftones, may be excited by
heat alone; though the generality of electric fubftances will not
act

act without friction. On the other hand, magnetism may be produced in the first instance by position alone, without either heat or friction.

' III. Insulation is a necessary part of almost every electrical experiment, and no good conducting body can retain even a small degree of this power without it : but nothing of a similar nature appears to have the least relation either to the retention or communication of magnetism.

' IV. A considerable degree of heat destroys both electricity and magnetism : and yet a moderate warmth, such as is found to be favourable to electricity in every respect, most certainly weakens a magnetic power, as appears from the late Mr. Canton's curious observations and experiments on the diurnal variation of the magnetic needle.

' V. Moisture is particularly unfavourable to electricity ; but magnetism is so far from being affected by it, that it is not in the least weakened by acting through water itself.

' VI. Electricity is capable of acting through electric substances, but with some diminution of power ; and this action is prevented by the interposition of every other body. Magnetism, on the contrary, cannot act through magnetic bodies, though it can through all others, and without the least diminution of power.

' VII. Every pointed conducting body weakens an electric power at some distance ; but nothing of the same kind has been observed in magnetism.

' VIII. No substances are capable of retaining any considerable degree of electricity in the exhausted receiver of an air pump : but a magnetic body retains the whole of its power, and acts with equal force, whether it be surrounded with air or not.

' IX. Electricity may be perceived by every one of the senses, either in its origin or communication : but the production and communication of magnetism are not attended with any sensible evidences ; neither can it be certainly known whether a body has received a magnetic power or not, without bringing it to the test of some experiment, and observing how that body and others of the same kind mutually act upon each other.

' X. Electricity appears to have no immediate relation to the poles of the earth : but polarity is the peculiar and distinguishing characteristic of magnetism.

' XI. The whole of any substance may be made electrical, either positively or negatively : but in every communication of magnetism, there will always be a north and a south pole in the same body, be it ever so small.

' XII. Electricity is either destroyed or weakened by every communication with other bodies : magnetism, on the contrary, is either preserved or strengthened by a communication of that power.

' XIII.

‘ XIII. In electricity the pofitive and negative powers will in fome cafes preferve, and in other cafes deftroy each other : but, in magnetifm, the poles of a different denomination will always preferve or ftrengthen each other.

‘ XIV. The ftrengthening a magnetic power in any body, will only enable it to lift a heavier weight, or to attract and repel the different ends of a magnetic needle at a greater diftance, or to communicate this power more readily to other bodies of the fame kind : but the greateft degree of magnetifm cannot produce the leaft refemblance to any of thofe various effects, which may be produced by the accumulation of an electric power. Electricity is fire itfelf, or fo intimately united with it, that when it is collected in a fufficient quantity, and properly difcharged, it becomes capable of firing different fubftances ; of rending fome bodies to pieces ; of melting and calcining metals ; of deftroying both animal and vegetable life ; and of producing all thofe wonderful effects, which have been obferved to be produced by lightning.

‘ Here it will be proper to ftate particularly, that a ftroke of lightning has given polarity to fteel ; and that the fame effect has been produced by fending a ftrong charge of electricity through a common fewing needle. This obfervation may help to eftablifh the famenefs of electricity and lightning, if it be taken in conjunction with a variety of other circumftances, in which they alfo agree : but as there is no other experimental proof of a real connection between electricity and magnetifm, and as thefe powers appear to be unlike in fo many other particulars, they ought certainly to be confidered as being effentially different, unlefs future difcoveries fhould produce fome other unqueftionable evidence of their connection, befides the folitary fact above mentioned ; which can prove but little in the prefent cafe, especially if it be confidered, that the ftroke of a hammer will alfo communicate to fteel the fame polarity.’

De Arte Medendi apud prifcos Muficcs Ope atque Carminum, Epiftola ad Antonium Relhan, M. D. Coll. Med. Lond. Soc. et Cenf. Editio altera & auctior. 8vo. 1s. 6d. Bowen.

THIS pamphlet is republifhed from the firft edition printed at Utrecht, with fome additions, and a flattering dedication to the earl of Shelburne, on his literary and political talents. It is the work of Michael Gafpar, well known on the continent for his claffical attainments ; but we never heard that he has attended to medicine as a fcience, and find no proof of it in the prefent epiftle. Since the days of the good Cornelius Scriblerus, we have heard no recommendation of he medical powers of mufic, except a confufed ftory of a ncing-mafter having been cured of the rheumatifm by it ; though

though the relief is to be attributed rather to the exercife and the perfpiration excited (for he was induced, as ufual, to dance), than to the melody. The boafted tales of its powers curing the tarantati are now well known to have been merely fictions.

Our author proceeds, from the earlieft periods, to bring proofs of the efficacy of this remedy; and we may prefume that he does not forget Saul and David, the double office of Apollo, as god of medicine and mufic, or the harp in the hands of Efculapius. The only remark which feems of confequence enough to deferve attention is, that Hippocrates produced another revolution in medicine, befides feparating it from philofophy, viz. difcarding the powers of mufic, in which he had little fkill. But this ftory has not the fhadow of foundation. Medicine was, at that time, ftudied as a branch of philofophy; though the philofophy of thefe ages was confined to vifionary fpeculations, and very feldom reduced to practice. If therefore we except the limited influence of one family, whofe powers were certainly inconfiderable, the practice of medicine, before the time of Hippocrates, was guided more by fuperftition than reafon, and the remedies were rather amulets than medicines.

In fact, the records of thefe remote ages are not worth the attention of a moment; but there is another and more evident error of our author, if he be really ferious in this defence, which we ought to mention. The greater part of his authorities fhow that *charms*, rather than *mufic*, were employed, fince the word 'carmen,' and its correfpondent word in Greek, 'ἐπῳδὴ,' are more frequently ufed in the former than in the latter fenfe. Cato's celebrated charm is ftill preferved; but our author attributes *his* cures to mufic, though his oppofition to every refinement and every elegant art is fufficiently notorious. If we except the credulous Pliny, all the authorities are adduced from the poets, and the hiftory of the fabulous ages. In the paffages quoted, Pliny fometimes means charms, and fometimes mufic; but he is a very uncertain authority in doubtful cafes, even though he fpeaks 'de re fibi haud incognita.' This is, we confefs, a character he is thought not to merit, for his own relations are fuppofed to be true: but let us hear his words; the paffage is not fingular :——— ' Ipfe in Africa *vidi* mutatum in marem nuptiarum die L. Copicium.' (Lib. vii. c. 4.)

Perhaps we have already been more diffufe than this author, though eloquent and learned, deferves. We may allow foft mufic to induce fleep, or, by exciting the attention, to draw it from pain; but we can go no farther : all beyond is

pre-

prejudice and fable. This Letter, as well as the dedication, is written with remarkable elegance, and chiefly on that account may be fufpected of irony. If fiction is the effence of poetry, we may fay with the author in his motto, ' hihil hic nifi carmina defunt.'

Flora Diætetica; or, Hiftory of Efculent Plants, both Domeftic and Foreign. By Charles Bryant, of Norwich. 8vo. 7s. White.

WE do not, in general, approve of methods which give the femblance of learning, without its weight and fubftance It is fcarcely an object worthy the attention of a botanift, to furnifh only the Linnæan names, or to enable any female precieufe, or her companion, to order the roots of the folanum tuberofum, or the leaves of the cichoreum endivia, as fauces for their dinner. It is lefs exceptionable to recommend a ' *competent*' knowlege of botany, to affift the travelling, or amufe and inftruct the ftationary gentleman; but this knowlege muft be fought at the fountain head, by patient ftudy and diligent inveftigation of the original language. Mr. Bryant, whom we refpect as a botanift, will excufe our freedom, when he perceives it is intended to promote the fcience which he cultivates and admires; but, though we fee little foundation in the reafons which feem to have induced him to undertake this work, yet we ftill think the attempt laudable, and the execution accurate. Every one will contemplate with eager curiofity the endeavours of different nations, either urged by the feverity of climate, or the accidental inclemency of feafons, in a purfuit fo effential to their exiftence: It raifes fuperior feelings to find that we can look above a failing harveft, or a deficient vintage; that we are protected by a Providence, which has fcattered food with a boundlefs profufion, fheltered it in woods, and even concealed it under the earth. It is ufeful alfo to collect the various facts, recorded by different authors into one view, and to examine the different pretenfions of each viand, which either folicits the appetite, or fcantily fupplies, in the hour of neceffity, the deficient meal. We might receive a philofophical repaft, by purfuing man from the fituation in which a mild climate furnifhes the proper food, and a contented mind aims at no more, to regions where nature on the one hand churlifhly denies, and, on the other, is lavifh of her bounties. Even one fpot, in the different æras and various ftates of opulence and fociety, might afford fufficient room for reflecting on the fmallnefs of our wants, and the profufenefs of our defires. But this is not the proper place to indulge fpeculations of

2   this

this kind; it is necessary rather to attend to the work before us.

Mr. Bryant has classed the esculent plants according to the parts which are the objects of our attention. He has given the generic and trivial names of Linnæus, with the concise and appropriated descriptions of Caspar Bauhine, in his Pinax; a method which we highly approve, and would recommend, instead of the string of synonyms which are sometimes added. He has next given a botanical description of the plant; and subjoined the methods of preparing it for food, with its effects on the body, when they are not purely alimentary. In this way he has collected a concise and comprehensive account of every dietetic vegetable, and there is reason to believe it will be generally acceptable. We have already said that the execution deserves our praises, yet ought to add, that there are some defects, and a few errors. The medical virtues of the different vegetables are sometimes exaggerated, though they are never materially misrepresented; and a few articles are less explicit than we had expected to find them. The sensible qualities also of many vegetables are omitted.

The defects however are by no means numerous, and seldom deserve the name of blemishes: we have chiefly mentioned them, to induce Mr. Bryant to review these parts of his work, in another edition. We shall insert, as a specimen, his account of the common onion; we have preserved it for the sake of our fair readers, who may avail themselves of the concluding advice.

' Allium cepa. Common Onion. Lin. Sp. pl. 431. Cepa vulgaris. Bauh. Pin. 71.

' From whence this was first brought into Europe is not known, but that it is natural to Africa is beyond a doubt, it being evident that onions were eaten by the Egyptians above two thousand years before Christ, and they make a great part of their constant food to this day in Egypt. Dr. Hasselquist says, it is not to be wondered at that the Israelites should long for them, after they had left this place, for whoever has tasted onions in Egypt must allow, that none can be had better in any part of the universe: here, he goes on, they are sweet, in other countries they are nauseous and strong; here they are soft, whereas in the North and other parts they are hard, and their coats so compact, that they are difficult to digest. They eat them roasted, cut into four pieces, with some bits of roasted meat, which the Turks call kebab; and with this dish they are so delighted, that they wish to enjoy it in paradise. They likewise make a soup of them in Egypt, which Hasselquist says is one of the best dishes he ever eat. The many ways of dressing onions in England are known to every family, but in regard

Z 4 gard

gard to wholesomeness, there is certainly no method equal to boiling, as thus they are rendered mild, of easy digestion, and go off without leaving those heats in the stomach and bowels, which they are apt to do any other way. Their nature is to attenuate thick, viscid juices, consequently a plentiful use of them in cold phlegmatic constitutions must prove beneficial. Many people shun them on account of the strong disagreeable smell they communicate to the breath; this may be remedied by eating a few raw parsley leaves immediately after, which will effectually overcome the scent of the onions, and cause them to sit more easy on the stomach.'

We think his account of the probable effects of the seeds of the dog-rose deserve attention, as we have frequently administered the cow-itch, sometimes called siliqua hirsuta, with success: we shall therefore transcribe it.

' Rosa canina. Dogs Rose. Lin. Sp. pl. 704. Rosa sylvestris vulgaris, flore odorato incarnato. Bauh. Pin. 483.

' The dogs rose is known to every one, by being so common in woods and hedges. These berries when mellowed by the frost have a very grateful acid flavour, which tempt many to eat them crude from the bush; but this is a bad practice, for the seeds are surrounded by a hairy, bristly substance, which if swallowed with the pulp, will, by pricking and vellicating the coats of the stomach and bowels, many times occasion sickness, and an itching uneasiness in the fundament. To avoid this therefore, the pulp should be carefully cleansed of this matter before eaten. There is a conserve of heps kept in the shops, which is deemed good in consumptions and disorders of the breast; and in coughs, from tickling defluxions of rheum.

' Notwithstanding what has been observed of the bad effects often attending the swallowing that bristly matter found in heps, yet it is probable this substance might be turned to advantage in some disorders, if judiciously managed; for it is nearly of the same nature to the celebrated cow-itch, so much in use among the Indians for killing of worms, and which they scrape off the pods of the dolichos urens. Their manner of giving the cow-itch, is to mix a small quantity of it with syrup or honey, and then eat it for two or three succeeding mornings fasting; this done, they take a dose of rhubarb, and if there be worms, it seldom fails to bring them away. It is plain from this, that the creatures receive their death by being stung and pricked with the cow-itch; and if this matter were given in the same manner, why should it not have the same effect, as it is much of the same prickly stinging nature?'

Mr. Bryant has mentioned the calla palustris, but observes, that he is not informed how it is usually eaten. Its insipid taste is commonly succeeded by a pungency, as from the arum; and as in the arum this stimulating quality is lost by boiling, though cold water has little effect in extracting it. It

‡   is

is more viscid than the arum, keeps better without turning to meal, and is more nutrient. It is eaten, we are informed, by some of the northern nations, after long boiling, and generally, if possible, after it has been kept for some time.

Mr. Bryant is commonly very short in describing different preparations of his esculent plants, though it would have rendered his book more valuable, if he had collected information of this kind. The best sources that we have met with are the Swedish and German authors.

We might enlarge this account with more specimens, but cannot easily give a better idea of a book, which consists chiefly of separate and detached articles. We may add, that it contains the several species of fruit-trees, described with accuracy from his own observation, and the best authorities; and even the humbler berries are considered with attention. We shall conclude this article with extracting some observations, which appear to us to deserve a very extensive circulation.

' Before I quit this article of wheat, I shall make an observation or two that may prove of some benefit to the generality of farmers. The common allowance of seed to sow an acre is not less than three bushels, a quantity, as Miller observes, which is certainly too much, but not perhaps altogether, for the reasons he gives. If the husbandman has ten coombs per acre, for his three bushels of seed, he thinks he has had an excellent crop, nor does he set himself about reflecting how much missed coming to perfection. Now if all the grain he sowed vegetated, and produced only two tolerable good ears each, and each ear contained only forty grains (which is rating them full low), the produce of one grain sown would be eighty, and the increase from the three bushels would be 240 bushels, or 60 coombs; consequently when he reaps but ten combs, he has the profit of only half a bushel of his seed. It stands the farmer in hand then to be careful about sowing his seed corn, and not throw it away to birds and other vermin, and which he frequently does, by sowing it too late. In order to prevent the ravages of these creatures, he ought to have all his wheat into ground by the end of October at longest, before the birds find a scarcity of food; for while there remains any part of the last year's offal on the fields, they will not trouble themselves much about the new sown grain; but as soon as they feel themselves pinched, they repair by flights to the fresh sown lands, and pick up all they can possibly get at; and though the seeds in general may have vegetated, yet if they be not strongly rooted, they make little difficulty of pulling them up by their leaves, and then twitch off the grain. Several sorts of birds are dexterous at this business, but larks in particular are quite adepts at at it; a fmall parcel of them will foon make a place as bare as it was before fown. Now this wafte never happens when there is plenty of food for thefe animals, nor can it be performed when the corn is much advanced, it then requiring more than their ftrength to draw it up, fo that if it be fown in time, and before thefe creatures are diftreffed, it fuffers little or nothing, but from the feverity of hard feafons. From what has been obferved it muft appear evident, that a much lefs quantity of feed fown early, properly fcattered, and well covered, will be productive of as large a crop as the ufual allowance is, and probably a larger, for the grains being lefs liable to be difturbed by the birds when ftriking root, and their roots ftanding more diftinct, they will be better fupplied with nourifhment, enabled to fupport their ftems, and bring their feed to greater perfection.'

Μετρικα Τινα Μονοστροφικα. *Metrica quædam Monoftrophica. Auctore Georgio Ifaaco Huntingford, A.M. e Coll. Nov. Oxon. Soc. 8vo. 2s.* Nichols.

THIS gentleman vindicates himfelf very ably, in his Preface, from any charge which might be brought againft him for the irregularity of meafure ('carmina ατακτα & αποτελυμενα') which he has adopted in fome of his poetical compofitions. To this purpofe he alleges the fanction of Ariftotle, the authority of old fcholiafts, and the example of fome eminent Grecian poets. Even modern ones, who have thought proper to difplay their talents in that language, and made ufe of a diverfified metre, are quoted on the occafion; though we cannot fee any great utility in their teftimony, and much lefs fo in that of Milton and Dryden, who are brought forward to depofe in favour of this mode of compofition. So much learning is indeed exhibited in its defence, that one would be almoft tempted to fuppofe, regularity of meafure had in fome cafes been purpofely avoided, to fhew by what high authority the neglect of it might be defended.

Thefe little poems are on various fubjects, and poffefs different kinds of merit. In fome the author emulates the daring flights of Pindar; in others, the *golden fimplicity* of the Teian bard. His irregular, or monoftrophic odes, as he choofes to ftyle them, are generally fublime without bombaft, and his Anacreontics fmooth and eafy without flatnefs or infipidity. Of the firft, we think the following ftanza on Peace a ftriking example. The laft line is peculiarly beautiful, and in its flow perfectly correfponds with the fcene it defcribes.

' Διος

" Διος Θρονω παρεδρος,
Ηκυσε πρωίον ὡς Χαος κελευσμαίος,
Ὁσα μυρια κειμεν' αβυσσω
Επι κοσμον παντα τελακίας.
Ει Φοβερος νεφελῶν δεινως σκολος ουρανον εἱλει,
Ει βροντη κτυπεει, σμαραγῆσι δε κυμαία πονίυ,
Σιγᾶν ὁταν κελευσῃς,
Ὑπερραῖη ασπίλος αιθηρ,
Κοιμῶντων ανεμων ρεε λεια θαλασσα γαληνη."

' When Chaos firft heard thy commanding voice, as thou
fateft on the throne of Jove, the innumerable elements in the
vaft abyfs were reftored to order. If the fearful darknefs of
clouds horribly involves the fky, if the thunder roars, and the
waves of the fea make a noife ; at thy bidding the pure extended æther is difclofed, the winds are lulled to fleep, and
the fmooth waters flow in tranquillity.'—In proof of our author's fuccefs in the familiar and lefs elevated line of metrical
compofition, we fhall annex his Ode to a mufical friend.

' Ω Φιλε, Θρεμμα Μυσων,
Καλως, καλως αειδεις.
Γηθει κεαρ μυ εντος,
Μελωδια γλυκιστη.
Σης εκχυθεισα γλωσσης
Ψυχην ερωσαν ὑμνων
Πεπληῖμευην δαμαζει.
Νυν, νυν παρ' ωτα χορδων
Ακυεία ετ' ηχος
Πας ἠδυς, ὁν Συ χερσι
Κεκασμευαισι ψαλλειν
Ετευξας. Ηχος ἠδυς
Ετ' ειν ακυετ' ωσιν.
Μελος παλιν δος αλλου,
Τελος τε μηποτ' εςω.

' Τι σοι θελων χαριζειν
Εγωγ' αμυσος ειπειν
Δυνωμαι ; Αλλα θυμος
Λυραν λαβειν ανηκεν,
Και βαρβιτου κρολησας
Ουκ αξιως περ αινῶν
Ποιῶ τα νευρα Φωνεῖν,
" Ω Φιλε, Θρεμμα Μυσων,
" Καλως, καλως αειδεις."

We

We hazard the following tranflation, to give fome idea of the fweetnefs and elegance which, with a few exceptions, diftinguifh the original.

> Friend, favourite of th'Aonian train,
> Sweet, fweetly flows thy vocal ftrain!
> My inmoft heart its tranfport owns,
> Whene'er thefe foft melodious tones
> Breathe from thy lips, whofe powers controul
> The feelings of th' enraptur'd foul.
> Now to thy voice the chords reply
> In mingled notes of harmony:
> Thefe chords, which fafhion'd by thy fkill,
> Refound obedient to the will.
> Hark, how the numbers, fweet and clear,
> Still vibrate in my lift'ning ear!
> Awake, awake thy voice again;
> Not ever ceafe the pleafing ftrain.
> Unfkill'd, unbleft with mufic's art,
> What meed can I to thee impart?
> My mind impulfive bids me feize
> The chorded lyre, to found thy praife:
> But to thy praife, and my defire,
> Unequal founds the chorded lyre.
> "How fweetly flows thy vocal ftrain,
> Friend, favourite of th'Aonian train!"

Though the author is not always perfectly correct, and fome few inftances occur of defective metre, his intimate knowlege of the Greek language, the ftudy of which he wifhes to promote, is fufficiently apparent. On the whole, the execution is entitled to our approbation.

A Treatife on the Immutability of Moral Truth. By Catharine Macaulay Graham. 8vo. 6s. Robinfon.

THE author of this Treatife is fo well known in the republic of letters, that it would be impertinent in us to make any remarks, at this time, on her literary abilities. It may be fufficient to obferve, that, though fhe now appears in a new character, that of a metaphyfician, fhe difcovers that comprehenfive mind, that ftrong imagination, and thofe virtues and liberal principles, which fhe has difplayed on former occafions.

In the Preface to this work Mrs. Graham feems to think ' that the decline of rational religion is, in a great meafure, owing to the doctrines of fome late writers, who have mifreprefented the true fource of moral differences; fome having fixed

the

the principles of moral virtue in mere human sentiment, on the subject of utility; whilst others have taught, that moral obligations are not founded on the real difference of things, but take their rise from the laws of God, as they are found in his revealed will, or as they are impressed on the consciousness of his rational creatures.'

The former opinion is attended with mischievous consequences, which lie open to the reason of every attentive and intelligent mind; and the latter, our author thinks (though veiled from common observation by a sentiment, which carries a seeming respect for the transcendent power of the Deity, and the allegiance which is due from the creature to the Creator) insensibly strips God of some of his most glorious attributes, and leads men into the worst kind of scepticism, if not into downright atheism, by weakening those strong principles of natural reason, which support the belief of revelation, the providential government of God, and the sanction of future rewards and punishments.

In opposition to these notions, our ingenious metaphysician endeavours to prove, that God is omnipotent in the most extensive sense of the word; and that his works and commands are founded in righteousness, and not in mere WILL.

The world has been represented by many distinguished writers, as being in a rapid state of progressive improvement; but our author shews, in a very lively manner, that if one vice has decreased, another has gained ground; that though men agree to spare one another, for considerations of mutual security, they immediately violate this agreement, whenever their interest tempts them to cut one another's throats; in short, that the present times have no reason to boast of having made any progress in that higher part of civilization, which affects the rational interest of man, and constitutes the excellence of his nature.

Having estimated the present state of morals, the author, in the second chapter, proceeds to examine archbishop King's hypothesis concerning the origin of natural evil.

' Dr. King, she says, sets out with a dogmatical denial of that catholic opinion in the creed of the moralist, viz. a necessary and essential difference of things, a fitness and unfitness, a proportion and disproportion, a moral beauty and a moral deformity, an immutable right and wrong, necessarily independent on the will of every being, created or uncreated; and thus, at one stroke, strips the Deity of the glorious attribute of wisdom.' For, she asks, of what use is wisdom, and in what manner can it be exercised, if there is such an ab-
     folute

folute indifference in the nature of things, as to leave no grounds for judicious election ?

' Dr. King, continues this writer, having thus robbed the Deity of wisdom, and reduced his attributes to those of a physical nature, accompanied with a kind of intelligent mechanical ability, proceeds to establish moral good and evil on the footing of will, dependent on the pleasure of God, and to be read by man through the medium of suffering and enjoyment; that is, upon the doctor's hypothesis, the moral colour of actions take their complection solely from their consequence ; and thus, if there were no punishment, there would be no vice.'

The archbishop having likewise asserted, that the terrestrial globe was necessary to complete the harmony and the perfection of the proposed system of creation ; that such a creature as man is a necessary link in the chain of gradation ; that what we call evil is not real evil, but only some want of a greater good : that sensitive existence, on any terms, is a blessing, &c. our discerning metaphysician observes, that this hypothesis is liable to the following objections :

' First, it introduces an uncertainty concerning the nature of virtue ; and by taking away the essential and eternal discriminations of moral good and evil, of just and unjust, and reducing these to arbitrary productions of the divine will, or rules and modifications of human prudence and sagacity, it takes away one regular, simple, and universal rule of action for all intelligent nature ; and thereby weakens those hopes of man, and that prospect of retribution and ultimate happiness, which receive their strongest support from the immutable nature of justice, and a determinate idea of this principle in the divine character.

' The second objection to be made to this hypothesis is, that it is highly derogatory to God to represent him as forming the creation, not for the only end which appears suitable to his moral perfections, viz. the bestowing happiness on sensitive existence, but the rendering this end in a manner subordinate to a motive of a very inferior nature, a certain kind of self-gratification, arising from the exertion of infinite intelligence and power, in the forming a complete system of creation, as far as it respects the principles of symmetry and harmony, on which the perfection of beauty is supposed to depend, and sacrificing to this end all that moral excellence which lies in the benevolent consideration of bestowing on all ranks of sensitive beings every happiness, of which their nature is capable. And, thirdly, it seems to weaken that notion of irresistible power, which forms one of the most exalted attributes of the Deity, viz. such a sufficient capability as is superior to every obstacle, but what implies a positive contradiction.'

The

The following obfervations feem to be founded in reafon and the nature of things :

' The queftion, therefore, whether it was more agreeable to infinite benevolence to create all creatures as perfect as the nature of a created being is capable of, will admit of a more fatisfactory anfwer, than that fuch a gradation is neceffary to that harmony which the divine mind conceived to form the beauty of his fyftem. God undoubtedly intended to beftow on all his fenfitive creatures the greateft poffible happinefs that their natures are capable of receiving ; and the harmony, therefore, of fuch a gradation, is a fubordinate caufe to the intended benevolent effect : nor can it be fuppofed, that fuch a benevolent intention can be an inferior confideration in the divine mind. No ; the more probable reafon to be affigned for fuch a gradation, becaufe more correfpondent to the ideas of perfect wifdom and perfect benevolence, is, that a being produced in the higheft degree of natural perfection which a creature is capable of, and ftill preferving the fame excellence, will not enjoy as much happinefs in the main, as if he was placed in a much inferior ftate at firft, by which he becomes capable of experiencing a perpetual acceffion of unknown pleafures, whereby the bleffings he enjoyed in a pre-exiftent ftate, by a comparative view, are made to add a fuperior relifh to the prefent more advantageous ftate, and thus enables him to enjoy a continued feries of frefh fatisfaction and new delights, whilft he is continually approaching nearer and nearer to that perfection, the excellence of which he has been thus taught to prize ; and to relifh a fupreme good by that rule of comparifon, whereby we learn to eftimate the worth of all poffeffions ; and as finites, however amplified, can never reach infinity or abfolute perfection, fo fome enraptured imaginations have fet no bounds to the inexhauftible power and goodnefs of God.'

The limits of our Review will not allow us to attend the author through all her obfervations on archbifhop King, lord Bolingbroke, and other writers, on the fubject of a future ftate, the doctrines of liberty and neceffity, the ftoic philofophy, &c. we muft therefore refer thofe readers, who wifh to enter more deeply into thefe difquifitions, to Mrs. Graham's performance. We fhall however fubjoin two fhort extracts, which contain her fentiments concerning liberty and neceffity.

' Dr. King, fays this learned lady, in endeavouring to emancipate the divine will from what he erroneoufly regards as a derogatory compulfon, degrades the divine attributes of wifdom and goodnefs into a principle of interefted action, and deftroys that principle of reafoning on which the immutability of God's counfels depends. But in him there is no variablenefs nor fhadow of turning ; and the reafon is plain, for, through all the wide extent of poffible differences in the nature of things, there

there can be but one best, and that one best will be perceived by infinite intelligence, and become the permanent election of infinite wisdom, and infinite goodness. The subjection to this necessity is the peculiar glory of the divine character; and as the nature of that absolute freedom which the doctor supposes, were it a possible quality, would reflect disgrace on every rational being who possessed it: so the nearer approaches which all finite creatures make to the perfections of their Creator, the more they will be brought under the blessed subjection of being necessarily determined in their volitions, by right principles of conduct.'

After she had finished this Treatise, Mrs. Graham observes, she had the pleasure to find, that her notions on this subject coincided with those of Dr. Clarke.

' That very learned divine, in treating on the subject of the freedom of the omnipotent agent, whilst he confutes the weak and shallow arguments used by Spinoza, in his attempt to prove that God created all things by the impulse of a physical necessity, strongly asserts, that the moral perfections of God subject him to a kind of moral necessity, to act, in all things, agreeably to the transcendent excellence of his nature. And, indeed, this is so necessary to every idea of immutability in the divine conduct, and so consonant to every comprehensive idea of infinite power and infinite perfection, that it is surprising that the heat of contention should ever have induced any intelligent reasoner to deny it.'

In the perusal of this work, the reader, who is not acquainted with metaphysical subjects, will sometimes find himself perplexed and embarrassed, like a traveller in one of the woods of America. But let him not be discouraged. His attention will be exercised, which is in itself a profitable employment; and he will find many observations, which will reward him for his trouble. The obscurity, for which some ignorant readers and lazy critics have censured this Treatise, will be attended with no inconvenience to those, who, like the author, can pursue a fugitive idea through ' periods of a mile.'

Dissertations, Moral and Critical. By James Beattie, LL. D.
4to. 18s. in Boards. Cadell.

THESE Dissertations, as the author tells us, were at first composed in a different form, being part of a course of prelections read to those young gentlemen, whom it was his business to initiate in the elements of moral science. This, he hopes, will account for the plainness of style; for the frequent introduction of practical and serious observations; for a
more

more general use of the pronouns I and You, than is perhaps quite proper in difcourfes addreffed to the public; and for a greater variety of illuftration than would have been requifite, if his hearers had been of riper years, or more accuftomed to abftract enquiry.

The reader, he fays, will be difappointed, if he expect to find in this book any nice metaphyfical theories, or other matters of doubtful difputation. ' Such things the author is not unacquainted with; but they fuit not his ideas of moral teaching, and he has laid them afide long ago. His aim is to inure young minds to habits of attentive obfervation; to guard them againft the influence of bad principles, and to fet before them fuch views of nature, and fuch plain and practical truths, as may at once improve the heart and the underftanding, and amufe and elevate the fancy.'

The fubjects of his firft effay are Memory and Imagination. In difcourfing on the former, he marks the difference between memory and imagination; fecondly, takes notice of fome of the more confpicuous laws and appearances of memory; thirdly, propofes rules for its improvement; and, fourthly, makes fome obfervations on the memory of brutes.

Among the methods propofed for the improvement of memory, the author recommends habitual attention, a methodical courfe of ftudy, recollection, writing, converfation, &c. Under this head he gives fome ufeful directions for committing fermons to memory. But, he thinks, that thofe preachers, who, after much practice, cannot commit a difcourfe to memory in lefs than two days, fhould never attempt it. ' If, continues he, I am to judge by my own feelings, and truft to the declaration of many perfons of candour and fenfibility, I muft fay, that fermons in the mouth of a good reader have a more powerful energy than thofe that are fpoken without book. The pathos may be lefs vehement perhaps, but it is more folemn, and feems better adapted to the place and to the fubject.'

In treating of memory, the author illuftrates his reafoning by examples: but he feems to pay too much deference to apocryphal ftories.

' I have read, he fays, of a learned author, who, on receiving a blow on the head by a folio dropping from its fhelf, loft all his learning, and was obliged to ftudy the *alphabet* a fecond time.'

' There goes a ftory of another great fcholar, who, by a like incident, was deprived, not of all his learning, but only of his *Greek*.'

' I know a clergyman, who, upon recovering from a fit of apoplexy, was found to have forgotten all the tranfactions of the *four* years immediately preceding, but remembered, as well as ever, what had happened before that period.'

On the memory of brutes he obferves, ' that the inhabitants of the water have memory, we cannot doubt, if we believe what Pliny, in his Natural Hiftory, Bernier, in his account of Indoftan, and Martial, in fome of his Epigrams, have mentioned *, of fifhes kept in ponds, that had learned to appear, in order to be fed, when called by their refpective *names.*'

We can eafily imagine that fifhes might appear, in order to be fed ; but we cannot fo readily believe that fifhes of any fort were ever acquainted with their refpective names.

Pliny and other ancient writers have tranfmitted us many fables. In this light we confider what is related of Mithridates in the following paffage : ' That four languages do not exceed the capacity of an ordinary man, will not be denied by thofe, who believe with Pliny and Quintilian, that Mithridates underftood *two and twenty.*'

Aulus Gellius tells us, that Mithridates perfectly underftood the languages of twenty-five nations ; ' Quinque & viginti gentium linguas percalluit.' Lib. xvii. 17. But the extent of his knowledge in this refpect is utterly incredible, unlefs we fuppofe that moft of thefe nations were the Ponticæ gentes†, and the languages only kindred dialects.

—We have fome doubts refpecting the accuracy of the following ftories :

' When a rider has fallen from his horfe in a deep river, there have been inftances of that noble creature taking hold with his teeth, and dragging him alive to land by the fkirts of the coat. And let me here, for the honour of another noble creature, mention a fact, which was never before recorded, and which happened not many years ago, within a few miles of Aberdeen.—As a gentleman was walking acrofs the Dee when it was frozen, the ice gave way in the middle of the river, and down he funk, but kept himfelf from being carried away in the current, by grafping his gun, which had fallen athwart the opening. A dog, who attended him, after many fruitlefs attempts to refcue his mafter; ran to a neighbouring village, and took hold of the coat of the firft perfon he met. The man was alarmed, and would have difengaged himfelf, but the dog regarded him with a look fo kind and fo fignificant, and endeavoured to pull him along with fo gentle a violence, that he began to think there might be fomething extraordinary in the cafe, and fuffered himfelf to be conducted by the animal, who brought him to his mafter, in time to fave his life.'

---

* Plin. x. 89. Mart. iv. 30. x. 30. † Florus.

The

The author fubjoins this note :

'The perfon thus preferved, whofe name was Irvine, died about the year 1778. His ftory has been much talked of in the neighbourhood. I give it, as it was told by himfelf to a relation of his, a gentleman of honour and learning, and my particular friend, from whom I had it, and who read and approved of this account, before it went to prefs.'

Stories, like this of the dog, fometimes arife from trivial circumftances, amplified and embellifhed every time they are told.

The author fpeaks too favourably of the following filly obfervation.

'Infants a month old fmile in their fleep : and I have heard good women remark, that the innocent babe is then favoured with fome glorious vifion. But that a babe fhould have vifions or dreams, before it has ideas, can hardly be imagined. This is probably the effect, not of thought, but of fome bodily feeling, or merely of fome tranfient contraction or expanfion of the mufcles. Certain it is, that no fmiles are more captivating.'

'Pull the old grandmother out of your entrails*,' ought to be the conftant and prevailing maxim of every philofopher, every author, and every man of fenfe. Apocryphical ftories may be cited, but they fhould be ftigmatized with marks of reprobation. This is a duty which a philofophical writer owes to reafon, to literature, to the fciences, and to the tafte and genius of an enlightened age.

In this differtation the author gives us many ingenious remarks on the affociation of ideas, on beauty, on tafte, and its improvement, and, laftly, on the regulation of the imagination.

The affociating principles, which he enumerates, are five, refemblance, contrariety, nearnefs of fituation, the relation of caufe and effect, and cuftom or habit.

With refpect to tafte, he fuppofes it to confift of thefe five qualities: 1. a lively and correct imagination; 2. the power of diftinct apprehenfion; 3. the capacity of being eafily, ftrongly, and agreeably affected with fublimity, beauty, harmony, exact imitation, &c. 4. fympathy or fenfibility of heart; and, 5. judgment, or good fenfe, which is the principal thing, and may not very improperly be faid to comprehend all the reft.

Speaking of the ornamental or mechanical rules of compo-fition, and particularly of the unities of time and place in tra-

---

* Beattie, p. 93.

A a 2

gedies,

gedies, the author makes these remarks, in justification of Shakspeare and other dramatic writers, who have neglected these unities.

' While we sit in the theatre, it is as easy for us to reconcile our minds to the shifting of the scene, from the town to the country, or from one country to another, as it is, at our entrance, to suppose the stage a certain place in Rome or Egypt. And if we can persuade ourselves that the player, whom we see, and whose name and person we know, has on a sudden become Cato, or Cæsar, or any other ancient hero; we may as well believe, that the evening which we pass in a playhouse comprehends the space of several days or years.

' But in fact there is not, in dramatical representation, that strict probability which the critics talk of. We never mistake the actor for the person whose character he bears; we never imagine ourselves in a foreign country, or carried back into the ages of antiquity: our pleasure is derived from other sources, and from this chiefly, that we know the whole to be a fiction. The unities of time and place are violated by Shakspeare, in every one of his plays. He often shifts the scene from one country to another; and the time of his action is not always limited to days or weeks, but extends frequently to months, and even to years. Yet these irregularities are not offensive to those who understand him. And hence, I think, we may infer, that the rule, which enjoins the dramatic poet to a rigid observance of the unities of time and place, is not an essential, but a mechanical rule of composition.'

The subject of our author's third disquisition is Dreaming. Without attempting to explore the efficient cause of this phenomenon, he contents himself with making a few unconnected remarks upon it, chiefly with a view to point out its final cause, and to obviate those superstitions in regard to it, which have sometimes troubled weak minds.

Baxter's hypothesis concerning dreaming has been favoured by some late writers. But Dr. Beattie thinks it improbable, for the following reasons.

' First, I see no reason for believing, that the Deity would employ " millions of spiritual creatures" in such an office, as that of prompting our ordinary dreams. Secondly, I cannot conceive how those creatures should be affected, in such an operation, by the external air, or by the state of our health, which are known to have great influence on our thoughts, both in sleep, and when we are awake. And, thirdly, from what we know of the rapidity of fancy when awake, we need not suppose any foreign impulse requisite to produce the various phenomena of dreaming; as the soul seems to possess in herself powers sufficient for that purpose. Fever, melancholy, and many other diseases, give a wildness to the thoughts of waking men, equal, or even superior, to what happens in sleep. If
the

the agency of unfeen beings is not fuppofed to produce the firft, why fhould we have recourfe to it, in order to account for the laft?—But it is urged, that in fleep the foul is paffive, and haunted by vifions, which fhe would gladly get rid of if fhe could. And it may be urged in anfwer, for it is not lefs true, that perfons afflicted with anxiety and melancholy too often find, to their fad experience, that their foul is almoft equally paffive, when they are awake; for that they are, even then, haunted with tormenting thoughts, from which all their powers of reafon, all the exertions of their will, and all the exhortations of their friends, cannot effectually relieve them.'

The difficulty, not to fay the impoffibility, of forming any rational hypothefis concerning the caufe of dreams, is a mortifying confideration. The phenomenon recurs to us almoft every night, yet it always eludes our comprehenfion. When it prefents itfelf, we find ourfelves incapable of reflection, and are hurried away by a power which we cannot controul. In this crifis we feem to refemble thofe perfons who are difordered in their intellects, and not mafters of themfelves. The imagination roves from fcene to fcene, and from one object to another, while our fenfes are locked up, and our reafoning faculty is oppreffed, and obftructed in its operations. We may throw ourfelves into a fimilar kind of reverie, if, when we lie down to fleep, we fix our attention on fome imaginary profpect, and travel over in idea fome well-known journey, or fome long track of country. While the imagination is thus occupied, we gradually lofe the command of our thoughts, and in a few moments perhaps feel ourfelves engaged in fome vifionary adventure, or under the influence of a real dream.

The chief difficulty is to account for the livelinefs of thofe exhibitions, which are prefented to the fancy in dreams. We find, that on the lofs of one of the fenfes, that of fight efpecially, many perfons have enjoyed fome of the reft in greater perfection. It is not improbable therefore, but that the imagination may be more active, when reafon, memory, and judgment, are fufpended. This, we find, is really the cafe with thofe who are in a delirium, or labouring under a fit of infanity. Their imagination is vivid, wild, and defultory; infomuch that it has been faid,

'Great wits to madnefs nearly are allied.'

On this principle we may perhaps, in fome meafure, account for the vivacity of thofe ideas which we conceive in our dreams, when the imagination purfues her excurfions through the ideal world, and is not checked in her flight by the underftanding.

A a 3

The

The subject of Dr. Beattie's third Dissertation is the Theory of Language, that is, of the Origin and Nature of Speech, and Universal Grammar.

In the former part of this essay the author very accurately examines the numbers or measures of English poetry.

It has been a question frequently debated, On what does the measure of English verses depend ? Some have said, on the quantity of syllables. But this, he observes, is not true : ' Since an English heroic line may consist of five short and five long syllables, or of nine short and one long syllable. In fact, this matter is regulated by the emphasis. In our verse there must be in every foot one emphatic syllable, whether long or short : and the alternate succession of emphatic and non-emphatic syllables, is as essential to English numbers, as that of long and short is to the Latin and Greek.'

On which he makes these two remarks.

' First, though our poetry derives its measure from the emphasis of syllables, and the Greek and Latin theirs from the quantity, we must not look upon the former as barbarous, and upon the latter as alone susceptible of true harmony. The only inference we can reasonably make is, that Greek and Latin verses are more uniform than our's in respect of time. The rhythm of sounds may be marked by the distinction of loud and soft, as well as by that of long and short.

' Secondly, though those terms in ancient grammar, trochæus, iambus, dactylus, anapæstus, spondæus, &c. do properly signify certain limited arrangements of long and short syllables, it can do no harm to adopt them in English prosody. For our emphatic syllables are often long, and our non-emphatic syllables are often short ; and where this is the case, we use these terms without impropriety. And where this is not the case, if we call that foot a trochee (for example) which consists of an emphatic and non-emphatic syllable, both of them short, as *body*, we do not depart from the original meaning of words more than is frequently done, without blame, on other occasions.'

The author, having given some account of various sorts of measure, which have been established in English poetry ; having explained what he considers as the proper nature and use of emphasis and accent, and made some remarks on the scripture history of Babel, the art of writing, the invention of printing, &c. proceeds to the subject of universal grammar.

The following observations on the tenses of past time, denoting two sorts of actions, complete or perfect, and incomplete or imperfect, deserve the attention of every classical reader.

' Eneas,

' Eneas, in Virgil, fpeaking of the deftruction of Troy, relates, that, after he had conducted his father and followers to a place of fafety, he returned alone to the burning city, in queft of his wife Creufa, who was miffing. He went firft to his own houfe, thinking fhe might have wandered thither : but there, he fays,

" ——— *Irruerant* Danai, et tectum omne *tenebant* ;"

" the Greeks *had rufhed* in, and *were poffeffing* the whole houfe." Obferve the effect of the plufquamperfect, and imperfect, tenfes. The Greeks *had rufhed* in, *irruerant* ; that action *was over*, and had been completed *before he came:* but the act of poffeffing the houfe, *tenebant*, was *not over*, nor *finifhed*, but *ftill continuing*. This example is taken notice of by Mr. Harris. I fhall give another from Virgil, and one from Ovid.

' In the account of the paintings, which Eneas is furprifed to find in the temple of Juno at Carthage, they being all, it feems, on the fubject of the Trojan war, the poet mentions the following circumftance :

" Ter circum Iliacos *raptaverat* Hectora muros,
Exanimumque auro corpus *vendebat* Achilles :"

which informs us both of the action of the picture, and of the event that was fuppofed to have preceded it. " Achilles *had dragged* the body of Hector three times round the walls of Troy ;"—this is the previous event ;—" and *was felling*," that is, was reprefented in the act of delivering, " the body to Priam, and receiving the ranfom." All this is eafily conceived, and an excellent fubject it is for a picture. But if, without diftinguifhing the tenfes, we were to underftand the paffage as Dryden has tranflated it,

" Thrice round the walls of Troy Achilles drew
The corpfe of Hector, whom in fight he flew," &c.

we fhould be inclined to think that Virgil knew very little of the laws, or of the powers, of painting. For, according to this interpretation, Achilles muft have been painted in the act *of dragging Hector three times* round Troy, and alfo in the act of delivering the body to Priam. Pitt, Trapp, and Ogilvie, in their tranflations, have fallen into the fame impropriety ; a proof, that the theory of tenfes has not always been attended to, even by men of learning.

' When Dido had juft ftruck the fatal blow, and lay in the agonies of death, the behaviour of her fifter, as defcribed by Dryden, is fomewhat extraordinary. Anna was at a little diftance from the pile, on which lay the unfortunate queen : but, hearing of what had happened, fhe ran in diftraction to the place, and addreffed Dido in a long fpeech. That being ended,

" ——— She mounts the pile with eager hafte,
And in her arms the dying queen embrac'd ;

A a 4

Her

Her *temples chafed*, and *her own garments* tore *,
To ftanch the ftreaming blood, and cleanfe the gore."

The fpeech is very fine, and very pathetic; in Virgil, at leaft,
it is fo; but, as it appears in Dryden (and Pitt commits the
fame miftake), never was any thing of the kind more unfeafonable. The poor lady was dying, the blood ftreaming from her
wound; and yet this affectionate fifter (for fuch we know fhe
was) would not attempt any thing for her relief, till fhe had
declaimed for fourteen lines together.—But, from Virgil's own
account we learn, that Anna did not lofe a moment. She *had
mounted* the lofty pile, and *was holding* her dying fifter to her
bofom, and weeping, and *endeavouring* to ftop the effufion of
blood, all the while that thofe paffionate exclamations were
breaking from her.

" ———— Sic fata, gradus *evaferat* altos
Semianimemque finu germanam amplexa *fovebat*
Cum gemitu, atque atros *ficcabat* vefte cruores."

This the Englifh poet would have known, if he had not confounded the imperfect tenfe with the perfect and plufquamperfect, and fuppofed them all to mark the fame fort of time and
of action. Similar blunders are frequent in Dryden, and in
all the other tranflators of Virgil that I have feen.

' In Ovid, when the flood was abated, Deucalion, having
concluded a very tender fpeech to Pyrrha with this fentiment,
" It has pleafed the Gods, that we are the only furvivors of
the whole human race;" the poet adds,

" *Dixerat*; et *flebant:* placuit celefte precari
Numen."——

" He *had done fpeaking*, and they *were weeping*; when it occurred to them to implore the aid of the goddefs of the place."
The fpeech had been for fome time concluded; then followed
a paufe, during which they wept in filence; and, while they
were weeping, they formed this pious refolution. The plufquamperfect, followed by the imperfect, is here very emphatical, and gives in two words an exact view of the behaviour of
this forlorn pair, which would be in a great meafure loft, if,
confounding the tenfes in Englifh, we were to tranflate it, as
is vulgarly done, " He fpoke, and they wept;" which marks
neither the continuance of the laft action, nor that it was fubfequent to the firft.——If children are not well inftructed in the
nature of the feveral tenfes, it is impoffible for them to enter
into the delicacies of claffical expreffion.

' The Latins elegantly ufe this imperfect tenfe to fignify actions that are cuftomary, and often repeated. Thus *dicebat*

———————————————————————————

* * Confidering Dido's condition, to *chafe her temples* was abfurd, if not
cruel: and to infinuate, that Anna on this occafion did not fpare *her own
clouth*, is ridiculoufly trifling. Virgil fays not a word of chafing temples,
or of tearing garments.'

may imply, *he was faying,* or *he was wont to fay*; the fame with *folebat dicere.* For actions that have become habitual, or which are frequently repeated, may be faid to be always going on, and may therefore with philofophic propriety be expreffed by the imperfect tenfe.

' It alfo deferves notice, that the ancient painters and ftatuaries, both Greek and Latin, made ufe of this tenfe, when they put their names to their performances.' On a famous ftatue of Hercules, ftill extant, are infcribed thefe words, *Glycon Athênaios epoiei,* Glycon Athenienfis *faciebat,* Glycon an Athenian *was making* it. The phrafe was thought modeft, becaufe it implied, that the artift had indeed been at work upon the ftatue, but did not pretend to fay that he had finifhed it, or made it complete; which would have been the meaning, if he had given it in the aorift *epoiefe, fecit, made* it. Some of our printers have adopted the fame tenfe at the beginning or end of their books; " *Excudebat* Henricus Stephanus : *Excudebant* Robertus et Andreas Foulis."

' Cefar, whofe narrative is not lefs diftinguifhed by its modefty, than his actions were by their greatnefs, often ufes the imperfect, in fpeaking of himfelf, where I think he would have ufed the perfect, if he had been fpeaking of another. This muft have been wonderfully pleafing to a Roman, who would be much more fenfible of the delicacy than we are. Indeed the beft ancient and modern critics, particularly Cicero, Quintilian, and Roger Afcham, fpeak with a fort of rapture on the exquifite propriety of Cefar's ftyle. And as to his narrative, though he pretended to nothing more than to write a journal or diary (for fuch is the meaning of the word, which is vulgarly tranflated *commentaries*)—as to his narrative, I fay, Cicero declares, that no man in his fenfes will ever attempt to improve it. The frequency of thefe imperfects in Cefar has, if I miftake not, another ufe; for it keeps the reader continually in mind, that the book was written from day to day, *in the midft* of bufinefs, and while the tranfactions there recorded might be faid rather *to be going on,* than to be completed.'

From thefe few examples it appears, that the imperfect and plufquamperfect are very ufeful, and may be the fource of much elegant expreffion; and that if we are not taught to diftinguifh, with regard to meaning as well as form, thefe tenfes from each other, and the preterit from both, we cannot pretend to underftand, much lefs to tranflate, any good claffic author.

This Differtation contains many other ufeful and ingenious obfervations on grammar, though not many, perhaps, that can properly be called new.

The fourth effay treats of Fable and Romance, and gives us an entertaining view of the feudal fyftem, the crufades, chivalry,

chivalry, the writers of hiftorical allegory, moral allegory, romances, and novels.

The following account of a very popular book, the Adventures of Robinfon Crufoe, will be acceptable to fome of our readers.

' Alexander Selkirk, a Scotch mariner, happened, by fome accident which I forget, to be left in the uninhabited ifland of Juan Fernandes, in the South Seas. Here he continued four years alone, without any other means of fupporting life than by running down goats, and killing fuch other animals as he could come at. To defend himfelf from danger during the night, he built a houfe of ftones rudely put together, which a gentleman, who had been in it (for it was extant when Anfon arrived there), defcribed to me as fo very fmall, that one perfon could with difficulty crawl in, and ftretch himfelf at length. Selkirk was delivered by an Englifh veffel, and returned home. A late French writer fays, he had become fo fond of the favage ftate, that he was unwilling to quit it. But that is not true. The French writer either confounds the real ftory of Selkirk with the fabulous account of one Philip Quarl, written after Robinfon Crufoe, of which it is a paltry imitation; or wilfully mifreprefents the fact, in order to juftify, as far as he is able, an idle conceit, which, fince the time of Roufféau, has been in fafhion amongft infidel and affected theorifts on the continent, that favage life is moft natural to us, and that the more a man refembles a brute in his mind, body, and behaviour, the happier he becomes, and the more perfect.—Selkirk was advifed to get his ftory put in writing, and publifhed. Being illiterate himfelf, he told every thing he could remember to Daniel Defoe, a profeffed author of confiderable note, who, inftead of doing juftice to the poor man; is faid to have applied thefe materials to his own ufe, by making them the groundwork of Robinfon Crufoe, which he foon after publifhed, and which, being very popular, brought him a good deal of money.

' Some have thought that a love-tale is neceffary to make a romance interefting. But Robinfon Crufoe, though there is nothing of love in it, is one of the moft interefting narratives that ever was written; at leaft in all that part which relates to the defart ifland; being founded on a paffion ftill more prevalent than love, the defire of felf-prefervation, and therefore likely to engage the curiofity of every clafs of readers, both old and young, both learned and unlearned.

' I am willing to believe that Defoe fhared the profits of this publication with the poor feaman; for there is an air of humanity in it, which one would not expect from an author who is an arrant cheat. In the preface to his fecond volume, he fpeaks feelingly enough of the harm done him by thofe who had abridged the firft, in order to reduce the price. " The injury, fays he, which thefe men do to the *proprietors* of works, is a practice all honeft men abhor; and they believe they may
challenge

challenge them to show the difference between that and robbing on the highway, or breaking open a houfe. If they cannot show any difference in the crime, they will find it hard to show why there should be any difference in the punishment." Is it to be imagined that any man of common prudence would talk in this way, if he were confcious that he himfelf might be proved guilty of that very difhonefty which he fo feverely condemns?

' Be this however as it may, for I have no authority to affirm any thing on either fide, Robinfon Crufoe muft be allowed, by the moft rigid moralift, to be one of thofe novels, which one may read, not only with pleafure, but alfo with profit. It breathes throughout a fpirit of piety and benevolence : it fets in a very ftriking light, as I have elfewhere obferved, the importance of the mechanic arts, which they, who know not what it is to be without them, are fo apt to undervalue : it fixes in the mind a lively idea of the horrors of folitude, and, confequently, of the fweets of focial life, and of the bleffings we derive from converfation, and mutual aid : and it fhows, how, by labouring with one's own hands, one may fecure independence, and open for one's felf many fources of health and amufement. I agree, therefore, with Roufleau, that is is one of the beft books that can be put in the hands of children.—The ftyle is plain, but not elegant, nor perfectly grammatical : and the fecond part of the ftory is tirefome.'

In the fifth Differtation the author points out the happy effects which arife from the matrimonial union, and the attachment of kindred. Among other queftions, which occur on this fubject, he confiders that of polygamy. The number of males which are born is found to be nearly equal to the number of females, being as 20 to 19, according to fome computations, or as 14 to 13, according to others. To keep the two fexes equal with refpect to number, and to provide for the cafualties, to which men are liable in war and by fea, a fmall fupply of males muft be neceffary. ' This exact proportion, fays our author, is a ftriking proof of the care of a wife Providence for the prefervation of the human race ; and is moreover a perpetual miracle (if I may fo fpeak) to declare, both that the union of the fexes is natural, and that polygamy is not.'

The laft Effay confifts of Illuftrations on Sublimity. On this fubject, as well as on every other, the author difplays great vivacity of imagination, and correctnefs of tafte and judgement.

Naval Architecture ; or, the Rudiments and Rules of Ship-Building, exemplified in a Series of Draughts and Plans. With Observations tending to the further Improvement of that important Art. By Marmaduke Stalkartt. Folio. 6l. 6s. Sewell.

NAVAL architecture being entirely foreign to literary pursuits, and yet a subject of great national importance, one of our friends, by means of his connexions, had an opportunity of procuring the opinion of a gentleman of extensive knowledge and approved judgment, to whom therefore we are indebted for the observations on this production.

YOU ask me for my opinion of Mr. Stalkartt's large work on Naval Architecture. I have perused the treatise and the plans with attention, and shall freely communicate to you my sentiments.

You need not be told, that in naval architecture there are no fixed principles and rules for all the dimensions and properties required in a ship, from which the artist must never depart. He is left, in a great measure, to his discretion ; and he naturally becomes by habit attached to his own plan, whatever it may be. This is a difficulty in the way of improvement, not easily to be surmounted ; and of this the author seems to be fully convinced.

'He is aware that there is a great deal to be wished, and much to be suffered, by trusting to the speculations of the theorist ; but in an art where there is so much avowed imperfection, and so great an object to be acquired by excellence, it will always be considered as wise and necessary to collect the opinions of men who have made the subject their study, that by reducing their inventions to experiment, it may be found whether they are merely ingenious chimeras, or valuable improvements.

'In the theory of the art there are no fixed and positive principles, established by demonstration, and confirmed by use. There is hardly a rule sanctified by common consent, but the artist is left to the exercise of his own opinion ; and this generally becomes so rooted by habit, as to resist innovation, however specious. Undoubtedly there is great reason for caution on the one hand, as there is for enterprize on the other. We ought to be as anxious to preserve the merits that are determined, as to overcome the acknowleged insufficiencies. It is our duty and our interest to trust with circumspection, and make fair trials of such propositions as are favourable in their appearance. This may surely be done with little danger, and with much benefit.'

The French have gone before us in naval architecture. We adhere, as a nation, to the practice which has so long obtained ;

obtained; and in all probability we adhere to it from the erroneous principle, that the fuccefs of our marine is as much to be imputed to the conftruction of our fhips, as to the bravery and difcipline of our men. The purpofe of Mr. Stalkartt, in the fplendid work before me, is to give a fet of rules for drawing and laying down all the effential timbers in a fhip; and he purfues his fubject in a regular feries, giving, in the commencement, his inftructions with ftudied minutenefs, and leading the artift forward in a gradual progreffion, from the fimple to the more difficult departments of the work. This is a thing which was very much wanted in the art of fhip-building. The treatifes publifhed before this were at once obfolete and defective. The laft and beft is that of Mungo Murray, which contained feveral ufeful propofitions; but the art had gone farther than the author. He was better acquainted with the theory of navigation than with the practice of fhip-building. He could teach his fcholars the art of trigonometry, and had the credit of being well verfed in the mathematics; but there requires fomething more than the mere philofophy of mechanics to enable a man to give practical inftructions for laying down the timbers of a fhip in the mould-loft. Mr. Stalkartt, in the whole of his treatife, fpeaks entirely as an artift, and his inftructions will no doubt be valuable. If he had joined the lights of philofophy to his practical knowledge, and had been as converfant with the principles of motion as he is with the mechanifm of a fhip, his treatife would have been more argumentative, but I do not know whether it would alfo have been more ufeful. He might have been tempted to wander too much from the folid ftandard of experience, and have fported with chimeras, which in this fubject, of all others, are dangerous and unwife. The whole of his work is not taken up with inftructions for the difpofition of the timbers merely. He propofes feveral new principles of material confequence in the fabric of a fhip, and which deferve the moft attentive confideration. His firft idea is, that of placing the midfhip-bend, or dead-flat, that is, the greateft breadth, at the diftance of one-third of the length of the fhip from the head, inftead of being, as it is now, near the centre. Another propofition is, that the water-lines fhould be fair, inftead of hollow. A third, that the fhip fhould be conftructed to fail on an even keel. There are feveral other alterations fuggefted, of inferior importance; but I fhall examine his work in its order.

His feries is regular and progreffive. He begins with the long-boat, for the purpofe of fhewing the principle of *whole-moulding*. From this he proceeds to the yacht, the floop, the forty-four-gun ship, and the seventy-four-gun ship. He then introduces the cutter, as being the most proper to explain a proposed method of drawing similar bodies; and he concludes his original design with a new and very ingenious rule for finding the true ending of lines.

The first book then treats of the art of whole-moulding, 'which', says he, 'is a method of forming the principal part of a ship, vessel or boat, by the use of a mould made to the midship-bend, and continued as far afore and abaft the same, as the form of the midship-bend and curve of the rising line are suitably disposed to each other, in order to make the body fair.

'Before the art of ship-building was brought to its present perfection, the method of whole-moulding was in great repute, and much practised by the unskilful, as well as by those whose business required expedition; but since some late improvements have been made by diligent study and application to the theory of the art, it has been less approved of in the construction of ships, whose form of the midship-bend has been required to be such, that if they were whole moulded well forward and aft, they would not only be almost incapable of rising in a heavy sea, but be deprived, in a great measure, of the proper use of their rudder; for, by whole moulding, no more is narrowed at the floor than at the main breadth; nor must the rising line lift any more than the lower height-of-breadth; which, according to the form of some midship-bends, would make a very disagreeable body at the foremost and aftermost floors, if the whole moulding were continued so far.'

Perhaps it would not have been necessary to be so minute as he is in this book on a principle which the good sense of the artist has exploded, if the author had not made it a sort of introduction to all that comes after. Here we have the first steps of ship-building; and he explains to the young artist the simplest and surest methods of taking off and transferring the square-timbers, water-lines, ribband-lines, cant and square bevellings, the square timbers, forming the boarding-lines, and bevelling the heels of the cant-timbers, &c. These directions are to be remembered through the more important parts, and are to be considered as the rudiments of the art. He has exemplified them in a plate, containing figures of the sheer-draught, the body plan, the half-breadth plan, &c. of the long-boat. These figures, as well indeed as all the plates, are executed with an uncommon degree of correctness and skill; and make, without question, his book truly valuable as a collection of plans, which, on account of their accuracy, may be referred to, in every possible case that can occur in ship-building.

Book

Book II. gives the conftruction of the yacht,——

' Defigned,' fays the author, ' to be an expeditious failer, without any other ftowage than is actually neceffary for accommodation ; but which is to be, at the fame time, what is termed a ftiff fea-boat, able to carry fail fufficient to fpeed her to fome place of fafety, and to keep her off from a lee-fhore. Thefe qualities in a yacht, when happily united, render her a moft ufeful as well as agreeable appendage to the more noble ftructures of naval architecture.'

Here it is that the author introduces his new principles, and applies them to the conftruction of this draught, as wel as the more important ones which follow. Mr. Stalkartt, as I have faid, does not indulge himfelf much in reafoning : he ftates his propofition with great humility and diffidence. The following are the author's words on the propofition of his new ideas.

' My prefent defign is not to fteer either by ancient or modern rules, unlefs where they are fupported by reafon and experiment. It was formerly the opinion of artifts, that the ftation of the midfhip bend fhould, in every inftance, be in the centre of the fhip, under the fuppofition that fhe would then pitch the leaft, and confequently ride the fafer at anchor. But experience, the only true guide, has taught the prefent age to move the midfhip-bend fomewhat forward, by which the fhip will meet with lefs refiftance, as the fluid will fooner pafs the greateft breadth, and thereby have the freer paffage to the rudder. As the preffure of water to the fides of the fhip is equal to the weight of the veffel, it follows that the more forward the midfhip-bend is placed, if the fhips begins immediately to narrow, the greater is the length, and confequently the effect of the preffure of water, to increafe her velocity. It feems alfo reafonable to believe, that the fhip will ride at anchor with more eafe if the midfhip-bend is placed forward ; fince, when it is fixed in the centre, and the form of the body is circular, inclining to be clean both forward and aft, the fhip will then be buoyed up in the middle, and for want of bearing forward and aft, muft unavoidably pitch. It would feem an inconfiftency to many, to conftruct a fhip to fail on an even keel, as it is termed, (that is, that the fhip, when trimmed for failing, fhould have her keel parallel to the furface of the water) and yet to place the midfhip-bend, or greateft breadth, very forward. For they imagine, that a fhip fo intended to fail, ought, when launched, to have an equal bearing fore and aft, in order that fhe may, before any ballaft is put on board, be on an even keel ; and they believe that the ballaft, if not placed equally fore and aft, muft inevitably ftrain the fheer of the fhip.

' Granting it may be fo, experience convinces us it is not materially detrimental ; for many fhips, when launched, will fwim four feet by the ftern, more or lefs ; and yet when trimmed

med for failing, are found to go fasteft on an even keel, or there-abouts, and I imagine they receive little or no damage, if care-fully ftowed.

' Some fhips are too clear abaft, and require to fail by the ftern, becaufe they have no bearing for fifteen or twenty feet from aft, till the buttock is bronght well in the water; and even then, for want of being fuller lower down, when the fea leaves the buttock, the overhanging of the ftern will ftrain the fhip, and occafions her to tremble, till the next fea, with re-doubled force, ftrike the buttock as the ftern is falling, and fhake the fhip, in which cafe it will be well if fome part of the maft is not carried away by the fhock: however, it is certain this kind of motion muft retard the velocity.

' This accident feldom happens, but, as it is a dangerous one, the more precaution fhould be ufed in the conftruction of a fhip.

' With refpect to fuch fhips as I have before mentioned, that ought to fail four feet by the ftern, on account of their infuffi-ciency abaft, it is my opinion, that if a line was drawn to be well with the lower fide of the keel, in the middle of the fhip, and two feet up at the aft part of the ftern-poft, from the lower fide of the keel, and that part of the keel and deadwood were to be taken off, and placed under the forepart of the keel, with the after end that was before, to be forward, fo as to make the lower part of the keel ftrait as before, the fhip would then fail fomething fafter, and be the better; for when a fhip is brought fo much down by the ftern, the keel not being parallel to the furface of the water (to which the fhip generally fails parallel), muft occafion a preffure at the under fide of the keel, equal to the weight of water difplaced by the breadth of the keel, and to the angle which the keel makes with the furface of the wa-ter in its own length. Though this may appear to be of little confequence with regard to obftructing the fhip's way through the water, yet, in part, it may prove the reafon that fo many fhips, differently conftructed, are found to fail beft on an even keel, although many of them were defigned by the builder, or draughtfman, to fail by the ftern.

' Having confidered every obftruction, and finding the refult rather in favour of an even keel, I fhall conclude upon con-ftructing the draught in fuch a manner as will moft likely anfwer the purpofe. By that means the water-lines will be parallel to the keel, and will thereby be lefs troublefome to the artift, as well as more properly placed to form the body; for when the fquare timbers, and the water-lines being fquare to the timber, pro-perly agree with each other, and are fair curves, the ribband-lines, or any other fection, will likewife be fair, or as fair as they fhould be, allowing the preference to the water-lines and fquare timbers.

' When the water-lines are not defigned to be parallel to the keel, the draught is generally formed by ribband-lines, becaufe the

the water-lines differing in height at every timber, require the square-timbers to be formed before the height can be set off; and, when the water-lines are run, if not approved of, much of the work must be done over again; it being the general opinion, to pay more regard to the water-lines than to the ribband-lines; for many ships are constructed by ribband-lines only, which seem to produce fair curves, yet, forward and aft especially, they make a very unfair body, which is detrimental to the ship.

'Having observed that the stationing of the midship-bend is at present entirely undetermined among the generality of ship-builder, I shall give my option for placing it one third from forward on the line A B, fig. 1. supposing that position to be the nearest to a medium that can be: for was it placed farther forward, the ship might have inconvenience from it when going to windward; by being too full to divide the fluid, she must consequently receive the whole shock of the sea; and if the midship bend were farther aft she might, when going large, by being too sharp forward, plunge and bury herself in the sea.'

This is the introduction of his new principles, which, I must acknowlege, as a professional man, appear to be rational, and to have probability. This is my opinion on the first view; but the author certainly has not gone so fully into the defence of his proposition as he ought to have done, considering that he has in this instance to combat with habits and prejudices, rendered sacred to the builders by the experience which they have had of the certainty at least of the old doctrine. I think Mr. Stalkartt to blame in this, because I am sure there are many arguments in his favour which he has omitted to use, and the modesty is scarcely pardonable, which, on such a subject, deters a man from advancing fairly, and discussing the merits of his opinion with the boldness which belongs to rational speculation. He should have shewn the mathematics of his plan, and tried how far he was supported by the rules and doctrines of general mechanics, and the philosophy of motion. Instead of this he has, with a few introductory thoughts, proceeded to delineate his idea on the plan annexed, and leaves it entirely to the test and reasoning of experiment. It is not my province to prove it in this letter, by experiment. To do that I must imitate Mr. Stalkartt himself, who, I understand, has built a boat, in which he has carried his doctrine to the extreme, and farther than he proposes to adventure in the Treatise before us. Let me for the present confine myself to reasoning on the subject.

It strikes the mind on the first view of the matter, that a vessel whose midship-bend is in the centre, is more liable to

accidents in bad weather ; for the extreme ends having inferior and both equal weight, she is likely to pitch, and to undergo an inceſſant ſee-ſaw motion, which muſt ſtrain her timbers, and keep her from the ſteadineſs which is ſo eſſential to
ſafety in an agitated ſea.   Place the great weight more forward, and you give ſolidity to the bow, where the action of
the waves is chiefly to be felt.   Were a ſhip to be conſtructed
ſolely for the purpoſe of lying at anchor, perhaps it might be
wiſe to give her uniform weight ; but when we conſider that
the two great objects in view are ſwiftneſs and capacity, we
ſhould enquire whether it is not neceſſary to ſwiftneſs that the
weight ſhould be forward.   The ſhip is to be impelled forward.   We call in all the powers of the wind to puſh her in
this direction ; and ſurely, if we argue from compariſon with
other bodies conſtructed to move in the fluid either of air or
water, we muſt conclude that it is neceſſary to the force and
evenneſs of her motion, that the principal weight ſhould be
near the head.   Could an arrow be darted forwards with equal
rapidity, if the weight was in the centre ? Would it not ſhi-
ver in the air ? Mr. Stalkartt ſays,

' By a philoſophical diſcuſſion it might be maintained, that
this diſpoſition of the midſhip-bend is clearly pointed out by
nature, in her formation of animals deſtined to move in the element of water.   It is not a novel obſervation, that the form of
a fiſh is the beſt calculated for velocity ; but though the obſervation has been made, the example remains yet to be followed.   We ſeem to require ſomething more than the evidence of
nature, to overcome the errors of prejudice.'

It has been contended that we ought not to truſt, in the
conſtruction of a ſhip, to the example ſet us in the formation
of animals ; and that if we were, there would be ſuch latitude
in the rule as to leave it ſtill to the diſcretion of the builder,
ſince animals differ ſo much in their forms as to afford no
preciſe pattern of the ſhape the beſt calculated for velocity.
This I peremptorily deny.   In all the diverſities of nature, the
principle which Mr. Stalkartt mentions is clearly obſerved to
prevail ; and it is an indiſputable fact, that the fiſh moſt
remarkable for ſwiftneſs are thoſe moſt remarkable for the
conſtruction which the author recommends ; on the contrary,
the ſluggiſh fiſh are the fartheſt removed from that form.   But
fiſh do not ſwim on the ſurface of the water, and therefore,
ſay they, we cannot draw any evidence from them.   This objection would be good if the queſtion depended ſimply on the
air ; but the object is to find the form the beſt calculated for
cutting its way through, and diſſipating the fluid of water ;
and it is perfectly indifferent whether the force is to be exerted,
                                                                    and

and the motion performed, at the bottom or at the surface of the water. But there are analogies in nature precisely the same. The nautilus, from which, if we believe history, the first idea of venturing on the deep was taken, sails with its extreme breadth forward ; and all animals remarkable for celerity in the fluid of air are equally distinguished for the fulness toward the head, rather than in the middle. What bird of flight can be mentioned as an exception to this rule ? Observe also how the plain sense and experience of the mariner, who acts without the light of philosophy, corroborates this opinion. If he has to take a mast, plank, or timber in tow, he drags it by the thick end ; a raft of timber is conducted in the same manner. The angle is more obtuse which cuts the fluid, but the weight is the great advantage ; and, as the author observes, the principal impediment lies in the distance from the head to the extreme breadth. To shorten that distance is therefore the first thing to be obtained, by which the water will pass more easily to the rudder.

A breadth in proportion to the weight, gives the ship a larger body of water for her support ; and this is an advantage which, in the present construction of bodies, cannot be enjoyed : I must therefore declare my full acquiescence in the proposition of Mr. Stalkartt, consistent with the various properties of the vessel.

In regard to the new principle of using fair instead of hollow water-lines, the advantages in my opinion are material. The curves described by the hollow water-lines must necessarily retard the ship, for as the water clings to the vessel, the unevenness of the sides makes the line longer, and the water is also more disturbed ; it is agitated in different ways by the inflections of the hollow lines, and this commotion is all against her speed. By fair lines she divides and leaves the fluid with more ease, the agitation of the waves being more simple, and all in a similar direction.

Mr. Stalkartt's argument for his proposal of making her on an even keel, are substantial. But this is not a new suggestion ; it has been practised in various instances, and found to succeed. The plate to this book contains ten figures ; the elevation or sheer-draught ; horizontal sections, or half-breadth lines ; the body plan, or view of the timbers which compose it ; the stern ; moulding of the fashion-piece ; cant-timbers ; the plan of the upper-deck ; the plan of the quarter-deck ; the plan of the lower-deck ; and the plan of the cabin-floor. In the construction of the yacht, Mr. Stalkartt proposes a square-tuck, but to be round forward at the ends. This kind of tuck has been generally considered

as

as difficult, from the method heretofore used ; but I think the author's plan is simple and easy.   He describes it in the following words.

' Observe then, says he, that the aft-part of the square-tuck, bounded by the wing-transom and fashion-piece, is meant to represent part of a cylinder ; the upper-side of the wing-transom, were it strait and square from the rabbet of the stern-post, would be part of the circumference of the end of the cylinder ; and the aft-part of the rabbet of the stern-post would be a strait line at the outside square from the end, and parallel to the middle line or centre.

' If the rabbet of the stern-post was perpendicular, the aft-side of the wing-transom and fashion-pieces would be likewise perpendicular, when properly fixed in their places ; otherwise all lines that should be drawn parallel to the middle-line of the stern-post, even to the end of the wing-transom, would be out of winding with the middle-line of the stern-post, just as strait parallel pillars, placed perpendicularly in the form of a cylinder, would all be out of winding with each other.'

The third book contains the plan for the construction of a sloop of war.

' The first thing, says he, to be considered in the plan of a ship of war is, the principal dimensions.   For the determination of this we have no fixed and certain rule, because the proportions of ships must always vary with the objects which they are intended to pursue ; and in all vessels the proportion must be calculated by the different services for which they are designed.   The yacht, plate II. was chiefly constructed for sailing, and for accommodating the requisites of pleasure ; on this account she admitted of being shallow above water : but as the sloop requires to have one deck reserved for guns, which must be disposed clear of the water during the action, with an allowance of moderate winds, there must be more depth of topside to answer that purpose.

' The principal dimensions, by being left unconfined to rules, so frequently lead artists into capital errors, that it is necessary to introduce some proportions to regulate their judgments, such as may be applicable to ships of the same class, whose experience has rendered them worthy of recommendation.   For the sloop then, let the extreme length be 98 feet 10 inches, breadth moulded $\frac{27}{3}$ of the extreme length ; height of the top-breadth at the lowest place $\frac{11}{16}$; height of the wing-transom $\frac{1}{9}$ of the extreme length ; and the height of the load-water-line be about $\frac{4}{7}$ of the top-breadth at the lowest place.'

In the construction of the sloop he follows his principle described in the yacht ; and the subject is illustrated by three plates, No. III. IV. V.—III. explaining the construction. IV. containing the fore and after-part of the former plate,

laid

1

laid off for the use of the mould-loft, in ten figures : the parts of the veſſel laid off are, the ſtern frame, the hawſe-pieces, the taffrail and quarter-pieces,—V. contains the bottom and top-ſide of the ſloop laid off, with the planks ſhifted, and clearly explained.

[*To be continued.*]

Poetical Remains of James I. King of Scotland. 8*vo.* 3*s.* Balfour, Edinburgh ; Cadell, London.

THIS volume begins with a Hiſtorical and Critical Diſſertation on the Life and Writings of James I. King of Scotland ; a prince who is celebrated by ſeveral of his contemporaries, as one of the moſt illuſtrious perſons of the age in which he lived. His natural and acquired endowments were equally conſpicuous. He is affirmed to have excelled in almoſt every branch of the learning of thoſe times, and in every accompliſhment of a gentleman. In all athletic exerciſes, particularly in the uſe of the ſword and ſpear, he was eminently expert. To his knowlege of the Greek and Roman languages, the latter of which he wrote with eaſe, he joined not only the philoſophy then received in Europe, but a proficiency in poetry and muſic. So much did he excel in the ſcientific as well as the practical part of muſic, that he is reckoned the firſt reformer, if not the inventor, of the Scottiſh ſongs. To uſe the words of an eminent hiſtorian of the laſt century, ' there was nothing within the circle of the liberal arts that he had not applied his mind unto, ſeeming rather born to letters than inſtructed.'

In the Diſſertation prefixed by the editor, we meet with a general account of the hiſtory of James, from his captivity by the Engliſh, at an early period, to the time of his barbarous aſſaſſination, on the 13th of February, 1436-7. But thoſe occurrences being generally known, we ſhall content ourſelves with ſubſcribing to the juſtneſs of the eulogium pronounced by the editor on this accompliſhed monarch, viz. that as a poet, patriot, and lawgiver, and the civilizer of the manners of his people, no prince in hiſtory deſerves more to be revered by his country than James I. king of Scotland.

The editor afterwards proceeds to take notice of the works of king James I. He obſerves, that the only poems extant of this royal bard, at leaſt thoſe which can with certainty be aſcertained his productions, are ' Chriſt's Kirk of the Green,' and that which is entitled ' The King's Quair.' The former of theſe poems has been aſcribed by ſeveral writers to James V. who was alſo a poet ; but the editor has, in our opinion,

refuted

refuted this idea, by clear and convincing arguments. To give our readers a full view of the controversy, we shall present them with what the editor has advanced on the subject. He begins with stating the authorities which ascribe this poem to king James V.

' The oldest of these, as far as I have been able to discover, is that of bishop Edmund Gibson, who, anno 1691, published an edition at Oxford of the poem of Christ's Kirk of the Green, with learned notes. The title which the bishop gave his book is " Christ's Kirk on the Green, composed, as is supposed, by king James V."—And in an elegant Latin preface to this poem, he thus writes, " Gratulor tibi lector, and Musis, regem in Parnasso, non infeliciter somniantem ; de Jacobi, ejus nominis apud Scotus Quinti, familia, eruditione, scientia militari, consulendi sunt historicorum annales ; principem autem hunc poesin deperiisse, nil mirum, commune id illi, cum augustissimis aliis viris, qui haud pauci carmen in deliciis habuere."

' The next authority is the editor of the last edition of Gavin Douglas's translation of Virgil's Æneis, published at Edinburgh anno 1710, who, in his preface, thus mentions this poem ; " with notes published at Oxford some years ago, by a celebrated writer on the famous poem of king James V, entitled Christ's Kirk on the Green."

' On the same side is Tanner, bishop of St. Asaph, who, in his Bibliotheca Britannico-Hibernica, sub voce Jacobi Quinti, regis Scotiæ, mentions the poem of Christ's Kirk of the Green as written by that prince, and adds, " Edidit, notisque illustravit cl. Edmond Gibson, Oxon. 1691." Tanner's Bibliotheca was published so late as the year 1748.

' These are the only ancient and positive authorities that I have seen, which attribute this poem to king James V. I shall sum up the whole arguments on that side of the question from an author of still greater weight than any of the above, that is, the learned sir David Dalrymple, lord Hailes, whose opinion, although he candidly does not decide, is on the same side with the above authors.

' Lord Hailes argues thus.—First, Major, in his life of king James I. mentions several pieces written by that prince, but says nothing of Christ's Kirk of the Green.—Secondly, The poem mentions " Peebles at the Play," which lord Hailes is of opinion relates to a more modern æra than the age of king James I.—And, lastly, bishop Gibson and bishop Tanner, and the editor of Gavin Douglas's Virgil, all agree in attributing the poem of Christ's Kirk of the Green to king James V.

' I shall attempt to answer these arguments in their order ; and to the first.—That Major, who mentions two or three pieces, said to be composed by king James I. does not mention the poem of Christ's Kirk, is an argument entirely negative,

tive, and can infer no direct conclusion that king James I. might not have been the author of that poem, as well as of several other pieces not mentioned by Major, of which, for certain, he was the author, viz. Rythmi Latine, et de Musica, mentioned by Dempster, and some other poems mentioned by other authors. Major does not pretend to give a full enumeration of the works of James, but, after mentioning two or three of his pieces, adds, Et plurimi codices, adhuc apud Scotus.— To the second, as to the æra of the plays of Peebles. The anniversary games or plays at Peebles are of so high antiquity, that, at this day, it is only from tradition, joined to a few remains of antiquity, that we can form any conjecture respecting the age of their inftitution, or even trace the vestiges of what these games were. Any argument, therefore, deduced from the æra of the inftitution of the plays at Peebles, inclines to the oppofite fide from lord Hailes. That this town, fituated on the banks of the Tweed, in a paftoral country, abounding with game, was much reforted to by our ancient Scottifh princes, is certain. King Alexander III. is faid to have had a hunting feat here; the place where it flood is ftill pointed out. We are told by Boetius, that the monaftery of Crofs Church, now in ruins, was built by that prince; and anciently our princes occafionally took up their refidence in the religious houfes. Contiguous to it is a piece of ground, of old furrounded with walls, and ftill called the King's Orchard; and on the oppofite fide of the river is the King's Green. The plays were probably the golf, a game peculiar to the Scots, foot-ball, and fhooting for prizes with bow and arrow. The fhooting butts ftill remain. Archery, within the memory of man, was kept up at Peebles; and an ancient filver prize arrow, with feveral old medallions appended to it, as I am informed, is ftill preferved in the town-houfe of Peebles. And to the laft argument, to wit, the authorities of bifhops Gibfon and Tanner, and the editor of Gavin Douglas's Virgil, all of whom attribute the above poem to king James V. All thefe writers are fo modern, and fo remote from the age of James I. or even of James V. that they can prove nothing. The oldeft of thefe writers, bifhop Gibfon, did not pnblifh his book till the year 1691, that is, 149 years after the death of king James V. and 250 years after the death of king James I. Befides Gibfon, upon whofe bare affertion the other two later writers profeffedly rely, fpeaks but dubioufly; his words, as on the title-page of the poem, are, "Compofed, as it is fuppofed, by king James V."—Having thus fhewn the infufficiency of the arguments and authorities which attribute this poem to king James V. I now proceed to prove that it was undoubtedly the work of king James I.

' The moft ancient teftimony for this opinion is that of Mr. George Bannantyne, to whofe tafte and induftry we owe a manufcript collection of many fine old Scottifh poems, prior to the year 1568, which is the date of his manufcript.

' In

' In Bannantyne's book, the first poem in point of antiquity is Chrift's Kirk of the Green, which at the end of it, as was the fashion of the time, bears this signature, "Quod King James I."—Bannantyne's manuscript was finished in 1568, within 26 years of the death of James V. Bannantyne may then be reckoned to have been contemporary with that prince. His teftimony, therefore, not only proves negatively that king James V. was not the author, but likewise, that univerfal tradition and report, in this laft prince's time, attributed this poem to his royal anceftor, king James I.—Further, although it may not be eafy to afcertain the age of any writing from its language, yet I apprehend there arifes ftrong internal evidence from the poem itfelf, that it belongs to an age more ancient than that of king James V.

' King James I. was carried to England in the year 1404, and remained at the courts of king Henry IV. V. and VI. until the year 1423, when he returned to his own kingdom; fome years after which we may conjecture this poem to have been written. If it is compared with any of the poems of the age of king James V. that is a century later, we fhall find the language of the firft much more antiquated and difficult to be underftood than that of the latter.'

The poetical genius difplayed in this beautiful ancient poem, might alone have been a fufficient incentive to the exertion of its royal author; but the editor, indeed with much appearance of reafon, confiders the defign of it as in great meafure political. He obferves that the poem is almoft one continued ironical fatire upon the aukward management of the bow, and the neglect into which archery had then fallen in Scotland. The opinion that the revival of archery may have been at leaft a fecondary object in the compofition of the poem, feems to be countenanced by the ftatutes enacted in the reign of James I. for diffufing among his fubjects the knowlege of that military exercife, which had for fome ages been cultivated in England with great fuccefs.

In the prefent edition of Chrift's Kirk of the Green, the editor has followed the manufcript of Bannantyne, made in 1568, and which appears greatly fuperior to the authorities adopted by bifhop Gibfon, in his edition of this poem printed at Oxford in 1691.

The poem entitled The King's Quair was compofed by king James, while a prifoner in England. The fubject of it is Jane, daughter to the earl of Somerfet, and afterwards the queen of this monarch; a princefs celebrated by the Scottifh writers for her beauty as well as for her virtues and conjugal affection. This poem, though well known in the time of James, and mentioned by feveral writers, has lain in obfcurity for the laft three centuries. The only copy of it preferved

has

has been discovered in the Bodleian library at Oxford ; from
an accurate transcript of which, obtained by the editor, it is
now for the first time printed. This poem, according to the
reigning taste of the age of James I. and the practice of his
contemporaries, Chaucer, Gower, and Lydgate, is written in
the form of an allegorical vision, and discovers not only such
purity of affection, but such richness of fancy, as does honour to the monarch, both as a lover and a poet.

The following stanzas, extracted from the beginning of this
poem, may serve as a specimen.

‘ Heigh in the hevynis figure circulare
　The rody sterres twynkling as the fyre :
And in Aquary Citherea the clere,
　Rynsid hir triffis like the goldin wyre,
That late tofore, in faire and fresche atyre,
　Thro’ Capricorn heved hir hornis bright,
　North northward approchit the myd nyght.

‘ Quhen as I lay in bed allone waking,
　New partit out of slepe a lyte tofore,
Fell me to mynd of many diverse thing
　Of this and that, can I not say quharefore,
Bot slepe for craft in erth myt I no more ;
　For quhich as tho’ coude I no better wyle,
　Bot toke a boke to rede upon a quhile :

‘ Of quhich the name is clepit properly
　Boece, efter him that was the compiloure,
Schewing counsele of philosophye,
　Compilit by that nobil senatoure
Off Rome quhilome yt was the warldis floure,
　And from estate by fortune a quhile
　Foringit was to povert in exile.

‘ And there to here this worthy lord and clerk,
　His metir suete full of moralitee ;
His flourit pen so fair he set a werk,
　Discriving first of his prosperitee,
And out of that his infelicitee ;
　And than how he in his poetly report,
　In philosophy can him to confort.

‘ For quhich thot I in purpose at my boke,
　To borowe a slepe at thilk time began,
Or ever I stent my best was more to loke
　Upon the writing of this nobil man,
That in himself the full recover wan
　Of his infortune, poverti, and distresse,
　And in tham set his verray feckerneffe.

　　　　　　　　　　　　　　　　　　‘ And

' And fo the vertew of his zouth before
  Was in his age the ground of his delytis :
Fortune the bak him turnyr, and therefore
  He makith joye and confort y^t he quitis
Of theire unfekir warldis appetitis,
  And fo aworth he takith his penance,
  And of his vertew maid it fuffifance.
' With mony a nobil refon as him likit
  Enditing in his fair latyne tong,
So full of fruyte, and rethorikly pykit
  Quhich to declare my fcole is over zong ;
Therefore I lat him pas, and in my tong
  Procede I will again to my fentence
  Of my mater, and leve all incidence.
' The long ny^t beholding, as I faide,
  Myn eyne gan to fmert for studying ;
My boke I fchet, and at my hede it laide,
  And down I lay, bot ony tarying
This mater new in my mynd rolling,
  This is to feyne how y^t eche eftate,
  As Fortune lykith, thame will tranflate.'

The prefent edition of thefe poems is illuftrated with notes and explanations, which muft greatly facilitate the perufal of them to a modern reader. The editor, whofe induftry in the prefent work merits great applaufe, has alfo fubjoined a Differtation on the Scottifh Mufic ; in refpect of which, befides evincing a good tafte, and an intimate acquaintance with the moft beautiful compofitions of that country, he makes feveral obfervations that bear ftrong marks both of ingenuity and critical reflection.——We cannot conclude our account of this production without informing our readers, that the editor pofitively denies the truth of a report which has long been circulated in the literary world, viz. that the celebrated dramatic paftoral of the Gentle Shepherd was not compofed by the poet Allan Ramfay, but by fome wits with whom he was connected. The editor therefore has the merit, not only of reftoring to James I. the laurels of which that monarch has been unjuftly deprived for fome ages, but of performing a fimilar act of juftice to the author of another of the moft admired productions in the Scottifh language.

A Criticism on the Elegy written in a Country Church-Yard. Being a Continuation of Dr. J———n's Criticism on the Poems of Gray. 8vo. 2s. Wilkie.

A Happy imitation of Dr. Johnfon's language, as well as of his modes of criticifm in the Biographical Prefaces. Perhaps prudence would dictate no more ; and the critic might reft

contented

contented with the character of carelefs and fuperficial, rather than incur the flighteft charge againft his fagacity and difcernment. If the author intended to perplex the world, he has fucceeded at leaft with a Reviewer; for this work would have been noticed more early, if we could have eafily feparated the ironical from the ferious, and the judicious criticifm from the fneer of ridicule. We have much reafon to fuppofe that the *whole* is not ironical ; and though we think our foundation is fometimes fecure, we feem frequently to totter, from its inftability.

This criticifm is written by a 'mafter's hand,' and, as we have already obferved, entirely in the manner of Dr. Johnfon. We need not remind the reader, that the fhape of fuch works is frequently queftionable. More than one fcholar, though every one is not ready to confefs it, at fome period of their lives have looked on the emendations of Scriblerus on Virgil as ferioufly intended to reftore erroneous readings ! If then the whole purpofe of the author be not ironical, we fhould fuppofe his chief aim has been, to point out how eafily the moft admired poetry may be *reafoned* into vague, trifling, and contradictory pofitions, or to correct the extravagance of panegyric, by pointing out fuperior paffages in other poets, from whom they were probably copied by Gray. Can we eafily avoid the laft opinion, in the following remarks on the three firft ftanzas of the poet ?

' If the images above recited are traced to the poets from whom they are taken, we fhall not always perceive them to have found their way into the Elegy written in a Country Church-yard, in an *improved* ftate. Of the curfew, as heard by a man of meditation, we have the following circumftantiation in Milton's Penferofo :

 ' Oft, on a plat of rifing ground,
 I hear the *far-off* curfew found ;
 Over fome wide-water'd fhore
 Swinging flow with fullen roar.

' To this characteriftical figuring Gray has thought proper to fubftitute the conceit of *Dante* ; according to which the curfew is made to toll *requiems* to the day newly deceafed : a fancy more fubtle than folid, and to which the judgment, if reconciled at all, is reconciled by effort.

' Of Evening, the approach is defcribed in the Elegy, as a profe-mufer would have defcribed it : " The glimmering landfcape fades on the fight ;" let us hear Thomfon :

 " A faint erroneous ray,
 Glanc'd from the' imperfect furfaces of things,
 Flings *half an image* on the ftraining eye ;
 While wavering woods and villages and ftreams

        And

And rocks—are all one fwimming fcene,
Uncertain if beheld."

Or, more compreffed in the thought, and invefted with the
fweetnefs of rhime :

" But chief, when evening fhades decay,
And *the faint landfcape fwims away,*
Thine is the *doubtful foft decline,*
And that beft hour of mufing thine."

And Collins :

" Be mine the hut that views
—Hamlets brown, and dim-difcover'd fpires.
And hears their fimple bell, and marks, o'er all,
Thy dewy fingers draw
The gradual dufky veil."

' The idea of making *founds* of a certain kind give a *relief* (to
fpeak in the language of artifts) to *filence,* is not new. Thus
wrote Collins in 1746 :

" Now air is hufh'd, fave where the weak-ey'd bat,
With fhort fhrill fhriek, flits by on leathern wing ;
Or, where the beetle winds
His fmall, but fullen horn."

The beetle of Collins and Gray is the "*grey fly*" of Milton,
that in the penfive man's ear " winds his fultry horn." Collins has changed the epithet into *fullen,* by a happy *mifremem-
brance.*

' In Parnell, in place of " ivy mantling a tower," we have
" yew bathing a charnel-houfe with dew." The ivy and the
tower might ftand any where as well as in a church-yard ; but
the charnel-houfe is characteriftic, and the yew is funereal. Of
Parnell's image, however, candour muft acknowlege the ftrength
to be fo great as to render it almoft offenfive.

' In Gray the introduction of the owl is proper. Parnell's
ravens might have found another place to croak in than a
church-yard, and another time than night. But the *part* the
owl acts in the Elegy is impertinent and foolifh, and exhibits
an example of a writer fpoiling a fine image, by *piecing* it. On
fome fine evening Gray had feen the moon fhining on a tower,
fuch as is here defcribed. An owl might be peeping out from
the ivy with which it was clad : of the obferver, the ftation
might be fuch, that the owl, now emerged from the mantling,
prefented itfelf to his eye in profile, fkirting with the moon's
limb. All this is well. The perfpective is ftriking : and the
picture well defined. But the poet was not contented. He
felt a defire to enlarge it : and, in execating his purpofe, gave
it accumulation without improvement. The idea of the owl's
complaining is an artificial one ; and the views on which it proceeds abfurd. Gray fhould have feen, that it but ill befitted
the *bird of wifdom* to complain to the moon of an intrufion,
which the moon could no more help than herfelf.'

There

There are some others of a similar kind.—That poetry,. though really excellent, will not always bear the cool examination of reason, is evinced by many paſſages of this criticiſm ; but the following is ſtriking and characteriſtic.

' In a ſeries of ſtanzas that follow, the author ſets himſelf to expoſtulate with. the proud, and undertakes to prove the abſurdity of the contempt which he ſuppoſes them ready to pour on the "unhonoured dead," for their want of more ſuperb monuments, from a regular ſucceſſion of *common places*.

' 1. It was no fault of theirs that they had them not.

' 2. They would have ſtood them in little ſtead.

' 3. Worth and genius may be without them.

' 4. It was the injuſtice of fortune that made them want them.

' 5. The account was balanced for them another way.

All which topics. are handled with decent plauſibility, and at decent length.

' X. It is in the tenth ſtanza that this train of thought commences. But the introduction is not clear of incumbrance. '" Impute not to theſe the fault," is an affected and inadequate expreſſion for '"don't treat them with ſcorn." The two laſt lines are the moſt majeſtic in the whole Elegy. But they contain an appeal to feelings, which none but thoſe who are ſo happy as to have been bred up in a veneration for the ſolemn forms and ſervice of the national church, can expect to poſſeſs. The palate of a ſectary, accuſtomed to the reception of ſlender foods, will nauſeate the full meal ſet before him in theſe lines :

' Where thro' the long-drawn iſle, and fretted vault, The pealing anthem ſwells the note of praiſe.

Of this laſt line, however, criticiſm muſt remark, that either the compoſition of the thought is faulty, or the arrangement of the expreſſion is inverted. It is not the anthem that ſwells the note, but the agglomeration of notes that ſwells the anthem. I am content to ſuppoſe this to have been his meaning : communicated in a mode of arrangement, unpleaſing to an Engliſh reader in his own language, but of which he admits the propriety in Latin compoſitions. I have ſeen this line moſt correctly transferred into that language in many different modes, all of them meritorious, in a collection of exerciſes written by the boys of the firſt form in Merchant Taylor's ſchool, and ſent to me with a view, of which I will not gratify my vanity with the publication ; though juſtice requires that of the worthy maſter I ſhould ſolace the labours, by recording the unwearied diligence, and by bearing teſtimony to thoſe abilities that are exerted in forming the riſing hopes of another age.

' XI. Fault has already been found with Gray for conforming to the affected uſe of participles in place of adjectives. "Honied ſpring;" "madding crowd, &c." "Storied urn ;" is of the ſame family, and even more exceptionable, becauſe

liable

liable to misapprehension. The meaning of the epithet is, "having stories figured upon it." In the Penseroso of Milton it is to be found as an epithet applied to windows, of which the panes are of painted glass. It is also used by Pope. "Flattery soothing the *ear* of death," is characteristical. What is said of "honour's voice" is not said happily. There is a want of appropriation. "Silent dust" is one of these expressions, which Voltaire used to denominate *des Suisses*; always ready at a call, and willing to engage in any service.

'XII. XIII. In the two following quatrains is well described the depression of genius under ignorance and poverty. But here too allowance must be made for a little of the *old leaven*. Hands are, *metaphorically*, said to "sway the rod of emire," and *literally* to bring forth sounds from the lyre. "Living lyre" is from Cowley ; and of his obligation to the royal poet of Judah, for the application of the idea "awake" to the eliciting of sounds from the harp or lyre, he has thought the acknowlegment deserving commemoration. In the whole of the Elegy, criticism has not been able to find two more happy lines than the following :

"Chill penury repress'd their noble rage,
And froze the genial current of the soul."

Here are really two ideas. Penury, in the character of frost, deprives the current of its heat, and checks its onward motion. I am unwilling to suppose the metaphor to be a broken one ; and that Gray jumbled into one, the images of horsemanship, and watery motion, as Addison has done in the following couplet :

"I bridle in my struggling Muse with pain,
That longs to launch into a nobler strain."

In illustrating our suspicions of the author's intention, we have given a sufficient specimen of his manner, which will probably induce the reader to recur to the work itself. It is executed so well, that even ' the sacredness of the critic's trust,' which 'imposes on him the exertion of self-denial, obliging him to range for blemishes, where his wishes are to find nought but beauties,' has not enabled us to perform more than half our task. We ought however to remark, that, if merely ironical, it is too long ; and the greater part of the world may, possibly with justice, look on it in no other light. The real good sense of the following remarks, as well as their very obvious ridicule, has induced us to preserve them.

' Reflections in a Country Church-Yard was the title by which this piece was first known ; a title plain, sober, and expressive of its nature, but too undignified in the apprehension of its author, who persuaded himself to think "Elegy" a nicer name. He should, however, have considered that, in adopting the new title, he subjected himself to severer rules of cri-

ticism

ticifm than before, and fhut himfelf out from many pleas in defence or palliation of its defultory ftyle, which would have been open to him from its old title of "Reflections;" a title in which little unity being promifed, there is little right to expect it. Being completely put together too, before the change of title took place, and fuffered, after the change, to remain in a great meafure as before, it became charged with incongruities too obvious to efcape obfervation. Though an elegy may be written in a church-yard as well as in a clofet, and in a *country* church-yard even better than in a *town* one; yet courtefy itfelf muft pronounce it fantaftical, if an elegy *is* to be written, to chufe out a place for writing it, where the conveniencies for that operation are a wanting, and even where the common implements either exift not at all, or exift by premeditation. Who is there that fays, or would be endured to fay, "I will take me pen, ink and paper, and get me out into a church-yard, and there write me an elegy; for *I do well to be melancholy?*" Parnell has carried the matter far enough, when he refolves to get out into a church-yard, and *think* melancholy thoughts.

'If the writers of ftudied ferioufnefs, and recorders of premeditated griefs, would employ one half of the time fpent in preparing their fadneffes for the public eye, in examining into the propriety of introducing them to the public at all, the journals of poetry would be lefs difgraced than they are with the balance of affectation againft nature. The ferioufnefs, which embraces the heart, is not the offspring of volition, but of inftinct. It is not a purpofe, but a frame. The forrow, that is forrow indeed, afks for no prompting. It comes without a call. It courts not admiration. It preffes not on the general eye, but haftens under covert, and wails its widowhood alone. Its ftrong hold is the heart. There it remains clofe curtailed, *unfeeing, unfeen.* Delicacy and tafte recoil at the publications of internal griefs. They profane the hallowednefs of fecret fadnefs, and fuppofe felected and decorated expreffion compatible with the proftration of the foul.'

The paffages which were more certainly intended to be ferious are, an elegant tranflation of one of Petrarch's fonnets, and, in our opinion, the Rondeau, though introduced in a ludicrous manner. The author fuppofes it to be contained in a letter of Gray to Dr. Curfon, which confifts of a lively explanation of the nature of this kind of compofition. It is well known that the fubject, in a rondeau, recurs at the end of every ftanza; the mufic is continued, and the voice flides imperceptibly into the 'return.' Our author is not contented with trufting this part to the powers of the finger, but contrives, that the final word of the verfe fhall be the firft that occurs in the burthen; fo that the difficulty to be overcome is, to finifh it with a word that will not materially alter the

fenfe

sense of the return, though it be substituted instead of that with which it originally commenced. We shall not consider this subject at length, because we apprehend the improvement is very trifling. It has been usual to adapt the words of a rondeau to this principle, by making the final and returning ones of easy pronunciation; and, by properly choosing mutes and liquids, to render the passage of the voice probably more easy, than by repeating the same word. But, after all, our ironical author may smile at a grave observation, on what may have been intended for ridicule. Poets, like the Gunner in the Critic, frequently think that they can never have enough of a good thing, and sometimes render the most striking beauties ridiculous, by an overstrained application. We can only add, that the accident by which this criticism was introduced to the press, is related by the author in the usual manner, and with great humour.

FOREIGN ARTICLE.

Winkelmann's Histoire de l'Art de l'Antiquité. (*Continued, from p. 143.*)

AFTER our author has considered every circumstance which relates to what he calls the essence of art, he proceeds to examine its progress. This may be more strictly called a history, as, in this part only, the influence of different circumstances and different states of society on the progress of arts are considered and detailed. The Abbé finds that the great hinge, on which their well-being depends, is liberty; for, though they are promoted by other fortuitous events, this is the leading principle which animates and supports them. But in this opinion he seems to be led by system to a partial and narrow view. The great spur to emulation, as we have already remarked, is the general attention of mankind; and, when art is connected with religion, it has a superior claim to respect, and even commands veneration. In every period, and in every country, religion, or its shadow, superstition, have prevailed; and in the different æras both of Greece and Rome, has contributed to promote the progress of art; but a general attention to works of taste and elegance cannot be expected during a civil war or a destructive pestilence. It is not therefore liberty alone which has the effect attributed to it by our author; it is a fixed, established, and flourishing government of any kind: it is a state of peace and harmony. The Peloponesan war, the effects of the rivalship between Athens and Sparta, is no objection to this opinion; the war was at a distance from the capital of either state: it was a rivalship in arts as well as arms, and carried on with so little animosity, that the enemies met, both at the Isthmian

mian and Olympic games, in harmony; or at leaft prepared to
carry on only the image of war, and to be ready for renewed
and real conteſts.

The hiſtory of art, before the time of Phidias, is ſcarcely
more than a chronicle of names; and the different ſchools of
Sicyon, Corinth, and Egina, are ſcarcely diſtinguiſhed but in
their appellations. It was after the deſtruction of the tyrants
of Greece, and the victories obtained over Xerxes, that the
arts flouriſhed in this country, and that Phidias aſtoniſhed the
world by his repreſentation of Jupiter. The only remains of
that æra now at Rome is the great Muſe, in the palace Barbe-
rini: this ſtatue, like all the early productions of Greece, diſplays a dignity and majeſty which is ſeldom obſerved in the
more finiſhed works of more enlightened ages. In the whole
period from Phidias to Alexander, the works of the artiſts,
without loſing their dignity, were executed with a purity and
ſimplicity which will always attract the admirers of nature.
' Refinement is as prejudicial to the cultivation of art, as to the
education of man.'

We cannot enter into a detail of the merits of Phidias, his
cotemporaries and pupils; but we ought to mention a curious
circumſtance, which is at once a flattering compliment to the
artiſts, and an incitement to thoſe who are capable of improving their ſeveral profeſſions. This was the period, during
which the preſent workmen were eſteemed more than their predeceſſors; but, as if art had been brought to perfection, from
this time the opinion of mankind was different.

When the war approached the ſeat of government, and Athens
ſubmitted to the arms of Lyſander, art declined with the proſperity of the ſtate, and ſeemed almoſt to expire with its diſtinguiſhed citizens; but it recovered when its tyrants were deſtroyed, and ſhone again with renewed luſtre, under the aufpices of Canachus and his cotemporaries, when Conon had
completed by ſea, what Thraſybulus had ſo ſucceſsfully began. It is obvious that the deſtruction of liberty had not ſo
much effect on this revolution, as the temporary humiliation,
and the diſtreſſes of the Athenians. The ſubſequent wars, as
they did not approach ſo near to the capital, had leſs effect on
the arts; and, even during the laſt war with Thebes, when
Epaminondas finiſhed his own life with a moſt glorious victory
in the 104th Olympiad, the impediments to their progreſs ſeem
rather imaginary than real. At this time, the ſun of Greece
was ſetting; but it ſat with a glory that had not diſtinguiſhed
even its meridian ſplendour. This was the age of Xenophon
and Plato, of Menander, of Praxiteles; and of Pamphilis,
the maſter of Apelles, Euphranor, Zeuxis, Nicias, and Par-
rhaſius.

It is a deciſive ſtroke againſt the ſyſtem of Mr. Winkelmann,
that the arts flouriſhed, with unimpaired vigour, under the
deſpotiſm of Alexander. The liberality and the taſte of this

prince had undoubtedly their fhare ; but they would have had a different effect, if the blaft of tyranny had been fo deftructive as our author fuppofed. The name of Lyfippus is well known, and he feems to have brought artifts back to a ftudy of nature, which they had neglected by aiming at the ideal and fublime beauties. Agefander, Athenodorus, and Polydorus, were the authors of the famous Laocoon, which ' demands the attention and admiration of pofterity, fince it has produced nothing comparable to, it.' Pyrgoteles was an engraver on precious ftones, of that age; Apelles, Ariftides, Protogenes, and Nichomachus, celebrated painters. The obfervations on the figures of Alexander and Demofthenes are fo interefting, that we wifh we could infert them entire. We muft however remark, that the figure of the orator, publifhed by Fulvius Urfinus, certainly reprefents fome other perfon. The prefent work prefents us with a reprefentation of one of his real bufts.

On the death of Alexander art feemed to languifh at Athens, from their peculiar fituation rather than from their new government ; and the words of Pliny, that art from this time languifhed and ' ceafed,' about the 155th Olympiad, our author contends muft be applied only to this ftate. It is not our bufinefs to recount their unfuccefsful attempts to efcape from defpotifm, nor the mean flattery which they lavifhly beftowed on their numerous and fhort-lived governors. Thefe are fufficiently underftood, and fhow that anarchy and confufion, rather than lofs of liberty, contributed to weaken the efforts of ingenuity. Yet every petty tyrant had his ftatues and medals, in which the value of the metal often made amends for the workmanfhip; but even thefe attempts, for a time, kept alive an art which they were not able to improve. A medal remaining of Antiochus is ftill one of the moft beautiful relics of ancient Greece; and the famous Farnefan bull is probably of this age. Of the numerous medals and ftatues faid to reprefent Pyrrhus, our author excepts to thofe which have the beard thick and long.

The arts of Greece, banifhed from their native climate, revived with luftre in Egypt under the Ptolemies ; and in Afia, under the Seleucidæ : ' transplanted to a new foil, they fet forward with new ftrength.'

We muft not confound thefe remains with what we have already obferved of Egyptian arts. The fcene only was changed, the artifts were the fame ; the materials were different, but the ftyle remained. The power, and the riches of Ptolemy Philadelphus, and his predeceffor Ptolemy Soter, are well known ; and it is rather our object to remark, that, after the difperfion of the Grecian artifts, Apelles was drawn to Egypt by the liberality and fplendour of the Egyptian fucceffor of Alexander, and almoft the rival of his greatnefs. Under the reign of the fecond Grecian king in Egypt, Euclid taught geometry, Theocritus wrote his Paftorals, and Callimachus his Hymns. But of all the Egyptian artifts the name of Satyrius only has reached the

prefent

present age. The works in porphyry and basalt are probably of this period; and the Alexandrian coins are still valued for the elegance of the workmanship. The poets, except perhaps Theocritus, did not equally support their former reputation.

The arts, when transplanted to Asia, did not flourish with the same luxuriance. Our author judiciously leaves his system to tell us, that this was owing to the distance from Greece, and to the faint recollection of what the artists had once seen, when a considerable interval had elapsed. It is one of the means of establishing a just taste, to review with care the most approved works; but this was sufficiently considered in our first article.

The period was not yet arrived, when the arts of Greece were to sink without recovery. The Achæan league was formed in the 125th Olympiad, and by the security and tranquillity which it established, restored in some degree the admiration of, and the value for, the more elegant works. The war between the Etolians and Achæans was carried on with a barbarous animosity, which for a time repressed what the league had a tendency to cherish. Every thing elegant and valuable was sacrificed to this rage of rivalship, during the temporary supremacy, which the chances of war gave to either party; and the existence even of art would have been forgotten, if the latent germ had not been cherished by the Grecians who had emigrated to Sicily, to Bithynia, and to Pergamus. The names of Hiero of Sicily, and Attalus of Pergamus, will recall to the reader's recollection the splendour of their courts, and the luxuries of their palaces. To this period, and particularly to Pergamus, our author attributes the different impositions of statuaries, who add the names of eminent masters to the copies of their works. This emulation, while it hindered the farther advances of art, contributed to prevent its decay; and it was of some consequence not to recede, if it was impossible, as the enthusiasm of a true antiquary will assure us, to go on. The return of public tranquillity in Greece, by the interposition of the Romans, and the various events related in different histories, dissipated the embers by which the spark had been hitherto concealed, and animated it with fresh vigour. This event happened the 4th year of the 144th Olympiad. To this æra our author attributed the famous relic styled the Torso of Belvidere. It is the trunk of a statue, without head, arms, or legs. 'The artist,' says our author, 'offers us, in this work, the sublime ideal of a body raised above human nature; of a constitution, arrived at the entire evolution of mature age; of a nature, exalted even to a degree which characterises divine content. Hercules appears here at the moment in which he is purified by fire from the grossness of humanity; at the instant in which he has obtained immortality, and is placed among the gods. He is represented without the necessity of tasting nourishment, without being again obliged to employ the force of his arms. You

C c 2

see no veins; his body is made to enjoy, not to nourish itself. His belly is full without being distended. By his attitude, he seems sitting with his right arm under his head, in a state of rest after his labours.'—What piercing eyes has an antiquary! All this is understood by the trunk alone; but every science has its weaknesses, and we must be silent. The other statues of Hercules our author describes with enthusiasm and eloquence. We eagerly wish to transcribe them; but in that case our article must remain another, though less valuable, Torso, without hands and feet.—The statuaries of this age were Glycon and Apollonius.

[*To be continued.*]

MONTHLY CATALOGUE.

POLITICAL.

An Argument to prove, that it is the indispensible Duty of the Creditors of the Public to insist, that Government do forthwith bring forward the Consideration of the State of the Nation, &c. By John Earl of Stair. 8vo. 1s. 6d. Stockdale.

THE zeal, the freedom, and the energy, with which the earl of Stair has repeatedly addressed the public on the state of the nation, are universally acknowleged. His lordship, we are sorry to observe, perseveres with unabated vehemence in urging the impossibility that the national revenues, or even resources, can continue much longer to preserve the government from bankruptcy. Admitting however the real danger of such an event, which we hope is at least at a greater distance than the noble lord seems to imagine, it is to be wished that so able and so diligent an enquirer into matters of finance would apply his talents towards restoring the prosperity of the nation, rather than overwhelm her with despondency by incessant predictions of inevitable and imminent ruin. The right honourable author's argument concludes in a strain remarkably emphatical.

' I am tired (says his lordship) with thinking—weary of conjectures, which, as they do not satisfy myself, cannot, I apprehend, satisfy the public; nor can I say what, or if any other aid than what she now affords, can be given by government's great ally the dubious source (as politicians hold) of good or ill; liable, perhaps, alike to use and to abuse; too much, alas! the fate of all human institutions.

' A peace is a proper epoch. Let the public creditors meet. In the multitude of counsellors safety resides. Interest is clear-sighted. They may, perhaps, discover that things are not as I represent them; or if they are, they may find issues from this labyrinth of distress unknown to me. My poor assistance, or any further information I can give, are heartily at their service. Let them

them depend upon themfelves, not upon minifters. Inveftigations of this kind are ever odious to minifters ; and our prefent great men, who tread the rounds of power in Lydian meafure, may think the public ought to be fatisfied, if they declare (as the generality of them fafely may) that they pay the fame attention to the interefts of the creditors of the public, as they do to thofe of their own creditors.

'During the courfe of this performance, I have fpoke of meafures and of men in the very manner they appeared to me, without fear or favour ; and I am fure without malice to any man, or connection of men whatever. I have fpoke of men, becaufe from men meafures muft flow. Was it not for this, I could have wifhed to have omitted this part of my fubject : for however guarded I have been in only cenfuring bodies and connections of men, leagued and arrayed to oppofe or promote public meafures, yet I apprehend, without making any friends, I create enemies to myfelf thereby.

'There is no wifdom in braving the private enmities of public men, and the difagreeable confequences of them even to the moft independent, where there are no hopes of public utility. My hopes of being of ufe, from paft experience, are not, cannot be very fanguine ; and on this ground I think I may be excufed from ftanding forth any more in the public fervice, and may without reproach wait with as much indifference as others, more immediately concerned than I am, do for the fatal cataftrophe, which feems to be approaching faft, without any body's caring or thinking about it. Even with thofe that are the moft anxious, the idleft delufions of hope and fpeculation ferve to overthrow the moft irrefragable demonftrations of figures ; which laft pafs for no more than the crude dreams of gloomy vifionaries.

'If, in treating of matters fo alarming, I have now and then let flip any thing too light and flippant, I humbly afk pardon of the public. It proceeds from a temper and difpofition of mind naturally chearful, that wifhes to beguile and make palatable to my readers, and to myfelf, the dry intricacies of figures. I am, notwithftanding, not the lefs in earneft ; nor was I ever more in earneft in my life than when I declare, that if the premifes that the conviction of the truth of them has compelled me to adopt are juft, or nearly juft, and nothing effectual is done to prevent their confequences, the infallible, inevitable conclusion that follows, is —

"That the ftate is a bankrupt; and that thofe who have trufted their all to the public faith, are in very imminent danger of becoming (I die pronouncing it) beggars."

In the prefent publication, the noble lord, with a franknefs becoming a loyal and affectionate fubject, declares, that fhould his majefty be pleafed to order a detailed ftate of the civil lift revenues to be laid before him, he will feparate the expence of his majefty and his family from the expences charged

on

on the civil lift, and publish an abstract of it as an appendix to this work. We are under no difficulty of agreeing with his lordship in opinion, that such a measure would be of service both to the k ng and to his people, by satisfying the latter that the profusions imputed to the crown are in a great measure not founded in fact and justice. By this means the earl of Stair perhaps might also be enabled to form, without prognostication, some important conclusions respecting the arcana of government.

Serious Considerations on the Political Conduct of Lord North, since his first Entry into the Ministry. By Nath. Buckington, Esq. 8vo. 1s. Stockdale.

The author of this pamphlet inveighs against lord North with an acrimony which evidently betrays prejudice. The first article of the charge exhibited by Mr. Buckington is, that when money was wanted for the public service, his lordship always had recourse to the practice of funding. This practice, no doubt, may justly be considered as pernicious in several respects. But lord North could not be particularly reprehensible for having recourse to an expedient which has been uniformly adopted by every administration for almost a century past; especially if, for raising the national supplies, no other method sufficiently practicable, and less disadvantageous, could be carried into execution.

Another charge produced against the minister by the author of the present pamphlet, is the choice of improper officers for military and naval commands. That, in some instances, the choice was unfortunate, is a fact that cannot be denied; but admitting that the mistake had even been voluntary, which we presume Mr. Buckington himself will not be so unreasonable as to affirm, it would be unjust to impute the blame entirely to any one member of the cabinet. The author is likewise sarcastic against some other persons in public life, respecting the supposed demerits of whom he is far from being singular in opinion.

Two Letters on Parliamentary Representation. By Jeremiah Batley, Esq. 8vo. 1s. 6d. Debrett.

The author of these Letters is a zealous, though we think an unprejudiced, advocate for parliamentary reformation. He professes a high opinion of the abilities and patriotic intentions of some of those who have been most forward in their endeavours to promote such a plan; but he expresses at the same time a disapprobation of the means which they have proposed for that purpose.

A general idea of his sentiments respecting the different methods of reform, is conveyed in the following extract:

‘ There are two modes of reform particularly contended for; and each is supported by individuals, very deservedly respected: I need not say, that I allude to the Yorkshire plan, and that of universal representation. The latter, most likely, will only

only ferve as a record both of the virtues and imperfections of
the human mind, for it required the greateft benevolence and
mental fortitude to conceive it to be practicable; and, confidering the circumftances of the country, an indifference, that is
nearly allied to infenfibility, in thofe for whofe relief it is propofed, not to endeavour to make it fo. But the other, very
different in its end and principle, is fo artfully contrived to attract powerful patronage, that, contrary to the fentiments of
many, I have always feared that it was likely to be carried into
execution. Should it fo happen, I fincerely wifh that our de-
fcendents may never have caufe to complain of that event; but
I cannot with equal truth add, that this is my expectation.

' Of the various fchemes that have been propofed for the me-
lioration of parliament, the moft eafy to execute, that will anfwer, in my opinion, the intention of the conftitution to give
univerfal protection, is either that which recommends an improvement of our prefent borough-reprefentation, by adding to the
voters the houfeholders of the town and of the neighbouring
hamlets; or that of the Weftminfter Committee of Affociation,
of dividing the kingdom into equal diftricts. The firft is the
moft fimple: the laft, were houfeholders only permitted to vote,
is more perfect, but will be far more difficult, I fhould fuppofe,
to obtain; and as either, I think, would anfwer our purpofe,
the moft practicable feems to be the beft entitled to a preference.
I may, perhaps, be too partial in afcribing to the propofal I
formerly recommended, fo much perfection; but certainly, if
boroughs can be made to anfwer the purpofe of reprefentation,
we fhould obviate many objections to a reform by retaining
them. Some muft undoubtedly be amputated, becaufe they
are fo unequally difperfed; but we may create others in their
ftead, and let all thofe remain that can be corrected.'

This author confiders a *diverfified reprefentation* as the beft
fecurity of public freedom; and intimates an apprehenfion left,
if the plan for adding a greater number of members to the counties fhould be adopted, the landed intereft might acquire too
powerful an influence in the legiflature.

This remark coincides with an opinion which we expreffed in
a late Review; but we cannot likewife acknowlege a fimilitude
of fentiment on the fubject of annual elections; a meafure tran-
fiently recommended, but in ftrong terms, by this fenfible
writer.

*A Defence of the Conduct of the Court of Portugal; with a full
Refutation of the feveral Charges alleged againft that Kingdom,
with Refpect to Ireland.* 8vo. 1s. 6d. Stockdale.

It appears from this pamphlet that the Irifh have expreffed
complaints againft the court of Portugal, for not admitting
them to trade in her ports with the fame freedom as the fubjects of Great Britain. In anfwer to thofe complaints the court
of Portugal, or fome perfon interefted in the meafures of that
nation, affures the Irifh that this conduct arifes from no partiality,

tiality, but merely from a neceſſary adherence to the terms of the commercial treaty made with Great Britain in 1703, in which the inhabitants of Ireland were not mentioned. It is added, that the court of Portugal has actually made application to the Britiſh miniſtry for a renewal of the treaty, in which it is their intention that the Iriſh ſhall be included.

A Letter to the Earl of Effingham on his lately proposed Act of In-ſolvency. By James Bland Burges, Eſq. 8vo. 2s. Cadell.

It ſeems that Mr. Burges, the writer of this Letter, had been deſired by lord Effingham to prepare the inſolvent act, which his lordſhip moved for, towards the cloſe of the laſt ſeſſion of parliament. Mr. Burges had formerly diſapproved of acts of that nature; but on attentively conſidering the ſubject, for the purpoſe above mentioned, he entirely changed his opinion; and he now endeavours to evince, by a variety of arguments, the expediency of paſſing ſuch an act. He begins with refuting ſome objections which have been made to the tendency of inſolvent acts in general, viz. that ſuch acts are improper, becauſe they give encouragement to fraudulent debtors; that they bear exceedingly hard upon creditors; that they have been productive of great evils; that they are founded upon narrow principles; that the act propoſed laſt ſeſſion differed from the inſolvent act of 1781, and was contrary to the principle of both houſes. After anſwering theſe ſeveral objections, Mr. Burges proceeds to give a general detail of the inſolvent and other acts relative to priſoners for debt, which have paſſed in England ſince the beginning of the laſt century.

As the author directs his obſervations to the underſtanding, not the paſſions of his readers, he is more argumentative than declamatory; and has, in ſupport of the meaſure he recommends, given only the two following facts, which humanity will not permit us to leave unmentioned.

' Not many months ago a poor wretch, who had been confined in the King's Bench for fifteen years, literally died of hunger: he was found in a ſequeſtered corner of the priſon ſtarved to death. One Grace Hooper is ſtill a priſoner in the county gaol of Devonſhire, where ſhe has been immured for one-and-forty years, for a debt of fifteen pounds, and a ſubſequent detainer on a writ *de excommunicato capiendo*, lodged againſt her in conſequence of a ſuit in the eccleſiaſtical court, with the rector of her pariſh, about a pew in the church.'

Upon the whole, the author urges very forcible conſiderations for the interpoſition of the legiſlature, in granting to impriſoned debtors that relief which he inſiſts is ſtrongly required, not only by humanity, but the principles of juſtice and wiſe government.

A Brief and Impartial Review of the State of Great-Britain, &c. 8vo. 1s. 6d. Kearſley.

We cannot avoid remarking an error committed in the title-page of this pamphlet, where we find mention made of the
' fourth

* fourth feffion of the fifteenth parliament of the prefent reign.*
—In refpect of this author's Review we meet with nothing that
merits particular attention. The principal drift of his obfervations feems to be, to pave the way for the affumption of the
Eaft India territories into the hands of adminiftration. His politics appear to be not untainted with perfonal prejudices ; unlefs indeed we miftake for prejudice a defire of gratifying thofe
who at prefent conduct the affairs of government.

*By Order of Congrefs. Addreffes and Recommendations to the States.
By the United States in Congrefs affembled.* 8vo. 2s. Stockdale.

In thefe papers, which are written with great energy, the
Congrefs urges the obligation of the United States to render
juftice to the public creditors ; and at the fame time points out
the refources from which a revenue for that purpofe may be obtained. The propriety of the expedients recommended by the
grefs is alfo enforced by a variety of documents.

*A Circular Letter from General Wafhington to William Greene, Efq.
Governor of the State of Rhode Ifland.* 8vo. 6d. Stockdale.

This Letter has already appeared in the public prints. The
author's defign is to rouze and confirm a fpirit of patriotifm and
unanimity in the American States. As a cautious, defenfive
general, Mr. Wafhington's military talents have formerly been
experienced ; and, on the prefent occafion, we muft acknowlege he appears to advantage in the capacity of a writer.

*Minutes of the Evidence at the Bar of the Houfe of Commons,
Proceedings of the Houfe, and hearing of Council, on reading the
Bill for inflicting Pains and Penalties on Sir Thomas Rumbold,
Bart. and Peter Perring, Efq.* Folio. 1l. 11s. 6d. Walker.

As this enquiry is not yet concluded, any obfervations upon
it would be reprehenfible.

DIVINITY.

*Eight Sermons preached before the Univerfity of Oxford, in the Year
1783, at the Lecture founded by the Rev. John Bampton, A. M.
By John Cobb, D.D.* 8vo. 3s. 6d. fewed. Rivington.

Woolafton, in his Religion of Nature delineated, propofes
this queftion :——How may a man qualify himfelf, fo as
to be able to judge for himfelf, of the other religions profeffed in the world, to fettle his own opinions in difputable
matters, and then to enjoy tranquillity of mind, neither dif-
turbing others, nor being difturbed at what paffes among them ?
Dr. Cobb keeps this queftion in view, and makes the fubject of
his firft difcourfe an Inquiry after Happinefs. Tranquillity in
life, he fays, is not to be maintained without prudence ; nor
without the perfuafion of the being and providence of God, nor
without religion. Rational happinefs is not to be found in
riches, honour, pleafure, or in contemplation. It is only to be
found in confcioufnefs ; yet not complete without the hope of
immortality.

8

He

He proceeds to examine the pretenfions of natural religion. ' Rational fyftematical religion, he obferves, is incompetent to the purpofes of the inquiry. Philofophy or rational fyftems being abftrufe and fpeculative, and alfo uncertain and various, prudence is the only rational religion, truly fo called. This is competent, as fuch, in itfelf to a moral agent. But man is a tranfgreffor; and this religion is not adapted to fuch a cha-racter.'

The next object of enquiry is the Gofpel. This, he fhews, is an act of grace, and the religion of finners. ' The Chriftian religion, he remarks, was not delivered in a fyftem; it does not add to the law of reafon, nor fuperfede the rational law. Yet it is not juftly defined as the reftoration of natural religion. The argument of its internal evidence is limited in its applica-tion. Chrift is the author of new methods of fanctification.'

The author then treats of repentance, of faith profeffional and practical, and of the Chriftian privileges; which, accord-ing to his account, are free inquiry, wifdom, prudence, fettled judgment, and peace.

On thefe topics he reafons in a cool, fedate, and fcientifical manner, as a learned and orthodox divine.

Vicarious Sacrifice; or the Reality and Importance of Atonement for Sin by the Death of Chrift, afferted and defended, againft the Ob-jections of Dr. Prieftley. By R. Elliot, A. B. 8vo. 2s. 6d. Johnfon.

This writer is a ftrenuous advocate for the doctrines of vica-rious facrifice, imputed righteoufnefs, and atonement for fin by the death of Chrift. He undertakes to anfwer thirty-three objections, which have been urged againft thefe tenets by fome late writers, particularly Dr. Prieftley. His manner of treating the fubject is calm and methodical. He ftates his arguments with great perfpicuity; and, though he generally contends againft the principles of human reafon, he appears to be actu-ated by a zeal only for truth, and the good of mankind.

The Explication of the Vifion of Ezekiel; which tends to unfold all Prophecy, and feveral other Parts of Scripture, which are not in general underftood. 8vo. 1s. Rivington.

A Continuation from the Firft Book, by the Author of the Explana-tion of the Vifion of Ezekiel: including Solomon's Song. 8vo. 2s. 6d. Rivington.

The Invifible Geography of the World, or an Explanation of the Bible, continued by the Explainer of the Vifion of Ezekiel. Book III. 8vo. 2s. 6d. Rivington.

As the intentions of this writer are pious, his faculties evi-dently diforded, and his lucubrations abfolutely unintelligi-ble, thefe three pamphlets muft be exempted from criticifm.

The Beauties of Methodifm. Selected from the Works of the Rev. John Wefley, A. M. 12mo. 2s. 6d. fewed. Fielding.

The Τὸ Καλὸν of Methodifm is here difplayed with zeal and oftentation, if not with colours fuitable to the native beauty afcribed

cribed to its doctrines by this writer. The compilation, however, we doubt not, will prove acceptable to the frequenters of the Foundery, and may likewife gratify the curiofity of fuch as defire to know the principles of this fect.

DRAMATIC.

Fatal Curiofity : a True Tragedy. Written by George Lillo, 1736. *With Alterations, as revived at the Theatre-Royal, Haymarket.* 8vo. 1s. 6d. Cadell.

This fcene of real diftrefs is one of thofe domeftic tragedies, which, as they require greater art in the poet, at leaft in the opinion of Horace, fo they are more interefting and affecting.—The practice of Lillo has conftantly been, to truft to the real effect of domeftic woe, with little poetical ornament, and lefs artificial management. His genius may not have been adapted to either, or he might have thought that they were unneceffary, when the heart muft have been fufficiently affected by a plain 'unvarnifhed tale.' He is certainly fupported by the practice of Shakfpeare, who, though he was able, from trifles light as air, to raife an apparent confirmation ftrong as holy writ; yet in fcenes of real woe is fcarcely fuperior in art or ornament to the author of the Fatal Curiofity. It will immediately occur, that we allude to a difputed play, the Yorkfhire Tragedy; but there is fufficient reafon to conclude, that it was really the production of Shakfpeare. We mean not to infer that Lillo was deftitute of a poetical genius, or ignorant of the beft methods of conducting his fables; though the former feldom foared to the fublimer flights; and in the latter, he commonly followed, and fometimes fervilely, the hiftory. In general his plays are the favourites of feeling hearts, and of thofe who do not difdain to be affected, becaufe their judgment or their tafte is not completely fatisfied.

Mr. Colman has again introduced this play to the attention of the public, with very flight alterations. We muft fuppofe the ftory to be generally known; the poftfcript only has the claim of novelty. It contains the original ftory, from a book commonly ftyled Frankland's Annals, and fome remarks on Mr. Harris's Commentary on this play, in his Philological Enquiries. The latter are not very interefting, as they are chiefly intended to correct fome miftakes, which Mr. Harris had fallen into by writing of this play from memory only. The former varies little from it, except that, in the Tragedy, the part of the Sifter is more interefting, from her office being given to a lady, whom the young man had formerly loved; and who, notwithftanding abfence and the report of his death, continued faithful to his memory.

The frequenters of the theatre were certainly obliged to Mr. Colman for refcuing this pathetic narrative from oblivion; and we ought not to forget our thanks, fince to recall the recollection, is frequently to renew the pleafure,

The

The Magic Picture, a Play. [*Altered from Massinger*]   *By the Rev. H. Bate.*   8vo.   1s. 6d.   T. Davies.

In altering 'The Picture' of Massinger, Mr. Bate has given freer scope, both to his judgment and invention, than is usual in such transmutations.   He has not only reformed the dialogue from those gross indelicacies with which it had been stained by its original author, but rendered the whole fable more confistent with dramatic probability, by substituting Jealousy, instead of Magic, as the principal agent in the piece. In several other circumstances, likewise, of sentiment and character, the Picture has received such improvement as justifies the applause bestowed upon it at the theatre.

M E D I C A L.

A Letter to Mr. Clare, upon the Prevention and Cure of the Siphilis, Gonorrhœa, Fluor Albus, &c. by Absorption.   By S. Freeman, M. D. Author of the Ladies Medical Friend, Good Samaritan, and Practical Midwifery.   4to.   1s.   Cornwell.

It is impossible to read a newspaper without having some acquaintance with Mr. Clare ; but we know little of the author of the Good Samaritan, &c.   We are, however, certain, that he sometimes 'follows truth', who really appears the goddess of his idolatry, for he has not even sent 'one copy of this *poor production* (truth again!—Would that every author was so much attached to it!) to the Reviewers, nor even one single guinea to puff for him.'   We must give our melancholy testimony to this assertion, and sigh in silence.

But who is Dr. Freeman ?—Do not be so impatient, reader, and we will inform you.   He is a man of credit and character, who has a great number of the genteelest patients, and does much good.   Hear his own words : 'I thank God there never was one single patient of mine ever *killed*, or their constitution the least injured by being *cured* in the manner proposed.'   It is lucky that nonsense is neither true nor false.   Mr. Clare, we are informed by the same authority, is a young man of great merit, to whom the '*whole world* is indebted for this valuable discovery.'   Indeed we did not think the disease, though general, had been universal.   The author informs him that, though he is so ingenious, it is possible that he may not be regarded, yet that this has been the lot of many ingenious men besides himself.   We are happy to find that Dr. Freeman has been more successful.

It is impossible to find room in our article for the many good things in this Letter ; as the virtue of fasting spittle for dropsies, scurvy, rheumatism, &c. or that a stone may be evacuated by masticated bifcuit being applied to the eyes.   It is a little unfortunate for this remedy, that fasting spittle must necessarily be swallowed every day, by every individual ; but it is probable that

that the Doctor imputes every death, as unfortunately there is a time when patients can no longer swallow, to this defect.

We may resume our acquaintance with Dr. Freeman from Mr. Clare's answer; — for he surely will not omit any occasion so favourable, who has adopted many, whose appearance was less flattering.

MISCELLANEOUS.

A Dissertation on the Preservative from Drowning; and Swimmer's Assistant. By R. Macpherson, Gent. 8vo. 2s. 6d. Murray.

The object of this Dissertation is to recommend a peculiar apparatus, as a preservative. The author is consequently induced to examine every machine of this kind, which has been hitherto recommended, and finds each of them unweildy, inconvenient and sometimes insufficient. His chief intention is to preserve the life of the seaman till some ship may happen to meet with him; or, if near the shore, till assistance from thence, or his own efforts, enable him to reach it. To enforce this plan, he has collected many histories of people who have been preserved by means of pieces of the wrecks, and has augmented the number, we think unnecessarily, by an account of almost every shipwreck or inundation he has been able to procure. We have examined his description of the preservative with the annexed plate, together with the principles on which it is recommended, and have little hesitation in pronouncing it equally simple, convenient, and safe. Yet it may never be much employed, and, like many other inventions, will be admired and neglected. It is probable that the very circumstance which may seem to make it generally necessary, will contribute to this neglect; the dangers which continually surround us we despise; and the inhabitants of a gunpowder mill think themselves secure, while the smallest spark would be their inevitable destruction. The guide, who conducts the traveller to the summit of Ætna, disregards an eruption; and the inhabitant below would despise a preservative, unless presented in the garb of religion, or the form of an amulet. We need not multiply instances of this nature; the conduct of every individual will recall our position to ', his own business and bosom.'

The experiments of our author differ a little, however, from our own. The water will certainly support us, though we have not found it easier to rest on our back, than in the opposite position. The hands are less exercised, but the neck is soon weary. When we trusted ourselves to the water without any effort, the constant consequence has been, that the face has turned downwards, and the head has sunk rather below the surface. This may seem to contradict the former opinion, that the supine position required less exertion of the hands; but it will be soon obvious, that, in this case, they are employed to greater advantage.

These

These hints may probably deserve the attention of our author, in adapting his principles to different persons, as different sizes and bulks must vary the events of these experiments.

Thoughts submitted to the Consideration of the Officers of the Army, respecting the Establishment of a Regimental Fund, for the Relief of the sick and necessitous Wives of the private Soldiers. By R. Hamilton, M. D. 8vo. 1s. Johnson.

This benevolent tract relates to the wives of the private soldiers, whose distress is considerable, and alleviated only by the cold, and often precarious, hand of casual charity. Our author proposes to raise a yearly fund for their more certain relief, from the vices of the common soldiers, and the subscription of the officers. The industrious workman, who is permitted to follow his labour, is also to contribute a penny per day from his small stipend. These taxes are trifling, and the utility material and certain; for the wives of the privates are important objects even to government, since the best soldiers are always those who have been bred in the army. The humanity of the author's intention, and the justice of his ' ways and means,' deserve our applause.

Maxims and Reflections. Small 8vo. 1s. Egerton.

A short but sensible preface served to conciliate our affections to this little piece : many of the Reflections are certainly shrewd and sagacious; more of them are trite, and we fear that some may be styled trifling ; yet they afford an agreeable amusement as well as some instruction, for an idle half hour ; and, if they had been arranged in a proper order, their merit would have been more conspicuous.

Joseph. In Five Books. By A. M. Cox. Small 8vo. 3s. Dodsley.

The favourable reception which this lady's first production, Burton Wood, met with from the public, has, she says, induced her to try the success of a second performance. The history of Joseph has been universally admired for its pathos and unaffected simplicity. Our author begins her narrative with the lamentation of Jacob for the loss of his son, and the return of Reuben and his brethren to the land of Canaan, after their first expedition into Egypt. She has embellished the story with some additional circumstances, as the love of Benjamin and Zaphna, the introduction of Asenath the wife of Joseph, &c. But, in general, she has adhered to the Mosaic history. The style, in which this work is composed, is a sort of measured prose. The following paragraph will be no improper specimen.

' At last he rose ;—and, speaking to the many present, " Depart (he said), I have farther business with these Hebrews."—Obedient, all retired ; when, ardent gazing through the medium of those tears impelled by powerful affection, he

struck

ftruck their fouls with this all-ftartling,—this awful declaration,——

" I AM YOUR BROTHER JOSEPH!"

' —Had fonorous thunder, in terrific peals, burft with tremendous horror o'er their heads, and fhaken the earth even to the loweft centre;—had Egypt's lofty towers in ponderous ruin fallen, all fhattered by the dire explofion,—they might have *felt* the fhock : but *this*,—*this* fudden ftroke, no fortitude could parry :—A gleam of joy, checked by the ftrongeft apprehenfion,—dread furprife,—hope, combating with fear,—conjunctive all, fhot fwiftly through their bofoms.—The youth, whofe artlefs plaints in vain implored their mercy, whofe tender years moved not their favage hearts,—whom (deaf to every foft fraternal claim, and thoughtlefs of a parent's deep diftrefs,) they ruthlefs fold to ftrangers;—this *youth* now ftood before them,—graceful,—majeftic.—The bloom of early years was loft in ripened manhood ;—his form athletic,—not inelegant,—covered with the richeft robes of ftate, fecond to none but Egypt's glorious king,—beloved,—refpected,—honoured !—Great God!—Imagination's force creative cannot form ideas adequate to fuch a fcene!'

This language has nothing of that fimplicity for which the original is diftinguifhed. It refembles Jofeph's coat of many colours.

Thefes, Graecae et Latinae, felectae. 12mo. 4s. Law.

A number of publications has lately appeared, containing the beauties of modern authors It was therefore natural to imagine, that fome perfon of learning would prefent the public with the beauties of the claffic writers, which are undoubtedly fufficient to make a very copious, and a very agreeable collection. Mr. William Baker, printer in Ingram Court, Fenchurch-ftreet, is the compiler of this volume. It is chiefly compofed of fhort fentimental obfervations, thrown together promifcuoufly. The want of a methodical arrangement, or an index, may in fome refpects leffen its utility ; but it will neverthelefs afford the claffical reader a great variety of rational amufement. Mr. Baker has made his extracts from both the Greek and Latin writers, and has difplayed no inconfiderable tafte and judgment in the felection.

The Magdalen : or, Hiftory of the firft Penitent received into that charitable Afylum. 12mo. 2s. 6d. fewed. Lane.

This narrative is faid to contain the hiftory of the firft penitent received into the afylum known by the name of the Magdalen ; with anecdotes of other penitents. It is written in a feries of letters, which are afcribed, with what truth the editor beft knows, to the late unfortunate Dr. Dodd. Whoever the author be, the ftory is not ill related, and may afford female readers fuch inftruction as is favourable to the cultivation of virtue, by fhewing the pernicious confequences of vice.

Fruit

Fruit Tables.   2s.   Stockdale.

These Tables exhibit in columns a description of the size, colour, shape, flesh, juice, and other distinguishing characteristics, as well as the various times of ripening, of the most esteemed species of peaches, nectarines, plums, and pears. Subjoined is a catalogue of the different sorts of esculent and herbaceous plants that are raised for the use of the kitchen, with the most common varieties, and a specification of the parts which are eaten. The Tables appear to be compiled with care; and the information contained in the catalogue may also prove not unuseful to private families.

Fables in Monosyllables, by Mrs. Teachwell. 12mo. 2s. Marshall.
Fables, by Mrs. Teachwell: in which the Morals are drawn in various Ways. 12mo. 1s. 6d. Marshall.

These fables are not only few, but many of them in reality the same, expressed in words somewhat different. The morals likewise are no less deficient in variety, and become insipid by the tedious dialogues in which they are often conveyed.

The Proceedings in the Court of King's Bench against Charles Bourne, Gent. on the Prosecution of Sir James Wallace. 4to. 3s. sewed.

A legal process by a gentleman of the sword, against another of the same profession, is an incident not very common; but an appeal to justice is certainly preferable, in every sense, to the Gothic substitution, which bids defiance both to reason and law.

Proceedings in the Cause, the King against the Dean of St. Asaph, on the Prosecution of William Jones, Gent. Folio. 1s. 6d. Gurney.

The subject which gave rise to this prosecution was an alleged libel, imputed to the dean of St. Asaph, and contained in a pamphlet entitled ' The Principles of Government, in a Dialogue between a Scholar and a Peasant.' The trial came on at the great session held at Wrexham, for the county of Denbigh, in September last, but was adjourned to the next meeting of that court. The Proceedings now published consist of the arguments of the court and lawyers, among which the speech of Mr. Erskine, counsel for the dean, is what principally commands the attention.

The Trial of a Cause between ——— Sutherland, Esq. Plaintiff, and General Murray, late Governor of Minorca, Defendant. Folio. 2s. Kearsley.

The allegation of the plaintiff, in this cause, was, that general Murray had illegally deprived him of an office which he held in Minorca. The trial ended in favour of the former, who obtained a verdict for five thousand pounds damages.

THE
CRITICAL REVIEW.

For the Month of *December*, 1783.

Notes and Various Readings of Shakespeare. *Three Vols.* 4*to.*
3*l.* 3*s. in Boards.* Walter.

'GRatiano fpeaks an infinite deal of nothing, more than
any man in all Venice : his reafons are as two grains
of wheat hid in two bufhels of chaff ; you fhall feek all day
e'er you find them ; and when you have them, they are not
worth the fearch.'—If we exhaufted both our patience and
our paper, we could give no better account of this voluminous commentary ; but, as antiquaries rather than poets have
lately deferved the title of a genus irritabile, we muft be more
explicit. The firft, and a great part of the fecond volume,
confift of notes and various readings. The former are generally trifling, and almoft always uninterefting. To fix the
removal of a fcene, or the propriety of a comma, to regulate
an exit and an entrance, are the objects of a little mind : yet
thefe occupy whole pages ; and we feek, in vain, for the developement of a latent beauty, or the elucidation of an obfcure or mutilated paffage. The gloffary, which attends the
notes, is, as far as we have obferved, an exact explanation of
words ; but this is frequently an unfaithful guide to the
fpirit which animates Shakfpeare. Even, in this part, there
are many trifling, and fome fufpicious interpretations ; but
thofe difcuffions are feldom either entertaining or ufeful. A
word in a former edition of this gloffary, occafioned a curious
remark from a manufcript before us, which, for its peculiar
humour, and the probable explanation of a difficult paffage,
we fhall infert.—' A late editor (Capel) interprets that paf-

fage in Shakſpeare, " I would land-damm him," to ſignify I would ſtop his mouth with earth ; that is, I ſuppoſe, bury him alive.'——Another equally fanciful has interpreted it, ' I would ſtop his water for him,' from lant urina & A. S. *demman* obſtruere, obturare flumen. But after all theſe conjectures, a Glouceſterſhire critic, who is better acquainted with the pro-vincial language of Shakſpeare, would conclude it to be only a cant phraſe, to which no certain idea is affixed : for hav-ing often heard in that county, *landan, lantan, rantan,* uſed in the ſenſe of ſoouring, correcting, rattling and rating ſe-verely, he would be apt to think that land-damm was one of theſe, which an affected nicety, reſpecting the final ſyllable, has corrupted to dan. It is indeed evident from the context, vol. iv. p. 325. of Mr. Steevens' edition, that the paſſion of the ſpeaker wiſhed to exaggerate the puniſhment even of dam-nation ; and the word of his native country immediately ſug-geſted ſomething more horrible, at leaſt in ſound.

The ſame critic uſed to remark, that in one of the old folios the hoſteſs ſays, ' the *tight* of a hair' was never loſt in her houſe ; but that the modern editors had improperly changed it to tithe. We uſe, ſaid he, at this moment, in Glouceſterſhire, the word tight for a very ſmall portion ; and the verb ' tight to weigh' is ſtill frequently employed. But to return to our author.

As we have little inclination to conteſt the diſputed paſſages in the gloſſary, we have as little to analyſe the notes. We would ſpare our readers the fatigue which we have endured for their ſakes ; and we can truly ſay, that we have not yet met with one which we wiſhed to preſerve. As a ſpecimen of the manner of our author, we ſhall ſelect the firſt which oc-cur ; we have not found many more intereſting.

1. 10.

' *rather than ſlack it*] The verb in the old edition is " *lack*;" but this, having no active ſignification,——that is, not implying action, cannot properly be oppos'd to " *ſtir up* :" " *ſlack*,"—— a reading of the three latter moderns,—is the very term the place calls for ; and ſo natural a correction, that he who does not embrace it, muſt be under the influence of ſome great pre-poſſeſſion.

4, 2.

' *O, that* had ! *how ſad a paſſage 'tis!*] Seeing Helena dis-order'd ; affected, as ſhe imagines, by the mention of her fa-ther. " *Paſſage*" has no extraordinary force in this place, but means ſimply —a paſſing over : " *how ſad a paſſage 'tis!*" how hard to be paſſ'd over without emotion and ſorrow ! — " *Play*," in l. 5, has been alter'd to —*play'd*; but very unneceſſarily, to ſay

7   ſay

ay no more of it : it is a fubftantive of known fignification, and oppos'd to another fubftantive—" *work.*"

D°. 23.

' *her difpofitions fhe inherits* &c.] The change of terms in this paffage, and the very uncommon fenfe that is put upon fome of them, have involv'd it in too much obfcurity. " *Difpofitions,*" mean—natural difpofitions ; by implication, good ones : and ' *gifts,*" the acquirements of education ; good ones, likewife : the firft he calls afterwards, *fimplenefs ;*" and then, " *honefty :*" the other, with too much licence, " *virtuous qualitie., virtues,*" and (finally) " *goodnefs :*" If the reader will carry this in his mind, he may be able to decypher the fpeech without a paraphrase ; and will fee too the propriety of changing "*their*" into ' *her,*" with the Oxford editor. But it fhould not be conceal'd from him, that the fpeech has fome other defeéts befides thefe which are mention'd ; fuch as will draw upon it the cenfure of the grammarian and logician too : the latter will fay of it,—that what the Countefs is made to urge, is no fit reafon for entertaining the " *hopes*" that fhe fpeaks of ; and the other will find a relative in it, that does not belong, as it fhould, to the fubftantive neareft at hand, but to another remote one ; and thefe circumftances too have their fhare in the fpeech's obfcurity.'

In the fecond note, we fhould have fufpeéted that the word ' paffage' was taken from ' paffagio' a term in mufic ; but we have been informed, that it was not formerly in ufe. It implies a part of a piece, on a preconcerted plan, which is not the charaéter of ancient mufic ; though, as the word was formerly applied to a part of any compofition, there is little occafion for the fanciful explanation of our author.

The various readings are, in our opinion, an important part of every edition ; as it is always of confequence to afcertain the probable text of the author, before we attempt to explain it. On this account we fhould have thought them valuable, if they had not been encumbered with fo many ufelefs additions. It will not be expeéted that we fhould afcertain their accuracy by a collation, but may obferve, that of the numerous reftored paffages in the edition, to which thefe notes relate, there are very few, and thefe by no means important, which have not been mentioned by other editors. Indeed there is a heavy charge againft Mr. Steevens in the Dedication, which we muft neceffarily tranfcribe.

' However, to fupply this omiffion, in fome degree, by pointing out the means of afcertaining the truth of what I have advanc'd, I muft beg leave to refer your Lordfhip to the edition of SHAKESPEARE, publifh'd in ten volumes, oétavo, 1773, and re-publifh'd in 1779, with notes by Dr. SAM. JOHNSON and Mr. GEO. STEEVENS, requefting you will take the trouble of comparing it with one publifhed by the Doctor alone, in eight volumes, 1765: You will then find, my Lord, a regular fyftem of plagiarifm, upon a fettl'd plan, pervading thofe later editions throughout, and that,—not the Doctor's former publication, as one would naturally fuppofe, but—Mr. CAPELL's, in ten volumes, 1768, is made the ground-work of what is to pafs for the genuine production of thefe combin'd editors, and is ufher'd to the world upon the credit of their names.   Either of their editions will afford full proof of this affertion, which is evidently deduc'd not only from the many conjectural emendations adopted into the text, or propos'd in the notes; but,— from the new Order in which the Plays are arrang'd; the new regulation of the Scene divifion, and fometimes that of the Acts; the new adjuftment of the metre, in many places; the changes made in the fcenical directions refpecting places, perfons, and actions, as well as in the pointing, &c. in all which particulars they differ from Dr. JOHNSON's firft work, as much as they agree with that of the prefent Author.   But the republication of their work, as it " is *revifed* and *augmented*," makes farther advances upon the fame plan, abounding with frefh matter and accumulated evidence in proof of the induftry with which the purloining trade has been purfu'd, and of the latitude to which it has been extended, in each of the abovemention'd particulars : For differing at it does from it's former felf in numberlefs inftances, in all of them it is ftill found to agree with that edition, which, we are gravely told in fo many words by the apparent manager in the bufinefs,—" has not been examin'd beyond one Play."   In fhort, every page of his work might be adduc'd in flat contradiction to his repeated affertions already refer'd to, the changes made even in the mode of printing, throughout his new production, being fuch as muft ftrike the eye of the moft fuperficial obferver, and can leave little doubt in any one at all converfant in fuch matters, from what original the text of it was form'd, or what copy was follow'd at the prefs.'

On this fubject we ought not to interpofe.   Mr. Steevens is fully capable of defending himfelf.   We may however obferve, if it were not for his acknowlegment that ' he had read but one play of that edition,' he might have refigned all the credit of thefe new arrangements with little lofs to his reputation.   In fact, the emendations complained of were fo obvious to an attentive reader, that it is more furprifing they efcaped one editor, than that they have been obferved by two. If Mr. Steevens be guilty, he is indeed an atrocious culprit, to have, in the midft of his riches, robbed the poor.—The charge has, however, been ferioufly and completely refuted in our Review, vol. xliii. p. 348.

The

The conclusion of the second volume contains an attempt to determine the order in which the plays of Shakspeare were written. Mr. Malone had engaged in a similar work ; and if the event is different, it must be ascribed only to their different methods. Our annotator depends chiefly on the entries in the stationers books: in a few doubtful cases, on the style, numbers, and conjecture. Mr. Malone's *attempt*, for so he has modestly styled it, comprehends every kind of evidence, which can now be procured. This may seem a trifling subject ; but there is usually some pleasure in pursuing the progress of genius, from its dawn to its meridian splendor ; and there is some instruction to be derived by tracing the gradual evolution of the mind, till it acquire its highest powers. In the present case it is of less importance ; since in the plays, in their various representations, were probably changed, and the imperfect flight of the poet corrected and supported, by the strength of maturer judgment.

The Essay on Shakspeare's Verse seems the effect of constant study and attention. Like Aristotle, our author probably draws rules from a poet that had none, and teaches native grace and untutor'd dignity to walk by method, or to move in time. But Shakspeare has irregularities, which distress the methodical, and excite the discerning critic : his anomalies are therefore carefully detailed, and his redundant and deficient syllables explained ; for

    ' When he happen'd to break off
In the middle of his speech, or cough,
H' has hard words ready to shew why,
And tell what rules he did it by.'

It might appear easy to select some observations as a specimen ; but to select with fairness would be too long either for our article, or the reader's entertainment. To the Essay on Verse are subjoined lists of words used as monosyllables, dissyllables, &c. words unusually accented and terminated :—from all which we are told may result ' the benefit following—that Shakespeare will (at last) be permitted the use of his own language, and of the numbers which he thought aptest.'

The third volume of this laboured work is styled the School of Shakspeare. It consists of ' authentic extracts from divers English books, that were in print in that author's time ; evidently shewing from whence his several fables were taken, and some parcel of his dialogue. Also farther extracts from the same or like books, which contribute to a due understanding of his writings, or give light to the history of his life, or to the dramatic history of his times.'—What may seem the duty of an editor, enthusiasm alone can recommend to an ordinary reader. Yet in this dunghill there is some gold : many passages are interesting and poetical ; and they frequently abound in that manly dignity of language, that nervous and expressive energy, which we admire in Shakspeare. He frequently indeed excels his copies in this respect, and is the golden star among lesser luminaries. We ought not to fill our page with extracts, because they contain occasionally a particle of brilliant metal among a heap of ore, but must chiefly attend to those circumstances which particularly illustrate our great dramatist. The names of Holinshed, Plutarch, and Stow, fill many pages ; and various other authors, ' such reading as was never read' are called in to contribute their assistance. We find, in this farrago, which frequently illustrates Shakspeare's language, and explains many of his words, passages that have been before quoted by Dr. Farmer and Mr. Steevens ; with some others, which we do not recollect to have been observed. But there are some important sources of intelligence to which other commentators have had recourse, that are not mentioned in the School, particularly the Italian novels.

As we have never met with the History of Hamblett, we were attracted by the account of it given in this volume. We confess that we greatly admire this play, though rather on account of particular passages, than the general conduct. But this extract will not require an apology.

CHAP. I.

' How *Horvendile* and *Fengon* were made Governours of the Province of *Ditmarse*, and how *Horvendile* marryed *Geruth*, daughter to *Roderick* chief K. of *Denmark:* by whom he had *Hamblet :* and how after his marriage his brother *Fengon* slewe him trayterously, and marryed his brothers wife, and what followed.   B. 3.

CHAP. II.

' How *Hamblet* counterfeited the madman, to escape the tyrannie of his uncle, and how he was tempted by a woman (through his uncles procurement) who thereby thought to underminde the Prince, and by that means to finde out whether he counterfeited madnesse or not : and how *Hamblet* would by no means bee brought to consent unto her ; and what followed.   C. 2.

CHAP III.

' How *Fengon* Uncle to *Hamblet* a second time to intrap him in his pollitick madnes : caused one of his counsellors to be secretly hidden in the Queenes chamber : behind the arras, to heare what speeches past betweene *Hamblet* and the Queen, and how

how *Hamblet* killed him, and efcaped that danger and what followed. C. 4.

CHAP. IV.

' How *Fengon* the third time devifed to fend *Hamblet* to the
king of *England*, with fecret Letters to have him put to death,
and how *Hamblet* when his companions flept, read the Letters,
and in ftead of them, counterfeited others; willing the king of
England to put the two Meffenger to death, and to marry his
daughter to *Hamblet*, which was effected, and how *Hamblet* efcaped out of *England*. E. b.

CHAP. V.

' How *Hamblet* having efcaped out of *England*, arrived in
Denmarke the fame day that the *Danes* were celebrating his funerals, fuppofing him to be dead in *England*, and how he revenged his fathers death upon his Uncle and the reft of the
Courtiers : and what followed. F. b.

CHAP. VI.

' How *Hamlet* having flaine his uncle, and burnt his Palace, made an Oration to the *Danes* to fhew them what he had
done : and how they made him king of *Denmarke*, and what
followed. F. 4.

CHAP. VII.

' How *Hamlet* after his Coronation went into *England*, and
how the king of *England* fecretly would have put him to death,
and how he flew the King of *England:* and returned againe into
Denmarke with two wives, and what followed. G. 4.

CHAP. VIII.

' How *Hamblet* being in *Denmarke*, was affailed by *Wiglerus*
his uncle, and afterwards betrayed by his laft wife, called *Her-
metrude*, and was flaine : after whofe death fhe married his ene-
mie *Wiglerus*. H. 3.

NOTE.

' Upon the woman, who, in *Chapter* II, is fet to tempt *Hamlet*, is grounded SHAKESPEARE's *Ophelia* ; and his deliverance
from this fnare by a friend, fuggefted his *Horatio* ; which deliverance is thus fpoken of,—and furely the poore prince at this
affault had bin in great danger, if a gentleman (that in Hor-
vendiles time had bin nourifhed with him) had not fhowne him-
felfe more affectioned to the bringing up he had received with
Hamblet, then deficous to pleafe the Tirant, * * * This
Gentleman bare the courtiers (appointed as aforefaide of this
treafon) company, &c. and these fame courtiers are likewise a
fhadow of SHAKESPEARE's *Rosincrantz* and *Guildenflern:* fee too
Chap. IV. Amidft all this refemblance of perfons and circumftances, it is rather ftrange—that none of the relater's expreffions have got into the play : and yet not one of them is to be
found, except the following, in *Chap.* III. where *Hamlet* kills
the counfellor (who is defcrib'd as of a greater reach than the

reft,

reſt, and is the Poet's *Polonius*) behind the arras: here, beating
the hangings, and perceiving ſomething to ſtir under them, he
is made to cry out,—a rat, a rat,—and preſently drawing his
ſworde thruſt it into the hangings, which done, pulled the
counſellour (halfe dead) out by the heeles, made an end of
killing him.— After which enſues *Hamlet*'s harangue to his mother; and the manner in which ſhe is affected by this harangue
is better deſcrib'd than any other thing in all the hiſtory; or,
more properly, is the only good ſtroke in it, and ſhould therefore be tranſcrib'd, Although the Queene perceiued herſelfe
neerely touched, and that Hamlet mooued her to the quicke,
where ſhe felt herſelfe intereſſed: neuertheleſſe ſhee forgot all
diſdaine and wrath, which thereby ſhe might as then haue had,
hearing her ſelfe ſo ſharply chiden and reproued, for the ioy ſhe
then conceaued, to behold the gallant ſpirit of her ſonne, and
to thinke what ſhe might hope, and the eaſier expect of his ſo
great policie and wiſdome.   But on the one ſide ſhe durſt not
lift up her eyes to behold him, remembring her offence, and on
the other ſide ſhe would gladly haue imbraced her ſon, in regard of the wiſe admonitions by him giuen vnto her, which as
then quenched the flames of vnbridled deſire, y[t] before had
mooed her to affect it. Fengon: to ingraft in her heart y[e] vertuous actions of her lawfull ſpouſe, whom inwardly ſhe much
lamented, when ſhe beheld the liuely image and portraiture of
his vertue and great wiſdome in her childe, repreſenting his
fathers haughtie and valiant heart: and ſo ouercome and van-
quiſhed with this honeſt paſſion, and weeping moſt bitterly,
hauing long time fixed her eyes vpon Hamlet, as beeing ra-
uiſhed into ſome great and deepe contemplation, and as it were
wholy amazed; at the laſt imbracing him in her armes (with
the like loue that a vertuous mother may or can uſe, to kiſſe
and entertaine her owne childe) ſhee ſpake vnto him in this
manner.   To ſpeak the very truth, perhaps, the *Geruthe* of this
picture is ſuperior to S H A K E S P E A R E'S *Gertrude*, in this one ſituation; allowance being made for the colouring, ſuiting the
time 'twas done in.   S H A K E S P E A R E purſues the hiſtory no farther than to the death of the tyrant; and he brings this event
to paſs by means different from what are there related: yet it is
eaſy to ſee, that *Hamlet*'s counterfeit funeral furniſh'd him with
the idea of *Ophelia*'s true one; as his harangue to the *Danes* did
the ſpeech of *Horatio*. This hiſtory, as it is call'd, is an almoſt
literal tranſlation from the *French* of B E L L E F O R E S T, (*v.* "*Hiſ-
toires tragiques*" in the index) and is of much older date than
the impreſſion from which these extracts are made; perhaps,
but little later than it's original, which was written in 1570,
and publiſh'd ſoon after.'

   Mr. Steevens has diſcovered the ſource of the machinery in
Macbeth, in an old play entitled the Witch; and Mr. Capel
informs us, that ſome of the circumſtances are to be found in
the

the first volume of Holinshed : they are there said to relate to the murder of king Duff. The same observation has also been made by Mr. Steevens.

'Here begins the history of king *Duffe's* murder, by *Donewald*, captain of *Fores*' castle, instigated by his wife : which murder is here related to have been performed by that king's chamberlains, with circumstances which SHAKESPEARE has taken and apply'd to king *Duncan*; who is only said by the Chronicler simply—to have been murdered at *Invernefs*, without telling the manner how. Both these histories should be perus'd by the curious, but cannot have a place here by reason of their length : they will find in them (perhaps, to their surprize) not only the general outlines of SHAKESPEARE's "Macbeth," but many minute particulars, and even some speeches; as—of the witches, *Banquo*, *Malcolm*, and *Macduff*: The first of them begins at the words above-mention'd, and ends with these that follow ;—

'Monstrous sightes also that were seene within the Scottishe kingdome that yeare were these, horses in Lothian being of singuler beautie and swiftnesse, did eate their owne fleshe, and would in no wife taste any other meate. In Angus there was a gentlewoman· brought forth a child without eyes, nose, handes, or foote. There was a Sparhauke also strangled by an Owle. Neither was it any lesse wonder that the sunne, as before is sayd, was continually covered with clowdes, for vi. moneths space : But all men understood that the abhominable murder of king Duffe was the cause hereof. D. b. *col.* 1; *c.*

'and *Duncan's* history, together with that of *Macbeth* with which it is connected, extends from signature P. 8, to signature D. 6. b inclusive.'

It is now time to leave these tiresome and sometimes disgusting volumes ; though an editor of Shakspeare will probably find some particles of useful information in the last—information which few would seek for in the original volumes, from which the different passages are extracted, and still fewer would probably be able to procure.

It is happy that some commentators are found, with whom to seek is itself an entertainment; and to find, though a single and probably useless word, a victory.—Let them enjoy their triumphs undisturbed and unmolested ; the glory will be theirs ; and the trophies, if by such victories they can be furnished, will glitter in the cars of more accessible and more entertaining annotators.

Philosophical

Philosophical Transactions of the Royal Society of London. Vol.
LXXII. Part II. For the Year 1782. (Concluded, from
p. 331.)

A RTICLE XXII. Proceedings relative to the Accident by
Lightning at Heckingham.——This article is embellished
with a very particular description of the Poor-House, as well
as with several plans and elevations of it. The accident attracted the attention of the Board of Ordnance, because the
injured house was armed with *eight* pointed conductors ; and
they referred the examination of it to the Royal Society, who
deputed Dr. Blagden and Mr. Nairne to enquire into the circumstances. The descriptions are very full and satisfactory ; but
the deputies have reported facts only, they have scarcely ventured to give any opinion relating to the cause of the failure of
the *armour*. We might therefore be easily excused from entering any farther into the subject ; but may be allowed to remark two very material errors in the construction, on which
much of the mischief depended. The first is, that the conductors were sunk only into a superficial drain, and terminated
in air : the second, that two of the conductors, from two neighbouring chimneys, united in a valley of the roof, which
was covered with lead : in this valley, the chief injury was
received. There were other circumstances which contributed
to the misfortune, and it will probably be explained by some
of the members of the society.——It would be impertinent in us
to anticipate their observations : we have only mentioned
these two defects, as hints for the preservation of other buildings. The clouds on that day were probably in a negative state.

Article XXIII.——Account of the Organ of Hearing in Fish.
By John Hunter, Esq. F. R. S.——It has been thought a question capable of puzzling a philosopher, to ask whether fishes
had ears ? If its terms are changed, and the question be,
whether they are sensible of sounds in the neighbouring air,
there would have been little doubt of the answer. We have
frequently tried experiments of this kind, and varied them in
different ways : the result has uniformly been, that vibrations
of the air must be considerable before they are communicated
to the water ; but those of the earth, by striking against it
with the foot, are very soon perceived. There are however
many circumstances relating to sound, and its different media,
which have been hitherto little considered. Mr. Hunter, in
this article, not only shows that fish are sensible of sound, but
has, in a general way, described their organs. Though the
former has been evinced with sufficient clearness, we have had
very

very little fatisfactory intelligence about the latter. A few loofe bones, and fometimes a fingle one, have been found in fome of the genera, which were fuppofed to anfwer this purpofe. Even thofe authors who have diffected fifh, and been copious in explaining the optic and olfactory nerves, never mention the auditory; though it is remarkable, that they frequently defcribe a large nerve going out at the fide of the head, which they obferve is *loft* in the neighbouring mufcles.

Mr. Hunter therefore, to whom anatomy and fcience have been formerly fo much obliged, gives new information on this fubject: we fhall follow him with pleafure, but may be allowed to exprefs our wifhes, that his other avocations will, at a future period, permit him to be ftill more explicit in his defcriptions. We have endeavoured to analyfe his general account, but cannot comprefs it within a lefs fpace than the original; we fhall therefore beg leave to ufe the author's own words.

‘ The organs of hearing in this latter order of animals, (viz. fifh) are placed on the fides of the fkull, or that cavity which contains the brain; but the fkull itfelf makes no part of the organ, as it does in the quadruped and the bird. In fome fifh this organ is wholly furrounded by the parts compofing this cavity, which in many is cartilaginous, the fkeleton of thefe fifh being like thofe of the ray kind; in others alfo, as in cod, falmon, &c. whofe fkeleton is bone, yet this part is cartilaginous.

‘ In fome fifh this organ is in part within the cavity of the fkull, or that cavity which alfo contains the brain, as in the falmon, cod, &c. the cavity of the fkull projecting laterally, and forming a cavity there.

‘ The organ of hearing in fifh appears to grow in fize with the animal, for its fize is nearly in the fame proportion with the fize of the animal, which is not the cafe with the quadruped, &c. the organs being in them nearly as large in the growing foetus as in the adult.

‘ It is much more fimple in fifh than in all thofe orders of animals who may be reckoned fuperior, fuch as quadrupeds, birds, and amphibious animals, but there is a regular gradation from the firft to fifh.

‘ It varies in different orders of fifh; but in all it confifts of three curved tubes, all of which unite with one another; this union forms in fome only a canal, as in the cod, falmon, ling, &c. and in others a pretty large cavity, as in the ray kind. In the jack there is an oblong bag, or blind procefs, which is an addition to thofe canals, and which communicates with them at their union. In the cod, &c. this union of the three tubes ftands upon an oval cavity, and in the jack there are

are two of thofe cavities; thefe additional cavities in thefe fifh appear to anfwer the fame purpofe with the cavity in the ray or cartilaginous fifh, which is the union of the three canals.

'The whole is compofed of a kind of cartilaginous fubftance, very hard or firm in fome parts, and which in fome fifh is crufted over with a thin bony lamella, fo as not to allow them to collapfe; for as the fkull does not form any part of thofe canals or cavities, they muft be compofed of fuch fubftance as is capable of keeping its form.

'Each tube defcribes more than a femicircle. This refembles in fome refpect what we find in moft other animals, but differs in the parts being diftinct from the fkull.

'Two of the femicircular canals are fimilar to one another, may be called a pair, and are placed perpendicularly; the third is not fo long; in fome it is placed horizontally, uniting as it were the other two at their ends or terminations. In the fkait it is fomething different, being only united to one of the perpendiculars.

'The two perpendiculars unite at one part in one canal, by one arm of each uniting, while the other two arms or horns have no connection with each other, and the arms of the horizontal unite with the other two arms of the perpendicular near the entrance into the common canal or cavity.

'Near the union of thofe canals into the common, they are fwelled out into round bags, becoming there much larger.

'In the ray kind they all terminate in one cavity, as has been obferved; and in the cod they terminate in one canal, which in thefe fifh is placed upon the additional cavity or cavities. In this cavity or cavities there is a bone or bones. In fome there are two bones; as the jack has two cavities, we find in one of thofe cavities two bones, and in the other only one; in the ray there is only a chalky fubftance.

'At this union of the two perpendiculars in fome fifh enters the external communication, or what may be called the external meatus. This is the cafe with all the ray kind, the external orifice of which is fmall, and placed on the upper flat furface of the head; but it is not every genus or fpecies of fifh that has the external opening.

'The nerves of the ear pafs outwards from the brain, and appear to terminate at once on the external furface of the fwelling of the femicircular tubes above defcribed. They do not appear to pafs through thofe tubes fo as to get on the infide, as is fuppofed to be the cafe in quadrupeds; I fhould therefore very much fufpect, that the lining of thofe tubes in the quadruped is not nerve, but a kind of internal periofteum.'

Article XXIV. Account of a new Electrometer. By Mr. Abraham Brooke.—This article cannot be abridged, nor can we properly form any judgment of its excellence, without fome experience. The principle on which it determines the force

of

of electricity, in any given charge, is, the *weight lifted* by *its* repulfive power. We may at leaft allow, with our author, that its language is generally intelligible ; but the inftrument is much more complex than thofe commonly employed.

Article XXV. A new Method of inveftigating the Sums of infinite Series. By the Rev. S. Vince, A. M. of Cambridge. —Mr. Vince, in this paper, informs us how we may inveftigate with great eafe the fum of fome infinite feries. The firft part extends to every cafe the rule which De Moivre difcovered in fome particular ones ; for, though his method appear general, it is frequently impracticable. The fecond contains the fummation of certain feries, the laft difference of whofe numerators become equal to nothing. The third relates to a correction which we muft explain more fully. Every converging feries, whofe terms, when infinitely extended, become equal to nothing, may be changed by collecting two terms into one ; but when the feries diverges, or converges to any affignable quantity, with the figns + plus and — minus alternately, this method is impracticable. The object then of the third part is to fhow the neceffity of a correction, and to determine its value. Propofitions of this kind cannot be eafily abridged ; thefe are diftinguifhed by their neatnefs, and even elegance, nor have we been able to detect any fallacy in the reafoning.

Article XXVI. A new Method of finding the equal Roots of an Equation by Divifion. By the Rev. John Hellings.—— This article relates only to thofe equations which have *equal* roots, and are chiefly ufeful in others, to obtain an approximation. Every method of facilitating our labour, in this intricate fubject, is undoubtedly valuable, and that recommended by Mr. Hellings feems to be remarkably convenient.

Article XXVII. Some farther Confiderations on the Influence of the Vegetable Kingdom on the Animal Creation. By John Ingen-houfz, F. R. S.—In the infancy of a fcience, when appearances offer themfelves which we cannot eafily explain, attended by many circumftances, either wholly unobferved, or neglected as trifling, it is not furprifing that the refult of experiments fhould be different, and frequently contradictory. Dr. Ingen-houfz formerly obferved, that leaves of plants meliorated phlogifticated air ; and produced, when put into water, and expofed to the fun, air remarkably pure. Dr. Prieftley contends, that the origin of the air is not the plant or the light, but that thefe are only agents to produce that effect from fomething elfe †. Indeed he feems to hint that

† Experiments and Obfervations on Nat. Philof. vol. ii. p. 27.

the

the air actually arifes from the water. Mr. Cavallo, in his volume, p. 824, has purfued this hint ; and by immerfing leaves in one jar, fome cloth well foaked in another, has found air produced from both in nearly equal quantities. Indeed he candidly obferves that the weather, as well as the pump-water and the plants, may have occafioned fome difference in the refult. Mr. Cavallo alfo obferves, that frefh leaves of plants did not improve phlogifticated air in a fufficient degree to be difcernible by the teft.

· Thefe objections Dr. Ingen-houfz, in the prefent article, endeavours to anfwer. He ufed the conferva rivularis, which was put in water deprived of its air by boiling ; in a fimilar veffel, full of boiled water, he put a piece of cloth foaked in the fame water ; and, as a ftandard, the plant was placed in common pump-water without boiling. The refults were conformable to his former opinion ; the firft, after fome time, yielded air, for the exhaufted water, in the beginning, abforbed it ; the fecond never yielded any ; and the third, in which the water was not exhaufted, yielded it copioufly. Though we are not fo prefumptuous as to decide always when doctors difagree, yet we may be indulged with a few reflections on this fubject. In Mr. Cavallo's experiments the air probably arofe from the water ; the difpute therefore chiefly relates to thofe of Dr. Ingen-houfz. There is certainly no criterion by which we are certain that we have deprived water of *all* its air ; fo that though the water was boiled two hours, it may ftill have retained fome portion. It is at leaft highly probable that water may contain air, as a component part ; for we are pretty certain that, in this way, it contains earth, an element more unlike to it than air. The water is decompofed and deprived of this earth by vegetation ; fo that it may be deprived of its air alfo. In either way, a very fmall quantity of air procured from the water will be confpicuous ; fince dephlogifticated air not only occupies a larger fpace than either fixed or atmofpheric air, but adheres very loofely to water, and is very foon feparated from it. It is no longer difputed that a *growing* plant will meliorate the air ; fo that probably, in the experiments, much will depend on the nature and ftate of the plant from whence they were taken. Dr. Ingen-houfz obferves, that the thick fucculent leaves afford more and better air than others ; and we know that many of thefe leaves poffefs an inherent power of their own, by which they are capable of vegetating, when taken from the plant. Others may poffefs this power in a lefs degree, and occafion a remarkable variety in the experiment. We have fuggefted thefe remarks as, in fome meafure, accounting for the dif-

ferent

erent conclusions, and to guard philosophers from inconclusive experiments. If they are not juft, they may probably occasion others that may be more fatisfactory.

Our author next proceeds to reafoning; but we cannot term it fatisfactory, though highly ingenious. The air, though it arife from the water, may ftick to different furfaces of the leaf, from the nature of thefe furfaces; a polifhed or a downy leaf will occafion a remarkable diverfity in thefe refpects. For other reafons, which will require farther examination, we muft refer to the work itfelf, but ought to tranfcribe an experiment, which appears more unexceptionable than thofe which we have already mentioned.

'Again: if the dephlogifticated air, obtained from plants in water, was air difengaged from the water, it would follow, that a plant fhut up in a tranfparent glafs veffel without any water would yield no air at all, nor increafe the quantity of air fhut up with the vegetable. The following experiment, I think, will be fufficient to convince any one that this is far from being the cafe. I placed in a glafs tube, hermetically fealed at one end, a piece of an American plant, called *cereus*; the extremity of this piece, where it was cut from the plant, was tightly fqueezed in a fmall glafs veffel, in which only as much water was kept as feemed to be required to keep the *cereus* in full vigour. I fmeared the vegetable, and the orifice of the glafs veffel all round with foft wax, fo that all communication between the air within the tube and the water within the fmall veffel was cut off. I placed this tube inverted in a veffel filled with quickfilver, keeping a column of fome inches of the metallic fluid in the tube, to allow the air within the tube to expand by the heat of the fun without efcaping. After this apparatus had ftood during a few hours, in a bright funfhine, I cooled the whole to the fame degree it poffeffed when it was expofed to the fun. This was done by plunging the whole in a tub filled with water, whofe degree of heat was reftored to the fame degree it had before. I found the quantity of air within the tube remarkably increafed, and fo far dephlogifticated, that a flame burned in it with an increafed brightnefs, and that one meafure of it joined to one meafure of nitrous air occupied 0.64; whereas the fame air, before it was fhut up with the *cereus* was of fuch a degree of goodnefs, that one meafure of it with one of nitrous occupied 1.06. Though this experiment may fully fhew that plants throw out air in the funfhine, yet if another plant, which does not by nature yield fo much air as the *cereus* commonly does, is fhut up in a fimilar tube, and expofed to the fun, the fame effect will not always be obtained. The reafon of it is, that plants abforb a good quantity of common air as their nourifhment at the fame time that they throw out dephlogifticated air. This fact, therefore, if confidered by itfelf, will not be looked upon as equally demonftrative

monftrative with the above mentioned ones. The refult of this experiment may depend on the more or lefs vigour of the vegetable employed, on the more or lefs brightnefs of the fun's light, on the more or lefs heat the vegetable receives, &c. A *cereus* being a plant of hot climates, may bear more heat than an European plant. All thefe circumftances, as well as many others, may make the iffue of this experiment fometimes ambiguous; but the fact, as I have related it, joined to the above mentioned analogous experiments of Dr. Hales and Mr. Boyle, will add ftrength to my affertion, viz. that vegetables really throw out air in the fun-fhine.

' If all what I have faid hitherto fhould not be thought fufficient to take away the prejudice which Dr. Prieftley's fifth volume, and Mr. Cavallo's book on Air, may have produced in the mind of fome philofophers, I fhould advife them to be prefent, at leaft once, at the moft beautiful fcene which they will behold, when a leaf of an *agave Americana*, cut in two or three pieces, is immerfed in a glafs bell or jar full of pump-water, inverted and expofed to the fun in a very fair day in the middle of the fummer, when this plant is in its full vigour; and when they fhall have feen thofe beautiful and continual ftreams of air, which rufh from feveral parts of this vegetable, principally from the white internal fubftance of it, I will be anfwerable for their laying afide all farther doubt about the truth of my doctrine.'

Dr. Ingen-houfz will not interpret our remarks to any defire of detracting from his reputation. His hafte has fometimes betrayed him into inaccuracies; but we ought to acknowlege our obligations both to his induftry and his ingenuity.

Article XXVIII. A Microfcopic Defcription of the Eye of the Monoculus Polyphemus Linnæi. By Mr. William André, Surgeon.—An enquiry into the nature and phyfiology of infects teaches not only to admire the goodnefs of the Creator, who has fitted them for their various fituations, but the accumulated advantages which are fometimes derived from fome organs to compenfate for the deficiency of others. The eyes of the king crab are very remarkable. It has feemingly four, two fmall ones almoft in front, and one larger at each fide of the head; but each of the large eyes is compofed of numerous cones, and each of thefe cones is a folid, tranfparent, and probably a complete organ of vifion. The contrivance is certainly admirable, and the execution truly beautiful.

The volume concludes, as ufual, with an account of the prefents made to the Society, and the names of the donors; which, though it has excited fome reflections, is certainly not an object of our criticifm.

The History of Henry III. King of France. 8*vo.* 6*s.* Dilly.

WHEN a writer employs his attention on a particular portion of hiſtory, which has already been co-
piouſly treated, it might juſtly be expected that he meant
either to deviate from the common repreſentation of his predeceſſors on the ſame ſubject, or at leaſt to place the characters, the intrigues, and the incidents, in a clearer and more
ſtriking point of view. Whatever may have been the deſign
of the author of the work before us, we do not find, upon
examination, that he has ſo much as once attempted to diſſent
from any preceding hiſtorian, or to affect, in the ſmalleſt degree, any novelty of ſentiment. But though he ſeems to have
implicitly adopted the ſyſtem of the generality of the French
writers on the hiſtory of Henry III. he has at the ſame time
avoided the imputation of thoſe prejudices with which ſome
of them appear to have been influenced.

The reign of Henry III. was one of the moſt active periods
in the French annals, and affords a cloſe ſucceſſion of occurrences equally extraordinary and important. The author of
the preſent hiſtory ſupports the narrative in a ſtrain of ſuch
uniformity, as ſeldom or never diſcovers languor or relaxation. The detail flows in a perpetual, and frequently even
with a rapid ſtream, far from being deſtitute of ſtrength of
expreſſion, but more diſtinguiſhed for intereſt than dignity.

As a ſpecimen of the work, we ſhall lay before our readers
the following extract.

‘ As the diſcontents, which at length ripening into open rebellion, plunged the realm of France for a ſerious of years into
all the miſeries incident to civil diſſenſions, are to be attributed
to the violation of the privileges of the princes of the blood
royal : it may not be improper to introduce this hiſtory with a
view of the firſt eſtabliſhment of that celebrated monarchy, and
its original inſtitutions.

‘ On the decline of the Roman empire, when its majeſty was
no longer ſupported by a vigorous adminiſtration, or defended
by the terror and diſcipline of its arms, ſwarms of barbarians
with dreadful havock, over-ran and took poſſeſſion of the de-
fenceleſs provinces of the weſtern world.

‘ The Franks, a fierce and warlike people inhabiting the
marſhes and foreſts of Germany, ſubdued and ſeized upon the
province of ancient Gaul. Here they fixed their empire, and,
conformable to the genius of barbarian tribes, tranſmitted to
the conquered country the name of its new poſſeſſors.

‘ As the conqueſt of Gaul was the general invaſion of a whole
people in ſearch of new habitations, the Franks, previous to
their emigration, digeſted a code of laws and inſtitutions with

a fagacity and penetration, which marks no fmall degree of improvement in the arts of civilization and fociety.

'Accuftomed from time immemorial to the dominion of a fingle perfon, they were attached to monarchy; but left that fpecies of government fhould degenerate into an abfolute defpotifm, by exprefs ftipulations they limited the power of the crown, regulated the fucceffion, and defined the various departments of the adminiftration of their future empire. At the fame time they refolved that this compact between the prince and people fhould be confidered as a perpetual and immutable obligation on both parties refpectively.

'To avoid the inconveniences of an elective crown, they further determined that it fhould be continued in the defcendants of their future fovereign, till on the extinction of the royal family, the right of nominating a new monarch fhould revert to the general fuffrages of the whole nation.

'Thefe original and fundamental inftitutions of the French monarchy are denominated Salic Laws, from the falii or priefts, who prefided over the deliberations of the general affembly; and from the river Sale in Germany, on whofe banks this national council was convened.

'Anxious to perpetuate their monarchy, and to preferve the crown from falling under a foreign dominion, the Salic legiflators declared females incapable of fucceeding to that rich inheritance.

'On this difpofition of the Salic law are founded the rights of the princes of the blood, who further claim in the abfence of the king, or during a minority, the exclufive right of reprefenting majefty, or of governing the realm. Nor are thefe important privileges fimply fanctioned by prefcription and time immemorial, but have been often ratified by the general eftates of the kingdom, in which affembly is united the abfolute authority of the whole French nation.

'The princes therefore of the royal family, lineally defcended in male line from the crown, poffeffing fuch invaluable and exclufive prerogatives, have, from the very foundation of the monarchy, preferved great weight and influence in all public deliberations. The people regard with veneration and refpect this diftinguifhed race, contemplating either in them or their defcendants a future fovereign: it having often happened, that by the failure of the reigning branch, the jurior has been called to fill the vacant throne. While thofe princes on the other hand are induced to watch over the public welfare with parental eyes, confidering the ftate as the inalienable property of the whole family.

'After various revolutions, the crown having paffed through the Merovian and Caroline race, was feized by Capet, from whom is defcended the prefent reigning family. Louis IX. furnamed the Saint, dying in the year of our Lord 1270, left two fons, Philip, who fucceeded to the crown, and Robert, count of Clermont.

'From

' From Philip is derived the houfe of Valois, which occupied the throne upwards of three hundred years. From Robert is defcended the houfe of Bourbon, fo ftiled conformable to the ufage of France, to affume, by way of diftinction, the appellation of that ftate or patrimony, fettled as a revenue on the collateral line. This royal branch, by its hereditary privileges, and proximity to the crown, by the acquifition of large territories and immenfe riches, acquired a degree of fplendour and power, little fhort of fovereignty. Being further fruitful in a progeny of princes, all poffeffing great abilities, popular manners, and royal munificence, it had captivated the efteem and veneration of the public. The profperity of this family excited the jealoufy of the court; to humble thofe formidable vaffals, became an invariable maxim of ftate policy.

' But, on the acceffion of Francis I. a total change of fyftem took place. Induced by juvenile ardour and generofity of fentiment, the young monarch began to carefs the princes of his blood. To inveft them with the higheft honours, to increafe their fplendour and magnificence, Francis conceived was to embellifh with additional luftre the dignity of his crown. Difcovering in Charles of Bourbon a noble and elevated mind, with talents equal to the moft arduous undertakings, he promoted him to the dignity of great conftable of the realm; and confided to the care of that nobleman and his connections, the whole management of the ftate. As the king advanced in years and experience, he began to perceive the caufes of that policy which had influenced his predeceffors; when, with a folicitude equal to the ardour with he had at firft exalted, he now defired to reduce the aftonifhing grandeur of that family.

' Fortune foon prefented the monarch with an opportunity admirably fitted for his fecret views. Louifa of Savoy, the king's mother, laid claim to the dutchy of Bourbon, which ftate conftituted the principal revenue of the duke. Francis imagined, that by procuring a fentence at law in favour of his mother, the houfe of Bourbon, deprived of the great fource of its riches, would naturally decay, and fall from its prefent envied ftate of fplendour and influence. Du Pratt, the chancellor, had fecret directions to conduct the procefs agreeable to the views of the fovereign. In the courfe of the litigation Bourbon difcovered the iniquitous proceeding. The fenfe of the injury, the dread of impending ruin, precipitated the perfecuted prince into the moft violent meafures. He fecretly confpired with the enemies of his country; but the treacherous correfpondence being detected, he was compelled to feek his fafety in a voluntary banifhment. He became one of the imperial generals, and, at the famous battle of Pavia, experienced the moft complete, though unnatural confolation, that could foothe the pride, or gratify the refentment, of an haughty and infulted mind. The army of Francis, was cut to pieces; the

E e 2 king,

king, who had so wantonly abused his power, found himself a prisoner in the camp of an offended and powerful vassal.

' Policy and resentment now united in the mind of Francis to depress the house of Bourbon. On his release from confinement, the angry and exasperated monarch involved the junior branches of that family in the disgrace of their guilty chief. But Charles, duke of Vendome, now become the head of that devoted race, by a dutiful and moderate behaviour, endeavoured to remove the prejudices, and assuage the resentment of the sovereign. This example of prudent moderation was wisely followed by the other princes of his blood. To demonstrate their abhorrence of the depraved counsels of their kinsman, their ready acquiescence in the king's desires, they voluntarily relinquished the pursuit of those honours and dignities, which were in some measure the prerogatives of their birth, and far from court lived unemployed, for the most part, in country retirement.'

We cannot avoid observing, as a mark of affectation in this writer, that he has often distinguished the pronoun *he*, and the conjunction *that*, with Italics, when, in respect of the former, there is no opposition of persons ; and, with regard to the latter, not any necessity for an emphasis.

The author draws, from the conduct and fate of Henry the Third, the following observation, which he terms a most useful lesson, viz. ' that, in the voyage of life, little avail the art and expertness of the mariner, if all his operations are not guided by the special protection of that Almighty Being whose eternal providence sustains and governs the universe.'—This remark is doubtless well intended, and impresses us with a favourable opinion of the piety of the author ; but besides that such direct moral illation seems foreign to the object, at least of profane history, the inference above deduced is both too trite, and too generally applicable, to be particularly specified.

Naval Architecture ; or, the Rudiments and Rules of Ship-Building, exemplified in a Series of Draughts and Plans. (Concluded, from p. 373.)

THE subject of the fourth Book is the forty-four-gun ship.

' A forty-four-gun ship, says he, designed to carry her guns upon two decks, is the most distant from good proportion of any two-deck ship that is built ; because the top-side must be too high above the water for the customary length and breadth, to enable her to carry her lower-deck guns sufficiently clear of the water. For the height of the lower-deck ports from the water, the height between decks, and consequently the depth in the waist, cannot be much less than in a ship of seventy-four guns,

and

and therefore it cannot be expected that such a ship can be duly proportioned in the water; that is, she cannot be brought down to nearly three-fifths of the height of the top-breadth, which is allowed to be the best sailing trim for ships in general, if their bodies are constructed suitable thereto.

' As ships of forty-four guns must of course labour under many disadvantages on account of their disproportioned height above water, even if their principal dimensions in every other respect are similar to those of ships in general, it is necessary that every inconveniency should be considered in the construction, in order to render them as useful as possible. For supposing ships to be constructed under water exactly similar in form as well as dimensions, it will appear improbable that the forty-four-gun ship should succeed in chacing a frigate of thirty-two or thirty-six guns ; and should the wind blow hard, the frigate may still have the use of her upper-deck guns, while the forty-four-gun ship is incapable of using her lower-deck tier, which are much nearer the water than those on the frigate's upper-deck ; the forty-four-gun ship also, by having a deep topside, will roll more than the frigate. When this is the case, it is beyond a doubt that the forty-four-gun ship may be taken by the frigate of thirty-two or thirty-six guns, because the latter would have the advantage, both in respect to number, as well as weight of metal.

' Considering, however, every obstacle likely to attend a forty-four-gun ship designed to carry her guns upon two decks, they may yet be very useful ships, on account of the weight of metal on their lower decks ; and as they may not be capable of chacing such ships as before mentioned, it is necessary they should be so constructed, as to be capable of using their lower-deck guns, at any time when the frigates can use their upper-deck guns, which will rescue them from the danger of being taken by ships of a smaller class. In order to this I shall propose the following dimensions :

		feet.	in.
Let the extreme length, from the fore-side of the stem to the aft-part of the stern-post, at the height of the wing-transom, be		143	0
The height of the wing-transom $\frac{3}{19}$ of the length,		22	7
The height of the top-breadth $\frac{5}{24}$ of the length,	29	9½	
But, if convenient, should be no more than $\frac{1}{5}$, which is		28	7
And therefore it is too high by		1	2¼
The load-draught of water should be $\frac{3}{5}$ of the top-breadth at least ; for then the ship is supposed to be in her best sailing trim, agreeable to the constructions of ships in general. This would be		17	10¼
But the ports will admit of its being no more than		15	6
Consequently she will be too high above water by		2	4¼

The

The ufual dimenfions for breadth is $\frac{7}{25}$ of the length, which is   —   —   } 40   0$\frac{1}{2}$

To which I fhall add $\frac{1}{4}$ of 2 foot 4$\frac{1}{4}$ inches, which is   —   —   } 0   7

And therefore the moulded breadth is } 40   7$\frac{1}{2}$

Add to this for the plank of the bottom on both fides,   —   —   — } 0   6

The extreme breadth for the tonnage therefore is   41   1$\frac{2}{4}$

And let the moulded breadth at the aft-part be about $\frac{3}{5}$ of the moulded breadth of the midfhip-bend,

' I fhould be fatisfied with the proportional breadth of $\frac{7}{25}$ of the length, if the fhip could be brought down in the water to $\frac{7}{9}$ of the top-breadth; but as fhe is fo much higher out of water than fhe ought to be, I think $\frac{1}{4}$ of that additional height fhould be added to her breadth, in order to make her more ftiff, and to enable her the better to ufe her lower-deck-guns.'

This plan would make a very formidable fhip of her clafs, with properties, I think, fuperior to thofe which they now poffefs. The body is conftructed by the ufe of a rifing line. The method of putting in the top-timbers in the draught is in fome refpect new, and preferable to that of the reconciler. This plan is exemplified in three large plates, No. VI. VII. and VIII.—In plate VII. the author fhews us how to find the proper form of the harpings, when placed to the fheer of the fhip: this is curioufly and correctly ftated in the plate.

His fifth Book contains the feventy-four-gun fhip, and is illuftrated by three plates, No. IX. X. and XI. which, for the correctnefs of the lines, and elegance of the workmanfhip, are truly beautiful. The author fays, in his introduction to this fubject,

' It is a maxim founded on experiment, that of the feveral claffes of fhips built upon fimilar principles, the largeft is always the moft eligible. Of all fhips that carry their guns upon one deck, the frigate of thirty-two or thirty-fix guns is acknowleged to be the beft; and, in the fame manner, of thofe that carry them on two decks, the feventy-four-gun fhip is moft approved of. The reafon is evident. The fhip whofe top-fide is the fhalloweft in proportion to her capacity under water, is the moft ftiff, and will hold the leaft wind. The guns of a floop fhould be as much above the water, as thofe of a large frigate, and, if poffible, rather more fo, if her dimenfions are fimilar; becaufe the larger the fhip, the more fail fhe will carry. For the fame reafon, with refpect to two-decked fhips, the feventy-four-gun fhip will require but little more top-fide than that of forty-four guns, in comparifon to the difference of their dimenfions; and therefore it may be rationally expected, that the feventy-four-gun fhip will work as eafy as the forty-four-gun fhip;

fhip ; and fhe muft fail fafter, becaufe fhe will bear a greater preffure of canvas.

' If we were to examine the ninety-gun fhip, we fhould find her very irregular and difproportioned ; for if the feventy-four-gun fhip can carry her guns upon two decks, the fhip of three decks may as well be calculated to bear one hundred guns as ninety guns. But fhips fo bulky in their dimenfions, though they may be ufeful in particular cafes, are far from being generally fo. Their fails are fo very heavy, that it is with the utmoft difficulty they are managed when the wind blows high. The feventy-four-gun fhip on the contrary, at once contains the properties of the firft-rate and the frigate. She will not fhrink from an encounter with a one-hundred-gun fhip on account of fuperior weight, nor abandon the chace of a frigate on account of fwiftnefs. The union of thefe qualities hath therefore, with juftice, made the feventy-four-gun fhip the principal object of maritime artention, and given her fo diftinguifhed a pre-eminence in our line of battle.'

The author gives in this book fome farther reafons for making the water-lines fair.

' The curves in the fheer-draught, fays he, and the water-lines in the half-breadth plan, are the principal lines to determine the fairnefs of the body. Thofe in the fheer-draught will fhéw how the fhip will eafe herfelf when pitching, and by the water-lines you can fee if the fhip has a good entrance forward, as you can likewife in the after-body, whether they are fo formed as to permit the water to pafs freely to the rudder. That the water, when agitated, acts in many directions agreeable to the form of the body, is an opinion of many artifts who approve of conftructing bodies by the ribband-lines, equally or preferably to the water lines ; a method by which, in the after-body efpecially, the ribband-lines are made fair curves, and the water-lines are hollow. This they imagine, becaufe they think the water acts fometimes in the direction of the ribband-lines ; but it feems that if the water was generally to rife in a diagonal direction at the buttock of the fhip, we fhould perceive it to fwell very much ; whereas, when the fhip is failing, it appears to be generally difturbed. The only determination is, to make the after-body as fair as poffible in every direction ; and though the ribbands at the after-ends may appear to be very full, (which cannot be altered without making the water-lines hollow) yet it will be neceffary for the curious, to lay down fections entirely oppofite to the diagonal lines.

' In the body-plan they will be firft drawn, and will be ftill diagonals, though reverfed to the others. In the half-breadth plan thefe will appear as much too hollow, as the others are too round ; and we muft fuppofe, that when part of the fluid rifes in the direction of the ufual diagonals, other particles muft defcend the contrary way, which fufficiently proves that

the

the water-lines are a mean between both, and are the moſt uſeful lines to conſtruct a draught, in order to make a fair body.'

The plates IX. and X. contain the ſheer-draught, half-breadth lines, the body-plan, the horizontal view of the ſtern-frame, and the head of the ſhip laid off, ſhewing the proper form of the rails and timbers when in their places. Plate XI. exhibits a full ſtern view of the ſhip, and alſo of the head and quarter gallery. The author introduces an account of the ornaments with which the view is embelliſhed in the following words :

' It would be needleſs in this work to be particular in deſcribing matters of mere ornament, ſince in general they are diſcretionary. They ſerve however to enrich the ſtructure, and without them the labour of the artiſt, directed and confined to the body of the ſhip, would in the end produce but a rude edifice. It might contain all the properties of ſtrength and uſe, but not the recommendations of dreſs and beauty. By the happy application of emblems and figures, well proportioned and ingeniouſly deviſed, the eye of the beholder is attached and gratified. Therefore, though ornaments are to be conſidered only as ſecondary objects, they merit attention. For when the devices are vague and unſuitable to the name and nature of the ſhip, inſtead of embelliſhing, they deform the work.'

And he concludes this book with an account of the method uſed in meaſuring the tonnage of ſhips.

' The methods for meaſuring the tonnage of ſhips are become final by uſe. They vary according to the modes of different places, but the principle is the ſame throughout, and the reſult is equally diſtant from the true burthen in all. It does not aſcertain the burthen for ſtowage, but is a mere agreement, rendered general by cuſtom, between builders and buyers. If it were neceſſary to trace the origin of this method, it would moſt probably be diſcovered that there was ſome certain, fixed, and known rule for determining the principle dimenſions for building, and the meaſurement when built. But now that the length and breadth are only conſidered, without paying any regard to the depth, the reſult is not only very undeciſive of the true tonnage, but exceedingly unfavourable to naval improvement. The addition of one foot to the breadth very much increaſes the tonnage in meaſurement, whereas two feet in the depth makes no alteration. This naturally directs the merchant-employer to order the ſhip to be built with a depth very much diſproportioned to the breadth, by which the ſtowage may be increaſed without additional expence. Many inconvenient and alarming evils ariſe from this practice, and, while it ſubſiſts, it muſt very much interrupt the progreſs of improvement in ſhip-building.

' To proceed and explain the method of caſting the tonnage of the ſeventy-four-gun ſhip in plate IX.'

' Take

Take the extreme length, from the fore-part of the main ſtem, to the aft-part of the main ſtern-poſt, at the height of the wing-tranſom, which is — — 172 0

The ſhip is moulded 48 ft. 2 in. to which add 8 in. for the thickneſs of the plank of the bottom on both ſides, which is called the extreme breadth of the ſhip, being — — — — 48 10

' To find the length of the keel for tonnage, proceed in the following manner :

Take the height of the upper-ſide of the wing-tranſom at the middle line, from the upper-ſide of the rabbet of the keel, on a perpendicular to the keel, which is — — — — 25 9¼

Allow 2½ inches for every foot of the laſt mentioned height, for the rake of the ſtern-poſt, which is 5 4½

Take ⅗ of the extreme breadth for the rake of the ſtem, which is — — — 29 3¼

Add the rake of the poſt and ſtem together, which is 34 8

The extreme length being given — — 172 0

From which take out the rake of the poſt and ſtern 34 8

The remainder is the keel for tonnage, which is 137 4

' The length of the keel for tonnage being found, the method for caſting the ſhip's tonnage is as follows :

' The extreme breadth, the half-breath, and the keel for tonnage, are to be multiplied together (either two of which may be multiplied firſt), and that product to be divided by 94 (the common diviſor), the quotient is the number of tons required, and the remainder are decimal parts of a ton.

The Operation.

Extreme breadth — — — 48 10

Multiplied by the half-breadth — — 24 5

Is equal to — — — 1192 4¼

Which product, multiplied by the keel for tonnage 137 4

Produces — — — 163749 0

Then divide this by 94 (the common diviſor), and the quotient will be 1742 1/94, which is the number of tons the draught of the ſeventy-four-gun ſhip in plate IX. meaſures, by the preſent method of caſting ſhips' tonnage.'

Book VI. is accompanied with a draught of a cutter, deſigned to explain the method of drawing ſimilar and diſſimilar bodies. The author ſays,

' To draw bodies ſimilar to any draught, where the principal dimenſions are all intended to be in a ſimilar proportion, can only be of uſe to ſuch as intend to make but little difference reſpecting the ſize of the veſſel ; becauſe large veſſels can diſpenſe with leſs breadth in proportion to the length and depth ; and the ſmaller ſhe is, the more breadth is required to enable her to carry a ſufficient quantity of ſail. Therefore, to make the moſt advantage of the preſent deſign, we ſhould ſuppoſe a veſ-

ſel

fel or cutter already built, and bearing all the good properties
required. Let it be likewise required to build another confiderably larger or fmaller, where of courfe the principal dimenfions fhould differ very much, but yet be conftructed by a fimilar
principle to that already built, whereby an equal degree of
good properties may be expected.'

Plate XIII. contains a new method for finding the true ending of lines.

' Various, fays he, are the methods ufed in ending the lines,
from the different opinions which prevail among the artifts. I
have introduced plate XIII. becaufe, like many other perfons,
I have a method peculiar to myfelf. Having found reafon from
experiment to difapprove of every mode I ever faw practifed, I
was obliged to refort to ftudy for a more certain and precife
plan. I humbly fubmit it to the world; at the fame time offering my reafons for difapproving of other rules, and preferring
my own. I truft the ftudent will alfo be convinced, as the
plate and the directions will be clear and fimple.

' Before I proceed to the explanation of the plate, it will
be neceffary to give the reader fome account of its defign. The
method of ending the lines by fome, is to fuppofe the rabbet of
the ftem to be trimmed all the way by the fame mould that is
made to trim the rabbet of the keel, which is an equilateral
triangle, each fide being equal to the thicknefs of the plank intended to be wrought on the bottom. At the height of either
ribband or water-lines, at the rabbet of the ftem in the fheerdraught, from thence the fore and aft-fides of the rabbet is
fquared down to the half-breadth plan; if it is a diagonal
line, the infide of the rabbet muft be fet off on the diagonal
line in the body-plan, and that height muft be transferred to the
fheer-draught, and from thence fquared down to the halfbreadth plan. Then take off the half-breadth from the bodyplan, in the direction of the diagonal line, for the infide and
outfide of the rabbet, and fet them off in the half-breadth
plan. This will give you the exact form of the rabbet, fuppofed to be cut agreeable to the diagonal line in the body-plan.
In order to end the line into the rabbet, it muft either end at
the after-part of the rabbet, or elfe at the infide angle, whichfoever of them fhall happen to be fartheft from the fore-fide of
the rabbet, agreeable to the direction of the half-breadth line.
This being performed, that part of the body (as in a full-bowed
fhip) which is fquare to the fide of the ftem, will bury the
proper thicknefs of the plank; and that part of the body, which
ftrikes in the direction of the aft-fide of the rabbet, fuppofing the
plank is 4 inches, will only bury 3½ inches; and lower down,
if the fhip fhould be very clean, it will nearly bury the thicknefs
of the plank. There are different methods befides this I have
mentioned, which it would be of no ufe to defcribe; all of
them are more or lefs erroneous. Some who approve of their
own method, allow that the ftem at the lower end is generally
fided

ided too small to receive the whole thickneſs of the plank on each ſide ; and that, if the plank be reduced half an inch at the foremoſt ends in ſome places, it is then ſufficient to do the ſervice required.   This may be allowed ; but if the ſtem at the lower end was ſided one inch more, and the plank wholly buried, it would certainly be better ; and the ſtem might be made the ſame bigneſs at the fore-ſide as before ; for the ſtem, if meeting with any accident, muſt fail at the rabbet, that being the weakeſt place.   However, as the artiſts are now become very curious and correct, to what purpoſe is it for the ſhip to be laid down to the greateſt exactneſs, if the form of the ſhip at the outſide of the plank is to be corrected by the workman ?

' The plate before us is not deſigned to contradict thoſe who are ſatisfied with reducing the plank, but to convince thoſe who, at the ſame time are of opinion that it really will bury the thickneſs of the plank, as well in one part of the ſtem as the other.   To ſuch as approve of burying the plank in every part, in order to reſerve the true form of the body, is this plate recommended.   It is performed ſo as to ſhew the work clearly, that, inſtead of burying a four-inch plank, it is ſuppoſed to be required to work ſtuff of three or four feet thick, which ſhall be exactly buried ; and the line for the fore-ſide of the rabbet of the ſtem, and the lower edge of the rabbet of the keel, ſhall be unalterably determined.'

Here the author's original work ended ; but he has been induced to lay before the public the draught of a frigate propoſed to be built on a plan of Benjamin Thompſon, eſq. F. R. S. late under-ſecretary of ſtate for the American department, on account of the coincidence which there appears to have been in their ideas.   The following letter from Mr. Thompſon introduces the draught.

" Sir.—Agreeably to your requeſt, I herewith ſend you my draught of a frigate, upon a new conſtruction, which you will make any uſe of you may think proper.   Though I have little doubt with reſpect to the principles upon which this drawing is made, yet I ſhould hardly have ventured to have propoſed it to be carried into execution ; nor ſhould I now have conſented to its being made public, had it not been for the very flattering approbation it has met with from ſome of the beſt judges of naval architecture in this kingdom.

" That curious and moſt important art has long been my favourite ſtudy ; and ſeveral ſea voyages, particularly a three months cruize in the Channel fleet, under the command of the late ſir Charles Hardy, in the year 1779, afforded me an opportunity of making many remarks upon the qualities of ſhips, which in all probability would not otherwiſe have occurred to me.   It was during this cruize that I amuſed myſelf with making the drawing which I now ſend you, and when I began it, I had little more than amuſement in view ; but after it was

finiſhed,

finished, it was so much approved of by many able and experienced seamen to whom I shewed it, that I could not refuse the pressing solicitations that was made me to offer it to the surveyors of the navy, to have a ship built after it, by way of an experiment; and several officers of rank in the navy, and high in the estimation of the profession, voluntarily engaged to do every thing in their power to get the measure adopted.

"I confess I never had very sanguine hopes of our being able to carry this point. Professional men are seldom disposed to allow others to meddle in their business; but thus recommended, I thought it rather probable that we should succeed, but it turned out otherwise.

"Having failed in this attempt, I afterwards endeavoured to get the plan carried into execution by private subscription, and several of my friends offered to subscribe very generously for that purpose; but so large a sum of money was wanted, and and so great a length of time was necessary in order to complete the undertaking, that these circumstances, added to the uncertainty of the continuance of the war, prevented my being able to accomplish my design. By the copy of my proposals, which accompanies the draught, you will see the grounds upon which I proceeded in this business; and by the certificates annexed to those proposals, you will see the manner in which I was supported.—With such respectable testimonies in favour of the plan, I think I cannot risque much in allowing it to be made public.

"Should those who have the direction of our marine, upon a re-examination of the draught, or out of respect to the opinions of those who have expressed their approbation of it, think proper so far to adopt it, as to give it a trial, I cannot help flattering myself, that the experiments will turn out of much importance to the public service; and should it answer, as I think there is reason to expect, I shall be amply repaid for my trouble, by the satisfaction I shall have in seeing my endeavours to be of use to my country, crowned with success.

"To describe fully the principle upon which this draught was formed, would be to write a Treatise on Naval Architecture, which is a work I have not leisure at present to undertake; but I would just observe, that my great object was to contrive a vessel, which, possessing all the qualities necessary for a ship of war, should at the same time be able to carry a great quantity of sail with little ballast.

"The stiffness of a ship depends upon her form, and the quantity and stowage of her ballast; but that vessel which is stiff from construction, is much better adapted for sailing fast than one which, in order to carry the same quantity of canvas, is obliged to be loaded with a much greater weight; for the resistance is, as the quantity of water to be removed, or nearly as the area of a transverse section, of the immersed part of the body at the midship-bend; and a body that is broad and shal-

low, is much ftiffer than one of the fame capacity that is narrow and deep.

" Another advantage attending fhips that are ftiff from conftruction is, they are much lefs liable to roll than thofe which
are obliged to carry a great weight of ballaft; they are alfo
much better fea-boats, and are lefs liable to be ftrained in bad
weather.

" Cutters, which are by far the ftiffeft veffels from conftruction of any that have yet been built, are remarkably eafy in
the fea at all times; and, I believe, are fafer than any other
clafs of veffels of the fame capacity; they certainly fail fafter,
and work better.

" You will fee by the draught, that I have totally avoided
hollow water-lines, and alfo that the line of extreme breadth is
every where confiderably above the line of floatation; the reafons for this conftruction you will immediately comprehend
without my mentioning them, as alfo many other particulars
refpecting the draught, upon which I have not time at prefent
to enlarge. To the draught therefore I fhall refer you, without adding any thing more to this letter, only to affure you,
that I really am, &c.

" Pall-Mall, March 4, 1781. B. THOMPSON.'

The propofals for building this fhip, with the teftimonies
of fome of the moft diftinguifhed officers and builders in the
navy, are curious; and ought furely to have weight with the
Navy Board, and induce them to make experiments of the
plan.

" As it may be proper to make fome explanation to fuch profeffional men as may have thefe propofals under their eye, of
the peculiar conftruction of this frigate, and of the manner in
which it is propofed to arm her, it will be neceffary to obferve,
that to *fail faft* being the great leading principle which governs
our whole conftruction, all the water-lines are perfectly fair, and
her body is formed in the moft exact and beautiful proportions.
This extreme delicacy of form, which is moft confpicuous near
the keel, will not, however, prevent her giving ample ftowage
for four months provifions, befides all her ftores; and her great
length and breadth above the water, will at the fame time furnifh more commodious room for the men's births, and better
accommodation for the officers, than any frigate in the navy.
Her great length, breadth upon the beam, and good bearings,
are qualities that will not only enable her to carry a prefs of
fail, but prevent her rolling and pitching too violently in a
rough fea.

' It is propofed to give her the mafts, yards, and fails of a
thirty-two-gun frigate, and alfo the fame cables and anchors;
and as it fometimes happens in calm weather, that very heavy-
going fhips make their efcape from the fafteft failors, under favour

vour of light airs, which often extend but to a small distance : to prevent so mortifying an event, and also to enable this frigate to avail herself of any of those favourable opportunities, which sometimes occur for attacking ships of force as they lie becalmed, she will be prepared for rowing with thirty oars, and one hundred and twenty men ; each oar to be twenty-five feet in length, and to be worked by four men ; all the oars are to be worked between decks, by running them out of the scuttles, that serve occasionally for airing the ship.

' Her length upon the main-deck being one hundred and fifty feet, it is proposed to pierce her for thirty guns on this deck, and she will carry ten guns upon her quarter-deck ; to which may be added two chace-guns upon her forecastle. All the guns upon the main-deck are to be thirty-two-pounders, upon a new construction, weighing twenty-six hundreds each ; and the quarter-deck guns will be light twelve-pounders.

' As thirty-two-pounder carronades, which are not half so heavy as the proposed thirty-two-pounders, have been proved with very large charges of powder, there can be no doubt that these guns may be made to stand fire with perfect safety ; and that they will do sufficient execution, and be manageable on shipboard, will appear evident, when it is considered, that many of the thirty-two-pounders now in use in the navy weigh no more than fifty-two hundreds, and that they may be fired with two bullets at a time with the greatest possible effect, and without rendering the recoil at all too violent : for it is experimentally true, that one bullet may be fired from a gun weighing twenty-six hundreds with the same velocity, and consequently to the same distance when the elevation is the same, as two fired at once from a piece weighing fifty-two hundreds ; and the velocity of the recoil will be the same in both cases. But when the velocity of the recoil is the same, the strain upon the breechings will be as the weight of the gun, The force of the recoil, therefore, of these new pieces, will be but half as great as that of the thirty-two-pounders now in use ; and therefore there can be no doubt but they may be easily managed.

' The quarter-deck guns are formed upon the same principle, and are just half the weight of the heaviest twelve-pounders in the service.

' In order to facilitate the working of the guns, it is proposed to mount them all on sliding carriages ; the bed upon which the carriage runs to be moveable upon a hinge fastened to the sill of the port, in such a manner that the bed may be always kept in a horizontal position, however the ship may lie along ; by which means the weather-guns may be fought at all times, and the lee-guns till their muzzles come down to the water, and that with as much ease and expedition, as if the ship was upright upon her keel.

' Instead of small arms for the tops, and for the quarter-deck and forecastle, it is proposed to make use of musketoons,

on

on fuch a conftruction as to mount on fwivel-ftocks, and to be ufed occafionally, either on fhip-board or in a boat. Thefe pieces having a bore of about three feet in length, and one inch and half in diameter, will carry a grape of nine mufket bul-lets, or eighteen or twenty-four piftol bullets, as the object is at a greater or lefs diftance; or occafionally a fingle leaden bullet of twelve ounces, if execution is meant to be done at a very great diftance.

' A comparative view of the dimenfions of the propofed fri-gate, and of the Lark frigate of thirty-two guns, which was built after a drawing of the late Mr. Bately.

	Propofed frigate.		The Lark.	
	feet.	in.	feet.	in.
Length of the keel —	128	0	111	0
Length on the gun deck	150	0	132	0
Extreme breadth —	39	6	34	0
Draft of Water { forward	15	9	15	6
{ abaft	15	9	16	6
Area of a tranfverfe fection of the immerfed part of the body, at the mid-fhip frame — }	315	0	378	0
Burthen in builder's tonnage	1000 tons		646 tons	
Real capacity of the im-merfed part of the bo-dy, to the load water-line — }	32784 cubic feet		32198 cubic feet	
Real burthen —	915 tons		898½ tons	

For the fatisfaction of thofe who are willing to encourage this undertaking, the author has annexed authentic docu-ments, in favour of the plan, from gentlemen whofe opinion muft be allowed to have great weight on a fubject of fuch a nature. The firft of thefe is the copy of a Letter, dated April 21, 1780, from captain Kempenfelt, admiral's captain in the grand fleet *. The fecond is the copy of a fimilar Letter, dated April 23, 1780, from fir Charles Douglas, baronet, cap-tain in the royal navy. Thefe are followed by three certifi-cates, dated in the fame month and year, and figned by fome of the moft eminent fhip-builders in the kingdom, viz. the firft by Mr. Wells, the fecond by Mr. Hallett, and the third by Meffrs. Barnard and Dudman. To this ample teftimony is fubjoined a certificate, equally decifive, from Dr. Hutton, profeffor of mathematics in the royal military academy at Woolwich.

---

* This gentleman was afterwards raifed to the rank of rear-admiral, and was loft in the Royal George, at Spithead.

The

This splendid work concludes with a dictionary of the technical terms in naval architecture.

I have thus gone through the whole of the Treatise, and my opinion is, that the undertaking has cost Mr. Stalkartt much time and attention; and that his endeavours to reduce shipbuilding to rules more fixed and certain than what they are at present, are truly laudable. He seems to have overcome the prejudices of education, and he treads in the new path with modesty indeed, but with the steadiness of a mind which perceives the certainty of its ground, and challenges the combat. As the work is dedicated to his Majesty by permission, I hope to see a line-of-battle ship built on the plan which he proposes; and if so, I will hazard all the credit that I have, as a professional man, on the success. At the same time I think, if he had made his operations less technical, and had used more argument in his suggestions, he would have pleased his readers more.　　　　　　　　　　　　　　　　　　*I am*, &c.

Observations on the Passage to India, through Egypt; and across the Great Desart; with occasional Remarks on the adjacent Countries, and also Sketches of the different Routes. By James Capper, Esq. Colonel in the Service of the Hon. East India Company. 4to. 6s. Faden.

IN an introduction to this volume, we are informed that the Letter, of which it chiefly consists, was written in India, at the request of a person of rank, who once had thoughts of returning to Europe by the way of Suez. The Letter was not at that time intended for publication; but since colonel Capper's return to England, many of his friends having desired a copy of it, to accommodate them in the easiest manner he has at last reluctantly consented to its going to the press. That the publication, however, may be rendered more acceptable, he has prefixed an account of the proper time, and most agreeable manner, of going from Europe to India by Suez; explaining first the cause of the prohibition lately issued, by the Turks, against any Europeans passing that way, and shewing that their objections against travellers going through Egypt may be easily removed.

It appears that, in the year 1774, the governor-general of Bengal proposed to some merchants in Calcutta to send a ship to the Red Sea, loaded with a proper assortment of goods for the Turkish markets, and instead of landing them as usual at Gedda, a sea-port within sixty miles of Mecca, to proceed with them directly to Suez. By this means the governor-general expected to establish a new trade, equally beneficial to us and to the Turks, and also to open a new channel for transmitting intelligence backwards and forwards between India and Europe. The sherreef or high-priest of Mecca, however, whose revenues would have been confiderably diminished by diverting the channel of commerce from Gedda, very foon took the alarm, and ufed all his influence, both fpiritual and temporal, to oppofe the governor-general's plan. In his negociation at the Porte for this purpofe, he was alfo zealoufly affifted by a large body of Turkifh merchants, who were apprehenfive of fuffering by the prices of India goods being lowered in their markets, which muft have ruined the old eftablifhed trade of Boffora and Aleppo. In confequence of this powerful oppofition, a firmaun was obtained from the grand fignior, exprefsly prohibiting the new commerce, under the penalty of confifcation of the cargo. No fooner was this edict procured, than fome acts of violence were committed upon Chriftian merchants, at the inftigation of the fherreef of Mecca.

Colonel Capper obferves, that in thefe circumftances, it may perhaps be deemed expedient to abandon the Suez trade, rather than involve ourfelves in a difpute with the grand fignior ; but that we ought not to renounce alfo the convenience of fending packets that way, to which neither the grand fignior, nor even the fherreef of Mecca, can offer the fmalleft reafonable objection.

' Every man, fays our author, acquainted with India muft know, that it is of the higheft importance to individuals, to the company, and to the nation at large, to have this channel of communication opened again. During the latter part of the late war, after the firmaun was iffued, the French regularly tranfmitted advices by Suez, to and from India, by which means they frequently anticipated us in intelligence, and thereby counteracted our operations. It is not neceffary to particularize every inftance of it, but it will doubtlefs be well remembered, that the news of the unfortunate defeat of Colonel Baillie came to England through France, where it was known in February, time enough to enable them to fend out reinforcements to Hyder Ally, before the beft feafon for paffing the Cape of Good Hope was elapfed; whilft we, who were ignorant of that difafter until April, could not fend out any fhips before the return of the infuing feafon, near fix months afterwards.

' Since then nothing lefs than the exiftence of our fettlements in India may fome time or other depend upon our poffeffing a right of paffing unmolefted through Egypt; and the prohibitory firmaun was only intended to prevent the trade of Gedda from being transferred to Suez, furely no time fhould be loft in demanding another firmaun explanatory of the firft, and declaring that no perfons dependent on, or connected with, the Turkifh government, shall impede or molest any British subject in passing up the Red Sea, or through Egypt, provided they have nothing but papers, and such baggage as travellers may be supposed to have occasion for on such a journey. The sherreef of Mecca may probably at first oppose our enjoying this privilege, in which also it is likely he will be secretly supported by the French; but can it be thought prudent in us to submit to the controul of the one, or to be dupes to the secret machinations of the other, especially, when consistently with justice, we can easily get the better of both.'

The author afterwards considers what is the best time for setting out from England for the East Indies, by the way of Suez.

'The season for undertaking this journey commences early in April, and ends early in June; during which time a person accustomed to travel will easily arrive at Alexandria from London in about a month, that is, supposing he has previously determined what route to pursue to the Mediterranean, and also has caused a vessel to be prepared for him on his arrival at the place where he intends to embark. The northerly and westerly winds prevail in the Mediterranean in May, June and July, and therefore in these months, the passage from Marseilles, Leghorn, or Venice to Alexandria, in a tolerable good sailing vessel seldom exceeds eighteen days, and is often performed in ten or twelve; from Alexandria he will easily get to Suez in eight days; and from thence to Anjengo is a voyage of twenty-five days; to Bombay twenty-eight; to Madrass thirty-five; and to Bengal forty; making the journey from England to India at the most seventy-eight days, at the least fifty-nine, and at a medium sixty-eight and an half. This perhaps to some people may appear too nice a calculation, considering it is an undertaking dependent upon many accidents of wind and weather; but in answer to this objection it must be remembered, that great part of the voyage is performed within the Tropic, where the winds and weather are as regular as any natural periodical revolution can be; and even in the Mediterranean, where only the winds are variable, they are never known in summer, to blow long between the S. and E. the only quarter of the compass unfavourable to the vessels bound from the ports of Italy and France, to the Levant.'

The manner of performing the principal part of the voyage is more fully explained in the Letter, of which we shall now proceed to give an account.

The colonel sets out with observing—that the principal objections he has heard mentioned against a voyage from India to Europe, by the way of Suez, are the expence, the inconvenience, and the danger of it; but all these, he thinks, may, by prudent management, be rendered easy.

'The

' The expence, fays our author, would be trifling to a man of fortune, or when divided between two or three perfons would be lefs to each of them than going round the Cape of Good Hope; the navigation of the Red Sea being now tolerably well known, can in a proper feafon no longer be deemed dangerous; and as to inconvenience, I know of none but what might be almoft entirely removed by means of a little money properly applied. In paffing from Suez to Alexandria, you may poffibly meet with fome difagreeable embarraffments from which a man of rank and fortune is generally exempt in a more civilized country, but moft of thefe are to be avoided, or at leaft greatly leffened by giving prefent of no great value to the beys and other leading men in Egypt.

' In all Arabian and Turkifh countries, efpecially in thofe near the city of Mecca, to avoid the infults of the lower clafs of people, an European fhould allow his beard and whifkers to grow, and always wear an Eaftern drefs; it is beft to make up a coarfe one in the Arabian fafhion for travelling, and another rather elegant in the Turkifh fafhion to wear at Cairo, and Alexandria. If you perform the journey in winter, a pellis will be both ufeful and ornamental, but it may be proper to remark that a Chriftian fhould not wear green clothes at any place in the Levant, for green is a colour deemed facred to thofe who have made the pilgrimage to Mecca, and to the defcendants of the prophet; nor do the Turks like to fee any European in red, which was alfo Mahomet's favourite colour.

' Thofe who undertake long journies in Europe are obliged to furnifh themfelves which bills of exchange, but on this they are not indifpenfably neceffary; a perfon of character may have credit to any amount the whole way for drafts upon England or India; but if you do not choofe to be without a fufficient fupply of ready money, you fhould take with you Venetian chequins, which are very portable, and at the fame time current in all countries between India and England.'

Among the various remarks and ufeful directions with which the author favours his correfpondent, he recommends to him, on his arrival at Cairo, to repair to the bagnio, as well for health as for pleafure. As a Turkifh bagnio or hummum muft be a new fcene to many of our readers, we fhall prefent them with the defcription of it, as accurately drawn up by our author.

' The firft room is the undreffing chamber, which is lofty and fpacious, about twenty-five feet long and eighteen wide; near the wall is a kind of bench raifed about two feet from the floor, and about feven or eight feet wide, fo that after bathing a perfon may lay down upon it at full length; the windows are near the top of the room, as well that the wind may not blow upon the bathers when undreffed, as for decency's fake. After undreffing a fervant gives you a napkin to wrap round you, and

alfo

also a pair of slippers, and thus equipped you are conducted through a narrow passage to the steam room or bath, which is a large round building of about twenty-five feet diameter, paved with marble, and in the centre of it is a circular bench, where you are seated until you find yourself in a profuse perspiration; then your guide or attendant immediately begins rubbing you with his hand covered with a piece of coarse stuff called keslay, and thereby peels off from the skin a kind of scurf, which cannot be moved by washing only. When he has rubbed you a few minutes he conducts you to a small room, where there is a hot bath about four feet deep and ten feet square, in which he will offer to wash you, having his hand covered with a smoother stuff than before; or you may have some perfumed soap given you to wash yourself: After you have remained here as long as is agreeable, you are conducted to another little side-room, where you find two cocks of water, the one hot, the other cold, which you may throw over you with a bason, the water being tempered to any degree of warmth, or perfectly cold if you prefer it. This being the last ablution, you are then covered with a napkin, and from hence again conducted to the undressing room, and placed upon the before mentioned bench with a carpet under you, and being extended upon it at full length, your attendant again offers to rub you dry with napkins. Some people have their nails cut, and also are shampoed*; the Turks generally smoak after bathing and the operation of shampoing, and in about an hour, a few minutes more or less, they commonly dress and go home.'

Colonel Capper appears to entertain a very favourable opinion of the use of the Turkish baths in preventing the gout and rheumatism; and he expresses a desire that some able physician would inform the public what would be the probable effects of them in England. The suggestion is worthy of an intelligent observer, and we should be glad to see it adopted. It is certain that bathing in general is too little practised in this country, though there is reason to think, from analogy, that it might be successfully used as a prophylactic.

Our author accounts, in a manner different from the common opinion, for the jealousy discovered by the Mahomedans

---

' * Shampoing is variously performed in different countries. The most usual manner is simply pressing the hands and fingers upon the body and limbs, particularly near the extremities, so as to compress, but not to pinch them. This is the general manner practised by the servants of the Asiatics, but the barbers and the guides at the baths make also the joints, and even the vertebræ of the back, crack by a sudden jerk, which to people unaccustomed to it in their youth, is rather a painful sensation. The Chinese and Malay barbers particularly excel in this art, which however is very well known, and generally practised all over Asia, being by them thought a necessary substitute for exercise during the hot weather.'

against

against European travellers, on seeing them examine the ruins of ancient cities.

' It is generally believed by them that all Europeans are deeply verſed in the abſtruſe and occult ſciences, which makes them conſider us in the ſame light as the vulgar and ignorant in Europe conſider our fortune tellers or conjurers, that is with a kind of admiration mixed with fear and deteſtation. Added to this prejudice, they are alſo thoroughly perſuaded from the ſtories they daily hear repeated out of the Arabian Nights Entertainments, that there are many ſubterraneous palaces in their country full of pearls and diamonds, in ſearch of which they ſuppoſe the Europeans are come to Egypt : we always acknowlege that we are looking after curioſities, which ſerves to confirm them in their error ; for as they have not the moſt diſtant idea of what we mean by curioſities, they naturally conclude we are looking for the pearls and diamonds ſuppoſed to be concealed in thoſe ſame palaces ; which opinion alſo is ſtrongly corroborated by the zeal and anxiety ſhews by our antiquarians in their reſearches.

' As the mean heat of a country is ſaid to be nearly aſcertained by the mean heat of the ſprings, ſo are the genius and character of a nation diſcovered by peruſing their favourite books ; for which reaſon I adviſe you by all means to peruſe theſe Arabian Nights Entertainments before you ſet out on your journey. Believe me, ſir, they contain much curious and uſeful information. They are by many people erroneouſly ſuppoſed to be a ſpurious production, and are therefore ſlighted in a manner they do not deſerve. They were written, as I have already hinted, by an Arabian, and are univerſally read and admired throughout Aſia by all ranks of men, both old and young : conſidered therefore as an original work, deſcriptive as they are of the manners and cuſtoms of the Eaſt in general, and alſo of the genius and character of the Arabians in particular, they ſurely muſt be thought to merit the attention of the curious ; nor are they, in my opinion, entirely deſtitute of merit in other reſpects ; for although the extravagance of ſome of the ſtories is carried too far, yet, on the whole, one cannot help admiring the fancy and invention of the author, in ſtriking out ſuch a variety of pleaſing incidents ; pleaſing I call them, becauſe they have frequently afforded me much amuſement, nor do I envy any man his feelings, who is above being pleaſed with them ; but before any perſon decides upon the merit of theſe books, he ſhould be eye witneſs of the effect they produce on thoſe who beſt underſtand them. I have more than once ſeen the Arabians on the Deſart ſitting round a fire, liſtening to theſe ſtories with ſuch attention and pleaſure, as totally to forget the fatigue and hardſhip with which, an inſtant before, they were entirely overcome. In ſhort, ſir, not to dwell any longer on this ſubject, they are in the ſame eſtimation all over Aſia, that the adventures of Don Quixote are in Spain ; and I

am

am perfuaded no man of any genius or taste would think of making the tour of that country, without previously reading the works of Cervantes.'

Our author's observations on the comparative state of Egypt and Hindoftan are juft and philofophical.

' It has long been a favourite opinion amongft the learned, both ancient and modern, that the Egyptians were acquainted with the arts and fciences, when all the other people were in a ftate of ignorance, We are told they difcovered geometry in making the divifions of land, after the annual overflowing of the Nile; that the clearnefs of their atmofphere enabled them to make aftronomical obfervations fooner than other people, and that the fertility of their country gave rife to trade, by enabling them to fupply all their neighbours with corn, and other necef-faries of life. Thefe arguments are, however, more fpecious than true, for if we owe the difcovery of geometry to the over-flowing of the Nile, of aftronomy to the clearnefs of the atmo-fphere, and of trade to the fertility of the foil, in that part of Hindoftan which is within the tropic, there are ftill larger ri-vers which overflow annually, a clearer fky, and a more fertile foil, The Nile only once a year affords a fupply of water to the countries on its banks, and the fmall quantity of rain that falls there at other times, does not furnifh moifture enough to keep up the fmalleft degree of vegetation : whereas the rivers in Hin-doftan, particularly thofe on the coaft of Choromandel, are re-gularly filled with water twice a year, firft from the rains which fall in June, July, and Auguft, in the Balagat mountains, where the fources of thofe rivers lie; and afterwards from the N. E. monfoon or rainy feafon, which continues on the Choromandel coaft during the months of October, November, and December. With refpect to the goodnefs of the climate, or the clearnefs of the atmofphere for the purpofe of aftronomy, there can be no comparifon between Egypt and Hindoftan ; for at night, during the greater part of the year, in Hindoftan, there is fcarcely a cloud to be feen in the fky, and the air, efpecially in the fouthern countries, is never difagreeably cold, fo that an aftronomer would have every opportunity and inducement to purfue his ftudies in the open air, whereas in Egypt the fky is often cloudy, and the air fo cold as to make it unpleafant to be out of doors after fun-fet.

' The Indians had alfo very evidently the advantage of the Egyptians with refpect to cloathing, which is one of the necef-faries, or at leaft one of the comforts of life ; for if we fuppofe men firft cloathed themfelves in the fkins of animals, India abounds in vaft forefts and extenfive fertile plains, where ani-mals of all kinds, both favage and tame, muft have bred infi-nitely fafter than in the barren deferts of upper Egypt ; but in a hot country the natives would naturally prefer garments made of woven cotton, Now the cotton fhrub is very rare in Egypt.

even

even at this time, and it is well known to have grown in India, and to have been fabricated into cloth ever since we have had any acquaintance with that country. From these premises, therefore, it is natural to suppose, that the Indians in the early ages were much more likely to supply the Egyptians with necessaries and comforts of life, than to be supplied by them; that the Indians would at least have as much occasion for geometry as the Egyptians, and that they had at least equal, if not greater advantages, for pursuing the study of astronomy.'

While colonel Capper represents Hindostan as preferable in point of climate to Egypt, he is also an advocate for its claim to superior antiquity in the cultivation of the arts and sciences; and, on a subject so hypothetical, it must be acknowleged that his arguments in general have a great degree of plausibility. His observations on various parts of Egypt, and other countries, must prove highly useful to travellers in those parts, at the same time that his topographical descriptions are agreeably blended with philosophical and ingenious remarks, which cannot fail of being interesting to every reader of taste.——The Letter is followed by the Journal of a voyage from Leghorn to Bombay, which appears very accurate, and is recited with great perspicuity.

An Essay on the Study of Antiquities. The Second Edition. 8vo. 2s. 6d. White.

IF the study of antiquity has been sometimes slighted or ridiculed, it may be attributed rather to the misconduct of the student, than the tendency of his object. An eager haste or partial fondness have frequently betrayed the attentive enquirer, or misled the learned professor; and the world has ridiculed both, without reflecting that, in similar circumstances, error is frequently respectable. The author of this Essay, to whom the world has been obliged for a more accurate edition of Mr. Dawes's Miscellanies, and a few chosen Greek tragedies, endeavours to defend the study of antiquity, by pointing out the various advantages which will result from it, both to the scholar and the gentleman; the various circumstances which it will elucidate, and the peculiar satisfaction which it frequently affords. He has supported the credit of this study by powerful arguments and persuasive language; for we can scarcely say whether we have received more information from the strength of the former, than pleasure from the elegance of the latter.

It has been observed, with great seeming reason, that antiquity of every kind is by no means equally valuable. Though

the

the remoter periods of Rome and Greece were distinguished by arts and elegance; though, in investigating their former state, the highest entertainment accompany the most solid instruction, yet in these western climes, the farther we go from our own times, we are more deeply immersed in rudeness and ignorance; the corruptions of a dark and barbarous age, without a ray of elegance or refinement. Our author combats this opinion, though he has not expressly mentioned it, by clearly showing, that the genius of a nation, and consequently its taste and acquisitions, are only to be learned from its language, its works, or even its amusements. But, as he has fully stated the connection between the several branches of the study of antiquity in his conclusion, we shall insert this part as a specimen.

' The study of antiquities thus useful and interesting is not more comprehensive, than it is connected in its several parts; by the great union and mutual comparison of which every particular branch derives additional lustre and utility.

' An accurate knowlege of the primitive manners and customs of a people tends much to illustrate the earlier periods of their language; while the investigation and analysis of language conduces to point out the genius of a people. But the first principles of a language can be thoroughly ascertained only from a diligent study of the most ancient marbles and coins. Thus also the ancient manners of a people are illustrated by their laws: and their laws reciprocally by their early monuments. Coins and marbles frequently throw great light on poetry: as poetry will sometimes reflect a similar light on the obscurities of a coin. Coins likewise as well as seals and medals, besides exhibiting specimens of their peculiar art, mark out the regular progress of architecture: the different stages of which are seen also in the various structure of sepulchral monuments.—But while they severally contribute to assist each other, all unite in the illustration and embellishment of history, poetry, and philosophy.

' To this union of the several branches in the study of antiquities perhaps is owing the success with which it is conducted in the present age. There have been those, who appear to have contented themselves with the laborious part of this study. They adored the precious rust which obscured their coins, and neglected the valuable information, which it concealed. Like those who form their opinions of ancient authors from the judgments of others. From whom they admire the vehemence and spirit of Demosthenes, the sweetness of Xenophon, the authority of Thucydides, the sublime poetry of Plato: and thus descant with warmth on the characters of their style from critics, many of whom understood not the language they were criticising. And here they stop short to contemplate those beauties at a distance. They admire the exquisite decorations that adorn the

7

shrine,

shrine, but have too much reverence for the divinity inclosed to withdraw the veil.

' Those lovers of antiquity therefore confined themselves to a necessary, but elementary part of the study, to which the collection and arrangement of their curiosities was only an introduction. Thus fixing themselves to one part of the antiquarian pursuits, by a consequence inseparable from too strict an attachment to any single art or science, their views in learning became partial and narrow, and their sentiments often bigotted and illiberal.

' To their labours however and industrious curiosity the present age has great obligations, for facilitating the acquisition of those materials which are now converted to their proper use.

' The study of antiquities once far removed from all the arts of elegance, is now become an attendant on the Muses, an handmaid to History, to Poetry, and Philosophy. From this united influence many are the advantages which have been derived to general knowlege. Particularly much of that obscurity, which overspreads the first periods in the history of every nation, has already been happily removed from our own by the diligence and sagacity of able antiquaries. And what indeed may we not expect further from an age in which every part of science is advancing to perfection : in which history has attained a degree of excellence unknown to any former period of English literature ; and poetry and philosophy have gained new honours : and lastly, in whose character that has so conspicuous a place, which is essential to the success of this study, an inquisitive curiosity and love of truth.'

The first edition of this elegant Essay appears scarcely to have emerged from its original situation. The second edition, considerably corrected and enlarged, seems to have been first advertised in the metropolis. The additional observations are equally elegant and useful. We were not surprised at his favourable account of Egyptian taste, since, as well as their learning and acquisitions, it has been the frequent theme of the learned scholar, and the superficial antiquary. Those who attributed the learning and arts of the more enlightened periods of Greece to the instructions of the Egyptians, admired in the scholar the excellencies of the master. Books however were more perishable than statues ; and the error, which the diligence of the antiquary has detected respecting their arts, seems to have remained with full force in regard to their literary attainments. We may on this occasion refer to our own Journal ; for, in reviewing the History of Winkelmann, we examined, with this intention, the early arts of Egypt, and found them rude and inelegant. Even at a more refined period the Egyptians were flattered by aukward

imitations

imitations of their original monuments; and only, after the dispersion of the Grecian artists, who carried with them their genius and address, were the productions of this admired country either agreeable or interesting. We have little hesitation in predicting, that, when the remains of their learning have been examined, it will deserve a censure equally severe.

Our author's observations on language, particularly the Greek, deserve attention, not only from their present merits, but from the dawn of future excellence. This promised day is, an Enquiry into the Origin and Formation of the Greek Language; and its principal purpose is

" An endeavour to trace the origin, progress, and connection of ideas, as expressed by the primitive language of Greece: to shew through the evidence afforded by language, that all ideas, communicated by words, not denoting particular sounds, and certain external adjuncts, or personal relation, were originally made known through the means of one general idea, which is the principle of every action; and which by the multiplex variety of its combinations is suited to the expressing of every action: that all verbs, not imitative of sounds, &c. are resolvable to that general idea: that the names of things are derived from verbs, and therefore return to the same universal origin: whence that general idea was formed, and how transferred to different and even opposite actions: and how far the elements, which will be there laid down as the principles of the Greek language may be supposed to have been the elements of universal language."

This general idea is *motion*; and the great trunk from which the several branches arise, seems to be the verbs of motion. He observes, with justice, that the properties of the several objects originally offered to the sight, probably influenced their appellations; so that verbs, or at least the words which were afterwards formed into verbs, seem to have been originally invented. It will be obvious, that he considers the Greek as an original or indigenous language: for this opinion he chiefly rests on the authority of Hemsterhusius, who was equally acquainted both with the Greek and the Oriental learning; but he observes that, when the origin of the language of Greece has been examined, this subject will be considered with more propriety and advantage.

We would beg leave to warn Mr. Burges against too much simplicity in his system, since this very circumstance has deprived lord Monboddo's excellent work on the Origin and Progress of Language of an attentive examination. Even the suggestion, that the Greek may have been derived from the duads, $\alpha\tilde{\omega}$, $\epsilon\tilde{\omega}$, $\iota\tilde{\omega}$, $o\tilde{\omega}$, and $v\tilde{\omega}$, or rather from a, e, i, o, u, has given the appearance of a trifling fancy to a work of judgment,

ment, learning, and ingenuity. It is not easy, in this state, to form an opinion of Mr. Burges's system; yet we are apprehensive that, from its too great simplicity, certainly not the first step in language, its real merit may not be sufficiently regarded. The different necessary adjuncts will certainly afford a considerable variety; and our author promises to raise the importance of these little words, which have been overlooked by philosophical grammarians, sometimes from their trifling, but more frequently from their inexplicable nature. We cannot resist the temptation of offering a very short analysis of this enquiry, in the words of its author.

' As to the first part of the enquiry, it will be sufficient for the present to mention, that the general idea alluded to is MOTION, the most general and comprehensive, that can be formed: that this idea was made use of as the interpreter of all others, not because, after a deliberate survey, its connection with every action was foreseen; but merely from the inexperience and imperfection of human knowlege, when, for want of sufficient discrimination, a new idea was most easily communicated through the assistance of one already known. This will appear the more natural, if we compare it with common practice even in these enlightened days, in which we may frequently observe those especially, who are unassisted with the knowlege of more than one language, having recourse to general terms, to express particular ideas. What action does not *to do* represent? and for what object is not *thing* a substitute? Indeed all knowlege is comparative, and all language, strictly speaking, metaphorical. All ideas of things were formed from the relation which objects and actions have to one another; and they were assimilated or distinguished only by comparison. According to the process of knowlege and experience, these relations become more and more remote; till at length a particular class of words and ideas may be found to preserve a strict connection between the individuals, which compose the class, and yet seemingly have lost all connection with another class though ultimately belonging to the same origin. The particular difference and general union of these classes of ideas and words, is like the composition of a picture composed of different parts, which have a relation to one whole. In a well-chosen and well-ordered historical subject, the general union of particular parts, and the harmony of the groups, exhibit to the eye even at the first view an attention to one end and one common interest. The two groups which are most distant are yet united by the middle group; and their common interest conspires to point out the principal character, who is the soul and spirit of the subject, and on whom depends the action of the subordinate parts. In the same manner two words, or two classes of words, may be expressive of ideas, unconnected in themselves, but yet united by an intermediate association, through which we ascend

cend to the general idea, which is the principle and essence of the rest, and from which they derive their several powers however variously modified.

' As to the second part of the enquiry, the primary and original sound by which the general idea was denoted, is supposed to have been arbitrary and symbolical, not chosen on account of any supposed relation to the nature of motion, but used, for its simplicity, to exprefs the original idea. From this element it is conceived that all other words were formed, and all ideas communicated, not by imitation or symbolically, for that were now unneceffary, but by derivation and metaphor, in reference to the general idea, the constituent and energy of every action. Except one clafs of words, which are imitative, denoting particular founds, &c. and another, signifying perfonal relation; neither of them formed by reference to the general idea, as they are not expreffive of action; but formed one by imitation of the thing fignified; and the other δεικτικως, or by pointing to the perfon and thing underftood. Inftances of which still exift, εδε fignifying ego, tu, ille. The proper names of places are alfo excepted, as being pofterior to the ftate of the language, which is the fubject of the enquiry; though they often appear to have become proper from general ideas of fituation, ftrength, &c.

' He therefore imagines that the names of things were not formed capriciously and by chance, but with fome view not indeed to their real nature and effence, but to their nature as obvious in external adjuncts, in their actions, effects, appearances, &c. and denoted by means of the general idea, and of the primary found expreffive of that idea.

' And laftly, (which is indeed the foundation of the firft part of the enquiry,) " That the names of things are derived from verbs; that all verbs in their primary and phyfical fenfe, (except fuch as have been particularly fpecified,) are fignificant of action; that all kinds of action are but different modifications of motion, which were expreffed by varieties of the primary found, by which the general idea was denoted.".

We ought to add, that the learning and abilities of the author give us the moft pleafing expectations of his future work. We wifh alfo to fuggeft, that, if the Greek be an original language, it has been probably formed in the fame method by which every other has been invented, by neceffity, and the ftruggles of a mind aiming at means to explain its own wants, and to procure inftruction. If that be the cafe, it would probably be better illuftrated by languages in various ftates of their progrefs, than by a philofophical enquiry. This is the method of experiment oppofed to hypothefis. This teaches us what really happens, inftead of what may have occurred. If we examine a polifhed language, we explain with a philofophical precifion, not the firft efforts of the favage, but the re-

finements

finements of civilization. If we attempt to afcend beyond it, we plunge into an ocean of obfcurity, with only the delufive fupport of a fancied etymology. Thefe are, in our opinion, real obftacles to the attempt ; and we have fuggefted them, not to depreciate the author's defign, but to warn him of the rocks and quickfands which furround him. Perhaps our apprehenfions have little foundation, or they may have probably occurred to the ingenious enquirer, and been already obviated. We have no doubt of his having examined the fubject with attention, and determined with propriety.

" *Vox Oculis Subjecta ;*" *a Differtation on the moft curious and important Art of imparting Speech, and the Knowlege of Language, to the naturally Deaf, and (confequently) Dumb ; with a particular Account of the Academy of Meffrs. Braidwood of Edinburgh.* 8vo. 4s. White.

THE principal channel, through which inftruction and knowlege are conveyed to the mind, is the ear. To thofe, in whom this organ is fhut up, or obftructed in its operation, by fome internal defect, improper formation, or material injury, all nature feems to be in profound filence. The confequence is, fuch perfons are dumb : for it is by the imitation of the founds we hear, that we ordinarily acquire the art of fpeaking.

It may well be fuppofed, that it is extremely difficult, if not impoffible, to teach fuch perfons to fpeak, to read, to write, to practife arithmetic, &c. But it is the defign of this effay to inform the world, that all this has been actually accomplifhed by Meffrs. Braidwood, in their academy at Edinburgh.

Mr. Thomas Braidwood, the fenior profeffor, firft engaged in this undertaking, with one pupil, in the year 1760. As the practical part of the art was then new to him, he made, comparatively fpeaking, but a flow progrefs : though in a few years he taught that pupil to fpeak and write with confiderable eafe and propriety. By degrees he augmented his number, and improved his method. About the year 1770 he took into partnerfhip Mr. John Braidwood, a young gentleman of abilities, and great application. The number of their fcholars, of both fexes, at the time when this Differtation was written, amounted to near twenty, including feveral who had only impediments in fpeech, without being deaf. They were of different ages, from five to upwards of twenty years ; but thefe gentlemen have inftructed feveral others, who did not begin till they were much older. Five years, it is faid, are neceffary

fary to give the deaf a tolerable general underftanding of their own language, fo as to read, write, and fpeak it with eafe.

' The manner in which this is effected is, by firft fhewing them how the mouth is formed for the production of the vowels, letting them fee the external effect that vocalized breath hath upon the internal part of the wind-pipe, and caufing them to feel with their thumbs and fingers the vibration of the larynx, firft in the teacher, then in themfelves. When they found any of the vowels, then they are fhewn the written form of what they have expreffed, till they are perfected in the knowlege of the vowels or vocal founds; to which fucceeds the formation of fyllables and words, then the meaning of common words, and finally the conftruction of a fentence or fentences, out of which all defcriptions of the mind or will are compofed, or every exhibition of perception or volition, which is the whole of language.'

Dr. Johnfon, in his Journey to the Weftern Iflands of Scotland, fays, the improvement of Mr. Braidwood's pupils is wonderful. They not only fpeak, write, and underftand what is written, but if he that fpeaks looks towards them, and modifies his organs by diftinct and full utterance, they know fo well what is fpoken, that it is an expreffion fcarcely figurative to fay, ' they hear with the eye.'

To conceive the theory of this art, ' we need only confider with a little attention the mechanifm of fpeech, and we fhall foon find, that there is required for fpeaking certain pofitions and motions of the organs of the mouth, fuch as the tongue, the teeth, lips, and palate, that cannot be from nature, but muft be the effect of art; for their action, when they are employed in the enunciation of fpeech, is fo different from their natural and quiefcent fituation, that nothing but long ufe and exercife could have taught us to employ them in that way *.'

The generality of the world, as the author of this tract remarks, are apt fuddenly, but erroneoufly, to combine the idea of idiotifm with that of the ftate of the deaf and dumb; whereas no greater error can fubfift, as may plainly appear by the inftances of perfection to which many of Mr. Braidwood's pupils have arrived in language and other arts, as well as in the fciences. The truth is, the fcale of intellectual comprehenfions or underftandings in them is as varioufly graduated, as in other perfons; many of them indeed poffefs a quicknefs of apprehenfion, a fcope of imagination and fagacity, above

' * Orig. and Prog. of Lang. p. 182.'

the

the common standard among those who are not naturally deaf.'

From what I have seen, continues this writer, ' it is my serious persuasion, that the operation of the mind in deaf persons, thus instructed, not being so liable to be diverted or disturbed by the noises or sounds that frequently occur, as in others, their application to any point in science may be more uniformly intense, and consequently their powers of abstraction greater than ordinary; and I have no doubt but that some of them, who are possessed of genius, will make mathematical discoveries of great importance, and carry their researches in philosophy beyond those of other men: and thus the ways of Providence, which, in many respects, are inscrutable, and past finding out, may, in a new instance, be justified to man.'

It is remarkable (notwithstanding all that had been written by Plato, Aristotle, Dionysius of Halicarnassus, Quintilian, and others of the ancients, who have investigated the principles of language, and the formation of the vocal and articulate sounds) that, until about the middle of the last century, we know of no attempts having been made in this extraordinary art, and at that time in only a few instances. It existed then indeed chiefly in theory. There were however some instances of successful practice. Bulwer, in his Philocophus, or Deaf and Dumb Man's Friend, published in 1648, relates an instance of a Spanish nobleman instructed by a priest. Dr. W. Holder taught one young gentleman in this country to make some proficiency, in 1659. Dr. John Wallis instructed two in some degree, about the year 1660. Dr. Amman, of Amsterdam, instructed a young lady at Haerlem, and several others in Holland, between the years 1690 and 1700. Some attempts had been made also by Van Helmont, a German, and by Monachus, a Spaniard. Mr. Baker professed the art in this country with some success, about twenty-five or thirty years since. But no regular academy was ever opened by any one. It was reserved for Messrs. Braidwood to bring this curious, important, and almost incredible art, to a much greater degree of perfection than all former professors.

The following authors have spoken with applause of this academy, viz. Mr. Arnot, in his History of Edinburgh; Dr. Johnson, in his Journey to the Hebrides; Mr. Pennant, in his Tour through Scotland; and Lord Monboddo, in his Origin and Progress of Language.

The latter part of this tract contains a proposal for extending and perpetuating this important art, by a public establishment, under the direction of proper governors.

Messrs.

Meffrs. Braidwood, we are told, have lately removed their academy to Hackney, near London.

Outlines of Mineralogy, tranflated from the Original of Sir Torbern Bergman. By William Withering, M. D. 8vo. 2s. 6d. Robinfon.

DR. Withering is fuch a tranflator as Bergman would have probably wifhed for, if he had been allowed to felect an interpreter. The fubjectis familiar to him; he is not unacquainted with the other works of the author, and he has himfelf made advances in the fame ftudies. The notes are confequently valuable and interefting. Dr. Withering has found the terra ponderofa aerata in a mine in this kingdom, and intends to prefent a more full account of it to the Royal Society. Bergman had never yet found it in this ftate; fo that the fpecific gravity, inftead of being 3.773, is now difcovered to be 4.338. We ought to have added, in our Review of the Sciagraphia, that Bergman fufpected this fubftance to be of a metallic nature, becaufe it was precipitated by a phlogifticated alkali; but its regulus has never yet been reduced.

Befides many ufeful notes, the tranflator has added fome new fpecies, either from Bergman's other works, or from his own obfervations. Of the former kind is the lithomarga or ftone-marrow, which confifts of clay united to other earths: of the latter, the fulphurated tin mentioned in Bergman's preface; an impure fpecies of alum, which fublimes from fome of the Staffordfhire coal-pits; and a fpecies of lead mineralized by vitriolic acid and iron, which exifts in immenfe maffes in the ifle of Anglefea. We fhall extract what Dr. Withering has added on the fubject of platina, as it increafes our knowlege of the properties of this curious metal.

'From fome late experiments made upon platina by the count de Sikengen, and publifhed in German by profeffor Succow, it appears that the fpecific gravity of pure platina is 27.500. When perfectly pure and in its metallic ftate it was not calcined by deflagration with nitre, it did not admit of being hardened or foftened by tempering, like fteel or other metals; it was drawn into a wire $\frac{1}{1040}$ of a line in diameter; this wire admitted of being flattened, and had more ftrength than a wire of gold or filver of the fame fize. This platina is not fufible by the ftrongeft fire, but melts in the focus of a burning glafs; its colour white, fhining like fine filver.

'From confidering the very interefting experiments of the count de Sikengen, I apprehend the following method to obtain pure and malleable platina will be found a good one.

'Diffolve

Diſſolve the grains of native platina that are leaſt magnetic, in aqua regia. Precipitate the iron by means of phlogiſticated fixed alkaly. Then precipitate whatever elſe will fall, by cauſtic vegetable alkaly. Saturate the liquor with cauſtic foſſil alkaly, and ſet it by to chryſtallize. The yellow chryſtals thus obtained are to be hammered together at a welding heat, and the metallic parts will unite.'

Beſides the other advantages of this tranſlation, the Engliſh names are added to the ſpecies ; and the properties of the different metals, as far as relate to their ſpecific gravity, melting heat, the quantity of phlogiſton neceſſary to their metallic appearance, and their attraction to that quantity, are included in an uſeful table.

The execution is in general valuable for its conciſeneſs and accuracy, rather than for ornament and elegance. In a ſubject of this kind the former are indiſpenſible, and the latter frequently unneceſſary or impertinent. Perhaps, however, without loſing the one, we might have attained a greater ſhare of the other ; but where we have received ſo many advantages we ought to be neither captious or faſtidious. On a careful compariſon we have found no real errors. Some little inaccuracies, either of Bergman or his Engliſh editor, are tacitly corrected ; and what is ſo conciſe in the original, as to be ſometimes leſs intelligible, is carefully explained. Dr. Withering will not complain if we ſuggeſt that ' principia proxima' are not adequately rendered by ' component parts,' but ſhould probably be the parts which *immediately* compoſe the body. Pyrites, § 152. of Cronſtedt, is at leaſt compoſed of the metal, phlogiſton, and vitriolic acid ; but its principia proxima are only iron and ſulphur. Again, we underſtand the laſt ſentence of § 12. in the following manner : ' In a ſyſtem of this kind, the advantages of both methods coincide.' Theſe are trivial errors, which we have marked from no invidious motive ; and we may be eaſily believed, when we obſerve, that we have detected none more material. We take this opportunity of expreſſing our wiſh, that the promiſed tranſlation of Cronſtedt may be enriched with the diſcoveries both of Bergman and his tranſlator.

Sacred Biography : Or, the Hiſtory of the Patriarchs from Adam to Abraham incluſively : Being a Courſe of Lectures delivered at the Scots Church, London Wall. By Henry Hunter, D. D. 8vo. 7s. Murray.

THESE ſermons were Sunday evening lectures, delivered at the Scots church, London Wall, in the year 1782, before a numerous audience of different denominations, who honoured them with a regular attendance, and a general approbation.

The subjects on which the author discourses are, the histories of Adam, Cain, Abel, Enoch, Noah, Melchizedec, and Abraham.

In this undertaking, his purpose, he says, is not to answer the objections and refute the cavils of unbelievers, but humbly to attempt to illustrate, enforce, and apply, Scripture truth to those who receive the Bible as the word of God, as the guide of their faith, the source of their hope, and the rule of their life. With this view, he chiefly confines himself to those pious and practical observations, which the more remarkable events in the lives of the patriarchs naturally suggest.

The theological notions which he adopts relative to sacrifices, atonement, imputed righteousness, &c. are Calvinistic. —A point on which he particularly insists is, the discovery of types in the history of almost all the patriarchs.—Such resemblances are, in general, merely imaginary, and may be increased to any number by an author of an inventive genius.

In the following passage, which casually presents itself, the author has been guilty of a slight inadvertency.

In commenting on Gen. xv. 5. he says, ' The stars are represented as innumerable, because this is apparently the case ; and justified by the ideas and language of all nations, though the fact be *philosophically otherwise.*'

This is not true. Derham speaks more philosophically when he says : ' When we view the heavens with our glasses, and discover many more stars than our naked eye could reach ; and when we again view them with better and better instruments, and still discover more and more of those starry globes ; when particularly we survey what they call the Milky Way, and see the prodigious number, I may almost say, clusters of stars, that fill that region of the heavens, and cause that remarkable whiteness there ; I say, when we see such prodigious numbers of those heavenly bodies, which *no art of man can number,* and when we farther consider, that in all probability we do not see the half, nay, perchance, not the thousandth part of what the heavens do contain, we cannot but be struck with amazement at such a multitude of God's glorious works.' Astrotheology, b. ii. c. 1.

The truth is, the stars, whatever their apparent number may be, are, in reality, innumerable. The blue expanse around us is, on all sides, without limits, and no human imagination can recount even the systems, which occupy those boundless regions.

Our

Our author's language, in thefe lectures, is, in general, perfpicuous and animated.

Forms of Prayer, and other Offices, for the Ufe of Unitarian Societies. By Jofeph Prieftley, LL.D. F.R.S. 8vo. 4s. Johnfon.

I N the introduction to this work, the author recommends the forming of Unitarian focieties, confifting of laymen only; and endeavours to remove every objection which may be aleged againft fuch a fcheme. In order to promote this defign, he has drawn up a fet of forms for baptifm, the Lord's fupper, funerals, and every other part of public worfhip.

' As there is nothing, he fays, peculiarly facred in the offices of baptifm, and the Lord's fupper, let the elders of fuch focieties, by all means, perform thofe fervices, whenever here fhall be occafion for them, without having recourfe to minifters of neighbouring places; and let thofe of the elders, who have moft leifure and ability, catechize the children, and inftruct young perfons belonging to the fociety.'

The moft formidable objection to fuch a fcheme as this, rifes from the ignorance or the abfurdity of thofe laymen, who may attempt to form and conduct thefe focieties. The folemnity, the dignity, the importance of public worfhip, and Chriftian congregation, are happily preferved by a grave and prudent minifter, regularly educated for that purpofe. But a congregation, under the direction of illiterate mechanics, can receive no edification, can command no refpect. Such minifters will expofe the fociety to ridicule and contempt.

The forms of prayer, which our author prefcribes, are calculated for Unitarian focieties; but breathe a fpirit of piety and philanthropy, becoming Chriftians of all denominations.

In the form for infant baptifm, the author confiders that rite, not as any thing done in the name of the child, that can lay him under any obligation, or properly entitle him to any privileges afterwards, but fimply as what belongs to the profeffion of Chriftianity in the parents. Having therefore directed the child to be fprinkled or immerfed, and ' baptized in the name of Jefus Chrift,' he recommends an addrefs to the parents, fetting forth their duty and obligation, with refpect to the religious and Chriftian education of their child, and fubjoins a prayer fuitable to the occafion.

He likewife prefcribes a form for the adminiftration of adult baptifm,' either by fprinkling, or, if the perfon to be baptized fhould choofe it, by immerfion.

In

In the form for the celebration of the Lord's supper, one of his directions is as follows : let the person who officiates, after eating of the bread himself, deliver it to those who distribute it to the communicants, saying, " Take and eat in remembrance of Christ.'

Whether these words are to be used only once, or are to be repeatedly addressed to every communicant, we are not informed. But however this may be, we conceive, that a far more solemn and pathetic admonition might be addressed on this occasion to each individual, separately and singly, with the greatest propriety, without any appearance of mystery or superstition.

Elements of Geometry, in which all the material Propositions in the first six, eleventh and twelfth Books of Euclid, are demonstrated with Conciseness and Perspicuity. By William Scott. 12mo. 3s. Robinson.

IT is a matter of much surprize, that, at a time when the sciences were yet in their infancy, a work should have been composed so perfect and complete, that all the efforts of later writers have not enabled them to add any thing either to its perspicuity, elegance, or precision. Euclid, the great father of geometry, must have compiled his Elements at least two thousand years ago; and, in all this long period, they have lost nothing of their orginal lustre, but, like the poems of Homer, still remain unparalleled and unrivalled. This work is, indeed, a master-piece. It may have, as all human productions must, some blemishes ; but if its object and design be properly attended to, its different parts compared, and the order and arrangement of the whole strictly examined, it must be considered as one of the greatest works of genius and judgment that ever appeared in the world. To every person, therefore, who would wish to obtain a perfect knowlege of the pure and genuine principles of Geometry, we would recommend either the original Elements of Euclid, or the late professor Simson's excellent translation of them, in preference to every other system that has yet been published.

The liberal encomiums we have bestowed upon this great work, and the advice we have given to the geometrical student, will, it is presumed, be not thought impertinent, or foreign to the purpose of a Review. They are neither the effect of partiality nor prejudice ; but are designed merely as incentives to emulation, and for the use of such young people as have a taste for this elegant science, but are yet unacquainted with the best and most effectual means of acquiring it. But, notwith-

withstanding the great superiority and eminence of the original
Elements, it must be confessed that a judicious abridgement
of them would be extremely acceptable. The present extensive circle of the sciences, as well as particular exigencies and
situations, makes it frequently necessary for the student to
content himself with such a knowlege of first principles only
as will enable him to proceed to those branches of mathematics or physics that are the more immediate objects of his
pursuit. Euclid's extreme rigour, and the length of some of
his demonstrations, makes him frequently appear tedious, and
irksome to young beginners. The nature of his plan likewise
make it necessary to introduce many propositions that have apparently no great practical application.

For these reasons, a book of the Elements, neither too much
relaxed in its principles, nor too scrupulously accurate, is a
thing much wanted. The work before us is said to have been
written with this view; and had the author's execution of it
been equal to the ideas we formed from the title-page, we
should have been happy to have given him the praise he would
have merited. But the impartiality necessary to be observed
upon these occasions, oblige us to acknowlege that, in this
respect, he is greatly excelled by many of his predecessors;
who have, notwithstanding, in our opinion, failed likewise in
their attempts of what might have been expected from them.
The author of the present performance appears to have been
unhappy as well in his arrangement as his choice of propositions, and the manner of demonstrating them. His treating
of triangles, parallelograms, circles, &c. separately, is puerile,
and what the nature of the subject does not admit. The propositions should have been the most useful and necessary; and
the demonstrations unembarassed, clear, and explicit. Geometry has always been considered as the most excellent logic; but
this author's free use of algebraic symbols entirely destroys
the sylogistic mode of reasoning, and, instead of simplifying
the demonstration, perplexes and obscures it.

His demonstrations respecting proportion and solids are, he
says, as short and simple as can be devised, and at the same
time founded on axioms that must satisfy the most scrupulous.
In this, however, we must beg leave to differ from him. His
doctrine of proportionality is confined to commensurable mag-
nitudes only; and is, besides, so inaccurately and obscurely
delivered, that we can discover no traces of that taste and
judgment which is necessary in the management of this delicate
subject. The axiom likewise upon which he builds his solid
geometry is extremely exceptionable. It is founded upon

Cavallerius'

Cavallerius' method of indivisibles, a doctrine almost entirely exploded, and which ought by no means to be used in demonstrating the first principles of geometry.

Observations on the Police or Civil Government of Westminster, with a Proposal for a Reform. By Edward Sayer, Esq. 4to. 2s. 6d. Debrett.

THE police of Westminster is universally acknowledged to be extremely defective; and a reform of it has long been an object of desire to all but the profligate and inconsiderate part of the inhabitants. Indeed the whole nation, as well as the metropolis and its neighbourhood, is deeply interested in the municipal government of this city; nor can there be any branch of domestic regulation which claims more strongly the attention of the legislature. Previous, however, to a parliamentary investigation of the subject, we are glad to find it treated with much clearness and ability by the present author; who seems to have been at no small pains both to obtain a distinct idea of the political constitution of Westminster, and to devise such means as are necessary, not only for correcting its abuses, but supplying its remarkable defects.

For rendering the subject more intelligible, Mr. Sayer has very properly introduced his observations with a general account of the church of Westminster. He takes notice that the abbey of Westminster, from which this great city has gradually extended itself, over a large tract of country, was founded originally upon the ruins of a temple of Apollo, situated in the island of Thorney or Thorns, A. D. 610; and an abbot and monks of the Benedictine order placed in it. This building being destroyed by the Danes, in 958, it was rebuilt with great splendor by Edward the Confessor, who, in 1049, endowed it with great additional revenues. From this period it continued in the possession of the black monks, until the general dissolution of monasteries at the Reformation. Devolving then into the hands of the crown, it was, in the thirty-second year of Henry the Eighth, erected into a bishop's see; and received, as its diocese, the whole county of Middlesex, except Fulham, the residence of the bishop of London. The bishoprick was abolished by Edward the Sixth, in 1550, leaving the dean and chapter by themselves as a collegiate church; and in 1556, under queen Mary, this establishment gave way to the restoration of the abbot and black or Benedictine monks. But in 1560, the collegiate church was reinstated by queen Elizabeth, with the same powers and emoluments which it now retains. The most important of these is the right to the franchise of Westminster, held under various charters of great antiquity. At the time when this extraordinary trust was first invested in an ecclesiastical body, the whole district was almost entirely a rural manor; the town consisting only of Tothil-street, and the adjoining alleys, with the sanctuary, then a refuge for even the most atrocious offenders.

The franchise is vested in the dean and chapter of the collegiate church of St. Peter, Westminster, and enjoys extraordinary privileges; many of which, however, have long been disused. Those remaining are, the holding a court leet, the custody of a gaol, and the return of all writs and process. The dean and chapter also claim, under their grant, all escheats, deodands, goods of felons, waifs, estrays, fines, whether imposed by the king's justices or others, within the franchise; and also the soil of the common, called Tothill-fields.

The chief officer of the dean and chapter, for assisting them in the exercise of the privileges incident to their franchise, is a high-steward, appointed for life; an office usually conferred upon one of the nobility. The chief duty of his office consists in holding and presiding at the several courts belonging to the dean and chapter; and of these he is the judge. The office, however, is executed by a deputy, appointed by the high-steward, with the approbation of the dean and chapter. The next officer is the high-bailiff, who is usually constituted for life. The business of his office requires him to execute all writs and process within the franchise, to preside at the election of members of parliament, and also to attend the courts of the dean and chapter. To this officer the dean and chapter generally grant a lease, during the time of his continuing in office, of all forfeitures, fines, and other profits and perquisites, to which they are entitled, as lords of the franchise, at a reserved yearly rent. The other officers of the franchise are a coroner, clerk of the market, and a keeper of the gaol; with a high-constable and eighty petty constables, chosen annually.

Mr. Sayer, after describing the constitution of Westminster more fully than our limits will permit, proceeds to point out the great defects under which its government at present labours. It appears, in particular, that the civil and criminal jurisdictions of this system are so unhappily constituted, that they tend to defeat the purposes of their own establishment. For instance, the high-steward in the court leet appoints the constables, and has a summary and discretionary right vested in him to punish them by fine; but has no right, as a magi-

G g 4

fary to give the deaf a tolerable general underftanding of
their own language, fo as to read, write, and fpeak it with
eafe.

' The manner in which this is effected is, by firft fhewing
them how the mouth is formed for the production of the vowels, letting them fee the external effect that vocalized breath
hath upon the internal part of the wind-pipe, and caufing
them to feel with their thumbs and fingers the vibration of
the larynx, firft in the teacher, then in themfelves. When
they found any of the vowels, then they are fhewn the written
form of what they have expreffed, till they are perfected in
the knowlege of the vowels or vocal founds; to which fucceeds the formation of fyllables and words, then the meaning
of common words, and finally the conftruction of a fentence
or fentences, out of which all defcriptions of the mind or will
are compofed, or every exhibition of perception or volition,
which is the whole of language.'

Dr. Johnfon, in his Journey to the Weftern Iflands of Scotland, fays, the improvement of Mr. Braidwood's pupils is
wonderful. They not only fpeak, write, and underftand
what is written, but if he that fpeaks looks towards them,
and modifies his organs by diftinct and full utterance, they
know fo well what is fpoken, that it is an expreffion fcarcely
figurative to fay, ' they hear with the eye.'

To conceive the theory of this art, ' we need only confider
with a little attention the mechanifm of fpeech, and we fhall
foon find, that there is required for fpeaking certain pofitions
and motions of the organs of the mouth, fuch as the tongue,
the teeth, lips, and palate, that cannot be from nature, but
muft be the effect of art; for their action, when they are employed in the enunciation of fpeech, is fo different from their
natural and quiefcent fituation, that nothing but long ufe
and exercife could have taught us to employ them in that
way *.'

The generality of the world, as the author of this tract remarks, are apt fuddenly, but erroneoufly, to combine the idea
of idiotifm with that of the ftate of the deaf and dumb;
whereas no greater error can fubfift, as may plainly appear by
the inftances of perfection to which many of Mr. Braidwood's
pupils have arrived in language and other arts, as well as in
the fciences. The truth is, the fcale of intellectual comprehenfions or underftandings in them is as varioufly graduated,
as in other perfons; many of them indeed poffefs a quicknefs
of apprehenfion, a fcope of imagination and fagacity, above

' * Orig. and Prog. of Lang. p. 182.'

the

imes by the rapacity, and at laft by the dawning tafte of the onquerors. Thus, while Rome was fuddenly enriched by reafures not its own, the original artifts were difcouraged by hefe repeated plunders. Amidft 'public mourning and defolaion,' tafte could be but imperfectly cultivated; and, though the fthmian games were ordered to be continued by the conquerors, hey were attended with little pleafure, and with lefs emulation. The arms of the Romans, by uniting the feveral different nations to their empire, carried defolation through different kingdoms, and contributed to deftroy the remains of the Grecian art. t languifhed in every nation, and every period; for their riches vere forcibly carried away to adorn the capital of the world.

Our author next purfues the Grecian art in Rome, and in Syracufe: what remained of it in Greece was carried on under Roman aufpices, and adorned the capital; but, after the Trimvirate, again enriched its native foil. During the republic, ve have few monuments of Roman artifts; the pretended bucker of Scipio, and his feveral portraits, are fuppofed by our auhor to be the productions of a different period, or to reprefent other events. At this time the arts, though underftood, were not remarkably encouraged, fince thefe Republicans valued hemfelves on the moderation of their manners, and an hoourable equality. When different citizens acquired an afcendency, it was announced by the fplendour of their public vorks; and Sylla, the deftroyer of art in Greece, was its chief upport in Italy. Cæfar was the fucceffor of Sylla in every hing but his moderation in the refignation of power. While fimple individual, the magnificenfe of his tafte diftinguifhed is buildings; and, when advanced to power, the afhes of Coiath fupplied ornaments which the art of Rome could not produce. The different victories of the triumvirs, of Pompey, nd at laft of Auguftus, introduced greater numbers of Grecian rtifts, at firft in the guife of flaves, and afterwards of freednen. Our author proceeds to mention the moft celebrated of hefe, whether in Rome or ftill in Greece, and to defcribe feeral works of that period; but, as we wifh to confine ourfelves to the influence of *events*, on the progrefs of art, we fhall proceed to mention his obfervation on the arts during the reign of Auguftus.

The tranquillity enjoyed in Rome, the riches, the fplendor, tafte, and liberality of its mafter, attracted the Grecian artifts from a country where they were funk by oppreffion, and not excited by any encouragement. Auguftus placed ftatues of illuftrious Romans in the Forum, repaired thofe already there, erected others to the gods, and appointed an officer to infpect, and probably to preferve them. But the works of a man who boafted that he had found a city of brick, and left one of marble, cannot be enumerated in this article. Our author's account is alfo extended by difcuffions of pretended relics, and enquiries about the perfons they reprefent. They are highly en-

entertaining; but, as we have endeavoured to purfue a continued narration, we muft leave his remarks to thofe who are able to read them in the work itfelf.

Tafte and ftyle feemed already to decline. Thofe, who wifhed to pleafe Mæcenas, are faid to have aimed at a lightnefs and effeminacy in their works, which he is reported to have admired. In painting, the tafte was already depraved by affected ornaments, and unnatural reprefentations. But thefe are always the attendants of a polifhed nation; for the fimplicity of nature and true tafte is unable to fatisfy the inceffant craving for novelty and fancy. Artifts, who muft follow rather than lead the public, will confequently fall into that ftyle which chiefly gratifies their patrons: ' thofe who live to pleafe, muft pleafe to live.' We need not apply thefe obfervations to the prefent age: the judicious reader will fpare us this trouble.

The harfh and fufpicious temper of Tiberius was not likely to advance thefe elegant amufements. Statues, at this time, were contemptible, as they were lavifhed on fpies and informers; and the brutal folly and childifh caprice of his fucceffors fcarcely furnifh a different picture. The characters of many of the fucceeding emperors will be a fufficient proof of their conduct in this refpect. The opulence, and the tafte of individuals, however, feems to have encouraged art, though it appeared ftill to decline; and our author, from the relics of this period, which were either the works of that time, or recent fpoils from the Grecian temples, is led into many amufing difcuffions. The defcription of the Apollo Belvidere, taken probably from his temple at Delphos, is elegant, and almoft fublime. The judicious parfimony of Vefpafian was of more advantage to art, than the oftentatious prodigality of his predeceffors. He encouraged artifts and philofophers by his attention, and his rewards; and the gardens of Saluft, the favourite refidence of the emperor, has afforded a great quantity of ftatues and bufts. His fucceffor was actuated by fimilar views; but, during the reign of Domitian, the columns worked at Athens for the temple of the Olympian Jupiter were little valued, till they had undergone fome change in their form;—a proof of ' a fenfible decay of tafte!'—Yet Domitian treated the Grecian artifts with greater attention than even Vefpafian and Titus; but the fhort and tumultuous reign of his fucceffor left him little leifure to improve this beginning change.

Rome and the Roman empire recovered new life under the dominion of Trajan, who practifed virtues, almoft unknown on the throne of the Cæfars. Liberal without prodigality, he received and encouraged artifts: without confining their labours to perpetuate the memory of himfelf, he communicated that honour to merit of every kind. We find that he even erected ftatues to youths of promifing expectations, who died in the flower of their age. The public works of Trajan were equally magnificent and elegant: his column, and the coloffal ftatue on the top of it, are frequently mentioned, and their remains share the attention of our antiquary. In this full tide of splendour and prosperity, when arts were both admired and cultivated, Greece seems to have been forsaken, and the plant decayed on its native soil. The Grecian cities seldom erected statues but to the emperor; and the representatives of a former hero or demi-god, with a change only of the inscription, exhibited the new objects of adulation, the present deity. While former emperors confined their regards to the Capitol, Adrian surveyed almost the whole of the empire; and, instead of depressing the country of art and artists, he excited their emulation, and encouraged their ingenuity; so that Greece had no period more happy, and no friend more warm, than the successor of Trajan, himself an artist. The temples, the mausoleum, and the villa of Adrian, are monuments both of his taste and magnificence; and even the statues taken from the last edifice, at present enrich almost all the cabinets of Europe. Yet the taste of Adrian is not unexceptionable. In his writings he affected obsolete terms and barbarous phrases. In his statues he followed the taste of different countries, with a facility which would disgrace a connoisseur: we have already mentioned the different imitations of the works of Egypt executed by the command of this weak and superstitious emperor.

But, as this is the last school, the last surviving spark of decaying art, we should be a little more particular. The different heads of Antinous still equal almost any of the more genuine remains of antiquity; the elegance and softness of the smaller figures, the grand sublimity of the colossal statues, are solid proofs of the capacity of the statuary. The portaits and medals of Adrian are also extremely beautiful. It may however be observed, that the piercing eyes of the antiquary finds defects in some of these representatives; the different parts are not always finished with accuracy and elegance.

It was the age of the Antonines which gave the mortal wound to art, though they possessed both genius and taste. The philosophers and sophists, who were pensioned by them, looked only on the artist as an experienced workman, and the emulation of a person who aimed at rivalling Phidias was considered by them as mean and contemptible. But, from the encouragement of the emperors, art still seemed to exist: it was, however, ' the apparent ease of a dying man, whose life hangs on a thread, and who thinks himself somewhat better, a little before his death; like the light of a lamp, which sparkles brightly, and exhausts itself in the effort.' The artists of the time of Adrian lived during the age of his successors, and retained their taste; but at their death their science sunk at once, with scarce a struggle to point out its remaining strength. Literature and art fell together; the Grecians, at the time of Commodus, scarcely knew their own language, and neglected Oppian as obscure, because he imitated the words and expressions

fions of Homer. The Hercules Commodus, which feems to
refcue this æra from the imputation of barbarity, carries on the
lion's fkin the young Ajax, the fon of Telamon, rather than
the emperor; and our author affures us, that it is a Grecian
work of antiquity, and one of the moft beautiful relics preferved at Rome. The gladiator is equally the work of another age,
and reprefents a very different perfon.

From Septimius Severus till the total extinction of art at
Conftantinople, we have a continued progrefs of decaying tafte,
and imperfect execution. It is ufelefs to defcribe them; and the
total extinction of art is fcarcely more interefting. In the year 663
the emperor Conftantius, grandfon of Heraclius, went to Rome,
to fave what had efcaped the fury of the barbarians, and depofited the remains at Syracufe; but, after his death, they
were feized by the Saracens, and carried to Alexandria. When
Conftantinople was taken by the Turks, under Baudouin, at
the beginning of the thirteeth century, the different ftatues
were melted to coin money. The Juno of Samos felt this fevere
deftiny; and we are told that the head of this ftatue, when broken
in pieces, loaded four carriages. To complete the picture, we
are prefented with a work of the lower empire, of an artift who
aims at gratifying a man raifed to dignity. He is feated on a
maffy pedeftal, without form or ornament; two young flaves
draw the curtain to exhibit him, when he confents to be fhown.
' O Grecians,' exclaims count Caylus, with honeft indignation,
' if you are already fallen into fo deplorable a ftate, and in
your own country, what will be our lot in a few years!'

We have thus at laft completed our account of this entertaining work; and if, in the laft volume, we have preferred giving
a feries of events to particular or occafional extracts, it was
chiefly to convey a more accurate and comprehenfive idea of
the labours of the antiquary. We need not add to our former
character of the work, and its author.—It is rich in entertainment and information; and thofe who have once perufed it,
will forget the labour in its gratification.

Frederici Wilhelmi Paffel Commentarii de Republica Batava. 8vo.
Lugduni Batavorum.

THE author of this excellent work, is profeffor of laws at
Leyden; and has defigned this publication for the ufe of
his auditors: but it will prove a very acceptable prefent to the
public at large, as it gives the firft complete and authentic account, hitherto publifhed, of the whole political conftitution
of the United Netherlands, and all their dependencies.

His tafk was a very delicate and difficult one; and he has acquitted himfelf with great fuccefs and credit. His intention
was, to form a juft idea of a whole, exceedingly complicated; to defcribe all its different parts, and their mutual relations to one another; to enter into the detail of the conftitution
of every particular province, fometimes even into that of particular

ticular cities and towns ; of the commerce of the republic and of her alliances ; to perform all this, unbiaffed by party-fpirit ; to comprize fuch a variety of fubjects in a fhort abftract, calculated for a courfe of lectures, without omitting any thing effential, and without admitting any redundancy.

In order to judge of the ftate of a country, he remarks, four things are to be confidered. 1. The advantages it has received, or not received from nature. 2. The effects of the induftry or neglect of its inhabitants, for improving the gifts of nature, for fupplying deficiencies, or for correcting natural defects. 3. The influence of laws and public eftablifhments on the nation, in order to excite and encourage her to improve the power and profperity of the ftate. 4. Finally, the affiftance wanted by that nation from foreign nations, in order to acquire what fhe wants, or to preferve her actual poffeffions.

Accordingly he divides his work into four parts.

In the firft, he treats of the country and its inhabitants. He begins with the origin of the commonwealth ; fhews by what degree and means fhe has attained her prefent ftate, and the extent of her dominions, including her colonies both in the Eaft and Weft Indies. He examines the nature of the foil of every province, her productions, and the produce of the colonies. He then proceeds to the confideration of the inhabitants, their numbers, their mode of living, the provifions made for the aged, the orphans, the poor ; the equality and differences between the feveral ranks of citizens, and their refpective advantages ; at the head of which he juftly places liberty, which he defines precifely, and then diftinguifhes it into public liberty, regarding the whole body of the nation, and particular liberty relating to individuals. The latter is founded on the natural liberty of living according to one's own choice, without infringing the rights of others : fo that, according to him, the liberty enjoyed by the Dutch, is natural liberty, limited only by the general good of the public, which the law muft determine. He enters into curious and interefting details on the nature of the laws, and the manner of propofing and enacting them.

Public liberty, according to him, confifts in the exemption of a nation from any fear of arbitrary power ; and this idea he illuftrates by faying that this liberty exifts wherever the advantages and mifchiefs refulting from a good or a bad adminiftration are common both to thofe who govern, and to thofe who obey. He fhews the precautions taken by the laws, in order to prevent any citizen's being wronged or injured, and to procure him redrefs and fatisfaction for any wrong he may have fuftained.

He next proceeds to the conftitution of religion, and the rights of the Dutch church. He confiders religion, not as a political engine, but as the moft effectual means for teaching people wifely to govern and to obey. This religion, according to the doctrine of Chrift and of his apoftles, confifts chiefly in

con-

conceiving juſt notions of the Deity; in a good conduct; in hurting no man, and in benefiting all who may need our aſſiſtance. He ſurveys the various religions tolerated by the Dutch government, and the police of the predominant church; and his poſitions on theſe ſubjects are drawn from the *placards* or edicts of the ſtates general, and of thoſe of each particular province.

Having noticed the univerſities, gymnaſia, and ſchools, for inſtructing youth, he proceeds to the various ſources from which the Dutch derive their ſubſiſtence and their wealth, viz. navigation, fiſheries, trade, manufactures, and the Eaſt and Weſt India companies. Theſe articles are treated ſo judiciouſly, that all the advantages reſulting from them either to the country at large, or to individuals, may be juſtly appreciated. His ſtatement of the proſperous or declining ſtate of the different manufactures, deſerves particular notice, and ſhews the true cauſe of the decay of many of them. The particular details given of the Eaſt India commerce, of its different objects, and the ſettlement of the company, are equally curious and intereſting. The firſt part concludes with ſhort, but judicious reflections, on the means employed by the republic for preſerving that proſperity ſhe enjoys, and by applying to her, what Tacitus obſerves of the *Chauci*: 'Populus inter Germanos nobiliſſimus, quique magnitudenem ſuam malit juſtitia fueri. Sine cupiditate, ſine impotentia, quieti ſecretique, nulla provocant bella, nullis raptibus aut latrociniis populantur.—Prompta tamen omnibus, arma, ac, ſi res poſcat, exercitus, &c.'

In the ſecond part, Profeſſor Peſtel treats of the form and adminiſtration of government in every particular province. ——This part muſt have coſt him a great deal of labour, as the Dutch republic is, next to that of the Swiſs, perhaps the moſt complicated government exiſting. Strangers have but very confuſed notions of her conſtitution, and even natives hardly know more of it than what relates immediately to that particular diſtrict in which they reſpectively live: there are but few among them whoſe knowlege extends to the conſtitution of the adjoining provinces, or to that of the whole body politic.

Previous to elucidating the ſubject of the part laſt mentioned, the author deſcribes the ſtate through which every province paſſed before ſhe arrived at her preſent conſtitution. He gives a conciſe, yet ſufficient idea, of the laws, the cuſtoms, the form of government: and always refers to the authorities and the reſolutions of the ſtate from which he has drawn whatever he aſſerts; and always illuſtrates the different adminiſtrations he treats of, by carefully comparing them with the principles of public law. He enlarges chiefly on the conſtitution of Holland, as the moſt conſiderable of the Seven Provinces: he carefully deſcribes the ſeveral boards or aſſemblies entruſted with the different parts of the ſovereign powers; he determines their reſpective functions, and the limits of their ſeveral juriſdictions. The article

rticle in which he exhibits the various taxes, and the manner of
aifing them, muft have likewife coft him great pains; he muft
have examined the voluminous collection of placards or edicts
ucceffively iffued by fovereign authority, on this fubject; and
where thefe informations were deficient, he was obliged to con-
ult the receivers of thofe refpective taxes.   This tafk, however, was neceffary for the inftruction of the young noblemen
nd gentlemen defigned to take a fhare in the future adminiftra-
ion of their country; and at the fame time its performance
annot but be very acceptable to foreigners, defirous of infor-
nation on thefe heads.

In the third part, he examines the rights which the feveral
provinces have referved to themfelves by the union of Utrecht,
and the duties in which they then engaged.   Here he explains
he functions and authority of the affembly of the ftates-ge-
neral, of the council of ftate, and the chamber of accounts of
he generality.   Thence he proceeds to the poft of the ftadtholder, as commander in chief of the army, under the title of
captain-general; and on this occafion, he juft touches on a very
delicate queftion concerning military jurifdiction.   That military delinquencies of foldiers are not to be punifhed but by
their officers, is generally agreed : the queftion here is of crimes
of a civil nature; would not the rights of each province be
infringed, if delinquents, in fuch cafes, were to be exempted
from their jurifdiction ? A great deal has been written on this
ubject, yet nothing has hitherto been clearly decided.   Our
author confines himfelf to report and ftate the arguments on
either fide of the queftion, but leaves his readers to judge for
themfelves.   After this, he treats of the Dutch navy, of the
functions of the admiralty, and of thofe of the ftadtholder, as
admiral-general.   The laft chapter treats of the adminiftration
of the territory belonging in common to all the United Provinces, and called the generality's country, *pays de la genera-
lité.*

The relation in which the republic ftands with regard to
other nations, are the fubject of the fourth part of this treatife.— Her conduct towards them in times of peace or war is
fuch, fays he, that, without leffening her dignity, it fhows
only her defire of offending none of her neighbours.   For this
purpofe, various meafures and precautions are taken.   He then
fpeaks of her ambaffadors, minifters, refidents, confuls in foreign countries, of their refpective functions, and the rights
enjoyed by them.   He concludes his work by an account of
the alliances of the United Netherlands with the different
powers of Europe.

That this laft part is lefs compleat than it was originally intended to be, is what Profeffor Peftel himfelf confeffes; but
he was obliged to publifh the work fomewhat abruptly, in order
to appeafe the impatience of his auditors.   He promifes, however, to treat the feveral fubjects which he has here pointed
out,

out, more fully hereafter; and finally declares himself ready and willing to avail himself of any effential correction or improvement that may be offered.

Such, however, is the firft edition of his work, which is one of the moft valuable performances publifhed in his age, and country. The fubject is generaly and highly interefting, the method accurate and perfpicuous, the diction elegant. The work may eafily be fuppofed to be ftill fufceptible of great improvements, which its judicious author will, no doubt, find ample opportunities to make in future editions.

Hiftoria Doctrinæ de vero Deo, omnium verum Auctore atque Rectore, confcripta a Chr. Meiners. 8vo. Lemgow.

THIS work was occafioned by a prize-queftion, propofed by the managers of Stolpe's Foundation; but it was not fent to Leyden, becaufe the author could not confine his enquiries within the prefcribed limits of forty pages.

The treatife is divided into two parts. In the firft, the author enquires whether the knowlege of one fole Creator and governor of the world exifted among the moft celebrated ancient nations, or their priefts; and in the fecond part, he ftates the doctrine of the great philofophers, concerning the origin of all things, and one fole and true God.

He begins with obferving, that all modern writers have conceived the acquifition of the knowlege of one fole true God, as either too eafy, or too difficult; and hence fallen into two oppofite extremes, equally erroneous. Some imagined that all nations have known the Creator of the world, either by revelation, or by inftructions and traditions from other nations, or by their own reflections; whilft other writers denied in general, and without exception, that man has ever rifen to the thought of one fole God, without being led to it by revelation. Yet, though both opinions are erroneous, that which trufts too little to the intellectual powers of mankind, left to themfelves, appears to the author to approach nearer to truth, than that which trufts too much to them. In his opinion, the idea of one fole univerfal Creator and God, is, by all hiftorical accounts, one of the moft difficult and lateft to be found by the human mind; and even the prefervation of that idea, when once conceived, is far from being fo eafy as is generally thought. To form that idea is a tafk as impracticable to uncivilized and rude nations, as it would be to them to produce at once a complete mafter-piece of art. He therefore, in the hiftory of that idea, paffes over all uninformed or half-informed people or tribes, and confines himfelf to thofe only to whom, on account either of their antiquity, or of their progrefs in arts and fciences, the knowlege of a fole true Deity has been or may be afcribed.

Of this knowlege, no traces are found in ancient Egypt, either in the popular religion, or among the priefts, whofe knownowlege in any branch of science was confined within their irst elements, and a very narrow sphere of their experience. This the author proves by a variety of instances and specimens of their ignorance or errors in history, physics, natural history, astronomy, geography; and finally, by the late rise and flow progress of scientific knowlege among the Greeks, who had a very intimate intercourse with the Egyptians for more than one hundred years before they ever began their philoso-phical enquiries, in which they afterwards made so very flow progress, as sufficiently demonstrate that they could not have imported, at once, any great store of knowlege, either from Egypt or any other country.

The ancient Phœnicians excelled, indeed, all other nations in useful arts, commerce, and navigation, but invented no science, strictly so called, nor ever attained a correct idea of the Deity. Both the name and the work of Sanchoniathon, are, by professor Meiners, considered as mere fictions of Philo-biblus ; but even supposing Sanchoniathon's work to be genu-ine, it contains no proof of any scientific knowlege, or any correct and pure notions of the Deity. The author quotes a variety of instances of the grossest and most cruel superstitions, of which the priests and chiefs of the Tyrians and Carthagi-nians were guilty. He considers the Chaldeans in the same light as the Egyptians and Phœnicians ; and thinks Berosus an impudent fabulist, who compiled his pretended History of Chaldea from fragments of the books of Moses, from Platonic allegories, Grecian mythology, and national traditions.

The section relating to the Indians begins with an examen of the accounts given of them by ancient and modern historians and travellers. From the very evidence of the attendants of Alex-ander, who extolled India, by way of compliment to its con-queror, he proves, that the regions between the Indus and Ganges were but very little cultivated at the time of the Greek invasion. He therefore ranks the inconsistent tales of Onesikri-tus and Megasthenes, about the doctrines and wisdom of the Brachmans, with those incredible stories with which these writers were reproached by all antiquity. After Alexander's time, the Indians actually became acquainted with the opi-nions which had been falsely ascribed to their ancestors : they received arts and sciences first from the towns built by Alex-ander in their country, afterwards from the Greeks of Bactria, whose sovereigns subdued a part of India ; afterwards from Christians, who either voluntarily, or being expelled by the bloody persecutions of the Persian kings, settled in great num-bers beyond the Indus, and finally from the Mahometans, who conquered Indostan.

The Chinese also were, in ancient times, polytheists, though they had no temples, nor statues, nor altars. They worshipped rivers, earth, heaven, and numberless fishes, as appears even from their own *Schu-king*. If, as the Jesuits pretend, the Chi-nese

nese had originally the pure religion of nature, they would not have adopted the abfurd worfhip of Lao-kiam and Fo-Confucius, fo far from attacking fuperftition and polytheifm, rather recommended and even enlarged them. Chinefe writers confefs, that even now the greater part of the mandarins know nothing of one true Deity; and that children and youth are inftructed from books which fay not a word of a creator and governor of the univerfe. But the authors of the few Chinefe books which contain purer notions of the Deity, were indebted for the notions, as the Chinefe in general were, for all their knowlege, to their intercourfe with the Bactrians; or to the early emigrations of Indians, Chriftians, and Arabs, into China.

In the laft fection of the firft part, the author proceeds to a furvey of the religion of the moft ancient Greeks, and of their moft celebrated poets. The religion of the firft inhabitants of Greece was very different from what it appears in Homer and Hefiod. Before their intercourfe with foreigners, the Greeks worfhipped ftars, winds, animals, trees, &c. and afterwards received the greater part of the names and human-like figures of the gods, from emigrants from Afia and Africa. Homer and Hefiod, therefore, already found notions of human-like divinities, male and female, their marriages, and generations; and enlarged the popular religion, only by inventing the epithets, relations, arts, and peculiar characteriftics of the figures of their gods.

In Homer, our author finds nothing of what may ftrictly be called cofmogony: and the few obfcure verfes in Hefiod, relating to that fubject, may feem to prove, that the queftion, not concerning the origin of the univerfe, but only concerning the origin of earth, air, feas, mountains, and rivers, was in his times, but of a recent date. Profeffor Meiners confiders Orpheus not as the civilizer of the Greeks, nor as the founder of their myfteries, nor as the inventor of mufic and poetry, nor even as older than Homer and Hefiod. He collects the teftimonies of Plato, Ifocrates, and other writers, concerning the Orphean poems which were circulated in their times, in Greece: he compares thefe with the fragments yet extant; and infers from this comparative view, and the contents and language of the latter, not only that the fragments are not genuine, but alfo that they are of a later date than the times of Ariftotle and Zeno. He concludes this article with confidering the religious notions of the Greeks, in their moft enlightened times; and fhews, that even their wifeft and greateft ftatefmen and commanders, entertained nearly the fame notions of Gods and religion, with thofe that are to be met with in the poems of Homer and Hefiod; that the doctrine of one God had never been ftarted before the time of Anaxagoras, and then in the Eleufinian myfteries; and that the fragments of the laws of Zaleukus are not genuine.

Is

In the first four sections of the second part, the author states and explains the opinions of the most ancient Ionians, of the Pythagoreans, the Eleatics, and of Heraclitus and Empedocles, on the origin and nature of all things; and denies that any one of all these philosophers ever had a knowlege of the true God. In the section of the Pythagoreans, he examines concisely, the original historical sources, and at the same time points out the real object of their alliance, their mysteries, and their symbols. Anaxagoras was the first in Greece who publicly announced the existence of one Creator and governor of the universe. His thoughts, and the sublime doctrines of Socrates, are stated and illustrated in the fifth section, with the beauties and defects of both. Plato differed from his master rather in the expression than in the substance of his notions of the nature of God. He demonstrated the providence of God, by arguments still more forcible than those of Socrates; he was more exempt from national prejudices and popular superstition, and attacked prevailing and pernicious errors with yet greater spirit than his master had done. He was also the first who may be confidently said to have conceived God to be an immaterial or incorporeal being. This idea of Plato's was adopted by Aristotle, who with him, maintained the doctrine of a divine providence, and who produced a new proof of the existence of an eternal and all-perfect Governor of the universe. In other respects he frequently contradicted Plato, as he contradicted himself in his doctrine of the fifth nature.

Of all the Greek philosophers, the Stoics entered into the fullest explanations and proofs of the doctrines of the nature of God; they justified providence with the greatest zeal; they asserted no necessity, yet in many opinions deviated from truth, but most so in their account of the divine substance, and the production and destruction of the world.

Epicurus thought chance, or a blind irrational nature, more powerful than any Deity; he denied the existence of an intelligent Creator and governor of the universe; yet spoke of gods, whom, for prudential reasons, he, as much as possible, assimilated to the gods of the Greeks.

MONTHLY CATALOGUE.
POLITICAL.

Impartial Considerations on a Bill now depending in Parliament, for establishing certain Regulations for the better Management of the Territories, Revenues, and Commerce of this Kingdom in the East Indies. 8vo. 1s. Debrett.

THE subject to which this pamphlet relates, is the East India bill, which at present so much agitates both the commercial and political world. The author of the Considerations endea-

vours

vours to fupport the bill upon the principle ufually urged, of the expediency, or rather abfolute neceffity of fuch a meafure. But, unfortunately for his argument, he has not produced any proof to corroborate his affertion. He infifts that the company is bank-rupt, though the idea of its infolvency appears to have been fa-tisfactorily refuted by authentic documents. He draws an inference in favour of the bill, from the legal practice of taking from lunatics the management of their own property; but he has not even attempted to infinuate that the company is in fuch a predicament. In his ftatement of affairs, he generally takes his premifes for granted; his illuftrations are inappofite; his con-clufions, when not evidently fallacious, are not eftablifhed on a folid foundation; and, what never can be admitted as decifive, he defends the utility of the projected board of direction, by appeal-ing to the unblemifhed characters of thofe who were intended to compofe it.

A Retrofpective View and Confideration of India Affairs, &c. 8vo. 2s. Debrett.

Though the late tranfactions in the Eaft Indies are of no fmall importance to Great Britain, yet a minute detail of them, efpe-cially when unfupported by authority, is little calculated to afford either ufeful information or entertainment to the public. We fhall therefore forbear giving any abftract of this narrative. Our referve on this fubject is rendered the more neceffary, as public events and meafures are intimately connected with perfonal characters, which it might be unjuft either to cenfure or approve, without evidence properly authenticated. We mean not, how-ever, by thefe obfervations, to infinuate the fmalleft degree of partiality againft the author of this Retrofpective View. He writes with the appearance of candour, and feemingly from good in-formation.

A Letter to the Right Hon. Charles James Fox, 8vo. 1s. 6d. Stockdale.

Major Scott, the author of this Letter, has avowed himfelf as Mr. Haftings's political agent; but a vindication of that gentle-man is not at prefent his only object. Befides juftifying the conduct of the governor, he endeavours to evince, by candid arguments, that the Eaft India bill, which lately paffed the houfe of commons, was founded upon pretexts that had no exiftence.

A Minifterial Almanack. By Recos Jeppbi. 8vo. 1s. 6d. Stockdale.

This author prefents us with farther obfervations on the per-nicious tendency of the celebrated Eaft India bill. The reafon for which he chiefly condemns it, is the vaft patronage it would have thrown into the hands of adminiftration. He divides this fource of corruption into three kinds, annual, contingent, and pecuniary, which, united, muft have produced a fecret influence dangerous to British liberty. The violation of the faith of par-liament might have eternally ftained the bill with the guilt of public injuftice; but the rejection of it by the houfe of lords,

there

there is reason to think, was no less favourable to the future interests than honourable to the virtue of the nation.

An authentic Copy of the Duke of Richmond's Bill for a parliamentary Reform. 8vo. 1s. 6d. Stockdale.

Several plans of a parliamentary reform have been proposed by different persons, of whom there are hardly two who entirely coincide in opinion with each other. Some declare in favour of annual, some of triennial parliaments; and, in respect of the mode of election, there is a yet greater diversity of sentiment. The duke of Richmond proposes that the number of representatives shall remain the same as at present; but that the privilege of voting at elections shall be extended to all persons (we presume his grace means only males), except infants, insane persons, and criminals incapacitated by law. He likewise proposes that the peers of Scotland shall elect sixteen of their number, in whom the right of sitting in parliament shall remain hereditary; and that when the male line of a parliamentary peer becomes extinct, the vacancy shall be supplied by a new election. How far this regulation would be acceptable to the majority of the Scottish peers, we know not; but we think, that by such a proposal, the duke of Richmond betrays a dereliction of those principles of justice, by which he professes to be actuated. If his grace should consider hereditary representation of the commons to be unconstitutional, as we doubt not he would, upon what principle does he recommend so exceptionable a mode to the Scottish peers? To qualify this restriction, however, he farther proposes, that all peers of Scotland, with their heirs apparent, shall be made capable of creation to *English* peerages; or of election to the house of commons.—We know of no creation of English peerages since the Union, they being all denominated British from that time.—In respect to the first of those privileges, if we are not mistaken, it was lately adjudged to them by the opinion of the twelve judges, delivered in the house of lords, relative to the title of the duke of Brandon; and with regard to a capacity in their heirs apparent of obtaining the same honour, it has also been recently confirmed by example. We have taken the liberty of making these few remarks, with the view of suggesting how much deliberation is requisite in forming such plans as are intended for the use of the legislature.

The Ministerialist. 8vo. 1s. Stockdale.

The avowed design of this writer is to delineate the character of some of those persons who formed the late administration. This he endeavours to accomplish by a display of their professions and actions, which, according to the authorities he produces, are certainly far from being consistent. The author makes little use of either declamation or argument; but he seems to have been a watchful sentinel on the departed ministers.

The Means of effectually suppressing Theft and Robbery, &c. 8vo. 2s. Debrett.

Besides the means of suppressing theft and robbery, the author

H h 3   delivers

delivers his sentiments on those likewise of suppressing vagrant beggars; of abolishing the poor-rates; of mitigating punishments for slight offences; and of relieving the great oppression of the labouring commonalty. For answering the several œconomical purposes here mentioned, he proposes, that the enormous sum now collected under the denomination of the poor-rates, but shamefully misapplied; and that which is bestowed on vagrant beggars, with the money annually expended on what he considers both as cruel and ineffectual means of reformation, such as jails and Justitia galleys; that all these sums, collected, should be applied towards placing the poor in a situation for earning their subsistence by industry, and for affording them employment. Such an institution as the author suggests, is, doubtless, highly desirable; but the plan of it will require to be more fully digested, before it can be carried into execution.

An Address to the Right Hon. the Lords Commissioners of the Admiralty, upon the degenerated, dissatisfied State of the British Navy, &c. 8vo. 2s. Stockdale.

The writer of this Address, we find, has served thirty years in the navy; and it may therefore be presumed, that his acquaintance with naval affairs is considerable. We are sorry to observe, that an officer of so much experience should have reason to describe the British navy, at present, as degenerate and discontented. These unfortunate circumstances he imputes chiefly to the partiality in the promotion of naval officers, whose connections and interest, more than personal merit, are too often the considerations which recommend them to the favour of those in power. We would respectfully submit to the attention of the board of admiralty, the ways and means proposed by this intelligent seaman, for putting the navy upon a formidable footing, both as to ships and men; as well as his proposition to establish a new mode of caulking the king's ships; his proposal for maintaining an extra-establishment of marines in time of peace; and for establishing also a general naval register-office. Besides these institutions, he recommends the appointing of commissaries on board the king's ships, as a measure which would be attended with great advantage. We meet likewise with many other plausible, and, we doubt not, just remarks, on subjects relative to the naval service.

Directions to the American Loyalists, in order to enable them to state their Cases to the Commissioners appointed to enquire into the Losses and Services of those Persons, who have suffered in Consequence of their Loyalty. 8vo. 1s. Flexney.

Containing forms of memorials, estimates, &c. for the information or convenience of those who may have occasion to apply to the commissioners, appointed by parliament to enquire into the claims of the Americans.

A Collection of Letters which have been addressed to the Volunteers of Ireland, on the Subject of a Parliamentary Reform, 8vo. 2s. 6d. Stockdale.

These Letters, on a parliamentary reform, are written by lord Effingham,

Effingham, Dr. Price, major Cartwright, and some other abettors of that measure. However they may be received by the majority of the nation, they evince at least the zeal of their authors.

An Abstract of the general Turnpike Act of George III. &c. &c. 8vo. 6d. Evans, Pater-noster-row.

The court of criticism is not a place for the explanation of statutes.

MEDICAL.

An Essay on the Use of the Red Peruvian Bark, in the Cure of Intermittents. By Edward Rigby. 2s. Johnson.

This candid and sensible Essay is written by the author of an ' Essay on Uterine Hemorrhages,' which it is not easy to praise too much, or to recommend too warmly. His present work by no means detracts from his character, though on a subject not equally calculated to display his skill, his humanity, or attention. We have not been inattentive to the red bark, since our account of Dr. Saunders's book: we have weighed the warmth of the admirers of novelty, with the prejudices of the obstinate or the interested, and have unremittingly observed its effects in actual experience. It is not now presumption to add our opinion; and, even an anonymous evidence may deserve some regard, when it is considered that he has never designedly misled, or been deaf to the remonstrances of sober or unprejudiced criticism.

We fully agree with Mr. Rigby, that the pale bark was in our hands frequently unequal to the cure of intermittents; and, in one epidemic, brought from some of the camps in the neighbourhood of Kent, it appeared to be a medicine almost wholly inert. It has frequently been said, that it would always cure if it was sufficiently continued; but those who have given this opinion must have felt little for the sufferings of their patient, or been unacquainted with the impatience of the sick. We also agree with our author, that the *red* bark has never yet failed, though tried on intermittents, which had resisted every remedy, and particularly the pale bark, for months, and for years. We have seldom given more than half an ounce, in the interval, in doses of one scruple, and have found that the fit was always so much mitigated, that it was more easily borne than a larger dose of the medicine. The taste, as Mr. Rigby observes, is generally more agreeable than that of the common bark; the bitter is more pungent or aromatic, and less nauseous. Our author seems uncertain in what parts the superior quality resides; but it is probable that the superiority is chiefly in those parts, in which it differs from common bark, that is, in the blackest brittle resin, about the middle. We have therefore constantly ordered that it be not pounded with too much

violence,

violence, and have preserved the first siftings, as of superior efficacy.

Mr. Rigby, in his evidence, confines himself to intermittents, and has produced some cases, in which it was successfully given, though they have been usually pronounced unfavourable to the success of the remedy. In a few of these he did not wait for a complete intermission, or the operation of an emetic; not because he thought it useless, but because when the fits appeared to increase in severity and danger, there was less mischief in being too precipitate than in being too slow. We own that we have never found any inconvenience from the former excess; though, whenever there is room for waiting, we think the physician would be no less wanting to his own credit than to the safety of his patient, to be too eager in administering the bark.

In other complaints, where the bark has been commonly given, we have found the red bark particularly useful. It has stopped violently spreading mortifications, corrected the putrescency of malignant remittents, and strengthened the bowels, in a remarkable degree. We would only observe, with respect to the remittents, that its virtues have been less considerable in some late epidemics, owing to a concurrence of particular circumstances, which have frequently prevented its exhibition.

We have only to add, that the present pamphlet deserves great attention, if its aim be only, as the author modestly professes, to recall the reader to that of Dr. Saunders; but he will also find it sensible and ingenious; he will recognise in it the attentive observer, and the humane practitioner.

An Essay on the most efficacious Means of treating Ulcerated Legs. 8vo. 1s. Nicoll.

This very candid author rather proposes questions for the consideration of surgeons, than dictates with confidence. A cautious reserve, more frequently the effect of modesty than ignorance, pervades this little tract; and we are led to believe that our author could have been more instructive, if he had been less diffident. He is aware of the whole state of the question, and speaks on the subject as if it was familiar. The only circumstances which struck us as uncommon, are the vulnerary virtues of dry powdered saffron, and elixir aloes, when applied to ulcers. These substances certainly deserve examination.

When we referred Mr. Underwood's treatise to future experience, we intended to take farther notice of it; we therefore take this opportunity to observe, that we have attended with care some trials of his method, which is mentioned also, by the present author, with respect. These experiments have been in general favourable to it; and we have little hesitation in saying, that, with some limitations, it promises to be really beneficial. The limitations chiefly relate to old ulcers, and those depositions

tions which nature, in the advanced stages of life, frequently endeavours to make. We therefore again caution Mr. Underwood against any attempts to oppose them.

An Improved Method of Opening the Temporal Artery. Also, a New Proposal for extracting the Cataract. 8vo. 4s. Johnson.

In this miscellaneous production the author, with a pardonable fondness, reviews and publishes the opinions of his youth. They are distinguished by the bold enterprising spirit of that period, and by an extent of knowlege, and depth of penetration, in general, beyond it. At this time they are not entitled to praises so considerable, though the chief subject of the volume is still important and useful. Dr. Butter recommends opening the temporal artery in all diseases of the head, or its various organs, and produces many instances of its success. We can add our own testimony, for we have frequently employed it, before the present publication, that it is always safe, and frequently salutary. We indeed thought that it was a boldness, bordering on rashness, to take twelve or sixteen ounces of blood, in this way; but our author seems to have no rule respecting the quantity, except a little faintness or the preceding sickness. One of his patients lost two pounds of blood before these symptoms appeared. In many instances this may be proper, but we fear the advice is too indiscriminate to be generally published. The new method, for which we refer to the book, depends on making a longitudinal incision into the artery, instead of a transverse one, by a lancet of a peculiar shape, and on applying a new and convenient bandage, which is called the star-bandage. This may be a sufficient specimen of our author's enterprize; yet it will be still more astonishing when we find him supporting, that ' *all accessible* arteries may be opened without danger.' He has indeed opened the carotid of a dog; and the cure, he observes, was complete; but he had also intended to open this artery in the human subject, when the managers of the infirmary at Edinburgh very properly interposed. It is remarkable, that he has not attempted this formidable operation since; and the greater number of the cases relieved by opening other arteries, are those which occurred in the infirmary of that city. We shall not enlarge, at present, on this subject, as the author informs us, that he is preparing some farther observations on it.

The next considerable object, in this little work, is the extract of hemlock, which we are informed still continues useful in the kinkcough. We are sorry to observe, that this remedy, though prepared with the utmost caution, and certainly possessed of at least the deleterious effects of the vegetable, has, in our hands, failed of success; and this disorder still continues one of the disgraces of medicine. The cases, which are related in this volume, and in which the extract was successfully administered, are a quartan and quotidian hemicrania, albugo, schro-

schrophulous weakness of the eyes, and ophthalmy, as well as the albugo and ophthalmia united. We are always happy to hear of any new resource, and can only wish that this remedy may be more successful with others than with us.

The other miscellaneous articles, in this volume, are chiefly intended to illustrate the subject of arteriotomy, or to collect his former efforts. For the remarks on, and description of his forceps, for extracting the lens in cataracts, and his new catheter, we must refer to the work itself, which is illustrated by a plate of the several instruments. His method of dissolving the stone, by injections into the bladder, is too slightly mentioned to engage our attention; and he will allow us to add, that, if his arguments, in support of his claim to the discovery of the lymphatics, as a system of absorbents, be allowed, Harvey must be also deprived of his honours, and the discovery of the circulation add a lustre to other names.

An Account of the Life and Writings of the late William Hunter, M. D. F. R. S. and S. A. By Samuel Foart Simmons, M. D. F. R. S. 8vo. 2s. Johnson.

While our author contributes his share to support the reputation of Dr. Hunter, he considerably increases his own. This little work is accurate, authentic, and sensible. It comprises the life of the Doctor, from his early youth; and, though it might be more extended by reflections, or adorned by the tinsel of flattery, yet we cannot think that either would add to its real merit. There are some anecdotes of different persons mentioned in the work, and particularly a short life of Mr. Hewson, drawn up with candour, elegance, and good sense, in a letter from his widow. We have read it repeatedly with pleasure.

It is not easy to make any extracts from a life; and, as the size of the work is small, we would not wish to deprive the reader of the pleasure of perusing the whole, by satisfying his curiosity with detached pieces. We shall, on some future occasion, endeavour to give a correct view of the character of Dr. Hunter: we can only now regret, that we are deprived of his work on the several concretions, in the very complete and extensive form which the author had purposed. The remaining works, which are ready for the press, would certainly be received by the public with avidity and gratitude.

Every Patient his own Doctor. By Lewis Robinson, M. D. 8vo. 1s. Cooke.

Whether an injudicious retailer of medical prescriptions be not as dangerous to society as any nostrum-monger, he certainly is equally despicable when he attempts to impose upon the credulous. That this Lewis Robinson, M. D. is notoriously guilty of such a charge, needs no other proof than his declaring, by direct implication, that the sick man, who follows his advice, shall triumph over death and the grave.

An

An Address to the Public, on the Subject of Insanity. By William Perfect, M. D. 4to. 1s. Dodsley.

A few years ago, this author published some cases on the subject of insanity; but the present performance seems only intended to make known, that Dr. Perfect practises in that branch, at West-Malling, in Kent, where his character may be sufficiently attested.

An Address to Persons afflicted with the Gout. By E. Bayley. 8vo. 6d.

This Address, like many others on the same subject, is designed to introduce a secret remedy; of the effects of which, we hope neither ourselves nor our readers will ever be qualified to speak from experience.

DIVINITY.

Essays on Suicide, and the Immortality of the Soul. Ascribed to David Hume, Esq. Never before published. Small 8vo. 3s. 6d. sewed. Smith.

These two Essays consist of some detached thoughts and arguments in favour of suicide and the mortality of the soul. They were undoubtedly written by Mr. Hume, and have been long circulated in a clandestine manner: but they have not been admitted into any edition of his works, as the proprietors of the latter honourably disdained to derive any advantage from publications which will disgrace the memory of the author.

These Essays are accompanied with notes, intended to expose the sophistry of the author's reasoning. And, in order to give the little manual of infidelity some additional weight and importance, the editor has subjoined Two Letters on Suicide (the second feebly obviating the pernicious doctrine of the first) taken from the Eloisa of Rousseau.

The principles, which Mr. Hume attempts to support, are mean and malignant, having a tendency to loosen the bands of society, to subvert the foundation of religion, to debase human nature, to extinguish all noble emulation, to cast a gloom over the whole creation, and to frustrate our sublimest views and expectations.

Supposing, what is contrary to the sentiments of the wisest men in all ages, that the author's arguments are conclusive, what shall we gain but the wretched prospect of annihilation? On the other hand, supposing them to be fallacious, suicide may be attended with such tremendous consequences, as we cannot at present either foresee or conceive.

A Letter to the Rev. Samuel Dennis, D. D. Vice-chancellor of Oxford, and President of St. John's College: in Reply to a Letter signed Vindex, in the St. James's Chronicle of the 16th of October, 1783. By the Rev. Philip Withers, D. D. 8vo. Dodsley.

This gentleman having been attacked by Vindex, and charged in direct terms with ignorance and methodism, appeals to the vice-chancellor of Oxford, in vindication of his honour, and makes this extraordinary requeſt:

' Communicate, Sir, the receipt of this Letter to the heads of houſes—inform them of the injury I have received—and make known my defire of meeting my adverſary, or any other member, on claffical ground. The language, time, and place, I leave to my opponent's choice; provided only that Greek be one of the languages—that the ſubject be previouſly concealed from both parties—and that the compofition be on the ſpot, with no aid from lexicons, grammars, or any other book whatever.'

This is a moſt heroic challenge, and muſt undoubtedly confound every puny antagoniſt. Some calumniators however will be apt to ſay, that the doctor ſhould have appealed, in vindication of his literary character, to the prefident of that learned ſociety in which he took the degree of D. D. and others may probably infinuate, that an appeal to the vice-chancellor of Oxford, in ſuch a cafe as this, can be of no ſervice; that he might, with equal propriety, have appealed to Hyder Ally or Tippoo Saib.

P O E T R Y.

Life: an Allegorical Poem. 12mo. 12s. Hogg.

This author profeſſes to write for the amuſement and improvement of youth. If he means in poetry, we would advife him to ſtudy rhime; if in morality, to be more perſpicuous, more coherent, and more practical.

Ode to Miſs Boſcawen. By the Rev. Mr. William Beloe. 4to. 1s. Wilkie.

If friendſhip with woman be nearly allied to love, the Rev. Mr. Beloe muſt certainly be happy in the confidence he entertains of Miſs Boſcawen's reciprocal attachment. But whether he ſacrifices at the altar of love or of friendſhip, we fincerely wiſh ſucceſs to an honourable paffion, expreſſed with ſo much ardor and ſentiment.

The Lobby. 4to. 1s. Cattermoul.

' Out-door converfation on the meeting of parliament,' in the meaneſt ſtrain of poetry, and in rhimes as diſſonant as the treafury-bench and the oppofition.

N O V E L S.

Peggy and Patty; or the Sifters of Aſhdale, 4 vols. 12mo. 10s. ſewed. Dodſley.

This novel, we find, is the production of a lady, and bears evident marks of a chaſtenefs and delicacy of imagination, as well as of pathetic and moral ſentiment. It refines while it moves the tender emotions of ſympathetic affliction; and where the narrative affumes a ſtrain lefs remote from gaiety, it is always by agreeable tranſitions, and with adventures that never fail to prove intereſting.

The

The Incognita ; or Emily Villars, 2 vols. 12mo. 5s. sewed. Lane.

We meet not here with any remarkable display of imagination; but as little does the author offend the judgment with any thing mean, indelicate, or immoral. So far is he meritorious as to inculcate to his readers the wholesome precept of filial duty ; and it would be unjust not to allow him likewise a talent superior to common novellists, in the contrivance of incident, the ingenuity of reflection, and the delineation of character.

The Double Surprize. 2 vols. 12mo. 5s. sewed. Hookham.

One well-imagined, well-conducted surprize would be fairly worth a thousand such duplicates as the present. These volumes consist of the common materials which are to be found in the store-room of every novellist ; but they are not manufactured with any degree of ingenuity. If they cannot afford much entertainment to the fancy, they are, however, not calculated to corrupt it.

The Ring. 3 vols. 12mo. 9s. Stockdale.

This novel, which is said to be the production of a lady, introduces us to the acquaintance of such a number of personages that we are almost bewildered in the crowd. The discrimination of character is lost in the multiplicity and mutual resemblance of the objects ; and we are every moment astonished with something marvellous. The language, nevertheless, is perfectly chaste, and the situations unexceptionable in point of morality.

The History of the Miss Baltimores. 2 vols. 12mo. 6s. Hookham.

A more frivolous and insipid production than these two volumes has, we believe, seldom issued from the press. Without incident, without sentiment, without passion, without character, that deserve to be called such ; and hardly less exceptionable in point of morality than of dullness.

The Portrait. 2 vols. 12mo. 6s. Hookham.

This is such a portrait as evinces the author to be no Apelles. It were well if he could even claim a rank among the menial servants of the dilettanti.

Female Sensibility ; or the History of Emma Pomfret. 12mo. 2s.6d. sewed. Lane.

This novel is not without merit, in point both of natural description and moral effect ; but its being printed in so close a manner, is a circumstance likely to render it less pleasing in the perusal.

MISCELLANEOUS.

Historical View of the Taste for Gardening among the Ancients. 8vo. 1s. 6d. Dilly.

In this work we find more learning than entertainment, which we can in some measure account for from the want of novelty. There are few circumstances in the historical part which have not been repeatedly mentioned, though perhaps to collect them into one view, with the different illustrations,

tions, may be no useless task. The author would probably have succeeded better, if he had expanded his subject, and by more particular and appropriated descriptions conveyed his reader to the several spots, and placed him now at Thebes and again at Athens.—On the contrary, his descriptions, though exact, are short; and left pleasing because they do not interest the feelings. The good sense of the concluding remarks on the different tastes for gardening, would compensate, however, for more errors than we have discovered. ' We should reflect, says our author, that if this style has subsisted from the earliest ages in warm climates, as we have reason to believe it has done, it affords a strong presumption that such a mode was suited to the climate, situation, condition, and manners of the people; and if this be the case, we may with equal propriety pronounce such a taste to be natural, as we may that any of their other customs are so.'

On this foundation, he endeavours to defend the different fashions of gardens with success, and has said so much, that, if we define a garden to be cultivated nature, we begin to suspect that more marks of cultivation should appear than we have lately allowed. If we extend our views to distant objects, and, under this title, include adjacent fields, our conduct will be proper; but it must then be owned, that we have abandoned the idea of a garden, and assumed that of something more extensive, the properties of which are consequently very different. But this subject is not likely to be settled by a philosophical investigation; so that we shall leave modern artists in their own tract, till nature can no longer supply the cravings of an enervated or a depraved appetite, but must in her turn yield to the refinements of art.

An Essay on Misanthropy. By Percival Stockdale. 8vo. 1s. Law.

Our literary veteran seems to have felt the force of neglect and disappointment. He has combated with various success; and, though seeming to retire from the contest to number his wounds, or to glory in his victories, yet he cannot forbear again to court danger in slight skirmishes, and the semblance of former fields. In this little work he endeavours to defend a character seldom regarded but with detestation.—If we were to indulge conjecture, we should suppose that, having incurred the imputation of misanthropy, instead of denying the charge, he endeavours to evade the guilt. In his view, misanthropy is by no means inconsistent with the warmest and most active benevolence; for the man who can look through human nature, and perceive its corruptions, will, with equal discernment, detect the various propensities which are conquered, and the power of those seducers which are unconquerable. Practical hatred then dies within his breast, and he becomes inclined to alleviate the sufferings, and assist the sufferer. This is a plausible, but we fear, a fallacious explanation: the character described

scribed is indeed amiable and benevolent; but is therefore not that of a misanthrope. In our author's endeavours to evade the crime, he changes the object; like some other systematics, he assumes the character which he proposes to analyse, and then triumphs in a discovery which must inevitably follow, because it is involved with his principles.

In the sequel of this little tract, he endeavours to defend, with some ardour, Swift's character of the Huynhnms, against the censures of Mr. Harris; but, in our opinion, with little success. We shall not expatiate on this subject, because our author does not consider it either at length, or in a proper light. On the whole, there is an originality in the sentiments of this piece, and it is written with clearness and precision.

Historical Account of the Prussian Army, and its present Strength, &c. By J. M. Baron de Helldorff. 8vo. 5s. in Boards. Cadell.

As in the whole corps of Reviewers, we have not even a ferjeant-major, we can form no very decisive opinion of this account. A great part of its merit must arise from its accuracy, of which we are unable to judge : we only know, that it is neither entertaining or interesting to general readers, as it consists chiefly of the names of officers commanding regiments, or in chief, the numbers of men in each regiment, battalion, &c. The little which is said of the constitution of the army is highly advantageous to the character of Frederick ; for, while it amply provides sources of men and provisions ; while it effectually secures obedience, and a due subordination, it preserves his own dominions from too severe exactions, and abundantly secures the properties of individuals. To contemplate this prince in various lights, is to raise our admiration of his greatness almost to idolatry. His goodness is more equivocal ; yet in this too ' much may be said on both sides.'

Dissertation on Gaming. By Richard Hey, LL.D. 8vo. 2s. 6d. Cadell.

This Dissertation has been published by appointment, as having gained a prize, last summer, in the university of Cambridge. The author who is Dr. Hey, describes, in strong colours, the pernicious effects of gaming, both on individuals and society. He considers the subject with precision and acuteness ; and though he seems not to have attended much to elegance of composition, his judicious observations and arguments carry with them the force of reason and of truth. Should the author's sentiments be read and adopted as generally as they deserve, he would be entitled to a rank among the greatest benefactors of his country.

The History of the Flagellants : otherwise, of Religious Flagellations among different Nations, and especially among Christians. The Second Edition. 8vo. 6s. in Boards. Robinson.

The History of the Flagellants was mentioned, at its first appearance, in our Review for May, 1777. It contains a
num-

number of ludicrous stories, and some curious information. This improved edition is adorned with cuts. The author is the ingenious Mr. De Lolme.

The Sheep, the Duck, and the Cock. A Dramatic Fable. 8vo. 1s. Meyler, Bath.

A dialogue between the three aëreal travellers lately sent up from Paris with the Air Balloon. 'Tis pity that Monf. Montgolfier did not send up this author at the same time.

Remarks on the Climate, Produce, and natural Advantages of Nova Scotia. 8vo. 1s. Debrett.

The author of this letter represents Nova Scotia as a country very far from being intemperate in point of climate. He informs us that, notwithstanding what has been said of the severity of the winter, few Europeans, in that season, change their ordinary clothing, except those who expect to be long exposed to the open air. Fuel of different kinds, we are also told, is in great plenty, and may be had at a small expence. The climate is even favourable to the production of all kinds of grain, roots, fruit, and vegetables, which Britain produces; and the country is particularly well situated for carrying on fisheries on the banks of Newfoundland. Such being the case, we hope that Nova Scotia will afford the American loyalists, and other emigrants, a more comfortable retreat than was generally imagined.

William Sedley: or the Evil Day deferred. 2s. 6d. Marshall.

Father's Advice to his Son. 2s. Marshall.

Both those productions are well calculated for the moral improvement of young children.

School Occurrences. 12mo. 1s. Marshall.

These Occurrences are supposed to have arisen among a set of young ladies. They are such as appear natural; and having, at the same time, a foundation in simplicity of manners, are calculated to afford profitable entertainment to young readers, especially of the female class.

Faithful Copies of Letters that have appeared in the General Advertiser, under the Signature of Scourge, and Mr. Binnet, Camberwell. 8vo. 1s. 6d. Debrett.

These Letters relate to the transactions of the commissioners of victualling, and Mr. Atkinson, their cornfactor, since convicted of perjury, and expelled the house of commons.

Address to the Public. By Christopher Atkinson, Esq. 4to. 6d. Clarke.

The present address, in behalf of a person so situated, is too weak and evasive to claim any attention from the public.

INDEX.

INDEX.

INDEX to the FOREIGN ARTICLES.

END OF THE FIFTY-SIXTH VOLUME.